Schriften zu Leben und Gesellschaft - Series on Life and Society

Volume 2

Über die Schriftenreihe Wissenschaft und Gesellschaft stehen durch zahlreiche Veränderungsprozesse und Krisen vor immer wieder neuen Herausforderungen. Technologisierung, Ökonomisierung, Ökologisierung und Globalisierung setzen das individuelle und gesellschaftliche Leben unter Gestaltungsdruck. Eine Vielfalt wissenschaftlicher Disziplinen und Akteure aus allen gesellschaftlichen Bereichen sind gefordert, die transformativen Prozesse der Gegenwart gemeinsam, kreativ und kritisch reflektierend zu gestalten. Die Schriften zu Leben und Gesellschaft stellen das Leben in den Mittelpunkt – das Leben nicht ausschließlich in einem biologisch-naturwissenschaftlichen Verständnis, sondern in allen Facetten des sich entfaltenden und entwickelnden Lebens. Es geht um das menschliche und das nichtmenschliche Leben, um das individuelle und das gesellschaftliche Leben, jenseits disziplinärer Grenzen. In ausgewählten Studien und Analysen präsentieren sie fachübergreifende und translationale Forschung, Debatten und Konzepte zur partizipativen Gestaltung unserer Zukünfte im globalen Kontext.

Jan Linhart

Science and the Other

An Inquiry into the Geopolitics of Knowledge, Potiguara Ontology and the Hard Problem of Modern Science

Springer

Jan Linhart
Center for Life Ethics
Rheinische Friedrich-Wilhelms-Universität Bonn
Bonn, Nordrhein-Westfalen, Germany

This work was submitted in 2021 as a PhD thesis for the degree of Doctor of Philosophy at the Faculty of Social and Cultural Sciences of the European University Viadrina Frankfurt (Oder), receiving the evaluation summa cum laude in 2022.
First reviewer: Prof. Dr. Harald Walach
Second reviewer: Prof. Dr. Hartmut Schröder
Date of defense: February 4, 2022

ISSN 3005-0901 ISSN 3005-091X (electronic)
Schriften zu Leben und Gesellschaft - Series on Life and Society
ISBN 978-3-032-03926-2 ISBN 978-3-032-03927-9 (eBook)
https://doi.org/10.1007/978-3-032-03927-9

Center for Life Ethics

This Springer imprint is published by the registered company Springer Nature Switzerland AG
The registered company address is: Gewerbestrasse 11, 6330 Cham, Switzerland

To the Potiguara

Acknowledgement

This work would not have been possible without the contributions of many different people, and in fact there are far too many persons who actively contributed to this work than I can mention here, but who certainly deserve my honest thanks.

I am especially grateful for the confidence and the support I received from the Potiguara, who allowed me to share so many pleasant and fascinating moments. In particular, I would like to thank Pedro Kaaguasu from Ybykuara who was so kind to help me initiate my research project, to introduce me to other Potiguara, provided me with shelter during my fieldwork, and who gifted me with his friendship. Likewise, Senhor João and Dona Maria and their whole family received me at their home like a family member, while the younger family members, like Iranilza, Iracilda, Leonardo, and Adriano, actively participated in our action research project. I am also very grateful for Dona Nilda's (who recently "ancestralised", but will continue in our memories) and "Caboquinho's" (Antonio Gomes) confidence, support, and friendship, who were among the first and the most active participants in our project; their outstanding knowledge and esteem as leaders of the indigenous movement were of decisive importance for our project. However, the active participation of all the other voluntary members of our research group (the *Coletivo de Pesquisa pelos Saberes Potiguara*) was of equally essential importance to the development and realisation of our collective goals. Moreover, I am indebted to the general chief (*cacique geral*) Sandro Gomes, as well as all the other local authorities, for accepting and supporting my presence and our research project. Among the more than 30 traditional healers and midwives who actively contributed to our autoethnographic work, I would like to express my particular gratitude to Dona Fatima and the young "*pajé*" Isaias, with whom I spent many hours philosophising about Potiguara cosmology, spirituality, medicine and history, and whose contributions were essential to the views presented in this work.

Fortunately, our work also received support from external academics with a special interest in indigenous activism. Professor Dr. Thiago Romero from the UFCG (*Universidade Federal de Campina Grande*) has been actively involved in our activities ever since 2016, and his dedication and commitment was certainly a key incentive for all the other participants. Personally, I am particularly indebted to Thiago for helping me shoulder this project, and for introducing me to the modernity/coloniality research project, which became a fundamental building block of the thoughts I am going to present herein. I also have to thank Professor Dr. Paulo Palhano, Professor Maika Zampier, Professor Dr. Wilma Mendonça, and Dr. Professor Estevão Palitot from the UFPB (*Universidade Federal da Paraíba*) for their backing of our joint activities with the Potiguara.

Apart from the many contributions during my research in Brazil, this work would probably not exist without the incentive and the assistance of Dr. Nikolaus von Stillfried, Professor Dr. Dr. Harald Walach, and Majella Horan. It was my old friend Nikolaus who, back in 2010, motivated me to develop a research project on the possible similarities between ontological models from Chalmers' debate on the "hard problem of consciousness" and quantum physics, and conceptions from indigenous cosmologies. Nikolaus also introduced me to Professor Dr. Dr. Walach, who was so kind to accept and supervise my Ph.D. project. And of course, it is only thanks to Majella Horan's magnificent (and entirely voluntary) lecturing that this text reads like proper English.

Last but not least, I apologise to my wife and to my little daughter for the many hours I spent with my laptop, writing these lines. The patience and the continuous support of my wife, Andrea, were of invaluable importance for my staying the course.

Contents

1 Introduction 1
References 15

Part I Scientific Universalism

2 What Is Scientific Universalism? 21
2.1 The Ideological Foundations of Universalism 26
2.1.1 The Modern Project 26
2.1.2 The Scholastic Heritage 29
2.2 The Institutional Foundations of Universalism 31
References 34

3 The Metaphysics of Scientific Universalism 37
3.1 The Scientific Method 38
3.1.1 The Epistemological Foundations of Method 39
3.1.2 The Natural Sciences 43
3.1.3 The Social Sciences 44
3.2 The Rationalist Heritage 47
3.3 The Empiricist Heritage 56
3.4 Pragmatism 62
3.5 Scientism's Universe 70
3.5.1 Mind-Stuff, the Matrix and Blind Matter 70
3.5.2 Causation, Linear Time, Determinism and Locality 79
3.6 Summing Up Universalist Metaphysics 88
References 92

4 The Geopolitics of Scientific Universalism 97
4.1 Science in Its Mirror 98
4.1.1 Between the Wars 98
4.1.2 From Cold War to Science Wars 112
4.2 Lessons Learnt so Far? 131
4.3 Decolonising Science 138

4.4 Should We Worry About the End of Truth? 160
References 166

5 The Scientific Construction of the Other 173
5.1 On Christians and Pagans 174
5.2 Of Noble and Barbarian Savages 175
5.3 Anthropology: The Science of the Other 181
5.3.1 From Evolutionism to Relativism 182
5.3.2 The Savage Mind and Western Science 183
5.3.3 The Western Scope of Rationality 192
5.4 The Ontological Turn: Beyond Nature and Culture 196
5.4.1 The End of the Great Divide? 197
5.4.2 Relational Epistemologies: Animism Revisited 199
5.4.3 Perspectivism and Cannibal Metaphysics 204
5.4.4 Political Ontology 209
References 226

Part II The Potiguara

6 On Method 237
6.1 Representing Others 239
6.2 Acting Rather than Representing 243
References 248

7 Research in Action 251
7.1 Some Challenges 255
References 263

8 Changing Potiguara Worlds 267
8.1 Ancestral Heritage and Changing "Traditions" 277
References 289

9 Contemporary Potiguara Cosmovision and Practice 293
9.1 An Enchanted Word 293
9.1.1 Tupã and Mother Nature 294
9.1.2 Earth, Sun and Moon 295
9.1.3 Living Beings 297
9.1.4 Enchanted Beings 300
9.1.5 The Enchanted Kingdoms and Their Patrons 301
9.1.6 Other Mythic Beings 305
9.1.7 Immaterial Agency 306
9.1.8 Birth and Death 308
9.2 Health and Sickness 309
9.3 Spiritual Practices and Healing Rituals 315
9.4 Recapitulating Potiguara Cosmovision and Practice 327
References 330

10 Potiguara Ontology 333
10.1 The Immaterial and the Material Realm 334
10.2 The Underdetermined Character of Consciousness and the Overdetermination of the Body 335
10.3 Intentionality and Relational Causation 337
10.4 Time and Space 340
10.5 Conclusive Remarks on the Potiguara and Their Cosmopractices 341
Reference 342

Part III The Hard Problem of Modern Science

11 The Hard Problem of Consciousness 347
11.1 The Hard Problem of Modern Science 347
11.1.1 The Ontological Bottleneck 349
11.2 Possible Solutions to the Hard Problem of Consciousness 366
11.2.1 Substance Dualism 368
11.2.2 Aspect Dualism 374
References 383

12 What Quantum Physics May Tell Us About Mind and Matter 387
12.1 Interpreting Quantum Physics in Search of Mind 394
12.1.1 Complementarity as a Fundamental Principle of Mind and Matter 400
12.1.2 Mind-Induced Collapse 404
12.1.3 Many Minds Instead of Many Worlds? 405
12.1.4 Mind and Matter as Unfoldings of a Multi-Dimensional Wave Function? 407
12.1.5 The Wave Function as the Intrinsic Mind-Side of Matter? 412
12.2 Generalised Quantum Theory 416
12.3 Summing Up Current Approaches to a Unified Theory of Mind and Matter 429
References 431

13 Of Ancestors and Wave Functions: A Tentative Comparability Analysis 437
13.1 Potiguara Cosmopractice Through the Lens of Quantum Physics 440
13.2 What Potiguara Ancestors Might Tell Us About Quantum Physics 448
13.3 The Mind-Body Problem Revisited from a Potiguara Perspective 453
References 463

14 Conclusion and Outlook 465
References 473

Chapter 1
Introduction

Modern science is the most powerful epistemological approach the world has ever seen. Thanks to science we are able to manipulate our material world in ways unimaginable for previous generations. Science provides us with fantastic technologies giving us abilities far beyond those of any other species. We can see stars and molecular microstructures invisible to any natural eye, detect sound and light of almost any frequency, go faster, fly higher, and dive deeper than any other living being. Science gives us superpowers! Today, we take it for granted that we can communicate with almost any other person on earth at any time, get all kinds of information within seconds, travel to other continents within hours, eat fresh fruit and crops from all over the world, move rivers and mountains as we please. Moreover, modern medicine provides cures for many formerly lethal injuries and diseases, and many of us would probably not be alive if there were no antibiotics, no vaccines, and no high-tech surgery. Science has changed our lives so profoundly, giving us such incredible powers, that it makes us dream of an even better future, a future where technology solves all our problems, where we can cure all maladies, where machines do all the hard work for us, and where we adventure to explore other worlds in outer space.

And yet, modern science has been the target of severe critique. Conspicuously, some of its most vigorous critiques come from within, from scientists and academic philosophers. In fact, scientific meta-discourse has been questioning the epistemological foundations of modern science ever since its beginnings. This may not be surprising, as sceptic self-criticism is the very core of modern science as a new, a *modern* epistemological approach intended to overcome the dogmas of religious and "traditional" knowledge in order to free our minds from oppression and superstition, the great promises of enlightenment. In other words, the end of self-critical scientific meta-discourse would mean the end of modern science, and a return to uncritical dogmatism. So, what are those critiques and why should we be concerned with them?

There are at least three major problems with modern science: First, there are some epistemological issues concerning the very fundaments of scientific method

J. Linhart, *Science and the Other*, Schriften zu Leben und Gesellschaft - Series on Life and Society 2, https://doi.org/10.1007/978-3-032-03927-9_1

that resist, and have been resisting for centuries, any attempt to solve them. This epistemological dilemma can be traced back to the *aporia* of the Cartesian subject-object-dichotomy and the representational model of perception, that is, the very core of modern epistemology itself. On the one hand, the modern subject, their perception and their rational deductions are the only source of truth; on the other hand, subjective experience is delusive and cannot be trusted. Scientific method is meant to avoid the pitfalls of subjective prejudice, substituting subjective judgment with quantitative and replicable procedures. However, subjective perception pertinaciously persists as the linchpin of modern epistemology. There have been uncountable attempts to loosen the Gordian knot of epistemology's intrinsic contradictions, but it seems the deeper we dig the darker it gets around us. As a result, science finds itself unable to provide a coherent epistemological legitimation for its truth claims. Moreover, modern science has failed to provide a coherent and unified theoretical framework for coping with subjective experience as a natural phenomenon underlying natural laws. These epistemological shortcomings have serious consequences, most strikingly demonstrated by the separation of the natural sciences from the humanities. However, the *aporia* of the subject-object dichotomy is a constant obstacle in all scientific disciplines. While the natural sciences continue by and large to simply ignore the whole epistemological quandary, going on with business as usual (producing new, profitable technologies), critical meta-discourses in the humanities have long proven positivism and objectivism to be unsustainable. But even the most fundamental theory of the natural sciences, quantum physics, has contributed more to the deconstruction of objectivism than to its substantiation. Furthermore, the natural sciences have not been able to answer some very fundamental questions. On the one hand, both relativity and quantum theory have revolutionised modern physics, but at the price of an utterly disunified fundamental theory of matter. On the other hand, the advances in neuroscience provide us with a detailed understanding of the physical processes concomitant with our subjective experience, but with no coherent explanation of what consciousness actually is and how it relates to physical processes. In other words, all the brilliant advances in the natural sciences notwithstanding, there is still no coherent theory of mind and matter. At the same time, the social sciences see themselves trapped in the dichotomous opposition between objective and subjective theories; the first trying to explain social phenomena in terms of objective social macrostructures constraining individual thought and behaviour, and the second focussing on the driving motivations of the individual subjects that constitute society. This theoretical dilemma might be most visible in sociology and its (failed) efforts to come to a coherent unified theory capable of integrating the active role of the individual subjects and the macrostructures they create and by which they are constrained. On the whole, it appears that science at large is trapped within the subject-object dilemma, unable to overcome this metaphysical bottleneck on its own.

Second, there are pragmatic concerns about Science (as a social institution) and its historical role as an essential element of the modern age—or even to the rise of a new geological era of human dominance over nature, the "Anthropocene", as some would phrase it. Beyond any doubt, thanks to the superpowers Science gave to us, it empowered us to shape the world as we know it. However, more than ever, this world is in crisis. The so-called Anthropocene, the "human age", threatens to become the age of human extinction precisely because of the planetary scale of our impact on nature. If we look at the roots of all those multiple existential crises, what we find are achievements of so-called scientific "progress". Without Science, there would be no nuclear weapons, no industrial mass production, and consequently, no over-exploitation of virtually all the natural resources our planet has to offer, including human labour. And it is by no means clear whether Science will provide the means to get us through these "catastrophic times"[1] and help us build liveable, post-anthropocenic futures.[2] Moreover, scientific discovery and technological development seem to benefit only a restricted part of our global modern society, while the majority suffers from its negative "side effects". Since this unequal distribution of boon and bane of modern Science clearly follows social, racial, and ultimately, colonial[3] dividing lines, Science appears to be in service of a global system of oppression and exploitation rather than of freedom and justice. One may get the impression that Science provides us (or at least the global elites) with superpowers, but unfortunately, not with wisdom.[4] The ongoing debates on climate change in the face of overwhelming scientific data, and the surprising resistance of our society to take the appropriate measures to prevent us from global disaster, are calling the social role of Science into question, once again. Does Science serve the ideals of an enlightened society, or rather the blind greed of global capitalism?

So, there are good reasons for having a deeper look into the intrinsic entanglement between Science and the social structure of our still quite colonial capitalist world system. And indeed, over the last 100 years, scientists and philosophers have been emphasising the essentially social character of Science and scientific knowledge. This social constructionist view has long become mainstream (at least in the social sciences), however, the resulting relativism led into the cul-de-sac of deconstructionism, and consequently, to a general critique of "truth". For if all different "truths" are equally socially constructed, there is no "truth" at all, but only different viewpoints, all of them based on equally unprovable presumptions. As a corollary, scientific "truths" are no better than any other "truth". Of course, philosophers and scientists involved in developing social constructionism and post-modern deconstructionism intended to advance Science by making it more conscious of its own constraints and more open to new ideas, and in a way, intended to free Science from its service to the elites, and thus, democratise scientific knowledge. Ironically, this relativisation of modern science's truth monopoly arguably contributed to the

[1] Stengers (2015).

[2] Isabelle Stengers (2018a) notes: "[…] the motto 'progress will repair the collateral damage that progress has occasioned' has lost all credibility" (position 1634). Or as Arturo Escobar puts it: "We cannot construct the postconflict (and postcarbon) world using the categories that created the conflict" (Escobar 2020: 125).

[3] Quijano (1992); Harding (1994, 2015); Latour (2001); Mignolo and Ennis (2001); Mignolo (2002); Wallerstein (2004); Maldonado-Torres (2007), among many others.

[4] Maxwell (2017, 2021).

current post-truth era, with new political players from the far right launching a counter-Enlightenment attack on reason and human rights.

In face of more than a century of frustrated attempts to put modern science on new epistemological fundaments we should better come to terms with the fact that modern academic discourse alone is evidently unable to go beyond its own conceptual limitations. So, why not initiate a dialogue with Other, non-"Western", non-"modern", non-hegemonic, subaltern kinds of knowledge? Maybe we could learn from the Other's views on Us "modern", "Western" academics and Our conception of "truth"[5]? Maybe we could think together about a new, truly universal science, or at least start thinking together about the world we would like to share and the knowledge we might need to have this vision come true?

This leads directly to the third problem: scientific universalism. Unfortunately, modern science crowned itself as the only universal method to find "the truth". It therefore radically discards any Other "truth" together with related practices of knowing and subjacent cosmological conceptions. As a consequence, modern science a priori delegitimises any Other way of knowing for being "unscientific", including knowledge from different cultural contexts. Due to this universalistic dogma, modern science is unable to learn from Other ways of knowing. Moreover, it disqualifies Other cultures and classifies them as inferior compared to Our modern industrialised "civilisation". Anthropology may be the scientific discipline which has contributed more than any other to visualise this hierarchisation of knowledge, giving rise to deeper reflections on this issue. Despite its inglorious onset as a tool of European colonialism, anthropology soon started to question the supposed inferiority of Other cultures. Aiming to establish a more horizontal relationship to the non-"modern"/"Western" Other, anthropologists subjected themselves to a radical self-critique, and developed more participatory and collaborative research designs. But even though considerable progress has been made, there still remains a deep epistemological gap between the hegemonic discourse of modern science and Other subalternised forms of knowledge. For an anthropological account of Other knowledge to be recognised as scientific "data", Other conceptions have to be translated into "scientific" terms. In practice this means that an anthropologist may participate in healing rituals, witness and even experience a successful cure, but when it comes to explain the cause of the healing effects they will have to stick to the current scientific paradigm and argue in terms of chemical components of the plants used and psychosomatic phenomena like placebo concerning the effect

[5] Conceptions of "Us" as representing a particular "modern", "progressive", "Western", "rational" and "civilised" "culture" or "society" in contrast to "Other" cultures representing the "non-modern", "primitive", "non-Western", "irrational" and ultimately "savage" are historical constructs rather than objective categories. Both the images of "Us" and of the "Other" can be understood as mutually constitutive elements of the dichotomous scheme known as the "Great Divide", which is also fundamental to the unequal global power-relations that have been prevailing for the last 500 years (for more details on this issue see Chaps. 4 and 5). In order to distinguish these historical constructs from objective categories, I will use upper case spelling for Us and the Other.

of ritual itself.[6] This, of course, is very far from taking Other, culturally different forms of knowledge seriously, since this kind of explanation completely dismisses the Other's own, *emic* explanations, which most likely would involve radically different kinds of healing concepts, simply because they (apparently) do not fit into the paradigmatic categories of modern science. For this reason, modern science, including anthropology, has been accused of being instrumental to cultural imperialism, colonialism, and more generally, to the maintenance of a modern/colonial world system based on racist distinctions.[7] From this point of view, the dogma of scientific universalism is co-responsible for the ongoing extinction of cultural difference and Other, alternative ways of knowing all over the world. Scientific universalism is clearly a dogma, since scientific metadiscourse quite unanimously proves science's own universal truth claims epistemologically untenable, simply because (from the viewpoint of modern representational epistemology) any kind of "truth" is ultimately a historically contingent social construction. Far from having the better arguments compared to Other kinds of knowledge, science's universalism is an expression of the same hegemonic global system of power that both supports Science and depends on it. The superiority of modern/colonial science is not simply based on a superior epistemological or methodological approach, as still claimed by many (especially natural) scientists, but most importantly on the economic, technological, and military power[8] of the dominant world system[9] as a whole, of which Science is an essential part.

From all this follows that it does not seem very promising to continue the never-ending debates about the epistemological and methodological superiority or inferiority of this or that system of knowledge. Instead of benchmarking different kinds of knowledge according to their epistemological premises and resulting truth values, which is impossible, it might be more straightforward to assume a more pragmatic stance and evaluate the actual effects of different ways of knowing.[10] Furthermore, it is impossible to evaluate modern science, or any other knowledge system, in isolation, because knowledge is just one element of a much wider, more holistic complex of historical, social, cultural, and economic structures.[11] Thus, science cannot be evaluated separately from technology, modernity, capitalism, and colonialism, since it is itself an essential part of this historical constellation. Of course, if we evaluate Science from the perspective of the "dark side" of modernity,[12]

[6] Of course, most anthropologists prefer to avoid referring to the (supposed) reasons for the efficacy of rituals and rather provide an *emic* account of the explanations provided by the cultural group they are working with. Their analysis will rather be concerned with the symbolic meaning or the social function of ritual than with the actual curing-principles.

[7] Quijano (1992, 2000, 2009); Dussel (2000, 2009); Escobar (2000); Lander (2000); Mignolo and Ennis (2001); Mignolo (2002); Wallerstein (2004, 2006); Santos (2007, 2009a, b).

[8] Aronowitz (1988); Harding (1994); Latour (2001), et al.

[9] Wallerstein (2004, 2006).

[10] Peirce (1878); Quine (1951); James (1981).

[11] Santos (2007).

[12] Mignolo (2011).

it suddenly appears in a different light, being related to quite negative effects, while Other, "ancestral", "animic", "perspectivist" or "relational" systems of knowledge may appear to be related to more sustainable ways of life. However, such a contrasted comparison entails the risk of a romantic essentialising of the Other, and thereby reproducing the stigmatising image of a "pre-modern" Other which is the very fundament of the Great Divide between Us and Them, and which sustains the "colonial difference"[13] between the "developed", "white", European decent, upper-class, male, metropolitan "Us" from the subalternised "underdeveloped", "coloured", non-European, working poor, female "Other" of the global peripheries. A critical analysis of modern science, therefore, demands a decolonised view[14] on both the modern/colonial character of Science and the modern/colonial character of the Other. From this vantage point, it becomes an important challenge to decolonise Our modern/colonial scientific gaze, to open Science for a horizontal dialogue with Other kinds of knowing-feeling-being, and start thinking together, to feel-think "in-between",[15] so to say, and to look at things from a new perspective inspired by different subaltern positionalities and practices of knowing. Such an *ecology of knowledges*,[16] *inverted anthropology*[17] or *pluriversal dialogue*[18] among diverging cosmovisions and practices—or *cosmopractices*[19]—might enable us to come to a differentiated understanding of the epistemological potentials and limitations and the overall effectiveness of Our modern/colonial way of doing science, and Other forms of knowing—particularly regarding their problem-solving capacities in view of the multiple global crises we are currently facing.

The problem is, however, that modern/colonial science does not seem to be able to enter into a horizontal dialogue with Other systems of knowledge precisely because of its universalistic dogma. Eventually, universalism derives from the foundationist notion of "truth" as a logical deduction from evidently "true" fundamental premises. Once the foundational premises are defined, there can be only one "truth". Accordingly, scientific universalism amounts to the claim that scientific knowledge, and only scientific knowledge is "true", since it derives from the only universally "true" premises. However, academic meta-discourse on the epistemological grounding of knowledge suggests that foundationalism is probably false, for all representations of reality are ultimately constructions. Hence, there are no "evident", universally "true" premises, but only historically contingent *metaphysical*

[13] Mignolo (2002).

[14] Mignolo (2011, 2021); Mignolo and Walsh (2018).

[15] Mignolo (2013) et al.

[16] Santos (2007).

[17] Castro (2015).

[18] Querejazu (2016); Dunford (2017); Hutchings (2019); Escobar (2020); Fitzgerald (2021); Behr and Shani (2021); Linhart et al. (2025).

[19] Castro (2004a, 2015, 2022); Cesarino (2006); Linhart et al. (2025).

presuppositions[20] that are largely agreed among a particular *thought collective*.[21] This set of metaphysical presuppositions are ultimately rooted in peculiar ideas about the ontological structure of the universe, that is, they reflect a particular cosmology. Of course, every system of knowledge is based on its own metaphysical framework, or cosmology (although several modern philosophers tried hard to get rid of metaphysics altogether), and it depends very much on the specific differences between those frameworks whether or not these different systems of knowledge will be able to "talk" to each other. For example, "scientific" knowledge is supposed to acknowledge specific notions of space, time, causation, mind, and matter. Other cosmologies, in contrast, may give rise to quite different notions of these fundamental categories, suggesting different metaphysical suppositions. From this vantage point, universalism amounts to the claim of a fundamental *incommensurability* between the *metaphysical presuppositions* assumed by science as "evident" and those suggested by Other cosmologies. As a result, (supposedly) incommensurable metaphysical notions are classified, a priori and without any further testing of their potential efficacy, as "unscientific", and thus, excluded from (hegemonic) scientific discourse on "truth".

This conclusion may, in part, explain why the relativising of modern science's truth monopoly by post-modern, post-colonial, feminist, and other critical strands in academic discourse did not result in abandoning the dogma of scientific universalism. Even though, *in principle*, Other kinds of knowledge may not be characterised by an inferior truth value, they are still *too different* to be meaningfully translated into scientific terms. Consequently, Other kinds of knowledge are held to be incompatible with scientific discourse on truth, since they describe a completely different "world" made up by ontic categories with all kinds of strange properties that apparently do not match with any of Our "scientific" conceptions of the natural principles that (supposedly) constitute the entire universe. How, for example, should we translate the conception of a "spirit" into scientific terms if there are no immaterial actants? Or, what could be the equivalent of "magic" if there is no evidence for such a "spooky action at a distance"[22]?

It is generally presumed that the metaphysical framework derived from scientific evidence precludes the existence of such "strange" phenomena. However, a closer look at the metaphysical concepts that are held to exclude such phenomena as immaterial actants or "spooky actions at a distance" are not quite as definitely imposed by empirical evidence as often assumed. Fundamental physics has long shown that common notions of time, space, causation, and matter are at best good approximations, but do not describe the actual ontic structure of the universe. In fact, relativity theory rather lump space and time together into a four-dimensional spacetime, and quantum physics quite clearly shows that, at least at the microlevel

---

[20] Collingwood (1998); Maxwell (2017).

[21] Mannheim (1954); Fleck (1983).

[22] Famous dictum of Albert Einstein used in a letter to Max Born dated March 3rd, 1947 (Einstein and Born 2005: 254).

of photons, electrons and atoms, "spooky actions at a distance" constitute the apparently causal reality of classical physics. The discovery of these strange properties at the very fundament of the physical nature of the universe has led physicists to speculate about the ontological implications of their empirical findings. In the course of the last 100 years, leading physicists developed a range of different ontological interpretations of quantum physics, however, without coming to an agreement about a single, coherent cosmological model. It turns out that scientific evidence can be interpreted in radically different ways, ranging from a universe made up by countless collapsing wave-functions,[23] to multiple universes (or multiple minds) emerging from a universal wave-function,[24] to a parallel existence of a multi-dimensional implicate order (represented by the wave-function) and an explicit order with a mental and a physical pole (represented by particles),[25] among other suggested interpretations. Each of these ontological interpretations implies a different notion of time, space, causation, and matter. Moreover, the intrinsic indeterminacy of physical events suggested by quantum physics is in conflict with both classical physics and relativity theory. As a result, there is currently no commonly agreed physical theory of matter; rather, there are several competing models, each with its particular shortcomings and incoherencies.

Furthermore, this lack of a coherent scientific theory of matter is paralleled by the lack of a coherent scientific theory of mind as well. It is true that neuroscience has greatly advanced our knowledge about the physical processes that correlate to cognitive states. However, it is by no means clear how those physical processes in our brains might be able to produce the phenomenal experience of "what it is like to be" in a particular cognitive state. David Chalmers[26] and others have emphasised the "hard problem of consciousness" resulting from the ontological difference between physical and phenomenal properties. In other words, the experience of seeing the different tones of red of a beautiful flower and smelling its perfume compared to their physical correlates of chemical neurotransmitters at synaptic clefts provoking electric potentials in neurons are of such radically different natures that they have to be conceived of as two irreducible, and thus, ontologically distinct categories. Hence, it is, at least, difficult to explain how phenomenal properties (like conscious experience of qualia) should emerge from physical properties, or how phenomenal properties (like our conscious decision to move our hand) might have a causal role in physical processes (like moving our hand). To date, no-one has been able to develop a convincing solution to the riddle of the century-old mind-body problem. Again, we are left with a range of different ontological models, but no coherent theory of consciousness.

---

[23] So-called Copenhagen interpretations, spontaneous collapse, Ghirardi–Rimini–Weber (GRW) model (Friebe 2015), Diósi–Penrose model (Penrose 1996).

[24] Everett (1957).

[25] Bohm (1980, 1990).

[26] Chalmers (1995, 2002, 2010, 2016a, b).

In sum, it turns out that there is neither a coherent scientific theory of matter, nor a convincing scientific theory of mind, let alone a unified scientific theory of mind and matter. Rather, there seem to be a lot of different competing interpretations of existing empirical evidence, allowing for a wide range of speculations about the possible ontological framework implied. Evidently, the epistemological question of how our mind may come to reliable knowledge about an outer physical world eminently depends on a clear definition of mind and matter, and the precise way the two relate to each other. This circular relation between the epistemological predicaments of representationalism and the lack of a coherent ontological model of mind and matter is what I will call the "hard problem of modern science". Moreover, the underlying metaphysical dichotomy between mind and matter, subject and object, human and nature, is also intrinsically related to the modern/colonial Great Divide between Us and the Other.[27] It follows, that scientific universalism can be understood as the tip of a giant iceberg of a much more fundamental "hard problem" of modern/colonial science. And due to its circular nature, it is difficult to see how modern science should decolonise itself by means of its own (colonial) categories. Thus, if we really want to advance science and make it fit for the challenges of maintaining our planet as a habitable place for our species, we are in urgent need of a common ground of understanding that allows us to think together with the Other, that is, a new kind of thinking in between.

The question is, thus, how do we break this vicious cycle of a notoriously self-referential scientific discourse? If, as I just said, scientific discourse is being "protected" from outside influence by scientific universalism, and if scientific universalism is ultimately hinging on the presumption of an a priori incommensurability between the fundamental natural principles suggested by scientific evidence and the principles entailed in Other cosmologies, then we should assume any proof to the contrary as an *in principle* possibility of a meaningful dialogue with Other kinds of knowledge. In other words, if it could be shown that one or more of the ontological models currently being discussed in terms of possible interpretations of quantum physics and/or those being discussed by philosophers and neuroscientists as possible explanations of consciousness are, at least in part, commensurable with at least one Other, subalternised cosmology, then universalism would fall. For even though there may be other examples of Other forms of knowledge that, in fact, may turn out to be completely incommensurable, this would have to be proven for every single case. That means, the burden of proof would be shifted from the Others to Our side of the table. Hence, subalternised kinds of knowledge could not be dismissed as "unscientific" simply for being a priori incommensurable, and thus, incoherent with scientific evidence. This train of thought is precisely what motivated the present work.

The main objective of the present enquiry is to explore the possibility of a pluriversal dialogue between modern science and Other, marginalised ways of knowing as a necessary precondition for decolonising Science. This demands a tentative

[27] Latour (1993).

comparison of ontological models from academic discourse with at least one example of those Other, subalternised kinds of knowledge. It goes without saying that there is no prototypical "Other" in terms of an essential category; rather there are religious, cultural, and ethnic groups of people that have been socially categorised, in the course of a colonial history and in the context of rising nation states, as representing the "underdeveloped" Other which is the necessary opposite of the "developed" modern self, and whose knowledge has been stigmatised as "primitive thought". Hence, if taking a real existing social group as an example of "the Other", this neither means these Others are not as modern as We are, nor that they necessarily share more similarities with other subalternised groups than they share with Us. Other kinds of knowledge differ from the hegemonic knowledge of our modern/colonial science primarily in respect to the subaltern position of their corresponding thought collective within global modern/colonial social structures, and in their resemblance to certain cosmological patterns that have been stigmatised as epitomes of 'primitive thought', such as 'magical' practices and beliefs in 'supernatural' powers and entities like 'spirits' and other enchanted beings. So, in principle, any subalternised group whose "traditional" knowledge displays such "supernatural" features should adequately qualify as a sufficient sample of the excluded "Other".

For various reasons, I opted to work with the Potiguara, who will play the role of the "Other" in the course of my investigations. Living in Paraiba for several years, I became friendly with some Potiguara. It was then that I came to realise that it could be very promising to work together with the Potiguara on my research project. The Potiguara are an Indigenous[28] group of about 25,000 individuals most of them living at the North-Eastern coast of Brazil, more precisely, in the North coast region of Paraiba state.[29] They are one of the biggest indigenous groups in Brazil and were amongst the first to be affected by European invasion as early as in 1501. As a consequence, they learned to live at the border, in-between the cultural and social lines that divide Us from Them. Not surprisingly, the Potiguara lost the use of their native language, Tupi—today speaking Portuguese as their mother tongue—and adopted a lifestyle quite similar to neighbouring non-indigenous rural communities. However, there are still many Potiguara who hold on to specific ancestral cultural practices and continue to live in an enchanted world full of mythological, spiritual beings, while at the same time practicing the Christian faith, going to school, and more recently, to university. This offered a very promising situation for this study for two reasons:

[28] The term "*indigenous*" has been widely criticized due to its historical and instrumental links to colonialism and the othering of the "primitive" Rest against the "modern" West (e.g., Chakrabarty 2007; Dussel 2013; Ingold 2000; Latour 1993; Mignolo 2000; Tanasescu 2022, among others). Despite these critiques, many marginalized communities still identify as *Indigenous* in order to reclaim their ethnic identities, ancestral heritage, cultural autonomy, epistemic justice, and land rights. I will use the term *Indigenous* (capital I) as a contested social category, acknowledging its complexities but for readability, without explicitly marking it in quotation marks.

[29] Tebet et al. (2023).

Firstly, the Potiguara do not fit the essentialist imagery of the "pre-modern" Other, which is constitutive to the othering of the subaltern, and ultimately for the whole system of modernity/coloniality. Although insisting on their ancestral, Indigenous identity, the Potiguara recalcitrantly refuse to adjust to racist and primitivist stereotypes of otherness. They constantly live "in between", are Them and Us at the same time—as are their world view, their habits, their cultural practices, their language, their belief-system, their physiognomy. This means that what can be extracted from their oral knowledge as some kind of ancestral[30] Potiguara knowledge is not fundamentally different to what one may find among other rural communities in Brazil, but still fundamentally different compared to the hegemonic world view of modern/colonial science. This observation, in a way, shifts the line between Them and Us from ethnic differences and identity politics to the *colonial difference*[31] between hegemonic modern/colonial scientific knowledge and subalternised, othered knowledge.

Secondly, the fact that many Potiguara entered university and became academics while at the same time being Indigenous activists and practitioners of what they consider their ancestral Potiguara culture, opened up the possibility to form a group of *organic border-intellectuals*[32] with a particular interest in, and skills for engaging in a collaborative research project.

In 2015, we founded the *Coletivo de Pesquisa pelos Saberes Potiguara* (Research Collective for Potiguara Knowledge), a group of about a dozen Potiguara activists, academics, and "traditional" authorities, assisted by several professors from neighbouring Federal Universities (UFPB/UFCG) serving as academic facilitators and mentors. During 3 years of participatory action research together with the Potiguara (2015–2018) the group published several papers, participated in academic events, organised annual seminars, founded a community library, and carried out ethnographic field research resulting in two schoolbooks, one on ancestral Potiguara cosmology and another on healing practices.[33] I then distilled these research results into a kind of "Potiguara ontology": a set of fundamental ontic categories with particular properties as entailed in the Potiguara's cosmopracticesl conceptions reported by the Potiguara.

Given this set of defined ontological categories and principles, it should be possible to compare their properties with those suggested by ontological models currently being discussed in modern/colonial academic discourse on the nature of mind and matter.

---

[30] The Potiguara themselves use the term "ancestral" to refer to their "own" knowledge, since they received it from their ancestors, not only through oral tradition, but also in dreams and mediumistic experiences.

[31] Mignolo (2002).

[32] Rappaport (2005) applies Gramsci's concept of organic intellectuals (Gramsci 1982) to indigenous activists who are living and acting at the border in-between dominant society and their own culture.

[33] Batista et al. (2021a, b).

As mentioned before, there are currently several different interpretations of quantum physics in the running, all of them more or less equally coherent with existing scientific evidence, and all of them equally facing their own conceptual problems. Likewise, there is still no agreed solution to the hard problem of consciousness, but rather different competing proposals for a coherent naturalist theory of mind. Moreover, it appears that quantum physics might contribute to a solution to the mind-body problem, since some ontological interpretations suggest a fundamental role of mind-like properties in the overall structure of the universe. Hence, there might be the germ of a coherent scientific theory of mind and matter at the intersection between quantum physics and philosophy of mind. It is this promising intersection and its focus on the mind-body problem that I shall explore and which shall serve as a sample of the most recent ontological models in academic discourse.

Of course, each theoretical approach comes with a set of (more or less) well defined ontic principles and corresponding properties that can be compared with those implied in the Potiguara's cosmopractices. If two ontological concepts share comparable properties, they may refer to the same ontic referent, that is, the two concepts may actually refer to the same sort of "thing". Hence, commensurability is given and a dialogue between the two is possible, even if the two respective cosmological frameworks attribute different meanings to such a shared ontic category. And since the ontology of mind and matter is also at the core of the epistemological pitfalls of modern science and philosophy, the attribution of alternative meanings may help Us see Our problems from a different perspective, and thus, discover new, formerly hidden aspects. In other words, a possible commensurability comes with the hope of genuinely new knowledge and new solutions for Our own problems.

I divided the text into three parts. Part I offers an analysis of scientific universalism in its different philosophical and social dimensions. While Chap. 2 provides a short introduction to the historical origins of scientific universalism, Chap. 3 discusses the epistemological, and ultimately metaphysical constitution of modern science and its universal truth claim. An analysis of the particular metaphysical presumptions that are responsible for the a priori exclusion of Other kinds of knowledge shows that most, if not all of them are either untenable or at least questionable, and thus, represent a scientistic creed rather than science proper. Since foundationalist epistemology leads into the *cul-de-sac* of relativism, I will particularly explore the pragmatic approaches of William van Orman Quine, William James, and Charles Sanders Peirce. Chap. 4 focusses on the social and ultimately geopolitical dimension of scientific universalism. It basically gives a short historical overview of the sociology of science and related research programmes like the history of science, science studies, and feminist, post- and decolonial studies. In sum, the whole debate quite unanimously shows a deep, and in fact, intrinsic link between the rise of modern science, colonialism, and capitalism, on the one hand, and the social construction of scientific knowledge, on the other. Furthermore, feminist, post- and decolonial studies from the global South emphasise the historical role of modern science as a means to stigmatise, subalternise, oppress, and exploit both nature and a major part of humanity from the peripheries, while sustaining the wealth and the hegemony of a white, male, bourgeoise, European descent elite at the global centres. The fifth and last chapter of Part I follows the changing anthropological gaze on the Others and their knowledge. Being an heir of the stigmatised image of the Other as either a noble or a barbarian savage, anthropology had a hard time to transcend this magic mirror of Eurocentrism and start seeing other cultures in their own right, and not just as the grimace of Our own desires and fears. While anthropologists soon began to emphasise the essentially rational and almost, but still not quite, scientific character of Other kinds of knowledge, it took a long while until anthropologists stopped asking why They are so different, and instead started to question what makes Us think We are "modern"? Bruno Latour, for example, analysed how We externalise the Great inner Divide between Us and nature, Our minds and Our bodies, which we carry in Our "modern" chests, and project onto the external Great Divide between Us and the Other.[34] More recent approaches envisage Other, "animist", "perspectivist" or "relational" worldviews as philosophical approaches with their own epistemological and ontological foundations. Anthropologists like Nurit Bird-David,[35] Bruno Latour,[36] and Eduardo Viveiros de Castro[37] not only hold that Other ways of knowing might not only be as "true" as Our scientific knowledge, but also entail some important news about Us. Following Eduardo Viveiros de Castro's turn towards ontology and Isabelle Stengers'[38] cosmopolitical proposal, authors like Marisol de la Cadena,[39] Mario Blazer[40] and Arturo Escobar[41] have been emphasising the political dimension of ontological diversion. Their call for a "cosmopolitical", "pluriversal" dialogue between different onto-epistemo-ethical practices or "worldings" reverberates Sandra Harding's[42] proposal of a standpoint epistemology-based "world of sciences" and Boaventura de Sousa Santos'[43] vision of an "ecology of knowledges" based on practices and "epistemologies of the South".

Part II is kind of an ethnographic research report. In Chap. 6, I discuss the methodological reasons for my option to realise a *participatory action research* (PAR) in line with Latin American intellectual activists Paulo Freire and Orlando Fals Borda.[44] It follows Chap. 7 with a short account of 3 years of action research together with the Potiguara and the results we yielded. Chap. 8 provides a brief ethnohistorical account of the Potiguara and their socio-cultural condition. Chapter 9 provides a detailed account of the Potiguara's "traditional" cosmovision

[34] Latour (1993).

[35] Bird-David (1999).

[36] Latour (1993).

[37] Castro (1996, 2004a, b, 2015).

[38] Stengers (2005, 2010, 2011, 2018a, b).

[39] Cadena (2010, 2015, 2019); Cadena and Blaser (2018).

[40] Blaser (2013, 2018).

[41] Escobar (2020).

[42] Harding (2015).

[43] Santos (2007, 2018).

[44] Borda (1981); Freire (1987, 1996)

and practice, their rituals, and their concepts of health and sickness. After more than 500 years of oppression and genocide, many Potiguara still live in an enchanted world, a nature representing God Tupã's emanation, populated by Ancestors and all kinds of other mythical beings. Health, disease, and cure all depend on immaterial principles related to plants and enchanted beings evoked by means of rituals. The tenth and last chapter of Part II presents a set of ontic principles and their particular properties entailed in Potiguara cosmovision and practices.

Part III gives a short account of the *hard problem of science*. Chapter 11 refers to the hard problem of consciousness, as discussed by David Chalmers,[45] and its peculiar difficulties. Chapter 12 provides a very short introduction into quantum physics and some of its most prominent ontological interpretations. Interestingly, many of the very founders of quantum physics soon began to associate their revolutionary findings in fundamental physics with the mind-body problem. Physicists like Bohr, Heisenberg, Pauli, and Bohm speculated that the wave-particle dualism displayed by quanta might be at the very basis of the mind-body dualism of our every-day experience. Recent investigations by Nikolaus von Stillfried[46] suggest that a modified interpretation of Bohmian quantum physics might pave the way to a unified naturalist theory of mind and matter. Based on these assumptions, Chap. 13 explores possible quantum physical interpretations of Potiguara ontology, as well as hypothetical Potiguara interpretations of Bohmian quantum physics. The overall results of these speculative comparisons between Potiguara ontology and recent academic ontologies strongly suggest a possible commensurability between certain ontological interpretations of quantum physics and Potiguara cosmopractices. Moreover, a Potiguara view on quantum physics might provide a fresh look at old problems, unveiling new perspectives, and possibly even new solutions to old and painfully tenacious problems.

If nothing else, this work creates a dialogue between several academic discourses concerning different aspects of scientific universalism, ranging from philosophy, history and sociology of science, feminist and decolonial studies, to anthropology, philosophy of mind, and quantum physics. Of course, due to the transdisciplinary character of the present study, I cannot dive as deep into each of these different and vast discursive fields as specialists would within their own individual fields. My hope is, however, that this inevitable lack of detail will be compensated by the advantages of providing a comprehensive introduction for non-specialists and an integrated consideration of these different fields. The resulting broad picture of modern/colonial sciences' "hard problem" delineates scientific universalism as a major obstacle on the way towards a decolonial, pluriversal science capable of tackling the challenges of our "catastrophic times".

And of course, I seek to provide a strong argument against universalism and the underlying a priori assumption of incommensurability it embodies, and in support of scientific practices that are based on an equitable, co-creative dialogue with Other

[45] Chalmers (1995, 2002, 2010, 2016a, b).

[46] von Stillfried (2018).

forms of knowing. My hope is that this piece will motivate further research and action in this direction.

References

Aronowitz S (1988) Science as power: discourse and ideology in modern society. University of Minnesota Press, Minneapolis

Batista MNF, Conceição FMd, Pereira PE (2021a) Cosmologia e Espiritualidade Potiguara. Sociedade Brasileira de Ecologia Humana—SABEH, Paulo Afonso, BA

Batista MNF, Conceição FMd, Pereira PE (2021b) Medicina Tradicional Potiguara. Sociedade Brasileira de Ecologia Humana—SABEH, Paulo Afonso, BA

Behr H, Shani G (2021) Rethinking emancipation in *a* critical IR: normativity, cosmology, and pluriversal dialogue. Millennium 49:368–391. https://doi.org/10.1177/03058298211031983

Bird-David N (1999) "Animism" revisited: personhood, environment, and relational epistemology. Curr Anthropol 40(Special issue Culture—a second chance?):67–91

Blaser M (2013) Notes towards a political ontology of "environmental" conflicts. In: Green L (ed) Contested ecologies: dialogues in the south on nature and knowledge. HSRC, Cape Town, pp 13–27

Blaser M (2018) ¿Es otra cosmopolítica posible? Anthropologica 36:115–144. https://doi.org/10.18800/anthropologica.201802.005

Bohm DJ (1980) Wholeness and the implicate order. Routledge & Kegan Paul, London

Bohm DJ (1990) A new theory of the relationship of mind and matter. Philos Psychol 3:271–286

Borda OF (1981) Aspectos teóricos da pesquisa participante: considerações sobre o significado e o papel da ciência na participação popular. In: Brandão CR (ed) Pesquisa participante. Brasiliense, São Paulo, pp 42–62

Cadena Mdl (2010) Indigenous cosmopolitics in the Andes: conceptual reflections beyond "politics". Cult Anthropol 25:334–370

Cadena Mdl (2015) Earth beings: ecologies of practice across Andean worlds. Duke University Press, Durham

Cadena Mdl (2019) An invitation to live together: making the "complex we". Environ Humanit 11:477–484

Cadena M, Blaser M (eds) (2018) A world of many worlds. Duke University Press, Durham

Castro EVd (1996) Os pronomes cosmológicos e o perspectivismo ameríndio. Mana 2:115–144

Castro EVd (2004a) Perspectival anthropology and the method of controlled equivocation. Tipití J Soc Anthropol Lowland South Am 2(1), Article 1

Castro EVd (2004b) Perspectivismo e multinaturalismo na América indígena. O que nos faz pensar 018:225–254

Castro EVd (2015) Metafisicas Canibais: Elementos para uma Antropologia Pós-Estrutural. Cosac & Naify, São Paulo

Castro EVd (2022) O medo dos outros. Concinnitas 23:28–52. https://doi.org/10.12957/concinnitas.2022.67434

Cesarino PDN (2006) De duplos e estereoscópios: paralelismo e personificação nos cantos xamanísticos ameríndios. Mana 12:105–134. https://doi.org/10.1590/S0104-93132006000100004

Chakrabarty D (2007) Provincializing Europe Postcolonial Thought and Historical Difference. Princeton: Princeton University Press

Chalmers DJ (1995) The conscious mind: in search of a theory of conscious experience. Department of Philosophy, University of California, Santa Cruz

Chalmers DJ (2002) Consciousness and its place in nature. In: Philosophy of mind: classical and contemporary readings. Oxford University Press, Oxford

Chalmers DJ (2010) The character of consciousness. Oxford University Press, Oxford
Chalmers DJ (2016a) The combination problem for panpsychism. In: Brüntrup G, Jaskolla L (eds) Panpsychism: contemporary perspectives. Oxford University Press, Oxford, pp 179–214
Chalmers DJ (2016b) Panpsychism and panprotopsychism. In: Bruntrup G, Jaskolla L (eds) Panpsychism. Oxford University Press, New York, pp 19–47
Collingwood RG (1998) An essay on metaphysics, revised. Clarendon, Oxford
Dunford R (2017) Toward a decolonial global ethics. J Global Ethics 13:380–397. https://doi.org/10.1080/17449626.2017.1373140
Dussel E (2000) Europa, modernidad y eurocentrismo. In: Lander E (ed) La colonialidad del saber: eurocentrismo y ciencias sociales—Perspectivas latinoamericanas. CLASCO, Buenos Aires, pp 41–54
Dussel E (2009) Meditações Anti-Cartesianas sobre a Origem do Anti-Discurso Filosófico da Modernidade. In: Santos BdS, Meneses MP (eds) Epistemologias do Sul. Coimbra, pp 283–336
Dussel E (2013) 'Europa, Modernidad y Eurocentrismo'. Revista de Cultura Teológica. ISSN (impresso) 0104-0529 (eletrônico) 2317-4307, no. 4 (March), 69. https://doi.org/10.19176/rct.v0i4.14105
Einstein A, Born M (2005) Alber Einstein Max Born, Briefwechsel 1916-1955. Nymphenburger Verlagshandlung, Munich
Escobar A (2000) Ciencias sociales: saberes coloniales y eurocéntricos. In: Lander E (ed) La colonialidad del saber: eurocentrismo y ciencias sociales—Perspectivas latinoamericanas. CLACSO, Buenos Aires, pp 11–40
Escobar A (2020) Pluriversal politics: the real and the possible. Duke University Press, Durham
Everett H (1957) "Relative state" formulation of quantum mechanics. Rev Mod Phys 29:454–462
Fitzgerald G (2021) Pluriversal peacebuilding: peace beyond epistemic and ontological violence. International Relations
Fleck L (1983) Zur Krise der Wirklichkeit. In: Schäfer L, Schnelle T (eds) Erfahrung und Tatsache. Gesammelte Aufsätze. Suhrkamp, Frankfurt a.M, pp 48–88
Freire P (1987) Pedagogia do Oprimido. Paz e Terra, Rio de Janeiro
Freire P (1996) Pedagogia da Autonomia. Saberes necessários à prática educativa. Pas e Terra, São Paulo
Friebe C (2015) Messproblem, Minimal- und Kollapsinterpretationen. In: Friebe C et al (eds) Philosophie der Quantenphysik. Springer, Berlin, pp 45–78
Gramsci A (1982) Os Intelectuais e a Organização da Cultura. Civilização Brasileira, Rio de Janeiro
Harding S (1994) Is science multicultural?: challenges, resources, opportunities, uncertainties. Configurations 2:301–330. https://doi.org/10.1353/con.1994.0019
Harding S (2015) Objectivity and diversity: another logic of scientific research. University of Chicago Press, Chicago
Hutchings K (2019) Decolonizing global ethics: thinking with the pluriverse. Ethics Int Aff 33:115–125. https://doi.org/10.1017/S0892679419000169
Ingold T (2000) The perception of the environment: essays on livelyhood, dwelling and skill. Routledge, NY/London
James W (1981) Pragmatism: a new name for some old ways of thinking. Hackett
Lander E (ed) (2000) La colonialidad del saber: eurocentrismo y ciencias sociales—Perspectivas latinoamericanas. CLACSO, Buenos Aires
Latour B (1993) We have never been modern. Harvard University Press, Cambridge
Latour B (2001) A Esperança de Pandora: Ensaios sobre a Realidade dos Estudos Cinetificos. Edusc, Bauru
Linhart J et al (2025) Reflecting on pluriversal dialogues on environmental ethics: decolonising scientific practice to build futures beyond 'development'. Conference proceedings & Publications, Social Solidarity Economy & The Commons International Conference ISCTE University of Lisbon 2024 Edition | 13th–15th November

Maldonado-Torres N (2007) On the coloniality of being: contributions to the development of a concept. Cult Stud 21:240–270. https://doi.org/10.1080/09502380601162548
Mannheim K (1954) Ideology and utopia: an introduction to the sociology of knowledge. Routledge & Kegan Paul, New York
Maxwell N (2017) In praise of natural philosophy: a revolution for thought and life. Kindle edition. McGill-Queen's University Press, Quebec
Maxwell N (2021) The world crisis — and what to do about it: a revolution for thought and action. Kindle edition. University College, London, UK
Mignolo WD (2000) Local histories - global designs: coloniality, subaltern knowledges, and border thinking. In: Princeton studies in culture, power, history. Princeton University Press, Princeton, NJ
Mignolo WD (2002) The geopolitics of knowledge and the colonial difference. S Atl Q 101:57–96. https://doi.org/10.1215/00382876-101-1-57
Mignolo WD (2011) The darker side of western modernity—global futures, decolonial options. Duke University Press, Durham
Mignolo W (2013) Geopolitics of sensing and knowing: On (de)coloniality, border thinking, and epistemic disobedience. Confero 1:129–150
Mignolo W (2021) The politics of decolonial investigations. Duke University Press, Durham
Mignolo W, Ennis M (2001) Coloniality at large: the Western Hemisphere in the colonial horizon of modernity. CR New Centen Rev 1:19–54. https://doi.org/10.1353/ncr.2003.0057
Mignolo W, Walsh CE (2018) On decoloniality: concepts, analytics, praxis. Duke University Press, Durham
Peirce CS (1878) How to make our ideas clear. Pop Sci Mon 12:286–302
Penrose R (1996) On gravity's role in quantum state reduction. Gen Relativ Gravit 28:581–600
Querejazu A (2016) Encountering the pluriverse: looking for alternatives in other worlds. Rev Bras Polít Int 59. https://doi.org/10.1590/0034-7329201600207
Quijano A (1992) Colonialidad y modernidad/racionalidad. Peru Indígena 13(29):11–20
Quijano A (2000) Coloniality of power, eurocentrism, and Latin America. Nepantla 1(3):533–580
Quijano A (2009) Cononialidade do Poder e Classificação Social. In: Santos BdS, Meneses MP (eds) Epistemologias do Sul. Coimbra, pp 73–118
Quine WvO (1951) Two dogmas of empiricism. Philos Rev 60:20–43
Rappaport J (2005) Intercultural utopias: public intellectuals, cultural experimentations, and ethnic pluralism in Colombia. Duke University Press, Durham
Santos BdS (2007) Para além do pensamento abissal: das linhas globais a uma ecologia de saberes. Novos estud CEBRAP 71–94. https://doi.org/10.1590/S0101-33002007000300004
Santos BdS (2009a) Um discurso sobre as ciências, 6th edn. Cortez, São Paulo
Santos BdS (2009b) Um Ocidente Não-Ocidentalista?: A Filosofia à venda, a douta ignorânçia e a aposta de Pascal. In: Santos BdS, Meneses MP (eds) Epistemologias do Sul. Coimbra, pp 445–486
Santos BdS (2018) The end of the cognitive empire: the coming of age of epistemologies of the South. Duke University Press, Durham
Stengers I (2005) The cosmopolitical proposal. In: Latur B, Weibel P (eds) Making things public. Atmospheres of democracy. MIT Press, Cambridge
Stengers I (2010) Cosmopolitics I. University of Minnesota Press, Minneapolis
Stengers I (2011) Cosmopolitics II. University of Minnesota Press, Minneapolis
Stengers I (2015) In catastrophic times: resisting the coming barbarism. Open Humanities, London
Stengers I (2018a) Another science is possible—a manifesto for slow science, Kindle-version. Polity Press, Cambridge
Stengers I (2018b) The challenge of ontological politics. In: Cadena Mdl, Blaser M (eds) A world of many worlds. Duke University Press, Durham, pp 195–260
Tanasescu M (2022) Ecocene politics. Open Book Publishers, Cambridge, UK

Tebet SN, Pereira CA, Stenner C, Cotovio CRP (2023) Censo Demográfico 2022 Indígenas Primeiros resultados do universo. Instituto Brasileiro de Geografia e Estatística—IBGE, Rio de Janeiro
von Stillfried N (2018) Vom Innen der Dinge: Das "Bewusstsein-Körper-Problem" und die "Welle-Teilchen-Dualität": Interdisziplinäre Impulse zwischen Quantentheorie und analytischer Philosophie des Geistes. Habilitation thesis, University of Trier
Wallerstein I (2004) World-system analysis: An introduction. Duke University Press, London
Wallerstein I (2006) European universalism: the rhetoric of power. New Press, New York

Part I
Scientific Universalism

Chapter 2
What Is Scientific Universalism?

Thou shalt have no other gods before Me.

Generally speaking, *scientific universalism* refers to the assumption that modern science is a universal system of knowledge; a system that is, *in principle*, able to generate true (or at least valid) propositions about every aspect of the universe. For such a universal knowledge to be possible one has to assume the existence of universal principles that govern the whole universe throughout time and space, and that modern science has developed the method to figure out those universal principles. In other words, scientific universalism holds that the scientific method is the only way to come to reliable, objective, and hence, *legitimate* knowledge about the world we live in.

The problem with universalism is that if science is the *only* way to produce reliable knowledge, automatically all other kinds of knowledge are said to produce false, illusive assumptions about reality. This is a very strong position, and of course, cannot be defended easily—actually, it might be virtually impossible to hold this assumption (and also unnecessary, as I will try to show later in this work).

While modern science is frequently perceived as representing a particularly European worldview,[1] its universalist pretensions are justified by its success in predicting and controlling physical events. However, historically, early European scientists built heavily on Chinese and Arabian knowledge,[2] and modern science has been imposed all over the world in the context of colonialism and globalisation, forcing other nations to accept it as the only officially legitimate form of knowledge.[3] However, scientific universalism justifies a truth monopoly, which has been instrumental to European cultural, political and economic predominance. This is why the concept of scientific universalism is at the very core of questions

[1] Zilsel (1942); Wallerstein (2006); Miettinen (2009); et al.

[2] E.g. gunpowder, fire-arms and the compass from China, algebra, Indian numbers and the experimental method from Arabian scholars, to name just a few examples (Needham 1993, 2006; Harding 1994).

[3] E.g. Feyerabend (1993); Castro-Gomes (2000); Lander (2000); Escobar (2003); Wallerstein (2004, 2006); Mignolo (2005); Quijano (2009); Santos (2009); Kuhn and Yazawa (2013); et al.

J. Linhart, *Science and the Other*, Schriften zu Leben und Gesellschaft - Series on Life and Society 2, https://doi.org/10.1007/978-3-032-03927-9_2

concerning the essence and legitimacy of modern science as well as the role it plays in the world we live in, especially how it regulates relations between *Us* and the *Others*.

In this first part I will sketch out what seem to me the most relevant aspects of scientific universalism concerning its legitimacy and its influence on relations between modern science and other kinds of knowledge. Of course, here I will only be able to give a brief account of the manifold discourses that have gathered around those questions during the last few hundred years. My main aim here is merely to expose the problem that gave birth to this research project.

* * *

The term *scientific universalism* has some quite ambivalent connotations, both positive and negative. For many, or maybe even most scientists, scientific universalism represents either an ideal or an inevitable reality, or both. This kind of feeling found one of its most famous expressions in Robert K. Merton's writings on the ethos of science. In his 1942 paper *The Normative Structure of Science* he proposed four principles[4] that would characterise scientific practice and distinguish scientific from non-scientific knowledge. The first and probably most fundamental of these Mertonian principles is *universalism*. Following this principle, the acceptance or rejection of a scientific truth claim should not depend on any social attribute of its author(s), such as race, nationality, religion or class, but should be evaluated solely based on objective scientific standards. Merton boiled his claim down to the phrase: "Objectivity precludes particularism".

While the Mertonian principles both describe and prescribe the ethos of science, they also follow from the methodological rationale of science, like the norm of empirical evidence or logical consistency, constituting the fundament of modern science as the only universal knowledge, applicable everywhere, regardless of local context or culture. Consequently, Merton proclaimed that universalism would be incompatible with any kind of ethnocentric particularism.

Of course, Merton's scientific ethos and its principles recall the ideals of Enlightenment, rationalism and humanism which gave birth to modern science. It follows the humanist view that all people, independent of class or origin, are equal in reasoning based on universal logical principles. The main aim of the founding fathers of modern science, such as Francis Bacon, René Descartes and Isaac Newton, was to create a new universal science based on a simple method available to everybody, not only to aristocratic and clergy specialists; they hoped to free people from hard labour by means of technical developments based on scientific research and mathematic calculus[5]; they aspired to uncover a new universal knowledge that

[4] (1) Universalism (see above), (2) Communism (collaboration and shared scientific findings), (3) Disinterestedness (altruism concerned with the benefit of humanity and scientific progress), (4) Organised Scepticism (objective analysis and resistance to dogmas of state, religion or economic groups).

[5] Grossmann (2009a, b).

would not only break with the unquestionable dogmas of the Catholic Church, but also transcend politics, religion and culture, a knowledge based on shared practices and international collaboration, free access to scientific findings through journals, finally founding a global community sharing the same ideals.[6] The idea of the *Republic of Letters* in the early modern period joined men of science under a shared ideal of fair, open and collaborative action, transcending religious and national boundaries, even during wartime.[7]

However, after the French revolution, in the context of the Napoleonic wars and the rise of nation states, scientific progress became related to national prestige and military victory. During the nineteenth century this association of science with national pride and culture became dominant, especially in Germany where many scientists actively fought for the country's reunification and nationalist feelings had become mainstream even in academic circles. Scientific success was now attributed to the greatness of the nation its authors belonged to. As a consequence, scientific progress was increasingly perceived as a kind of "Olympic"[8] competition between nations and the cosmopolitan community of letters developed into an international scientific community of national associations. The first World War contributed to a rapid decline of the principles of fair play and science was quickly confused with politics.[9] With the rise of Nazi-totalitarianism in Germany, science would be radically nationalised and reframed to represent Aryan racial superiority. Furthermore, the Nazi-regime kept its scientific work secret and began to exile and persecute Jewish scientists. In Britain, influential leftist scientists reacted to the Nazi-German Aryan chauvinism by promoting scientific internationalism during the 1930s, militating against any kind of nationalism in science. Merton's principle of scientific universalism was formulated in this context of World War II and as a reaction to the violation of the core values of modern science committed by Nazi-Germany.[10] Universalism, in this sense, followed the internationalist, and ultimately humanist, ideals of science as a universal enterprise of all humankind aiming to enhance consciousness and conditions of life all over the globe.

However, after World War II internationalism (being related to socialism) was widely abandoned by western academics and universalism began to serve as a paradigm to foster international scientific collaboration under US leadership.[11] The world was invited to engage in the universal endeavour of modern science. But in practice this meant that other cultures, especially those from the so-called Third World, should adopt modern science as their new dominant knowledge without having a real chance to introduce their own epistemological and ontological concepts

---

[6] Whitehead (1925); Whitesides (2019).

[7] Somsen (2008); Whitesides (2019).

[8] Idem.

[9] This became highly visible with German scientists' manifesto "An die Kulturwelt" and the subsequent exclusion of German scientists from international scientific associations and events (idem).

[10] Whitesides (2019).

[11] Kuhn and Vessuri (2016).

and engage in a meta-scientific debate concerning science's paradigmatic framework. On the contrary, those other epistemologies, ontologies, cosmologies and kinds of knowledge were excluded for being "unscientific", since they do not fit the norms of scientific ethos and methodology. Scientific universalism, therefore, has been criticised for being instrumental to the promotion and justification of "Western" or "European" domination, globalisation and World Capitalism.[12]

> Universalism sustains a reckless drive for power, for the domination of other men and other civilisations, driven by the belief of its own righteousness, and its universalist pretensions (Segesvary 2004).

Subsequent sociological studies on scientific practice showed that universalism and scientific ethos as proclaimed by Merton are not sufficient criteria to distinguish science from other kinds of knowledge. Research results not only pointed to the fact, that similar principles could be found in other systems of knowledge, too, but that it was also doubtful to which extent those principles were really put in practice in modern science itself.[13] Another criticism was, that since the Mertonian principles themselves represent genuine "European" or "Western" concepts and therefore are ethnocentric, too, they thus violate their very own principle of universalism.

Interestingly, Merton[14] himself famously demonstrated that modern science arose in the cultural climate of seventeenth century reformation and benefited from shared values of Protestant ethics in a way similar as suggested by Max Weber[15] for early capitalism. In other words, the development of modern science was a result of specific social conditions, it was a child of historical processes deeply embedded in the European culture, philosophy, religion, economy and social structure.[16]

> The universal science view--that modern sciences are uniquely successful exactly because they have eliminated cultural fingerprints from their results of research--incorporates some assumptions that are probably false, [...] (Harding 1994: 304).

There is actually not much reason to believe that modern science represents some kind of culturally, or ideologically "neutral", and thus "universal" knowledge. On the contrary, there are many reasons to understand it as a genuine European, colonial or modern phenomenon. For example, Merton himself showed that the emergence of modern science was not only related to Protestantism, but also to economic and political interests of colonialism and early capitalism.[17] The

---

[12] Harding (1994); Segesvary (2004); Wallerstein (2004); Kuhn and Yazawa (2013); et al.

[13] Zuckermann (1988); Cole (1995); Shapin (1995).

[14] Merton (1968).

[15] Weber (2006).

[16] "Thus while science is said to need a supportive social climate in order to flourish, the particular form of that climate is claimed to leave no distinctive cultural fingerprints on science's results of research" (Harding 1994: 308).

[17] See Merton (1968) concerning research and funding of the Royal Society and its relations to technological problems of navigation, transport and warfare.

expansionist project of the new dominant class of merchants as well as the British Empire needed better navigation instruments, bigger ships that could be built quickly and new weapons. Therefore, they invested in scientific research to enhance their technological resources.[18] Modern science both drew a new worldview and provided the necessary technologies to spread it over the world. Science would become essential for the success of colonialism, global capitalism, and ultimately for the establishment of bourgeois hegemony, with the democratic nation state as its new political order. It was this European expansionist project that both financed scientific progress and brought modern science to its new colonies. From this point of view, modern science became "universal" by being forcefully imposed on other cultures, violently eliminating all "traditional" forms of knowledge—in Europe as much as in its colonies.[19] We are told that, despite all existing doubts concerning its epistemological superiority, modern science proved to be superior due to its success in predicting, controlling and manipulating the physical world. But in fact, modern science's apparent success as a kind of knowledge that works better than other kinds of knowledge results from its focus on projects that benefited European expansion and consequently eliminated other rival kinds of knowing. The problems and aspects of nature modern science focuses on were determined by the needs of European expansion and techno-capitalist "progress"; other aspects remained largely untouched.

Moreover, the benefits of this success, as well as its negative impacts, are distributed over the globe in an extremely unequal manner. Modern science solved problems of transport, mining, production, and the exploitation of natural resources for the benefit of European upper and middle class and their descendants but was never concerned about accounting for the costs it has been generating for the majority of all those other people living in the global peripheries. While the dominant classes of people of European descent enjoy the benefits of science and technology, most of its environmental and social costs are left to the marginalised classes and world regions. Furthermore, the own, *emic* accounts of these marginalised classes and regions are invisibilised by scientific account as being "unscientific", thus eliminating any alternative view that might unveil science's intrinsic shortcomings and reveal alternatives beyond "progress".Universalism, from this perspective, appears to be a subtle ideological justification of European and/or capitalist expansion.[20] Moreover, universalism follows a tautological justification, based on a truth monopoly, which

[18] "European sciences advanced because they focused on describing and explaining those aspects of nature's regularities that permitted the upper classes of Europeans to multiply and thrive, especially through the prospering of their military, imperial, and otherwise expansionist projects. […] The British needed better navigation, so they built observatories, funded astronomers, and kept systematic records of their voyages. […] Thus European expansionism has changed the "topography" of global scientific knowledge, causing the advance of European sciences and the decline or underdevelopment of scientific traditions of other cultures" (Harding 1994: 314).

[19] Feyerabend (1993); Harding (1994, 2015); Castro-Gomes (2000); Dussel (2000); Lander (2000); Segesvary (2004); Kuhn and Yazawa (2013); Kuhn and Vessuri (2016); et al.

[20] Wallerstein (2006).

itself is justified by its self-declared universal validity and humanism, while at the same time concealing its function as a means to global expansion and rampant violation of fundamental human rights.[21]

2.1 The Ideological Foundations of Universalism

Although scientific universalism has long been criticised, it still dominates the image of science for a majority of scientists[22] as well as for the public at large. It is commonly accepted that modern science is the most efficient way of explaining and describing the world, in spite of all evidence to the contrary and epistemological doubts concerning the objectivity of the scientific method.[23] Why? What makes us believe in the absolute superiority of modern science compared to any other possible way of knowing?

The history of modern science is a very extensive issue and has been recounted in many different ways. In what follows, I would like to sketch out just a few of these narratives to shed some light on the manyfold historical aspects of universalism.

2.1.1 The Modern Project

To a certain extent, modern science can be understood as a core element within a whole civilisational project, the so-called *modernity*. As the (mainstream) story goes, modernity has its historical beginnings somewhere between the Renaissance and Enlightenment, when European intellectuals dreamed of a new *civitas* of rational men seeking truth based on logical reason, critical research and freedom of speech. Thomas More's *Utopia*, Campanella's *Civita Solis* and principally Francis Bacon's *New Atlantis,* a society governed by the scientists of the Salomon's House, exemplify the modern dream of a new golden age of reason, science and technology.

The roots of these utopian visions can be traced back some 2600 years to Greek philosophy, beginning with the Pre-Socratics, and later Plato, Aristotle and the Neoplatonists in late antiquity, all of whom established rational discourses on what the best foundations both of truth and society would be. It was this utopian project of a society based on the faith in rationality and objective truth that fascinated early humanists of fourteenth century Italy and which ultimately contributed to the emergence of the Renaissance and Enlightenment movements in subsequent centuries.[24]

---

[21] Kuhn and Vessuri (2016).

[22] Somsen (2008).

[23] See next chapter.

[24] Miettinen (2009).

Following this narrative, the European history of ideas would eventually give rise to modern science as a new, alternative way of knowledge production, but also to a new dominant world view and a new world order.

The modern subject was construed as an essentially rational being, with its rational mind, the *cogito,* naturally following the logical rules of the universe. The concept of the autonomous subject, which is at the very basis of rationalism, empiricism and objectivism, the idea of man as the single rational being capable of understanding the logical principles of the universe, is of course a special form of anthropocentrism. Along with its roots in Greek philosophers, such as Protagoras' famous dictum on "man as the measure of all things", religion may have played an important role in the formation of this notion, too. The rise of the Judaeo-Christian faith in God as the one creator of nature who made man in his own image was favourable for the modern notion of a universe ruled by logical laws, accessible to man's understanding and control[25] (while other cosmologies would not provide much space for such an idea).[26] Not only the mind was rational, but also the universe itself. Thus, rationality really became universal in a very deep sense.[27] And the newly-educated European upper class had found the key to the secrets of God's creation, the logic behind appearances, by cultivating their logical minds and overcoming the weakness of the flesh through discipline and reason.[28] Given that logical reason was a universal God-given human faculty, human history appeared as a progressive evolution of mankind's cognitive capacities, with European culture representing the peak of this evolutionary process. And Europe would bring reason and progress to all people and free them from barbarism and irrational superstition. To be "European" or "Western", therefore, was to be rational, educated, disciplined, in other words, civilised, while other cultures were considered not to have yet reached this evolutionary stage.[29]

---

[25] Early Christian gospels praised the denial of oneself and the respect for the anonymous other, emphasising the universal equality of humankind. However, the unification (Greek: *katholou* = in general) of the Catholic Church soon got an exclusive character, demarcating Catholicism against "heretic" and "orthodox" beliefs. Later, Protestantism promoted universal salvation against Catholic particularism. Christian universalism was essentially based on the assumption of a universal human faculty of reason, providing the most fundamental supposition of humanism and Enlightenment (compare also Miettinen 2009).

[26] Harding (1994); Segesvary (2004); Varela and Shear (2002).

[27] "However, the theological view of writing developed by Christianity and the epistemological view of knowledge provided by Socrates and Plato (where God is not only the archetype of the writer but also the archetype of wisdom), joined forces during the Middle Ages and extended to the Renaissance. Nature is the book God wrote, and to know nature is the best way to know God" (Mignolo 2005: 82). "The laws of nature could now be declared universal, precisely when a Christian God no longer could, and the law of nature (the cosmos) provided the basis for an idea of cosmopolitanism: the law of the cosmos discovered by Man displaced the law of the orbis regulated by God" (Mignolo 2021: 200). Compare also Mignolo 2000 and 2011.

[28] Böhme (1980).

[29] See also Hornbacher (2005).

However, to become truly instrumental for European expansion and for distinguishing *Us* from the *Others*, yet another element had to be universalised: physicalism.[30] Scientific cosmic universalism (or *scientism*) considers only the physical and psychological aspects as they are appropriate for applying empirical methods. The worst distortion of universalism extends scientific claims from the physical elements to the whole cosmos, and thus also to non-physical, mental, and spiritual aspects.[31] Modern science's physicalist image of nature resulted from a general shift from the European medieval view of nature as God's creation, representing the inscrutable mystery of God, to the modern view of a disenchanted[32] nature disposable to calculus, from feudalism to capitalism, from a religious to a worldly power.[33] There seems to be a link between the parallel shifts during early modern history in the concepts of man, nature, religion and political ideals. As a result of this shift, any "traditional" knowledge containing any kind of non-physical, non-causal, or so-called spiritual concepts is a priori false, and hence, has to be remedied by rational, scientific thought.[34] Therefore, our modern concept of being "civilised" not only entails being rational, but also being rational physicalists.

This string of narratives around the history of ideas may illustrate how scientific universalism developed as a fundamental ideological instrument for European expansion. It shows how *We* came to see ourselves as rational beings, and consequently the *Others* as irrational. Science represents the utopian essence of *Us*, as "western", "modern", "rational", "civilised" "citizens" in contrast to the *Others* who are "traditional", "savage", "irrational" or "uncivilised".[35] Hence, it is the duty of educated European men to colonise and "civilise" other people in order to help them to get on their way to progress. Scientific universalism, therefore, is fundamentally based on the assumption of the universality of reason and logic both as the essence of human mind and of the universe.

---

[30] Many authors rather speak of materialism in this context (e.g. Segesvary 2004; Harding 1994; Walach 2019; Whitehead 1925; et al.), however, for reasons I will explain in the next chapter, I prefer to refer to physicalism in this respect.

[31] "Western scientific universalism followed in the footsteps of the reductive conceptualization of physis elaborated by the Sophists who separated from it the moral and aesthetic domains; this imprint of Greek antiquity remained, then, embedded in Western scientific thought. For science, universalism means universalism of the functioning of materially existing things, of the physical universe, in accordance with the mechanical laws of nature demonstrated by scientific methods." (Segesvary 2004: 10). See also Voegelin's (1987) critique of scientism as a "gnostic movement" and instrument of "Westernization": "Scientism has remained to this day one of the strongest Gnostic movements in Western society; and the immanentist pride in science is so strong that even the special sciences have each left a distinguishable sediment in the variants of salvation through physics, economics, sociology, biology, and psychology" (ibidem: 127).

[32] Weber (1919).

[33] Harding (1994); compare also: Zilsel (1942); Linhart (2008); Walach (2019).

[34] "To gain would, for modern man, violate no moral or religious principles" (Harding 1994: 316).

[35] "Since the Enlightenment, science has been associated with modernity, and modernity with 'civilization', 'Christendom', and 'Europe'" (Somsen 2008: 374). See also Segesvary (2004); Böhme (1980); Harding (1994); et al.

2.1.2 The Scholastic Heritage

After World War II, western historians of science (like Koyré and Butterfield) abandoned socialist materialist views and predominantly concentrated on the history of ideas that lead to the development of modern science, starting with Scientific Revolution in the sixteenth century. As a consequence, the role of the Middle Ages was largely neglected.[36] Hence, the emergence of modern science was attributed to a radical change in European society, strictly opposed to the values and ideas of the *ancient regime*, and therefore eradicating all medieval heritage by reviving the ideas and values of Greek antiquity. The Middle Ages appeared only as an empty gap in history, merely representing the *Other*, the antitheses of humanist values and European civilisation, the "Dark Ages" of European history.[37] But this view conceals the important contributions from different cultural origins, such as Arabian interpretations of Aristotle and mathematics or Chinese technologies like the magnetic needle and gunpowder, all of them indispensable for the Scientific Revolution.[38] It also draws a quite unrealistic picture of European history and underestimates the importance of the social, cultural, political, intellectual and economic developments during the Middle Ages. If we want to better understand the foundations of scientific universalism, we have to take some of these developments into account as well.

So, there is another narrative which concerns the scholastic heritage in the historical context of the power-relations prevalent during the Middle Ages. Although, following the first narrative, science would be a continuation of Greek philosophical tradition based on free discourse, the power of the better argument and fact-based proof, science was also an heir to scholastic tradition, a system of knowledge that had been legitimating the power of the Roman Catholic Church for centuries. It might seem contradictory to assume that science emerged out of a process motivated precisely by a desire to overcome the exclusive hegemony of Catholic dogmatism only to take over exactly the same exclusive hegemonic position of its predecessor. How did it happen that science eventually failed to represent the new, open discourse of truth it always pretended to be, where any sound proposal about how things work would be discussed and evaluated regardless its implicit metaphysical or cosmological pre-assumption or cultural background?

First of all, the picture of the Middle Ages as an intellectual gap of about 1000 years between late antiquity and the sixteenth century Renaissance seems to be too simple. Neoplatonism, which was one of the dominant philosophical schools in late antiquity until the sixth century and influenced Christian religion in the Roman Empire, spread to the East and influenced Arabian philosophy and interpretations of Aristotle. After the fall of Rome, Byzantium became the new capital of the Roman Empire, preserving the fundaments of its political and intellectual heritage for another 1000 years. Due to its extensive sea-borne trade, the Byzantine Empire

[36] E.g. Somsen (2008); Polanyi (1946).

[37] E.g. Voegelin (1987); Latour (1993).

[38] Whitehead (1925); Harding (1994); Needham (1993, 2006).

remained in close contact with Western Europe throughout the centuries, influencing the first medieval kingdoms as a kind of civilisational reference.[39] As early as the eighth century, during the Carolingian Renaissance,[40] Christian *literati* in Western Europe read the ancient texts and their Arabian interpretations, giving continuity to an intellectual tradition which in the thirteenth century would eventually culminate in the foundation of the scholastic theologies of Albertus Magnus and his disciple Thomas Aquinas, introducing Aristotelian philosophy as a complementary element into the official theology of the Catholic Church. Additionally, the Turkish attacks on the Byzantine Empire resulted in the migration of numerous Greek intellectuals to Italy and further translations of Arabic transcriptions of texts from Greek antiquity contributed to the rise of humanism in fourteenth century Italy, paving the way to Renaissance, Enlightenment, and thus, modernity. There was no real gap; there were changes, but no fundamental rupture, no "Dark Ages", but an ongoing historical process of reinterpretation and resignification within a millenary European intellectual tradition based on Greek antiquity as well as important influences from other civilisations.

Like Greek philosophy before and early modern scientists after the Middle Ages, scholastic discourse was also based on comparing and pondering the best logical arguments of different scholars. And scholastic scholars were the first to introduce Aristotle's writings and his Arabian interpretations as a central part of their theoretical reasoning. Inspired by the writings of Abū ʿAlī al-Ḥasan ibn al-Ḥasan ibn al-Haytham, an Arabian scholar from eleventh century also known as Alhazan, the English Franciscan friar Roger Bacon was probably the first medieval scholar to propose the empirical method based on observation and experiment as early as the thirteenth century—some 300 years before the Enlightenment movement of the sixteenth century.[41] However, scholastic discourse continued to concentrate on text interpretation rather than methodological observation, and this would change only during the Renaissance, and most notably, with Francis Bacon's principles of inductive method. Francis Bacon, his later scientific colleagues and his scholastic predecessors were all searching for the one principle that governs the universe, and Bacon's method sought to discover precisely this universal principle. What had fundamentally changed was the method of knowing, adding mathematical predictions and systematic, empirical observation to the interpretation of theoretical texts. But what did not change was the assumption that there is a fundamental principle governing the universe: since it was created by the one God, there is only one viable way to find out the "truth" about it. And while many of the great pioneers of science, like Newton, Descartes and Leibniz, had explicitly introduced the notion of God into their theoretical systems, others, like Kant[42] and Laplace, would show that God

[39] Wolf (2010).

[40] Riché (1985).

[41] Walach (2019); Whitehead (1925).

[42] Kant (1787, 1922) had shown that the idea of God could not be proven to be an ontological principle, but rather a necessary idea for ethical reasoning. However, he criticised Descartes' and

was no longer a necessary concept to explain the physical universe. With the arrival of evolutionary theory, and modern sciences explaining ever more natural phenomena, even the creation of humankind and the universe itself seemed to be explainable by scientific theory. Nature's laws and human reason, although initially understood as God's creation, were now seen as the universal principle to explain everything, and eventually substituted the notion of God as the one principle that governs the universe. And as religion before, science now would never accept any rival explanatory approach besides its own. Modern science, thus, inherited religious universalism resulting in a distorted metaphysical vision of science as a worldview,[43] often called *scientism*.[44]

2.2 The Institutional Foundations of Universalism

However, the scholastic heritage of modern science is not only ideological, but also institutional. Universities are the institutional pillars of Science and probably the most important heritage Science received from the Middle Ages.[45] Universities were not created by modern science. Rather, they were taken over by modern science hundreds of years after the first universities had been created under the rule of Pope Gregory VII during the eleventh century. The universities provided, for the first time, exclusive and relatively autonomous spaces for intellectual work and maintained a pan-European network for intellectual exchange.[46] Initially, philosophy, theology, canonical law and medicine were the only subjects to be taught and academic titles were of marginal importance in society. But with growing bureaucratic structures, titles slowly grew in importance to access high level positions within the church and the feudal states. And with this growing demand for academic titles universities flourished and spread all over Europe. A class of intellectual professionals emerged competing with innovative ideas for chairs and positions within the academic system. Slowly, dogmatism decreased and intellectual innovation was unleashed, especially within philosophic faculties, which were less important initially and therefore more open to change. Philosophical faculties became more prominent and philosophy developed into an independent discipline. But during the

---

Newton's approaches in natural philosophy for being based on the notion of God. A few years later, Laplace, would explicitly advocate a purely secular, deterministic explanation of nature.

[43] Miettinen (2009); Segesvary (2004); Voegelin (1987); Walach (2019); Latour (2017).

[44] Compare also Miettinen (2009).

[45] Collins (2009).

[46] Thomas Aquinas, for example, first studied at the university of Napoli, from 1239 to 1244, then at the university of Paris from where he followed his master Albertus Magnus to Cologne before he returned back to Paris where he started to teach as a professor. After four years in Paris he went back do Napoli for another three years before he was called to Rome, where he would stay for seven years. He died in 1274 during a journey from France to Italy (http://www.zeno.org/Philosophie/M/Thomas%20von%20Aquin/Biographie; Accessed: 22.11.2023).

fourteenth century the inflation of titles forced academics to work outside Catholic universities and relocate their intellectual interests towards secular studies. The old theocentric dogma began to decline and humanism emerged as a new anthropocentric world view, making way for the Renaissance movement of the fifteenth century. The secularisation of science made room for a whole range of new research fields, like arts, technology, mathematics, astronomy and alchemy. Growing conflicts between church and state during the reformation, religious wars, colonial and economic expansion, and new state bureaucracies all contributed to a separation of science from the church. The Royal Society was founded, followed by the Academie des Sciences, the Berlin Academy and the St. Petersburg Academy of Sciences.[47] The sixteenth and seventeenth centuries saw a wave of new universities and scientific academies due to the practical value of natural sciences for colonial expansion and industrialisation. Modern science was born.

Here we have yet another little historical narrative that may help understand why the relationship between the academic system and modern science is so intimate, that the one cannot be even conceived without the other. An interesting fact about this story is that while modern science resulted in very profound changes in the structure of knowledge, the academic system continued surprisingly unchanged. Today we use the same academic titles that once had been used at medieval universities more than 800 years ago. And also their primal social functions remained basically the same: they work as symbolic capital for the dominant elites, a means to maintain and regulate social hierarchy, stratification and distribution of structural resources like social status, important positions, economic and political power.[48] Of course, the social system and its elites changed, feudalism was substituted by nation states and capitalism, clergy and nobles by bourgeoisie; but the role of the academic system in regulating access to fundamental social and economic resources is still very similar, though it has been adjusted to current demands. The same goes for its truth monopoly. Only "scientists" with academic titles granted by universities have the right to participate in the official discourse about what is true or not. Only "scientific" knowledge is legitimate knowledge and can be accepted in economic and political decision making, just as canonical knowledge had been the only legitimate knowledge in medieval times.

This kind of *institutional* or *structural universalism* also justifies capitalist expansion as a neo-colonial, modern mode of European colonisation. The theological narrative about the righteous "mission" of Christians to fight and catechise pagans was substituted by the duty to bring "progress" to the "underdeveloped", "uncivilised" and "savage" people of this world. This is the same spirit of missionary racism that drove the Crusades, the Iberian *conquista* and the invasion of the new world, slaughtering millions of people just for being "pagans"; that justified colonialism, black slave capitalism and fascism during the modern age. There are frightening parallels and there is no doubt that scientific universalism is

[47] Merton (1968).

[48] Bourdieu (1992).

fundamental to the maintenance of the current world order with its unequal distribution of centres and peripheries following the lines of racial differences between those "moderns" of European decent and the "non-modern" Others.[49]

Modern science not only inherited most of its social structure from the medieval universities of the Catholic Church, but also its central functions within modern society. Considering its social function, modern science is what God and the church were for medieval society. And its truth monopoly, that is, scientific universalism, is essential to this role.

In summary, the different narratives about the historical origins of scientific universalism I tried to trace so far indicate two important arguments: First, rationalism, as the prime philosophical fundament of modern science, has been ideologically instrumental to the project of European and subsequent capitalist expansion. Second, the universalistic claim and social function of modern science as holder of a truth monopoly has its roots in its medieval heritage. However, if scientific universalism has its origin in the monotheistic truth monopoly and the social structures of the medieval academic system, the fact that rationalism was instrumentalised as an ideological means to sustain modern universalism does not *necessarily* imply that rationalism in itself has to be universalistic. It could be the case, but it does not follow as a necessary corollary. Actually, in antiquity there was no universalistic hegemonic cosmological model at all, precisely because philosophical discourse was rational, critical and open to any cosmological approach as long as it could be sustained by sound logical arguments.[50] This would only change with the rise of monotheism as a hegemonic, and in fact totalitarian system of power,[51] as it was institutionalised by the Roman Catholic Church in late antiquity and the early Middle Ages. So, if there was a rupture between antiquity and the Middle Ages, this rupture went along with the end of cosmological pluralism, but unfortunately this change would not be reversed with Enlightenment or modernity. Modern science may justify its universalism by ideologically instrumentalising philosophical ideas from Greek antiquity, humanism and Enlightenment, but the institutional and ideological foundation of its universalism are also rooted in the medieval structures of domination related to the Catholic Church.

[49] Wallerstein (2004, 2006).

[50] "Rather than presenting us what could be called a universalised particularism—as in the case of modern theories of natural law, the assumed universal applicability of certain particular dogmas—the Greek universalism provides us with a counter-motive, namely, the de-absolutisation of all particularisms" (Miettinen 2009: 1).

[51] Also compare Jan Assmann's (1996, 2003) famous thesis of the 'Mosaic distinction' between 'primary' (polytheistic, cosmotheistic) religions and the exclusive universalism of later 'secondary' (scriptural, monotheistic) 'counter-religions', which drew a hard distinction between followers of the one universal truth and 'othered' all 'non-believers' as 'pagans'. "Ancient polytheisms", in contrast, "functioned as such a technique of translation within the "ancient world" as an ecumene of interconnected nations. […] Whereas polytheism or rather, 'cosmotheism,' rendered different cultures mutually transparent and compatible, the new counterreligion blocked intercultural translatability. False gods cannot be translated" (Assmann 1996: pp 49–50).

Scientific universalism, therefore, may not be a necessary consequence of the ideals of humanism or Enlightenment, like human freedom and rationality, or scientific method, but rather appear as an obscured heritage of the dogmatic system of the Middle Ages that resulted in an ideologically distorted vision of science as the only legitimate ontological approach—*scientism*.[52] However, this is not to say that the philosophical and methodological principles of science would not have an important role for universalism. As shown above, they serve as ideological justifications of Science's truth monopoly; but this ideological misuse might not *necessarily* follow from the metaphysical premises modern science is based on. So, there is reason for hope that we may not need to abandon logical reasoning and the ideals of Enlightenment altogether, just to overcome the "darker", colonial side[53] of Science's universalist truth monopoly.[54]

References

Assmann J (1996) The mosaic distinction: Israel, Egypt, and the Invention of Paganism. Representations, Autumn, 1996, No. 56, Special Issue: The New Erudition (Autumn, 1996), pp 48–67

Assmann J (2003) Die Mosaische Unterscheidung – oder der Preis des Monotheismus. Carl Hauser Verlag, Munich, Vienna

Böhme G (1980) Alternativen der Wissenschaft. Suhrkamp, Frankfurt a.M

Bourdieu P (1992) Homo academicus. Suhrkamp, Frankfurt a.M

Castro-Gomes S (2000) Ciencias sociales, violencia epistémica y el problema de la "invención del otro". In: Lander E (ed) La colonialidad del saber: eurocentrismo y ciencias sociales—Perspectivas latinoamericanas. CLACSO, Buenos Aires, pp 145–162

Cole S (1995) Making science: between nature and society. Harvard University Press, Cambridge

Collins R (2009) Quatro Tradições Sociológicas. Editora Vozes, Petropolis JR

Dussel E (2000) Europa, modernidad y eurocentrismo. In: Lander E (ed) La colonialidad del saber: eurocentrismo y ciencias sociales—Perspectivas latinoamericanas. CLASCO, Buenos Aires, pp 41–54

Escobar A (2003) Mundos y Conocimientos de Otro Modo. El Programa de Investigación de Modernidad/Colonialidad Latinoamericano. Tabula Rasa. Bogotá, Jan–Dec, pp 51–86

Feyerabend P (1993) Against method: outline of an anarchist theory of knowledge. Verso, London

Grossmann H (2009a) The social foundations of the mechanistic philosophy and manufacture. In: Freudenthal G, Mclaughlin P (eds) The social and economic roots of the scientific revolution: Texts by Boris Hessen and Henryk Grossmann. Springer, Dordrecht, pp 103–156

Grossmann H (2009b) Descartes and the social origins of the mechanistic concept of the world. In: Freudenthal G, Mclaughlin P (eds) The social and economic roots of the scientific revolution: Texts by Boris Hessen and Henryk Grossmann. Springer, Dordrecht, pp 157–230

Harding SG (1994) Is science multicultural?: challenges, resources, opportunities, uncertainties. Configurations 2:301–330. https://doi.org/10.1353/con.1994.0019

---

[52] "Our point is: scientists who believe in Science, i.e. in the future superiority and the universality of the current scientific approach, do not practise science but profess a creed" (Walach 2019: 25).

[53] Mignolo (1995, 2011).

[54] I shall come back to this question in the final chapter of this work.

Harding S (2015) Objectivity and diversity: another logic of scientific research. University of Chicago Press, Chicago
Hornbacher A (2005) Zuschreibung und Befremdung: Postmoderne Repräsentationskrise und verkörpertes Wissen im balinesischen Tanz. Reimer, Berlin
Kant I (1787) Kritik der reinen Vernunft, ungekürzte Ausgabe nach der zweiten, hin und wieder verbesserten Auflage. Paderborn
Kant I (1922) Kritik der Urteilskraft, 5th edn. Felix Meiner, Leipzig
Kuhn M, Vessuri H (2016) Contributions to alternative concepts of knowledge. Ibedem, Stuttgart
Kuhn M, Yazawa S (2013) Theories about and strategies against hegemonic social sciences. Center for Glocal Studies. Seijo University, Tokyo
Lander E (ed) (2000) La colonialidad del saber: eurocentrismo y ciencias sociales—Perspectivas latinoamericanas. CLACSO, Buenos Aires
Latour B (1993) We have never been modern. Harvard University Press
Latour B (2017) Facing Gaia: eight lectures on the new climatic regime. Polity Press, Cambridge, UK; Malden, MA
Linhart J (2008) Universidades Indígenas: Programas de Educação Indígena Superior na América Latina: A Caminho de uma Ciência Intercultural? Master Thesis, LMU
Merton RK (1942) The normative structure of science. https://www.panarchy.org/merton/science.html. Accessed 09.01.2024
Merton RK (1968) Social theory and social structure. Free Press, New York
Miettinen T (2009) On the philosophical foundations of universalism: reason, task, critique. In: Conference of the Network of European Studies and the Center for European Integration at Freie Universität. Berlin
Mignolo WD (1995) The darker side of the renaissance: literacy, territoriality, and colonization. University of Michigan Press, Ann Arbor
Mignolo WD (2000) Local histories/global designs: coloniality, subaltern knowledges, and border thinking. Princeton University Press, Princeton, NJ
Mignolo W (2005) El Pensamiento Des-Colonial, Desprendimiento y Apertura: Un Manifiesto. Tristestópicos
Mignolo WD (2011) The darker side of western modernity: global futures, decolonial options. Duke University Press, Durham, London
Mignolo WD (2021) The politics of decolonial investigations. Duke University Press, Durham, London
Needham J (1993) Poverties and triumphs of the Chinese scientific tradition. In: Harding S (ed) The "racial" economy of science: toward a democratic future. Indianapolis, Bloomington
Needham J (2006) Science and civilisation in China. In: Kaptchuk T (ed) Das große Buch der chinesischen Medizin: Die Medizin von Yin und Yang in Theorie und Praxis. Frankfurt a.M, pp 280–281
Polanyi M (1946) Science, faith and society. Oxford University Press, London
Quijano A (2009) Colonialidade do Poder e Classificação Social. In: Santos BdS, Meneses MP (eds) Epistemologias do Sul. Coimbra, pp 73–118
Riché P (1985) Die Karolinger. Eine Familie formt Europa. dtv, Munich
Santos BdS (2009) Um Ocidente Não-Ocidentalista?: A Filosofia à venda, a douta ignorânçia e a aposta de Pascal. In: Santos BdS, Meneses MP (eds) Epistemologias do Sul. Coimbra, pp 445–486
Segesvary V (2004) From illusion to delusion: globalization and the contradictions of late modernity. Mikes, The Hague
Shapin S (1995) Here and everywhere: sociology of scientific knowledge. Annu Rev Sociol 2:289–321
Somsen GJ (2008) A history of universalism: conceptions of the internationality of science from the enlightenment to the Cold War. Minerva 46:361. https://doi.org/10.1007/s11024-008-9105-z
Varela FJ, Shear J (eds) (2002) The view from within: first-person approaches to the study of consciousness, 2. reprint. Imprint Academic, Thorverton

Voegelin E (1987) The new science of politics: an introduction. University of Chicago Press, Chicago, London
Walach H (2019) The Galileo Commission Report: beyond a materialist worldview: towards an expanded science. Scientific Medical Network
Wallerstein I (2004) World-system analysis: an introduction. Duke University Press, London
Wallerstein I (2006) European universalism: the rhetoric of power. New Press, New York
Weber M (1919) Wissenschaft als Beruf. In: Kaesler D (ed) Max Weber—Schriften 1894–1922. Kröner, Stuttgart
Weber M (2006) Die protestantische Ethik und der Geist des Kapitalismus: Textausgabe auf der Grundlage der ersten Fassung von 1904/05 mit einem Verzeichnis der wichtigsten Zusätze und Veränderungen aus der zweiten Fassung von 1920. Munich
Whitehead AN (1925) Science and the modern world. Cambridge University Press, London
Whitesides G (2019) Science and American foreign relations since World War II. Cambridge University Press, Cambridge
Wolf E (2010) Europe and the people without history. University of California Press, Berkley
Zilsel E (1942) The sociological roots of science. Am J Sociol 47:544–562
Zuckermann H (1988) The sociology of science. In: Smelser NJ (ed) Handbook of sociology. Sage, Newbury Park, pp 511–574

Chapter 3
The Metaphysics of Scientific Universalism

There can be little doubt about the ideological character of scientific universalism. Philosophy of science and science studies have been debating possible criteria to distinguish science from non-science for many decades, and as far as I can see these "science wars" have been won by the anti-universalist camp—at least on the level of sustainable arguments. So it would not make much sense to go over the whole debate once again to "prove" the ideological character of universalism. However, it appears that scientism and scientific universalism continue to dominate the hegemonic discourse on legitimate "truth". So, we are confronted with the historical fact that a huge portion of modern science persistently ignores its own meta-discourse about its epistemological foundations in favour of an ideologically motivated myth of objective truth and scientific superiority. Accordingly, we should try to come to a better understanding of this strange—and blatantly unscientific—resistance to adjust the theory to the facts.

The whole issue is very complex, and a satisfactory analysis would include an extensive discussion of the vast literature on metascience, the philosophy, history and sociology of science, and science studies, which is clearly something I do not intend to do here. However, for my present purpose, I feel it necessary to shed some light on at least three dimensions of this question:

1. How is scientific universalism being justified?
2. What is the role of Science—both as an ideology and a social institution—in the context of our globalised world?
3. How does modern science define itself in relation to other ways of knowing?

This chapter concerns the first of the three questions. My main argument concerning this topic will be that although scientific method and its epistemological principles are generally championed as being more objective than other ways of knowing because they focus on avoiding value judgments and metaphysical suppositions, the real argument for the rejection of alternative ways of knowing follow from the negated metaphysical presuppositions classical modern science (and current scientism) is based upon.

J. Linhart, *Science and the Other*, Schriften zu Leben und Gesellschaft - Series on Life and Society 2, https://doi.org/10.1007/978-3-032-03927-9_3

My aim is to make my thoughts assessable to readers with no specific proficiency in the history and philosophy of science, which means that some of my explanations may lack the details and the depth other readers might expect.

3.1 The Scientific Method

Following the predominant official narrative, the main argument for Science's superior attitude to Other ways of knowing is justified by its alleged objectivity guaranteed by the scientific method of knowledge production. The superiority of science over other modes of reasoning is taken for granted and its epistemological foundations are rarely seriously questioned during scientific practice. Most scientists simply apply the methods they learned without reflecting too much on their underlying epistemological principles. Methods are used like well-established tools[1]—like a hammer which serves to hit the nail and drive it into the wall—unproblematic as long as they work. And science works, no doubt.

This mainstream notion of scientific method is typically exemplified by contemporary textbooks.[2] Accordingly, the difference between scientific and other kinds of knowledge (e.g. religious, philosophical, "common sense", "practical" or "traditional") is that the former is objective while the latter are subjective, and hence, biased and based on value judgements. Scientific knowledge, on the other hand, is produced under the strict rules of scientific methodological standards, excluding subjective bias (at least as much as possible). Typically, such methodological standards of objectivity are: deduction based on logical and mathematical reasoning, induction based on systematic observation, and testing of falsifiable (non-metaphysical) hypotheses through controlled experiment or other reproducible empirical evidence.

Of course, in practice there is no such thing as "the" scientific method, but rather many methods gathered around a common set of central epistemological principles.[3] In fact, there are as many different definitions of "the" scientific method as there are textbooks and encyclopaedic entries on this subject matter. This fuzzy character of "the" scientific method is also exemplified by the muddled way many textbooks define central concepts like "theories", "hypotheses", "laws" or "models", and the simplistic descriptions of induction, deduction and falsifiability. In many cases, these issue are treated with an almost total lack of reference to the complex epistemological problem of induction, the fundamental shortcomings of falsificationism, and the frequent reduction of "the" method to the methods typically used in natural sciences, ignoring the existence of social sciences and their

[1] Kind of "black boxes", in the sense of Latour (1987).

[2] Chalmers (1993); Gower (1997); Laville and Dionne (1999); Lakatos and Marconi (2003); Blachowicz (2009); et al.

[3] E.g. Collingwood (1998); Hacking (1999).

particular methods. In fact, the methodological difference between the natural and the social sciences are so huge that we often speak of the "two cultures".[4] Some authors have even tried to show that the latter are not sciences at all,[5] while other authors emphasise the common epistemological and methodological bases of all modern sciences.[6] Be this as it may, there is certainly no consensus on what scientific method is or should be. And finally, Feyerabend famously showed that scientific knowledge is not even produced following any rigorous method whatsoever, but on the contrary, proceeds according to a creative methodological "anarchism", just as any other type of social construction of knowledge. However, I did not refer to Feyerabend here to follow his radical relativism, but to take him as an example of the power of a critique of method to smash any kind of universalism. Now, the important point here is, that Feyerabend not only showed that scientific practice lacks any uniform methodological rules, but also that it necessarily has to bypass its own rules in order to make any substantial progress. In other words, his argument questioned the epistemological foundations of scientific method. This is, of course, a much stronger argument than the mere critique of method, as scientific method has always been construed and justified following specific epistemological models around the best viable way to come to reliable knowledge about "reality". It follows, that it is not the method of knowledge production which qualifies as distinctive character of science versus non-science, but the epistemological principles from which the method actually is a result.

3.1.1 The Epistemological Foundations of Method

The set of fuzzy ideas and routine practices we often call "the scientific method" is frequently depicted as being a direct result of a linear progress beginning with sixteenth century European natural philosophy. Following this narrative, science is the outcome of the revival of Greek logic and mathematics together with systematic empirical observation and experimentation. These two basic methodological strands, logical reasoning and empirical observation, represent the two complementary epistemological principles of deduction (reasoning from the general to the particular) and induction (particular observations leading to general natural laws).[7] As the story goes, logical reasoning and mathematical models based on empirical data lead to new hypotheses predicting causal relations, which will be tested in con-

[4] E.g. Collingwood (1998) Hacking (1999) argues that the differences in methods are due to the different kinds of questions of both sciences. While natural sciences focus on prediction (How?), humanities would aspire to understanding (Why?).

[5] E.g. Popper (1970).

[6] E.g. Knorr-Cetina (1981) observes that although the social sciences reject the prevalent positivism of natural sciences, they still share similar methods. See also Gadamer (1978).

[7] See Blachowicz's (2009) review of simplistic textbook explanations of basic epistemological concepts.

trolled experiments and "verified" or "falsified", and so on. In this fairy-tale for naive positivists, induction and deduction work together in perfect harmony, and they lived happily ever after.

Of course, there is nothing harmonic or unproblematic about deduction or induction, and the relation between the two is more of a Bohr-type complementarity in the sense of maximal mutual exclusiveness, but tied together by their shared constitution, since empiricism rests on rationalism.

> The theory of Induction is the despair of philosophy—and yet all our activities are based upon it (Whitehead 1925: 30).

Actually, the two-fold epistemological foundations of modern science have been problematic right from its beginning. Although both rationalism and empiricism emerged as critical responses to the dogmatic scholastic interpretations of Aristotle, the two strands came to different and mutually incompatible solutions.

The empiricist tradition initiated by Francis Bacon[8] rejected the scholastic way of seeking truth through logical speculation and contemplation, proposing induction as a new method to come to universal axioms based on systematic observation and experimental testing of hypotheses.[9] Moreover, Bacon changed the whole purpose of knowledge from a mere intellectual or theological enterprise to a powerful tool to serve his utopian project of social transformation, which he called "the Great Instauration". Now, acquiring knowledge about God's creation was not only a means to get closer to Him, but meant power to control nature and regain man's rule over God's creation.[10] The experiment was a tribunal where nature was interrogated, if necessary, even tortured, to reveal its secrets to be put in man's service.[11] But the experimental method also eliminated mere opinion and sophistic speculation, as it submits theoretical predictions to rigorous testing. This is important, for the intellect cannot be trusted as it is misted by the *idols*, biased presumptions inducing us to distorted perceptions and wrong interpretations.

The rationalism of René Descartes,[12] on the other hand, was also sceptical about the authority of scholastic scholars, but did not trust the senses either. In his view, our sensual perceptions were far more unreliable than mathematics and logical reasoning. Hence, experience could not be the source of certainty, and consequently, the first metaphysical principles could not be established by evidence alone, but only by means of logical inquiry. Accordingly, his solution was to go back to the only undeniable certainty he could find, which he thought would be the existence of his mind, the *cogito*, as proven by the fact that he was thinking about such questions, and then deduce further certainties as necessary logical consequences from this first

---

[8] Bacon (2017).

[9] Francis Bacon himself was not an empiricist in the contemporary sense, as he followed to his namesake, Roger Bacon, not only in promoting experience and the experimental method, but also defended divine intuition and faith as the prime sources for true knowledge (Walach (2019, 2020).

[10] See also Weber (1919); Collingwood (1998).

[11] Merchant (2006, 2018).

[12] Descartes (2017).

one. This radical scepticism towards the senses almost automatically led to solipsism, opening an unbridgeable epistemological gap between the inner and the outer world, since there was no causal way to explain how the mind may know about the world of objects. Descartes' solution was to take recourse to God, assuming that our mind was an emanation of Him, and hence, our perceptions were true intuitions, since God would not lie.[13] Without these ad hoc hypotheses, rationalism cannot say anything about the world of objects.

However, Descartes's dualistic model of the autonomous subject's mind here, and the outer world of objects there, called on the empiricists to explain how experience could reveal anything true about the "real" world. Locke[14] may have been the first to look for foundations of knowledge in the realm of the senses,[15] but his mind-as-mirror model was soon refuted by Hume's (2017 (1739)) sceptical inquiry, leaving little more than open questions. Hume showed, quite convincingly, that deduction (although in principle allowing for absolute truth claims) alone could not get anywhere without starting from some empirical ground; empirical observations, on the other hand, are neither objective (as experience is a constant conjecture, presupposing uniformity of nature) nor sufficient to establish any general rule. Most importantly, Hume based his argument on an inquiry on causation, showing that there is no way to "prove" causation based on empirical evidence. Hence, induction, the main pillar of empiricism, falls, and with it, the experimental method—at least as a method to come to absolute universal truth.

Soon after, Kant[16] tried to put things together, joining the teachings from Descartes, Hume and Locke to a new fundamental theory of knowledge. In his transcendental inquiry on reason and perception, knowledge is the result of a complex process of mental construction, based on unprovable a priori (that is, innate, non-empirical) perceptive intuitions and schemata (time, space, causation, etc.) shaping the inner representations of sensual perceptions, before conceptualising them and assembling the concepts into conjectures ("judgments" in Kant's terminology). However, the "glue" between our inner mechanism of reasoning and our perceptions of the outer world are a priori modes of perception, like time, space and causation, which can neither be logically derived from any more fundamental truth nor induced from evidence; they are absolute presuppositions necessary to enable experience in any meaningful way. Thus, although it may be reasonable to trust these a priori intuitions for the lack of any alternative, we will never come to any absolute truth about the world of things-in-themselves. Our consciousness, and thus, our

[13] "The core of the argument is this: I couldn't exist with the nature that I have—that is, containing within me the idea of God—if God didn't really exist. By 'God' I mean the very being the idea of whom is within me—the one that has no defects and has all those perfections that I can't grasp but can somehow touch with my thought. This shows clearly that it is not possible for him to be a deceiver, since the natural light makes it clear that all fraud and deception depend on some defect" (idem, Meditations III).

[14] Locke (1690).

[15] Rorty (1979).

[16] Kant (1787).

knowledge about "the world" will always remain within the cognitive and perceptual limits of our mind. This means that we ultimately do not know with certainty whether linear time, extended space and deterministic causality actually exist apart from our perception. Here, Kant clearly deviates from Newton's[17] conception of absolute space, time and causation—with important consequences: with Kant, Newton's laws of nature became rather laws of perception, constructing principles of representations within our minds.[18] Of course, Kant assumed it logically necessary to trust our a priori intuitions of perception, as his transcendental analysis showed that there are no other more fundamental or more reliable foundations we could draw on. But now the assumption that these representations have anything to do with the world of objects was nothing more than a good working hypothesis (although it actually is an unfalsifiable metaphysical presupposition). This rather pragmatic solution was more a gesture of surrender than of victory. He finally confirmed Hume's doubts concerning the possibility of deriving knowledge solely from induction as well as the empiricists critique of Descartes' purely deductive approach, suggesting that the only way to define the epistemological foundations of knowledge is to come to a better understanding about the mental processes responsible for the construction of our inner representations.[19] As a consequence, modern philosophy defined epistemology as its central problem. Epistemology was now understood as a theory about the foundations of knowledge[20] and the legitimacy of method would depend on the coherence of its epistemological principles. However, this view already entails the assumption that knowledge needs to be based on foundations and that these foundations are problematic. It is this sceptical stance of modern discourse on truth that conditions the legitimacy of knowledge to its epistemological foundations[21] and it is its representational model which makes these foundations so problematic, since it defines epistemology as a study of man as knower and man's knowledge as an inner representation of an intangible outer world of objects. In this sense, Kant redefined the role of modern philosophy as epistemology precisely by demonstrating the inevitableness of the aporia implied in Cartesian dualism and the resulting representational model of mind.[22]

This move fostered the division of natural philosophy into science, on the one hand, and philosophy on the other, the former dealing exclusively with empirical evidence and the latter with epistemological foundations and other metaphysical questions.[23] In the course of the following three centuries, science would make incredible progress, while modern philosophy kept on trying to solve the predica-

[17] Newton (1846).

[18] Actually, Newton anticipated this problem by articulating his theories in terms of models (Maxwell 2017).

[19] Compare also Maxwell (2017).

[20] Rorty (1979).

[21] Idem. Also Lyotard 1986.

[22] Rorty (1979).

[23] Maxwell (2017).

ments left behind by Descartes dualism and Kant's constructionism, without substantial success and largely ignored by science.

3.1.2 The Natural Sciences

All the philosophers' epistemological doubts notwithstanding, modern science flourished greatly under the positivist paradigm, transforming the world profoundly in every aspect of life. Since Newton's breakthrough work on gravity one fantastic scientific "discovery" had been following the next, and the world was frenzying in a delirium of joy and despair in face of the astonishing promises and the dramatic transformations of the industrial age. Most natural scientists were under the spell of their own success, more or less ignoring philosophical discourse, pursuing Newton's anti-metaphysical empiricism. Contrary to Kepler and Galileo, who had openly referred to their metaphysical presumptions about a harmonious structure of the universe, Newton maintained that he derived his law of gravity from evidence alone.[24] Many continental natural philosophers continued to defend Cartesian foundationalism, insisting on the necessity of coherent metaphysical explanations for gravity. The British scientists of the Royal Academy, however, quickly adopted Newton's method and his pragmatic anti-metaphysical approach, warranted by their technological progress, the Industrial Revolution and the expansion of the British Empire. Throughout the nineteenth century, the massive amount of new scientific findings seemed to fit nicely into the framework of Newton's physics, explaining ever more natural phenomena in an apparently coherent manner, giving little reason for scientists to lose time with questioning its metaphysical principles.[25]

Classical physics and positivism would only reach its limits in the course of the twentieth century. Einstein's relativity theory implied some major adjustments concerning basic physical concepts, like space, time and gravity. However, it did not question the deterministic principle of causality, and thus, the positivist paradigm would not be shattered by his theory. Serious metaphysical questions would only come to the stage with the findings of quantum physics, which led to abstract mathematical formalisms that not only contradicted classical physics, but also questioned its most fundamental metaphysical presumptions, like causality (determinism, locality), physical materialism, and ontological dualism (which was the reason why

---

[24] Actually, in his first edition of the *principia*, Newton still referred to the metaphysical character of his rules. In his third edition, however, he explicitly holds to have derived his laws from evidence alone (probably as an attempt to protect his laws from the heavy criticisms coming from other natural philosophers like Huygens and Leibniz). Ironically, gravity contradicts Newton's own definition of causality, as it is a non-local phenomenon with no coherent metaphysical explanation, and even Newton himself had to admit how absurd his newly invented principle was (Maxwell 2017).

[25] Whitehead (1925); Maxwell (2017).

Einstein insisted on refuting quantum physics[26]). Some of the pioneers of quantum physics (e.g. Bohr, Schrödinger, Pauli[27]) soon called attention to the possible implications of their findings concerning the mind-body problem, which could also entail considerable epistemological consequences. However revolutionary, these ideas have been by and large ignored by mainstream science for almost a century, having near to zero effect on scientific practice.[28] Much to the contrary, the advances made in the neurosciences during recent decades have fostered a materialistic concept of mind, equalling consciousness with brain-functions.[29] This raises the question how zombie-scientists who only think they think while their thoughts are actually only meaningless epiphenomena of deterministic brain-activities, can possibly come to the strange idea that zombie-scientists are capable of doing science[30]? But this is a matter to be treated later in more detail.

3.1.3 The Social Sciences

Motivated by the great success of the natural sciences and challenged by the collateral damage of the Industrial Revolution, scientists went on to apply their universal all-in-one method on social and human affairs, too. The nineteenth century witnessed the foundation of a range of human and social sciences, initially under the positivist paradigm.[31]

But it soon turned out, that the new subject matter also demanded new methods. Humans simply do not behave according to deterministic laws; neither do societies, cultures, languages or history—they are moved by meaning, values, power-relations, beliefs, passions, hopes, desires and fears. It was necessary to *understand* humans' conscious and unconscious feelings, ideas and intentions in order to explain their behaviour both on the individual and collective scale. Wilhelm Dilthey's definition of the *Geisteswissenschaften* (humanities) was one of the first attempts to ground a scientific theory of understanding in the hermeneutic method and was ultimately rooted in a critical extrapolation of Kant's constructionism from the individual to the social sphere. The hermeneutic tradition was also influential for Max Weber's *verstehende Soziologie* (understanding/interpretative sociology) and later interpretative approaches, eventually fusing with phenomenology, and leaving little or no space for objectivity in the strong sense as common to the natural sciences. To

[26] Einstein et al. (1935).

[27] von Stillfried (2018); Walach (2020).

[28] Only recently, these ideas have been rediscovered by a group of philosophers and scientists concerned with the hard problem of consciousness and related matters. I will come back to this later in this work.

[29] E.g. Dennett (1991) or Edelman (2004). In Part III of this work I will offer a more detailed discussion of the different ontological models of mind and consciousness.

[30] Rorty (1979).

[31] E.g. Comte's vision of sociology as the study of social "laws" (Comte 1974).

understand subjects is not an objective business, but rather a subjective interpretation based on lived, synaesthetic, bodily experience (especially in the case of anthropology and ethnomethodology). To paraphrase Clifford Geertz[32]: by describing people's behaviour we know nothing about the meaning of their action—we need to interpret their expressions within their particular socio-cultural context.

Nonetheless, the social sciences define themselves as empirical sciences. However, the empirical evidence one encounters in social science is made up of subjective "realities", meanings, symbols, patterns of collective behaviour, discourses, rituals, social relations, and stuff of the kind, by no means comparable to the kind of evidence we find in the natural sciences. These, mostly immaterial, objects of study are not objectively observable but themselves the product of abstractions and interpretations of observables, which are not always[33] reproducible or quantifiable.[34] As a consequence, experiments are difficult to conduct in the social sciences, and most often useless, as people react differently to the artificial situation of experiment.

In fact, the social sciences differ so deeply from the natural sciences concerning both their methods and their theoretical approaches that it has been argued that the social sciences are not sciences at all[35]—but of course this is nonsense. Social scientists are still seeking to be as "objective" as possible, and they make use of quantitative methods wherever useful. Actually, the social sciences are in permanent crisis precisely because the current paradigm of "scientific method" obliges them to give an "objective" account of subjects, while evidence in their field of inquiry requires qualitative, that is, subjective methods. This conflict ultimately reflects the more fundamental contradictions implied by Cartesian dualism, which in the humanities results in an artificial distinction between people as subjects of inquiry, on one side, and people as objects, on the other.

Even if we take "societies", "cultures", "structures" or "systems" as objects of inquiry, this is an equally artificial definition,[36] as these entities are in fact conceptual abstractions representing nothing other than aspects of collective human behaviour. So, while the individual behaviour is constrained by social and cultural factors, individual action and its motives have to be understood to explain collective

---

[32] Geertz (2008).

[33] People do not act in a deterministic way and their behaviour is highly sensitive to context and depends heavily on individual experience, socialisation and cultural background, rendering any kind of generalisation a tricky business.

[34] In fact, in social sciences, quantitative methods often do not lead to more objectivity, but to the contrary, to a loss of objectivity. The reason is that many of the most important data are of subjective character, like opinions or experiences collected by means of interviews or questionnaires. But these means of quantification almost inevitable produce biased data, as they predefine the issues and questions in a decontextualised manner. Hence, in social science, more openness, confidence, and empathy are essential for the production of qualitative data.

[35] E.g. Popper (1970); Foucault (1974); Habermas (1988).

[36] Actually, there is neither a consolidated definition of "culture" in anthropology nor a definition of "society" in sociology.

behaviour.[37] Thus, there is a circular, or dialectical, relation between the individual and the collective dimension, demanding a more complex, holistic approach. However, here, again, the problem is rooted in Cartesian dualism, dividing the human and social realm into its subjective aspects on one side and its objective aspects on the other by creating artificial entities (e.g. "societies", "cultures", "structures", "institutions", "social facts", etc.), which are treated as objects. Especially in sociology, this problem has been debated for decades in terms of the exclusiveness of micro- and macro-theories, and many attempts[38] have been made to overcome this fundamental predicament, with little success.

As a consequence, even objectivist, materialist or systemic approaches in social sciences, like functionalism, Marxism, structuralism and system theory, ended up adopting a constructionist view, and thus, defining "reality" in terms of socially construed belief systems.[39] The individual and their subjective "reality" is constrained by the objective social reality ("social facts", as Durkheim[40] called them), which in turn, is the result of the collective behaviour of individuals acting according to their subjective "realities", and so on. Hence, from the social sciences' point of view, there is no "true reality", but many "truths" and many "realities", which are socially construed within the context of symbolic systems of meaning and changing power-relations.

The whole situation became even more confusing, when social scientists started to apply their methods to modern science, that is, to their colleagues, and ultimately, to themselves. Now, scientists were simultaneously subjects and objects of their own inquiry—so, how could they be "objective"? Moreover, approaching modern science as just another social practice, they "discovered" that scientific knowledge was socially constructed, just as any other kind of knowledge; a belief system equally subject to all kinds of social and economic constraints, unconscious

---

[37] Compare Horkheimer (1937) for a discussion of this problem concerning the relation between scientific theorising and social practice. He shows how the modern individual perceives themself as part of an unreasonable organism they cannot change, and to whose rules they have to submit themself as if they were natural laws. Hence, a critical theory of society is necessary to unveil the ideological character of accepted theories and to unleash the liberating potential of reason. For Foucault (1974), this double nature of subjectivity is related to the "discovery" of subconsciousness by Russel and Freud. The humanities did not emerge in order to understand the biological nature of the human being, but to explain that part of the subject's reality which lies between his positive existence and her understanding of it, and which has been conceptualised with terms like "function", "norm", "rule", or "system". Hence, for the social sciences, representation is not the same as consciousness, but rather related to the unconscious, exterior social realities.

[38] E.g. Bourdieu's (1985, 1987) *habitus* concept, Giddens' (2003) *structuration* or Elias and Scotson's (2000) *configuration.* Actually, the predecessor of sociology, historical materialism, already conceptualised this problem of circularity in terms of the dialectical relation between infra- and superstructure, objective material relations on one side and alienation and ideology on the other Marx (1962).

[39] The *social construction of reality* was most famously discussed by Berger and Luckmann (1991), but this view has been equally stated, more or less explicitly, by most other social scientists for at least a century.

[40] Durkheim (2007).

presumptions and personal interests. So, how can science be more "objective" than other kinds of knowledge?

I will come back to the important findings of the sociology of science and science studies in more detail in the next chapter. For now, I would just like to call attention to the divergent developments of the social and the natural sciences, and their strange relation to each other.

The two branches of modern science are rooted in the same epistemological principles, namely deduction and induction both methodological corollaries from Cartesian dualism and representationalism. However, natural sciences hold on to naive empiricism, thereby legitimating scientific universalism, while social sciences propagate a relativistic constructionism, completely delegitimising universalism, empiricism, natural sciences and ultimately, "truth" in general. Here is not the place for a conclusive analysis of this situation, but I take the risk of preempting that one reason for this situation is that the humanities were forced to maintain an ongoing dialogue with philosophy as they were trapped together within the same epistemological predicaments implied in dualism, while large parts of natural science could afford to enjoy the luxury of celebrating their steady progress instead of losing time with epistemology. However, this view also entails that the natural sciences depend on the maintenance of dualism to continue treating nature as an object.[41] Once the subject-object distinction is questioned, naive empiricism is not feasible and the natural sciences lose their epistemological legitimation. This is the reason why the natural sciences *have* to ignore such unpleasant epistemological reflexions to be able to go on with their business as usual.

3.2 The Rationalist Heritage

Meanwhile, modern philosophy took its own path apart from science, trying to tackle Descartes' and Kant's legacies in different ways.[42] After Kant, philosophy split into different movements, offering a wide range of radically diverging

[41] I was still a young student of biology when I first recognised how rigidly we were drilled to treat life as an object. Part of the curriculum for the first semester in biology was the anatomic practicum, where we had to dissect all kinds of different animals, despite this activity offering little benefit in this early stage of our studies. The course deliberately aimed at selecting those students who would feel uneasy with the useless killing of countless living beings just for slicing them up into little pieces, and the professors would openly suggest to those students to abandon the course, since biology was no business for soft-hearted animal lovers, but serious science. I did not mind dissecting the animals (although I would have preferred to dissect animals we could have eaten instead of throwing them away), but I could not identify myself with a science of life which treats life as if it was just a dead thing. Thus, I left the course and decided to become an anthropologist instead—but this is another story.

[42] One cannot say modern philosophers would not have been inventive; there is an enormous amount of radically different approaches and I personally find it difficult to make any generalisations without being unfair, unprecise and incomplete. However, for the current purpose, I will lean

approaches, although all of them in some way continued to refer to the problems entailed by dualism and representationalism. While some philosophers followed Kant in his attempt to furnish the project of enlightenment with solid metaphysical foundations, others rejected an all too rational, mechanistic and reductionist approach to nature.

The romantic movement criticised the cold mathematical abstractions natural philosophers like Newton and his colleagues extorted from nature by means of brutal force—a view Max Weber[43] would later coin with his concept of "disenchantment". Instead of accepting Descartes' radical rationalism with his mechanistic view of nature, romantics like Schelling and Goethe[44] rejected dualism, assuming the unity of man and nature, and defending an organic, animated view of nature. Contemplation, admiration and respect rather than dissection and calculus should be the way to a profound understanding of nature and man, aiming to reunite us with nature rather than to dominate her, harmonious coexistence rather than manipulation. Goethe's holistic-humanistic approach to a science based on aesthetic contemplation, whose main instrument of inquiry is the human being itself, was fundamental to Rudolf Steiner's anthroposophy. This movement, however, albeit promising, had little influence on mainstream epistemology.

Schelling attempted to reconnect Kant's isolated world of perceptions with the world of objects, taking both as equally real, but with his insistence on defining the "absolute" as a fundamental connecting principle he inspired the development of further "bombastic metaphysics",[45] like those of Hegel, Schopenhauer, Husserl and Heidegger. The idealists' philosophical systems tried to get around the cul-de-sac of dualist representationalism by postulating absolute metaphysical principles[46] to bridge the gap between inner reality and the world of outer objects, while concentrating on the transcendental inquiry into the constitution of our inner reality. However, none of these highly elaborated systems was able to offer a viable alternative to representational epistemology, nor did they really overcome dualism.

Although both Edmund Husserl and his treacherous disciple, Martin Heidegger, initially intended to escape metaphysics, they finally ended up accepting its inevitableness.[47] Husserl's[48] phenomenological approach sought to overcome the two-faced predicaments of dualism, namely realism and relativism, by separating the pure universal aspect of phenomena (their *eidos*) from its biased, individual inter-

on Nicolas Maxwell (2017), who traces a train of thought quite similar to the one I would like to propose here, while offering some additional observations.

[43] Weber (1919).

[44] Compare also Gernot Böhme (1980) on Goethe's polemic rejection of Newton's objective method.

[45] Maxwell (2017).

[46] E.g. Schopenhauer's *tat twam asi* or Will-to-Be, or Hegel's *Idea* and the *absolute Geist* (mind/spirit).

[47] Heidegger (1975) criticised Husserl's eidetic reduction for still remaining within the universal ontology of the cartesian *cogito* and its kantian transcendental analysis (see also Cristin 1999).

[48] Husserl (1962).

pretations by means of what Husserl called *epoché,* or *eidetic reduction.* Nevertheless, phenomena in Husserl's sense were still inner perceptions, and thus, phenomenology a kind of transcendental psychology. Despite its vague metaphysical fundaments,[49] however, Husserl's phenomenology provided important methodological impulses to the social sciences, since his ideas of *eidetic* inquiry and *epoché* entail similar questions about the objectivity of observations to those encountered in participatory observation.[50] But it was far from providing a solid epistemological foundation for an aprioric scientific philosophy, as Husserl would have hoped,[51] nor did it change the way the natural sciences worked.

Heidegger understood the shortcomings of his former mentor, and therefore, used phenomenology (that is, detecting how things reveal themselves instead of deducing them) to go behind the foundations of metaphysics.[52] But in order to understand the historical relation between modern subject and world he ended up postulating a new ontology based on metaphysical conceptions of "being". His legacy was to call attention to the temporality of metaphysical foundations and the impact the particular metaphysical presuppositions entailed in modern science, technology and worldview concerning our disposition towards life and world in terms of changes in the ways of "being" reveals itself. Following Heidegger, by approaching the world from the perspective of the Cartesian subject, modern science and technology has "being" reveal itself as an object ready for manipulation, but not its meaningful essence.[53] Hence, the particular disposition of modern science and technology towards "being", which is related to a loss of the meaningful essence of "being", is the consequence of its specific subject-centred ontology.[54] Science and technology are themselves particular metaphysical forms of apprehension, serving as a behavioural matrix (which he calls "scaffold"—"*Ge-stell*"[55]) of an

---

[49] Husserl initially based his phenomenology on Brentano's concept of intentionality, which Husserl understood as a means to separate mental acts from pure phenomena.

[50] Geertz (2008).

[51] Husserl (1962).

[52] See also Habermas (1988) on Heidegger.

[53] "Wenn also der Mensch forschend, betrachtend der Natur als einem Bezirk seiner Vorstellung nachstellt, dann ist er bereits von einer Weise der Entbergung beansprucht, die ihn herausfordert, die Natur als einen Gegenstand der Forschung anzugehen, bis auch der Gegenstand in das Gegenstandslose des Bestandes verschwindet" (Heidegger 1954: 26).

[54] "Gegenstand im Sinne von Ob-jekt gibt es erst dort, wo der Mensch zum Subjekt, wo das Subjekt zum ich und das Ich zum ego cogito wird, wo dieses cogitare in seinem Wesen als 'ursprünglich synthetische Einheit der transzendentalen Apperzeption' begriffen wird, erst dort, wo der höchste Punkt der 'Logik' erreicht wird (in der Wahrheit als der Gewissheit des 'Ich denke'). [...] Subjektivität, Gegenstand und Reflexion gehören zusammen. Erst wenn die Reflexion als solche erfahren ist, nämlich als der tragende Bezug zum Seienden, erst dann wird das Sein als Gegenständlichkeit bestimmbar." (idem: 84/85).

[55] "Im Ge-stell ereignet sich die Unverborgenheit, demgemäß die Arbeit der modernen Technik das Wirkliche als Bestand entbirgt" (idem: 28). And: "Wenn die Physik in zunehmendem Maße sich damit abfinden muß, daß ihr Vorstellungsbereich unanschaulich bleibt, dann ist dieser Verzicht nicht von irgendeiner Kommission von Forschern diktiert. Er ist vom Walten des Ge-stells herausgefordert, das die Bestellbarkeit der Natur als Bestand verlangt. Darum kann die Physik bei allem

objectifying practice, while both apprehension and practice dialectically result from each other.

Anyhow, by pointing to the interdependence of historical changes in fundamental metaphysical suppositions and its related lifeforms, Heidegger also revealed the perspectivist character of reality in general. This move towards a historical, life-based and finally perspectivist concept of truth was influenced by Nietzsche's radical anti-rationalist critique of foundationalism. Nietzsche mistrusted the Christian narratives of goodness and truth as universal principles of being. While Hegel had still struggled with the contradiction between the transcendental perfection of the absolute (which he had borrowed from Spinoza) and the imperfection of the contingent forms, the ultimate problem how a good Absolute or God could be unified with apparent evil events, Nietzsche championed the Dionysian exuberant a-morality and irrationality as the real spirit of existence. From Nietzsche's point of view, Christian morality was just a perverted, hypocritical version of the universal will-to-power (*Wille zur Macht*),[56] and rationalism and truth were only ideological narratives of legitimation. The will-to-power did not simply follow an alternative rationality, it was essentially irrational, following rather aesthetic principles between the antagonistic poles of Dionysian, dark, ecstatic wildness against the Apollonic dream of reason, clarity and beauty.[57] Hence, truth-claims, whatever their propositions, have to be mistrusted, as they always aim to justify a particular aesthetic form of enacting the will-to-power, that is, historical life-forms striving for their total realisation.[58] There is no "truth" in any metaphysical sense, but only changing truths legitimating moral systems as products of historical realisations of the will-to-power. In his anti-metaphysical,[59] anti-rationalist, anti-realist, anti-everything! rage, Nietzsche dismantled the autonomous subject together with its myth of rationality, logical reasoning and objective truth.[60] Instead of insisting on a useless quest for truth, we would do better to accept the phantasmagoric character of being, assuming

Rückzug aus dem bis vor kurzem allein maßgebenden, nur den Gegenständen zugewandten Vorstellen auf eines niemals verzichten: daß sich die Natur in irgendeiner rechnerisch feststellbaren Weise meldet und als ein System von Informationen bestellbar bleibt" (idem: 28).

[56] "- Leben selbst ist Wille zur Macht -" (Nietzsche 2002: 20). With his concept of will-to-power, Nietzsche heavily leans on Schopenhauer's world as will.

[57] Compare also Habermas (1988).

[58] "[…] - das meiste bewußte Denken eines Philosophen ist durch seine Instinkte heimlich geführt und in bestimmte Bahnen gezwungen. Auch hinter aller Logik und ihrer anscheinenden Selbstherrlichkeit der Bewegung stehen Wertschätzungen, deutlicher gesprochen, philosophische Forderungen zur Erhaltung einer bestimmten Art von Leben" (Nietzsche 2002: 9).

[59] Nietzsche's concept of will-to-power is, of course, also a metaphysical principle (compare e.g. Heidegger 1954), although Nietzsche would never accept this view. But contradictions did not seem to bother Nietzsche too much.

[60] "[...], jenes 'ich denke' setzt voraus, daß ich meinen augenblicklichen Zustand mit anderen Zuständen, die ich an mir kenne, vergleiche, um so festzusetzen, was er ist: wegen dieser Rückbeziehung auf anderweitiges 'Wissen' hat er für mich jedenfalls keine unmittelbare Gewißheit" (idem: 23).

that we are all notorious liars, and stopping overestimating our supposedly rational mind.[61]

> With Nietzsche's metaphysics, philosophy has been concluded. That is to say: it trespassed the perimeter of its predestined potentials (Heidegger 1954: 83).[62]

Obscure, complex and contradictory as he was, Nietzsche would have an extremely powerful influence throughout the twentieth century both on philosophy and social sciences. His revolt against Hegelian rationalism of the philosophical establishment would also be followed by George Bataille, who called for a complete inversion of traditional views. Bataille's surreal, highly provocative works explored the irrational essence of the human mind as well as life in general, which he painted as an exuberant, ecstatic celebration of life-energy expenditure.[63] Both Nietzsche and Bataille stood at the beginning of a profound critique of the modern subject and rationalism, which would be further explored by authors like Lacan, Horkheimer, Adorno, Foucault, Deleuze and Derrida.[64]

Faced with the destructive forces of modern science and technology unleashed during the two great wars, with racism and its scientific justification, and finally, with the tragic lapse of enlightenment into totalitarism, Horkheimer and Adorno[65] submitted modern rationalism and the role of science to a critical analysis of its ideological fundaments. Following their analysis, fascism was not the result of counter-enlightenment, a mere return to the obscurantism of the myths and pure barbarism, but of a self-destructive element intrinsic to enlightenment itself. Following Max Weber's concept of disenchantment[66] as resulting from the abstract view of nature as calculus, which makes nature disposable to exploration, Horkheimer and Adorno hold that Cartesian dualism and its resulting subjectivism is instrumental not only to the domination of nature, but also the objectification of human subjects. Under the sway of positivist sciences, technology and capitalist production, subjects are reduced to manipulable masses. Hence, the instrumental character of science together with its universalistic pretension[67] finally betrays its original promise of liberating the human race from the burden of nature's tyranny,

---

[61] Nietzsche (1887).

[62] My translation from the original: "Mit Nietzsches Metaphysik ist die Philosophie vollendet. Das will sagen: sie hat den Umkreis der vorgezeichneten Möglichkeiten überschritten".

[63] Bataille (1972, 2001).

[64] Compare also Habermas (1988).

[65] Horkheimer and Adorno (1969); Horkheimer (1937).

[66] Weber (1919).

[67] Horkheimer (1937) had already referred to the instrumental and ideological character of scientific theorising for technological progress and the maintenance of capitalism and the hegemony of the bourgeois class: "Soweit der Begriff der Theorie jedoch verselbständigt wird, als ob er etwa aus dem inneren Wesen der Erkenntnis oder sonstwie unhistorisch zu begründen sei, verwandelt er sich in eine verdinglichte, ideologische Kategorie. [...] Dass eine Entdeckung die Umstrukturierung vorhandener Ansichten veranlasst, ist nie ausschließlich durch logische Erwägungen, des näheren durch den Widerspruch zu bestimmten Teilen der herrschenden Vorstellungen begründbar. Es sind immer Hilfshypothesen ausdenkbar, durch die eine Änderung der Theorie im ganzen vermieden

transforming, instead, humans into objects and submitting the manipulable masses to the demands of technological development and capitalist economy. Though legitimating itself as grand demystifier of myth, by objectifying both nature and the inner nature of the subject, enlightenment had itself become a grand myth. Now, the myth of a positivist fact-based world view would justify social reality as a necessary result of naturalised economic forces. In so arguing, Horkheimer and Adorno built on Nietzsche's definition of reason as a means of domination and his unmasking of the dominant classes' false morality. In the hands of Horkheimer and Adorno, however, Nietzsche's sceptical view concerning the intrinsic relatedness of truth and power is instrumental to an anti-materialist, more dialectical critique of modern capitalism and the ideological faith in technological progress.

All their harsh critics notwithstanding, Horkheimer and Adorno emphasised that they did not aim to abolish enlightenment, but on the contrary, to salvage its liberating ideals by means of a critical reflection on its relations to power and domination. However, by demystifying enlightenment as myth and accusing reason itself of being ideological, their argument remains within the typical demystificationalist attitude of enlightenment's logical scepticism, which their critique actually pretended to unmask.[68]

This tricky contradiction would also haunt Michel Foucault,[69] a brother in mind and heir to Nietzsche, Heidegger and the critical school.[70] His "archeology" traced the genesis of the modern subject by browsing between the lines of history and tracking the formative processes of its constitutive normative discourses about the body, sexuality, health or madness. Foucault's method is an expression of an entirely constructionist, and hence, relativist notion of perception and truth, which is explicitly objecting positivist and biological concepts of sexuality, gender or the subject. Far from being natural categories, they are naturalised historical figures, patterns of intellectual, aesthetic and moral notions, and institutionalised disciplinary practices. As such, they are an expression of omnipresent subtle power-relations which, together, form epochal *dispositives* of social and cosmological order. The autonomous subject, as the decisive instance for truth is the central idea of the modern *episteme*, its representational reality, and its cosmological narcissism. But the subject is just an ephemeral chimera in western history, which appeared with Cartesian dualism, becoming problematic with Kant's transcendental subject, to disappear with the emergence of the human sciences and their "discovery" of the unconscious and its social constitution.[71] However, the human and social sciences are bound to

---

werden könnte" (idem: 7); and further: "Die Beziehung von Hypothesen auf Tatsachen vollzieht sich schließlich nicht im Kopf der Gelehrten, sondern in der Industrie" (idem: 9).

[68] Habermas (1988).

[69] Idem.

[70] Actually, Foucault developed much of his early work in parallel to the Frankfurt school, without making reference to it, but later emphasised his debts to the critical theory.

[71] Following to Foucault (1974), the aporia of the modern subject resulted from the Kantian epistemological principle for unlimited cognisance based on transcendental conditions of a limited subject. However, it also followed from the modern will to know, which is ultimately also a will to

the same contingent changes in modern *episteme* and social practices as the autonomous subject itself, and hence, are not able to overcome the aporia of the subject-object-dilemma and its narcissistic self-objectification. For Foucault, therefore, in order to free the human subject from its own tyranny, it is necessary to go beyond the anthropologic philosophy of humanism, that is, to become anti-humanistic in a political sense (a project which would be further developed by Deleuze and Guattari[72]).

However, the most influential legacy of Foucault's work was probably his "methodological toolbox",[73] containing discourse-analysis, the archaeological and genealogical method, and most notably, his particular concepts of power and knowledge. Power, as Foucault understood it, is an intrinsic aspect of any social relation, not only of dominance or oppression, and truth in a way orients these relations as a kind of "perceptive matrix".[74] However, knowledge and truth are themselves the results of power-relations and the related disciplinary practices. Together they constitute regimes of truth which accept certain discourses as true while excluding others as illegitimate. Thus, power and knowledge co-emerge in the course of changing social relations; they are the two sides of the same coin, both equally contingent and historical in character. As a consequence, there is, by definition, no absolute truth nor any neutral knowledge—every discourse and every proposition is always bound to particular power-relations, either reinforcing them or putting them at stake, always trying to impose their own normative truths.[75] Hence, knowledge is always built on the systematic exclusion of other knowledge. This is especially true for the modern sciences, which are identified as an institutionalised form of such an exclusion mechanism. In his later works, Foucault turned his gaze from the dominant to the disqualified forms of knowledge. His genealogical method[76] was meant to make these struggles between opposing power-knowledge-complexes visible, to question the legitimacy of the established scientific discourses, to be an "anti-science"[77] in defence of subaltern modes of knowing and being, and finally, to empower them in their struggle against the dominant theoretical, uniform scientific discourse[78]—in other words, to be a weapon against scientific universalism.

Foucault's work received wide acceptance and provided important impulses to queer theory, feminism, post-colonial and science studies, and was fundamental to

power, a will to overcome its own limitations; and the humanities (as a kind of pseudo-sciences) would have the function to mystify the structural will to self-understanding modern power is based upon. For details on the discussion of Foucault's dictum of the "death of the human subject" and his "anti-humanism" see also Améry (1982); Marti (1988); Schädelbach (1989); Kögler (2004); Sarasin (2005); Kammler et al. (2008); Keller (2008a, b).

[72] Deleuze and Guattari (2000).

[73] Keller (2008b).

[74] Idem.

[75] Foucault (1978).

[76] Foucault (1978, 1981).

[77] Foucault (1978: 62).

[78] Idem: 64.

the entire post-modern discourse. However, he did not overcome subjectivism, but rather intensified the work of the social sciences in showing, once again, that the autonomous subject is an "incurable rupture",[79] a yawning gap between the two sides of the one essence, our inner and outer reality, mind and body, culture and nature, meaning and logic, perception and being, thus, reaffirming Hegel's "*Entzweiung*", Marx's "alienation", Nietzsche's "nihilism", Weber's "disenchantment", Husserl's "crisis of modern sciences" and Heidegger's "*Seinsvergessenheit*". After noting that structuralism had not destroyed the subject (as he had initially assumed in his archeology of human sciences[80]), Foucault himself completed the work he had foreseen for the social sciences. Eventually, he ended up following Nietzsche's suggestion to content ourselves with our illusions, for they are all we have,[81] and thus motivating authors like Baudrillard[82] and Taussig[83] to declare the character of reality to be essentially symbolic, mimetic, simulative or phantasmagoric—in a word: an illusion. Foucault killed the modern subject without offering any substitute. In this sense, his "toolbox" contained the weapons for the final destruction of "reality", and he would be heavily criticised for his supposedly pessimistic and anti-revolutionary outlook.[84]

Foucault's work has not only been fundamental for post-modern discourse, it is also emblematic of what post-modernity stands for: it was the attempt to end or transform modernity by demystifying its meta-narratives[85] in order to open ways for new alternatives, to give enlightenment a second chance by transcending its metaphysical foundations. However, it was not only the end of modernity's grand narrative, the autonomous subject, but also the end of truth, ethics and identity, and hence, did not end modernity, but rather deconstructed the very fundaments of human orientation in an inexplicable world. In the "liquid"[86] post-modern world there are only simulacra and hybrid identities. Postmodernism is so diluting that we are still not even sure how we should name it or whether it actually existed! Is it not

---

[79] Deleuze and Foucault (1977).

[80] Foucault (1974).

[81] "Gesetzt, wir wollen Wahrheit: w a r u m n i c h t l i e b e r Unwahrheit? Und Ungewissheit? Selbst Unwissenheit?" (Nietzsche 1887: 7). "Die Unwahrheit als Lebensbedingung zugestehen: das heißt freilich auf eine gefährliche Weise den gewohnten Wertgefühlen Widerstand leisten; und eine Philosophie die das wagt, stellt sich damit allein schon jenseits von Gut und Böse" (idem.: 10). "[…] wir erdichten uns den größten Teil des Erlebnisses und sind kaum dazu zu zwingen, n i c h t als "Erfinder" irgendeinem Vorgang zuzuschauen. Dies alles will sagen: wir sind von Grund aus, von alters her—a n s L ü g e n g e w ö h n t. Oder, um es tugendhafter und heuchlerischer zu sagen, kurz angenehmer auszudrücken: man ist vielmehr Künstler, als man weiß" (idem: 102).

[82] Baudrillard (1982).

[83] Taussig (1997).

[84] E.g. Améry (1982); Habermas (1988); Ndjodo (2013). Of course, Foucault himself saw the contingent character of knowledge also as a chance for change.

[85] Lyotard (1986).

[86] Bauman (1998).

rather an "unfinished project"[87] or "late modernity"[88]? Or why not better call it "post-truth" instead, referring to its radical relativism?

In essence, post-modern discourse was the consequent continuation of enlightenment and its sceptical demystification reflexively applied to itself.[89] Hence, while attacking the subjectivist metaphysical foundations of modernity, the post-modern critique continued to hold on to most of these same metaphysical presuppositions.[90] Rather than overcoming dualism and subjectivism, by dissolving the autonomous subject into unconscious and contingent social structures, and thus, becoming ever more constructionist and relativist, it further widened the gap between subjective and objective reality, rendering it practically unbridgeable. As a result, postmodernism deepened Kant's dilemma instead of solving it,[91] while maintaining representationalism. In the same way, it destroyed rationalism together with the autonomous subject by means of rational arguments. Furthermore, it proclaimed the contingent character of truth, while tacitly assuming this to be a sufficient reason to deduce its complete relativity, too, thus reproducing metaphysical foundationalism. And last but not least, the postmodern critique of modernity aimed to transcend enlightenment in order to overcome its shortcomings and finally open ways to a better, "post-modern" world, thus, holding on to typically modern ideas of progress and linear time.[92]

This circularity[93] in post-modern thought had several serious consequences. First of all, post-modern philosophy became more and more sociological, anthropological and historical, and eventually, almost fused with social sciences while departing ever more from the natural sciences. Moreover, by unveiling the contingent character of the rational subject and debunking the irrational aspects of scientific knowl-

---

[87] Habermas (1988) argues, against post-modernism, that modernity has not been overcome, but instead, still needs to be concluded. True, modernity is based on the enlightenment ideal and the autonomous subject, however, in contrast to traditional world views, modernity does not find its reason in religious dogmas, but has to create it from itself (Hegel would be the first to realise that). Therefore, we should radicalise the enlightenment project of freedom through rationality rather than returning to irrationalism. Habermas' theory of communicational action suggests cultivating open dialogue based on rational argument, but his attempt to rescue enlightenment fails, for he has no answer to the question of power.

[88] Giddens (1991).

[89] Latour (1993).

[90] Most notably, it attacked the autonomous rational subject by means of rational scepticism and within the framework of representationalism, which was tacitly taken for a universal. Postmodern critique debunked truth based on the autonomous subject to be only a contingent, construed, and hence, illusive representation and then concluded that truth in general is illusive. The possibility of an alternative, non-representational concept of truth has never been seriously considered within postmodern rationale. So, in effect, it said: The modern concept of truth was an illusion (and of course we assume this concept to be only admissible as we cannot think outside this framework), hence, truth in general is an illusion.

[91] Strong constructionism actually completely abolishes objective reality, leaving only the subjects isolated inner world.

[92] Stengers (2000).

[93] E.g. Ndjodo (2013); Habermas (1988).

edge, post-modern critique promoted relativism instead of valorising other kinds of knowledge. Much to the contrary, by declaring knowledge to be irrational and contingent, it rather downgraded knowledge in general, stating that scientific knowledge is as irrational and illusive as non-scientific knowledge, instead of cherishing other ways of knowing as kinds of alternative scientific traditions.[94]

Nonetheless, Foucault's works and post-modern critique in general have contributed to a new understanding of our modern world, and its findings, as well as its powerful "toolbox", have become essential elements of current research on science and knowledge. It would make little sense to throw it into the historical dustbin of failed paradigms, rather we should learn from its failings. The principal pitfall of postmodernism was to adopt the anti-metaphysical bearing of its predecessors,[95] which made it blind towards its own metaphysical basis and kept it trapped within the solipsistic cage of representational epistemology. So, the most important lesson from this experience is, I think, that we have to go back to metaphysics. Instead of declaring the end of truth and falling into radical relativism, we should continue the postmodern inquiry into the different ways in which knowledge systems are related to particular social structures and ask about the concrete effects of their metaphysical presumptions in terms of the social realities they produce. I will come back to this point later.

3.3 The Empiricist Heritage

While the rationalist or idealist strand in modern philosophy culminated in post-modern discourse and its fusion with the social sciences, it practically abandoned the natural sciences, declaring their objectivist, universalist stance to be ideological. But of course, there were also philosophers to defend the natural sciences from constructionists' attacks and organise their ideas under what would become known as philosophy of science and analytical philosophy.

After Kant, Newtonian natural philosophers, mainly in Britain, would not only attack Cartesianism, but also German metaphysical idealism. Following Francis Bacon and Newton's anti-metaphysical empiricism,[96] scholars like William Whewell, John Herschel and John Stuart Mill tried to solve the epistemological riddles left behind by Hume and Kant. Their attempts to defend the inductive method and to provide a solid epistemological legitimation for the natural sciences would finally result in the dogmatic positivism which predominated during the nineteenth and early twentieth century. However, instead of eliminating metaphysical presumptions and solving the epistemological problems set by Hume and Kant,

---

[94] Harding (1994).

[95] Namely Nietzsche, Bataille, Husserl, Heidegger. Although being critical of the dominant positivism of their times, interestingly, they shared anti-metaphysicalism with their opponents.

[96] Wilson (1974); Maxwell (2017).

positivists followed Newton in masking their own metaphysical presumptions as generalisations induced from empirical evidence.[97] Albeit accepting representationalism and the resulting inevitably phenomenal character of reality, they finally concluded that our perceptions would necessarily fit with the natural order of the universe, as clearly shown by the predictive power of Newton's laws.[98] As a consequence, metaphysical presuppositions like linear time, absolute space, deterministic causality, uniformity of the universe or the mathematical essence of natural laws were justified as necessarily true by virtue of evidence. The natural laws discovered by Newton and his colleagues were as true as any knowledge could possibly be, and the principles of mechanics were moving every aspect of the universe. Hence, inductive knowledge was not limited by perception, but the limits of mathematics and logical reasoning. Newton's first rule of reasoning, that only true and sufficient causes are admissible in science, was adopted as the defining principle of the new natural sciences. Consequently, positivism relocated the epistemological question from the transcendental problem of perception to the problem of logical reasoning and true propositions.

This move became ever more explicit with Ernst Mach's critical conception of positivism. He not only criticised Newton's mechanics and his concept of absolute time and space (Mach's principle)[99]; Mach also carried the unresolved transcendental questions of former positivism to their logical consequences. In accepting the impossibility of distinguishing between perception and perceived object, between self and world,[100] Mach rejected any kind of metaphysical speculation about a hypothetical non-experiential reality as well as naturalistic and materialistic equations of theory with reality. Following Mach's anti-realist view, empirical evidence was simply data to be organised as economically as possible into theoretical models with

[97] In his 1843 work *A System of Logic*, John Stuart Mill introduced his inductive method arguing, that although the uniformity of the universe is a metaphysical presumption, it has to be true as it is fundamental for the natural sciences, which provide true predictions, and can be induced from observation. In so arguing, Mill transforms an absolute presupposition into a generalisation (induction of second order), which is, of course, a completely circular argument. Collingwood (1998) further observes that nineteenth century positivism was an expression of Oxford platonism, which was based on an inverse interpretation of Plato that made him agree with Mill. And Collingwood concludes that positivism was "the attempt to justify by appeal to observed facts the absolute presuppositions of our thought".

[98] Although Whewell held to Kant's apriorism while Herschel defended Hume's radical empiricism both agreed that our perceptions and logical reasoning would finally have to match with the natural order of things, as both the mind and the universe were created by God, and hence, would follow to the same principles, with man's mind necessarily being in harmony with the hidden realm of natural laws (Wilson 1974). In so arguing, Whewell and Herschel not only fell back behind Kant in assuming Locke's naive psychologism (in the case of Whewell) or Hume's radical empiricism while ignoring its sceptical consequences (in the case of Herschel), they also returned to Descartes' theological argument to sustain their unsustainable beliefs.

[99] Heller (1964).

[100] Brentano (1988).

maximal predictive power.[101] Science can, at best, offer coherent, albeit provisional models based on available data and logical conjectures.[102] Mach's relativistic conception of time and space would be important for the groundbreaking theories of physicists like Albert Einstein and Max Planck, influencing not only their ideas concerning the physical principles of the universe, but also their positivist notion of science.[103] However, Einstein and Planck would also object to Mach's critical stance toward science as ultimately following standards of human subjectivity and artificial measurements rather than universal objective constants and natural laws.[104]

Moreover, and may-be more importantly, Mach would also inspire a group of philosophers to engage in yet another endeavour to finally put modern science on solid epistemological grounds. This group of philosophers, many of whom belonged to the so-called Circles of Vienna and Berlin, later joined in a wider movement often termed logical empiricism, logical positivism or neo-positivism.[105] Other important impulses came from Bertrand Russell and Ludwig Wittgenstein and their anti-metaphysical approach of logical atomism.[106] In a sense, logical positivism, as derived from Russell, "developed into the following syllogism. 'Any proposition which cannot be verified by appeal to observed facts is a pseudo-proposition. Metaphysical propositions cannot be verified by appeal to observed facts. Therefore, metaphysical propositions are pseudo-propositions, and therefore nonsense.'[107]" Inspired by new developments in non-Euclidean geometry, Einstein's relativity theory and the growing importance of mathematics in scientific reasoning, it seemed promising to explore mathematical logic as the ultimate arbiter to distinguish between scientific certainty and metaphysical blunder. Based on the works of

---

[101] Mach's radical reductionism is a direct result of his evolutionary and biologistic concept of science as a pragmatic means for orientation in rather than true explanation of the universe. "As is typical for Mach, widely accepted biological principles become uncritically held cornerstones of his epistemology" (Pojman 2019).

[102] Vorländer (1902).

[103] Although both would later critique Mach's denial to accept their new theories (Pojman 2019).

[104] "Wirklich ist, was sich messen läßt." (Max Plank, quoted in Heidegger 1954: 58). Compare also Pojman (2019).

[105] The nineteenth century had witnessed the funding of a serious of new scientific disciplines, like physics, chemistry, biology, sociology, anthropology of psychology, advancing with astonishing velocity while philosophy seemed to be trapped within a bubble of metaphysical pseudo-problems; with each new scientific discipline philosophy seemed to lose another field of reasoning, raising the question what would actually be left for philosophy? Faced with an unprecedented outbreak of chaos and irrationality during the 1930s and the failure of continental philosophy (both metaphysical idealism and anti-metaphysical approaches as those of Nietzsche or Heidegger) to fulfil the promises of enlightenment, philosophers related to logical empiricism once again, aspired to make Francis Bacon's dream of a rational society led by scientific evidence come true. Logical reasoning, mathematics and empirical evidence alone should guide the human race, instead of dogmatism, religion and political fanaticism (Creath 2022).

[106] Logical atomism tried to avoid metaphysical assumptions by dividing assertion about reality into logically independent facts. However, it would turn out that there are no such independent facts (Maxwell 2017).

[107] Collingwood (1998): position 1866.

Russell, Gödel, Frege and Wittgenstein's non-content theory of logic, meaningful sentences could be analysed to verify their truth value in respect to both their empirical proof and logical coherence. Verificationalism appeared to be the perfect tool against metaphysicalism. However, it soon turned out that under such rigorous standards not only any ethic, aesthetic or religious claims were nonsense, but even the most important natural laws of modern science would be rendered metaphysical, and thus, unscientific. Many attempts were made to solve this logical riddle (particularly by Rudolf Carnap), without the desired success. After finally having to accept verificationalism to be a flop, most philosophers who had participated in logical empiricism went different ways, some of them founding new philosophical schools. Many had fled to the United States during World War II, where their particular analytical thought style, later known as analytical philosophy, had influenced a new generation of philosophers who were basically concerned with defining truth following strictly logical rules (in opposition to continental philosophy, as discussed above). Others, like Wittgenstein, Quine, Putnam or Popper, turned more or less radically against the principles of logical empiricism.

Wittgenstein's[108] radical turn not only outraged his former teacher, Bertrand Russell, for its complete contradiction of his former position exposed in the *Tractatus;* by analysing language as lived activity or *form of life*[109] and relativising the meaning of sentences as contextually related to particular *language games*, Wittgenstein also made a general critique of any language-based logical analysis of truth values. While broadly rejected by his former colleagues from the Vienna Circle, his approach would be welcomed by postmodern authors like Lyotard,[110] receiving by and large an anti-naturalist, relativist reception.

Karl Popper,[111] in contrast, remained faithful to the idea of providing science with a solid methodological fundament. However, he rejected both verificationalism and inductive empiricism as untenable. Instead of verifying new hypotheses, Popper suggested falsifying them. As long as a hypothesis is consistent with known facts and has not yet been falsified by evidence, it can be treated as a valid model within a wider theoretical framework. This proposal entailed, as a necessary condition, that any hypothesis must be testable in the face of facts, that is, empirical evidence and

---

[108] Wittgenstein (1958).

[109] "[…] to imagine a language means to imagine a form of life" (idem: § 19). "But how many kinds of sentence are there? Say assertion, question, and command?—There are countless kinds: countless different kinds of use of what we call "symbols", "words", "sentences". And this multiplicity is not something fixed, given once for all; but new types of language, new language-games, as we may say, come into existence, and others become obsolete and get forgotten. (We can get a rough picture of this from the changes in mathematics.) Here the term "language-game" is meant to bring into prominence the fact that the speaking of language is part of an activity, or of a form of life" (idem: § 23). ""So you are saying that human agreement decides what is true and what is false?"—It is what human beings say that is true and false; and they agree in the language they use. That is not agreement in opinions but in form of life" (idem: § 241).

[110] Although Wittgenstein would hardly agree with Lyotard's use of his concept of language-games (Lyotard 1986).

[111] Popper (2005).

an established theoretical framework. Hence, a hypothesis which cannot be falsified by evidence is, by definition, unscientific. However, Popper's principle of falsification and his evolutionary model of scientific progress was more a repetition of Ernst Mach evolutionism and Charles Sanders Peirce's fallibilism than a real innovation. Moreover, with insisting on his demarcationalism[112] based on the dogmatic a priori exclusion of non-falsifiable claims, Popper incriminated himself in all kinds of contradictions, in some respect falling back behind Peirce's earlier pragmatic approach. Popper claimed he had solved the problem of induction with his falsificationism. However, he actually only pretended to circumvent it, while tacitly presuming some kind of correspondence between the object and its perception (despite his anti-empiricist and anti-naturalist attitude), as well as universal uniformity of nature (otherwise the hypothetical assumption of any general rule would be as meaningless as its falsification).

Moreover, Willard Van Orman Quine had shown that hypotheses cannot be tested in isolation. Following Quine, the relation between analytic sentences and their empirical basis was circular, because empirical data in themselves were under-determined and needed to be interpreted within a wider theoretical framework based on unprovable,[113] and hence, ultimately relative metaphysical presumptions about the ontological constitution of the universe (e.g. it is impossible to provide evidence for the existence or non-existence of unobservable entities like the Greeks' "Gods" or electromagnetic "waves", although there may be phenomena that could be described using such metaphors)[114]; or to put it in a nutshell, all experience is theory-laden and ultimately based on metaphysical, non-falsifiable presumptions.

[112] Stengers (2000).

[113] "The totality of our so-called knowledge or beliefs, from the most casual matters of geography and history to the profoundest laws of atomic physics or even of pure mathematics and logic, is a man-made fabric which impinges on experience only along the edges. Or, to change the figure, total science is like a field of force whose boundary conditions are experience. [...] Having re-evaluated one statement we must re-evaluate some others, whether they be statements logically connected with the first or whether they be the statements of logical connections themselves. But the total field is so undetermined by its boundary conditions, experience, that there is much latitude of choice as to what statements to reevaluate in the light of any single contrary experience" (Quine 1951: 39).

[114] "As an empiricist I continue to think of the conceptual scheme of science as a tool, ultimately, for predicting future experience in the light of past experience. Physical objects are conceptually imported into the situation as convenient intermediaries—not by definition in terms of experience, but simply as irreducible posits comparable, epistemologically, to the gods of Homer. Let me interject that for my part I do, qua lay physicist, believe in physical objects and not in Homer's gods; and I consider it a scientific error to believe otherwise. But in point of epistemological footing the physical objects and the gods differ only in degree and not in kind. Both sorts of entities enter our conception only as cultural posits. The myth of physical objects is epistemologically superior to most in that it has proved more efficacious than other myths as a device for working a manageable structure into the flux of experience" (idem: 41). "Total science, mathematical and natural and human, is similarly but more extremely underdetermined by experience. The edge of the system must be kept square with experience; the rest, with all its elaborate myths or fictions, has as its objective the simplicity of laws" (idem: 42).

Additionally, Thomas Kuhn's[115] critique of Popper's evolutionary model of scientific progress had shown how deeply scientific knowledge is rooted in contingent historical belief systems. Rather than being a continuous evolutionary progress resulting from methodological testing and selecting of hypotheses, scientific theory appeared to be subject to revolutionary changes in its theoretical frameworks, or *paradigms* in Kuhn's terminology, while facts would be either ignored as anomalies or reinterpreted in a way to make them fit the current paradigm. Despite Kuhn's own commitment to science, his approach has been largely interpreted as a strong argument in support of social constructionism and relativism.

Although equally rejecting Popper's methodological falsificationism, Imre Lakatos[116] did his best to reconcile it with Kuhn's critique. In his *method of scientific research programmes*, Lakatos holds that even if hypotheses cannot be falsified in isolation, the research programmes (his version of Kuhn's paradigms) they belonged to could be evaluated as a whole according to their predictive power.[117] While progressive research programmes would anticipate still unobserved fact, degenerating research programmes would increasingly depend on post hoc explanations of observed anomalies. However, Lakatos himself points to the equally conventionalist character of his approach and then goes on to justify it anyway, arguing that the internal history of scientific progress (e.g. Newton's defence of inductive positivism) would be related to, but not determined by, external historical events and changes in worldview. In effect, Popper's demarcationism turned out to be untenable, since there is no strictly objective knowledge independent of contingent historical events.

It seems that all attempts to establish a clear line between scientific and non-scientific knowledge based on methodological or epistemological criteria are doomed to fail. Neither idealism, nor positivism, logical empiricism or falsificationism finally managed to solve the problem of induction or to escape some sort of regression to metaphysical presumptions, and hence, to the contingency of scientific knowledge as defended by social constructionism and its implicit relativism.[118] To maintain that scientific knowledge is "objective", giving a more realist account of nature because it excludes value-judgments and metaphysical presumptions, or because it is falsifiable while other types of knowledge are not, is simply wrong.

---

[115] Kuhn (1970).

[116] Lakatos (1977).

[117] "[…] before Newton the problem was whether it is possible at all to arrive at episteme; after Newton the problem became how it was possible to arrive at episteme, and how one can extend it to other spheres of knowledge [...] The influence of Newtonian success was then possibly the most powerful influence on modern thought" (idem: 221).

[118] Maxwell (2017) points out that the origins of this failure appears to be grounded in the strange fact that despite all the harsh critique against Descartes' rationalism and the predicaments implied in his dualism, philosophy after Descartes "rather preoccupied itself with the problems Cartesian dualism generates even though Cartesian dualism itself is rejected" (idem: 97). However, as I tried to show earlier, the natural sciences depend on the maintenance of dualism to continue treating nature as an object, which may be the reason for this "fundamental failure of philosophy" (ibidem).

This failure to provide modern science with a solid epistemological fundament stands in stark contrast to its general acceptance as a hegemonic knowledge system and its undeniable predictive power. In other words, science's universalist pretensions cannot be justified on methodological or epistemological grounds, but, if ever, only with respect to its ability to predict and control physical events. However, from a foundationalist point of view, its effectiveness does not necessarily prove a higher truth-value or explanatory power of science compared to other kinds of knowledge.

3.4 Pragmatism

There has been yet another approach which tried to find a middle ground to avoid both the shortcomings of empiricism as well as those of rationalism. During the last decades of the nineteenth century, Charles Sanders Peirce[119] and William James[120] proposed a more pragmatic way to handle the epistemological predicaments arising from representationalism and foundationalism. The ideas of Peirce and James were influential to a wide range of epistemological approaches throughout the twentieth century, such as logical empiricism, critical realism, analytical philosophy and neo-pragmatism, but many of pragmatism's original core tenets got lost in those subsequent receptions.

Pragmatism followed Mach's anti-realist instrumentalism in casting out metaphysical speculations about the relation between subject and object,[121] but extended the instrumental character of theoretical models beyond the scope of prediction and control. Peirce[122] defined truth in terms of belief as "a rule for action" essentially aiming at the "establishment of habits".[123] In other words, for us as human beings, truth is what we believe firmly enough to orient our decisions and our actions. Hence, the truth-value of a theory would not only be defined by its not being falsified by evidence, but first and foremost concerning its practical implication for human life.

---

[119] Peirce (1878).

[120] James (1981).

[121] Rorty (1979).

[122] Peirce was not only the first to introduce the concept of falsification, he also coined the term Pragmatism for this new train of non-representational epistemology.

[123] "The essence of belief is the establishment of a habit, and different beliefs are distinguished by the different modes of action to which they give rise. […] What the habit is depends on *when* and *how* it causes us to act. As for the *when*, every stimulus to action is derived from perception; as for the *how*, every purpose of action is to produce some sensible result. Thus, we come down to what is tangible and practical, as the root of every real distinction of thought, no matter how subtile it may be; and there is no distinction of meaning so fine as to consist in anything but a possible difference of practice" (Peirce 1878). Peirce habitual definition of truth showed certain parallels with Max Weber's interpretative sociology as applied in *The Protestant Ethics and the Spirit of Capitalism*, Heidegger's concept of the *Ge-stell* or Bourdieu's *habitus* as more or less unconscious perceptive matrix based on naturalised conventions that orient our behaviour.

However, Peirce still tried to square his pragmatic theory of truth with the idea of applicability in terms of prediction and control[124] on one hand, and a purely conventionalist theory of truth[125] on the other. While James explicitly built on Peirce's pragmatic maxim,[126] he took a more radical approach towards ontological and epistemological relativism. Although in James view the pragmatic method of asking about the concrete consequences of believing in a particular hypothesis is a means to distinguish true problems from idle disputes, this does not exclude metaphysical questions.[127] Much to the contrary, James shows that ultimately there is no fundamental difference between empirical and metaphysical issues, and once the pragmatic method is applied, "science and metaphysics would come much nearer together, would in fact work absolutely hand in hand".[128] He explicitly discusses the

---

[124] For Peirce, the more operational applicability (prediction and control) a theory provides, the closer it comes to truth. As an example, he refers to the idea of force which had been developed from the idea of cause during the seventeenth century, especially by Newton, and which had not only been essential for modern science, but also for the subsequent deep changes in the whole modern world. However, although force had been conceptualised as an effect describable by mathematical law, it would be nonsense to ask about the cause of this effect. Such metaphysical speculations about the ontological status of phenomena would have no practical result, and thus, be meaningless. In the same vein, Peirce criticised Descartes' sceptical maxim to doubt everything and the rationalists attempt to construe the foundations of truth starting with first, self-evident a priori certainties. Since there are no neutral grounds free from metaphysical presupposition it does not make any sense to doubt everything, but to the contrary, doubt is justified only as long there is reason for doubt, which is settled as soon as there is nobody left to doubt. Hence, certainty is an idle issue and cannot be attained individually, but only collectively by a consensus between well informed researchers. Inquiry and falsification rather than certainty, knowledge seeking rather than knowing should be the aim of science and philosophy. Following Peirce, scientific inquiry is not merely based on induction, but rather a cycle starting with the creative "invention" of a problem, which he called abduction, followed by deduction of theoretical implications and inductive testing (Peirce 1878).

[125] "The opinion which is fated to be ultimately agreed to by all who investigate, is what we mean by the truth, and the object represented in this opinion is the real. That is the way I would explain reality" (EP1: 139; in Legg 2020). Peirce's conventionalist theory of truth imputed a notion of "being constrained by reality" which by virtue of continuous inquiry would necessarily result in a convergence of opinion. However, Russell and Quine criticised this teleological convergence theory and scientific progress, and Peirce himself later relativised it as kind of "regulative hope" (Legg 2020).

[126] "Consider what effects, which might conceivably have practical bearings, we conceive the object of our conception to have. Then, our conception of these effects is the whole of our conception of the object" (Peirce 1878: 6).

[127] "The pragmatic method is primarily a method of settling metaphysical disputes that otherwise might be interminable. Is the world one or many?--fated or free?--material or spiritual?--here are notions either of which may or may not hold good of the world; and disputes over such notions are unending. The pragmatic method in such cases is to try to interpret each notion by tracing its respective practical consequences. What difference would it practically make to anyone if this notion rather than that notion were true? If no practical difference whatever can be traced, then the alternatives mean practically the same thing, and all dispute is idle. Whenever a dispute is serious, we ought to be able to show some practical difference that must follow from one side or the other's being right" (James 1981: 11).

[128] Idem.

consequences of metaphysical hypotheses like the belief in God, free will, spiritualism, the Absolute, matter and energy.[129] James argues that, like in magic, such words would primarily serve the illusion of holding the secret principles of the universe in one's hand. However, from the pragmatic point of view, the only thing that counts is a belief's "practical cash-value, set it at work within the stream of your experience. It appears less as a solution, then, than as a program for more work, and more particularly as an indication of the ways in which existing realities may be CHANGED".[130] For James, the cash-value of a hypotheses is relative to its costs and benefits in relation to its direct effects in life as well as to its implications on other valuable beliefs. A hypothesis may prove to have great results, but contradict another, even more vital belief, and therefore be dropped for being too "expensive".

> If there be any life that it is really better we should lead, and if there be any idea which, if believed in, would help us to lead that life, then it would be really BETTER FOR US to believe in that idea, UNLESS, INDEED, BELIEF IN IT INCIDENTALLY CLASHED WITH OTHER GREATER VITAL BENEFITS (James 1981: 18).

This radically instrumental conception of theories in terms of decision-orienting beliefs also renders the fact-value-dichotomy untenable, for any decision or action has an intrinsically ethical dimension. If a hypothesis is, by definition, only valid if it has practical implications, this means that it necessarily has to be based on value-judgements to be meaningful. Moreover, although truths emerge from facts, facts are theory-laden, since they are always born out of previously produced facts and themselves imprint on future facts, and so forth.[131] The reason for this is our loyalty to our established beliefs, the conservative principle following which even radical changes in our beliefs will leave the core of our theoretical framework and its fundamental conceptions, like time, space, matter or causality, largely untouched. There is simply no reason to question or change our beliefs as long as they do not result in an unacceptable clash with experience or other, more vital beliefs. So,

---

[129] In his discussion concerning the practical effects of metaphysical belief James also contrasts materialist belief in deterministic natural laws with the spiritualist belief in spirit as active mover. James argues that the difference between materialism and theism or spiritualism is that the first denies that moral order is eternal, eliminating any hope for a better future, and hence, the consequences are rather emotional but still very important (idem). However, this is only true for a philosophical God who created the universe to abandon it thereafter, but not for the God or the Gods of real religions, and even less for animist creed in a living world full of entities to whom one can call for support in daily life. Moreover, if nature is entrenched with spirit, if objects become persons, the world changes radically in all its aesthetic, emotional and ethical aspects, and hence, urges us to completely change our behaviour as well. Similarly, James argues that Darwinian theory changed everything and made God obsolete. But the real question is why Darwin could possibly form his idea of an origin other than God?—this was only possible, because God had already become obsolete for the modern worldview. These examples show to what extent not only Peirce, but also James were still involved with the positivistic spirit of their times.

[130] Idem.

[131] "Truths emerge from facts, but they dip forward into facts again and add to them; which facts again create or reveal new truth (the word is indifferent) and so on indefinitely. The 'facts' themselves meanwhile are not true. They simply are. Truth is the function of the beliefs that start and terminate among them" (idem: 50).

despite the non-existence of any clearly definable objective reality, the overall framework of our established beliefs constitutes a very stable reality based on reliable truths.

James' pragmatic ontological relativism has been further developed by Quine,[132] showing how empirically-based hypotheses and metaphysical presumptions are related to each other by their interdependencies within the same theoretical framework, differing gradually concerning their position within the system rather than being essentially different in character. He follows the conservationist principle held by Peirce and James in arguing that recalcitrant experience leads to adjustments in the most peripheral parts of the system, which are closer related to direct experience, while central beliefs are more difficult to change because of empirical facts, as they are much more abstract and remote from direct experience. However, the more central a belief is, the more important it is for our sense of life, and hence, to our attitude. In other words, metaphysical beliefs are both more stable and more effective concerning their concrete consequences in real life than falsifiable, evidence-based hypotheses.[133]

Nevertheless, pragmatism was born out of positivism and sought to justify modern science by virtue of its undeniable efficacy, and hence, underestimated the implications of metaphysical beliefs. To make science a thinkable and desirable endeavour, one has to believe in certain metaphysical presumptions first. Modern science was not a result of empirical inquiry, as held by empiricism, but on the contrary, empirical inquiry was a consequence of certain beliefs held by seventeenth century's natural philosophers. Different sets of presuppositions not only correspond to different kinds of knowledge, but also to different cultural styles and social structures; they are elements of worldviews, a *Zeitgeist* or *episteme* born out of the lived experiences of a generation of intellectuals in the context of particular historical moments.[134]

Philosophers like Robin George Collingwood[135] and more recently, Nicholas Maxwell,[136] have been urging reintroduction of metaphysics into science. In order to overcome the untenable epistemological presumptions of "standard empiricism", and thus become more objective, science has to be conscious of the fundamental presuppositions implicit in its methods and epistemological theories to be able to

---

[132] Quine (1951).

[133] In fact, Quine does not make this logical consequence of his approach explicit. Instead he reaffirms his empiricist stance: "As an empiricist I continue to think of the conceptual scheme of science as a tool, ultimately, for predicting future experience in the light of past experience" (idem: 41). However, this is exactly the attitude which leads into materialism, since physical macro-events accessible to our experience are the only deterministic events, and hence, the only ones susceptible to experimental method and reliable prediction and control.

[134] As shown by a range of philosophers and social scientists like Weber (1919); Whitehead (1925); Merton (1968); Horkheimer and Adorno (1969); Kuhn (1970); Foucault (1974); Bachelard (1978); Böhme (1980); Knorr-Cetina (1981); Latour (1993); Collingwood (1998); Stengers (2000); Fleck (2008); Maxwell (2017); among others.

[135] Collingwood (1998).

[136] Maxwell (2017, 2021).

eliminate untenable contradictions in its theoretical framework.[137] However, the problems implied in modern science's metaphysical presumptions are not merely epistemological, they are also responsible for the current state of our world. The fantastic progress in science and technology not only endowed us with countless great benefits, it is also responsible for most of, if not all, the big problems of our time.[138] Without modern science, there would be no world wars, no weapons of mass destruction, no Industrial Revolution, no capitalism, no environmental disaster, no climate change. The categoric exclusion of value-judgments and metaphysical reasoning, which are generally held to be basic scientific standards for "objectivity", has blinded science not only concerning its epistemological untenability, but also its actual consequences. Enlightenment's dream of a new, better society based on logical reasoning, scientific and technological progress finally got lost in its blind and ultimately frustrated quest for the one, only true "theory for everything". All subsequent radical transformations of our world notwithstanding, the initial aims of science have never been adjusted to the new realities it has been creating.

However, the problem with science's blindness regarding its metaphysical presumptions and its consequences is not exhausted with the direct effects of the knowledge and technology it produces; the real hard problem of modern science lies in the motivating and orienting power of its underlying fundamental (and vastly unconscious) beliefs about the essence of the world, ourselves and our place within the world. These beliefs are responsible for our particular disposition towards the world, orienting all our decisions, aims and actions. The particular "modern" disposition of an autonomous rational subject towards a world of blind matter, which made modern science and technology thinkable, was exactly the target of counter-enlightenment's critique from Goethe to postmodernism,[139] which was also an expression of a fundamental discomfort in our modern culture.[140] For science to

[137] Maxwell (2017) advocates a "[…] new conception of science, which I call aim-oriented empiricism. This view provides methods designed to facilitate the articulation, critical assessment, and improvement of metaphysical assumptions of science. It is the methodological framework for synthesizing metaphysics and empiricism, science and philosophy, and thus recreating something close to seventeenth-century natural philosophy. […] The basic idea is that, in order to give ourselves the best chance of improving the metaphysical assumption accepted by physics, we need to represent this assumption in the form of a hierarchy of assumptions which become, as one goes up the hierarchy, less and less substantial, and more nearly such that their truth is required for science, or the pursuit of knowledge, to be possible at all" (idem: 28).

[138] Idem.

[139] E.g. the romantic movement (Goethe, Schelling), German idealism (Hegel, Schopenhauer), Marx, Nietzsche, Weber, Heidegger, critical school (Horkheimer & Adorno), post-structuralism/-modernism (Foucault et al.), as discussed above.

[140] In his famous abstract about the libido-suppression imposed by culture Freud's (1993) emphasises the failure of technological progress and control over nature to compensate the auto-oppressive imperative of the super-ego. The final question will be, says Freud, whether humanity will use its technological power for self-extermination, and the consciousness about this existential threat may be the reason for the modern's agony.

become conscious[141] of itself and its role in the world it has to understand its metaphysical presuppositions not only in terms of internal coherence and empirical evidence, but first and foremost in terms of a worldview, a belief-system with immediate effects on our way of being in the world.

Interestingly, from the early days of the modern era, European philosophers like Montaigne and Rousseau used alien cultures and their exotic habits for reflections about the shortcomings of their own culture.[142] However, while they concluded that the "savages'" habits might tell us something about how to improve our society, they never considered learning from their knowledge or worldview. But in the face of the above it should be arguable that any change in our social relations as well as concerning our relation to our natural environment is necessarily related to corresponding changes in our knowledge.[143] During the last centuries, none of the endless attempts of modern philosophy to solve or escape the predicaments of dualism and representationalism were blessed with the desired success, so there is little hope that future attempts will succeed, at least not without some external input.[144] It would be interesting, then, to engage in a dialogue with other kinds of knowledge, to analyse their impacts on being and acting in the world and to explore their underlying conceptions of the world.[145]

Unfortunately, science's universalist pretensions forbid such a dialogue with supposedly "unscientific" types of knowledge. But how, after all, can this prohibition be justified if no clear distinction can be drawn between science and non-science, neither on methodological nor on epistemological grounds? Why should it be impossible for science to learn something, let's say for example, from magic? Well, most (especially natural) scientists would probably argue that the effectiveness of magic cannot be proven by evidence, that its effects are not reproducible or that its basic assumptions are not falsifiable. However, as discussed above, science is equally based on non-falsifiable metaphysical assumptions, with inductive empiricism being one of them, and even worse, an untenable one. So, we are still going in circles. Other, epistemologically better-informed scientists might respond then, that some basic assumptions of magic contradict those basic assumptions science is

141 Compare also Edgar Morin's (2005) appeal to a new, more complex sociology of science as conscious metascience.

142 I will come back to this issue in more detail later.

143 I do not pretend to enter the long-lasting debate about the dialectical or howsoever characterised relation between material conditions and ideology, social structure and individual behaviour, etc., also because I think that this question may well be a product of cartesian dualism and might possibly disappear or radically change once different metaphysical presumptions are assumed. For the present purpose I would like to suggest that our fundamental beliefs and our ways of being in the world are "somehow" co-related in a way that both aspects mutually inter-depend on each other, so that changes in our beliefs inevitably imply correlated changes in our way of being and vice versa—or to put it in a nutshell, that they are the two sides of the same coin.

144 Morin (2005).

145 E.g. Varela et al. (1993); Varela and Shear (2002); Linhart (2008); Kuhn and Yazawa (2013); Gutierrez and Esteves (2016); Kuhn and Vessuri (2016); Charbonnier et al. (2017); Walach (2020); among others.

based upon, like say, causality or physicalism. So now, the problem would not be some supposed lack of "objectivity" in terms of methodological or epistemological inferiority compared to modern science, but *incommensurability* between distinct metaphysical presumptions. With this move, the argument switches over to another language game. Now, the argument would go something like this: although science cannot be said to be more "objective" (since there is no objectivity in any strong sense) it provides an undeniable (and highly desirable) power of prediction and control which is based on certain metaphysical presuppositions and resulting methodological practices, and which would have to be violated if magic was accepted to be true. The *foundationalist* argument of being "truer" than other kinds of knowledge has now been abandoned in favour of the *pragmatic* argument of being more effective *and* the *logical* argument of non-contradiction. But the *pragmatic* argument only holds in respect to science's predictive power, which is largely limited to physical events and is weak on the explanatory side. More importantly still, considering the overall costs of scientific progress in terms of modernity's negative fallout, a pragmatic (in a holistic sense) evaluation of science might not necessarily justify the maintenance of all its metaphysical presumptions. Rather it might even indicate the need to reconsider at least some of them for the sake of urgent improvements regarding our performance as a species that needs social peace and nature for survival. And in respect of the *logical* argument of non-contradiction there are equally several objections to be made. First of all, non-contradiction is a rule itself derived from other metaphysical presumptions about the uniformity of nature and its simplicity, which are not only arbitrary, but also not equally applicable to all modern sciences. This is true for the social sciences, where social reality changes with time and place, and were the intrinsic complexity of human affairs calls for holistic theoretical solutions rather than reductionism; but it is also true for physics, which is currently based on three mutually exclusive theoretical approaches about the structure of matter, namely classical mechanics, relativity, and quantum theory. Modern science in its current state is itself theoretically and methodologically disunited. Hence, if one decides to strictly hold on to non-contradiction, most social sciences and physics would be rendered "unscientific" and "incommensurable" as well.[146]

However, this does not mean that non-contradiction and parsimony may not be desirable heuristic ideals or that modern science would not have any beneficial effects we might want to keep. But it does say that these assumptions are metaphysical and value based, and hence, *negotiable*. And suppose we decide to hold to non-contradiction (which I still think is an appealing ideal), there still remains a lot to be

[146] This may sound pretty much like relativism, but as I tried to show above, social constructionism, cultural relativism and the postulated incommensurability between different worldviews have been instrumental for the maintenance of universalism: if "anything goes", why not hold to our own views? Why change our most fundamental beliefs in exchange for no change at all? So I am definitively NOT arguing in favour for relativism, but much to the contrary, trying to find a way out of it. This is precisely what the present work is all about.

improved in science concerning its internal incoherencies,[147] before using incoherence or incommensurability as an argument for judging other kinds of knowledge as inferior.

Nonetheless, incommensurability is a problem, since it is an obstacle once we try to make sense of other views. The problem of translating or interpreting apparently incommensurable ways of being is, of course, a central problem in cultural anthropology. For more than a century now, anthropologists have been attempting to overcome, or at least, to somehow tackle the problem of incommensurability and to come to an understanding concerning the differences between Our and the Others' ways of being in and conceiving the world. I will come back to the scientific construction of the Other and the problem of incommensurability in Chap. 4 of this first part. For now, I would simply like to assume that, while incommensurability and contradiction is no argument for judgments concerning the truth-value of other kinds of knowledge, it is an important obstacle on the way to a real dialogue between modern science and other ways of knowing.

What does all of this tell us about *scientific universalism*? Well, quite simply, that universalism is *ideological* in the classical sense of the term. It is a false belief aiming to motivate collective behaviour favourable for the reproduction of a certain socio-economic system,[148] or to put it in less Marxist terms, particular forms of life or being in the world. It is false for neither being true in the foundationalist sense of being the only purely evidence based, and hence, objective knowledge, nor in the pragmatic sense of guaranteeing better results in our lives. It is, however, effective in reproducing in us the particular disposition towards the world which makes us go on with business as usual, and to believe that other ways of knowing are either inferior or too different to be taken into account when we try to make sense of ourselves, the world, and our place in it. This ideological belief in science as the only viable means of making sense of the world, usually called *scientism*, is the fundament of universalism. Unfortunately, as with all institutionally strong ideologies, it appears that scientism has been internalised by a majority of both scientists and non-scientists,[149] which of course, is the reason for its effectiveness. Thus, in order to overcome universalism and to recognise other ways of knowing in their own right and as possible partners in a fertile dialogue about good ways of making sense of and being in the world, we need to overcome scientism.

To start with, we should get to a better understanding about the metaphysical arguments for the a priori exclusion of so-called non-scientific kinds of knowledge.

---

[147] Compare also Maxwell's (2017) analysis of the hierarchy of presumption of standard empiricism and its internal incoherences.

[148] I will come back to the role of science as hegemonic system of truth within the global geography of knowledge in the next chapter.

[149] This seems to also include philosophers, as indicated by a recent survey by Bourget and Chalmers (2013). However, as this survey also shows, "scientism" is no fixed set of beliefs, but rather a pattern of related bundles of beliefs held by different individuals in varying combinations. However, there are some typical assumptions which are fundamental to the current understanding of scientific method, as well as to the a priori exclusion of so-called non-scientific beliefs.

So what exactly are the metaphysical presuppositions scientism is based on and why and how do they conflict with other kinds of so-called non-scientific beliefs?

3.5 Scientism's Universe

So far there has been a lot of talk about foundationalism, representationalism, Cartesian dualism, rationalism, empiricism, and abstract philosophical concepts of this kind. But exactly what kind of ideas about ourselves, the world and our place in it do those concepts stand for? What kind of being in the world do they imply? What does it feel like to be in the world in such a way as induced by these ontological conceptions? What kind of universe do we need to be part of to believe in scientism? In other words, what kind of ontology is necessary to make scientism thinkable?

When we read ethnographic accounts about magic rituals, shamanism and exotic cosmologies other people in other parts of the world or in other times used to hold for "real", we may ask how any reasonable person may ever have believed in such weird ideas about the world. However, if we turn our eyes on the ontological presumptions implicit in scientism's metaphysics we might be surprised at the strange kind of universe we ought to live in following this doctrine.

In what follows I would like to go over some of what may be the most fundamental ontological notions of scientistic cosmology and analyse how and why they exclude certain alternative views.[150] So let us dive into the world of scientism and pretend, just for a moment, to be part of its universe.

3.5.1 Mind-Stuff, the Matrix and Blind Matter

In many ways, rationalism is at the very roots of scientistic cosmology. The reason is that it entails at least two even-more fundamental ontological principles, which are reflected in most other metaphysical presumptions scientism is based upon.

The *first* is the idea that there is a *mind* capable of *logical reasoning*, an autonomous thinking and conjecturing *subject*, which Descartes called the *cogito*

[150] Of course, there may be other important ideas and some of those ideas I will discuss may not necessarily pertain to every imaginable variety of scientism, but I hope it will provide a kind of draft topography of universalism's metaphysical mechanisms of exclusion. Also, I will present some ideas as being prior to or following others, but I do not insist here on any strict hierarchy of necessary logical implication. The overall constitution of scientism's metaphysics is certainly a contingent result of historical processes and can probably be better understood in terms of confluence than in terms of causal or logical relations between its elements. Some very fundamental ideas may also entail other possible ideas than those which have been associated historically, but this does not make much difference for my purpose here. I would also like to remind the philosophers among my readers that I am an anthropologist. My aim is NOT to provide a coherent logical system, but a cosmology, that is, an imagination of the universe.

("thinking self") or *res cogitans* ("thinking stuff"). However, to come to the sceptical (and extremely bold) conclusion that possibly the whole world and even our own bodies could be just an illusive imagination of our mind, we have to believe that our senses may be completely delusive while our logical reasoning is capable of deducing absolutely true conclusions. This assumption, which by no means can be derived from any evidence, entails the foundationalist idea that there *is* some absolute truth *and* that our mind-stuff somehow *reflects* the principles of this truth, which we call *logic*, with mathematics representing the abstract language of logical reasoning. Without these assumptions scepticism would make no sense, since logical reasoning would give no hope of finding any truth, let alone a truth truer than lived experience. Moreover, the only place to find this marvellous true-thinking mind-stuff is within our human bodies. Well, the latter is not actually a logical consequence of the aforesaid, but it is the only way to escape the absolutely absurd idea of solipsism, that is, the negation of the existence of the whole physical universe together with our own body.

We are so accustomed to these ideas that we may not find anything strange about them. But to realise how arbitrary they are, let me just remind you that medieval cosmology assumed God as well as nature, His creation, to be an eternal mystery impossible to be understood by means of the limited capacities of our all too simple minds. Given the fact that after more than two centuries of scientific inquiry we still do not have a clue what the universe or our own minds actually are about, the mystery thesis does not seem less plausible than rationalism.

Be this as it may, once the existence of the world and our physical bodies is assumed, it is imagined as something distinct, essentially different from our mind-stuff, a physical realm of blind objects following deterministic laws. *Cartesian dualism* has been established, and with it, representationalism, empiricism, naturalism, physicalism, causality and linear time. It is like a metaphysical big bang, having everything emerge in an instant, together with the metaphysical "anti-matter" to annihilate half of it immediately thereafter. But let me try to look at each element one by one and see what it means for our cosmology and how these ideas are related to each other.

Actually, dualism is far from being the only possible answer to rationalism. Monistic answers have been proposed, for example, by Spinoza and Leibniz, but for some reasons in the course of history they did not become mainstream in modern thought.[151] Anyhow, once dualism is accepted, *empiricism* is a consequence, and with it, representationalism, because the only connection between our mind-stuff and the outer world is via our senses, providing an image, that is, a representation of the physical realm. This move, which was not logically necessary but a contingent

[151] One reason, among others, was that Newton and his British colleagues were supported by the Royal Academy enjoying the protection of the King, while continental natural philosophers still were on their own and moreover had to fear ideological persecution. Another, closely connected reason probably comes from the technological success of science, its importance for British expansionism and science's need to treat nature as an object in order to manipulate it and make it disposable for technological and industrial progress.

historical event, came with all kinds of contradictions, as exemplified by the problem of induction. But as good adherents of scientism we do not care too much about such details. Instead, we simply assume these representations to be roughly faithful, although grossly incomplete and deficient, so we can test all *thinkable* hypotheses comparing them with empirical evidence. In order to reduce the limitations of our senses we conduct experiments to reduce nature to measurement and tests, using technical protheses to augment our senses, and thus, compare our logical deductions with the empirical facts we gained from our experiment. This is possible because we assume that not only our mind-stuff follows the rules of logic, but physical stuff follows them, too. We call those rules natural laws, and with them, we invented naturalism.

Naturalism is the *second* grand presupposition underlying rationalism.[152] With this move we also made quite profound assumptions concerning the nature of nature, namely that it is ordered and that this order is comprehensible, that is, that its order follows the same logic principles as our mind-stuff, and that it is uniform, so that those laws will rule everywhere and for all times. These are a lot of presumptions, none of which can be derived from empirical evidence.[153]

Considering the *ontological* suppositions we made so far, they tell us that we are rational mind-stuffs encapsulated in physical bodies which are part of a physical universe that we do not know with certainty exists, since we cannot trust our senses; but supposing the physical world exists, it necessarily obeys the same logical principles as our mind-stuff. Strange enough, but now we add the even bolder assumption, that the laws of nature follow mathematical equations. We can assume this to be true, being a logical consequence of the parallelism between mind-stuff's logic and nature's principles, with mathematics representing the essence of mind-stuff's logic. Hence, the mathematical nature of nature's laws are just a logical corollary of our previous assumptions (though neither of them can be empirically proven to reflect the real structure of the universe).[154] It follows that the mathematical equations representing natural laws are more "real" than our sensible perception of the world. Thus, the more mathematical a scientific theory is, the more it can possibly tell us about reality, for the true nature of the universe lies in its mathematical code.

Today, most people might see mathematical models as a reasonable way to describe the physical world. It's simply the way things are: nature obviously follows mathematical natural laws as clearly shown by their predictive power. But in fact, this is a quite weird idea. For in nature, as we experience it, there are no numbers at all.[155] Numbers are an abstraction of our mind, they are not part of the phenomenal world we live in. This naturalisation of a mathematical model of reality may be the

[152] Whitehead (1925).

[153] Whitehead (1925); Walach (2019); Collingwood (1998); Maxwell (2017).

[154] "The principle that natural science is essentially an applied mathematics is thus by no means an indispensable presupposition for any science of nature. A presupposition it certainly is, and an absolute presupposition. It could not possibly be learnt from experience or justified by research" (Collingwood 1998: position 2815); compare also Whitehead (1925) and Maxwell (2017).

[155] Compare also Walach (2019).

strangest aspect of modern science, and one of the most characteristic aspects of the whole modern *episteme.*[156]

Historically, the use of mathematics has been by no means restricted to Western society, modernity or modern science. Other cultures at different times and places have used mathematics in order to calculate the movement of the stars and to construct sophisticated buildings; however, they did not base their whole worldview on mathematical principles.

In the European context we may find a first step towards a mathematical explanation of reality in early Greek philosophers, like Pythagoras, and later, Aristotle, Archimedes and Euclid. Although their mathematical knowledge was based on previous Egyptian and Babylonian concepts, those Greek philosophers were probably among the first to create a new philosophy built on the mystical power of numbers.[157] But still, numbers had either a mystical, symbolic meaning or an instrumental function to solve specific problems of geometry and logic. It took some additional 2000 years until natural philosophers like Kepler, Copernicus, Galileo, Bacon and Newton came to explain nature in terms of mathematical laws.[158] Now, finally, numbers could explain more than the Holy Bible. The key to understanding the mysteries of God and His creation were no longer to be found in the sacred texts, but in the discovery of mathematical laws, God's secret code that ruled the universe. Now it was all a question of *calculus*[159]; there were no angels or daemons, no spirits or any other mystical power at work, just blind matter following mathematical equations. This new view not only *disenchanted*[160] our world, but it also transformed it into an

[156] Compare e.g. Collingwood (1998): "All modern scientific work rests on the absolute presupposition that nature is one and that science is one: that the different realms of nature are in part governed by one and the same code of absolutely identical laws, the laws of mathematics, [...]" (idem: position 2317).

[157] Whitehead (1925) argued that mathematical generalisation was a fundamental step in human thought towards the notion of abstract, general principles. The Greek philosophers and especially Pythagoras draw a connection between nature and its hidden principles. "The Platonic world of ideas is the refined, revised form of the Pythagorean doctrine that number lies at the base of the real world.[...]In a sense, Plato and Pythagoras stand nearer to modern physical science than does Aristotle" (idem: 36)..

[158] Collingwood (1998) held that Galileo's dictum that God writes in the language of mathematics was not only an absolute presupposition, but also a declaration of war against scholastic Aristotelianism, which had been a qualitative science of nature. However, Maxwell (2017) emphasises that Newton, despite his insistence that he discovered the law of gravity by induction alone, "[…] rejected the thesis that the universe has a harmonious mathematical structure, and that all natural phenomena are the outcome of particles interacting in accordance with precise physical law", favouring a creationist view instead (idem: 37).

[159] Although most natural philosophers during the Renaissance and enlightenment firmly believed in God, the overall effect of confirming mathematical models by empirical evidence eventually reduced the function of God to that of the Creator. However, once the universe had been created, natural laws would rule it and God would not have to interfere to make things happen. Curiously, however, Newton himself did not think his laws would be sufficient to explain all events and believed that God would still have to intervene in order to keep the universe moving (Maxwell 2017).

[160] Max Weber (1919) famously criticised this highly abstract, mathematical model of reality for disenchanting our world. For Weber, science is part of a historical millenary process of intellectu-

illusion, for all we see and feel is just a delusive curtain of impressions and feelings, while in "reality", behind this curtain works an invisible matrix of numbers, a never-ending computing process we cannot see, but which we can discover by using our logical mind. Quite like in the well-known movie entitled "The Matrix",[161] just with the difference that there is no "blue pill" to get out of it, because matter itself *is* this matrix; there is no other more "real" reality behind it (at least not unless we stop being materialists).

The assumption of mathematical natural laws being more real than our sensible perception has many serious implications concerning the character of the universe we live in. Perhaps most importantly, it implies a deterministic, causal behaviour of matter and energy. It is often held that causality is based on assumptions about the uniformity of nature, linear time and extended space,[162] which of course, is not wrong. But without believing in the mathematical nature of nature's laws, and thus, believing that causal relations follow precise mathematically predictable principles, it would not make much sense to submit causal relations to experiment. Only if we believe that nature is governed by hidden *mathematical* laws can causal relations be conceived as being completely determined, and thus, predictable by means of mathematical equations that can be tested in experiment to discover those laws.[163]

---

alisation and rationalisation. While the "savages" still live in a world full of supernatural beings, magic and mystery, the intellectualisation of the modern world makes us believe that we do not need any magic to invoke spirits or God in order to control nature, but only what he calls the calculus. And Weber immediately alerts us, this does not mean that we would know more than the "savages", but on the contrary, we understand very little about details of our highly technological world and the scientific models behind them, while the "savages" dominate and know their world. Moreover, we (moderns) lost the sense of life and death. In the old times people died peacefully, feeling they had fulfilled the purpose of their lives. Today, in contrast, a person would die "tired" of life, but not "satisfied". The mathematical abstractions of modern science cannot grab the blood and flesh of real life. Like Plato, we end up seeing our phenomenal world just as a kind of shadows at the wall, while the "real" reality is made up of abstract eternal ideas.

[161] The Matrix is a 1999 science fiction film by Lena and Lilly Wachowski. It basically paints the picture of a distopic future where mankind is being bred by machines for energy supply, while their minds are connected to a virtual world, called "The Matrix", where they live and interact as if it was the real world. People do not know they are within the Matrix as long as they do not exit to the real world.

[162] Hume (2017) famously brought the problem of induction down to the question of the uniformity of nature as a basic precondition for induction and causality. But suppose we knew causality to be true, what would this knowledge provide us without mathematics somehow resembling the principles of causality? We would only be able to make general propositions and predictions like: "once an apple is dropped it falls to the ground", or maybe even: "the higher the distance to the ground the greater the velocity and the damage caused by hitting the ground". But we would not be able to come to mathematical equations exactly quantifying the velocity of the apple and the impact it is exposed to when hitting the ground, and neither would we be able to formulate a general law of gravity and calculate the exact orbits of the planets using the same formulae we used to calculate the velocity of the falling apple.

[163] Compare also Stengers (2000) or Maxwell (2017): "This metaphysical view is not just psychologically important, important in suggesting fruitful hypotheses—important in the context of discovery, as philosophers of science would put it. The view is methodologically important—indeed

However, we should not forget how artificial this assumption is. In order to discover and experimentally prove natural laws, to unveil the hidden mathematical nature of nature, it first has to be transformed into numbers. The quantification of a purely qualitative phenomenal world requires arbitrary numerical scales to enable quantitative measurements. Only if we can translate, for example, the observation of something being "quite cold" into quantitative data such as "5.23 °C", "very hot" into "189.8 °C", "quite small" into "1.45 mm", "very, very far away" into "5,210,000 light-years", or "green" into "553 nm wave length", only if we artificially quantify all phenomena, transforming them into objects completely describable by numbers, only then can we submit nature to the total control of the *calculus*,[164] only then, suddenly, the matrix appears behind the curtain of our sensual experience.

Of course, once we quantify these phenomena and submit them to calculus everything appears to be governed by equations and mysterious numbers, like π, or physical constants like e, h, or c. But the resulting description of the world will differ from our perception in a quite radical way. Take time as an example: Imagine you are waiting for a bus at the station. You look at your watch and half an hour later you look again, but your watch tells you that only five minutes have passed. Now consider the same situation reading a book. After reading a few pages and estimated five minutes passed your watch tells you that half an hour has gone. Who is wrong, you or your watch?! Does measurement really represent reality more faithfully than our perception? Is time really so absolute and linear as suggested by quantitative measurement?

Calculus does not tell us anything about the world we experience, but it makes fantastically precise predictions and it provides us with an incredible power to control nature, or at least, its physical aspects. Science's predictive power (not its epistemological truth value) has convinced us that the universe is physical in its very nature and following deterministic, mathematical principles.[165] However, while the calculus' predictive power seems to suggest that the universe is comprehensible, its mathematical abstractions do not provide any coherent or at least imaginable ontological notion of the universe. This is especially true, empirically, for most successful theories in physics, like relativity and quantum theory, whose predictions are

---

essential. It is vital in the context of verification, the context of accepting and rejecting hypotheses" (idem: 272).

[164] This particular aspect of the modern scientific world view is part of a much wider modern epistemic concept, which ultimately transforms every aspect of life into calculi. Not only scientific objects, but also plants, animals, stars, even human beings, their health and wellbeing, and even more importantly, power are now being quantified and measured in numbers. Typically, in our modern age, we do this in terms of money, or as we use to say, economic figures. It is at least suspicious, that the rise of a generalised use of money and a bank system in northern Italy and England during the fifteenth century coincides with the humanist movement, renaissance, and ultimately with the beginning of the modern age, colonialism and early capitalism. From this perspective, the intellectualisation and rationalisation of nature appears not exactly as a result of modern science, but as an aspect of the modern age's episteme, which called for a new systematic quantitative approach of "truth": modern science (compare also Zilsel 1942).

[165] Heidegger (1954).

leading to completely counter-intuitive and incoherent patterns of facts, offering no comprehensive, unified ontology at all.[166]

From the perspective of other, non-scientific ways of knowing, scientism's matrix-world may be interpreted as a kind of metaphysical "*Hinterwelt*" comparable to the invisible realm of the spirits, some immaterial principle or God who governs both the visible and the invisible realm of the world. Scientists' mathematical formulae may be seen as magic spells, a secret language encoded by mystic numbers, completely incomprehensible for any layman, but imbued with some fundamental truth about the universe. And in fact, from an anthropological view, such a comparison of science with magic would not be too misleading.[167]

However, from the scientists' point of view, there is a fundamental difference between magic spells and scientific predictions based on mathematical equations. The reason is that the concept of magic is based on the idea of communication, and hence, presumes entities to behave according to the relations one establishes with them, typically, by some kind of ritual or incantation. Of course, the communicative establishment and manipulation of relations will never produce any precisely *determinable* reaction of the target entities, but rather dispositions of *probable* behaviour. Quite obviously, the absolute determinism entailed in the precision of mathematical predictions is explicitly meant to be the total opposite of magic. The scientist does not (at least not in their own perception) communicate with their *objects*, instead they observe and analyse them, manipulating them during experiment, forcing them to reveal their mathematical principles, and finally, aiming to precisely predict and totally control their deterministic behaviour.

From an ontological point of view, these contrary intuitions and dispositions towards the objects of inquiry are related to some, but not all, of the metaphysical suppositions mentioned so far.

Dualism is frequently identified as the most striking ontological difference between scientism and other cosmologies. However, in such general terms this finding is not necessarily true. The mere assumption that there might be two distinct realms with a visible, material world on the one hand, and an invisible, immaterial world on the other, appears to be quite compatible with a whole range of different cosmologies. Descartes himself assumed that his mind-stuff originated from God, who would also be the creator of the material universe. Moreover, his naturalist assumption concerning the comprehensibility of the "extended stuff" of the physical world was justified precisely by having been created by God, and hence, following the same principles as his "thinking stuff". So far there is no fundamental contradiction between dualism and non-scientistic cosmologies.

---

[166] Maxwell (2017) criticises quantum theory exactly for being unable to provide any comprehensive ontological explanation about the nature of quanta and their apparently contradictory wave- and particle-aspects, and thus, being unacceptably disunited. However, there might be alternative interpretations of quantum theory that permit a more unified ontological picture of the universe. I will discuss some of such alternative interpretations in the last part of this work.

[167] Compare Chap. 5.

The problems start with Descartes' additional supposition that mind-stuff is *exclusively* related to the living human body, reducing dualism to a mere *mind-body dualism*, while negating the existence of any immaterial thinking stuff outside human bodies. This obviously precludes the existence of mind-stuff related to other-than-human beings or objects, and hence, renders any attempt to communicate with those entities pure nonsense. Furthermore, it equally precludes both the existence of any free-floating mind-stuff, as suggested by the notion of "spirits", "souls" or else immaterial entities, and the existence of an invisible, immaterial realm where those entities might dwell, and to where the mind may travel during dreams or trance.

Moreover, following a *second* additional presupposition, mind-stuff is supposed to have *no direct connection* with the physical realm, being a completely different substance, entirely separate from physical substance, merely passively receiving sensual information of doubtful content. In other words, Cartesian dualism is a type of ontological or substance dualism, in contrast to epistemological or aspect dualisms (sometimes also called dual aspect monism), where mind and body are conceived as two aspects of one single underlying substance, resulting in two different kinds of perceptive modes. It follows, that mind-stuff is completely deprived of any possibility to act on the physical world, except on the living body in which it happens to be imprisoned during a lifetime (and it remains to be explained how this should be possible under the presumed conditions). In fact, the exact relation between our subjective experience and the concomitant physical processes in our neurones, that is, between mind and body, is still subject to intense scientific and philosophical debating. Far from having been solved, the predicaments of Cartesian dualism have fostered materialist views and attempts to explain consciousness as a mere epiphenomenon of neuronal processes in our brains. This solution not only evades the mind-body problem by simply eliminating the idea of "mind-stuff", it is also a necessary consequence of reductionism and parsimony, yet another pair of additional, rather heuristic principles associated with scientism.[168] However, the resulting materialist monism not only renders our lived experience, together with our free will, an illusion; by deconstructing the autonomous subject, materialism also ultimately deprives science of its most essential epistemological concept, the rational *cogito*.

Anyhow, even if we hold to Cartesian dualism, its *second* additional supposition precludes any kind of direct mental action on physical objects. It therefore contradicts other cosmologies, like those related to "magic" or "shamanism", where the mental powers of the practitioner are supposed to produce effects in the material realm (typically illness or cure).

Similarly, *naturalism* does not necessarily conflict with other worldviews, since most cosmologies suppose nature and the whole universe to follow some kind of general principles. Actually, any cosmology represents a narration aiming to make those universal principles understandable in the first place. However, in non-scientistic cosmologies, these principles are rarely based on mathematics and they

[168] Walach (2019).

may change with time (for example in the course of periodical cataclysmic ends and rebirths of the world). But once the matrix of calculus is proclaimed to be the only universal principle governing the entire physical universe for all times, absolute determinism is the result. Supposing we knew the exact position of every quantum at the moment of the Big Bang, and were given the necessary computational capacities, we could calculate any future state of the entire universe. No space for any arbiter, any unmoved mover, or any wilful being or free will to make any difference to the inevitable destiny of the universe. Now, the world is made up solely of blind, soulless matter with no spiritual or subjective aspects whatsoever. Any event is determined by the laws of physics; naturalism has gone *physicalist*.[169]

This most radical supposition not only renders any attempt to act upon things by communicating with them an expression of childish "animism"; it also changes our deepest feelings, our *aesthetical* and our *ethical* disposition towards the world and ourselves. The world has been disenchanted and transformed into dead, soulless matter.

To sum it up in a nutshell, neither dualism nor naturalism are per se incommensurable with other cosmologies—even if their notions of mind, matter and their causal roles may differ significantly. The exclusive character often attributed to naturalism and dualism in general is, in fact, related to certain additional presuppositions entailed in the specific *Cartesian* type dualism, and even more radically so in materialist monism. The problem of incommensurability arises when dualism goes subjectivistic, and thus, representational, when naturalism is equalled with physicalism and physicalism with the "mathematicalism" of pure calculus, and finally, when the world we live in is reduced to an epiphenomenon of the matrix, to a mere manifestation of calculus in form of tasteless, colourless, blind matter.

---

[169] Historically, physicalism as currently hold by a majority of philosophers (Bourget and Chalmers 2013), is the refined version of enlightenment's mechanistic theory of nature, which probably goes back to Ionian philosophers' concept of matter as being located in space and time. However, the problems involved in this view would soon become apparent and philosophers like Bergson would protest against this "intellectual spatialisation of things". Whitehead (1925) called it the "fallacy of misplaced concreteness" or the mistaking of the abstract for the concrete which characterised seventeenth century materialism: "Nature is a dull affair, soundless, scentless, colourless; merely the hurrying of material, endlessly, meaninglessly. However you disguise it, this is the practical outcome of the characteristic scientific philosophy which closed the seventeenth century" (idem.: 69). Whitehead also called attention to the ethical implication of materialism, since it entails valuelessness: "the assumption of the bare valuelessness of mere matter led to a lack of reverence in the treatment of natural or artistic beauty", and hence to two fundamental evils: "ignoration of the true relation of each organism to its environment" and "ignoring the intrinsic worth of the environment". Moreover, materialistic determinism denies the free mind and responsibility, leading to fatalism. In the vein of Marx' and Weber's critique of capitalist exploration, Whitehead concludes: "It may be that civilisation will never recover from the bad climate which enveloped the introduction of machinery. This climate pervaded the whole commercial system of the progressive northern European races. It was partly the result of aesthetic errors of Protestantism and partly the result of scientific materialism, and partly the result of the natural greed of mankind, and partly the result of the abstractions of political economy" (idem: 253).

3.5.2 Causation, Linear Time, Determinism and Locality

Once the universe has been reduced to blind matter governed by a matrix of calculus, causality has to follow its deterministic rules. The determinist view has become so dominant that we almost automatically associate causality with determinism. However, determinism is actually just one of several possible concepts of causation. The scientific notion of causality had been developed out of Aristotle's concept of "efficient" causes in contrast to the scholastic preference for his concept of "final" causes. Aristotle's four causes[170] had been reorganised by Thomas of Aquinas in a hierarchical order, with "final" causes now being the "first" causes, representing God's will, followed by "secondary" causes, including Aristotle's "efficient" causes, representing instruments intrinsic to nature created and endowed by God with their own creative power to act independently, as a kind of natural law. Arguing for his inductive method, Francis Bacon[171] would criticise this primacy of final causes over natural laws. Building on Bacon's empiricist endeavour, Hume[172] eventually defined causation as a result of the repeatedly observing temporal succession of particular causes followed by particular effects in close local and temporal relation. This laid the fundaments for the scientific concept of causation, as well as its refutation, highlighting the problem of induction. Ever since, philosophers have been trying to solve Hume's riddle and provide a solid concept of causation. However, there is still no consensus about the real nature of causation—not even on Hume's initial question whether it actually exists apart from our perception, or not.[173]

[170] Aristotle distinguished between four different types of causes: "material" or "essential" causes (concerning the reason of a thing being the way it is as a result of its material nature), "formal" or "logical" causes (concerning an objects function as a result of its intrinsic inner nature), "efficient" or "moving" causes (concerning an external cause or force acting upon an object to move or change), and "final" causes (concerning the ultimate reason for something to happen) (Metaphysics, Book V).

[171] Bacon (2017).

[172] Hume (2017).

[173] Causation is a very deep and complex philosophical issue, and it would certainly outstrip both my capacities and the scope of this work to give a complete account of the vast literature and the countless different interpretations concerning the problem of causation (compare e.g. Cartwright 1983; Collingwood 1998; Schaffer 2016; Walach 2019; Meyering 2020; among others). However, due to its importance for the present purpose, I feel it necessary to highlight at least a few aspects and ideas concerning causation, which are co-responsible for the a priori exclusion of alternative cosmologies.

Nevertheless, causation continues to be one of the most central concepts of modern science and most (natural)[174] scientists will probably not hesitate to acknowledge[175]:

1. That *every* event has a cause
2. That any cause *precedes* its effects
3. That to be effective a cause has to be a *physical* event or entity
4. That all physical events are completely *determined* by *mathematical natural laws*
5. That (macro-)physical events are always *local*[176] events and
6. That *physical causes* might have *mental effects*, but never the other way round

Once again, we are confronted with a whole bunch of metaphysical presumptions with all kinds of ontological implications. The whole issue of causality is a very complex one, so let me go through the listed points one by one and analyse what they actually mean, the metaphysical presumptions they are based on, the ontological view they imply and the alternative ontological views they preclude.

1. Every Event Has a Cause

This very basic supposition may seem too obvious to be further discussed. However, at a closer look, it reveals itself to be based on several additional assumptions. Moreover, the question whether causation actually really exists gets increasingly difficult the more we think about it. Hume[177] had already shown that the very notion

[174] In fact, in the social sciences many observed phenomena can be said to be "caused" by decisions, attitudes, beliefs and other subjective, non-deterministic factors. However, concerning the (supposed or not) physical basis of subjective phenomena, the "mental" is treated as a black box. Social scientists are primarily concerned with the phenomenology of mental states, the social factors influencing them and the social consequences they produce, leaving the investigation of the internal processes within the black box, that is, of the correlation between mental states and neuronal activities, to the neurosciences, and hence, to physicalist explanations.

[175] Of course, this is an idealised list of ideas which will certainly change depending on a scientist's individual philosophical and meta-theoretical background. Some of the listed ideas may not be supported by some scientists while other ideas someone might hold to be important, too, are not listed here. However, based on both the literature I am aware of and my personal experience of colleagues from different academic fields, I argue that the listed points are part of a pattern of ideas very common especially between natural scientists. Moreover, the list contains those ideas containing implicit ontological arguments for an a priori delegitimisation of alternative views.

[176] *Locality,* in this context, refers to the necessary condition of a cause being effective by directly producing its effect with no laps of time or space separating the two, including effects caused by signals transmitted by some physical force, wave or radiation with maximum speed of light (e.g. Walach 2019).

[177] "It is a general maxim in philosophy that whatever begins to exist must be caused to do so. […] But if we examine this maxim in terms of the idea of knowledge that I have explained, we shan't discover in it any mark of any such intuitive certainty. Quite the contrary: we'll find that it is of a nature quite foreign to what can be known intuitively" (Hume 2017: 45). Hume refutes previous arguments of Hobbes and Locke who tried to prove the necessity for everything to have a cause due to the impossibility of something causing itself out of nothing. These arguments are circular since they already presuppose the necessity of something being caused, in this case, by itself. "An object that exists absolutely without any cause is certainly not its own cause; and when you assert that the one follows from the other you are taking for granted the very point that is in question" (idem: 46).

of causation cannot be proven, neither by logical deduction nor by evidence, to be an ontological principle of the universe. In order to assume the existence of causation outside of our perception, we would have to make at least two ontological ad hoc assumptions: first, our repeated empirical observation of apparently causally-related phenomena would need to give a reliable account of the external world of physical objects. Second, nature would have to uniformly follow to the same causal rules everywhere and for all times. However, even if we simply assume these two presumptions to be true, how can we distinguish causes from their effects or mere background conditions? Following Hume and Kant, the very notion of causation is intimately related to our perception of time as change, and change as a temporal succession of related events, giving us the impression that the present state of affairs has been "caused" by previous events. So, a cause differs from its effect by preceding it. However, for different reasons, temporal succession has not proven to be a reliable criterion to define causal relations.[178] It also turns out that the causes we may identify as being responsible for a certain effect may change depending on how we ask for them. Different conditions for one and the same effect may be treated as "causes", depending on intention and scope, making it impossible to objectively determine *the* decisive cause(s) responsible for a particular event.[179] Any object or event depends on countless conditions, rendering the identification of one or several of those conditions to be its sole "cause" an arbitrary business. Given the ultimate interconnectedness of the universe, it seems even possible to argue that everything is the result of everything else, so that the very concept of causal relation might be

---

Hence, there is no a priori deductive proof for causality to be a general immanent rule of nature. "So the opinion of the necessity of a cause for every new production isn't based on ·a priori· knowledge or scientific reasoning, and must therefore arise from observation and experience" (idem: 47). Our notion of causation is the result of memorised repeated observation of the constant conjunction of two particular objects we thus identify as the previous being the cause of the latter, which we call its effect. However, without the additional presupposition that nature is unified we have no reason to assume this to assign to a general rule accountable for future events. "Thus, not only does our reason fail to reveal to us the ultimate connection of causes and effects, but even after experience has informed us of their constant conjunction we can't through our reason satisfy ourselves concerning why we should extend that experience beyond the particular instances that we have observed. We suppose, but can never prove, that objects of which we have had experience must resemble the ones that lie beyond the reach of our discovery" (idem: 52).

[178] See next section.

[179] E.g. if an apple falls from a tree, was it gravity which caused it to fall (cause = natural law), or was it the wind (cause = force/"effective" cause), the apple's ripening (cause = natural process), its increase in mass (cause = change in physical properties), God's will (cause = wilful power), my having it seen falling in last night's dream (cause = divination of future event), the natural necessity or the apple's desire to drop in order to spread its seeds and renew the cycle of life (cause = teleological/"final" cause)?

questionable.[180] Collingwood[181] even suggested the very notion of causality to be an anthropomorphic, and thus, ultimately an animistic concept derived from the social idea of compulsion, rather than from observed deterministic causal effects.

To my knowledge, none of these (or other) fundamental problems have been solved.[182] It turns out, that the simple assumption that everything has a cause, no matter what kind of cause, may encounter serious metaphysical predicaments.

Be this as it may, the mere notion of universal causation does not necessarily preclude diverging cosmologies as long as no additional assumptions are made concerning the particular conditions which qualify causal relations.

2. A Cause Always Precedes Its Effects

Causes are generally assumed to precede their effects in time. However, this presumption actually already presumes the additional metaphysical presuppositions that time follows a linear, progressive flux and that causal relations exclusively follow a temporal succession along this linear time-flow, from the past to the future. Without these additional ontological assumptions about the nature of time, it is difficult to draw the line between cause and effect. Moreover, Hume's conditions of contiguity and constant conjunction ultimately amount to a reduction of the time and space separating cause and effect to zero.[183] As a result, the two assumptions of temporal succession and contiguity produce an inconsistency by saying that, on the one hand, a cause has to precede its effects, while on the other, both have to coincide. Of course, once causation is conceived as a succession of effective processes,

[180] E.g. Max Verworn's (1928) critique of causation and his systemic conditionalist approach:"Es ist seltsam: Obwohl man mit dem Ursachenbegriff auf allen Gebieten menschlicher Geistestätigkeit täglich und stündlich zu operieren gewöhnt ist, scheint es doch kaum möglich, eine scharfe und allgemein anerkannte Definition dieses Begriffes zu geben" (idem: 4). "Kein Vorgang oder Zustand in der Welt ist von einem einzigen Faktor allein abhängig. [...] Die Tatsache, daß es keine isolierten Teilsysteme in der Welt gibt, daß vielmehr jedes von uns für praktische Zwecke isoliert gedachte System in Wirklichkeit die mannigfaltigsten Zusammenhänge hat mit anderen isoliert gedachten Systemen, ist eine der fundamentalen Tatsachen unserer Erkenntnis überhaupt. Wenn auch die elektive Tätigkeit unserer Sinnesorgane der naiven Betrachtung die Welt als eine Summe von einzelnen isolierten Dingen vortäuscht, so weiß doch die kritische Naturwissenschaft längst, daß in Wirklichkeit ein kontinuierlicher Zusammenhang der Dinge nach allen Seiten hin besteht. Jeder Zustand oder Vorgang in der Welt wird daher in seiner spezifischen Existenz durch zahlreiche andere Zustände und Vorgänge bestimmt und würde beim Fehlen auch nur eines der Faktoren, von denen er abhängig ist, in seiner spezifischen Form nicht vorhanden sein" (idem: 6). "Der Kausalismus ist ein primitiveres Stadium der Weltanschauung, der Konditionismus ein weiter vorgeschrittenes" (idem: 15).

[181] Collingwood (1998).

[182] Schaffer (2016).

[183] Compare also Collingwood (1998): "In order to illustrate the implications of sense III [causality in theoretical natural sciences], I will refer to the contradiction between the traditional denial of actio in distans (which, I suppose, would hold as against action across a lapse of time no less than across a distance in space) and the assumption, commonly made nowadays, that a cause precedes its effect in time. [...] The denial of actio in distans, spatial or temporal, where the 'agent' is a cause in sense III, is therefore not a 'prejudice' but is logically involved in the definition of sense III [causality in theoretical natural sciences]" (idem: position 3479–4502).

each of which take a period of time, some however short, this contradiction can be relativised.[184] However, the concept of time in terms of a linear succession of causal events is not compatible with current physical theories about spacetime, which are suggesting a much more relative concept of time,[185] including the possibility of temporal symmetry and time loops.[186] Hence, the phenomenological structure of our perceived reality as a succession of causally related events along linear time may not reflect the ontological structure of time, space and causality. Once again, we are confronted with Hume's empirical definition of causation and its related problems. Similarly, Kant came to the conclusion that time, space and causality cannot be defined in terms of noumenal properties of nature but only as transcendental a priori categories of our perception. Rather than objectively determining the successive order of cause and effect, the perception of time itself is the result of a synthetic apprehension based upon the a priori notions of endurance, causal relation and coincidence.[187]

Despite its metaphysical character and its intrinsic predicaments, the temporal definition of causation persists and continues to be one of the most fundamental presuppositions of scientific method. Unluckily, it is incompatible with a wide range of different cosmologies, and consequently, responsible for the a priori disqualification of diverging views and practices. Most notably, the temporal conception of causation precludes *divination*, since it denies the possibility of any kind of events, including mental states like dreams, visions or intuitions, being caused or induced by future events.

3. To Be Effective, a Cause Has to Be a Physical[188] Event or Entity

This is, of course, a very bold and far-reaching assumption, and some readers (especially social scientists) may immediately object that the causes of a whole range of events are *not* physical, but rather subjective decisions and wilful acts of persons, that is, caused by *mental* states[189]—and I (as a social scientist) totally agree!

---

[184] E.g. Kant refers to the problem of causal coincidence with his well-known example of a ball's impression on a pillow, holding that while cause and effect coincide, the causal event would start previously to its effect, the latter only following as a result of the first. The argument is obviously circular, since Kant explicitly confirms that temporal succession is the only empirical criteria for causal relations, while holding that the experience of time is an indirect impression resulting from our a priori notion of causal relation (Kant 1787: 225).

[185] E.g. special relativity suggests that events might be perceived by a certain observer as coinciding while appearing to occur at different times for another.

[186] Collingwood (1998).

[187] Kant (1787: 204).

[188] I chose the term "physical" rather than "material" to include immaterial physical phenomena like gravity, fields or waves as well as abstract "laws" as possible causes. In so doing I also suggest that materialism, although still frequently identified as being part of scientism, is actually a notion too restricted and too outdated to be held by a majority of scientists and philosophers today. However, physicalism, being a much wider notion, can certainly be said to represent the mainstream view in current science and philosophy.

[189] E.g. if Peter throws a stone at a window, its breaking is primarily "caused" by his decision to throw the stone and the following wilful action, while the physical parameters involved, like

However, the notion of physical causation amounts to *physicalism*, thus, reducing mental states to neuronal states caused by bio-chemical processes in our brains. Consequently, even if an event is caused by a person's wilful action, their decision to act has been caused by (or at least supervenes on) neuronal processes, that is, ultimately physical events. So while we may have the impression that we consciously ponder our options and then freely decide how to act, in "reality", our thinking and pondering is just an epiphenomenon of physical events, which are the "real" causes responsible for our deciding and acting.

Physicalism, therefore, is often regarded as rendering consciousness an illusion, and thus, precluding free will. However, this is only true if physical events are conceived as mechanically following deterministic laws. As long as physical events are not completely determined by mathematical laws, they might follow unpredictable probabilities or even some kind of inherent intentionality. For example, if quanta were free or intentional, the activities of our brains might be free and intentional, too.

Similarly, at first sight, physicalism may appear to be incompatible with notions of immaterial intentional actants, like "souls", "spirits" or "God". However, at a closer look the cosmos described by physical theory reveals itself to be made up of all kinds of invisible, immaterial actants, like energies, waves and fields, and ultimately reduces matter to something like informed, condensed energy. Where does this information come from? What if it was the manifestation of an immanent intentionality inherent to energy, or waves, or quanta, or the cosmos? Would such invisible, immaterial, intentional cosmic stuff be ontologically incompatible with notions of "souls", "spirits" or "God"?

So here again, for physicalism to become incommensurable with other cosmologies and so-called "spiritual" notions, additional assumptions are necessary.

4. All Physical Events Are Completely Determined by Mathematical Natural Laws

As already discussed above, the predictive power of Newtonian physics was fundamental for the breakthrough of physicalism. Now that nature's mathematical laws had finally been uncovered, everything appeared to be completely determined by this hidden matrix. However, for Newton, his discovery of nature's laws alone would not necessarily imply a deterministic view. For example, Newton had shown the predictive power of his mathematical laws of gravity and motion, but he did not understand these laws as "causes". A "cause", in Newton's view, was an external "force impressed upon bodies",[190] but movements following the laws of motion "freely" were not caused by any external force at all. So once every event would completely be explainable by natural laws there would be no causation, which in a way, anticipated modern physics. Curiously, Newton himself did not think his natural laws alone would explain all events. Quite the contrary: he explicitly emphasised

Peter's physical strength, the stones kinetic energy, its inertia, its material properties of density and rigidity, together with the windows material properties, etc. are only background conditions of this event.

[190] Newton quoted in Collingwood (1998: position 3609).

the utterly "absurd" character of gravity, which completely contradicted basic conditions of causation, stating that physical bodies were endowed with an inherent force acting upon other objects at a distance, instantaneously and with nothing mediating between the two. Actually, Newton appears to have thought nature and her laws so fantastic they should convince any sound mind that only God could be the ruling cause behind them.[191] Although Newton convincingly demonstrated how natural events could be modelled and precisely predicted using mathematical equations, he did not believe nature to be governed by a hidden matrix, but by an "intelligent and powerful being".[192]

At the turn of the nineteenth century, however, this view would have changed, as exemplified by Kantian physics. Now, causes were understood as physical events determined by natural laws, and Kant emphasised that once every event was governed exclusively by natural laws, determinism must be the consequence. However, he had also followed Hume in showing that causation could neither be deduced logically nor derived from experience. Hence, even if natural deterministic causation was accepted as a necessary a priori principle of our perceived world of phenomena, this would not automatically preclude the existence of a free, intelligible, wilful causation as a principle of the unobservable world of things-in-themselves. While the human being and its actions were empirical phenomena subjected to deterministic causation, the wilful acts of reason would not belong to the domain of observable phenomena, and thus, were not subject to deterministic causal rules either. Hence, all empirical evidence for deterministic causation would not be enough for ruling out the possibility of free will.[193]

All these arguments notwithstanding, a neo-Kantian deterministic interpretation of physicalism apparently ended up dominating the mainstream view between both scientists and philosophers.[194] This generalisation is justified by the methodological principles of reductionism and parsimony, for if the whole observable universe can be sufficiently explained as a result of deterministic events, there is no need for any further additional causal principles.[195] Given the evident deterministic behaviour of all observable events, Kant's argument of non-preclusion of free will amounts to

---

[191] Maxwell (2017).

[192] Newton quoted in Maxwell (2017: 37).

[193] "Da Vernunft selbst keine Erscheinung und gar keinen Bedingunen der Sinnlichkeit unterworfen ist, so findet in ihr selbst in Betreff ihrer Causalität keine Zeitfolge statt, und auf sie kann also das dynamische Gesetz der Natur, was die Zeitfolge nach Regeln bestimmt, nicht angewandt werden" (Kant 1787: 455). However, Kant's conclusion that deterministic causality might be just a transcendental, and hence, epistemological a priori perceptive principle is tacitly based on other presuppositions, such as excluding the possibility to come to an understanding about the world other than by empirical observation and deductive reasoning, such as spiritual experience as a possible source or knowledge. It seems that determinism was not a consequence of logical reasoning, but rather a performative aspect of the nascent modern episteme. Heidegger (1954) suggested that the modern performative, instrumental, goal-oriented logic focusing on prediction and control implied causation in the technical, deterministic sense.

[194] Collingwood (1998); Bourget and Chalmers (2013); Walach (2019).

[195] Walach (2019).

overdetermination, and hence, imposes the reduction of all causes to sufficient observable rules. However, this argument is both circular and internally incoherent. First, it is circular for judging intentionality and consciousness as dispensable causal concepts simply based on the ungrounded preference for empirical evidence over subjective perception. Next, it is incoherent, since both empirical induction and logical deduction, while being the preconditions for producing any "evidence", are exactly an expression of subjective experience and intentional conscious reasoning.[196] So how can evidence possibly prove consciousness to be an illusion?

Moreover, quantum physics suggest that the universe at its micro-level never behaves in a deterministic way, but instead probabilistically. At each quantum event, the involved quanta "choose" between their options. Although this does not imply an intentional behaviour of quanta, it does not rule it out either. Of course, the infinite number of probabilistic quantum events may eventually add to something like a quasi-determinism, but this is a bit like saying that the individual behaviour of countless people under given social constraints may amount to relatively predictable collective behavioural patterns. The ontological difference between strict determinism and added probability is clear and undeniable.

Anyhow, the generalisation of deterministic causation, albeit a purely metaphysical (and actually unsustainable) presupposition, has very far-reaching ontological implications, since it narrows the range of possible cosmological models down to a very restricted selection of alternatives. In particular, it reduces consciousness to an epiphenomenon of *deterministic* physical processes within the nervous system, and thus, renders the idea of free will an illusion. Moreover, it radically rules out the existence of consciousness and any intentional force or being in general. In effect, determinism implies some kind of mechanic, materialist monism, a universe solely consisting of soulless matter blindly following mathematical equations. Any cosmology suggesting the existence of conscious subjects or intentional properties whatsoever, let alone immaterial entities like "souls", "spirits", or "God", are a priori doomed inadmissible for scientific consideration.

As a consequence, determinism works as one of the most powerful arguments for the a priori rejection of diverging cosmologies.

5. Physical Events Are Always Local Events

Locality, one of physics' fundamental principles, states that any causal relation between two objects has to be either the result of physical contact between the two or of some physical agent (typically particles, waves or fields) mediating between them. As emphasised by Newton himself, his law of universal gravitation violated the principle of locality. However, Newton hoped the missing physical agent that would explain gravity while preserving the principle of locality might be found later. This would be accomplished by Einstein's general relativity, explaining

[196] One can even argue that epiphenomenalism deepens the cartesian cut and the subsequent problem of induction: "Technically speaking: the assumption that consciousness is a purely brain-derived activity precludes any introspective knowledge that reaches beyond the cognitive system" (Walach 2019: 31).

gravity in terms of spacetime curvature. His special relativity had already re-defined locality in terms of causation through signal transmission with maximum speed of light, so that under no circumstances any causal action at a distance might occur in less than the speed of light, no matter their relative velocity or position in spacetime. However, quantum theory predicts non-local behaviour of particles under certain circumstances (e.g. entanglement). Although, depending on the various currently existing interpretations of quantum theory, this does not necessarily imply the possibility of faster-than-light communication; quantum theory certainly does not sustain locality, but rather challenges it.[197]

In sum, locality appears to be an additional metaphysical ad hoc assumption about the ontological constitution of the universe, based on inconsistent evidence, and not important enough to disqualify any fundamental theory in physics. For two centuries, physics had been thriving grandiosely based on Newton's law of gravity, albeit radically violating the principle of locality. After Einstein had finally elaborated a theoretical solution to this problem, it took another hundred years to provide experimental evidence for the gravitational waves his theory had predicted. And quantum theory has been the most fundamental theory of matter for a century now, although it violates local causation.

Curiously, though, locality is an argument strong enough to disqualify diverging views as being "non-scientific" and to explain away a whole range of knowledge practices, observed phenomena and experiences reported by countless witnesses all over the globe. This includes non-local perception of distant events during visions, dreams or trance, as well as any kind of non-local effect provoked by magic or psychokinesis. Such events are commonly declared to be impossible since there is no detectible signal mediating between brain activity and distant events, so these phenomena would violate the principle of locality, and hence, cannot be real.

Anyhow, in the face of the inherent weakness of locality and the unequal weighting of this principle depending on the subject of application, the ideological character of its use as an a priori disqualifier for diverging views is quite obvious.

6. Physical Events May Have Mental Effects, but Never the Other Way Round
The assumption that mental acts are not accountable for causing any direct physical effects is generally understood as a corollary of the previous causal conditions. If a cause has to be a physical event or entity to be effective, determined by natural laws, and the causal relation has to occur locally, obviously volitional acts of the mind cannot be the cause of anything. However, once the metaphysical character of these preconditions is unveiled, it remains to be explained why this should be so. Take the relation between consciousness and brain activity as an example: Why should the first not be the cause of the latter, or the latter in some other way supervene on the first, or both phenomena be somehow entangled effects of yet another cause? Isn't my decision to lift my arm the cause responsible for my nerves to fire and have my muscles lift my arm (as John Locke once suggested[198]). Or to put the question the

[197] E.g. Walach (2020).

[198] Locke (1690).

other way round: Why should it be so obvious that physical processes in my brain produce an immaterial, objectively unobservable phenomenon we call consciousness? Why is there anything like the experience of seeing a beautiful blue, of smelling the flagrance of flowers or of hearing the wonderful sound of a violin, if in fact there are only waves of sound or light and molecules provoking neurons to fire? Why is there something it is like to be myself, and something else it is like to be a bat (to use Thomas Nagel's example[199])?

These kinds of questions point to what David Chalmers has coined "the hard problem of consciousness".[200] The whole issue is highly complex and amounts to a variety of possible ontological interpretations of theories and evidence from a range of scientific fields, including neurosciences, quantum theory and philosophy of mind. I will come back to the different ontological models which are currently being discussed in this context in the last part of this work. For now, I would just like to hold that current scientific evidence and theoretical frameworks do not necessarily impose the conclusion that causal relations between physical and mental events always have to be one way, leading from physical causes to mental effects and never the other way round. On the contrary, as the discussion advances, epiphenomenal approaches seem to be ever more difficult to be defended, while other alternative models are gaining terrain.

Be this as it may, mainstream physicalism categorically denies any possible direct effect of mental events in the physical world. This view not only greatly exacerbates any attempt to come to a coherent theory of mind, it also precludes a number of notions that are essential to many subalternised, so-called "traditional" cosmologies. In its weakest interpretation, it states that even if we consider our mind to be free, our thoughts will not have any physical effect apart from our own body. Consequently, any kind of prayer, magic spell, ritual or trance seeking to provoke effects in the physical world are nonsense, since there simply is no such thing as "mental power", "spiritual energy" or "supernatural" causes originating from our mind.

3.6 Summing Up Universalist Metaphysics

Once the inherent predicaments and the metaphysical underpinning of all those methodological and epistemological arguments in defence of empiricism and scientific objectivity have been clarified, there can be little doubt about the ideological character of universalism. Moreover, social sciences and critical strands in philosophy, from Nietzsche to post-modernism, have repeatedly debunked knowledge and truth in general, including scientific knowledge, to be contingent, historical, socially construed, power-laden, and hence, inseparably related to particular power

199 Nagel (1974).

200 Chalmers (1995).

relations. The resulting relativistic stance is quite convincing and comparatively easy to defend, since it represents the consequent application of scientific scepticism to itself by turning modern science into just another object of scientific scrutiny. However, relativism comes with at least two major problems: First, relativism seems to equalise all kinds of knowledge, but not by upgrading diverging ways of knowing to scientific level of credibility; instead it downgrades science to the level of illusive myth. Second, relativism does not solve the problem of incommensurability, but rather escalates it into an insuperable barrier. Albeit its liberating self-understanding, relativism, therefore, ends up supporting universalism rather than valorising Other, subalternised ways of knowing.

In search for a way to overcome relativism in support of an equitable dialogue between science and subalternised views I proposed to revisit pragmatism and its suggestion to explore the impact of metaphysical presumptions as a possible non-epistemological yardstick for a qualitative comparison of different kinds of knowledge. However, in the face of modernity's "dark side", impact-assessment should transcend mere performative reaches in terms of prediction, control and technological applicability, and rather ask about the mental and behavioural dispositions induced by particular worldviews and the ways of being in the world they tend to produce. In order to enable such a comparative assessment of the particular effects of different metaphysical presumptions and resulting cosmologies, universalism has to be overcome. And since universalism is an ideology that takes its legitimation from naive scientism, the universalistic arguments for the a priori delegitimisation of diverging views are to be found between scientism's metaphysical presuppositions.

In the speculative analysis of scientism's ontology discussed above, I focused on two aspects: First, I tried to offer a comprehensive exploration of its ontological implications in terms of a scientific worldview or cosmology, and second, to identify those metaphysical presumptions responsible for the a priori disqualification of particular notions typically to be found between the essential elements of Other, subalternised cosmologies.

The metaphysical presumptions I proposed as being those most essential to scientistic cosmology were: Cartesian dualism, naturalism, physicalism, mathematicalism, determinism, and several ontological presumptions concerning causation, time, space and matter. The analysis of these presumptions showed that:

1. Dualism does not necessarily preclude alternative views, but Cartesian dualism does. Specifically, its additional presumptions concerning the exclusive existence of mind-stuff within living human bodies only and its purely receptive relation to the physical world turned out to be problematic in several aspects. First, the reduction of dualism to a mind-body dualism precludes the existence of any immaterial, intentional actant other than human minds within human bodies, as well as the existence of an immaterial realm beyond physical phenomena. Second, by reducing the mind-stuff to pure cognition with no direct connection to the physical realm other than through receiving sensual impressions, Cartesian dualism produces not only representationalism, but also the classical mind-body

problem with all its terrifying predicaments. Moreover, it precludes any kind of direct mental action on physical objects, as suggested by “magic”, “shamanism” or “parapsychological” experiences.

2. Similarly, naturalism does not necessarily conflict with other worldviews as long as nature’s laws are not held to be mathematical equations, transforming the universe into an illusive appearance governed by an invisible matrix of infinite calculi. The mathematical conception of nature’s hidden “true” nature not only disqualifies subjective, sensual perception for being illusive; it also transforms the universe into blind matter completely determined by mathematical laws. The matrix view of nature and the resulting deterministic physicalism is responsible for the so-called disenchantment of the world, and thus, renders any attempt to act upon things by communicating with them an expression of childish “animism”.
3. Although deterministic physicalism historically led to a deterministic concept of causation, causation itself has to be regarded a metaphysical presupposition in its own right (probably rooted in anthropomorphic notions of compulsion). An analysis of scientific standard notions about causation reveals that some, but not all, of these notions are incommensurable with certain concepts or classes of events and entities which are conceived as possible causes by different cosmological traditions. In particular, the following standard notions were shown to function as arguments for an a priori delegitimisation of diverging views:

   (a) The temporal definition of causation as a succession of causes followed by their effects precludes *divination*, since it denies the possibility of any kind of events, including mental states like dreams, visions or intuitions, to be caused or induced by future events.
   (b) The deterministic physicalist notion of causation, that any cause to be effective has to be a physical phenomenon *and* completely determined by natural laws strictly following to mathematical calculi, is probably the heaviest weapon against diverging cosmologies. In sum, it reduces consciousness to an ineffective epiphenomenon of physical processes within our nervous-system, and thus, radically rules out the existence of mind-stuff or any other intentional force or being in general, such as “souls”, “spirits”, or “God”.
   (c) The principle of locality, albeit too weak to refute major theories in physics, is frequently used to reject “traditional” ritual practices and observed phenomena like non-local perception of distant events during visions, dreams or trance, as well as any kind of non-local effect provoked by magic or psychokinesis.
   (d) Finally, the categorical denial of any possible direct effect of mental events in the physical world not only greatly exacerbates any attempt to come to a coherent theory of mind, it also renders any kind of prayer, magic spell, ritual or trance seeking to provoke effects in the physical world pure nonsense.

It is important to keep in mind that the notion of causation as well as all those additional conditions are metaphysical assumptions, not necessarily following from evidence, and most of them do not even follow as a necessary corollary from each other. Moreover, all of these notions, including the apparently simple assumption that everything is caused by something else, are subject to serious objections for being internally incoherent or inconsistent with fundamental scientific theories and/or evidence.

The overall result of this analysis suggests that universalism's exclusion mechanism is based on a limited number of identifiable metaphysical presuppositions[201] which turn out to be incommensurable with certain alternative concepts. Moreover, many of these presumptions are themselves problematic for being incoherent and producing epistemological dilemmas, like the problem of induction or the mind-body problem. As a result, current scientific practice and meta-discourse have already shown the need to rethink those metaphysical concepts as a necessary precondition for the solution of existing incoherencies and shortcomings within science's theoretical frameworks. Actually, critique of some of these presumptions has been so severe that they have to be regarded untenable, which is the reason why I identified them as part of *scientism* and not of science proper. And last but not least, the metaphysical presumptions in question seem to be also responsible for the so-called disenchantment or objectification of the world, that is, for the aesthetic and ethical disposition towards ourselves and nature typically associated with the modern way of being and its destructive side-effects.

These findings have several important corollaries:

1. In order to overcome incommensurabilities with a particular cosmology or tradition of knowing, it is *not* necessary to give up the scientific method as a whole, but merely to relativise a few metaphysical presumptions and their epistemological implications.
2. Since the metaphysical presumptions identified as being responsible for the a priori preclusion of diverging views are also among the most problematic ones, they will have to be reviewed and adjusted anyway for the sake of scientific progress and inner coherence.
3. This raises the hope that adjustments concerning problematic metaphysical presumptions will not only contribute to the solution of inconsistencies inherent to scientific theory and practice, but also relativise incommensurabilities with other, subalternised views.
4. Moreover, by adjusting these problematic metaphysical presumptions, scientific theory and evidence may not only come closer together, but also lead to ontological interpretations which may positively alter our worldview and eventually our way of being in the world. Considering the pragmatic evaluation of knowledge proposed above, such a change may result in a qualitative progress of

[201] Of course, the list offered here is the result of a speculative analysis and may be extended or else modified. I leave it to further works on this subject to explore alternative interpretations discussing other metaphysical presumptions. However, the important point here is that the list of presumptions identified as those precluding alternative views only contains a relatively small portion of the metaphysics science is based on.

scientific knowledge in terms of its objective overall positive effects for us and our planet.

Following this rationale, it would be interesting to analyse to which extent current scientific evidence based theories about the fundamental structures of the universe are in fact incommensurable with Other, so-called "traditional" or "animistic" cosmologies. Supposing there are no fundamental incommensurabilities between these ontological models, this would render any a priori rejection of Other ways of knowing inadmissible. Moreover, not being fundamentally incommensurable, an equitable dialogue between science and Other ways of knowing would become possible. This also includes the possibility of a comparative assessment concerning the objective effects of particular metaphysical presuppositions subjacent to both different knowledge traditions and concomitant ways of being. Assessing different kinds of knowledge and "truth" as essential ingredients in the unfolding of more or less desirable futures could provide an alternative yardstick for measuring their objective value, and thereby, relativise relativism.

To explore the possible conditions needed to overcome universalism and facilitate such an interscientific, transcosmological, or "pluriversal"[202] dialogue is precisely the aim of this work. For this purpose, I will offer a comparative analysis of Potiguara cosmology (in Part II) and ontological interpretations of quantum physics currently being discussed as possible solutions to the "hard problem of consciousness" (in Part III).[203] However, before I turn to the Potiguara and their way of being, there still remain some open questions concerning the socio-ecological, geopolitical, and anthropological aspects of scientific universalism.

References

Améry J (1982) Wider den Strukturalismus: Das Beispiel des Michel Foucault. In: Lindemann G (ed) Améry, Jean: Weiterleben—aber wie?: Essays 1963-1978, Stuttgart, pp 101–125

Aristotle Metaphysics: Book V. https://www.perseus.tufts.edu/hopper/text?doc=Perseus:abo:tlg,0086,025:1. Accessed 12.01.2024

[202] Pluriversality, as an onto-political counter model to universality, will be discussed in detail in the last Chap. 5 of Part I.

[203] In so doing, I basically follow the argument that if at least one of those recently discussed ontological models is both coherent with current scientific theoretical framework and evidence, and also with at least one alternative model cosmology containing metaphysical concepts conventional scientism would preclude, then it is in principle possible to find metaphysical "hinges" to enable a dialogue with alternative systems of knowledge currently held to be incommensurable, and thus, "unscientific"—and universalism has fallen. Obviously, there are countless different cultures and traditions, all of them with their own ways of knowing and cosmological underpinning; and the Potiguara do by no means represent some kind of generic "indigenous" or "traditional culture" that might represent all those others. However, the Potiguara's way of knowing and being is based upon cosmological ideas concomitant with ontological concepts conventional scientism would judge unscientific. And this is a feature Potiguara cosmology has in common with countless other traditional views.

Bachelard G (1978) Die Bildung des Wissenschaftlichen Geistes, Frankfurt a.M
Bacon F (2017) The new organon: or true directions concerning the interpretation of nature. https://www.earlymoderntexts.com/assets/pdfs/bacon1620.pdf. Accessed 03.01.2024.
Bataille G (1972) Das obszöne Werk (Die Geschichte des Auges, Madame Edwarda, Meine Mutter, Der Kleine, Der Tote). Rowohlt
Bataille G (2001) Die Aufhebung der Ökonomie. Matthes & Seitz, Munich
Baudrillard J (1982) Der symbolische Tausch und der Tod. Matthes & Seitz, Munich
Bauman Z (1998) O Mal-Estar da Pos-Modernidade. Jorge Zahar Editora, Rio de Janeiro
Berger PL, Luckmann T (1991) The social construction of reality: a treatise in the sociology of knowledge. Penguin, London
Blachowicz J (2009) How science textbooks treat scientific method: a philosopher's perspective. Br J Philos Sci 60:303–344. https://doi.org/10.1093/bjps/axp011
Böhme G (1980) Alternativen der Wissenschaft. Suhrkamp, Frankfurt a.M
Bourdieu P (1985) Praktische Vernunft: Zur Theorie des Handelns. Suhrkamp, Frankfurt a.M
Bourdieu P (1987) Sozialer Sinn: Kritik der theoretischen Vernunft. Suhrkamp, Frankfurt a.M
Bourget D, Chalmers DJ (2013) What do philosophers believe? Philos Stud 170:465–500
Brentano F (1988) Über Ernst Machs "Erkenntnis und Irrtum". Mit zwei Anhängen, Kleine Schriften über Ernst Mach, Der Brentano-Mach-Briefwechsel, Rodopi, Amsterdam
Cartwright N (1983) How the laws of physics lie. Oxford University Press, New York
Chalmers AF (1993) O que é Ciência Afinal? Editora Brasiliense
Chalmers DJ (1995) The conscious mind: in search of a theory of conscious experience. Department of Philosophy University of California, Santa Cruz
Charbonnier P, Salmon G, Skafish P (2017) Comparative metaphysics: ontology after anthropology. Rowman & Littlefield, London
Collingwood RG (1998) An essay on metaphysics, revised. Clarendon Press, Oxford
Comte IMAX (1974) Die Soziologie. Die positive Philosophie im Auszug ("Cours de philosophie positive"). Kröner, Stuttgart
Creath R (2022) Logical empiricism. Stanford Encyclopedia of philosophy. First published Mon Apr 4, 2011; substantive revision Wed Apr 5. https://plato.stanford.edu/entries/logical-empiricism/#Rel. Accessed 22.11.2023
Cristin R (1999) Edmund Husserl—Martin Heidegger—Phänomenologie. Berlin
Deleuze G, Foucault M (1977) Der Faden ist gerissen. Merve, Berlin
Deleuze G, Guattari F (2000) Anti-edipus: capitalism and schizophrenia. University of Minnesota Press, Minneapolis
Dennett DC (1991) Consciousness explained. Little, Brown, Boston
Descartes R (2017) Meditations on First Philosophy in which are demonstrated the existence of God and the distinction between the human soul and body. Bennett J (ed). http://www.earlymoderntexts.com/assets/pdfs/descartes1641.pdf. Accessed 22.11.2023
Durkheim E (2007) As Regras do Metodo Sociologico. Martins Fontes, São Paulo
Edelman GM (2004) Das Licht des Geistes: Wie Bewusstsein entsteht. Zürich, Düsseldorf
Einstein A, Podolsky B, Rosen N (1935) Can quantum-mechanical description of reality be considered complete? Phys Rev 47:777–780
Elias N, Scotson JL (2000) Os Estabelecidos e os Outsiders: Sociologia das relações de poder a partir de uma pequena comunidade. Jorge Zahar, Rio de Janeiro
Fleck L (2008) Genesis and development of a scientific fact, Repr, 11th edn. Univ. of Chicago Press, Chicago
Foucault M (1974) Die Ordnung der Dinge: Eine Archäologie der Humanwissenschaften. Suhrkamp, Frankfurt a.M
Foucault M (1978) Dispositive der Macht: Über Sexualität, Wissen und Wahrheit. Merve, Berlin
Foucault M (1981) Überwachen und Strafen: Die Geburt des Gefängnisses. Suhrkamp, Frankfurt a.M
Freud S (1993) Abriß der Psychoanalyse: Das Unbehagen in der Kultur, Frankfurt a.M
Gadamer H-G (1978) Seminar: Die Hermeneutik und die Wissenschaften. Frankfurt a.M

Geertz C (2008) A Interpretação das Culturas. LTC, Rio de Janeiro
Giddens A (1991) The consequences of modernity. Polity Press, Cambridge
Giddens A (2003) A Construção da Sociedade. Martins Fontes, São Paulo
Gower B (1997) Scientific method: an historical and philosophical introduction. Routledge, New York
Gutierrez JPV, Esteves PR (2016) Towards a dialogue between knowledge systems: learning experience in indigenous contexts in Mexico. Beyond Soc Sci 4:21–40
Habermas J (1988) Der Philosophische Diskurs der Moderne. Frankfurt a.M
Hacking I (1999) The social construction of what? Harvard University Press, Cambridge
Harding SG (1994) Is science multicultural?: Challenges, resources, opportunities, uncertainties. Configurations 2:301–330. https://doi.org/10.1353/con.1994.0019
Heidegger M (1954) Vorträge und Aufsätze. Tübingen
Heidegger M (1975) Die Grundprobleme der Phänomenologie: Gesamtausgabe. Klostermann, Frankfurt a.M
Heller KD (1964) Ernst Mach: Wegbereiter der Modernden Physik: Mit ausgewählten Kapiteln aus seinem Werk. Springer, Wien
Horkheimer M (1937) Traditionelle und kritische Theorie. http://lesekreis.blogsport.de/images/MaxHorkheimerTraditionelleundkritischeTheorie.pdf. Accessed 10.03.2019
Horkheimer M, Adorno T (1969) Dialektik der Aufklärung: Philosophische Fragmente. Frankfurt a.M.
Hume D (2017) Treatise of human nature. Book I. Bennett J (ed). https://www.earlymoderntexts.com/assets/pdfs/hume1739book1_4.pdf. Accessed 01.12.2023
Husserl E (1962) Hesserliana. Köln
James W (1981) Pragmatism: a new name for some old ways of thinking. Hackett, Indianapolis
Kammler C, Parr P, Schneider J (2008) Foucault-Handbuch: Leben—Werk—Wirkung. Weimar, Stuttgart
Kant I (1787) Kritik der reinen Vernunft, ungekürzte Ausgabe nach der zweiten, hin und wieder verbesserten Auflage. Paderborn
Keller R (2008a) Wissenssoziologische Diskursanalyse: Grundlagen eines Forschungsprogramms. Wiesbaden
Keller R (2008b) Michel Foucault. Konstanz
Knorr-Cetina K (1981) The manufacture of knowledge: an essay on the constructivist and contextual nature of science. Pergamon, Oxford
Kögler H-H (2004) Michel Foucault. Stuttgart
Kuhn T (1970) The structure of scientific revolution. In: Neurath O et al (eds) International encyclopedia of unified science 2:2. University of Chicago Press, Chicago
Kuhn M, Vessuri H (2016) Contributions to alternative concepts of knowledge. Stuttgart
Kuhn M, Yazawa S (2013) Theories about and strategies against hegemonic social sciences center for glocal studies. Seijo University, Tokyo
Lakatos I (1977) The methodology of scientific research programmes. Cambridge University Press, Cambridge
Lakatos EM, Marconi MdA (2003) Fundamentos de metodologia científica. Atlas, São Paulo
Latour B (1987) Science in action: how to follow scientists and engineers through society. Harvard University Press, Cambridge
Latour B (1993) We have never been modern. Harvard University Press, Cambridge
Laville C, Dionne J (1999) A construçao do saber: manual de metodologia da pesquisa em ciencias humanas. Artmed, Porto Alegre
Legg C (2020) Pragmatism. Stanforfd Encyclopedia of Philosophy. First published Sat Aug 16, 2008; substantive revision Tue Apr 6, 202. https://plato.stanford.edu/entries/pragmatism/#MeanPragJame, Accessed 3.01.2024
Linhart J (2008) Universidades Indígenas: Programas de Educação Indígena Superior na América Latina: A Caminho de uma Ciência Intercultural? Master thesis, LMU

Locke J (1690) An essay concerning human understanding. http://www.pinkmonkey.com/dl/library1/book1284.pdf. Accessed 22.11.2023
Lyotard J-F (1986) Das Postmoderne Wissen: Ein Bericht. Vienna
Marti U (1988) Michel Foucault. Munich
Marx K (1962) Das Kapital: Kritik der politischen Ökonomie. Dietz, Berlin
Maxwell N (2017) In praise of natural philosophy: a revolution for thought and life, Kindle. McGill-Queen's University Press, Quebec
Maxwell N (2021) The world crisis—and what to do about it : a revolution for thought and action. University College, London
Merchant C (2006) The scientific revolution and the death of Nature. Isis 97:513–533
Merchant C (2018) Science and nature—past. Present and Future, Routledge
Merton RK (1968) Social theory and social structure. Free Press, New York
Meyering TC (2020) Causation. Encyclopedia of science and religion. https://www.encyclopedia.com/philosophy-and-religion/eastern-religions/buddhism/causation. Accessed 05.08.2020
Morin E (2005) Ciência com Consciência. Editora Bertrand Brasil, Rio de Janeiro
Nagel T (1974) What is it like to be a bat. Philos Rev LXXXIII(4):435–450
Ndjodo L-MN (2013) Léon-Marie Nkolo 2013: Philosophies and Ideologies of Globalization: Postmodernism, Postcolonialism and How to Go Beyond Them. In: Kuhn M, Yazawa S (eds) Theories about and strategies against hegemonic social sciences center for glocal studies. Seijo University, Tokyo, pp 7–30
Newton I (1846) Newton's principia: the mathematical principles of natural philosophy. Daniel Adee, New York
Nietzsche F (1887) Die Fröhliche Wissenschaft (La Gaya Scienza). Verlag von E.W. Fritzsch, Leipzig
Nietzsche F (2002) Jenseits von Gut und Böse. Genealogie der Moral, Stuttgart
Peirce ChS (1878) How to make our ideas clear. Pop Sci Mon 12:286–302
Pojman P (2019) Ernst Mach. Stanford encyclopedia of philosophy. First published Wed May 21, 2008; substantive revision Sun Mar 3, 2019. https://plato.stanford.edu/entries/ernst-mach/#Sci. Accessed 22.11.2023
Popper K (1970) Die Logik der Sozialwissenschaften. In: Adorno TW (ed) Der Positivismusstreit in der deutschen Soziologie (9.Aufl.). Neuwied, Berlin, pp 103–122
Popper K (2005) The logic of scientific discovery. Routledge, London
Quine WvO (1951) Two dogmas of empiricism. Philos Rev 60:20–43
Rorty R (1979) Philosophy and the mirror of nature. Princeton University Press, Princeton
Sarasin P (2005) Michel Foucault zur Einführung. Dresden
Schädelbach H (1989) Foucault und der anthropologische Schlummer. In: Honneth A (ed) Zwischenbetrachtungen: Im Prozess der Aufklärung. Frankfurt a.M, pp 231–261
Schaffer J (2016) The metaphysics of causation. Stanford encyclopedia of philosophy. First published Sun Feb 2, 2003; substantive revision Tue Jul 5, 2016. https://plato.stanford.edu/archives/spr2022/entries/causation-metaphysics/. Accessed 03.01.2024
Stengers I (2000) The invention of modern science. University of Minnesota Press, Minneapolis
Taussig M (1997) Mimesis und Alterität: eine eigenwillige Geschichte der Sinne. Europäische Verlagsanstalt, Hamburg
Varela F, Shear J (eds) (2002) The view from within: first person approaches in the study of consciousness. Imprint Academic, Thorverton
Varela FJ, Thompson E, Rosch A (1993) The embodied mind. Cognitive science and human experience. MIT Press, Cambridge
Verworn M (1928) Kausale und konditionale Weltanschauung. Verlag von Gustav Fischer, Jena
von Stillfried N (2018) Vom Innen der Dinge: Das "Bewusstsein-Körper-Problem" und die "Welle-Teilchen-Dualität": Interdisziplinäre Impulse zwischen Quantentheorie und analytischer Philosophie des Geistes. Habilitation Thesis, Univerisity of Trier
Vorländer K (1902) Geschichte der Philosophie, Solingen
Walach H (2019) The Galileo Commission Report: beyond a materialist worldview: towards an expanded science. Scientific Medical Network

Walach H (2020) Inner experience—direct access to reality: a complementarist ontology and dual aspect monism support a broader epistemology. Front Psychol 11:640. https://doi.org/10.3389/fpsyg.2020.00640
Weber M (1919) Wissenschaft als Beruf. In: Kaesler D (ed) Max Weber—Schriften 1894–1922. Kröner, Stuttgart
Whitehead AN (1925) Science and the modern world. Cambridge University Press, London
Wilson D (1974) Herschel and Whewel's version of Newtonianism. J Hist Ideas 35:79–97
Wittgenstein L (1958) Philosophical investigations. Blackwell, Oxford
Zilsel E (1942) The sociological roots of science. Am J Sociol 47:544–562

Chapter 4
The Geopolitics of Scientific Universalism

Once the metaphysical, and ultimately ideological, nature of scientific universalism has been unveiled, the problem of modern science's nature and purpose shifts from its epistemological grounding towards its social embedding and its role within our globalised, modern world. If Science's purpose is, supposedly, exclusively to seek unbiased truth, and if there is no objective reason to reject other ways of knowing for methodological or epistemological reasons, what then is the real purpose of its universalistic claims? Why does Science insist on denying the truth value of other ways of knowing, against all logical epistemological arguments? What is the real sociopolitical role of Science and to what extent is Science involved in the maintenance of our current world order?

There can be no doubt that modern science has long achieved global hegemony, and yet its own meta-discourse does not sustain its methodological or epistemological superiority. The result of this situation is a rampant clash between our lived global reality in which Science and scientifically-produced technology have taken a central role in almost all aspects of our lives, and the surprising insight that apparently there is no sustainable argument for its universal truth claims. If scientific knowledge does not have a higher truth value than any other form of knowing, why then has it been adopted all over the globe? Isn't the reason for its success its efficacy in predicting and controlling natural events? Why is it, then, that science (and not magic or Taoism) enabled white men (and why still no women or Black men?!) to fly to the moon, if science and other kinds of knowledge are equivalent?

This chapter is an attempt to summarise some of the many answers which have been proposed to these kinds of questions. The first section of this chapter provides an overview of the different approaches in the social sciences to conceptualise the social aspects of Science concerning both the production of scientific knowledge and the role Science plays in modern society.[1] The second section focusses on the

[1] Of course, this is a story which has already been told countless times, but I feel that the field is still too marginal to assume it common knowledge among scientists, let alone the general public. I therefore opted for providing a little history of the development of social theories on science, following the most influential contributions within their historical context over the last 100 years or so. There is nothing substantially new to tell about this issue; however, in order to come to a better understanding of the geopolitical dimension of scientific universalism, it is important to have the main points of this debate in mind.

J. Linhart, *Science and the Other*, Schriften zu Leben und Gesellschaft - Series on Life and Society 2, https://doi.org/10.1007/978-3-032-03927-9_4

geopolitical dimension of scientific universalism, and its significance for the construction and maintenance of global inequalities.

4.1 Science in Its Mirror

> It does not matter that the scientific community ritualistically denies its alliance with economic/industrial and military power. The evidence is overwhelming that such is the case (Aronowitz 1988: 20).

In fact, Science has itself been an object of scientific inquiry for a century now. Accordingly, scientists have been investigating virtually all imaginable aspects of Science and scientific knowledge production, its role and bearing in society, and to what extent scientific knowledge is itself determined by social factors.

Robert Merton is often credited with being the "founding father" of the sociology of science. In his 1936 thesis Merton[2] showed how seventeenth century Protestant ethics together with the Industrial Revolution and British expansionism were influential on the development of early modern science. However, his own contributions to the field were based on a number of works that had already been written on the social aspects of Science. His thesis not only hinged heavily on Max Weber and Emile Durkheim, he also emphasised that he was deeply indebted to Boris Hessen[3] and Karl Mannheim[4] (although submitting the latter to a harsh critique for his "Marxist" conceptions and his theoretical eclecticism).

4.1.1 Between the Wars

The 1920s and 1930s saw a number of pioneering contributions to the study of science and knowledge, among which the work of Karl Mannheim certainly played a central role. Mannheim's *Wissenssoziologie* (sociology of knowledge) emphasised the social, and hence, essentially political character of knowledge. He argued that the collective experiences of different social groups within their particular historical situation and their position within social relations of power would result in different perspectives or *thought styles*. Concepts, meanings and values entail the "crystallisation of the experience" of a particular group, providing a largely unconscious perceptive matrix. The individual reality of a group member is, thus, determined by the thought style they inherited, which would guide their perception, their thinking, their behaviour, and their decisions. Mannheim explicitly argued against any subject-based epistemology or absolutist concepts of truth, since these were

[2] Merton (1970).

[3] Hessen (2009).

[4] Mannheim (1954).

themselves offshoots of a particular thought style, typical of early capitalist bourgeoise's extreme individualism. These irrational foundations of the rational concept of knowledge were rather rooted in the labour division of industrial society into different classes living in extremely diverging realities, which would result in a plurality of radically different worldviews. Accordingly, each social group would also have its own intellectuals[5] to rationalise their particular views. As a result, science would also be reflected in politics, as exemplified by socialist (e.g. Marx and Engels) and liberal (e.g. Adam Smith) theories. Thus, any kind of knowledge represents a particular thought style and is imbued—at least to a certain degree—with the political demands of a certain group, with their ideologies and their utopian visions. In this sense, knowledge in general is ideological (or utopian)[6] in a broader or "total" sense. For Mannheim, this general formulation of *total ideology* led directly to his sociology of knowledge. But Mannheim was also painfully aware of the danger of slipping into relativism, which he saw as a main cause of the fundamental crisis of thought of his times, and hence, would have to be avoided at any cost. He argued, however, that relativism was itself bound to an outdated foundationalist notion of truth that equated the historical contingency of knowledge and the plurality of possible perspectives with falsity. To prevent his theory from falling into this epistemological pitfall, Mannheim proposed his concept of *relationism* instead. According to relationism, the elements of a thought system only become meaningful in relation to each other and to the entire system of meaning within its particular historical and social context.[7] Mannheim proposed a dynamic concept of ideology and reality

---

[5] In fact, Mannheim adopted Alfred Weber's concept of *unattached intellectuals* (*Freischwebende Intelligenz*), a social stratum of its own characterised by a relatively independent mindset, compared to other class members who were basically trapped within their class-specific ideologies. Mannheim held that from its beginning the bourgeoise class has been internally divided into capitalists and educated men, the latter being bound together by their education rather than by their economic situation, and hence, being obliged to their intellectual "mission" of attaining a "total view", revealing the ideological bias of certain ideas rather than class interests (Marx and Engels may represent the epitome of such unattached intellectuals). Accordingly, these "unattached" intellectuals might choose more or less consciously to take the side of a particular class. The hazy character of this concept of "unattached" intellectuals and its obvious incoherence with the rest of Mannheim's theses of the ideological, socially determined, and historically contingent character of knowledge has been heavily criticised (e.g. by Merton). Retrospectively, it is a pity that Mannheim did not have the opportunity to include Gramsci's (1982) studies on intellectuals into his account, which certainly would have been a valuable contribution to his approach. Unfortunately, by the time Mannheim had published *Ideology and Utopia* in 1929, Gramsci would be in jail, after having been arrested by the fascists, writing his famous theses on the role of organic and traditional intellectuals within class struggle.

[6] Mannheim introduced the distinction between ideology and utopia, each reflecting opposite political and social positions. While ideology refers to the unconscious belief in distorted views that justify the status quo, and thus, the position of the dominant groups, utopia refers to the unrealistic vision of a better future for dominated classes, however, without any correct analysis of current conditions (Mannheim 1954).

[7] Of course, the question arises here, how to evaluate the truth value of a particular set of knowledge. A non-evaluative study of ideology would certainly come to a better understanding about the relation between particular thought styles and the social conditions from where they arose, but not

beyond the concept of absolute truth with its static relation between knowledge and existence in an unchanging universe. Ethical norms, theories, and meanings change with time, culture and social position; but they also adapt to changing historical situations, allowing for adequate behaviour and sound decisions in a concrete situation. However, once a norm or theory proves unable to comply with a given historical setting, obscuring rather than revealing its meaning, it has degenerated into an ideology. Instead of relativising knowledge, sociology of knowledge should come to a better understanding concerning the historical development of the relation between thought and existence, that is, between the objective social reality and the conceptual apparatus we use to interpret our experience.

> In view of this, the sociology of knowledge has set itself the task of solving the problem of the social conditioning of knowledge by boldly recognizing these relations and drawing them into the horizon of science itself and using them as checks on the conclusions of our research (Mannheim 1954: 237).

For Mannheim, this "total view" implies the assimilation and transcendence of the different perspectives, aiming at enlarging the horizon of knowledge, rather than the pursuit of the one universal truth.[8] This perspectivist stance of his sociology of knowledge was meant to respond to the extreme heterogeneity and disunity of perspectives that characterised the beginning of the twentieth century by seeking to attain "unity on a higher level" beyond any absolutism.

Mannheim was well aware that his sociological approach to knowledge had deep epistemological consequences for science and truth in general. He concluded that even though the sociological conception of knowledge might not imply judgments on truth values, its findings would still be relevant for epistemology, since its very application to science and epistemology would not only put the presuppositions of science into question, but also those of the critical analysis of epistemology itself. However, epistemology would not be relevant to the question of validity anyway, for knowledge grows out of concrete collective life situations and not out of epistemological considerations.[9] Rather than depending on epistemological legitimation, knowledge is justified post facto once a field of empirical knowledge has been established. "Truth" as such, Mannheim argued, is a philosophical construct related to Cartesian dualism, itself a result of a particular historical life situation of a certain social class, which should not be the basis for any sociological analysis of

---

about their absolute truth value. However, a non-evaluative approach would itself inevitably be bound to particular metaphysical presuppositions. Moreover, by questioning the ideological bias of certain ideas we are also constructing a new ideological framework, although the consciousness about our own metaphysical suppositions may contribute to our understanding (idem).

[8] "Relationism does not signify that there are no criteria of rightness and wrongness in a discussion. It does insist, however, that it lies in the nature of certain assertions that they cannot be formulated absolutely, but only in terms of the perspective of a given situation" (idem: 254).

[9] "New forms of knowledge, in the last analysis, grow out of the conditions of collective life and do not depend for their emergence upon the prior demonstration by a theory of knowledge that they are possible; they do not therefore need to be first legitimized by an epistemology" (idem: 259).

knowledge.[10] Instead of denying the contingent and situated character of knowledge in the name of a non-existent absolute truth, we should rather develop the appropriate epistemological instruments to cope with the existing plurality of truths within the limits of our human perspectives.[11]

In his critique on Mannheim, Merton[12] accused him of being eclectic, mixing up different theoretical approaches in an incoherent manner. Of course, it is true that Mannheim could hark back to a range of previous theories, like Dilthey's hermeneutic method, Husserl's phenomenology, Heidegger's critical approach to modernity, science and technology, Max Scheler's *Wissenssoziologie*, Weber's interpretative sociology, Durkheim's concept of collective unconscious, just to name a few of the many theoretical influences notable in Mannheim's thinking. Mannheim himself, however, stated that "[t]he sociology of knowledge actually emerged with Marx, whose profoundly suggestive *aperçus* went to the heart of the matter.[13]" And indeed,

---

[10] Mannheim (1954) suggested two possible directions for solving the problem: The first would be to accept the relational, situated, and contingent character of knowledge. This would neither exclude objectivity nor render all knowledge an illusion. Rather knowledge can be objective within a particular perspective, just like the different visual perspectives of an object in space seen from different angles. Objectivity would just get another meaning. However, to be able to make any judgment about the objectivity of a particular view a "common denominator" would be necessary to make the different perspectives commensurable, and thereby, comparable. In this way, different perspectives might be evaluated concerning their problem-solving capacity (a fairly pragmatic solution). The second option proposed by Mannheim was not to absolutise the situated and contingent character of knowledge, but instead to integrate the different viewpoint within a new, overarching ontology. This would probably lead to increasingly abstract and formalised higher-level models of reality. Moreover, the construction of such a universal ontology would be limited by the fundamental problem of interpretation and commensurability. Anyhow, Mannheim reasoned that it was far too soon to come to any definitive solution.

[11] "We are thus implicitly called upon to find an epistemological foundation appropriate to these more varied modes of thought" (idem: 260). "The problem is not how we might arrive at a non-perspectivistic picture but how, by juxtaposing the various points of view, each perspective may be recognized as such and thereby a new level of objectivity attained" (idem: 268).

[12] Merton (1968).

[13] Mannheim (1954). It may be worth noting that the importance of Marx for the sociology of knowledge is not limited to the concepts of ideology or class, which, as Mannheim himself discussed, had already been in use before Marx introduced them into his theory. As Bernal observed: "The relevance of Marxism to science is that it removes it from its imagined position of complete detachment and shows it as a part, but a critically important part, of economic and social development" (Bernal 1939: 415). In fact, Marx was ambivalent concerning the influence of social relations on scientific knowledge. His positivist stance towards his own scientific objectivity is contradicted by his theory about the determination of superstructure by infrastructure. On the other hand, Marx himself made no clear exception for science in his analysis. "Marx understands science in terms of the domination of capital over labor. Science is subsumed under capital in the period of the transformation of the labor process from manufacturing to modern industrial production" (Aronowitz 1988: 32). Since science is a social practice under capitalist rule, Marx did not see the need to develop an epistemology. However, in the *German Ideology,* Marx and Engels hold that science appeared in the context of growing importance of technology, not as pure knowledge. Marx's greatest contribution to the social sciences in general was certainly to develop a scientific method to study social phenomena. Recurring to Vico's distinction between natural history and human made human history, Marx concluded that this difference would have to be reflected in dif-

Mannheim's use of Marxist concepts is striking, especially the preeminent role of *ideology* and *class* in his theory (although he claimed to have developed these concepts further, transcending the original meaning in Marx's writings). Anyhow, at that time Mannheim was by far not the only one employing Marxist concepts in the social study of knowledge and science. In fact, during the interwar period, Marxism had great influence on early science research.

As the story goes, in 1931 a delegation of Soviet scientists attended the Second International Congress on the History of Science in London. It turned out that compared to their British colleagues, the Russians were well ahead with their theoretical work on Science and its social aspects.[14] Boris Hessen's paper on *The Social and Economic Roots of Newton's Principia* in particular attracted great attention and became a turning point for the British studies of science. His article was a consequent application of Marxist theory,[15] analysing both material and ideological aspects of early modern science as exemplified by Newton's thematic focus and the ideological underpinning of his theory. In sum, the text argued against an idealist image of science in terms of a history of ideas by showing (1) how technical and economic developments had anticipated and oriented scientific research, (2) how the political and religious context of the Glorious Revolution had influenced Newton's theoretical conceptions, and (3) how Science developed into a sine qua non for industrial capitalism. According to Hessen's proposal the scientific revolution was not the result of a cosmological "Copernican" revolution, but rather of a technical and social revolution resulting in a mechanistic worldview.[16] He provides

ferent scientific methods—decades before Wilhem Dilthey's publications on the *Geisteswissenschaften* and Durkheim's insight that (contrary to the ideas of Auguste Comte) "social facts" constituted an object of their own, being qualitatively different from the natural phenomena. Hence, to study them would demand a method of their own, too. Following Marx's analysis, science and technology were primarily part of the productive processes that constituted social relations and class divisions as well as the relation between humans and nature, resulting in particular world views. Accordingly, natural science and its materialist methods were ideological, reflecting a bourgeoise world view, and therefore, inappropriate to study human affairs. Marxism provides a method to identify metaphysical presumptions intrinsic to modern science. This is why, in a sense, all subsequent theories that hold to social constructionism (sociology of science, post-structuralism, etc.) can be understood as derivations of Marxism (Aronowitz 1988).

[14] Freudenthal and Mclaughlin (2009).

[15] In the introduction of his article Hessen explicitly recites the principles of historic and dialectical materialism as exposed by Marx in the *Capital* and in *German Ideology*: "Society exists and develops as an organic whole. In order to ensure its existence and development society must develop production. In the social production of their life men enter into definite relations that are independent of their will. These relations correspond to a definite stage of development of their material productive forces. The sum total of these relations of production constitutes the economic structure of society, the real foundation, on which rises a legal and political superstructure and to which correspond definite forms of social consciousness. The mode of production of material life conditions the social, political and intellectual life process of society. It is not the consciousness of men that determines their being, but, on the contrary their social being determines their consciousness" (Hessen 2009: 42).

[16] "The dazzling flowering of natural science during the 16th and 17th centuries resulted from the disintegration of the feudal economy, the development of merchant capital, of international maritime relations and of heavy (mining and metallurgical) industry" (idem: 44).

many examples of different technical problems craftsmen had been working on during the fourteenth and fifteenth century, including water pumps for mining, ballistic calculations for artillery, as well as hydrodynamics, astronomy and optics for navigation. These technical developments had been paralleled by an ever-growing importance of cities, merchant capital and the industrialisation and mechanisation of production, finally resulting in a shift from feudal to capitalist economy and the rise of bourgeoisie as the new dominant class. During the sixteenth and seventeenth century educated scholars, who were associated with the bourgeoise class, would increasingly engage in research on technological issues and further develop theoretical approaches to explain the mathematical laws behind mechanics. While the official sciences at the Catholic universities were openly opposed to the study of such worldly matters, the new sciences represented by scholars like Kepler, Galileo, and later by Newton, were addressing the whole range of technical problems of their time concerning communication, navigation, and industries and war, thus clearly serving bourgeoise interests to enhance industrialisation and merchant expansionism.[17] Moreover, the intimate relation between early modern science and class interests transcended the mere ideological realm, manifesting at the very personal level of the scholars' social backgrounds, most of whom were themselves members of the bourgeoise class.[18] These were also the men who joined forces to set up the first scientific academies to openly oppose the then hegemonic scholastic sciences at the universities.[19] Hence, the topics Newton treated in his *Principia* not only resembled all the technological problems of his time, but also the interests of the new bourgeoise class.

[17] "If we compare these principal themes with the physical problems that emerged from our analysis of the technical demands presented by communications, industry and war, it becomes quite clear that these physical problems were mainly defined by those demands" (idem: 52). "When Galileo invented the telescope and discovered the phases of Venus, the scholastic university philosophers did not even want to hear about these new facts, whereas the trading companies requested his telescope, which was superior to those made in Holland" (idem: 54). "The struggle between the university and the extra-university science that served the needs of the rising bourgeoisie was a reflection in the ideological realm of the class struggle between the bourgeoisie and feudalism" (idem: 55). Hessen points out that previous accounts of science's history exclusively examined the ideological superstructure while ignoring its material basis. However, the superstructure can only be understood in the context of the historical processes that gave birth to the social relations it sustains. "In class society the ruling class subjects the productive forces to itself and thus, becoming the dominant material force, subjects all other classes to its interests. The ideas of the ruling class are, in every historical age, the ruling ideas, and the ruling class distinguishes itself from all its predecessors by presenting its ideas as eternal truths. It wishes to reign eternally and bases the inviolability of its rule on the eternal nature of its ideas. In a class society the dominant ideas are separated from the relations of production, thus creating the notion that the material basis is determined by ideas" (idem: 43).

[18] For example, Boyle was a director of the East Indian Company, and Newton was a Member of Parliament.

[19] In Italy, the Florentine Accademia del Cimento was founded around 1650 (by the Medici), while British gentlemen joint the Invisible College, which in 1661 resulted in the foundation of the Royal Academy.

However, Hessen explicitly emphasised that it would be "a gross oversimplification to derive *every problem* studied by various physicists, and *every task* they solved, directly from economics and technology".[20] Neither would historical materialism hold that "the economic factor is the *sole* determining factor".[21] Economic and social structures rather constitute the historical background (material infrastructure) for the development of particular philosophical ideas, worldviews, and related scientific theories (ideological superstructure).[22] Again, taking Newton as an example, Hessen suggested that the introduction of God and the related notion of absolute space (as *sensorium dei*) into the theoretical framework of his *Principia* was due to Newton's identification with Puritan Protestantism rather than for logical reasons. Following Hessen's argument, the mechanistic determinism of Descartes's physics had already established a coherent materialist system which would not depend on the notion of God.[23] Newton seems to have forcefully introduced God into his physics (by separating space from matter and omitting the law of the conservation of energy) to justify his religious worldview, which was typical of the British bourgeoisie in those days.

Finally, Hessen proposed a new view of the role of the steam engine in both the industrial revolution and the theoretical development of thermodynamics. Drawing on Marx's analysis of the importance of machines for the emergence of industrial capitalism and the proletarian class, he showed how thermodynamics would only appear at the agenda of science once industrial production had reached a point when the steam engine had become necessary for its further development. Hessen argued that Newton had, arguably for ideological reasons, deliberately omitted the logical step of developing a theory on the conversion of energy, although the first steam engine had already been invented in his days (Ramsey's patent in 1630). However, merchant capitalism in Newton's time had no use for the steam engine, since it was based on international trade and manufacturing production. Only with the rise of industrial capitalism, which depended on cost efficient production, did the pressure

---

[20] Idem: 61.

[21] Idem.

[22] "The economic situation is the basis. But the development of theories and the individual work of a scientist are also affected by various superstructures, such as political forms of the class struggle and its results, the reflection of these battles in the minds of the participants—in political, juridical, and philosophical theories, religious beliefs and their subsequent development into dogmatic systems" (idem: 62).

[23] Of course, Descartes, too, needed the notion of God in his system, However, Hessen argued that here the role of God was an entirely different one compared to Newton's approach: "Descartes, like Newton, also introduced God, but he needed God only to prove that the quantity of motion in the universe remains constant. He not only refused to admit the conception of an external impetus imparted by God to matter, but, on the contrary, considered that constancy is one of the principal properties of the deity; hence, we cannot assume any inconstancy in his creations, since by assuming inconstancy in his creations we also assume inconstancy in him. Thus Descartes' reason for introducing a deity is different from Newton's, but his conception also requires a deity since Descartes, too, does not maintain an entirely consistent view of the self-movement of matter" (idem: 70).

to lower labour costs by mechanising production create the need for a universal motor. When James Watt and Matthew Boulton began to optimise the steam engine for these new demands during the second half of the eighteenth century, sophisticated machines made up a large part of industrial production and had reached the limits of water-driven power supply. A new, powerful and water-independent motor was now an essential precondition for the further development of industrial production. To make the steam engine fit these new demands complex technical problems had to be solved, which made it necessary to engage in the theoretical development of thermodynamics. In this sense, the study of thermodynamics was a direct result of developments in industrial production. Conversely, and probably even more significantly, with the introduction of the steam engine scientific research had definitively become an indispensable element of capitalist production.

On the social side, the mechanisation and the use of machines in industrial production led to an increasing exploitation of labour. Instead of reducing working hours, machines dramatically extended the working days of the workers, who became a mere appendage to the machines. Following Marxist theory, Hessen suggests that the machine became a means to exploit and dehumanise the working class only because it was in the hands of the bourgeoise class.[24] But, he maintained, once the relations of production would be reorganised under proletarian rule, technology would serve to the benefit of all men. And in the course of these social changes, science, being a part of the productive processes, would change, too.

> The great historical significance of the method created by Marx lies in the fact that knowledge is not regarded as the passive, contemplative perception of reality, but as the means for actively reconstructing it (Hessen 2009: 88).

Hessen concluded triumphantly that in socialist society, finally, science would "belong to all mankind". It might be questioned, however, whether the same machine technology and materialist sciences born to enslave humankind for the most part in favour of a tiny elite may ever serve the ideals of freedom and equality.

Be this as it may, the social constructionist views of the Soviet delegation greatly impressed the participants of the conference in London and were decisive for later works of British scholars like microbiologist J. D. Bernal and biochemists Joseph Needham, as well as for Robert Merton,[25] and sociological approaches to science in

[24] "The worker was indeed becoming an appendage to the machine, not because machines had been invented, but because these machines served the interest of the class that owned the means of production" (idem: 85). "It is not the improvement in the means of production that causes the impoverishment and unprecedented sufferings of the masses. It is not the machines that transform the worker into a blind appendage of a mechanism, but those social relations that exploit machinery in such a way as to turn the worker into a mere appendage to it" (idem: 87).

[25] Merton's thesis concerning the link between Puritan Protestantism, technological requirements of early capitalism and British expansionism, and the rise of modern science, can be understood as a further development of Hessen's approach. Actually, Merton explicitly refers to Hessen and even defends him against Clark's superficial critique, which had (erroneously) accused Hessen of economic determinism (Merton 1968: 664). However, while Merton's first thesis on Puritanism (with reference to Weber rather than to Hessen) was widely acknowledged, his second thesis on the

general. Interestingly, there are also astonishing similarities between Hessen and other authors of his time, like the Austrian philosopher Edgar Zilsel[26] and the Polish economist and historian Henryk Grossmann.[27] These two had developed their own Marxist theories on the social aspects of Science, largely independently from Hessen. In sum, all these authors agreed on some fundamental points:

1. That modern science is a social institution, and thus, cannot be understood in terms of a history of ideas alone or as a result of individual genius, but only within the historical context of the social and economic dynamics it has been a part of.[28]
2. That scientific research and method was inspired primarily by mechanical developments of craftsmen, and not by humanist or scholastic discourse, ultimately resulting in a mechanistic cosmology.[29]
3. That the rise of modern science was concomitant with merchant expansionism, industrialisation and capitalism, the first scientists being members of the bourgeoisie, thus serving bourgeoise interests and representing bourgeoise values and worldviews, which were also related to Puritan Protestantism.[30]

---

economic and military influences has been almost completely ignored—probably due to ideological reasons (Freudenthal and Mclaughlin 2009).

[26] Zilsel (1942).

[27] Grossmann (2009a, b).

[28] Boris Hessen (2009) particularly argued against Whitehead's expression that modern culture is based on the genius of Newton and Galileo, since society is an organic whole determining individual relations as well as superstructure, including social consciousness, according to development of productive forces. Henryk Grossmann (2009a, b) showed in great detail how Descartes' mechanistic worldview had been influenced by technical developments as well as by a general fascination for machines, which had been present in the writings from Thomas Aquinas, over DaVinci, Morus, to Copernicus, Galileo, Hobbes, and Francis Bacon. Bernal (1939) emphasised that the image of science as a contemplative activity seeking for truth is a myth. Science is a social institution, although an extremely powerful one, dependent on social order. The development of science was driven by material needs and new instruments. Since Roger Bacon, and more explicitly so in Francis Bacon, science has been understood as a means to gain power over nature. Edgar Zilsel (1942) came to the conclusion, that science has to be studied as a social phenomenon. And finally, Robert Merton would establish the Sociology of Science as a new discipline. The basic tenets concerning the social and economic foundations of science are, of course, already to be found in Marx's writings (as mentioned before).

[29] This was a central thesis of Boris Hessen's (2009) paper, as well as that of Grossmann (2009a, b), and Edgar Zilsel (1942). The three authors apparently developed their incredibly similar approaches independently, which can be explained by the fact that Marx had already traced the basics of their argument. For example, in the *Capital* he described in detail how the development from simple tools used in early manufacturing to the machine tools of industrial production demanded the steam engine, guiding scientific research rather than being a result of it.

[30] The concept of science as part of the productive processes, and hence, a product of and important element within social structure, which had emerged together with capitalism and its technological and ideological demands, goes straight back to Marx (1962). Marx extensively quotes liberal authors like Adam Smith and Ure who blatantly glorified science and technology as a means to subdue the working classes, transforming the worker into a mere appendix of the machine. "Sie [the self acting mule] war berufen, die Ordnung unter den industriellen Klassen wiederherzustellen... Diese Erfindung bestätigt die von uns bereits entwickelte Doktrin, daß das Kapital, indem es

4. That although Science and technology, whilst in the hands of the ruling classes, contributed to the enslavement of humankind, the ruthless exploration of nature, and the slaughter of the millions during World War I, it still bears the potential to free men and serve to their benefit.[31]

These Marxist views were paralleled by further social constructionist contributions to the study of science, such as those of the Polish Jew and microbiologist Ludwik Fleck, and French philosopher Gaston Bachelard. During the late 1920s, Fleck had begun to develop a radically constructionist view on scientific knowledge. He attacked the positivist insistence on objective truth, which at that time was being defended by the Vienna Circle, pointing to the epistemological implication of relativity and quantum theory. In a paper published in 1929,[32] Fleck called for extending the notion of entanglement between the observer and observed phenomenon, as implied by quantum physics, to scientific observation in general, and to relinquish the idea of absolute truth. A few years later, his ideas had ripened into a fully-fledged theory on the social construction of scientific knowledge. Fleck adopted Mannheim's concept of thought style and further developed it, disentangling it from class relations using theoretical approaches from ethnology, sociology and philosophy. In the *Genesis and Development of a Scientific Fact*[33] Fleck fused concepts of authors like Mannheim, Durkheim, Lévy-Bruhl, Malinowski, Bergson and Carnap into a single, coherent theory of pluralistic thought styles.[34] The text argues that science, just like any other kind of knowledge, is equally determined by traditions, social constraints, and thought styles, reflecting particular world views or living

die Wissenschaft in seinen Dienst preßt, stets die rebellische Hand der Arbeit zur Gelehrigkeit zwingt" (Ure *apud* Marx 1962: 460). The scientist, or engineer, becomes a worker within the productive process, although a privileged one, separated from the former craftsmen who now were reduced to mere labour forces—after having passed their technical expertise to the professional scientists. Marx also pointed to the fact that the Puritan Protestants from the Netherlands and Britain were characterised by their particularly cruel exploitation of the workers both in their European homelands as well as in their colonies, transforming all workers in their factories into "slaves". The role of Protestant Ethics would be further elaborated by Max Weber, and later by Merton in relation to seventeenth century science. It had, however, also been Hessen's major argument to illustrate the ideological character of Newton's theoretical concepts. The material relation between science and capitalism as well as the personnel already highlighted by Marx was equally reiterated in more detail by Hessen, Grossmann, Zilsel, and Bernal. They all show how scientific research follows economic and military interests, that modern science was actually founded by members of the bourgeoise class, and that the first scientific academies were funded by rich bankers like the Medici, or by the state as a form of investment into military expansion and economic development. Moreover, Bernal (1939) observed that science failed to comply with its essential promises to democratise knowledge and to free all people from the burden of hard labour, thus, contributing rather to the diametral opposite historical unfolding. Hence, the real social function of science is to serve capitalism and the ruling classes.

[31] This point is especially highlighted by Hessen (2009) and Bernal (1939), but also present in the works of Merton (1942) who, like Mannheim, defended science's importance for democracy.

[32] Fleck (1983).

[33] For the present research I used the English translation from 1981.

[34] Werner (2014).

worlds, and defended by certain *thought collectives*. Since any thought basically represents an aspect of a particular thought style, perception and understanding are entirely determined by that thought style, too, and so are also scientific facts. Actually, Fleck argued that the perception of phenomena as *Gestalt*, that is, as meaningful objects of a certain kind, is only possible within the perceptive matrix of a thought style. Since only such "stylised" Gestalt perceptions constitute our normal experience of what we perceive as "objective reality", the thought style determines what we "see" as well as the problems and questions that may arise from it. Hence, there cannot be any objective, neutral scientific account of "reality", as there are multiple "realities", each entailed within the perspective[35] of the respective thought style. To illustrate his thesis, Fleck provided a detailed analysis of the evolution of the concept of syphilis and the role of the Wassermann reaction in the construction of related scientific "facts" (in this case the supposed proof for "syphilitic blood") following epistemological interests of certain thought collectives. Probably, Fleck's most important finding was that scientific "discovery must be regarded as a *social event*".[36] Facts are the result of complex processes of social interaction and changing conceptions resembling historical shifts in the fundamental viewpoints that characterise a particular thought style—or to put it simply: facts are historically contingent, theory-laden and biased.[37] The same goes for science and the scientific method in general, which are likewise determined by the historical changes in the thought styles they represent, and hence, contingent historical phenomena.[38] Thus, compared to other kinds of knowledge, there is no objective differentiator that would justify science's universal truth claims.

> Whatever is known has always seemed systematic, proven, applicable, and evident to the knower. Every alien system of knowledge has likewise seemed contradictory, unproven, inapplicable, fanciful, or mystical. May not the time have come to assume a less egocentric, more general point of view and to speak of comparative epistemology? (Fleck 1981: 22)

The stability of a thought style arises from its noological structure[39] on the one hand, and its social embedding on the other. Its property as a closed system of opinions

---

[35] Fleck uses the concept of *perspective* or *view point* in a similar way as (and probably following) Mannheim.

[36] Fleck (1981: 76).

[37] "For the time being we can define a scientific fact as a thought-stylized conceptual relation which can be investigated from the point of view of history and from that of psychology, both individual and collective, but which cannot be substantively reconstructed in toto simply from these points of view" (idem: 83). "A fact always occurs in the context of the history of thought and is always the result of a definite thought style" (idem: 95).

[38] "Current research techniques, after all, are also the result of historical development. They are the way they are because of just this particular history. Even the modern concept of disease entity, for example, is an outcome of precisely such a development and by no means the only logical possibility" (idem: 21).

[39] "A universally interconnected system of facts is thus formed, maintaining its balance through continuous interaction. This interwoven texture bestows solidity and tenacity upon the 'world of facts' and creates a feeling both of fixed reality and of the independent existence of the universe" (idem: 102).

provides it with multiple layers of vindicatory narratives to protect the whole system against inner contradiction and external objections, thus maintaining its "harmony of illusions". More importantly, however, thought styles are sustained by thought collectives. We are all born into such thought collectives and we may become part of other, more esoteric, elitist collectives by initiation rites (e.g. Science).[40] In any case, we are socially constrained to accept and perpetuate the thought style of our group, thus, determining what can be thought and even what can be asked. Such processes of socialisation are only rarely consciously perceived, as are the compulsive forces thought styles exert upon our perception and cognition.[41] Within the logic of a thought style, there is normally only one solution to a problem that is accepted as "truth". Hence, truth is not "relative" or "subjective", since it is determined by the inner logic of a thought style and the social dynamics of a collective. Truth is, however, procedural, contingent and contextual, as it is bound to a particular thought style which changes with time.[42]

Of course, the socially conditioned nature of thought and knowledge was not Fleck's discovery, but had long been discussed in the social sciences by authors like Weber, Durkheim, Lévy-Bruhl and Malinowski. However, Fleck emphasised that none of these authors had applied this insight to science, or to their own theories; instead, they continued to believe in the objectivity of scientific facts and purely theoretical, dispassionate reason. He further observed that natural scientists and positivist epistemologists tend to believe in pure reason while admitting the relative character of empirical facts, whereas social scientists rather believe in objective facts while relativising thought. Both epistemological strands, thus, relegate the supposedly fixed aspect of reality to the realm of the unknown and to prejudice instead of embracing the insights of both viewpoints and, finally, accepting the non-existence of any fixed point of reference.[43] According to Fleck, rather than doing

---

[40] "The initiation into any thought style, which also includes the introduction to science, is epistemologically analogous to the initiations we know from ethnology and the history of civilization" (idem: 104).

[41] "Although the thought collective consists of individuals, it is not simply the aggregate sum of them. The individual within the collective is never, or hardly ever, conscious of the prevailing thought style, which almost always exerts an absolutely compulsive force upon his thinking and with which it is not possible to be at variance. [...] The presence of thought style makes it necessary and, indeed, indispensable to construct the concept 'thought collective'" (idem: 41).

[42] "Such a stylized solution, and there is always only one, is called truth. Truth is not 'relative' and certainly not 'subjective' in the popular sense of the word. It is always, or almost always, completely determined within a thought style. [...] Truth is not a convention, but rather (1) in historical perspective, an event in the history of thought, (2) in its contemporary context, stylized thought constraint" (idem: 100).

[43] "To these epistemologists trained in the natural sciences, for instance, the Vienna Circle including Schlick, Carnap, and others, human thinking—construed as an ideal, or thinking as it should be—is something fixed and absolute. An empirical fact, on the other hand, is relative. Conversely, the philosophers previously mentioned with a background in the humanities construe facts as something fixed and human thought as relative. It is characteristic that both parties relegate that which is fixed to the region with which they are unfamiliar. Would it not be possible to manage entirely without something fixed?" (idem: 50)

justice to the state of the art in scientific discourse, objectivism reflects the over-simplified view of popular science or scientism, aiming to provide a vivid world-view rather than an exact picture of scientific findings. This worldview, however, would reflect back to and determine the thought style of the scientific community itself, and thus, legitimate the scientists' belief in the universality of science.

Similar to Fleck, Bachelard[44] argued that experience, including scientific observation, is construed according to the particular aesthetic moods and psychological dispositions that characterise the observer's epoch. Moreover, he emphasised that knowledge is always construed upon previous knowledge, and though changes would often occur in a discontinuous fashion leading to epistemological breaks, at least some linkage between the new and the old view would remain. Bachelard's psychoanalysis of the scientific mind traced shifts and breaks in the observer's experience throughout history in a way that would strongly influence Foucault's archaeology of knowledge. However, although Fleck also saw thought styles as (*Gestalt-*) psychosociological phenomena, his approach focussed on the explanation of the social dynamics and the collectives behind them, in a sense, providing a blueprint for a micro-sociology of knowledge. Bachelard, in contrast, painted a macro-picture of grand historical movements in collective consciousness (following Comte's evolutionist model) aiming to identify *epistemological obstacles* to scientific progress, and finally, suggesting that the modern idea of reason would hinder science from advancing beyond its current limits. Instead of relating changes in the collective mindset to concrete social relations, Bachelard's constructionism drew a history of embodied perceptions and passions reflecting into the history of ideas. In sum, Bachelard's constructionism was a critic of rationalism with a flavour of historical contingency, but it did not question science's superiority compared to previous stages or other kinds of knowledge. Since Bachelard allocated science within a progressive history of mind, emphasising the differences rather than the general epistemological equality of all knowledge, he did not even catch the problem of relativism, let alone suggest any solution.

In many ways, compared to Bachelard, Fleck addressed much more of the crucial questions that would later bother sociologists of science. Curiously, although his works would have a considerable impact on the sociology of scientific knowledge through the writings of Thomas Kuhn in the 1960s, Fleck's contributions to the field would receive very little attention during his lifetime. Bachelard, in contrast, would soon be widely recognised, especially in France, and in 1940 he assumed a chair of History and Philosophy of Science at the Sorbonne. Disregarding all the unpredictability of life, there are two diverging aspects between the two scholars that might explain, at least in part, the disparity and the timing of their success: First, while Fleck's approach was immediately perceived as a radical attack on scientific universalism, Bachelard did not question science's superior position within the established hierarchy of knowledge; second, Fleck was a Polish Jew born in the former Austrian Empire who tried to ascend in the academic community by

[44] Bachelard (1978).

publishing in German, while Bachelard was a member of French petty bourgeoise, living and publishing in France.

All the differences notwithstanding, what united all these aforementioned authors was not only their attention to the social aspects of Science, but also the shared experience of general crisis that was shaking the interwar period. Europe had just been destroyed (thanks to scientific progress) by modern weapons of mass destruction, by air strikes, poison gases, flamethrowers, machine guns and tanks, butchering almost 20 million people; meanwhile, science could not avoid the death of tens of millions caused by the Spanish flu; the social and economic crisis unmasked, once again, the dehumanising side of world capitalism, dooming millions to starvation while the bourgeoisie celebrated "the Golden Twenties"; the ongoing Russian Revolution, despite the millions it was killing, seemed to be an option for the working class who would organise socialist revolutions and insurgencies in Germany, Spain and elsewhere; however, the new and still fragile European democracies were threatened not only by proletarian revolutions and Trotsky's Red Army, but also by the rise of fascism, thus putting all the achievements of the Enlightenment into question; and last but not least, new revolutionary developments in science had shattered the secure and comprehensible fundaments of the Newtonian universe, with relativity theory, quantum physics, and non-Euclidean mathematics thrusting humankind into a chaotic, unpredictable, and incomprehensible future. Many of the aforementioned authors explicitly referred to these multiple crises.[45] The same goes for philosophers like Horkheimer and Adorno,[46] Edmund Husserl,[47] and A.N. Whitehead,[48] who equally urged the rethinking of science and its epistemological premises in the face of this generalised crisis.

In a way, the historical context which gave birth to those theories was comparable to the days when Marx and Engels developed their social theories. The failure of the French Revolution to fulfil its utopian promises of freedom and justice had unveiled the deep cleavage between the bourgeoise and the working class, and thence, gradually developed into a new kind of class struggle, which in 1848 would culminate a series of revolutions all over Europe and the slaughter of the Parisian population. But the working class had also been betrayed by the bourgeoise utopia of a better world based on scientific and technological progress, being degraded into mere exploitable human material instead of being freed from hard labour. It was this general crisis that called out to be explained by a new social theory, which happened to be written by Marx and Engels (and a few decades later rewritten by sociologists like Weber, Simmel and Durkheim).

[45] For example, Bernal (1939); Grossmann (2009a, b); Hessen (2009); Mannheim (1954).

[46] Horkheimer and Adorno (1969).

[47] Husserl (1962).

[48] Whitehead (1925).

4.1.2 From Cold War to Science Wars

After World War II, the world was split into East and West, not only politically and economically, but also scientifically speaking. While Soviet theories on science would strictly have to follow the official doctrine of orthodox Marxism-Leninism, in Western scientific discourse Marxism, and social constructionism in general would be banned from the agenda.[49] Moreover, the economies of the "free" capitalist world were driven by the development of ever-new products based on scientific progress as well as on the ideas of "development" and scientific superiority. Consequently, there was no space for any talk on the historical contingency, social construction, or relativity of scientific knowledge in official Western discourse. The Cold War was, after all, eminently an ideological war.

The political and intellectual climate would only change in the 1960s,[50] calling social constructionism back on stage. This would substantially advance during following decades. During the 1980s and 1990s a vast inventory of literature would

[49] After WWII the old and outdated history of ideas approach to pure science became dominant in the West once again, while any kind of linking science to worldly interests had been banned from the agenda. In the US, leftist scientists were persecuted and many left the country. Likewise, in Europe former leftist scientists were substituted by aesthetic modernists, epistemologists, and metaphysicists, like Bachelard, Butterfield, Koyre, and Kuhn, or by Mertonian functionalists (Whitesides 2019).

[50] At first sight, the situation after WWII was radically different compared to the interwar period. Unlike the economic disaster after WWI, economic growth and rising salaries had led to an unprecedented state of well-being among Western working classes. However, there were some parallels, too. Similar to the interwar period, which had been dominated by the shockwaves of Versailles and the forceful imposition of a new world (dis-)order on the nations of the entire planet, the world revolution of 1968 was a reaction to the new world order of the post-war period. Of course, the reasons for people to go out on streets in Prague were different from those in Paris or the United States, which differed from those of Vietnamese or Cuban peasants engaging in socialist revolutions. Interestingly, however, much of what culminated in the events of 1968 had its antecedents in the so-called third world of the global south. Decolonisation in Asia and Africa, and the subsequent foundation of independent states, led East and West to dispute hegemony in those new states. The Cold War would soon get very hot in Korea and Vietnam, but also in Cuba, Chile, and Brazil, were socialist governments had come to power. US interventions in Vietnam and South America (especially in Cuba, Chile, and Brazil), together with the domestic repression of women, Afro-Americans, labour unions, and progressive socialism, unmasked the hypocrisy of US imperialism, which was killing millions in the name of freedom while oppressing its own minorities at home, driving young Americans and Western Europeans on to the streets. They would join the fight of the oppressed, Black people, workers, women, and the marginalised countries of the South, seeking global freedom and justice. Meanwhile, workers and students in European countries under Soviet rule, like Hungary, East Germany, Yugoslavia, Poland, and Czechoslovakia, had been disappointed by the authoritarian version of socialism under Stalinist doctrine. And last but not least, the Cuba crisis would demonstrate to the world the eminent danger of complete nuclear destruction in the name of imperialism and ideology. Consequently, the post-war world order, in all its different aspects, would be questioned and criticised, often by taking recourse to inter-war theories (especially critical school), Marxism, or theories of the south (Ho Che Min, Mao, Decolonialism, etc.). So, although at least in Western countries there was no economic crisis, there was still a systemic global crisis going on (Wallerstein 2004 even speaks of a "world revolution").

appear, highlighting multiple social perspectives on Science, including feminism, post-structuralism, and post-colonialism.

Commonly, three books are mentioned as starting points for this revival of social constructionism: Thomas Kuhn's 1962 *The Structure of Scientific Revolution*,[51] Peter Berger and Thomas Luckmann's 1966 *The Social Construction of Reality*,[52] and Paul Feyerabend's 1975 *Against Method*.[53] All three of them were greatly indebted to the aforementioned works of the interwar period, as well as to Marxism, although this has not always been made explicit.

Kuhn's essay resumed the main tenets of previous constructionists, especially those highlighted by Fleck,[54] stating that experience, including scientific observation, is fundamentally based on metaphysical presuppositions about the essence and structure of the universe. Moreover, Kuhn followed Fleck's central point that "facts" have an inner history, being products of complex social interaction within a particular historical context. Consequently, all "facts" and scientific theories are only true and meaningful from the perspective of a particular, historically contingent world view and the corresponding theoretical framework, or *paradigm*.[55] Most impor-

---

[51] Kuhn (1970).

[52] Berger and Luckmann (1991).

[53] Feyerabend (1993).

[54] In the introduction to his famous work on scientific revolutions, Kuhn (1970) emphasised how impressed he was by Fleck's work. In fact, there are so many parallels to Fleck that the reader may get the impression Kuhn's book was rather an attempt to further develop Fleck's ideas than to propose his own, genuine approach. This becomes apparent particularly in Kuhn's social constructionist tendencies, which were responsible for most of the attention Kuhn's work received, and the impact it had on later conceptions of science. "[…] Fleck's work made me realize that those ideas might require to be set in the sociology of the scientific community" (Kuhn 1970). In the foreword to the English translation (1981) of Fleck's book Kuhn, at first, reiterated his debt to Fleck, but then relativised the influence on his own approach, criticising Fleck's concept of thought collective. Once more, he highlights the importance of Fleck for his understanding of the social dimension of science, and especially the sociological concept of collective mind, of which Kuhn himself had been unaware before. Other shared aspects, however, like the Gestalt character of theoretical models of nature and related "facts", would have been based on Kuhn's own ideas, and thus, rather be coincidences than direct influences. Moreover, in the absence of an English translation, Kuhn had to read Fleck's book with his poor German skills, and therefore, missed many of Fleck's basic insights. Only later, said Kuhn, would he grasp the full range of Fleck's ideas, which in some aspects transcended his own work. This is especially true for Kuhn's rudimentary understanding of social aspects, as also apparent in the literature he referred to in his book back in 1962. While Fleck extensively referred to sociologists and anthropologists of his times (like Durkheim, Lévy-Bruhl, Malinowski, Scheler, Mannheim, and Simmel), Kuhn almost exclusively referred to historians of science (like Koyré, Cohen, Metzger, and Maier).

[55] Kuhn's use of the term "paradigm" has led to extensive critique and considerable confusion, as Kuhn (1970) himself stated in the postscript of the second edition of his essay. Quite obviously, however, Kuhn's "paradigm" refers to something comparable to Fleck's "thought style". My own impression is that Fleck's concept of thought style is eminently aesthetical in character, referring to a particular "style" of perceiving the world and a correspondent intellectual "mood" to conceptualise things in a very particular manner, much in the sense of Bachelard's aesthetic approach to knowledge. Kuhn's "paradigm", in contrast, draws on a much more rational overtone, while mixing in aesthetic and ethic notions indistinguishably. In the postscript of his 1970 edition, Kuhn tried

tantly, paradigms are subject to historical changes in the scientists' perception. Kuhn followed Fleck and Bachelard maintaining that such paradigmatic changes are not the result of a continuous accumulative process of scientific progress towards "truth".[56] He showed that history of science is rather characterised by epistemological breaks, paradigmatic "revolutions", resulting in different Gestalt perceptions (e.g. to identify oxygen instead of phlogiston while analysing the same gas),[57] and incommensurable metaphysical presuppositions. Since different paradigms are mutually incommensurable, they are unable to make judgments about the truth-value of other, diverging paradigms and corresponding theories and "facts".[58] The idea of accumulative scientific progress is rather derived from what Kuhn calls "normal science", that is, long periods during which a community of experts holds to a shared paradigm.[59] During normal science, scientists are engaged in a kind of "puzzle solving", pretty much following a game of testing or falsifying, trying to get evidence ever closer to their theories by forcing nature into the conceptual boxes of the ruling paradigm. Since paradigms predict all possibly existing phenomena and their behaviour, they not only determine the agenda of problems to be solved, but also exclude all diverging phenomena and questions for being "metaphysical", and

to unscramble this confusion by distinguishing a number of different meanings he had attributed to "paradigm" in his 1962 essay, including "something shared" by the members of a group, or a "disciplinary matrix" composed by "symbolic generalisations", "metaphysical paradigms", "values", or a "groups shared commitment" to "exemplars". From my own point of view, the problem with Kuhn's "paradigm" is that it mingles the general notion of worldview with the rationalist notion of a coherent theoretical framework, or research programme, thus (tacitly) presuming a rational worldview instead of conceptualising rationalism as a particular thought style, or aesthetic intellectual mood (although Kuhn would probably not agree with this critique).

[56] "[...] the view of science-as-cumulation is entangled with a dominant epistemology that takes knowledge to be a construction placed directly upon raw sense data by the mind" (Kuhn 1970: 96). "We may, to be more precise, have to relinquish the notion, explicit or implicit, that changes of paradigm carry scientists and those who learn from them closer and closer to the truth" (idem: 170).

[57] "What a man sees depends both upon what he looks at and also upon what his previous visual-conceptual experience has taught him to see" (idem: 113).

[58] Kuhn (1970) pointed to the problem that any argument in favour of a particular paradigm argues within that particular paradigm, and hence, is necessarily circular. However, this would not make the argument worthless, but its value would be merely persuasive, and thus, only reach those who are willing to step into the logical circle of that paradigm. Accordingly, paradigm choice can never be settled by logic or evidence.

[59] To explain the stability of a paradigm during such long periods Kuhn took recourse to social cohesion and Gestalt psychology (much like Fleck before him) as well as to Michael Polanyi's (1962) concept of "tacit knowledge". Like Fleck's thought styles, paradigm's are essentially a perceptive matrix allowing the identification of different objects or problems immediately as *exemplars* of a certain category. A student would become part of the thought collective or group of experts by adopting its thought style or paradigm, and thus share its particular Gestalt perception. Now, Kuhn argued (following Polanyi's approach on tacit knowledge), that this learning process is based on practise and practical examples rather than on theoretical abstractions. Actually, Polanyi had been working on his approach since the 1940s, arguing against objectivist and rationalist accounts of scientific progress (Polanyi 1946). He maintained that scientific discovery could not be explained as a result of the mechanical application of a fixed method, nor would theories be abandoned due to contradiction. Instead, discovery would only occur by "spontaneous emergence".

thus, not admissible for scientific scrutiny. On the other hand, Kuhn argued, this restrictive character is a precondition for scientific progress, as it provides the necessary theoretical framework for any meaningful interpretation of observables, allowing for a progressive integration of ever more detailed solutions and precise predictions. This progress, however, is not to be equalled with an increase in the truth value of facts and theories, since all solutions are restricted to the problems raised by that particular paradigm, and not by "nature" itself, as many scientists would have it. Even the most accurate measurements are paradigm-determined, since they depend on the development and interpretation of sophisticated instruments that only make sense within the realm of the corresponding paradigm.[60] Thus, "facts" can, by definition, neither prove nor disprove a paradigm.[61] Moreover, anomalies will always occur and continuously increase with scientific progress, since every solution leads to further problems and further anomalies, forcing scientists to make more and more additional ad hoc assumptions to save their paradigm. As a result, evidence supporting a paradigm will decrease in the course of its own progress, eventually giving rise to crisis. However, Kuhn emphasised, debates on alternative paradigms are not about problem-solving. What is at stake are alternative ways of doing science, different research programmes leading to different ways of understanding the world we live in, and finally, the decision to ask different questions. "A decision of that kind can only be made on faith".[62] This, of course, contradicts the common expectation of science as provider of an ever-growing degree of "truth". So, although paradigm changes may generally be preceded by an accumulation of anomalies, increasing inconsistency between theory and evidence, finally resulting in a crisis of the old paradigm, the choice in favour of a new paradigm is ultimately a question of value, and thus, related to external factors.

All his own protests notwithstanding, Kuhn's 1962 book has largely been received as a relativist approach.[63] In Kuhn's own eyes, however, there seemed to be

[60] Similarly, Bachelard (1978) emphasised that instruments, like a microscope or telescope, are basically theories, and that the more precise a measurement, the more indirect it would be.

[61] Kuhn (1970) reminded us that Western epistemology over the last 3000 years has been based on the distinction between an unchanging nature contrasted by changing ideas, a view which has long been shown to be untenable. In fact, neither verification, nor falsification may ever work as a rule, for if all anomalies would lead to the dismissal of a theory, there would be no scientific theories at all. Moreover, since falsification of a theory implies verification of another, it would almost equal to verification anyway.

[62] Idem: 157.

[63] In the introduction of his 1962 essay, Kuhn explicitly states that "[o]bservation and experience can and must drastically restrict the range of admissible scientific belief, else there would be no science. But they cannot alone determine a particular body of such belief" (idem: 4). This is a position which he would further specify in his postscript (1970), desperately exclaiming: "I am a convinced believer in scientific progress" (idem: 206). Indeed, the comparison of different theories with different language cultures, applied to culture, would be relativistic, but applied to science might not need to be. "Though the values that they deploy at times of theory-choice derive from other aspects of their work as well, the demonstrated ability to set up and to solve puzzles presented by nature is, in case of value conflict, the dominant criterion for most members of a scientific group" (idem: 205). Following Kuhn, there are clear criteria that distinguish new paradigms

no contradiction between the historically contingent social construction of scientific knowledge, and its objectivity.

This is not the place to discuss in detail to what extent Kuhn actually went beyond Fleck's approach. In any case, Kuhn has the merit of having found an interested readership for the debate Fleck had attempted to establish 30 years before (apart from making his book accessible to an international audience by promoting its English translation). After all, Kuhn's essay definitely had a decisive impact on the subsequent development of theories and research on science and scientific knowledge both in the social sciences and in philosophy of science.

The "Treatise in the Sociology of Knowledge"[64] Peter Berger and Thomas Luckmann would publish a few years after Kuhn's essay had quite different pretensions. Their book was meant to resume and rethink the sociology of knowledge as proposed by Mannheim and others before, offering a general approach to the social construction of "reality". Accordingly, their focus was not on theoretical or scientific knowledge, but on the social micro-mechanisms that generate the knowledge that orients us in everyday life, that is, the social interactions that bring into being what we perceive as "reality". In fact, Berger and Luckmann explicitly refused to draw any conclusions about epistemological implications from the empirical study of the social origin of knowledge; questions about the truth value of scientific knowledge, they argued, would have to be fought out beyond the scope of empirical evidence, being a subject of philosophical debate rather than sociological theorising.[65] Like Mannheim, they put much emphasis on the central problem of the dia-

---

from older ones for being the "better" choice. Moreover, scientific development would follow undirectioned evolution just like in biological species. However, the notion of new theories being better in terms of representing nature more correctly, and thus, being closer to "truth", would not hold, since the supposed match between theory and "reality" would be an illusive notion. Rather, Kuhn emphasised, it would be necessary to do more research on the particular social characteristics of scientific community. "Scientific knowledge, like language, is intrinsically the common property of a group or else nothing at all. To understand it we shall need to know the special characteristics of the groups that create and use it" (idem: 210).

[64] Subtitle of "The Social Construction of Reality" (Berger and Luckmann 1991).

[65] Of course, they redefined the focus of sociology of knowledge by focussing on social processes responsible for the establishment of certain sets of knowledge and their legitimation as "realities", regardless of the ultimate truth-value of its content. Berger and Luckmann pointed out that their definition differed from the original definition of *Wissenssoziologie* as coined by Max Scheler and Karl Mannheim. Moreover, they argued the discipline would have become marginalised and later contributions from Merton, Parsons, and others, had not reached beyond Mannheim. Generally speaking, sociology of knowledge had concentrated on certain epistemological implications of empirical investigation of ideas, theoretical thought, and intellectual history. However, the full theoretical significance of sociology of knowledge would not have been acknowledged, so far. Although epistemological questions about the relativity of thought implied in sociology of knowledge would, indeed, be of concern also for social and natural sciences, sociological empirical research would not be able to answer these questions. It could, however, provide data for a philosophical discussion of such questions. In this sense, Berger and Luckmann suggested excluding epistemological questions from the sociological debate. They also emphasised that their approach would "*not* imply that sociology is not a science, that its methods should be other than empirical, or that it cannot be 'value-free'" (idem: 221).

lectics between the objectivity and the human origin of "reality", which had been first conceptualised in Marx's infra- versus superstructure distinction, and which continues to be one of the most troubling *topoi* of social theory. However, Berger and Luckmann would base their approach on quite different theoretical premises, taking recourse not only to Mauss's *total social fact*, but also to Husserl's phenomenology, Mead's social interactionism, and Schutz's emphasis on the role of everyday life (Lebenswelt) in the foundation of knowledge. Knowledge, Berger and Luckmann argued, is the result of the social construction of reality based on social interaction reinforcing shared beliefs. Our everyday reality is primarily based on the "here and now" of face-to-face encounters, providing what we perceive as "reality par excellence". Other kinds of knowledge, like religious or theoretical knowledge, are rather "enclaves" or "provinces of meaning", yet enveloped by the paramount reality of everyday experience. Given the coexistence of different "realities", legitimation is of important concern in the maintenance of a shared frame of reference to regulate social relations. What makes us believe in a certain "reality" instead of another, or what makes us take anything for "real" anyway?! According to Berger and Luckmann, we are all socialised within a given *symbolic universe* providing meaning to institutionalised roles we learn to enact and accept as parts of a given "reality", and which are thus *objectivised* or even *reified*, making us apprehend those human-made phenomena "as if they were things". Institutions like marriage, for example, together with related roles of gender and kinship are thus naturalised, inverting the true relation between us and the world we incessantly produce by enacting these very roles.

> Typically, the real relationship between man and his world is reversed in consciousness. Man, the producer of a world, is apprehended as its product, and human activity are an epiphenomenon of non-human processes (Berger and Luckmann 1991: 106).

However, since this inherited reality is untransparent to us, and because socialisation is never complete, the institutional order and the symbolic universe[66] society is based upon have to be legitimated by *conceptual machineries of universe maintenance*. Note that the ultimate legitimation is based on cosmological and anthropological models determined by the symbolic universe, which is itself a human product rooted in our concrete individual lives, and hence, "has no empirical status apart from these lives".[67] This is also true for esoteric and theoretical frameworks created by "full-time legitimators" who may develop such conceptual machineries against attacks from deviant "heretical" groups, or in the face of radically different cultural alternatives.[68] In a way that remembers Mannheim's total ideology, Berger and

[66] Berger and Luckmann define symbolic universe as a "[...] matrix of *all* socially objectivated and subjectively real meanings; the entire historic society and the entire biography of the individual are seen as events taking place *within* this universe" (idem: 114).

[67] Ibidem: 146.

[68] Berger and Luckmann proposed a number of different types of such symbolic universes, distinguishing between mythology, theology, philosophy, and science. Although they emphasised that they do not follow an evolutionary scheme, they still found it analytically helpful to allocate them in a hierarchical scheme, with mythology representing the most "archaic" and "naive" level (sic!).

Luckmann pointed to the ideological character of symbolic universes since their conceptual machineries are built to legitimise institutions bound to political group interests.[69] Accordingly, the social construction of "reality" is not the result or the function of some sort of social equilibrium, but to the contrary, an expression of antagonistic interests which are intrinsic to any social order.[70]

Berger and Luckmann's relaunch of social constructionism in terms of a phenomenological research programme was emblematic of a general paradigmatic change in the social sciences going on at that time.[71] And despite their ostensive refusal to apply their method to science, it was an implicit invitation for others to do so—and indeed, many would follow this path.[72] Moreover, in order to describe the complex social processes of generating and legitimating "reality", Berger and Luckmann had mobilised an arsenal of powerful concepts (including *objectivation*, *reification*, *habitualisation*, *roles*, *institutionalisation*, *legitimation*, *semantic field*, *symbolic universe*, among others) that would be further developed and applied to the study of Science by social scientists like Bourdieu and others.

Paul Feyerabend's[73] critique of scientific method stands out against the aforementioned works in a number of points. As is well known, his book is one of the most provocative contributions, and deliberately so, as Feyerabend himself emphasised. According to his own narration, the idea for the book had been suggested by his close friend Imre Lakatos (a declared rationalist) as a kind of funny game of polemic dispute between the two friends. So, originally, the text was drafted as a kind of provocative letter to his friend, Imre, who would add his

In contrast to higher levels, mythology would allow for the coexistence of inconsistent traditions. Moreover, due to the relatively easy access to the esoteric knowledge of the elites, its institutionalisation would have to be maintained by means of secret knowledge: "Unlike mythology, the other three historically dominant forms of conceptual machinery became the property of specialist elites, whose bodies of knowledge were increasingly removed from the common knowledge of the society at large. Modern science is an extreme step in this development, and in the secularization and sophistication of universe-maintenance. Science not only completes the removal of the sacred from the world of everyday life, but removes universe-maintaining knowledge as such from that world" (idem: 130). However, they concluded that "[t]he interesting problems posed by this situation belong to an empirical sociology of knowledge of contemporary society and cannot be further pursued in this context" (ibidem).

[69] "Traditional definitions of reality inhibit social change. Conversely, breakdown in the taken-for-granted acceptance of the monopoly accelerates social change. It should not surprise us, then, that a profound affinity exists between those with an interest in maintaining established power positions and the personnel administering monopolistic traditions of universe-maintenance. In other words, conservative political forces tend to support the monopolistic claims of the universal experts, whose monopolistic organizations in tum tend to be politically conservative" (idem: 140).

[70] In defending a theory of social conflict, Berger and Luckmann also made a clear commitment to Marx's social theory and against structural functionalism.

[71] For example, Clifford Geertz (2008) interpretative approach would resemble a similar move in anthropology.

[72] Their phenomenological approach would become especially influential to ethnographical contributions to the study of science from Garfinkel and Latour (Shapin 1995).

[73] Feyerabend (1993).

equally polemic counter arguments and publish the whole thing in one single volume. Unfortunately, Lakatos would die before he could write his response and Feyerabend ended up publishing his part as a monograph. Another reason for the polemic style of his essay was grounded in Feyerabend's motivation, which was more moral and political than intellectual. Once a convinced disciple of Karl Popper, Feyerabend had come to a critical view of the political dimension of scientific universalism as a means for cultural imperialism and political dogmatism. From this new viewpoint, rationalism and methodological monism were obstacles on the way to a free society. Feyerabend was deeply concerned about the oppression and subsequent extinction of other cultures in the name of "progress and civilization" as well as about the institutional entanglement of state and Science, which he saw as a threat to democracy. Accordingly, his book can be understood as an effort to deconstruct scientific universalism and pave the way to a new, more democratic and pluralistic science.

His essay, which admittedly showed some parallels to Kuhn's approach, basically followed a two-fold argument. On the one hand, Feyerabend showed that scientific method was a myth, being neither theoretically possible nor historically evident. Particularly, he argued that neither falsification, nor exclusion of ad hoc hypotheses, nor consistency were warranted. On the theoretical side, he emphasised that apprehension, and thus, also facts were theory laden, and that theories were ideological and based on metaphysical presuppositions. Moreover, in practice scientists would frequently "rescue" falsified or inconsistent theories by means of ad hoc hypothesis. On the other hand, the same would also be true for new theories, which would generally appear as ad hoc hypotheses and only become reasonable in the light of a new corresponding cosmological framework (as exemplified by Galileo's "evidence" for the Copernican world view). As a result, Feyerabend argued, a strict application of fixed methodological rules would actually make scientific progress impossible. Only an anti-inductive practice of "anything goes" would be capable of true innovation. It follows that there is no sustainable argument for scientific superiority compared to other kinds of knowledge. Science had not become the dominant knowledge all over the world, and hence, "universal", because its rational arguments were more convincing, but through violent imposition in the course of colonialism and global expansionism. So, instead of simply dismissing the rain dances of the Hopi as a priori ineffective, since unscientific, Feyerabend suggested that social scientists should rather provide statistical data to evaluate the efficacy of Hopi rain-dancing. And instead of declaring laymen to be unqualified for engaging in scientific discourse, science should abdicate from its esoteric elitism and engage in an open discourse with the public at large, and particularly with those citizens affected by its findings.

Of course, Feyerabend's approach heavily hinges on a quite radical relativism. In his later contributions, however, he further qualified his concept of an "ontological" or "cosmological" relativism. Since culture and nature are inseparably entangled, one determining the other, resulting in different forms of being, each representing a particular way of approaching the world, there would naturally also be different responses depending on the way reality is being approached.[74]

Regardless, Feyerabend's book has by and large been received as a call for extreme relativism and certainly later motivated strong programmes in the Sociology of Scientific Knowledge.[75] On the philosophical side, Feyerabend provided powerful (albeit polemic) arguments against falsificationism and rationalism in general. But by catching great heroes of science while blatantly breaking fundamental rules of scientific method, he also gave reason for further empirical investigations into scientific practice. And finally, his general critique of scientific universalism as an instrument of control and oppression can be seen as part of a critical discourse, reaching back to the critical school (e.g. Horkheimer, Adorno, Marcuse), which would also be represented in different ways by intellectuals like Louis Althusser, Michel Foucault, Immanuel Wallerstein, Edward Said, Homi Bhabha, Stuart Hall, Antonio Negri and Michael Hardt, among others.

Together with Foucault's entangled notion of power and knowledge, Derrida's deconstructionism, and encouraged by the anti-establishment spirit of the 1970s, the books of Kuhn, Berger and Luckmann, and Feyerabend contributed to a revival of social research on science.

In Britain, a group of sociologists around Barry Barnes and David Bloor called for a new sociology of scientific knowledge, arguing that modern science as well as its main product, scientific knowledge, were social phenomena amenable to sociological research just as any other kind of knowledge. In contrast to Mertonian sociology of science, which basically acknowledged scientific objectivism, their "strong programme" held that modern science was not a set of universal standards to find out the "truth" about nature, but rather represented a specific culture with its own context-dependent forms of rationality. Accordingly, scientific knowledge was the result of social norms and hierarchies, and a particular local form of reasoning rather than of some universal rationality or methodological rules.[76] Moreover, fun-

[74] Feyerabend (1980).

[75] Which he, following Kuhn's expression, explicitly rejected as an "absurd" example of "deconstruction gone mad" (Feyerabend 1993: 200).

[76] "Science is not a set of universal standards, sustaining true descriptions and valid inferences in different specific cultural contexts; authority and control in science do not operate simply to guarantee an unimpeded interaction between 'reason' and experience. Scientific standards themselves are part of a specific form of culture; authority and control are essential to maintain a sense of the reasonableness of that specific form. Thus... science should be amenable to sociological study in fundamentally the same way as any other form of knowledge or culture" (Barnes 1982: 10). "[The relativist] accepts that none of the justifications of his preferences can be formulated in absolute or context-independent terms. In the last analysis, he acknowledges that his justifications will stop at some principle or alleged matter of fact that has only local credibility. For the relativist there is no sense attached to the idea that some standards or beliefs are really rational as distinct from merely locally accepted as such. Because he thinks that there are no context-free or super-cultural norms of rationality he does not see rationally and irrationally held beliefs as making up two distinct and qualitatively different classes of things" (Barnes and Bloor 1982: 27/28). For Steven Shapin (1995), science, like any knowledge system, is based on trust, and the norms of trustworthiness change historically. Thus, "scientific knowledge is a local and mundane affair" (idem: 304).

damental categories of knowledge, truth, and rationality were not only historically contingent, but also bound to the interests of particular social groups. In sum, the British "strong programme" basically followed a relativist interpretation of Kuhn's approach, while also reiterating the main tenets of Mannheim's *Wissenssoziologie* and Fleck's relativism, thus joining internalist with externalist views on Science. However, all the emphases on empirical social research notwithstanding, the main concerns of British sociology of scientific knowledge were epistemological rather than merely sociological, following a philosophical agenda against uncritical positivist notions of rationalism, foundationalism, realism, and any universal truth claims in general. It abandoned traditional normative philosophical notions of knowledge and truth in favour of a descriptive concept of what and why people hold something to be "true". According to this relativist constructionism, all beliefs are equally true or false, but also equally problematic concerning the local causes of their credibility. On the other hand, the whole argument continued hinging on a naturalistic account of Science as an observable social phenomenon, and on rational arguments within Western epistemological discourse. This obvious contradiction, which appears to be intrinsic to relativism, and which had already been of great concern for Mannheim and his own approach, would expose the British strong programme to harsh criticism.

Meanwhile in France, sociologist Pierre Bourdieu and anthropologist Bruno Latour set out to launch their own research programmes in the study of science. While Bourdieu defended his own strong programme, Latour would oppose anti-realist views and propose an alternative theory of science and technology.

Albeit alluding to Bachelard, Bourdieu's sociology of science was by and large an application of his own social theory and corresponding concepts like *social fields* and *habitus*[77] together with the characteristic *capital* metaphors he used for tagging different kinds of value. Accordingly, in Bourdieu's sociology science appears as a social field producing its own habitus among scientists, that is, a particular set of habitualised behavioural dispositions together with its particular perceptive matrix of tacit knowledge about the symbolic values of objectivised phenomena. Each field would be governed by a set of socially attributed values, different forms of "capital" in Bourdieu's terminology, regulating social relations. Thus, scientists do what they do in order to accumulate "symbolic capital" or "scientific profit". However, such "capital" is not only related to financial gains, but primarily to status within the academic hierarchy and resulting access to resources (e.g. laboratories, scientific journals, academic chairs, research funding, etc.). Ultimately, symbolic capital would authorise certain persons or groups to speak legitimately on scientific

However, for Shapin, the study of these historically grown norms does not necessarily need to lead to anti-realism. Although no particular account is capable of judging other accounts of truth (for being equally "local" and for to do so it would only reaffirm its own premises), all knowledge-systems are causally connected to reality. Once the myths of unique method or norms are put aside, new questions about the way scientists construe their authoritative system of knowledge arise.

[77] Bourdieu (1985, 1987).

matters, while excluding others from this privilege.[78] As a consequence, Science represents a particularly closed, and thus, self-referential field, which is construed around the arbitration of the "real".[79] In other words, Science is an immense apparatus of collective construction of legitimate "truth", governed by a particular set of rules of truth production and methods of validation. These rules, however, are not epistemological but rather social rules determined by inner hierarchies and the distribution of symbolic capital within the field. It follows that "epistemological conflicts are always, inseparably, political conflicts: so that a survey on power in the scientific field could perfectly well consist of apparently epistemological questions alone".[80] The truth value of scientific findings has its basis solely in the collective belief in science and its methods, being reproduced by the habitualised processes of the scientific field itself. The belief in the objectivity and disinterestedness of science, however, is also an expression of the interests of the dominant classes, which would grant an exceptional autonomy to the natural sciences in exchange for profitable technological applications.[81]

It is debatable to which extent Bourdieu actually succeeded in overcoming the subject-object dichotomy by transferring the object of sociological research from either interacting individuals or coercive social macrostructures to the *habitus* as new locus where the individual crosses the collective sphere. One could also criticise that his objective description of the social mechanisms of reality production is delegitimated by the illusive character of "reality" which is unveiled by his very own "objective" analysis. However, Bourdieu's approach has the advantage of being based on a consistent, generic theory of social conflict, which can be applied to

---

[78] "The distinction which Merton makes (with reference to the social sciences) between 'social' conflicts (over 'the allocation of intellectual resources between different sorts of sociological work' or 'the role appropriate to the sociologist and intellectual' conflicts, 'oppositions between strictly formulated sociological ideas', itself constitutes a social and intellectual strategy which tends to impose a delimitation of the field of objects of legitimate argument. This distinction is in fact a form of one of the strategies through which American official sociology tends to secure academic respectability and to impose a demarcation of the scientific and the non-scientific which is designed to forbid any inquiry liable to question the bases of its respectability as a breach of scientific decorum" (idem 1975: 22). Consequently, American (Mertonian) functionalism would take the interest of the dominant classes as "function", thus actually concealing these interests.

[79] Compare also Luhmann (1990).

[80] Bourdieu (1975: 21).

[81] "Science never has any other basis than the collective belief in its bases which is produced and presupposed by the very operation of the scientific field" (idem: 34). "This raises the question of the degree of social arbitrariness of the belief which is produced by the functioning of the field [...]" (idem: 35). "[T]he dominant class grants the natural sciences an autonomy corresponding to the interest it finds in the economic applications of scientific techniques [...]. The idea of a neutral science is a fiction, an interested fiction which enables its authors to present a version of the dominant representation of the social world, neutralised and euphemised into a particularly misrecognisable and symbolically, therefore, particularly effective form, and to call it scientific" (idem: 36). "The thesis that productivity and competition are directly linked is based on a functionalist theory of competition which is a sociological variant of belief in the virtues of the 'free market economy'" (idem: 37).

pretty much all different aspects of human coexistence—including Science and scientific knowledge,[82] symbolic violence against women,[83] or the reproduction of class inequalities.[84]

Together with his British colleague, Steve Woolgar, Bruno Latour set out to do field work among a "strange tribe" populating an environment yet untouched by anthropological research: natural scientists in their laboratories. In their 1979 book *Laboratory Life*[85] Latour and Woolgar followed the construction of scientific facts through the techno-jungle of mysterious laboratory equipment built to transform observables into cryptic quantitative inscriptions to be published and disputed in scientific journals by a handful of experts. In what at times appears to be an ironically exaggerated follow-up to Fleck's call for a more detailed social study of thought collectives, Latour and Woolgar showed, once again, that "facts" do not resemble "nature", but rather networks of resources mobilised by scientists in order to accumulate a kind of "credibility capital".

This kind of ethnographic approach to science studies was soon taken up further by researchers like Karin Knorr-Cetina,[86] Michael Lynch,[87] and Sharon Traweek,[88] and laboratory studies quickly developed into an important research programme. By and large, these contributions stressed the local and situated character of Science and scientific knowledge by tracing the processes of scientific knowledge production through scientists' daily routines, unveiling the importance of embodied, tacit knowledge,[89] and their struggles for recognition by means of persuasion and resource mobilising. However, they also called attention to the problems posed by anti-realist relativism, suggesting alternative solutions for bringing together social constructionism and realism.[90]

---

[82] Bourdieu (1975, 1992, 2001).

[83] Idem 2002.

[84] Idem 2006

[85] Latour and Woolgar (1986).

[86] Knorr-Cetina (1981).

[87] Lynch (1985).

[88] Traweek (1988).

[89] Just to remember, "tacit knowledge" had already been coined by Michael Polanyi (1946, 1962) and highlighted by Thomas Kuhn (1970) as a main feature of scientific knowledge production.

[90] For example, Knorr-Cetina (1981) showed how scientific knowledge is produced as part of an "economy of power", driven by interested decisions and selective social action, pointing to the resulting indeterminacy in the selection and validation of "facts", and the contextual contingency inherent to scientific operations. Scientific knowledge, Knorr-Cetina argued, is therefore "indexical", that is, intrinsically localised, situated, and based on social methods of localised practice, and on an indexical logic of opportunistic "tinkering" rather than on fixed methodological rules. Hence, scientific findings, albeit being sold by scientists as universal "facts", are actually interpretations which obtain their validity exclusively from their local practices. She therefore attacks the distinction between natural and social sciences for being based on an outdated mechanistic worldview, assuming that matter is passive, causation is external, fundamental entities are atomic, and qualitative diversity is secondary; rather, events should be re-conceptualised as active things and laws as mere observable tendencies, since in our lived (phenomenal) world there are no natural laws at all.

Latour and Woolgar not only emphasised the essentially social and contextual character of scientific knowledge, but also its dependence on sophisticated and expensive technological apparatus for the production of mathematical inscriptions, indispensable for the maintenance of the "objectivity" and credibility of scientific findings. The active role of such "non-human actants" as certain technical objects, "facts", laboratories, or papers, indicated a shift from pure social constructionism to an enlarged concept of a network of different kinds of actors, which inspired Latour and his colleagues from the Centre de Sociologie de l'Innovation to develop what would become known as Actor-Network Theory. In subsequent publications,[91] Latour argued that the whole problem with social constructionism, as well as with the positivist notions of science as the only universal representation of nature, is based in a one-sided view of two complementary aspects of science; one concerning the social process of making science, and the other concerning its outcome, which would be represented as ready-made "black boxes" of working theories and technologies. Once debate on a theory has been settled, it becomes a simple tool in the process of knowledge production, and its history will disappear inside the darkness of a closed black box. The same principle would equally apply to social sciences and their fundamental concepts, like "culture" or "society". Accordingly, neither "nature" nor "society" would serve to explain the other. Hence, to overcome the predicaments of relativism both aspects, the context of production and the use of scientific knowledge, would have to be conceptualised together. Rather than separating "social" factors from "natural" ones, technoscience would represent a network of human and non-human actors, hybrid entities, who would gain "in reality if related to many other 'real' entities, which can be seen as its 'collaborators'". These scientific networks have been spreading on a global scale, however, in a structurally unequal manner, dividing the world into centres and marginalised economies, world regions, social and ontological classes. Along these networks, data is being transferred from all over the world to the calculation centres, where the information is mathematically codified and formalised, making the peripheries accessible and controllable to the global centres of power. So, the official rhetoric about "rational", and hence, "universal" scientific versus "irrational", and thence, "local" knowledge would only be part of the modern narrative about the Great Divide between Us, "modern" "Westerners", and all the Others.[92] Consequently, in terms of resource

---

And if causal agency was not limited to the social realm, she concluded, the distinction between natural and social sciences would cease to make any sense.

[91] Latour (1987, 1993, 2001).

[92] "In other words, all this business about rationality and irrationality is the result of an attack by someone on associations that stand in the way. They reveal the extent of a network and the conflict between what will stay inside and what will fall through its mesh." "[I]t seems that there is an absolute divide between, on the one hand, all the cultures that 'believe' in things, and on the other hand, the one culture, ours, that 'knows' things […] between 'Them' and 'Us'" (Latour 1987: 205). "[I]t has nothing to do with a divide between belief and knowledge. It has simply to do with the scale at which the enrolling and controlling of people occurs" (idem: 211). "All the distinctions one could wish to make between domains (economics, politics, science, technology, law) are less important than the unique movement that makes all of these domains conspire towards the same

distribution and information flow within these global networks, contemporary technoscience would primarily appear as a business of industries dominated by the US, and particularly by its war industry. It follows that Science and scientifically-produced technology indeed "work" in the real world. However, they only work within the infrastructure of these networks (just like a train only works on railways).[93] Latour emphasises that his understanding does not render scientific knowledge an illusion, but rather traces its universal truth claims back to the context and extension of the networks that gave birth to and continue to sustain it. In other words, facts and theories, just as technologies, are "true", since functional, in relation to other such hybrid entities that constitute the network they are part of. They "work" in the real world, no doubt, but in a specific, qualified way, contributing to the construction and totalising of the networks that divide the world into centres and peripheries, "developed" and "under-developed" countries, "rational" and "irrational" minds, "Us" and "Them".

Together with Foucault, Feyerabend and Bourdieu, Latour pointed to the political dimension of Science. In a way, their contributions broke with the post-war silence about the ambivalent social and political role of Science, technology and scientific universalism. After World War II, sociology and history of science had focussed on the history of ideas and the internal social structure of Science, only slowly returning to social constructionist views concerning the internal and, to a lesser extent, also to external social and economic factors involved in the production of scientific knowledge. However, although social constructionism had re-opened the Pandora's Box[94] filled up with the frightening predicaments of modern epistemology, it left questions about the social and political dimension of modern science largely untouched. This would change when the social movements discovered their stakes in the question about scientific authority. The 1980s and 1990s witnessed a considerable production of critical analyses of Science's role as a vehicle of colonialism, racism, global capitalist exploration, social stratification, and masculine domination. The sheer amount of rich and valuable texts of this period simply makes

goal: a cycle of accumulation that allows a point to become a centre by acting at a distance on many other points" (idem: 222).

[93] "'Still, is not the application of science outside of the laboratories the best proof of its efficacy, of the quasi-supernatural power of scientists? Science *works* outside and its *predictions* are fulfilled.' Like all the other claims we have encountered in this chapter they are based on no independent and detailed study. None has ever observed a fact, a theory or a machine that could survive *outside* of the networks that gave birth to them. Still more fragile than termites, facts and machines can travel along extended galleries, but they cannot survive one minute in this famous and mythical 'out-thereness' so vaunted by philosophers of science" (idem: 248). "The predictable character of technoscience is entirely dependent on its ability to spread networks further" (idem: 249). "Facts and machines are like trains, electricity, packages of computer bytes or frozen vegetables: they can go everywhere as long as the track along which they travel is not interrupted in the slightest" (idem: 250). This core of Latour's argument, however, had already been articulated earlier, e.g. by Fleck and Kuhn concerning the paradigm dependency of scientific facts and measurements (see above).

[94] Latour (2001).

it impossible to do justice to all the contributions which would deserve to be mentioned here. Roughly speaking, most of these works built on Mannheim's *Wissenssoziologie* and other Marxist approaches, but this time equipped with an amplified conceptual toolbox, containing powerful instruments like Foucault's discourse analyses and his power-knowledge equation, Derrida's deconstructionist grammatology, Kuhn's paradigm concept and his revival of Fleck's social concept of Science, Feyerabend's critique of universalism, Berger's and Luckmann's phenomenological version of social constructionism, Bourdieu's capital metaphors and his concept of symbolic violence, just to name a few. Despite many obvious differences between the primary political agendas represented by those voices, there were some common points of convergence.

Feminists like Sandra Harding and Donna Haraway sought a feminist epistemology based on situated,[95] non-heteropatriarchal standpoints,[96] making androcentric bias transparent, and thus, providing scientific knowledge with a "strong(er) objectivity".[97] However, they also emphasised the similarities between the marginalised standpoints of non-hetero-male gender groups compared to any other kind of Others, who are equally defined and marked as "anomalous" by the supposedly "neutral" gaze of the unmarked standard of white middle-class hetero men of European-descent. Far from being based on value-free objectivity, the natural sciences succeeded in replacing Other scientific traditions not because they (and only they!) unveiled the universal laws of nature; but rather because they succeeded in "describing and explaining those aspects of nature's regularities that permitted the upper classes of Europeans to multiply and thrive, especially through the prospering of their military, imperial, and otherwise expansionist projects".[98] Following the footsteps of Marxist scholars like Hessen, Grossmann, Bernal, and Zilsel, Harding shows how the natural sciences were fundamental to the solution of technical requirements for both the Industrial Revolution, which gave rise to the bourgeoise class and global capitalism, and to the development of military forces to subdue and colonise the Others. Its success in promoting colonialism and capitalism, not its universal truth value, led to the imposition of modern science as the only "universal", since "rational", and hence, legitimate knowledge, thus, delegitimating any alternative way of understanding.

> Thus European expansionism has changed the 'topography' of global scientific knowledge, causing the advance of European sciences and the decline or underdevelopment of scientific traditions of other cultures (Harding 1994: 314).

Since the aspects of nature modern science focuses on are defined along the needs of European expansion, other aspects would either remain unnoticed or be treated as anomalous phenomena resulting from false perception. The outstanding clear-sightedness of modern science concerning the law-like regularities in the behaviour

---

[95] Haraway (1988).

[96] Harding (1986).

[97] Harding (1992, 2008, 2015).

[98] Harding (1994: 314).

of the material aspects of nature stands against its blindness concerning all other aspects of life. Moreover, its great potential in advancing global capitalist exploration of human (particularly women, poor, and non-whites) and natural resources is counter-balanced by its inability to stop the resulting ecological disaster and the structural under-privileging of the global marginalised. This incapacity to grasp nature other than in terms of dead matter blindly following universal laws, in turn, would be the expression of a particular interpretation of what commonly is held as "Western" philosophical and religious thought. The resulting disenchanted image of nature provides the moral legitimation of undamped exploration, since "[t]o gain power over nature would, for modern man, violate no moral or religious principles".[99] Particularly, ecofeminists have been insisting that the same epistemic violence that forbids the non-white, non-male, non-European Other to speak is also responsible for the reckless exploitation of nature by means of scientifically produced technology in the hands of modern capitalism.[100] The core of this theses is that dichotomies of nature/culture, male/female, and We/Other are all part of the same set of binary oppositions that constitute the foundational framework of modern mechanistic cosmology as well as of its mechanistic sciences.[101]

> To recapitulate, certain dualisms have been persistent in Western traditions; they have all been systemic to the logics and practices of domination of women, people of colour, nature, workers, animals—in short, domination of all constituted as others, whose task is to mirror the self. Chief among these troubling dualisms are self/other, mind/body, culture/nature, male/female, civilized/primitive, reality/appearance, whole/part, agent/resource, maker/

[99] Idem: 316. Compare also Donna Haraway (1988): "But the difficulty and loss are not necessary. They derive partly from the analytic tradition, deeply indebted to Aristotle and to the transformative history of 'White Capitalist Patriarchy' (how may we name this scandalous Thing?) that turns everything into a resource for appropriation, in which an object of knowledge is finally itself only matter for the seminal power, the act, of the knower. Here, the object both guarantees and refreshes the power of the knower, but any status as agent in the productions of knowledge must be denied the object. It—the world—must, in short, be objectified as a thing, not as an agent; it must be matter for the self-formation of the only social being in the productions of knowledge, the human knower" (idem: 592).

[100] In her 1983 book *The Death of Nature*, Carolyn Merchant famously charged Francis Bacon for his rhetoric on the domination and control of nature: "Francis Bacon advocated extracting nature's secrets from 'her' bosom through science and technology. The subjugation of nature as female, I argued, was thus integral to the scientific method as power over nature" (Merchant 2006: 515). Merchant's polemic text suggested that Bacon's method of interrogating nature had been derived from practices of torture as common in witch trails in his days. The domination and exploitation of nature followed, thus, the same logic as the domination and exploitation of women: "My own efforts to deal with the problems of essentialism and nature/culture dualism led me to develop a form of socialist ecofeminism rooted not in dualism but in the dialectics of production and reproduction that I had articulated in The Death of Nature. There I had argued that nature cast in the female gender, when stripped of activity and rendered passive, could be dominated by science, technology, and capitalist production" (idem: 514). Compare also Merchant (2018).

[101] "Nature is only the raw material of culture, appropriated, preserved, enslaved, exalted, or otherwise made flexible for disposal by culture in the logic of capitalist colonialism. Similarly, sex is only matter to the act of gender; the productionist logic seems inescapable in traditions of Western binary opposition" (Haraway 1988: 592).

> made, active/passive, right/wrong, truth/illusion, total/partial, God/man. The self is the One who is not dominated […]. To be One is to be autonomous, to be powerful, to be God; but to be One is to be an illusion, and so to be involved in a dialectic of apocalypse with the other. (Haraway 1991: 178).

Anything or anyone on the Other side of this binary divide is reduced to an object and subjected to "Western"/male domination and exploitation in the name of "progress".[102] The disqualification of "non-scientific" knowledge, therefore, also prevents Us from learning from Other, potentially less (self-)destructive forms of being and knowing. Scientific universalism is not only an ideological instrument to oppress the Other, but also the main obstacle towards a sustainable future. We *need* to learn from the Others since Our own way of life will not only lead to the extinction of any Other form of life, but also to ecological disaster, and consequently, to our own extinction as well. To overcome universalism is, thus, a question of survival—not only the survival of other cultures and the "environment", but also our own survival.

In other words, modern science, its particular "gaze from nowhere"[103] and its content, together with the modern interpretation of "Western" philosophy and religion, are part of the ideological apparatus destined to sustain "Western" expansionism in the form of global capitalism. Science's claims to value-neutrality and universality are a core instrument of this "Western" cultural, economic, and political imperialism—just like white or male invisibility is instrumental to racism and masculine oppression. Of course, the cultural specificity of modern science would not imply that natural laws only work in "Western" culture, but to the contrary, that other, equally universal sciences may possibly discover and explain some of the vast blind areas in the knowledge about the universe left out by modern science. This would raise the possibility of a different, more inclusive, and thus, more objective future science; but it also raises the question whether we should "continue to develop sciences that, intentionally or not, succeed by extinguishing or obscuring all other scientific traditions, directing limitless consumption of scarce and unrenewable resources, distributing their benefits internally and their costs externally, and so forth?"[104] Instead of a single, universally "objective" scientific "truth" we might do

---

[102] Also Harding (2008, 2015).

[103] Donna Haraway (1988) speaks of the god's eye "trick" of the "gaze from nowhere", pleading for a reflexive situated knowledge instead, as a new form of feminist objectivity: "This is the gaze that mythically inscribes all the marked bodies, that makes the unmarked category claim the power to see and not be seen, to represent while escaping representation. This gaze signifies the unmarked positions of Man and White, one of the many nasty tones of the word 'objectivity' to feminist ears in scientific and technological, late-industrial, militarized, racist, and male-dominant societies, that is, here, in the belly of the monster, in the United States in the late 1980s. I would like a doctrine of embodied objectivity that accommodates paradoxical and critical feminist science projects: Feminist objectivity means quite simply *situated knowledges*" (idem: 581). "The moral is simple: only partial perspective promises objective vision" (idem: 583). "Only the god trick is forbidden" (idem: 589).

[104] Harding (1994: 320).

better in doing research and rethinking science "from below",[105] from the epistemological and socio-political standpoints of the marginalised, hitherto excluded Others. Since from the naturalized standpoint of the supposedly "objective" "gaze from nowhere" we will never be able to analyse and conceptualise our own standpoint and its intrinsic limitations, "strong objectivity" demands assuming multiple standpoints, that is, a "world of sciences"[106] rather than a single universal science. Exactly by rejecting the ideal of (supposedly) value-free research and in deliberately and reflexively assuming one's particular standpoint, a higher degree of objectivity can be achieved. However, taking marginalised standpoints into account does not amount to relativism; nor does it idealise marginalised standpoints as incorrigible. Standpoint methodology, as understood by Harding, is simply about recognising that knowledge is situated and that different kinds of knowledge practices lead to different results, different forms of life, and thus, different possible futures. The question is: "What kinds of sciences do we want for today's multicultural, democratic societies?"[107]

> We can commit ourselves to a new kind of "world of sciences" through strategizing how to maximize and harmonize the scientific and political benefits of multiple scientific questions, conceptualized from multiple social perspectives, with a multiplicity of useful methods. Such harmonizing must never aim for a single "theory of everything"; it must not aim for a "singularity," […] (Harding 2015: 50)

However, doing science from below not only demands other standpoints, other methods and practices; it also demands alternative research collectives with different scientific selves. The scientific self that does science from below is a hybrid, intersectional self, representing multiple (subaltern) standpoints (Black, women, from the South, working class, etc.). Hence, "[…] the success of standpoint methodology and strong objectivity projects depend upon just such socially embedded, multiple, and contradictory subjects of the production of knowledge".[108]

Declarations of War

The political drive of ecofeminist and other radical critiques of modern science rose the pitch of the debate, which at times showed quite polemic overtones. By the 1990s, some natural scientists felt it was time to launch a counterattack against what they perceived as a fierce attack against modern science, and which they feared might threaten reason as the basis of modern society and democracy. In their 1994 book *Higher Superstition*, biologists Paul Gross and mathematician Norman Levit accused the "academic left" and its "eclectic brew of postmodern radicalism" of promoting a "muddleheaded", "pseudoscientific" apology to "irrationalism". They argued that under the influence of postmodern deconstructionism, science studies had degenerated into a field of unqualified speculation driven by Afrocentric racism, environmentalist mysticism, feminist fundamentalism, and other irrational

---

[105] Idem 2008.

[106] Idem 2015.

[107] Idem: 49.

[108] Idem.: 163.

fantasies, finally, equalling a "rejection of the strongest heritage of Enlightenment".[109] Their ardent defence of realism would soon gather further "science warriors" on their side, but also call social scientists for a response to what they saw as a declaration of war, on the other. In 1996, the academic journal *Social Text* would strike back issuing a "Science Wars" edition, joining articles in defence of critical social studies of science. To the great delight of Gross and Levit, the volume also contained a fake article by the physician Alan Sokal.[110] The paper was intentionally salted with unsound ideas about quantum physics and meant to expose the journal's lack of scientific rigour together with the whole field of science studies. Of course, Sokal's hoax was like gasoline to the burning lands of science wars, provoking further attacks and counterattacks from the two hostile camps, and guaranteed press coverage for a couple of years. The public representation obviously privileged the more polemic voices, drawing an oversimplified picture of the conflict, with cartoon "scientists" fighting against cartoon "postmodernists". On both sides, however, all kinds of theoretical and political positions were lumped together indifferently, rounding up natural scientists, objectivists, positivists, rationalists, empiricists, realists, naturalists, analytical philosophers, and conservatives in one camp, while gathering social scientists, constructionists, relativists, anti-realists, postmodernists, anti-rationalists, together with feminists, anti-racist activists, environmentalists, (and you name it!) in the other camp. In fact, science wars were the outbreak of a century-long latent conflict between idealist and empiricist traditions, the two contradictory aspects of Cartesian dualism, finding their expression in a number of antagonistic epistemological models of realism/positivism/rationalism on the one hand, and nominalism/constructivism/relativism on the other; which is also reflected in the division between the "two cultures" of natural and social sciences, respectively.[111] Not surprisingly, the arguments on both sides were often flat and did not really meet the point of their adversaries, instead shooting at the shadows of an imaginary enemy. For example, Sokal's main arguments against science studies targeted constructionism for its supposedly inherent relativism, which would inevitably lead to anti-realism, thus abolishing the distinction between true and false propositions, ultimately justifying irrational arguments (recently re-coined as "alternative facts") against important scientific facts (e.g. global warming). However valid this argument may seem in a hypothetical world dominated by radical relativists, in our world the vast majority of social constructionists explicitly reject relativism and anti-realism.[112] Even the most radical critiques of modern science did not hold to

[109] Gross and Levitt (1998: 3).

[110] Sokal (1996).

[111] As discussed in the previous chapter. Compare also Harris (2020).

[112] For example, Bruno Latour (2001), who had been among those who were explicitly attacked by Gross and Levit, particularly protested against being put into the relativist corner. He emphasised his own objections to social constructionism, which would extend the problem with Descartes's isolated mind to the social realm, finally leading to the predicaments of relativism and incommensurability. Constructionism, therefore, only repeated the old question of modern epistemology about the reality of the real, which otherwise would not even appear. His own view, in contrast, was an attempt to abandon the hopeless disputes between realism and relativism, by including both

irrationalism in any way, but to the contrary, rather advocated for a more reflexive science in order to enhance its objectivity. It is precisely because modern science and technology are so effective in changing our world that we should better understand the underlying power-relations. Natural scientists, on the other hand, may not all be naive positivists, as some social scientists seem to suggest, but rather hold to Popperian falsificationism or to pragmatist views of theories in terms of sufficient models of an ultimately inscrutable reality.

Be this as it may, after a few years of hot combat, science wars apparently cooled down again, resuming its previous latent form as a kind of intellectual cold war between the "two cultures". However, the recent incident of "Sokal Squared", which could be considered Sokal's hoax reloaded, where in 2018 a group of three professors published seven fake articles in different scientific journals, shows that little has changed since the 1990s.[113] Anyhow, apart from Quixotesque wars against the spectre of naive positivism on one side, or the spectre of radical relativism on the other, there seems to be a solid discourse both in philosophy of science and in the social sciences showing that neither of the two extreme positions appears to be tenable.

4.2 Lessons Learnt so Far?

> […] the meaning of 'hegemony' consists precisely in its presence within the discourse of opponents of the dominant ideology (Aronowitz 1988: 22).

Looking back on a century of social research and theorising on modern science, I personally feel particularly struck by the tenacity of the main tenets being discussed again and again, generation by generation, decade after decade. This Sisyphus-like going in circles notwithstanding, I also feel, however, that beside this recounting of old stories some valuable progress has also been made.

The pioneering works of the interwar period already pointed to the most fundamental questions raised by a sociological gaze on Science. Not surprisingly, from the very beginning social sciences had shown that "reality", "truth" and "knowledge" at large are both socially construed in the course of social practice and at the same time dialectically determined by historically inherited cultural norms and social structures. This conclusion was predetermined by the very question about the

human and non-human actors in a symmetrical explanatory model. His aim was not relativism, but exactly the opposite, a more real realism. In fact, his approach would defend science against the humanists' attempts to exclude all non-human factors from the field. However, natural scientists seemed to be unable to recognise their own friends. In search for an explanation for this strange behaviour, Latour took recourse to Socrates's dialogue with Callicles, suggesting that rationalism represents an ideology of power exploiting reason as a means to exclude the masses from the discourse on truth. Instead of bringing people from the cave to the light of reason, Plato's philosopher would lock them up in the darkness forever to nurture themselves with shadows. Finally, Latour concluded that the easiest way to escape the aporias of modern epistemology would be to abandon it once and for all together with its toxic notion of an autonomous mind observing dead matter.

[113] Harris (2020).

(then newly invented) "social" and "cultural" aspects of human life. And it took only one logical step to turn this sociological gaze on modern science, too, and treat it as a social and cultural phenomenon. Consequently, Science appeared as a social institution deeply embedded in historically contingent social structures and power relations, while scientific knowledge would reflect the interests and particular worldviews of the social groups involved in its production. And a closer look at the social conditions of scientific knowledge production showed, quite obviously, that scientific knowledge was a result of social interaction, and hence, intrinsically local, situated, and embodied, just like any other kind of knowledge (how should a social study of Science come to a different result? In the end, if the only tool you've got is a hammer, anything will look like a nail!).

So, once the social sciences applied their theoretical framework and their methods to science itself, a whole bunch of far-reaching theoretical consequences came to the fore. Generally speaking, these findings reach into two dimensions: *Epistemological* questions concerning the truth value of scientific knowledge, and questions concerning the socio-*political role* of modern science, particularly in the contexts of capitalism, (neo-)colonialism, and environmental disaster.

What Social Studies of Science Tell Us About Epistemology
First of all, from the social sciences' point of view, knowledge is not the product of some disembodied, isolated mind, but of social construction, as is scientific knowledge. Accordingly, the Kantian problem of a constructed "reality" is transferred from the individual to the collective, and from the natural, supposedly unchanging *a priori* to the contingent cultural and historical realm, with all its symbolic meanings, value systems, social constrains, hierarchies, and worldly interests. Instead of being a superior substitute for theological knowledge, now "scientific knowledge is a local and mundane affair".[114] Here, again, the argument goes into two directions: First, on the macro-level, being related to the interests of particular social groups, scientific knowledge is inescapably biased and ideological. Second, research on the micro-level of social practices of scientists revealed that scientific knowledge is unlikely to be the result of "scientific method", being rather based on social action, tacit, embodied, and habitualised knowledge, symbolic belief and value systems. Taken together, research on both the macro- and the micro-level suggest that scientific knowledge does not reveal the "true" nature of the universe, but instead reflects a particular set of moral values, unprovable metaphysical presuppositions, and social practices.

While some social researchers of science focussed on linguistic aspects of scientific discourse, linking to Wittgenstein and explaining "facts" and "theories" in terms of situated *language games*, others would highlight the role of social interaction, disputes, hierarchies, or networks of actors (including non-human agents).[115]

[114] Shapin (1995: 304).

[115] In a sense, the collapse of logical empiricism and the resulting revision by some of the former participants of the Vienna Cycle had paved the way for both kinds of analysis. On the one hand, Popper's consensualist model of truth pointed to the importance of groups of experts and their

However different in many aspects, both approaches were complementary in leading to the conclusion that scientific "facts" reveal more about the particular gaze of the observer, that is, their research interests and the theoretical framework (or *thought style, paradigm, research programme, language game* of a particular *form of life*, the *habitus* maintaining the *illusio* inherent to the *field*, etc.) employed to define the object, than about the object itself. In other words, "facts" are answers to specific questions being asked, rather than universally valid representations of a passive nature.[116] So, once the myths of unique method, and value-free universal truth are put aside, new questions arise about the way scientists construe their authoritative discourse on truth. From this vantage point, universalism has the ideological function of detracting attention from its local, situated, and thus, essentially biased (Eurocentric, masculine, racist, class-determined, etc.) character of science, and thereby, to legitimise its authority.[117] At this point the methodological argument meets again with the ideological argument, rendering internal and external factors analytically inseparable.[118]

In fact, the very history of the scientific discourse on science itself is a quite revealing example of the contingent character of scientific theories.[119] There is a clear parallel between historical events, changing political climates and intellectual moods, and the theoretical tendencies in the study of science, leaving little doubt about the influence of external factors on scientific content. If Karl Mannheim would still be alive, he might well analyse the disputes in the study of science along the twentieth century in terms of ideological and utopian thought styles. Universalist and functionalist approaches would represent the conservative, backward, and hence, ideological camp, while social constructionism and relativism emphasise social change and the possibility to think in radically different ways, standing for the utopian camp. Moreover, in the context of modern thought, social constructionism is walking in the footsteps of the Enlightenment, which was fundamentally

---

interests. And since Lakatos's attempt to rescue internalism did not withstand evidence from social sciences, group interests and cultural bias would soon enter the scene, leading more or less directly to external interests, too. On the other hand, Carnap's failed effort to construe a logically coherent linguistic system and Wittgenstein's insight that language and meaning are both intrinsically situated and bound to tacit knowledge about context, inspired some authors to transfer Wittgenstein's language game metaphor to their social analysis of science.

[116] In this respect, Knorr-Cetina (1981) also spoke about "problem-input" based models of science.

[117] Shapin (1995).

[118] Knorr-Cetina (1981).

[119] Compare also Harding (2015): "Thus an exceptionalist and triumphalist philosophy of science was propagated precisely at the moment when research in the United States and Europe was becoming more deeply directed by nationalist, military, and corporate economic and political values and interests. The logical empiricist philosophy of science helpfully aligned itself with economic and political projects of its era. This is the philosophy of science that we all learned in the 1960s and '70s. It still is found compelling by most scientists and educated citizens of the West today, as well as by people around the globe. Yet it was grounded in political and intellectual contradictions and tensions at its very birth. Faith in its standards for objectivity was crucial to its continuing to receive taxpayer dollars without excessive congressional or public oversight" (idem: 10).

based on the idea that society is created by men, and consequently, can be changed by men, too. Like the ideas of the seventeenth century bourgeoise gentlemen of natural philosophy, who had challenged the Catholic Church's truth monopoly, constructionism can be understood as an attack on conservative legitimising narratives. By debunking the ideological character of scientific universalism, different forms of life and new utopian projects become thinkable. Actually, many authors more or less explicitly related their views on science to certain political projects. While authors during the interwar period predominantly defended socialist ideals, and hence, developed Marxist approaches to science, post-war authors either naturalised the established order by defending universalism, or developed their critical views of science as part of their engagement in the political demands of different social movements: Marxists emphasised Science's role as an instrument of capitalist exploitation; Feyerabend debunked the universalist pretensions of scientific method in support of a more democratic and pluralistic way of doing science; Foucault[120] had shown how the historical formation of truth regimes regulate power relations by establishing and naturalising social boundaries (e.g. by means of conceptions of sexuality, rationality, sanity, etc.); feminists discovered masculine bias in modern science and sought for a more objective, i.e. more self-conscious science; eco-feminists held masculine bias responsible for the objectifying gaze of modern science and its destructive side-effects; and so on.

However powerful these critiques may have been—and I hold they still are—they critically depend on an epistemological argument against modern science that entails some non-trivial problems. Particularly, these critiques delegitimate scientific authority by relativising the universal truth claims of scientific knowledge. Like cultural relativism in anthropology before, this scientific relativism is key for questioning naturalised "truths" and giving a chance to alternative views. The problem with relativism is, of course, that it (apparently) implies an anti-realist notion of knowledge, rendering any "objective" proposition about "reality" a kind of a collective dreamworld with no traceable relation to really real reality, so to say. As a consequence, this implicit anti-realism would also apply to the critical analysis of science itself, and thus, make the whole argument circular, since these scientific analyses of science would equally lack any objective truth value, telling nothing about science at all, but rather pointing exclusively to their own political and philosophical agendas.

The problem of circularity implied by relativism has been addressed in many different ways, with Karl Mannheim certainly being one of the first and most

[120] Foucault's power-knowledge concept was key to the rediscovery of the political importance of science. Once knowledge is not only construed, but construed in order to control others by defining what is true and what is not, science and scientific knowledge are pitched into the eye of the hurricane of power disputes. In a way, Foucault was to the social movements of the 1980s what Marx had been for the intellectual left before World War II, and what F. Bacon had been to the gentlemen of the seventeenth century. All three of them emphasised the importance of knowledge as a means of domination—not any kind of knowledge, but of the particular thought style able to subdue reality under its truth regime and to have people look at the world in such a way that they would support and reproduce a specific sociocultural project.

emphatic voices in this respect. Conspicuously, all the critical analysis notwithstanding, constructionist authors have been virtually unanimous in emphasising their ambition to enhance science—none of them would want to do away with it! So, the ambivalent relation of constructionism towards science is also rooted in this desire to transcend the limitations of science by means of a critical, reflexive examination of its social conditions.

Some authors pointed to the operational closure of science, arguing that precisely because scientific authority is exclusively derived from self-referential confirmation, thus, categorically excluding all external judgments, to be effective critical analysis would have to come from science itself.[121] However, such a self-reflexive account of science would have to go beyond subject-based epistemology and Cartesian dualism. Of course, this is not an easy thing to do—although some social scientist might claim that they did it. Anyhow, for the moment I do not see any fully developed constructionist solution to this problem. As to my own understanding, the most auspicious proposals follow the path precast by Mannheim's relationism in abandoning the old notion of universal truth in favour of a more perspectivist view, shifting the problem of "reality" from the relation between subject and object to the different ways we relate to other entities, the world, and life in general. Once the question about the subject's limits of understanding is put aside, there is no reason why different perspectives resulting from relating to other entities in different ways

[121] Niklas Luhmann (1990), for example, described science as an auto-poetic, operationally closed, and therefore, self-referential subsystem of society whose function is to define the system's entanglement with its environment in terms of a binary code of true-false-distinctions. However, according to Luhmann, science is by no means the most reliable knowledge system, but instead quite the opposite; it raises uncertainty and maintains it at the edge of supportability. But due to its operational self-referentiality, scientific findings can only be legitimised in a circular manner, and not by external factors, nor by any other discourse on truth. Since any external critique is by definition excluded from the scientific communication system, it can only be studied by itself, as a kind of third order observation. A self-referential system, like science, implies the observation of observation, or second order observation, so that the observation of such a system would equal to a third order observation. However, Luhmann remarks that for such a third order observation to become feasible, the notion of truth as representation would have to be substituted by a concept of world built up of the difference between system and environment. Within the old limits of Cartesian dualism, no third order understanding would be possible, for once the object is taken for real, the subject disappears and vice versa, never allowing for a holistic picture. Hence, to overcome its own limits, any universalistic system (like science) would have to take itself as an object of investigation, which means that the subject-object-dichotomy has to be abandoned for self-referentiality to be interrupted, making science able to learn from its insights about itself. However, as Karen Knorr-Cetina (1981) observed, system theoretical approaches always depend on a relation between environment and system, but since science is an operationally closed subsystem, its relation to the environment with respect to its reconstruction becomes obscure. Moreover, I do not see how the notion of "environment" could be divorced from the notion of "objective reality", with the social system standing for the construed, and hence, "subjective" aspect of a dualist relation. Similar observations also hold for Bourdieu's description of science as a closed field, dialectically producing and being reproduced by the unconscious behavioural matrix of *habitus*. Here, too, the knowing subject is substituted by an abstract intersubjective structure, reducing the subject to a "medium" (decoding symbolic meanings according to the rules of the field etc.) of more or less autonomous communicative processes.

should not reveal equally "true" aspects of "reality", leading to equally effective practices. Accordingly, constructionism, understood in these terms, does not necessarily entail anti-realism, since different kinds of knowledge can, at least in principle, be equally "true" and "objective", even if they suggest mutually exclusive descriptions of the one world we all share. Moreover, since all kinds of knowledge can be assumed to be equally related to a shared world, they can also be expected to be equally effective in orienting the way we relate to the world and to each other. So, although the constructionist model does not provide any reliable yardstick for measuring or comparing the truth-value of different kinds of knowledge, it is still not necessarily relativistic, as it allows for distinguishing different kinds of knowledge regarding its objective effects on both our outer and our inner "worlds". In philosophical terms, of course, this solution points to pragmatism (as discussed in the last chapter), while its political implications corroborate ideological readings of science, highlighting its political and economic dimension.

What Social Studies Tell Us About the Role of Science in Modern Society

The blueprint for any critical analysis of the role Science has been playing in modern society is, of course, the dialectical historical materialism of Karl Marx and Friedrich Engels. Accordingly, most critical studies on the social, economic, political and ecological implications of Science would follow the twofold model of intra- and superstructure, examining its ideological and material dimension, and the dialectical relations between the two of them. On the whole, all studies (even conservative ones like Robert Merton's) have shown that Science emerged as an integral part of the utopian societal project which had been pushed forth by the seventeenth century's bourgeoise intellectuals.

On the material side, Science has been intimately related to the rise of capitalism, European expansionism, and the Industrial Revolution. Here, again, the relation between the intellectual and the material dimension has been shown to be dialectical (or entangled[122]) rather than a simple one-way determinism. On the one hand, Marxist analysis emphasised that modern science not only emerged in the course of a changing *Zeitgeist*, following a movement from a theological to a mechanistic worldview, but that this mechanistic view of nature had been anticipated by technological developments driven by industrial, economic, and military demands. The appropriation of mechanics and mathematics by bourgeoise intellectuals would then give rise to early modern science and related utopian visions of a new society based on Science and technology. And once scientific findings showed they could be applicable to the development of new technologies, external demands oriented most of its research agenda. Thus, Science was not the result of some free-floating history of ideas, but of quite worldly affairs. On the other hand, Science has been fundamental to the development of new technologies which would prove essential to modern capitalism and colonialism, providing the means of production and the weapons for global domination and exploitation. So, while Science has, ever since its beginnings, been driven by economic factors related to rising capitalism, it is also

[122] Aronowitz (1988); Rieppel et al. (2018).

an indispensable precondition for the success of capitalism and the current world order.

So far, this train of thought does not question the efficacy of scientific knowledge, but to the contrary, reassures its power to predict and control nature. Orthodox Marxists held to an objectivist notion of science, defending that science, notwithstanding the historical roots it shared with capitalism, would entail the potential to contribute to the freedom and wellbeing of all people once it had been freed from bourgeoise control. In other words, in its essence scientific knowledge is objective, morally neutral, and ultimately superior to "religious" and "traditional" knowledge, however, the bourgeoise class has been misusing its great potential to enslave and exploit the proletarian class.[123] At this point, the majority of the more recent authors would split from orthodox Marxism, instead insisting that scientific knowledge is far from being "neutral" or "unbiased", since it is not only put in service of the societal project and to the sole benefit of the European bourgeoise class; far more importantly, science and its methods also represent the God's-eye view of a hyperstaticised subject arrogating to treat anything else out there as mere objects, completely disposable to its will and virtue. From this point of view, the Marxist faith in science and technology as a means of universal freedom and wellbeing is just another example of naive belief in "progress". The very idea of "progress", however, is itself an ideological element of the modern worldview, aiming to delegitimate "traditional" forms of life, to justify colonialism and global capitalism (or communism), and to promote technological development as an end in itself. Of course, this school of thought, which may have found one of its most emblematic expression in ecofeminist critiques of Science, hinges not only on Marx, but also on Max Weber, and particularly on Martin Heidegger, whose works transcended the Marxian concept of ideology, emphasising science's role as a perceptive and behavioural matrix mediating our relation to the world and even to ourselves.[124] And once again, the old villain Cartesian dualism is held responsible for the distinction between "nature" and "culture", and for the resulting disenchantment and reification of the world.[125] This deep analysis of Science's entanglement with the general constitution of modern society, modern world order, and the modern way of being in general, obviously points back to the epistemological implications of constructionism as just mentioned. However, the epistemological problem of "truth" has

---

[123] Aronowitz (1988).

[124] However, Aronowitz (1988) shows that Marx himself had come to quite similar views, and he quotes the following passage from the *Grundrisse*: "Capital creates the bourgeois society, and the universal appropriation of nature as well as of the social bond itself by members of society. . . . For the first time, nature becomes purely an object for humankind, purely a matter of utility; ceases to be recognized as a power for itself; and the theoretical discovery of its autonomous laws appears merely as a ruse to subjugate it under human needs" (Marx, *Grundrisse*, *apud* Aronowitz 1988: 40). Aronowitz concludes that "even though science discovers the 'autonomous laws' of nature, this activity is not for the sake of knowledge but for the sake of utility; nature becomes nature 'for us'" (ibidem). Hence, from Marx's point of view, science objectively describes natures laws, but in a way and from a perspective that serves capitalist needs.

[125] Latour (1993); Knorr-Cetina (1981); Merchant (2006).

now been identified as being fundamentally a problem of human existence. For to *know* is to *be* in a particular way. And to know from the perspective of the Cartesian cogito is to be in a self- and life-negating manner. This is why Cartesian dualism and ultimately modern epistemology in general have been identified as the main obstacles towards real freedom, equity, and sustainability. This reading not only converges with the analysis of the epistemological shortcomings of modern thought, but also points to its possible solution. The shift from the epistemological question of universal "truth" to the concrete effects of different thought styles in our lived reality also reveals why science is so efficient in dominating nature, and why it could become universally dominant all over the globe, albeit not necessarily being "truer" than any other way of knowing: modern science has always been a vital element of the "Western", bourgeoise utopia of a global society based on universal truth and the domination of nature; and accordingly, it provided the necessary knowledge to have this dream come true—at least for the white, European descent, male, upper class members of the global "community", while externalising its "dark side"[126] to the unfortunate global "Rest".

On the whole, social studies of science left little doubt about the socially-construed constitution of scientific knowledge and its structural relation to global capitalism, finally debunking the ideological function of scientific universalism as a legitimating narrative of masculine, capitalist models of "Western" domination and exploitation. However, once scientific universalism has been uncovered as an instrument of "Western" domination on a global scale, this geopolitical dimension of scientific knowledge raises new questions about the relations between the "West" and the "Rest", and Science's role in this story.

4.3 Decolonising Science

Alongside with those self-critical reflections from within the global centres of scientific knowledge production, critique has also been articulated from the peripheries. Although initially representing two separated discourses, findings of social studies of science, particularly feminist approaches, have increasingly been converging with post- and decolonial approaches.

For many decades, post-colonial and subaltern studies have been unveiling the colonial perspective behind images of the Others and how "Western" cultural knowledge has been instrumental in subjugating the subaltern by drawing the line between Us and Them. The othering of women and "Black" people through the naturalisation of "white" men as the "neutral" social norm had long been denounced by feminists like Simone de Beauvoir, Afro-American intellectuals like W.E.B. Du Bois, and negritude activists like Aimé Césaire and Frantz Fanon. Du Bois, who had

[126] Mignolo (1995).

identified the "color-line"[127] that disguises and sustains white dominance as the central problem of the twentieth century, also showed how white racism and male dominance were intrinsically related to capitalism. Writing from the perspective of the colonised, Aimé Césaire accused European colonialism of hypocrisy for selling its reckless, de-humanising exploitation of other nations as a benevolent civilising mission, ostensibly aiming to help those "underdeveloped" "savages".[128] Frantz Fanon not only further radicalised Césaire's critique of colonial violence as ultimately justifying counter-violence[129]; he also carried his critical analysis of the underlying colonial and racial differences to its existential dimension. "Black" men and women have not only been divested of their right of self-representation, but also of their metaphysics; being forced to adopt "white" metaphysics, there is no space for any "Black" ontology either, that is, no self-determined way of being. The idea of man can only be thought of within the boundaries of hegemonic "white" ontology, but this ontology already distinguishes between different kinds of men along racial lines.[130]

The representation of the Others and the social construction of truth in the context of colonialism would also be central questions of Edward Said's[131] foundational text on Orientalism. Based on a critical application of post-structuralist methods, Said showed that the "Orient" had been invented by Western authors based on a

[127] Du Bois (2007).

[128] Césaire (1978).

[129] "The violence of the colonized, we have said, unifies the people. [...] At the individual level, violence is a cleansing force. It rids the colonized of their inferiority complex, of their passive and despairing attitude. [...] When they have used violence to achieve national liberation, the masses allow nobody to come forward as 'liberator'" (Fanon 2004: 51). "The people in arms, the people whose struggle enacts this new reality, the people who live it, march on, freed from colonialism and forewarned against any attempt at mystification or glorification of the nation. Violence alone, perpetrated by the people, violence organized and guided by the leadership, provides the key for the masses to decipher social reality" (idem: 96). "Now, comrades, now is the time to decide to change sides. We must shake off the great mantle of night which has enveloped us, and reach for the light. The new day which is dawning must find us determined, enlightened and resolute. We must abandon our dreams and say farewell to our old beliefs and former friendships. Let us not lose time in useless laments or sickening mimicry. Let us leave this Europe which never stops talking of man yet massacres him at every one of its street corners, at every corner of the world" (idem: 235). "When I look for man in European lifestyles and technology I see a constant denial of man, an avalanche of murders" (idem: 236). "For Europe, for ourselves and for humanity, comrades, we must make a new start, develop a new way of thinking, and endeavor to create a new man" (idem: 239).

[130] Fanon (2008) (1952). According to Fanon (2008), this ontological distinction is the result of sociogeny, the social process of bringing into being a "massive psychoexistential complex" of different ontological categories of human "races". Drawing on Fanon's notion of sociogeny, Sylvia Wynter (2015) traces the social construction of otherness even further down to the human condition, to the "sociogenic replicator code symbiloc life and death". For Wynter, being defined as certain kinds of "human" by means of naturalising and institutionalising our own narrations is precisely what defines us as "humans" or "Homo Narrans", as a species fundamentally different in htis respect from any other living species.

[131] Said (1978).

colonial concept, producing images of the Others servile to imperial power. Accordingly, orientalist narratives would conflate people, times, and places to exotic, essentialised images. This essentialising discourse bears on the construction of an epistemological distinction between "Occident" and "Orient" that acts as powerful political instrument disguised as academic discourse. The resulting image of the Others as essentially "traditional" and backward, then, justified European colonialism and developmentalism as necessary steps towards "progress". Essentialised cultural representations of the ("irrational", "inscrutable", "exotic", "traditional") Others, therefore, are nothing but an ideological means of Western domination. The scientific concept of truth as genuinely non-political knowledge serves, thereby, to obscure the political circumstances of knowledge production, thus authorising these stereotyped images of the Others as valid arguments to justify political decisions.

Said's concept of Orientalism has been further generalised by post-colonial authors like Homi Bhabha and Gayatri Chakravorty Spivak. According to Bhabha,[132] this kind of othering, typical of colonial discourse, is nothing less than the operational mode of imperialism and should be the focus of post-colonial inquiry. However, colonial discourse is situated *in-between*, producing hybrid identities along hierarchies of colonial power and as a product of negotiation between colonisers and the colonised. The omnipresence of colonial structures of thought forces the colonised to adopt dominant concepts and representations, even if they intend to fight colonial discourse. This paradoxical phenomenon of *mimicry* produces a form of being "almost the same, but not quite", a domesticated Other admissible to representations within authoritative discourse. As a result, counter-discourses of Others, from Black intellectuals like Fanon, to African, Asian, and Latin American authors, speak to the "West" using and reinterpreting "Western" categories, however, aiming at "transforming the conditions of enunciation at the level of the sign".[133] Like Said, Bhabha, and other post-colonial authors, Spivak[134] made extensive use of post-structuralist theory (particularly of Derrida's deconstructionist approach and Foucault's concept of *epistemic violence*) to describe the silencing of the subaltern Others and their knowledge by "Western" philosophical discourse. She criticised, however, that even post-structuralists like Foucault and Deleuze ended up reintroducing the modern subject through the backdoor of (apparently subject-free) power and the totalising of "the worker", while ignoring the particularities of labour in the centres and the peripheries. Foucault located epistemic violence in the construction of the subject within European history, while invisibilising the subaltern Other which, in fact, would be the target *par excellence* of epistemic violence exerted by the disavowed construction of the colonial Other, and which would also be constitutive for the European subject.[135]

---

[132] Bhabha (1994).

[133] Bhabha (1994: 247).

[134] Spivak (1993).

[135] Ibidem.

These rather philosophical critiques of Eurocentrism were paralleled by economic explanations for global inequality in the post-colonial era. Based on the economic models of Prébesch and Singer concerning the economic pitfalls of primary commodity-producing countries, Latin American authors like Anibal Pinto Santa Cruz, Celso Furtado, and Eduardo Galeano developed a powerful theory of structural dependence between the underdevelopment of the former colonies of the "Third World" and the wealth of the "First World". Dependence theory gained considerable power during the 1970s, and for all the critique it has been subjected to, it still plays an important role in decolonial theory.

In his influential 1971 book *Open Veins of Latina America*,[136] Galeano portrayed the history of Latin American underdevelopment as a history of the development of global capitalism. "Development", as defined by the global imperialist system, Galeano argued, only develops inequalities. This systemic violence would have emerged with the European conquest of the New World, initiating the great killing of Indigenous nations for the Europeans' lust for gold and silver. Galeano's report drastically depicts the rise and fall of the legendary silver city of Potosi, whose silver mountain devoured Indigenous workers by the millions, and in the end, financed European bankers and industrial capitalism.[137] This structural connection between the depletion of the New World and the original accumulation of modern capitalism in Europe had, of course, already been mentioned by Marx.[138] However, Galeano showed how these historical processes directly led to the contemporary international division of labour, with rich industrialised nations at the centres exploiting cheap labour and natural resources from the peripheries of one and the same global economic system. To the eyes of Galeano and Latina American social movements, liberalists' talk about the invisible hand of free markets is nothing but a myth designed to conceal the brute reality of Euro-American imperialism. While global economic institutions under US rule (like the IMF and World Bank) are hassling "Third World" countries to open their markets, leading imperial powers, like Britain and the US, gained their hegemony exactly by protecting their markets, and through military intervention against "inconvenient" governments to guarantee access to cheap labour and primary commodities for their industries. It followed that "underdevelopment" is not a step towards "development", but its permanent consequence and a structural element of global capitalism.

---

[136] I used the Portuguese edition from 2010.

[137] Although all the silver initially went to Spain, its Catholic Crown would spend this incredible wealth for luxury-goods imported from Italy, Holland, England, and France, and in endless wars against the rising Protestant bourgeoisie of these very nations. Soon, only 5% of oversea commerce would be left in Spanish hands, and the Spanish economy would rapidly decay, while, particularly, Britain and Holland would take the lead in the exploitation of the New World as well as in European industrialisation. Spain had lost its fight for the old feudal system and against bourgeoise capitalism. Meanwhile, satellite metropoles like Potosí would rapidly appear and decay according to the current demand for sugar, rubber, coffee and other commodities at the global markets (idem).

[138] See Marx (1962), Capital, Chap. 24, on the "so-called primitive accumulation", and Chap. 25, on the "modern theory of colonisation".

Economic dependence theories like Galeano's have been of great influence for socialist governments and social movements throughout Latin America, but also for critical theorists elsewhere, like American sociologist Immanuel Wallerstein.[139] His *world-system* approach provides an economic analysis of modern capitalism as a global system of unequal division of labour, wealth and power, while introducing the inherent epistemic violence—as issued by post-colonial and subaltern studies—as an equally important analytical dimension. Tracing back the historical origins of the modern world-system, Wallerstein discovered its beginnings in the sixteenth century, when the European Renaissance coincided with early capitalism and the conquest and successive exploitation of the New World; the confluence of these historical events, then, accelerated capitalist accumulation, industrialisation, and liberalism. Economically, Wallerstein re-dated the birth of capitalism by redefining infinite accumulation as its differentiator, in contrast to the Marxian definition of capitalism on the basis of its labour relations. While wage labour, in fact, has been an important feature of European industrialisation, it has not been so in many other parts of the modern world-system. Independently of its different modes, however, labour has been exploited more ruthlessly in the peripheries, accumulating ever more wealth in the centres while impoverishing and deteriorating the peripheries. Apart from its material basis, the modern world-system has been sustained by an intellectual "scaffold", a kind of superstructure composed of universalistic norms, liberalism, and the epistemological divide between the "two cultures". Wallerstein insists that the latter has been of fundamental importance, since it obscured the social and historically contingent nature of the system, thus, sustaining developmentalism as a driving ideology of globalisation. Particularly, liberalism has been propagating empirical sciences and their supposedly value-neutral method as the only universally valid knowledge system. Meanwhile, social sciences adopted the liberal model of society as an assembly of separated spheres of market, state, and civil society, developing from the most "primitive" "savagery", over to "pre-modern" "oriental" "high civilisations", until, 1 day, finally reaching the state of "modern civilisation". Imbued with these liberal, and thus, ultimately ideological categories, the social sciences did more to sustain the modern world-system than to understand it.[140] Although the humanities had already cautioned about the fundamental crisis of the modern episteme in the early twentieth century, World War II and the subsequent Cold War provided a truce to the competition between the "two cultures" and empiricists would win the field for a couple of years, basically due to

[139] Wallerstein (2004, 2006).

[140] All his critique notwithstanding, Wallerstein did not argue against science, but only against universalist versions of scientism. He emphasises that "[t]o be against scientism is not to be against science" and "[t]o be against particularism disguised as universalism does not mean that all views are equally valid and that the search for a pluralistic universalism is futile" (Wallerstein 2004: 21). The modern world-system's ideological structure is based on a paradoxical coexistence of the positive norm of universalism and anti-universalist norms like racism, sexism and nationalism. However contradictory these norms may be, both justify inequalities as a "antinomic duo" and are fundamental to sustain the global division of labour.

the central importance of technological development. However, the growing disappointment about the capitalist world-system and the increasing gap between the "West" and the "Rest" under US hegemony would provoke the World Revolution of 1968. People would no longer believe in the myth of inevitable progress towards a better world, and the establishment therefore abandoned developmentalism in favour of a neoliberal concept of "globalisation", that is, free markets to lower costs and rise profits. With the end of the Cold War the counter movements of the global left began to articulate alternative proposals, and to reorganise their resistance on a global scale. In 2001, they met at the World Social Forum in Porto Alegre to declare that "another world is possible", expressing the hope of billions for a better future beyond the dogma of infinite growth.

While the Cold War ended with the liberation of many European and Asian countries from Soviet hegemony and its puppet communist parties' dictatorships, for many Latin American countries, the 1980s and 1990s were marked by the end of US imperialism and its puppet military dictatorships. However, in Latin America, the comeback of democracy was perceived as a victory of civil society and minority groups who had been fighting against violent oppression since the 1960s. Now, the causes of industrial and rural workers, women, LGBTGIA+, Black and Indigenous movements, would finally come into their own in the new democratic constitutions. By the turn of the millennium, many countries elected socialist progressive governments which would implement a series of public policies aiming at social and political inclusion and protecting minority rights. As a result, tens of millions would be freed from extreme poverty, and suddenly, poor, Black, and Indigenous students could study at public universities, side by side with the sons and daughters of the old oligarchies. Indeed, another world seemed to be possible!

The Modernity/Coloniality Research Project (M/C)

Spurred by this wind of change, a group of Latin American intellectuals decided to embark on a new research programme aiming to review four decades of post-modern theorising, post-colonial studies, and world-system theory, but this time, from a situated, Latin American point of view. During the year 1998 they organised a number of meetings under the leadership of Edgar Lander, with the participation of Enrique Dussel, Walter Mignolo, Arturo Escobar, Aníbal Quijano, and Fernando Coronil. The group would soon attract further members to join their discussions and begin publishing on what would receive the (somewhat cumbersome) label "*modernity/coloniality research project*"[141] (M/C).

Conceptually, their approach linked to Wallerstein's historical and structural association of capitalism and modern rational discourse with the conquest of the New World, colonialism and racism, and the idea of *decoloniality*[142] as a necessary consequence. In a pioneering paper, Aníbal Quijano[143] had conceptualised this

[141] Escobar (2003); Mignolo and Walsh (2018).

[142] "Decoloniality" was originally coined by Asian and African countries at the Bandung Conference in 1955 (Mignolo 2013; Mignolo and Walsh 2018).

[143] Quijano (1992).

inherent colonial aspect of modernity as an expression of *coloniality of power,* a matrix of power relations that would constitute structural hegemony of the centres over the peripheries based on global division of labour along racial classifications. Coloniality of power works as a kind of epistemic violence, instrumenting rationality to justify colonial order in the name of "progress" and to impose disciplinary policies to "civilise" the "irrational", and thus, incommensurable "primitives", while ultimately betraying the modern promises of liberty and equity. As a consequence, for a better world to become possible, it would be necessary to "delink"[144] from modern/colonial epistemology, that is, to *decolonise* one's terms of reasoning.[145]

A first step towards decolonising one's own perception would be to review modern history from a situated, subaltern, and in this case, Latin American perspective. From this vantage point, not only capitalism and the modern world-system, but also modernity at large had emerged as a consequence of the conquest of the Americas, since modernity can only be thought of in contrast to the "pre-modern" Other, stigmatised in terms of evolutionist and racial categories. Hence, modernity was not a genuinely European phenomenon which had been spread around the globe in the course of colonial and capitalist expansionism; rather modernity is, and has always been, a genuinely *colonial* phenomenon.[146] Moreover, the very idea of "Europe" as

[144] Idem.

[145] This decolonial project was a post-cold-war result of post-colonial studies, however, seeking to overcome the post-colonial focus on post-structuralist European discourse, departing from the rich decolonial thought all over the globe, and the "second De-colonisation" which would begin after the Cold War, with Indigenous movements like the Zapatista, the Social Forum in Porto Alegre, and the election of the leftist governments of Hugo Chaves, "Lula" da Silva, Rafael Correa, and Evo Morales (idem).

[146] Much like Wallerstein, Quijano (2000) argued that globalisation began with the constitution of the Americas and colonial/modern capitalism as a new system of global power, with racial classifications as its fundamental pillar. However, it was not in Europe, but in America that the new order of global power and also the first modern identities emerged. These modern identities were based on two fundamental axes: 1. the construction of racial differences; 2. the control of labour focussing capital accumulation and global market. The modern idea of race did not exist before the invasion of the Americas, and the notion of colour was a posterior attribution to the concept of race emerging in British controlled America a century later. During the colonial era, the notion of race was exported to the whole world to naturalise and justify European domination. The colonial control of labour was organised along racial classifications, with paid labour being reserved for white Europeans, and non-paid labour attributed to non-European races. However, although colonialism has come to end, the same distribution of modes of labour along racial categories still determines the geography of capitalism. Particularly in the colonial/modern Americas people are socially classified in terms of work, race, and gender. Racist organisation of power relations and geo-cultural identities has been the fundament of Eurocentrism. European/occidental hegemony established new global cultural standards to exert control over cultural and knowledge production along binary categories like orient-occident, primitive-civilised, magic-scientific, irrational-rational, traditional-modern. In sum, Eurocentrism would be based on three basic ideas: 1. the articulation of dualism and evolutionism in terms of binary oppositions (We, European, modern <> They, pre-modern, etc.); 2. the naturalisation of cultural differences in terms of race; 3. the identification of the Others with the past. Moreover, Cartesian dualism had transmuted the theological concept of "soul" into "reason" as the only source of knowledge, while transforming the body into a mere object of knowledge, leading to the objectification of the body as a part of nature. As a consequence, the

a cultural space rooted in Greek antiquity had only emerged a century after Columbus' discovery of the New World, as a reaction to the colonial situation.[147] It follows that "Europe" is itself a rhetoric element of the modern/colonial legitimating narrative about the Great Divide between "West" and "Rest", Us and Them, and to justify "Western" domination of the "Rest". In other words, the supposedly "European" origin of modernity is a modern/colonial myth based on the negation of the co-constitution of modernity and colonialism, and its persisting colonial, racist, Eurocentric structural and epistemic violence. In the face of this colonial re-definition of modernity, M/C proposes a decolonial perspective of a global and empirically testable modernity based on a critical visualisation of its disclaimed dark, colonial side,[148] most of which is externalised to the peripheries.

From this new, de-centred perspective, Western expansionism and capitalism, as well as modern philosophy and science are all part of the same colonial/modern matrix, conjointly contributing to its structural and epistemic violence.[149]

inferior other races are conceptualised as irrational, and thus, closer to nature, mere objects of knowledge, too. "Estas modalidades de representación, estructuradas en términos de oposiciones binarias, oscurecen la mutua constitución de "Europa" y sus colonias, y del "Occidente" y sus postcolonias. Ocultan la violencia del colonialismo y del imperialismo detrás del embellecedor manto de misiones civilizatorias y planes de modernización" (Coronil 2000: 90). Compare also Chakrabarty's (2007) influential book *Provincializing Europe*.

[147] Enrique Dussel (2000, 2009) asserts that "Europe" is an ideological construction of German romanticism. According to Dussel, before the sixteenth century the "Occident" had never been a centre, since until the Iberian *conquista* there was no global centre anyway, but only regional empires. However, Spanish victories against Indigenous nations constituted the myth of universal superiority, and finally, established Europe as a new global centre. Hence, Europe is a modern myth that defines its periphery as the other side of modernity. This myth of modern/European superiority justifies violence against the Others in the name of "progress/development". Modernisation, therefore, is neither necessarily desirable, nor an inevitable destiny, but a contingent, irrational expression of structural violence that has to be demystified to open ways to envisage the modern peripheries. Only if the subalterns are envisaged as the victims of an irrational act of modern/colonial violence, the "trans-modern" project of global liberation based on recognition of subaltern, and neglected alterity become possible. However, the Eurocentric myth is deeply embedded within modern/colonial knowledge, as exemplified by Hegel's definition of Descartes as the first truly "modern" philosopher. Dussel shows that, in fact, Descartes had derived his views from his meditations during his time as a Jesuit, but also from his study of the Mexican philosophers Antonio Rubio and Francisco Suarez. At the time of Descartes, these Latin American authors were widely read in Europe and had also been fundamental to the works of Leibniz, and all other posterior ontologies. Suarez's work represented a sceptic current of Ibo-American Jesuit scholastics, also known as second scholastic, with great influence in early modern philosophy. It follows that modern philosophy was not the genuinely European business Hegel and others would later paint. Compare also Greaber and Wengrow (2021) on the constitutive role of Indigenous critique for European Enlightenment.

[148] Mignolo (1995, 2011).

[149] The Portuguese sociologist Boaventura de Souza Santos (2009a), who has been closely related to M/C, points to the "abyssal" character of modern/colonial thought that radically divides reality into two interdependent, yet mutually exclusive realms, invisibilising what is at the other side of the abyss as the neglected Other of excepted "normality". This neglected Other, however, is the disavowed foundation of the official, visible side of modernity. While at the official, metropolitan

Accordingly, the expansion of colonialism and capitalism went with the expansion of the modern/colonial episteme, thus, establishing a particular modern/colonial *geopolitics of knowledge.*[150] As a result, subaltern populations have been deprived of their "traditional" knowledge and forced to adopt the hegemonic Eurocentric perspective with its particular forms of perception and knowledge production. This is why coloniality of power inevitably entails *coloniality of knowledge*,[151] demanding the decolonisation of knowledge and practices of knowing. The need for a decolonial epistemology that "delinks"[152] and goes beyond modern/colonial categories of thought and perception would, therefore, occupy a central role within the decolonial project.[153] This epistemological turn not only called for a critical analysis of modern/colonial episteme and its ideological facets, but also for a quest for alternative

side regulation and emancipation are mandatory norms, at the neglected, colonial side depletion and violence dominate the scene, which would be unthinkable in the metropolitan realm. Like Aimé Césaire (1978) said, the holocaust perpetrated by Nazi Germany did not outrage the modern world because of its unprecedented atrocity, but because its victims were white Europeans, while, in contrast, the enslavement and slaughter of millions of non-whites in the peripheries were simply accepted as an unfortunate "normality". Santos also argues that the colonial condition of the peripheries is conceived as the condition of nature, the ultimate Other, where civilised institutions cannot exist. From the very beginning of modern social and political theory, leading authors like Hobbes, Locke, and Rousseau positioned this absolute difference in a chronology of human development, from nature to civilisation, with the New World and its inhabitants representing the initial state of nature. However, this temporal difference is transmuted into a permanent difference, denying the Others' "humanity", and thus, divesting their right to further develop, and finally, to have a future of their own. This radical absence of humanity at the other side of the abyss constitutes the invisible, but necessary Other of modernity and its humanitarian discourse at this side. At this side of the line, the truth monopole has been assigned to modern science, including its disputes with philosophy and theology, while on the other side there is simply no truth at all, since the Others' humanity, and hence, also their knowledge (Indigenous, Popular, "traditional") is radically denied. In sum, Western modernity could only expand on a global scale by systematically violating the very principles it defends, and the same goes for modern science and its truth monopoly. So, on the one hand, scientific universalism is the result of impositions forced by colonialism and capitalism, while on the other, it is itself a colonial project sought to homogenise the world epistemologically and culturally, radically silencing and suffocating any diverging way of being, thereby legitimating the modern/colonial project as the only viable alternative.

[150] Mignolo (2002); Mignolo and Tlostanova (2006).

[151] Lander (2000).

[152] Mignolo (2000b).

[153] In a way, M/C turns Marxism from its materialist feet back on Hegel's idealist head, so to say. As Ramón Grosfoguel (2011) explains: "The old Marxist paradigm of infrastructure and superstructure is replaced by a historical-heterogeneous structure (Quijano 2000[b]), or a 'heterarchy' (Kontopoulos 1993), that is, an entangled articulation of multiple hierarchies, in which subjectivity and the social imaginary is not derivative but constitutive of the structures of the world-system (Grosfoguel 2002). In this conceptualization, race and racism are not superstructural or instrumental to an overarching logic of capitalist accumulation; they are constitutive of capitalist accumulation at a world-scale. The 'colonial power matrix' is an organizing principle involving exploitation and domination exercised in multiple dimensions of social life, from economic, sexual, or gender relations, to political organizations, structures of knowledge, state institutions, and households (Quijano 2000[b])" (Grosfoguel 2011: 13). M/C seeks to come to a holistic view beyond culturalist or materialist reductionisms.

concepts and decolonial epistemologies. Of course, analysis would soon reveal that "Western" academic discourse is almost entirely contaminated with Eurocentric concepts and categories. Particularly, social sciences have been naturalising colonial categories, and thereby, providing the scientific knowledge to legitimate the imposition of modern/colonial order.[154] But even critical and highly valuable post-modern approaches like Foucault's microphysics of power cannot explain how the disciplinary power/knowledge is connected to the capitalist world-system, since his conception ignores that the invention and disciplining of the modern subjects is bound to the invention and disciplining of the colonial Other. This lack of consciousness concerning inherent colonial aspects of modernity shows the conceptual limitations of (post-)modern academic discourse. Modernity and rationalisation have been construed as processes inherent to European history, independently from other histories and intellectual currents in the Americas, Africa, or Asia. However, Foucault's disciplinary power also emerged from colonial experience, and thus, has to be understood from a geopolitical perspective, taking these silenced histories into account as well.[155]

To avoid the epistemological pitfalls of "Western" academic discourse, M/C takes recourse to a localised, situated, and embodied conception of knowledge. Since non-locality is a central supposition of modern/colonial universalism and globalisation, locality, particularly in its geopolitical dimension, has been widely omitted in modern discourse.[156] However, once the geopolitics of knowledge are envisaged, Eurocentrism and Occicentrism will crystallise along the lines of the *colonial difference*,[157] showing the limits of any abstract universalism, however, without suggesting relativism. Colonial difference qualifies the distinction between

---

[154] Castro-Gomes (2000).

[155] Walter Mignolo (2000a, b) also criticises Wallerstein's world-system theory for its failure to articulate the coloniality of power, as demonstrated by Quijano. Like post-modern discourse, world-system theory would ignore the colonial difference between subaltern and dominant realities, reducing the subaltern Other to a passive, irrelevant, naturalised historical fact. The consolidation of the concept of the "occident" is intimately related to the emergence of the Atlantic commercial circuit. American white criollo elites needed to re-define their geopolitical position in-between Europeans and other races, finally constructing their self-consciousness as (pseudo-) Europeans of the peripheries of "Western Hemisphere". Wallerstein's concept of *geo-culture*, however, would be based on the formation of bourgeoise citizenship during the French revolution, ignoring revolutions in the peripheries (US-independence wars, Haitian revolution, Bolivarian revolutions, etc.). It, therefore, re-enforces the invisible white matrix which excludes the idea of proactive Black or Indigenous citizenship. But, Mignolo emphasises, it is exactly this naturalisation of racial difference which has always been constitutional for modern/colonial reality. However, Francisco Segrera (2000) opens an exception for Latin American social sciences, since they developed a number of alternative concepts, expressing the subaltern perspective, including *colonial capitalism, centre-periphery, sub-imperialism, dependency, participatory action research, coloniality of power and knowledge, pedagogy of the oppressed, liberation theology, border thinking*, to name just a few. Problems indicated by Wallerstein, therefore, would not apply to Latin American social sciences in the same way as to their hegemonic counterparts.

[156] Escobar (2000).

[157] Mignolo (2000b, 2002).

the reality of the colonised and the reality of the coloniser, which is always also an epistemological difference. The fundamental difference, however, is not the incommensurability between "Western" and "non-Western" cosmologies (as supposed by modern/colonial discourse), but the colonial difference imposed by colonial power relations. In this sense, post-modern debates in Latin America have been discussing European problems, not their own ones. Consequently, intellectual decolonisation cannot come from existing "Western" scholarship, nor from Latin American debates using (post-)modern/colonial concepts. Latin American social movements, in contrast, have long been fighting for a reintroduction of locality into political discourse, claiming the recognition of local knowledge, local culture, and local economy as key resources for a fair and sustainable future.[158] M/C is also an attempt to translate these experiences from social movements and subaltern groups into academic discourse. It is an important element of its self-conception, that M/C not only emerged from a critical review of academic discourses from a Latin American standpoint, but also that it bequeathed grassroots militancy and its most powerful resources: subaltern (Popular and Indigenous) knowledge, liberation theology, and participatory action research. Militant intellectuals, like Orlando Fals Borda, have long called for delinking from hegemonic epistemologies.[159] But the history of subaltern voices reaches far beyond the 1960s, right back to the first century after the European invasion of the lands of proud nations like the Incas, the Aztec, the Tupi, or the Guarani. One of the first decolonial authors was Felipe Guaman Poma de Ayala, a Peruvian descendant of the Incas. In his *New Chronicles and Good Governance* (*Nueva crónica y buen gobierno*) from 1616, Poma set out to inform the Spanish king about the crude and unchristian deportment of his majesty's subjects, followed by Poma's own suggestions for a better, a "good", and more Christian government.[160] Guaman Poma was also an early example of those hybrid identities incessantly emerging from modern/colonial social relations, a border subjectivity uniting Indigenous (subaltern) heritage and identity with European (hegemonic) intellect. In his critique of the colonial society of his times, Guaman Poma appropriated Christian ethics as a yardstick to denounce the double standard of the Spaniards, their talk on Christian values and their unchristian attitudes. A "good government", in contrast, should be truly based on Christian principles of mutual respect, as had been practiced by the Incas in the *Tawantinsuyu*, before the arrival of the European conquerors. Of course, historically Poma's argument seems absurd; however, his point is not historical, but rather one of standpoint, a shift across the colonial difference, using and reinterpreting colonial categories to express his own point of view in a language understandable to the coloniser. The modern/colonial condition is identified with hell, while the Tawantinsuyu is associated with an authentic Christian society, a locus of respectful co-existence beyond colonial difference. With this rhetorical move, Poma pictured an alternative *topia* (not a *utopia*, since it is precisely bound

[158] Escobar (2000, 2003, 2020).

[159] Borda (1981); Mignolo (2002).

[160] Poma (1616); Mignolo (2005); Dussel (2009); Walsh (2013).

to a particular location, the Tawantinsuyu) for a good life based on a respectful living together of different ethnic groups, acknowledging both the colonizer's Christian values as well as his own Indigenous heritage. Of course, Guaman Poma's messianic interpretation of Christendom within Indigenous cosmogonical categories seems to allude to a form of liberation theology. However, the decolonial critique of Guaman Poma differs, for example, from Las Casas's critique, since he spoke for himself, from a subaltern standpoint, albeit adopting Christian arguments to make his point more comprehensible. The critiques of Poma and Las Casas are distinguished by the colonial difference. This is also the reason why Las Casas' critique was appreciated by both the Pope and the Spanish king, while Poma's writings would disappear in history's dustbin. The decolonial view has always been there, but it has been neglected and muted all the time.

Being situated at the other side of colonial difference, and thus, exposed to epistemic violence, subaltern groups readily perceive modern/colonial science as a means of oppression.[161] This is why decolonial resistance against the epistemological violence exercised by modern/colonial science and its universalist pretensions generally comes from the borders, being articulated in the interstices of colonial difference, in-between hegemonic and subaltern realities. In fact, decolonial thinking can only be *border thinking*. Walter Mignolo defines border thinking as "epistemology from the subaltern perspective".[162] Border thinking recognises that the politics of knowing are anchored within its local histories, in the context of global modern/colonial differences, and the resulting embodied and bodily classified experiences. It identifies the points of origination and traces its routes of dispersion within the geopolitical body-politics of knowledge.[163] Border thinking seeks to delink from imperial epistemology, from their grounding in theological and egological politics of knowledge, in the suppression of the sensing, of the body, and of the geo-historical location, which was actually the basis for its universalistic claims. To delink requires epistemological disobedience. Fanon's concept of sociogeny already implied the logic of being classified as ontologically, and thus, epistemologically inferior. However, to think and act differently is not to go backwards, not to become "pre-modern" again, but to think in a *non-modern* way, as an alternative, legitimate way of thinking of a future beyond the coloniality of modern narratives. The decolonial perspective is an anti-paradigm to modern/colonial hegemony and its unilinear history of supposedly inevitable "development". Border thinking means "thinking from non-Western categories of thought through Western categories of thought"[164] by means of a pluriversal, cosmopolitical dialogue. Decoloniality does not simply aim to negate modernity, but to transcend it, making different futures possible. Decolonial projects like Mignolo's border thinking, Dussel's "transmodernity" or Santo's "post-abyssal thought" aim to realise what modernity alone is not

---

[161] Meneses (2009).

[162] Mignolo (2002: 71).

[163] Mignolo (2013).

[164] Mignolo (2021: 330).

able to: the realisation of its emancipatory potential as a global project to free the negated Other.[165] In its quest for an alternative to the hegemonic modern/colonial discourse, border thinking adopts subaltern perspectives together with their own rationalities and practices. From these subaltern vantage points the colonial difference, which had been disguised by the universalisation of eurocentrism, and therefore, could not be seen (or sensed) from the hegemonic standpoint, comes to the fore. However, current academic discourse does not offer much space for a horizontal, equitable dialogue between different, non-colonial ways of knowing and sensing, since it categorically excludes subaltern views. M/S pursues creating alternative, decolonial spaces, "cracks"[166] in the colonial structures, where it is possible to think differently, to construe Other paradigms, border epistemologies beyond any universalisation of particularism, "new institutional and non-institutional locations from which the subaltern can speak and be heard".[167] However, the construction of such border epistemologies is about "changing the terms of conversation and not only its content".[168] The aim is not to come to another universal epistemology, but to substitute scientific monoculture with a *pluriverse*[169] of different forms of sensing, thinking, and knowing. It seeks *ecologies of knowledges*[170] that allow for a horizontal, cross-fertilising dialogue between modern scientific and other kinds of knowledge. Due to the colonial difference and the modern/colonial geopolitics of knowledge, ecologies of knowledges have to be a counter-hegemonic project, and therefore, be advanced from the borders, from the peripheries, from subaltern forms of being, from where the colonial character of modernity and its outrageous oppression of subaltern knowledge are crystal-clear facts. In a way that recalls Harding's *strong objectivity*, Santo's *ecologies of knowledges* do not disqualify modern science or deny its obvious effectiveness, but puts science in service of a counter-hegemonic project that acknowledges our infinite ignorance and seeks to know as much as possible about other epistemologies instead of allocating them within a hierarchical system of supposed truth values. Rather than devaluing or relativising science, or any other kind of knowledge, ecologies of knowledges enhance self-awareness about the limitations inherent to any particular way of understanding. No single system of knowledge can give a complete account of "reality" anyway, and no knowledge system is able to evaluate its own limitations without reference to other, external systems.[171] Only from the distance of the epistemological difference that

---

165 Garbe (2012).

166 Walsh (2017, 2023); Mignolo and Walsh (2018).

167 Grosfoguel (2011); compare also Escobar (2003, 2020).

168 Mignolo (2013: 133).

169 Blaser (2013, 2016); Cadena (2015); Cadena and Blaser (2018); Escobar (2020); Mignolo (2021).

170 Santos (2009a, b, 2018, 2022). "Ecologies of knowledges, intercultural translation, and the artisanship of practices are based on the idea of a mutual encounter and reciprocal dialogue that supports cross- fertilization and reciprocal exchanges of knowledges, cultures, and practices fighting against oppression. They promote prismatic perspectives between knowledges, cultures, and practices" (Santos 2018: 251–252).

171 Compare also Edgar Morin (2005) on this point.

divides one form of knowing from the other can its metaphysical framework come to the fore, showing both its epistemological and its transformative potential. Knowledge, in any universal sense, can only exist as a plurality of different interconnected forms of knowing, mutually learning from each other's limitations. The more a form of knowledge understands about its own limitations concerning its understanding of other forms of knowledge, the more it understands about its own limits as well as its real potentials. However, epistemological asymmetries are always also political, and in the case of modern/colonial science, involving a kind of *epistemological fascism*[172] that maximises differences and negates the existence of other epistemologies to impose its own hegemony. Accordingly, ecologies of knowledges can only become possible based on political and epistemological solidarity between different systems of knowledge, jointly working to overcome differences and maximise commensurability. However, complete commensurability or translatability can never be accomplished, since this would imply a reduction of epistemological difference to zero, thus, eliminating diversity. The only alternative, apart from relativism, is the pragmatic comparison of the concrete applicability of each kind of knowledge, and its translation into social practice. Boaventura de Souza Santos[173] draws a comparison between Pascal's pragmatic question concerning the benefits of believing in God or being an atheist, and our uncertainty concerning the possibility of a better world: is it better to believe or not to believe in a better world? Santos concludes, that to become really human, we need utopias. Once we define our priority in these terms, the demands shift from the truth value of knowledge as a representation of reality towards the effectiveness of knowledge as an intervention in reality. Since any knowledge is intrinsically incomplete, revealing only certain aspects while obfuscating others, any particular form of knowledge will also permit only certain interventions while inhibiting others. Incommensurability, therefore, does not preclude mutual enhancement within ecologies of knowledges, since a certain degree of incommensurability is actually necessary to maintain epistemological difference as an inventive resource—incommensurability is, however, invoked as an argument to defend abyssal thinking.

To get started on the decolonial project, Santos proposes a new research programme to evaluate different kinds of knowledge concerning their interventions in the real world and their usefulness as tools in the struggle against oppression within particular contexts.[174] Such a pragmatic evaluation invokes an understanding of knowledge in terms of social practices, "ways of knowing, rather than knowledges".[175] Hence, "knowledge-practices" are always embodied and political—although the modern/colonial sciences tend to disavow this fact, claiming to represent value-free theories. However, there is no theory without practice, just as there is no practice

---

172 Santos (2009a, b, 2018).

173 Santos (2009b).

174 Idem 2018.

175 Idem: 3. Of course, this conception of knowledge in terms of a situated social practice goes back to Marxist, constructionist, and particularly, feminist theories of knowledge and science as discussed earlier in this chapter.

without theory.[176] Moreover, subalternised *epistemologies of the South*[177] do not distinguish between theory and practice, nor between the true, the good or the just, since they are born out of practices of resistance and struggle against oppression; they rather deliberately emphasise their performative, local and contextual character as well as the importance of oral tradition, emotional, mystical or spiritual experiences. The construction of a post-abyssal science by means of a dialogue between different knowledge practices therefore demands methods and spaces for intercultural translation enabling reciprocal dialogue and cross-fertilising exchange of thoughts and experiences. In other words, the decolonisation of modern/colonial sciences—be it in terms of a *world of sciences*,[178] *border thinking*,[179] *decolonial investigation*,[180] *ecologies of knowledges*,[181] *post-abyssal sciences*,[182] or *pluriversal politics*[183]—crucially depends on new (embodied) practices of knowing, sensing and doing.

Decolonial Practices of Knowing

Advocates of decolonial projects frequently refer to existing "epistemologies of the South" and decolonial practices that have been developed and enacted by subaltern groups in the global South.[184] Among the most cited examples are experiences led by Latin American Indigenous movements like the Zapatistas, their educational programmes ("*escuelitas*", Unitierra) and their dictum of a "world where many worlds fit", or the Andean conceptions of *buen vivir* (good living) and *Pachamama,* and the subsequent establishment of rights of Nature/*Pachamama* and for a "good living" in the new constitutions of Bolivia and Ecuador, as well as the Indigenous concept of *interculturality*.[185] The intrusion of these alternative ontological, epistemic and ethical conceptions and practices into hegemonic political discourse may well be seen as a game changer in the geopolitics of knowledge.[186] However, decolonial authors also emphasise that truly transformative theory and practice can only emerge from lived experiences of struggle against oppression and systemic violence.

[176] Mignolo and Walsh (2018).

[177] Santos (2009a, 2018, 2022)

[178] Harding (2015).

[179] Mignolo (2002).

[180] Idem 2021.

[181] Santos (2009a, b, 2018).

[182] Idem 2021.

[183] Escobar (2020).

[184] e.g. Walsh (2013, 2017); Solano et al. (2018a, b, c); Santos (2018); Escobar (2020).

[185] ETSA 1996; López 1996; Rappaport 2005; Ramos & Rappaport 2005; Little 2005; Linhart (2008); Walsh (2009, 2013, 2017, 2021); Harding (2015); Cadena and Blaser (2018); Santos (2018); Escobar (2020); Mignolo (2021).

[186] Arturo Escobar (2020) speaks of examples of "pluriversal politics", Boaventura de Sousa Santos (2009a, b, 2018) calls them "epistemologies of the South" and Walter Mignolo (2021) even evokes the beginning of a "third nomos of the earth".

In fact, Latin American Indigenous movements have long been developing their own decolonial projects in the course of their struggle for recognition, autonomy and land rights. From the 1960s onwards, Indigenous groups received significant support from liberation theologists and leftist intellectuals, contributing to the theoretical conception of their fight against colonial/modern epistemic violence in terms of a counter-hegemonic project. The pedagogical approach of Paulo Freire[187] and Orlando Fals Borda's[188] method of *participatory action research* (PAR) have been of particular significance for Indigenous and other grassroots movements in Latin America as well as in other parts of the global South.[189] Both approaches explicitly establish alternative local practices for the collective construction of counter-hegemonic knowledge. *Indigenous intercultural education* (IIE) is one of the most vivid examples that epitomizes the importance of these alternative practices.

While, initially, Indigenous movements had focussed on civil and land rights, education soon gained a central role in their struggle for cultural autonomy. What began with local programmes for *bilingual school education* gradually advanced into a complex conception of *Intercultural Indigenous Education (IIE)*, gaining a crucial role for the reviving of Indigenous identities, languages and ancestral knowledge and the collective construction of their own visions of "good living". During the last three decades, Indigenous populations not only gained their own Indigenous schools and their own university courses in Indigenous education, but some of them also engaged in the construction of their own *intercultural Indigenous universities*.[190]

The concept of *interculturality*,[191] which had been developed by Latin American Indigenous movements during the 1990s, has been central to IIE. Although initially not being directly related to M/C, interculturality stands for a decolonial project with striking parallels and overlaps to M/Cs aims and concepts such as border (feel-)

[187] Freire (1987, 1996).

[188] Borda (1981).

[189] E.g. Walsh (2013, 2017); Harding (2015); Mignolo and Walsh (2018); Santos (2018); Escobar (2020). "At the intellectual level, the epistemologies of the South would not have been possible without two major proposals that revolutionized pedagogy and the social sciences at the end of the 1960s and during the 1970s: Paulo Freire's pedagogy of the oppressed and Orlando Fals Borda's participatory action research (PAR). These two powerful proposals helped in decisive ways to formulate the epistemologies of the South" (Santos 2018: 253).

[190] These "universities" are characterised by a huge variety of different approaches, ranging from independent small-scale local initiatives (like the UNCIA in Ecuador, the Universidad Indígena de Venezuela, the Yutsilal Bahlumilal Pluriversity in Mexico), autonomous Indigenous universities led by regional Indigenous organizations (like the UAIIN in Colombia), public Indigenous universities (like the Amawtay Wasi in Ecuador, the three UNIBOLs in Bolivia, and various intercultural Indigenous universities in Mexico), national programmes for Indigenous post-graduate students at public universities (like the PROLIND in Brazil), reformulation of the national educational system for a pluri-cultural society (like in Bolivia under Evo Morales), and international post-graduate programmes for Indigenous leaderships (like the PROEIB Andes). For a detailed discussion of Indigenous higher education in Latin America see Linhart (2008) and Soto (2019).

[191] Ramos et al. (2004); Ramos and Rappaport (2005); Linhart (2008); Walsh (2009, 2013, 2017); Harding (2015); Mignolo and Walsh (2018); Santos (2018); Soto (2019); Escobar (2020).

thinking, epistemic violence/equity and ecology of knowledge. Interculturality, however, emerged from lived practice, not from an intellectual discourse about practice.

On the one hand, interculturality points to the societal project of a pluri-national state that goes beyond multiculturalism, that is, beyond tolerating cultural diversity within the nation state. Interculturality envisions a society that defines itself as a plurality of co-equal cultural and ethnic groups, who not only tolerate each other, but who enter into a "dialogue of knowledges" governed by "epistemic equity".[192] On the other hand, interculturality has always been the lived Indigenous practice of survival and organizing resistance. In fact, most, if not all Indigenous organisations and educational programmes—as well as most of their theoretical underpinnings—were an achievement of intercultural dialogue and collaboration between different Indigenous groups together with non-Indigenous activists and intellectuals (typically liberation theologists and anthropologists).[193] In this sense, Indigenous organizations and educational programmes have not only been practicing interculturality for the last 50 years or so—they can be understood as an offspring of intercultural practices. Interculturality, thus, appears to be rather a post hoc conceptionalisation of existing practices rather than a theoretical concept.

IIE, as understood by autonomous Indigenous universities like the *Universidad Autónoma Intercultural Indígena* (UAIIN) in Colombia and the *Pluriversidad Amawtay Wasi* in Ecuador, represents a radical counter-paradigm to the universalist self-understanding of modern/colonial sciences.

As a political project, IIE envisages a plurinational society based on an equitable dialogue between different, self-determined cultures as a precondition for a utopian vision of a radically inclusive democracy and a civilisational transformation towards a sustainable living in cosmic harmony.[194] As a pedagogical paradigm within this socio-political and spiritual utopia, IIE creates epistemic spaces for the collective construction of counter-hegemonic visions and knowledge practices based on a critical dialogue among diverging cosmovisions. As an alternative research paradigm, it puts the local communities at the control of research agendas to help them understand their situation from their own perspectives and develop their life projects (*proyectos de vida*) for a good living *(buen vivir)*, however within a global context and based on both hegemonic and ancestral knowledge, but fit for current and future challenges.

Research frameworks like the CRISSAC (*Crianza y Siembra de Sabidurías y Conocimientos*; Nurturing and Sowing of Wisdom and Knowledge), such as those being developed and employed by the UAIIN, deliberately invert the logic of conventional modern/colonial education and research and install their own

---

[192] Linhart (2008, 2012); Walsh (2009, 2021, 2023); Harding (2015); Macas et al. (2017); Macas (2018); Soto (2019); Escobar (2020); CRIC (2021); Mignolo (2021).

[193] Ramos and Rappaport (2005); Rappaport (2005).

[194] Ramiro Huanca Soto (2019) analysis different approaches to IIE concerning their capacity to bring about onto-epistemic *pachakuti*, referring to a cyclical renewal of the *pacha* (space-time/nature/cosmos/unity of dualities) through the re-establishment of cosmic harmony.

counter-hegemonic knowledge practices within the academic sphere. Rather than seeking another universal epistemology or method, CRISSAC is a pragmatic approach to knowledge as a tool for enhancing the self-determined flourishing of each community—including past and future generations, human and non-human beings—in cosmic harmony with life in general. Each community defines its own CRISSAC according to its needs and cosmovisions along a common set of shared principles, such as: reciprocity, relationality, complementarity, communality, spirituality, care of life and cosmic harmony, mindfulness and attentiveness to Nature and the Ancestors, intercultural dialogue, unity of theory and practice, reflexive auto-research, mutual teaching and learning through unlearning, just to name some of them.

> CRISSAC is a feel-living process of nature, family and community for recreating, deepening, visualising, constructing, reproducing and sharing wisdom and knowledge, keeping in mind the spiritual, cultural, territorial, autonomous and identitary principles of the peoples' and cultures' life plans (CRIC 2021: 10).[195]

CRISSAC is a preliminary result and part of a long-lasting living process of collective, reflexive self-investigation among different communities from different Indigenous nations, Indigenous and non-Indigenous activists and academics. Accordinly, it has been built around a complex mesh of ontological, epistemic, methodological and axiological conceptions. Its cosmological embedding in a reality made up by a living fabric of relations between visible and invisible beings implies introducing spiritual, bodily and collective practices as essential research methods together with a scientific ethos based on an ethics of respect, care, attentiveness and reflexive mindfulness.

However, this radically different way of knowing and co-creating is neither new nor limited to Indigenous universities. Often cited Indigenous conceptions like *buen vivir*, *Pachamama,* rights of Nature or a "world where many worlds fit" have all been elaborated in the course of some kind of CRISSAC-like procedures—even though they might not have been conceptualized in these terms.

Intercultural Indigenous education is, therefore, much more than education for Indigenous children; it is a central pillar of a decolonial project against epistemic violence; it is the vertebral dispositive for the construction of a radical transformation based on an epistemic shift from a colonial, oppressive logic towards a liberating, dialogical practice—which is also a shift from a representational model of truth towards a pragmatic notion of knowledge as lived practice.

Some Critical Remarks on M/C

Unfortunately, the history of the last decades painfully shows the dependence of these noble utopian projects on political reality. The cyclic returns of the empire, the

---

[195] My translation from the original: "La CRISSAC es un proceso sentivivencial de la naturaleza, familia y comunidad, para recrear, profundizar, visibilizar, construir, reproducir y compartir las sabidurías y conocimientos, teniendo en cuenta los principios espirituales, culturales, territoriales, autonómicos e identitarios de los planes y proyectos de vida de los pueblos y culturas" (CRIC 2021: 10).

rise and fall of Latin American socialist governments resulted in a harsh drawback for all those who presumed to dream of a different, better, more decent world. However, these recent historical developments only confirmed the theoretical core of counter-hegemonic approaches like decoloniality and interculturality: the entanglement of systemic and epistemological violence. Meanwhile, many intercultural educational projects have either been co-opted by national governments or returned to the resistance mode so typical of the Indigenous survival strategy—like the first Indigenous Bolivian president, Evo Morales, once said: "What counts is to resist" (*"Basta resistir"*).[196] But the progress that has been made during the last three decades in constructing intercultural education also unsheathed some fundamental conceptual and practical limitations inherent in approaches like decoloniality and interculturality.

One major problem is related to the contradictory role of essentialism as invoked by these approaches. On the one hand, essentialist constructions of "cultural" and "racial" difference are fiercely attacked for their crucial role as epistemic dispositives for the maintenance of the colonial difference and the epistemic violence that both sustains and disguises the dark, colonial side of modernity.[197] On the other hand, however, decoloniality assumes colonial difference to be the essential denominator for distinguishing between hegemonic and decolonial standpoints, delegitimating the first, while ultimately essentialising the latter.[198] In this sense, M/C has

[196] Quoted in Walsh (2009: 234).

[197] For example, Mignolo (2021) notes: "Replacing "cultural differences" with "colonial and imperial differences" helps change the terms, and not just the content, of the conversation. The first term, "cultural differences," hides power differentials, that is, hides coloniality. The second, "colonial and imperial differences," exposes it. "Culture" is the term that in the eighteenth century and in the Western secular world replaced "religion" in a new discourse of colonial expansion. The notion of cultural relativism transformed the coloniality of power into a semantic problem. If we accept that actions, objects, beliefs, and so on are merely culturally relative, we hide the coloniality of power from which different cultures came into being in the first place" (idem: 219). "Pluriversality instead requires changing the terms of the conversation, to imagine and act toward abandoning (delinking from) the concept of "culture" to focus on decolonial "projects" that no given "culture" could contain." (idem: 223).

[198] Ramón Grosfoguel (2011) explicitly addresses the dilemma of essentialism implied both in Eurocentrism and in "third-world fundamentalism", as he calls it, and its "rhetoric of an essentialist 'pure outside space' or 'absolute exteriority' to modernity". Since the modern/colonial world-system did not leave any ethnic group, no matter how remote their homelands, unaffected by its epistemological imperialism, all existing kinds of knowledge, including modern/colonial hegemonic knowledge itself, are kind of modern/non-modern hybrids. Border thinking, on the other hand, would acknowledge this inescapable hybrid co-presence of modern/colonial episteme. "Instead of rejecting modernity to retreat into a fundamentalist absolutism, border epistemologies subsume/redefine the emancipatory rhetoric of modernity from the cosmologies and epistemologies of the subaltern, located in the oppressed and exploited side of the colonial difference, towards a decolonial liberation struggle for a world beyond eurocentered modernity" (idem: 27). But, what is it exactly that distinguishes "subaltern" from "hegemonic" cosmologies? If the only distinction is defined by its situatedness on either side of colonial difference, dividing the "oppressors" from the "oppressed", why should the "oppressed" necessarily be the keeper of a "non-modern" or howsoever "counter-hegemonic" knowledge? Grosfoguel himself asserts that it "is important here

been accused of being a post-occidental reductionist construction that idealises certain groups, like "Indigenous" people, "Afro-Americans", or the "subaltern" in general, as having a special "decolonial" potential.[199] This inconsistency also manifests in conflicting internal relations between the participants of decolonial and intercultural projects. For example, most members of the group associated with M/C are Latin American academics, and therefore, essentialised as "subaltern" intellectuals. However, some of them, like Walter Mignolo (ironically the author who most emphatically defends colonial difference as the decisive criterium to define the decolonial standpoint) work and live in the US, while others, like Boaventura de Souza Santos and Immanuel Wallerstein, have been marginalised within the group for being from Europe and the US, respectively, and thus, not quite representing "subaltern" views.[200] Similarly, Indigenous activists have been questioned by their communities for not representing the "authentic" ancestral traditions, since many of them are forced to live in the cities (due to their work as activists or academics), and because their intellectual projections include "Western" concepts, albeit reinterpreted from an "Indigenous" standpoint. However, concepts like standpoint epistemology, interculturality, border thinking and ecology of knowledge suggest that Other kinds of knowledge may serve as a resource for reflecting on one's own knowledge. Of course, such reflections may, and actually intend to alter all kinds of knowledge involved in the process. Change and mutual exchange is not necessarily negative—all knowledge is subject to constant change anyway—as long as the encounter between different kinds of knowledge is based on an equitable dialogue, where unavoidable epistemic power-relations between different positionalities are made explicit. The problem is rather rooted in the very distinction between ones "Own" in contrast to "Other" knowledges, be it "hegemonic" versus "subaltern", or

---

to distinguish the 'epistemic location' from the 'social location.' The fact that one is socially located in the oppressed side of power relations does not automatically mean that he/she is epistemically thinking from a subaltern epistemic location. Precisely, the success of the modern/colonial world-system consists in making subjects that are socially located in the oppressed side of the colonial difference, to think epistemically like the ones on the dominant positions" (idem: 7). So, by means of what criteria should we distinguish merely "socially" subaltern from "epistemically" subaltern views, if not along ethical and cultural identities or diverging cosmological conceptions, that is, without ultimately essentialising the "Others" as "non-moderns" or "non-Westerners"? However, Grosfoguel insists: "I am not claiming an epistemic populism where knowledge produced from below is automatically an epistemic subaltern knowledge. What I am claiming is that all knowledges are epistemically located in the dominant or the subaltern side of the power relations and that this is related to the geo- and body-politics of knowledge" (ibidem).

[199] Garbe (2012).

[200] Curiously, Mignolo finally accepted Santos' argument, that Portugal is kind of a European periphery, which would qualify him to participate in the "subaltern" discussions of M/C: "Granted, Santos is not focusing on Colombia or Latin America. However, the marginality of Portugal, as the south of Europe, allows for a perception of the social sciences different from that which one might have from the north" (Mignolo 2002: 64). So, I might, then, ask myself about my own position between my "hegemonic" origin as a white European (albeit being the son of an (subaltern?) immigrant) and my later life as a "subaltern" lower class immigrant and indigenist activist in Latin America: Am I qualified to speak from a "subaltern" standpoint?!

"Western" versus "Indigenous", any of these categories ends up reproducing essentialist notions of "Us" and the "Others". However, once knowledge is conceived of in terms of situated, embodied practices that are positioned along classifications of the body (gender, race, etc.), social and geopolitical position within the modern/colonial world-system, epistemological differences are inextricably bound to the identities being incessantly produced by this system. Hence the difficulty in overcoming identity politics.

Another criticism is that M/C's conceptions lag behind its radical rhetoric.[201] Although many authors of M/C claim a radically new and non-modern, decolonial position towards modernity/coloniality, their own discourse is deeply rooted in modern academic discourse and does not overcome logocentrism. All the rhetoric rejection of "Western", Eurocentric, hegemonic discourse notwithstanding, M/C extensively refers to Marxist concepts and post-structural authors like Foucault, Derrida, Deleuze and Guattari as well as to other European philosophers like Heidegger, Husserl, and Levinas. And while Mignolo rejects Wallerstein's world-system theory for representing the hegemonic side of colonial difference, after adding the adjective "modern/colonial" to "world-system", he continues using Wallerstein's theory as if the relabelling would have "subalternised" it. It is true that M/C also draws on genuinely Latin American currents, like liberation theology, dependence theory, participatory action research, and pedagogy of the oppressed; however, these approaches were already quite radical in themselves, and one may doubt whether M/C really managed to be even more radical. Actually, these previous approaches either derived from practice or had already accomplished the transformation from theory into practice, which M/C is still rather talking about.[202]

These critiques notwithstanding, M/C deserves the merit of having successfully merged counter-hegemonic theories and practices from both the centre and peripheries, "North" and "South", from Marx to feminist, subaltern and post-colonial studies, into a consistent theoretical framework with a solid hold in lived practices. However, although M/C only refers to and conceptually informs already-existing

[201] Garbe (2012).

[202] In an attempt to bridge this gap, Mignolo and Walsh (2018) argue that by conceiving their theorizing as part of the "praxis of living", they are thus "delinking" it from the modern conceptual distinction between theory versus praxis. "For us, theory is doing and doing is thinking. Are you not doing something when you theorize or analyze concepts? Isn't doing something praxis? And from praxis—understood as thought-reflection-action, and thought-reflection on this action—do we not also construct theory and theorize thought? By disobeying the long-held belief that you first theorize and then apply, or that you can engage in blind praxis without theoretical analysis and vision, we locate our thinking/doing in a different terrain. This terrain is rooted in the praxis of living and in the idea of theory-and-as-praxis and praxis-and-as-theory, and in the interdependence and continuous flow of movement of both. It is in this movement that decoloniality is enacted and, at the same time, rendered possible" (idem: 7). However, writing academic texts about the unity of "theory-and-as-praxis" still is a knowledge practice quite different from the lived, embodied, spiritual practices that are common "praxis-and-as-theory" among Indigenous and other grass-roots movements.

practices and methods, and has not yet converted its theoretical findings into a concrete methodological proposal or lived practical experiences.[203]

Meanwhile, experiences in the field of Indigenous intercultural education have been crystallising practical challenges concomitant with the construction of spaces and methods for a collective construction of such border epistemologies.[204] While multiple difficulties are encountered, differing according to each particular context, most of them gather around two general issues: one being related to the geopolitics of knowledge, that is, the inevitability of colonial difference and the resulting hegemony of modern/colonial science; the other, even more tricky problem results from the body-politics modern/colonial geopolitics of knowledge are based upon, and which emerge from the situated, embodied character of knowledge. The first issue complicates the establishment of a truly horizontal dialogue between the subaltern Indigenous, and the not-quite-as-subaltern non-Indigenous participants. No matter how many times all participants affirm their honest respect for the Others' views, modern/colonial sciences will always be the "universal" point of reference for any construction of (local) counter-hegemonic alternatives. Although the terms of enunciation are definitively changed, guaranteeing mutual respect and recognition, the ruling modern/colonial geopolitics of knowledge keep on impinging on any epistemological discussion, irrespective of the enunciator's intention. Moreover, since Indigenous education envisages the formation of a new generation of *border intellectuals*[205] (professionals both in modern/colonial "scientific" discourse and "traditional", "ancestral" knowledge practices) prepared to cope with the challenges of our globalised modern/colonial reality, the knowledge necessary for any effective intervention in this scenario will always have to be translatable through the terms of "Western" hegemonic discourse. The second issue, concerning the bodily situatedness of knowledge, has deep implications for the construction of alternative spaces and methods of knowledge production. Strictly speaking, "knowledge" as an abstract something with its own existence apart from practice does not exist; instead, knowledge exists exclusively through lived practices of knowing, learning, and being related to the world. Consequently, knowledge cannot be separated from the practices and spaces of knowledge production. How, then, could it be possible to

---

[203] This bad habit of writing hundreds and thousands of pages about the voidness of abstract theory and the urgency of putting all those noble worlds into lived practices is not limited to the authors of M/C, but unfortunately, something they share with all of us, critical modern/colonial intellectuals. Sometimes, when I am writing page after page about the necessity of establishing new practices instead of yet another theory, I feel like an alcoholic who, after one of those terrible hangovers, declares they will never drink again, and like him, I swear I will never ever waste my time again with writing theoretical treatises about the need to start off with just doing things. However, like the alcoholic who would grab the next bottle as soon as his headache eases, we modern/colonial theory-junkies will grab our pen again the next day, writing once again about the need to get up and start doing things instead of just talking and writing about them. Of course, we may argue that writing is part of the practice of knowledge production, too. But, deep in our souls we all know this is like drinking the next beer the following morning to "cure" our hangover.

[204] Linhart (2008).

[205] Rappaport (2005).

transform a "school" or a "university" into a space for the construction of "Indigenous" forms of border knowledge, or ecologies of knowledge where Other, non-modern/colonial forms of knowing are practiced and put into dialogue? The conceptions of what a "school" or a "university" is or ought to be are deeply rooted in European history. These spaces are related to very particular forms of body-politics aiming to reproduce discipline and obedience to modern/colonial order.[206] Is it possible to teach, for example, ancestral practices in a classroom, or in an auditorium? And if not, would it help to reshape the architecture, say, building an Indigenous "pluriversity"[207] in the design of a traditional *maloca*[208]? Or is it necessary to relocate the whole process of knowledge construction to its places of origin, into the Indigenous community, the family or remote places in the forest or mountains? What would it take to transform our current monocultural universities into "pluriversities"[209]? To my knowledge there are no ready answers to such questions; there are, however, countless experiences from subaltern grassroots movements, popular and Indigenous intercultural schools, uni- and pluriversities experimenting with innovative methods and spaces of (un-)learning and knowing seeking to enable the construction of border epistemologies, and aiming to transcend the limits of modern/colonial science and its methodological and epistemological impositions.

4.4 Should We Worry About the End of Truth?

In 2004, after 25 years of intensive publishing on the construed nature of scientific facts, Bruno Latour wrote a paper in which he puts all his work to the test:

> Was I foolishly mistaken? […] Was I wrong to participate in the invention of this field known as science studies? (Latour 2004: 227)

In our current "post-truth" era—which had been heralded by the blatant lies of the Bush administration, finally culminating in Trump's coinage of "alternative facts" to cover his lunatic distortions of otherwise crystal-clear facts—well established scientific findings seem to be the last stronghold of reason. So, why should we debunk science's supposed objectivity and put it at one benchmark together with any other spiritual, religious, or whatever "unproven belief"? Is this iconoclasm not a welcome gate for all kinds of unsound and blatantly ideological claims to invade the sacred halls of wisdom? When conservatives use the supposed relativity of scientific knowledge to promote "alternative facts" to "prove" that, in "fact", there is

---

[206] Foucault (1981).

[207] For the discussion of these challenging contradictions and the answers Indigenous uni- and pluriversities have been developing compare for example Linhart (2008); Macas et al. (2017); Soto (2019); CRIC (2021).

[208] As has been done by some Indigenous schools and universities (e.g. the Universidad Indigena de Venezuela).

[209] Santos (2018).

no climate change at all; when Protestant fundamentalists demand the suspension of evolutionary "theory" and gender "ideology" from school curricula in exchange for creationism and geo-centric cosmology; when neo-fascist conspiracy theorists flood social media with outlandish stories about secret societies of devil-worshipping Jews of alien descent planning a new world order; finally, in these dangerous times, facing the advance of irrationality and violent fundamentalism, can we account for putting science's credibility at risk, for our questioning of scientific universalism, or for divulging the epistemic violence wielded by modern rationality? Or in the words of Latour: "Has knowledge-slash-power been co-opted of late by the National Security Agency? Has *Discipline and Punish* become the bedtime reading of Mr. Ridge"? Are we responsible for people's run on conspiracy theories because we have been insisting on showing the way in which power is based on the production and control of "truth"? Have we written a Machiavellian manual for the manipulation of the masses[210]? Latour's answers are, as usually, a lot more indigestible than his questions. Of course, Latour reiterated his defence of his own approach as an attempt not to do away with empiricism, but to enhance it.[211] He detected the problem rather in our modern type of criticism, which either debunks subjective experience (as a mere epiphenomenon of determinism) or the objectivity of facts (as a mere construction of our minds). Since we always use only one of these two modes of criticism selectively, depending on whose view we aim to expose as "fetishism", their obvious incoherence never becomes apparent. Accordingly, any accusation of fetishism (be it against science or any other kind of knowledge) would simply be an act of barbarism.[212] Latour followed Whitehead's notion of the bifurcation of nature as imposed by the factual gaze of modern science, producing "totally implausible, unrealistic, unjustified definitions of what it is to deal with things", and urged us to turn our attention away from "matters of fact" and towards "matters of concern".[213] The limitations of "matters of fact" as well as of modern criticism result from a

[210] "Of course, conspiracy theories are an absurd deformation of our own arguments, but, like weapons smuggled through a fuzzy border to the wrong party, these are our weapons nonetheless. In spite of all the deformations, it is easy to recognize, still burnt in the steel, our trademark: *Made in Criticalland*" (idem: 230).

[211] "My argument is that a certain form of critical spirit has sent us down the wrong path, encouraging us to fight the wrong enemies and, worst of all, to be considered as friends by the wrong sort of allies because of a little mistake in the definition of its main target. The question was never to get away from facts but closer to them, not fighting empiricism but, on the contrary, renewing empiricism" (idem: 231).

[212] Actually, this observation had already been made by Ludwik Fleck (1981), some 70 years before Latour published his paper (compare the first section of this chapter).

[213] "It is not the case that there would exist solid matters of fact and that the next step would be for us to decide whether they will be used to explain something. It is not the case either that the other solution is to attack, criticize, expose, historicize those matters of fact, to show that they are made up, interpreted, flexible. It is not the case that we should rather flee out of them into the mind or add to them symbolic or cultural dimensions; the question is that matters of fact are a poor proxy of experience and of experimentation and, I would add, a confusing bundle of polemics, of epistemology, of modernist politics that can in no way claim to represent what is requested by a realist attitude" (Latour 2004: 245).

muddling of questions about what we perceive with questions about how we know. What we would need instead, Latour recommended, is another kind of constructive criticism leading to a *multiplication of views* instead of exposing all views as equally illusive. But what exactly does this tell us about our initial problem concerning the misuse of constructionist approaches to "truth" in the hands of those "bad guys"? Ultimately, Latour's argument indicates that the whole quandary with post-truth politics is rooted not only in post-modern deconstructionism and constructionist accounts of science, but rather in the very epistemological/ontological (bifurcated) constitution of modern knowledge/being. Accordingly, post-structuralism and constructionism have been part of the problem, but not its origin. In addition, these theories demonstrated the limits of modern epistemology, not only by criticising it, but eventually by failing to transcend it by means of criticism.

Once again, we arrived at the point of departure for research programmes like M/C, and the need for an ecology of knowledge able to transcend the limitations of Our modern/colonial, universalist thought prisons; that is, we need to engage in an equitable dialogue with Other, subaltern knowledges. However, now we are faced with an even more desperate problem: In order to sincerely take the Others' views seriously, we need to assume that, in principle, their views are as valid as Our "scientific" findings. But what if creationists, Jihadists and neo-fascist "conspirationists" take a seat at our round table, claiming their right to be taken seriously as well? Are they not subalternised groups, being demonised and oppressed by hegemonic discourse all the time? Do they not deserve to partake in our ecology of knowledge? No? Why not? Because they are fundamentalists and our aim is to fight any kind of fundamentalism? But can we be sure that other subaltern or Indigenous groups do not aspire to hegemony? Of course, we may establish non-universalism as our most fundamental norm, arguing that intolerance cannot be tolerated, and maybe we convince the creationists to stay on their flat earth while leaving us in peace on our global planet. But would this mean taking them seriously? Of course not! But why not take them seriously? Isn't science as construed as the Bible? Obviously, such a naive relativism would hardly get anywhere, let alone transcend the limits of modern science. The problem is not that theological knowledge is per se inferior or not as "true" or "objective" as scientific knowledge (although this might be the case). The problem is rather that we might not want to live in a world governed by religious fanaticism, fascism or any other form of totalitarianism. For most of us, creationism, jihadism or racial hatred simply do not appear to be promising ingredients in our recipe for constructing a better world. Nobody can seriously claim to know with certainty that God does not exist, not even the most stubborn positivist, but few of Us moderns would like to return to the ancient regime of a theocracy. We do not reject creationism because we know it can only be wrong (although many things we believe tell us that it might not be the most convincing theory), but because it stands for a worldview, an ethics, an aesthetic, a way of life we simply cannot identify with. We instinctively fear the possible results of believing and adopting such views because of the *impact* it would have on our lives.

The problem of relativism (and its misuse by the "bad guys") only arises if we try to deconstruct universalism by disclaiming scientific knowledge as a social construction—that is, by a transcendental critique which ultimately leads to iconoclasm and the end of truth. But once universalism is debunked as an instrument of power, the truth value of scientific knowledge ceases to be the central question—what counts, instead, are its concrete effects; in other words, an immanent analysis of modern science and Other kinds of knowledge understood as particular kinds of body-politics and practices of power/knowledge will reveal the kind of worlds each of them produces, or promises/threatens to produce. Now, from this pragmatic viewpoint, the differences between modern/colonial science, religious fundamentalism, and Other subaltern kinds of knowledge are not relative at all, since they represent radically different *possible futures*.

The whole question about the validity or acceptability of different "truths" is thus put down to a question of decision. But, which decision is the right one? Although pragmatism offers a solution to epistemological relativism, it is challenged by the problem of moral relativism. In James'[214] pragmatism, this problem is solved by accepting that conventions are not reducible to, or derivable from any foundational, general principles—they are rather solutions to particular problems. Isabelle Stengers[215] illustrates this solution with the decision for or against modern scepticism (as discussed by Latour 2004): in engaging sceptical reasoning about witches as well as about witch hunters, we inherit the witch hunter's operation of eradicating the (supposedly) irrational Other.

> Certainly the witch hunters are no longer among us and we no longer take seriously the accusation of devil worshipping that was once levelled at witches. Rather, our milieu is defined by the modern pride in being able to interpret both witches and witch hunting in terms of social, linguistic, cultural, or political constructions and beliefs. What this pride ignores, however, is that we are the heirs of an operation of cultural and social eradication—the forerunner of what was committed elsewhere in the name of civilization and reason. Anything that classifies the memory of such operations as unimportant or irrelevant only furthers the success of those operations.
>
> In this sense, our pride in our critical power to 'know better' than both the witches and the witch hunters makes us the heirs of witch hunting (Stengers 2012: 6).

According to Stengers, we are obliged (with James) to accept this effective option to be some kind of "Us", demanding to situate ourselves through the decisions we take. Instead of criticising its epistemological shortcomings as a transcendent approach to truth, Stengers's outlook presents science in terms of an immanent *ecology of practices*,[216] with each practice having its particular situated effectiveness. However, the practitioners are not necessarily aware of the whole range of the effectiveness of the processes they are operating, often including unintended effects, always being at risk of good intentions leading to disaster. In a globalised world

[214] James (1981).

[215] Stengers (2009, 2012); Debaise and Stengers (2022); Stengers et al. (2023).

[216] Stengers (2005a, b, 2010, 2011, 2018b). "Ecology is, then, the science of multiplicities, disparate causalities, and unintentional creations of meaning. The field of ecological questions is one where the consequences of the meanings we create, the judgments we produce and to which we assign the status of 'fact', concerning what is primary and what is secondary, must be addressed immediately, whether those consequences are intentional or unforeseen" (Stengers 2010: 34–35).

facing multiple global crises, in these "catastrophic times",[217] each decision affects a lot of potential victims while excluding them from the making of those decision. Our inevitable decisions in the face of a particular problem of concern to become a certain "us" and not another, therefore, have to be taken "in the presence of" the muted victims of our decisions. However, Stengers's[218] concerns about the ethical and highly political character of knowing go much deeper. In our "dangerous world, where nothing stands to reason, where any proposition may be falsified, where we who 'invented politics' also produced the means to reduce it to a largely empty game, leaving outside what was at work, producing, or destroying, our worlds",[219] we are too quick in taking our decisions about the world we might aspire to, about our desirable utopias. This is because Our politics depart from the assumption that we know about the cosmological foundations of the world (while the Others don't). However, there is no such cosmos in terms of a fixed, knowable entity, no foundations for universal truth, and thus, no universal grounds for universally "good" decisions. Rather there are different forms of worldmaking each based upon utopian cosmovisions, unknowns rather than knowns. Hence, Stengers's "cosmopolitical proposal"[220] urges us to "slow down" before blindly opting for a particular cosmos to serve as the stage of our utopian politics for a "better" world.

> […] the idea is precisely to slow down the construction of this common world, to create a space for hesitation regarding what it means to say "good" (Stengers 2005a: 995).[221]

Reflecting on what kind of being we might become through our choices "in the presence of" the victims might help us become another being than we would have become otherwise, and thus, help us envisage other modes of existence, other worlds, diverging cosmoi, each with their particular matters of concern and pregnant with different possible futures.

However, becoming in the presence of other, diverging cosmoi and their matters of concern does not mean coming to a common understanding about some kind of shared foundations. Much to the contrary, cosmopolitics is about accepting the irreducibility of divergence and coming to terms with the absence of a universal foundation once and forever. The question would thus not be to eliminate divergence, but

[217] Stengers (2015); Stengers et al. (2023).

[218] Stengers (2005a, 2010, 2011, 2018a, b); Stengers et al. (2023).

[219] Stengers (2005a, b: 999).

[220] Stengers (2005a, b).

[221] "But slow science is not about scientists taking full account of the messy complications of the world. It is about them facing up to the challenge of developing a collective awareness of the particularity and selective character of their own thought-style. This, however, should not be confused with a call for lucid reflexivity to be developed inside thought collectives. It is rather a matter of collective learning through the test of an encounter with dissenting voices around issues of common interest. Such a learning process demands of modern collectives what I would characterise as a 'becoming-civilised'. So slowing down the sciences means civilising scientists […]" (Stengers 2018b: position 1644).

to negotiate local concerns and obligations[222] without insulting diverging views by questioning their truth value. Rather than coming to a common understanding about "truth", the aim would rather be to avoid war, to find a way towards peaceful coexistence—despite all the irreducible divergences—and, eventually, letting oneself be transformed in the process of becoming in the presence of the Other. The "truth" that might be the outcome of these negotiations is "what succeeds in producing a communication between divergent parties".[223] The pragmatics of ethics is, thus, about bringing diverging views and demands to the test concerning their capability to bring about "better worlds" in the sense of "new modes of composing, maximizing the possibilities for coexistence of what in every epoch seem destined to exclude each other".[224]

So, maybe we should give up being experts and start becoming cosmopolitical diplomats[225] and negotiate all the diverging cosmovisions "in the presence of" all those hitherto muted Others?

Now, that we (my scientific network collaborators and I, in Latour's sense) have given so many reasons for engaging into an open-minded, cosmopolitical dialogue with Other, non-hegemonic forms of knowing and being, what exactly do we think we can expect from the Others' knowledge? What is it that makes these forms of knowledge so different from Our science, or from "Western" thought in general? Where and by which criteria should we draw the line between "Us" and "Them", "scientific" and "non-scientific" knowledge, without reproducing the abyssal divide between the "West" and the "Rest"? And finally, what can We, or Science, learn from Other ways of knowing? Are there really any alternatives to Our "modern/colonial" worldview, or do we only project our fears and hopes into Our "Others"?

Of course, these are a lot of tricky questions, and I certainly do not pretend to provide the answers here. In the next chapter I will offer a brief summary of the scientific construction of the Other, and some of the more recent attempts to figure

[222] "I use the term 'obligation' to characterise what it is to know that you belong. Practitioners have obligations. Not all they can do has the same value. This is the primordial fact for an ecology of practice, and if you make it relative to something you can identify and relate it to more general categories, you insult practitioners. Indeed obligation also communicates with indebtedness. Because of the fact I belong, I am able to do what I would not be able to do otherwise" (Stengers 2005b: 190).

[223] Stengers (2005b: 194).

[224] Stengers (2009: 18).

[225] "I call experts those who give voice to a position that is able to accept the constraints of the political procedure, that is, those who are called to contribute to a relevant decision representing a group that will not be existentially threatened by this decision, whatever it may be and whatever the way their contribution is taken into account by it. The experts' role requires them to present themselves, and to present what they know, in a mode that does not preempt how that knowledge should be taken into account. By contrast, diplomats are there to provide a voice for those whose practice, mode of existence, world, or what is often called identity, may be threatened by a decision: 'If you decide that, you'll destroy us.' The diplomats' role is therefore above all to force experts to think about the possibility that an envisaged course of action may effectively amount to an act of war" (Stengers 2018b: position 2410)

out what might be the "real" differences between Our and Other ways of being and knowing.

References

Aronowitz S (1988) Science as power: discourse and ideology in modern society. University of Minnesota Press, Minneapolis
Bachelard G (1978) Die Bildung des Wissenschaftlichen Geistes, Frankfurt a.M
Barnes B (1982) T. S. Kuhn and social science. MacMillan, London
Barnes B, Bloor D (1982) Relativism, rationalism and the sociology of knowledge. In: Hollis M, Lukes S (eds) Rationality and relativism. Blackwell, Oxford, pp 269–285
Berger PL, Luckmann T (1991) The social construction of reality: a treatise in the sociology of knowledge. Penguin, London
Bernal JD (1939) The social function of science. Routledge, London
Bhabha H (1994) The location of culture. Routledge, London
Blaser M (2013) Notes towards a political ontology of "environmental" conflicts. In: Green L (ed) Contested ecologies: dialogues in the south on nature and knowledge. HSRC, Cape Town, pp 13–27
Blaser M (2016) ¿Es otra cosmopolítica posible? Anthropologica/Año XXXVI(41):117–144
Borda OF (1981) Aspectos teóricos da pesquisa participante: considerações sobre o significado e o papel da ciência na participação popular. In: Brandão CR (ed) Pesquisa participante. Brasiliense, São Paulo, pp 42–62
Bourdieu P (1975) The specificity of the scientific field and the social conditions of the progress of reason. Soc Sci Info 14:19–47. https://doi.org/10.1177/053901847501400602
Bourdieu P (1985) Praktische Vernunft: Zur Theorie des Handelns. Suhrkamp, Frankfurt a.M
Bourdieu P (1987) Sozialer Sinn: Kritik der theoretischen Vernunft, Frankfurt a.M.
Bourdieu P (1992) Homo Academicus. Suhrkamp, Frankfurt a.M
Bourdieu P (2001) Para uma Sociologia da Ciência. Edições, Lisboa
Cadena Mdl (2015) Earth beings: ecologies of practice across Andean worlds. Duke University Press, Durham
Cadena Mdl, Blaser M (eds) (2018) A world of many worlds. Duke University Press, Durham
Castro-Gomes S (2000) Ciencias sociales, violencia epistémica y el problema de la "invención del otro". In: Lander E (ed) La colonialidad del saber: eurocentrismo y ciencias sociales—Perspectivas latinoamericanas. CLACSO, Buenos Aires, pp 145–162
Césaire A (1978) Discurso sobre o colonialismo. Livraria Sá da Costa Editora, Lisboa
Chakrabarty D (2007) Provincializing Europe postcolonial thought and historical difference. Princeton University Press, Princeton
Coronil F (2000) Naturaleza del poscolonialismo: del eurocentrismo al globocentrismo. In: Lander E (ed) La colonialidad del saber: eurocentrismo y ciencias sociales—Perspectivas latinoamericanas. CLACSO, Buenos Aires, pp 88–112
CRIC CRIDC (2021) La Crianza y Siembra de Sabidurías y Conocimientos (CRISSAC): Sentir, Pensar y Hacer para Trascender la Investigación Convencional. Grupo Estelar Impresores, Popayán
Debaise D, Stengers I (2022) An ecology of trust? Consenting to a pluralist universe. Sociol Rev 70:402–415. https://doi.org/10.1177/00380261221084794
Du Bois WEB (2007) The souls of black folk. Oxford University Press, Oxford
Dussel E (2000) Europa, modernidad y eurocentrismo. In: Lander E (ed) La colonialidad del saber: eurocentrismo y ciencias sociales—Perspectivas latinoamericanas. CLASCO, Buenos Aires, pp 41–54
Dussel E (2009) Meditações Anti-Cartesianas sobre a Origem do Anti-Discurso Filosófico da Modernidade. In: Santos BdS, Meneses MP (eds) Epistemologias do Sul. Coimbra, pp 283–336

Escobar A (2000) Ciencias sociales: saberes coloniales y eurocéntricos. In: Lander E (ed) La colonialidad del saber: eurocentrismo y ciencias sociales—Perspectivas latinoamericanas. CLACSO, Buenos Aires, pp 11–40

Escobar A (2003) Mundos y Conocimientos de otro Modo. El Programa de Investigación de Modernidad/Colonialidad Latinoamericano. Tabula Rasa. Bogotá, Jan-Dec, pp 51–86

Escobar A (2020) Pluriversal politics: the real and the possible. Duke University Press, Durham

ETSA (1996) Los alcances de la noción de „cultura" en la educación intercultural: Exploración de un ejemplo: sociedad y cultura bora. In: Godenzzi AJ (ed) Educación e Interculturalidad en los Andes y la Amazonia, Cusco, pp 187–294

Fanon F (2004) The wretched of the earth. Grove, New York

Fanon F (2008) Black skin white masks. Pluto Press, London

Feyerabend P (1980) Erkenntnis für freie Menschen, Veränderte Ausgabe. Suhrkamp, Frankfurt a.M

Feyerabend P (1993) Against method: outline of an anarchist theory of knowledge. Verso, London

Fleck L (1981) Genesis and development of a scientific fact. University of Chicago Press, Chicago

Fleck L (1983) Zur Krise der Wirklichkeit. In: Schäfer L, Schnelle T (eds) Erfahrung und Tatsache. Gesammelte Aufsätze. Suhrkamp, Frankfurt a.M, pp 48–88

Foucault M (1981) Überwachen und Strafen: Die Geburt des Gefängnisses. Suhrkamp, Frankfurt a.M

Freire P (1987) Pedagogia do Oprimido. Paz e Terra, Rio de Janeiro

Freire P (1996) Pedagogia da Autonomia. Saberes necessários à prática educativa. Pas e Terra, São Paulo

Freudenthal G, Mclaughlin P (eds) (2009) The social and economic roots of the scientific revolution: texts by Boris Hessen and Henryk Grossmann. Springer, Dordrecht

Galeano E (2010) As Veias Abertas da America Latina. L&PM Etitora, Montevideo

Garbe S (2012) Das Projekt Modernität/Kolonialität in Gegenüberstellung mit postkolonialer Theorie und als Herausforderung für die Kultur- und Sozialanthropologie—Eine theoretische Übersetzungsarbeit anhand interkultureller Teamarbeit in Argentinien. Master thesis, University of Vienna

Greaber D, Wengrow D (2021) The dawn of everything: a new history of humanity. Signal/Penguin Random House, New York

Geertz C (2008) A Interpretação das Culturas. LTC, Rio de Janeiro

Gramsci A (1982) Os Intelectuais e a Organização da Cultura. Civilização Brasileira, Rio de Janeiro

Grosfoguel R (2011) Decolonizing post-colonial studies and paradigms of political-economy: transmodernity, decolonial thinking, and global coloniality. Transmodernity J Peripher Cult Prod Luso Hispanic World 1. https://doi.org/10.5070/T411000004

Gross PR, Levitt N (1998) Higher superstition: the academic left and its quarrels with science. Johns Hopkins University Press, Baltimore

Grossmann H (2009a) The social foundations of the mechanistic philosophy and manufacture. In: Freudenthal G, Mclaughlin P (eds) The social and economic roots of the scientific revolution: texts by Boris Hessen and Henryk Grossmann. Springer, Dordrecht, pp 103–156

Grossmann H (2009b) Descartes and the social origins of the mechanistic concept of the world. In: Freudenthal G, Mclaughlin P (eds) The social and economic roots of the scientific revolution: texts by Boris Hessen and Henryk Grossmann. Springer, Dordrecht, pp 157–230

Haraway D (1988) Situated knowledges: the science question in feminism and the privilege of partial perspective. Fem Stud 14:575–599

Haraway D (1991) A cyborg manifesto: science, technology, and socialist-feminism in the late twentieth century. In: Simians, cyborgs and women: the reinvention of nature. Routladge, New York, pp 149–181

Harding S (1986) The science question in feminism. Cornell University Press, London

Harding S (1992) After the neutrality ideal: science, politics, and "strong objectivity". Soc Res 59:567–587

Harding SG (1994) Is science multicultural?: Challenges, resources, opportunities, uncertainties. Configurations 2:301–330. https://doi.org/10.1353/con.1994.0019

Harding S (2008) Science from below: feminisms, postcolonialities, and modernities. Duke University Press, Durham

Harding S (2015) Objectivity and diversity—another logic of scientific research. University of Chicago Press, Chicago

Harris M (2020) Science wars: the next generation. Sci People 2(11). https://magazine.sciencefor-thepeople.org/vol22-1/science-wars-the-next-generation/. Accessed 08.01.2024

Hessen B (2009) The social and economic roots of Newton's principia. In: Freudenthal G, Mclaughlin P (eds) The social and economic roots of the scientific revolution: texts by Boris Hessen and Henryk Grossmann. Springer, Dordrecht, pp 41–102

Horkheimer M, Adorno T (1969) Dialektik der Aufklärung: Philosophische Fragmente. Frankfurt a.M.

Husserl E (1962) Hesserliana. Biemel W (ed), Bd. VI: Die Krisis der europäischen Wissenschaften und die transzendentale Phänomenologie, Köln

James W (1981) Pragmatism: a new name for some old ways of thinking. Hackett, Indianapolis

Knorr-Cetina K (1981) The manufacture of knowledge: an essay on the constructivist and contextual nature of science. Pergamon, Oxford

Kuhn T (1970) The structure of scientific revolution. In: Neurath O et al (eds) International encyclopedia of unified science, vol 2, no. 2. University of Chicago, Chicago

Lander E (ed) (2000) La colonialidad del saber: eurocentrismo y ciencias sociales—Perspectivas latinoamericanas. CLACSO, Buenos Aires

Latour B (1987) Science in action: how to follow scientists and engineers through society. Harvard University Press, Cambridge

Latour B (1993) We have never been modern. Harvard University Press, Cambridge

Latour B (2001) A Esperança de Pandora: Ensaios sobre a Realidade dos Estudos Cinetificos. Edusc, Bauru

Latour B (2004) Why has critique run out of steam? From matters of fact to matters of concern. Crit Inq 30(2):225–248

Latour B, Woolgar S (1986) Laboratory life: the construction of scientific facts. Princeton University Press, Princeton

Linhart J (2008) Universidades Indígenas: Programas de Educação Indígena Superior na América Latina: A Caminho de uma Ciência Intercultural? Master thesis, LMU

Linhart J (2012) A interculturalidade no contexto do ensino superior e as suas implicações epistemológicas. Cadernos de Educação Escolar Indígenas 10(1):35–51. https://doi.org/10.17851/2175-0998.2.0.268-285

Little P (2005) Indigenous people and sustainabililty development subprojects in Brazilian Amazonia: the challenges of interculturality. In: Law & policy, vol 27, no 3, pp 450–470

López LE (1996) No mas Danzas de Ratones Grises: Educación y Interculturalidad en América Latina. In: Godenzzi AJ (ed) Educación e Interculturalidad en los Andes y la Amazonia, Cusco, pp 23–82

Luhmann N (1990) Die Wissenschaft der Gesellschaft. Suhrkamp, Frankfurt a.M

Lynch M (1985) Art and artifact in laboratory science: a study of shop work and shop talk in a research laboratory. Routledge, London

Macas LFS (2018) Interculturalidad y acceso a la Universidad. Cuadernos Americanos 163:45–58

Macas LFS et al (eds) (2017) Kapak Ñan Pedagógico-Filosófico de la Pluriversidad "Amawtay Wasi": El Gran Camino de los Aprendizajes. Pluriversidad "Amawtwy Wasi," Kitu

Mannheim K (1954) Ideology and utopia: an introduction to the sociology of knowledge. Routledge & Kegan Paul, New York

Marx K (1962) Das Kapital: Kritik der politischen Ökonomie. Dietz, Berlin

Meneses MPG (2009) Corpos de Violência, Linguagens de Resistência: As complexas teias de conhecimentos no Mosambique contemporâneo. In: Santos BdS, Meneses MP (eds) Epistemologias do Sul. Coimbra, pp 177–214

Merchant C (1983) The death of nature: women, ecology and the scientific revolution. Wildwood House, London

Merchant C (2006) The scientific revolution and the death of nature. Isis 97:513–533

Merchant C (2018) Science and nature—past, present and future. Routledge, London
Merton RK (1942) The normative structure of science. https://www.panarchy.org/merton/science.html. Accessed 09.01.2024
Merton RK (1968) Social theory and social structure. Free Press, New York
Merton RK (1970) Science, technology and society in seventeenth century England. Howard Fertig, New York
Mignolo WD (1995) The darker side of the renaissance. Literacy, territoriality and colonization. University of Michigan Press, Ann Arbor
Mignolo WD (2000a) La colonialidad a lo largo y a lo ancho: el hemisferio occidental en el horizonte colonial de la modernidad. In: Lander E (ed) La colonialidad del saber: eurocentrismo y ciencias sociales—Perspectivas latinoamericanas. CLACSO, Buenos Aires, pp 55–86
Mignolo WD (2000b) Local histories—global designs: coloniality, subaltern knowledges, and border thinking. Princeton University Press, Princeton
Mignolo WD (2002) The geopolitics of knowledge and the colonial difference. South Atl Q 101:57–96. https://doi.org/10.1215/00382876-101-1-57
Mignolo WD (2005) El Pensamiento Des-Colonial, Desprendimiento y Apertura: Un Manifiesto. Tristestópicos
Mignolo WD (2011) The darker side of western modernity: global futures, decolonial options. Duke University Press, Durham, London
Mignolo WD (2013) Geopolitics of sensing and knowing: On (de)coloniality, border thinking, and epistemic disobedience. Confero 1:129–150
Mignolo WD (2021) The politics of decolonial investigations. Duke University Press, Durham
Mignolo WD, Tlostanova MV (2006) Theorizing from the borders: shifting to geo- and body-politics of knowledge. Eur J Soc Theory 9:205–221. https://doi.org/10.1177/1368431006063333
Mignolo WD, Walsh CE (2018) On decoloniality: concepts, analytics, praxis. Duke University Press, Durham
Morin E (2005) Ciência com Consciência. Editora Bertrand Brasil, Rio de Janeiro
Polanyi M (1946) Science, faith and society. Oxford University Press, London
Polanyi M (1962) Personal knowledge: towards a post-critical philosophy. Routledge, London
Poma FG (1616) El Primero I Nueva Crónica I Buen Gobierno. https://poma.kb.dk/permalink/2006/poma/titlepage/en/text/. Accessed 25.11.2023
Quijano A (1992) Colonialidad y modernidad/racionalidad. Peru Indígena 13(29):11–20
Quijano A (2000) Coloniality of power, eurocentrism, and Latin America. Nepantla 1(3):533–580
Ramos A, Rappaport J (2005) Una Historia Colaborativa: Retos para el Diálogo Indígena-Academico. Historia Crítica 39–62
Ramos A et al (2004) ¿Que pensaria si la escuala ...?: 30 años de construcción de una educación propia, Bogotá
Rappaport J (2005) Intercultural utopias: public intellectuals, cultural experimentations, and ethnic pluralism in Colombia. Duke University Press, Durham
Rieppel L, Lean E, Deringer W (2018) Science and capitalism: entangled histories. Osiris 33
Said EW (1978) Orientalism. Pantheon, New York
Santos BdS (2009a) Para além do Pensamento Abissal: Das Linhas Globais a uma Ecologia de Saberes. In: Santos BdS, Meneses MP (eds) Epistemologias do Sul. Coimbra, pp 23–73
Santos BdS (2009b) Um Ocidente Não-Ocidentalista?: A Filosofia à venda, a douta ignorânçia e a aposta de Pascal. In Santos BdS, Meneses MP (eds) Epistemologias do Sul. Coimbra, pp 445–486
Santos BdS (2018) The end of the cognitive empire: the coming of age of epistemologies of the South. Duke University Press, Durham
Santos BdS (2022) Poscolonialismo, descolonialidad y Epistemologías del Sur, CLACSO, Buenos Aires / Centro de Estudos Sociais - CES, Coimbra
Segrera FL (2000) Abrir, impensar, y redimensionar las ciencias sociales em América Latina y el Caribe. ¿Es posible una ciencia social no eurocéntrica en nuestra región? In: Lander E (ed)

La colonialidad del saber: eurocentrismo y ciencias sociales—Perspectivas latinoamericanas. CLACSO, Buenos Aires, pp 177–200
Shapin S (1995) Here and everywhere: sociology of scientific knowledge. Annu Rev Sociol 2:289–321
Sokal AD (1996) Transgressing the boundaries: towards a transformative hermeneutics of quantum gravity. Soc Text #46/47:217–252
Solano XL et al (eds) (2018a) Prácticas otras de conocimiento(s): entre crisis, entre guerras, Primera edición electrónica. Tomo I. CLASCO, Mexico
Solano XL et al (eds) (2018b) Prácticas otras de conocimiento(s): entre crisis, entre guerras, Primera edición electrónica. Tomo II. CLASCO, Mexico
Solano XL et al (eds) (2018c) Prácticas otras de conocimiento(s): entre crisis, entre guerras, Primera edición electrónica. Tomo III. CLASCO, Mexico
Soto RRH (2019) ¿El entretejido de la pluriversidad?. Conocimientos en tensión y diálogo en universidades indígenas de Abya Yala: Amawtay Wasi (Ecuador), UAIIN-CRIC (Colombia) y Tupak Katari (Bolivia). PhD thesis, Universidad Andina Simón Bolívar
Spivak GC (1993) Can the subaltern speak? In: Williams P, Chrisman L (eds) Colonial discourse and post-colonial theory—a reader. Colombia University Press, New York, pp 66–111
Stengers I (2005a) The cosmopolitical proposal. In: Latur B, Weibel P (eds) Making things public. Atmospheres of democracy. MIT Press, Cambridge
Stengers I (2005b) Introductory notes on: an ecology of practices. Cult Stud Rev 11(1):183–196
Stengers I (2009) William James—an ethics of thought? Radic Philos 157:9–19
Stengers I (2010) Cosmopolitics I. University of Minnesota Press, Minneapolis
Stengers I (2011) Cosmopolitics II. University of Minnesota Press, Minneapolis
Stengers I (2012) Reclaiming animism. E-Flus J 36:1–10
Stengers I (2015) In catastrophic times: resisting the coming barbarism. Open Humanities, London
Stengers I (2018a) Another science is possible—a manifesto for slow science, Kindle version. Polity, Cambridge
Stengers I (2018b) The challenge of ontological politics. In: Cadena Mdl, Blaser M (eds) A world of many worlds. Duke University Press, Durham, pp 195–260
Stengers I, Higgins M, Wallace M (2023) In conversation with Isabelle Stengers: ontological politics in catastrophic times. In: Tolbert S et al (eds) Reimagining science education in the anthropocene, vol 2. Springer, Cham, pp 363–387
Traweek S (1988) Beamtimes and lifetimes: the world of high energy physics. Harvard University Press, Cambridge
Wallerstein I (2004) World-system analysis: an introduction. Duke University Press, London
Wallerstein I (2006) European universalism: the rhetoric of power. New Press, New York
Walsh C (2009) Interculturalidad, Estado, Sociedad: Luchas (de)coloniales de nuestra epoca. Ediciones Abya Yala, Quito
Walsh C (ed) (2013) Pedagogias Descoloniales: Prácticas insurgentes de resistir, (re)existir y (re) vivir—Tomo I. Ediciones Abya Yala, Quito
Walsh C (ed) (2017) Pedagogías decoloniales: Prácticas insurgentes de resistir, (re)existir y (re) vivir. Tomo II. Ediciones Abya Yala, Quito
Walsh C (2021) "Outros" saberes, "outras" críticas: reflexões sobre as políticas e as práticas de filosofia e decolonialidade na "outra" América. Revista X 16:54–79
Walsh CE (2023) Rising up, living on: re-existences, sowings, and decolonial cracks. Duke University Press, Durham
Werner S (2014) Wissenschaft und Magie: Ethnologische und wahrnehmungspsychologische Motive in Ludwik Flecks Epistemologie. NTM 22:31–48. https://doi.org/10.1007/s00048-013-0103-3
Whitehead AN (1925) Science and the modern world. Cambridge University Press, London
Whitesides G (2019) Science and American foreign relations since World War II. Cambridge University Press, Cambridge

Wynter S (2015) The ceremony found: towards the autopoetic turn/overturn, its autonomy of human agency and extraterritoriality of (self-)cognition. In: Ambroise JR, Broeck S (eds) Black knowledges/black struggles. Liverpool University Press, pp 184–252. https://doi.org/10.5949/liverpool/9781781381724.003.0008
Zilsel E (1942) The sociological roots of science. Am J Sociol 47:544–562

Chapter 5
The Scientific Construction of the Other

> *All people must distinguish at least two categories, a 'we' and a 'they'.*
>
> *— Langness (1974: 13)*

As already discussed in the previous chapters, scientific universalism has contributed to European expansion and continues to contribute to the maintenance of the unequal relations that sustain the current global social, economic and political order. It should also have become clear that scientific universalism is sustained by a dichotomist image of Us and the Others, where We, "moderns" are rational and the Others are irrational or underdeveloped.

In this chapter, I will offer a closer look at the way in which modern science constructed its own self-image in relation to the culturally different Other. Well, in fact modern science in general did not even consider being compared with other kinds of knowledge, as its universalistic dogma puts it on top of humanity's intellectual evolution. "Traditional" and "common-sense" knowledge are simply synonymous with "unscientific", and therefore not to be taken into scientific account by definition. But one scientific discipline did try to compare modern science with other, so-called "traditional" kinds of knowledge and to figure out what, in the end, is really the difference between modern science and other, non-modern modes of knowing. This scientific discipline is, of course, anthropology.

It is a well-known fact that anthropology emerged in the context of colonialism[1] and was initially meant to help the colonial powers to better understand their colonies in order to facilitate colonial administration. This is not the place to repeat too much of this part of the story, so I will just sketch out some well-known examples from the history of anthropological thought before I proceed to those anthropologists who made an effort to understand the particularities of modern science and

[1] E.g. Wolf (2010).

J. Linhart, *Science and the Other*, Schriften zu Leben und Gesellschaft - Series on Life and Society 2, https://doi.org/10.1007/978-3-032-03927-9_5

other, culturally different modes of reasoning by going beyond Eurocentric exceptionalism.

In what follows, I will offer a kaleidoscopic overview with no pretension of being a complete account or deep analysis of the vast landscape of anthropological attempts to understand and conceptualise the Other. My intention is merely to provide a brief overview of the historical development of anthropological conceptions of the difference between Our scientific and Other ways of knowing.

5.1 On Christians and Pagans

Our image of Us and the Others has been shaped in the context of European expansion and the unequal social relations which sustained the colonial system for centuries, and which fundamentally continue to characterise our current model of globalisation, too. As has been famously described by Eric Wolf,[2] European expansion was neither an accident, nor did it start with Christopher Columbus' arrival at the Caribbean islands in 1492. A long time before, Portuguese and Spanish Christians fought the Muslim conquerors who had been controlling the Iberian Peninsula since the eighth century. While the Portuguese managed to reconquer their lands during the twelfth and thirteenth century, the Spanish kingdoms of Castile and Aragon would have their final victory only in the year 1492, winning the battle of Granada (the same year the Spanish Crown had sent Columbus to discover a new sea route to India). This *reconquista* was conceived as a war against the Godless pagans, much in the spirit of the Crusades into the Orient, and was fought with unleashed cruelty in the name of Christendom and the Holy Church. However, having gained their lands back, the Portuguese still did not stop fighting the pagans. In 1415 they crossed the Strait of Gibraltar, seized the African port of Ceuta and continued raiding the African coast, finally rounding the Cape of Good Hope in 1487 before proceeding to East Africa and India. And while, in 1497, Vasco da Gama went out to conquer the East, at around the same time Pedro Álvares Cabral went to the West, landing at the Brazilian coast in the year 1500. The Iberian *Reconquista* almost seamlessly merged into the *Conquista* of the New World and initiated an age of European expansion. As a consequence, the *Conquista* was also conceived as a holy war against the Godless pagans for the sake of God (although it

[2] Erdheim (1990); Niess (1991); Galeano (2010); Wolf (2010).

was actually driven by economic and political needs[3]). The conquered Others, therefore, were seen as the non-Christian pagans who had fallen from God's grace and who would have to be either converted to the Christian faith, or die so at least their souls would be redeemed.[4] In fact, it was not even clear whether those "Indians" could be converted, as it was still to be decided whether they were real humans or not. Scholastic intellectuals, like Sepúlveda and Las Casas, would debate this question for decades. It took some 45 years after Columbus' first encounter with the "Indians" until, in his encyclical *Sublimis Deus* from 1537, Pope Paul III finally declared that all human beings, including the "Indians", actually were humans capable of receiving the Christian faith, and therefore, should not be enslaved or deprived of their property. However, this holy declaration of universal human rights did not change much for America's Indigenous population, which would be enslaved and slaughtered anyway by their European conquerors. The European invaders clearly saw themselves as a superior race, calling themselves "*gente de razón*" (people of reason), while the Others were seen as morally and intellectually inferior, childlike savages.[5]

5.2 Of Noble and Barbarian Savages

However, while there was no doubt about the superiority of the Europeans compared to any other people, the moral status of the Others was evaluated in an ambivalent manner, depending on the political and philosophical viewpoint.

Christopher Columbus himself first described the inhabitants of the Caribbean islands as kind and handsome persons, ideal to serve their new European masters (when he praised the greatness of his newly "discovered" lands), but then belittled them as despicable, cannibalistic savages (when he justified their enslavement and slaughter). Indeed, different observers would paint quite different images of the Others, some of them describing them as brutal, rude, soulless cannibals, and some of them emphasising their nobleness, peacefulness, strength, beauty, and moral virtues.

---

[3] The rising Western European states were running out of bullion. Feudal crisis and the holy wars against the pagans had emptied the treasuries and the access to the treasures of the Orient were blocked by the Muslim Empires. Furthermore, the expansion to the exterior served as a means to consolidate these new states: "Seizure of external resources was the main strategy followed by the Iberian powers of Portugal, Leon-Castile, and Aragon in their Reconquista of Muslim Spain. Another attempt to use this strategy took the form of the Crusades, carried on by the kings of France and England not long after their initial consolidation of power (1096–1291). The announced motivation for the Crusades was the reconquest of the Holy Land from the infidels. On another level, however, the Crusades were efforts to consolidate still incipient political systems through an attack against greatly weakened enemies" (Wolf 2010 (1982): 105). See also Galeano 2010.

[4] Erdheim (1990); Wolf (2010); Mendonça (2014).

[5] Wolf (2010); Erdheim (1990).

The first view was clearly the dominating one and may be best exemplified by Hans Staden's famous travelogue about the "wild, naked, grim cannibals" he had lived with for some time during his capture around 1550. Staden's description of the Tupinambá provides some interesting observations of the life and ritual of those people at that time, while holding to the common image of the Others as fierce pagans (in his case quite understandably, as he really had to fear being ritually eaten by his hosts).[6] He repeatedly refers to his faith in God and explicitly attributes the plague that struck the Tupinambá during his presence and which eventually contributed to his rescue to God's grace and his own unshakable faith. Hans Staden was a simple soldier with no clear political interest. His descriptions are based on the common beliefs of his time and only confirmed the image of the Others as Godless cannibals.

Another author, the Franciscan missionary Bernadino de Sahagún, gives us quite a different picture of the "Indians". Sahagún came to Mexico in 1529, soon becoming a kind of ethnologist and linguist of Aztec culture and the language, Náhuatl. His prime interest was to convert the "Indians" to Christianity, following the Franciscan mystic doctrine which interpreted the conquest of the New World as a sign of the oncoming end of the world, when all people would be Christians and history would be concluded. While the Europeans and the Jews had failed to live the Christian ideals, the Christian utopia would now become possible in the New World and finally bring salvation to all people. Furnished with this eschatological faith, Sahagún would dedicate his life to study the "Indians" in order to understand and catechise them. While initially only interested in learning the vernacular and the Indigenous habits as a means for his mission, Sahagún gave a voice to the view of the victims of the European invasion. For years he interviewed Indigenous representatives who had been chosen and indicated previously by their communities, and finally gathered the results of his ethnographic work in the bilingual *Historia general de las cosas de Nueva España*, also known as *Florentine Codex*. Although Sahagún clearly did not share the views of his Aztec interlocutors, but on the contrary, aimed to convert them to Christian faith, he provided a unique *emic* description of their culture as it appeared to the Aztec themselves. Not surprisingly, the church did not allow him to publish his work and forced him to hand over all his material so it would not fall into the wrong hands. Fortunately, Sahagún made several copies and hid them so others could have access to his work, and the Florentine Codex would reappear in the Biblioteca Medicea-Laurenziana in Florence some decades later. However, it remained largely unknown until the eighteenth century and therefore had no influence on the image of the Others during previous centuries.

The authors who had a fundamental influence on the European discourse on alterity mainly followed one of two opposed schemes, which later became known as the "Noble" or the "Barbarian Savage". The dominant scheme, which demonised the "Indians" as pagan savages, was defended by those who were interested in

[6] Staden (1557).

taking their lands and in exploiting their labour, mainly for mining gold and silver, and in maintaining the feudal system. Those authors were men like Juan Ginés de Sepúlveda and Fernández de Oviedo, great defenders of colonisation justified by European superiority and the duty to civilise the pagan savages. The "Indians", in their opinion, were not really human, but mere *homunculi*, irrational half-humans, not even suitable to live close to the civilised Europeans. Cultural or racial difference was interpreted as the result of the moral degeneration of those nations who had fallen from God's grace. The Others, therefore, were inferior because they had been abandoned by God. The image of the Others Sepúlveda and Oviedo maintained were meant to legitimate the brutal *encomienda* system, slavery, and the "*guerra justa*" (just war) against those savages who would not let themselves be subdued under the rule of their European masters.[7] These pejorative representations of the Others were also a reaction to the *Leyes Nuevas* (New Laws), which had been pronounced by the Spanish king Charles V in 1542, and which abolished both the *ecomienda* as well as slavery, guaranteeing basically the same rights and duties to the "Indians" as to the European settlers.

The *Leyes Nuevas* were a result of Bartolome de Las Casas' efforts to protect the "Indians" from the abusive mistreatment and slaughter committed by the Europeans. Despite being a member of a family of *conquistadores* which actively participated in the invasion of the Canary Islands and Columbus' second voyage to the New World, Las Casas would become one of the greatest defenders of the "Indians" against the cruel abuses they suffered under their European oppressors. He came to the New World in 1502 and initially lived the life of a *conquistador.* But after having assisted the cruelty of his Spanish fellows over 10 years, he became a Dominican priest and began to militate in defence of the "Indians'" rights. In 1515 he went back to Spain and denounced the crimes committed by the *conquistadores* to the Spanish king. He was named *defensor universal de los indios* (universal procurator of the Indians) of the crown and was assigned to implement his plans for a peaceful colonisation in the territory today known as Venezuela. Although his plans failed,[8] he went back to Spain in 1539 and persuaded king Charles V to proclaim the *Leyes Neuvas*.

Las Casas' descriptions of the "Indians" were written in explicit opposition to Oviedo's image of the cruel, rude, pagan, savages, half-human-half-beasts. In Las Casas' writings, in contrast, the "Indians" were kind, noble, beautiful, and intelligent, while the Spaniards were cruel, rude, and greedy. Accusations of sodomy (homosexuality), cannibalism, and human sacrifice, as can be found in Oviedo's

[7] Erdheim (1990); Wolf (2010); Mendonça (2014).

[8] After Las Casas' failed trial to colonise the area peacefully, it was entrusted to German bankers, the Welser, in 1529, in exchange for the gigantic debt which King Charles V was unable to pay back to them. The Welsers were accused of horrendous crimes against both "Indians" and the Spanish settlers, and in 1546 the king cancelled their contract, leaving only the name the Welsers had given to their lands: Venezuela, "little Venice". Moreover, the *leyes Neuvas* were revoked in 1545, and Las Casas' further efforts in Chiapas to realise his dream of a peaceful New World were rendered unsuccessful (Erdheim 1990).

texts, are either completely denied or downplayed. While Oviedo claimed the "Indians" were lazy and did not like to work, Las Casas responded that they simply managed to get everything they needed with little time and effort, so they could spend the rest of the day playing, dancing and singing. The greedy Europeans, in contrast, were possessed by the devil, and thus, never stopped piling up wealth and enlarging their lands without any need.[9] In doing so, Las Casas acted in the spirit of his Dominican Order, which rejected the idea that the mission would imply the right to enslave non-Christian people, defending equal rights for all people and nations. The ideals of human equality and equal rights which Las Casas maintained were based on Cicero's image of man, all born equal and gifted with the same universal reason and sensational experience, but different in virtue of their social experience as a member of a specific society and culture. He is, therefore, also seen as a humanist and precursor of enlightenment.

The two opposing legal views for and against the right to explore and enslave the "Indians" are based on two different anthropological models, one maintaining the fundamental racial, cognitive, and moral difference, and the other defending the fundamental equality and unity of the human race. Furthermore, these opposing anthropological notions are also related to two opposing social models, which are philosophically legitimised by particular corresponding anthropological notions. Sepúlveda and Oviedo defended their inequality-based anthropological model in order to justify a violent mode of colonisation which would reproduce the European feudal structures in the New World, and hence, justify the continuity of the old feudal system in the Spanish motherlands, too. Las Casas, however, defended a new equality-based anthropological view in order to justify a different, peaceful mode of colonisation, which would help to solve the ongoing feudal crisis in Spain by changing the old social structures of the feudal system. The growing misery of peasants in Spain and many other European countries during the fifteenth and sixteenth century led to numerous riots and peasant wars. Las Casas' solution was to relocate poor landless farmers into the New World to have them live in peaceful coexistence with the "Indians", and finally, found a new society based on the fundamental Christian values of equality and brotherhood. However, both parties created their own image of the Others for the purpose of legitimating their own socio-political projects in the context of European problems.[10] None of them was able to perceive the Others in their own right. This image of the Others as either Noble or Barbarian Savages would become one of the most important themes of the nascent modern discourse.

The Noble Savage soon became an important figure in European literature. In his *La Araucana*, published in 1569, Alonso de Ercilla y Zúñiga transformed his experiences during the war against the Mapuche in southern Chile into a critique against the brutality of his Spanish fellow *conquistadores*. The Indigenous chief Caupolicán and his wife Fresia are depicted as heroic defenders of their people, being brutally

[9] Las Casas *apud* Erdheim (1990).

[10] Erdheim (1990).

slaughtered by their Spanish enemies. While the "Indians" fight for the sake of their life and liberty, the Europeans only seek gold and wealth. This literary figure of the noble "Indian" fighting the cruel and greedy European invaders would become a permanent genre of modern literature,[11] and later also in cinema.[12]

But more importantly, the Noble Savage would become a central element in early modern philosophy and fundamental for the entire modern political discourse. In his *Essays*, the French philosopher Michel Eyquem de Montaigne also refers to the nobleness of the savages compared to European society.[13] Unlike the previously mentioned authors, Montaigne never went to the New World. His interest in the Others was of philosophical concern. Montaigne not only construed his image of the Others as purer and closer to nature when compared to the depraved European society; the fact of cultural and moral differences also led him to a relativistic stance, serving as a dispositive for his cultural scepticism. What was true and good here, could be wrong and ugly there. "Barbarism", therefore, was everything one would not be accustomed to, a result of blind ethnocentrism, as we would say today. In this way, the Noble Savage became instrumental for a general critique of European society, turning an ethnological eye to the European self.[14] However, the Noble Savage continues to be a savage, a primitive human being, still living in a more "natural" way, while European society had developed in the opposite direction, away from nature, and hence, represented a process of decadence.[15] It is not difficult to associate this view with the biblical Genesis and the fall of the first humans from the Garden of Eden. Adam and Eve, first living much like animals, naked, innocent, and without any moral notion, eat from the forbidden tree of the knowledge of good and evil, suddenly becoming aware of their nakedness, and finally are thrown out of Eden, being cursed by God to live a painful life of hard labour. As a consequence of their new hard life, their son, Cain, commits the first murder, killing his brother Abel, and initiates the history of

[11] Another important author to be mentioned here is Jean de Lery (1580, 1992).

[12] A classical example is Karl May's *Winnetou*; a recent example would be the film *Avatar* from 2009.

[13] In his essay *Of Cannibals*, Montaigne (1877) even defends the Tupinamba's habit of eating their enemies, emphasising that for the Tupinamba to be eaten was a symbol of honour, and that European habits of torture and supplication were much worse than cannibalism (see also Erdheim 1990).

[14] Montaigne also reported the observations made by Brazilian "Indians" who had been brought to the French court, that there would be two kinds of people in France, some very healthy and well nurtured, and others hungry and poor, and wondered why those poor would not kill the rich ones (Erdheim 1990; Mendonça 2014).

[15] "These Nations then seem to me to be so far Barbarous, as having receiv'd but very little form and fashion from Art and Human Invention, and consequently to be not much remote from their Original Simplicity. The Laws of Nature, however, govern them still, not as yet much vitiated with any mixture of ours: but 'tis in such Purity, that I am sometimes troubled we were not sooner acquainted with these People, and that they were not discovered in those better times, when there were Men much more able to judge of them than we are" (Montaigne 1877: 237).

human sin and depravation. In Montaigne's anthropology, the Others represent humankind before the fall from Eden, and thus serve as a general critique of cultural degeneration as a process against nature.[16]

Two centuries later, this image of the Noble Savage as a representative of a still pure, pre-cultural, natural state of humankind advanced to a powerful political dispositive through the works of Jean Jacques Rousseau. In response to Thomas Hobbes' misanthropic view of the initial state of humankind as a "war of all against all", Rousseau maintains that the human being is essentially good, although obviously humankind as we observe it today is fundamentally evil. But this evil is a result of the pernicious societal process. Men in the hypothetical State of Nature had been free and moved by an innate repugnance to see others of his kind suffer.[17] Living together in a society, however, men would compare themselves with others and strive for more honour, wealth, and power to distinguish themselves from others, finally building societies based on inequality, injustice, and oppression. While Rousseau referred to existing "savages" as being more egalitarian, he did not identify them with men in the State of Nature, nor did he use the term "Noble Savage". However, the idea of the Noble Savage, as previously drawn by Montaigne, was clearly influential for Rousseau's project, as it opened the stage for the possibility of a different humanity. Man in the State of Nature was a cipher for the human potential to build a better society, given his intelligence which would allow for an understanding of the principal pitfalls that would have to be avoided. His *Social Contract*, therefore, intends an egalitarian society where social and economic differences would be obviated as much as possible. Rousseau was not only of utmost influence on the French Revolution, but also on the intellectual formation of socialism as a new ideological stance opposing bourgeois society and capitalist exploitation.

The ciphers of the Noble and the Barbarian Savage, hence, played an essential role in the formation of the leading political ideas of modern society. The Barbarian Savage, on the one hand, justifies conservative projects, inhibiting self-reflexion, and therefore, legitimating the maintenance of given structures in one's own society as well as the domination of other nations for the sake of "progress". The Noble Savage, on the other hand, serves as a vehicle for self-reflection and critique of one's

---

[16] But this view also inverted the logic of the degenerative process as it had been understood in his times, where the others would be de degenerated ones who had fallen from God's grace and therefore became pagan barbarians, while the Christians were the only ones to conserve the original faith in God.

[17] "There is besides another principle that has escaped Hobbes, and which, having been given to man to moderate, on certain occasions, the blind and impetuous sallies of self-love, or the desire of self-preservation previous to the appearance of that passion, allays the ardour with which he naturally pursues his private welfare, by an innate abhorrence to see beings suffer that resemble him. I shall not surely be contradicted, in granting to man the only natural virtue, which the most passionate detractor of human virtues could not deny him, I mean that of pity, a disposition suitable to creatures weak as we are, and liable to so many evils; a virtue so much the more universal, and withal useful to man, as it takes place in him of all manner of reflection; and so natural, that the beasts themselves sometimes give evident signs of it" (Rousseau 2020: 8).

own society, justifying social changes and at the same time de-legitimating the forced transformation and exploitation of other nations.

However, the image of the Noble Savage, as an unreal, romantic construction, not only continues to stigmatise the Others as "primitive", resembling humankind's remote origins, but also reproduces the idea of the childlike, "irrational" savage and the "rational" European. Nevertheless, the spectres of the Noble and the Barbarian Savage still haunt contemporary discourse on alterity and identity as well as the political discourse in general[18].

5.3 Anthropology: The Science of the Other

Anthropology emerged, together with other social sciences during the nineteenth century, in the context of colonial expansion and the deep social transformations of the beginning of the modern age. While sociology tried to make sense of the contradictions of modern society, with its great scientific and technological progresses on the one hand and the unconceivable misery it created between the working classes on the other, anthropology set out to make sense of "racial" and cultural differences, and what they meant to humankind in general.

Initially, self-declared "anthropologists" basically reproduced much of the prejudices about the Noble and/or Barbarian Savages and it was very common to associate cultural differences with supposed "racial" differences. The concept of "race" was actually new, as prior to the sixteenth century the demarcation lines between Us and the Other had been either between Christians and pagans or between human and non-human (e.g. *homunculi*), as discussed above. Along with various phenotypical differences, "racial" difference was conceived fundamentally as one of intellectual and moral capacity, thus giving continuity to the prejudices contained in the *homunculi* concept of Sepulveda and Oviedo.

[18] See also Greaber and Wengrow (2021) on the role of the cipher of the "Noble" and "Barbarian" "Savage" in early modern political theory. They show that the Indigenous critique of European society—famously articulated by the Huron-Wendat leader Kandiaronk during his exchanges with French interlocutors—had a direct influence on European Enlightenment thinkers. Thus, they reject the view that Indigenous perspectives shaped European thought only through the "myth of the noble savage," understood as a "romantic projection of European fantasies". In fact, the very expression "noble savage" emerged later as a right-wing caricature of Enlightenment social critiques such as Rousseau's, which themselves drew inspiration from Indigenous critiques and reflections on humanity's state of nature.

5.3.1 From Evolutionism to Relativism

A fundamental change in Christian cosmology occurred with the consolidation of Darwin's theory about the evolutionary origin of species, since it contradicted the creationist cosmogony as described in the Book of Genesis. Now, man would no longer be created by God nor would he necessarily be his image. From now on, it would be natural science which explained man's origins. However, despite all initial outrage between Christian intellectuals, evolutionary theory soon became mainstream in scientific discourse and it did not take long until it was adopted in other fields of study, too. Actually, it took only a small step to transform the narration about the "primitive" savage into a theory of cultural evolution, where cultural and "racial" difference was equated with backwardness, with European modern culture standing at the peak of cultural evolution, just as the human species would represent the peak of natural evolution.[19] Evolutionism also reverted to the old degenerative view, substituting it with "progress". The Others would no longer have abandoned God's path and degenerated into *homunculi*, but on the contrary, monotheism was a result of an evolution that had begun with "animistic savagery", passing through the stage of "polytheistic barbarism", "monotheist civilisation", and finally, into the enlightened state of scientific knowledge.[20] The Others now represented a past stage of our own history, they were a kind of "living fossils" which would help us understand more about the evolution of the human species in general. The more "racial" (=phenotypical) and cultural differences compared to white, "civilised" Europeans they would represent, the more "primitive" they would be.

Although some great evolutionists like Henry Morgan and Edward Tyler were dedicated defenders of the Indigenous cause, being fascinated by all those different ways to live and view the world, they never completely stripped away the racist ideas that governed their time. Cultural difference, therefore, was not only translated into a chronological order from "savagery" through "barbarism" to "civilisation", but also into a ladder of intellectual capacities from irrationality to rationality. Following Morgan and Tyler, the "primitive" mind would not be able to distinguish between subjective and objective experience, constantly mixing up imagination and reality, unable to think like a Western scientist. James Fraser argued that "magic was an early form of science based upon incorrect notions of cause and effect—basically that things which were similar or had once been in contact with each other could affect or continue to affect each other at a distance".[21] But with time, modern science would inevitably result from experience as the only correct, and consequently, the most successful way to cope with reality.

Evolutionism, therefore, brought very old prejudices about the Barbarian Savage into modern concepts, while maintaining its symbolic function as a means to legitimate European expansionism. The former degenerated pagan savage was translated

[19] See also Langness (1974); Harding (1994); Wolf (2010).

[20] According to Auguste Comte (1974) and evolutionist scientists.

[21] Langness (1974: 24).

into the underdeveloped "primitive"; while the pagan would have to be conducted to Christian faith and reason, the "primitive" would have to be conducted to progress and scientific rationality. Once again, Europe was called to "save" the Others by subduing them under her rule.

Things would start to change with Franz Boas' relativistic approach. His personal experiences with the Kwakiutl had left him with a positive impression of those people and he began to ask himself "what advantages our 'good society' possesses over that of the 'savages'".[22] In the middle of a pandemic outbreak of racism and nationalism at the turn of the century, Boas, once again, invoked the image of the Noble Savage to relativise and question the idea of Western superiority. His aim was not to explain human evolution, but to understand the Others in their own right. And this could only be achieved by living together and sharing the experiences of those Others. Contrary to his evolutionist colleagues, whose work had been mainly based on bibliographic research and comparing all kinds of different cultural elements throughout time and space, Boas demanded that his students do field work among the Others and collect as much material as possible about the disappearing Indigenous cultures.

Probably the most influential legacy of Boas' relativistic anthropology was to think of "culture" in the plural, as manifold "cultures", each having their own history, internal logic and beauty. Formerly, "culture" was more of a synonym for "civilisation"—either you have it or you are a "savage"! Now, every culture would have a value in its own right, a value worth being defended. The Others, therefore, ceased to be necessarily inferior, they were just different, but there was no fixed point of reference for any objective judgment concerning their value, inner logic, or beauty.

But what may look like a solution in fact only frames an old problem in a different way. While the former problem had been to explain why the Others were so different, now it would have to be explained why We are so modern. Anyhow, the *Great Divide* between the "West" and the "Rest" continued as the defining demarcation line of the anthropological question.[23]

5.3.2 The Savage Mind and Western Science

Evolutionists who had been handling the "primitive's" way of understanding the world simply in terms of deficiency and lack of intellectual development were now attacked by a new generation of anthropologists. Lucien Levy-Bruhl identified

[22] "The more I see of their customs, the more I realize that we have no right to look down on them. When amongst our people would you find such true hospitality? Here, without the least complaint people are willing to perform every task demanded of them. We have no right to blame them for their forms and superstitions which may seem ridiculous to us. We 'highly educated people' are much worse, relatively speaking" (Boas *apud* Langness 1974: 46).

[23] See also Harding (1994).

"primitive mentality" not with a deficient, but a completely different, "mystical", "pre-logical" mode of thinking and perceiving, which was oriented by collective ideas that became manifest through myths and rituals. The "primitive mentality", said Levy-Bruhl, would be governed by other principles, such as *mystic participation*, making no distinction between reality and dreams, neither between past, present, or future, cause and effect, living and non-living objects, the one and the multiple. Levy-Bruhl's "primitive mentality", thus, represented a logic of its own, completely incommensurable to our rational logic, and therefore, could only be studied from an objective perspective. The differences between those thought styles would resemble differences in the social structures of a society, or in other words, each social system would produce its particular thought system, and vice versa. Moreover, Levy-Bruhl insisted that "primitive mentality" would not be restricted to non-Western cultures, but exist within every human being, although in modern society it might be more restrained than in other societies. He emphasised its fundamental and important role in different domains of human life like arts, poetry, philosophy, and creativity in general.[24]

Magic as Pseudo-Science

Levy-Bruhl's view was criticised by Bronislaw Malinowski,[25] who argued that "primitive" societies actually do have copious experiential knowledge based on observation and logical reasoning, and that they do distinguish quite rigidly between profane and sacral knowledge, although magic and profane knowledge may be closely associated. And he went on to ask whether such "primitive knowledge" could be called science:

> If by science be understood a body of rules and concepts, based on experience and derived from logical inference, embodied in material achievements and in a fixed form of tradition and carried on by some sort of social organization—then there is no doubt that even the lowest savage communities have the beginnings of science, however rudimentary (Malinowski 1948: 17).

Furthermore, Malinowski claimed that these rudimentary sciences would even satisfy some of the most fundamental epistemological requirements of modern science, such as open control of experiment, critique by reason, theoretical laws, and disinterestedness. Following Frazer, he maintained that magic could be called a "pseudo-science" for it would share inner coherence, one of science's most fundamental attributes. However, unlike modern science, which was based on everyday experience and logical reasoning, magic was based on specific subjective experiences and desires in ritual contexts. Of course, Malinowski never considered magic to really work in the same sense as modern science does and merely interpreted magic concerning its social function "to ritualize man's optimism, to enhance his faith in the victory of hope over fear".[26]

---

[24] Lévy-Bruhl (1927). See also Tambiah (1990) about Levy-Bruhl.

[25] Malinowski (1948).

[26] Idem: 70.

Nevertheless, Malinowski contributed to the consolidation of the concept of a universal *psychic unity of mankind*, as suggested earlier by Adolf Bastian and Franz Boas, thereby excluding racial inferiority as an explanation for cultural differences and emphasising the intellectual capacities of "primitive" men to think in terms of coherent logical abstractions.

Bricolage and the Symbolic Capacity of the Savage Mind

The *psychic unity of mankind* was also the cornerstone of Claude Lévi-Strauss' structuralist approach. Like Malinowski, Lévi-Strauss made an attempt at directly comparing modern science and the "savage mind",[27] criticising previous accounts which had characterised the "primitives" as irrational and intellectually inferior. Magic and science should be seen as two parallel, equally valid forms of reasoning, although differing in their theoretical and practical outcome. While modern science would be more successful in practical terms, magic would work as a symbolic system to order and classify things, making sense of them. Lévi-Strauss emphasises that both science and magic are based on the same universal cognitive abilities and processes, and that both aim to establish order, assuming deterministic principles of cause and effect. However, one important difference between magic and science was that while the former assumed a global and integral determinism, the latter distinguishes between different degrees of determinism, of which it accepts just some particular forms.

As a metaphor, Lévi-Strauss compared the mythical thinking of the "savage mind" with an intellectual *bricolage* or tinkering, making do with what is at hand by assembling and reassembling what it finds in its surrounding to solve the problem of perceived chaos. The "scientific mind", in contrast, would be comparable to the work of an engineer, who first analyses and calculates, and then provides the best materials to do the job. While the "savage mind" or *bricoleur* uses signs and images, fusing signifier and signified together, the "scientific mind" or engineer works with concepts, which are completely transparent in respect to their meaning. However, despite its limitations, the "savage mind" or mythical thinking would manage to make sense of a chaotic universe which science ended up accepting, contenting itself with the explanation of limited phenomena.[28]

To put it in a nutshell, and at the risk of oversimplifying Lévi-Strauss' highly eloquent work, both "savage" and "scientific mind" aim to establish order by means of a system of classifications and signs aiming to enable orientation, and ultimately, survival—and both modes of reasoning and classifying equally manage to attain this task. But while the "savage", "magic" or "mythical" mode of reasoning provides a deeper sense of meaningfulness, the "scientific" mode is more efficient in manipulating the material world. This deep sense of meaningfulness that characterises the "savage mind" is a result of the fusion of signifier and signified, sign and assigned object, thus constituting a world of comprehensible and manifest symbols. Science's success in manipulating the material world, on the other hand, is due to its

---

[27] Lévi-Strauss (1973).

[28] See also Lévi-Strauss (1995).

use of abstract concepts instead of symbols. Lévi-Strauss understood culture as a system of symbols, and as a corollary, the "savage mind" would do wonderfully in this respect, therefore representing a mode of reasoning as valid as modern science.

Consensual Versus Competitive Modes of Theorising
Symbolist approaches, however, have been criticised by authors like Robin Horton.[29] According to Horton, symbolists "divided human thought and discourse into two great categories: the expressive, which involves the production of symbolic imagery as an end in itself; and the instrumental, which involves the use of literal, discursive thought and language to achieve the ulterior end of practical control of the world".[30] Although both modes were universally present in all cultures, the *expressive* mode would be the dominating mode in non-Western contexts and the *instrumental* mode in the modern West. This view enabled symbolists to obviate value judgments about the inferiority of non-Western thought systems. But in fact, members of non-Western cultures would not agree to this external interpretation and state that their reasoning is equally meant to explain, predict, and control the objective world, just as Western science does. Horton now argues that instead of explaining non-Western thought, the symbolist view reveals more about Western ideology, where the *instrumental* had been separated from the *expressive* sphere in a process of secularisation, the first becoming the domain of science and the latter the domain of religion. According to Horton, this separation was a crucial distinctive feature of the modern Western thought-system, while in virtually all non-modern-Western contexts, including the pre-modern West, those two domains would have never been separated. Horton also introduced the distinction between *primary* and *secondary theory* as a substitute for the common opposition of empirical/practical versus theoretical knowledge. While the former explains the material world of our everyday experience, the latter provides a metaphysical framework to explain the hidden structure of the universe that governs the world we live in. Now, another difference between the modern West and non-Western traditional thought would lie in their secondary theory. Traditional non-Western secondary theory would tend to more spiritual explanations, while the modern West would tend to impersonal, materialistic, or secular theory. This difference in secondary theory, again, corresponds to different modes of theorising: traditional thought would be based on a *consensual mode of theorising* and a *traditionalistic concept of time*, therefore not becoming aware of possible alternative secondary theories; modern thought, in turn, would be based on *a competitive mode of theorising* and a *progressivistic concept of time*, therefore allowing for changes in secondary theory and moreover for the development of a meta-theory to compare and balance different alternative secondary theories against one another.

In sum, Horton provides us with several objective distinctive aspects which would separate the "West" from the "Rest", or more precisely, the modern "Western" thought from "non-modern" "traditional" thought (including pre-modern Western

[29] Horton (1967, 1993).

[30] Horton (1993: 6).

thought). Following his analyses, those distinctive features of modern thought would be bound to:

1. A process of secularisation based on the separation of the *expressive* and *instrumental* knowledge
2. A more impersonal, materialistic secondary theory (=metaphysical framework)
3. And the combination of a progressive concept of time and a competitive mode of theorising, as manifested in scientific meta-discourse on alternative secondary theories

True, this comparison of objective features of "modern" and "traditional" thought systems does not make any judgment concerning their particular truth values. However, this is also due to the fact that Horton avoided touching on this point as much as the symbolists did. What are compared are exclusively the different modes of knowing; neither their epistemological foundations nor their objective results are put into question.[31] Furthermore, it can be doubted whether modern science is really as "competitive" or "open" to changes in its secondary theory as Horton seems to suggest. And finally, one could question whether those diacritical aspects as demonstrated by Horton would also be identified as such by the Others (in his case African "traditional" communities), and if not, whether this sample of aspects does not merely reflect a particular "Western" self-image and the epistemological model that legitimises the dominant geopolitical position of the "West".[32]

Oral Knowledge and Western Logocentrism

Horton also associated oral tradition with more "closed" thought systems or consensual modes of theorising, while written tradition would tend to foster "open" or competitive thought systems. He argued that oral knowledge was perceived as unchangeable, representing the ancestral wisdom, while in fact it was constantly changing due to different interpretations and adaptations made by each generation, and even by each individual narrator. However, since those changes went unnoticed for both narrators and believers, no comparison between those different versions was possible, and would continue to be conceived as timeless and absolutely valid. With literacy this situation would change radically, since the transcription of oral knowledge into written text would "freeze" its content, so that different interpretations could be checked against the original text. This, in turn, would be favourable for the establishment of a more "open" and competitive mode of theorising.[33]

[31] Actually, in his earlier work, Horton (1967) proposed a distinction between "open" Western and "closed" non-Western thought-systems, following Popper. Here he lists a number of differences that would prove his view, including the power of words in magic, the relation between "idea" and "reality", degrees of reflectiveness, divination versus diagnoses, experimental method, concepts of coincidence and probability, written versus oral tradition, etc. But in his 1993 work, Horton relativises his former views and switches to the more "neutral" version of consensual versus competitive mode of theorising.

[32] Tambiah (1990).

[33] Horton (1967).

Horton's argument follows Jack Goody's[34] work on the influence of literacy on the development of Western culture and modern science. More than just "freezing" and accumulating knowledge, Goody holds that written language decontextualises knowledge and facilitates the use of abstract concepts. While oral speech is perceived as a continuous flux of rhetoric figures, written text falls into single words, each representing an idea or concept. Written text, thus, facilitates logical analysis and, as a consequence, logical thought.[35] Literacy, therefore, would represent an important "technology of the intellect" and heavily influence the form and use of language as well as our cognitive operations. Goody emphasises that the invention of letters represented a decisive step in human evolution. Without an alphabetical writing system, logical operations like Aristotle's syllogism would be difficult to imagine. This is not to say that there would be no logical reasoning without writing, as reasoning is always a logical operation, but there would be different kinds of logic, and written cultures tend to develop a particular form of logical reasoning different from oral cultures. In a way, writing might be just another form to enact the magical power of words,[36] and science, like magic, could be seen as a "set of procedures for changing the world".[37]

Other authors[38] have urged some caution against such overestimations of the importance of literacy, as they could be a result of Western scholars' own logocentrism. Maurice Bloch, for example, holds that cognition is not affected by the use of writing as much as Goody would have it. He argues that culture is more than language, and consequently, cognitive concepts do not follow linguistic concepts, but on the contrary, language would be based on non-linguistic concepts. Although people commonly refer to their knowledge using language, most of knowledge is non-linguistic, non-linear, or embodied. However, embodied knowledge should not be confused with the linguistic expressions referring to it. Written, oral, and embodied knowledge, therefore, simply represent different kinds of knowledge. As a consequence, the transcription of oral and performative knowledge into written accounts may not change its content, but still results in a new set of knowledge, different in character and meaning compared to its original non-linguistic model.[39] Moreover, social scientist's logocentric accounts would not be approved by the people whose view they pretend to represent.[40] For quite a time now, a growing number of authors

[34] Goody (1977, 2000).

[35] See also Hornbacher (2005).

[36] Very much like Lévi-Strauss' Nambikwara chief who tried to imitate the white anthropologist's magic of writing to impress his community (Lévi-Strauss 1999).

[37] Idem 1973: 149.

[38] Münzel (1986); Bloch (1998); Lévi-Strauss (1999); Hornbacher (2005).

[39] "If the anthropologist is often attempting to give an account of chunked and non-sentential knowledge in a linguistic medium (writing), and she has no alternative, she must be aware that in so doing she is not reproducing the organisation of the knowledge of the people she studies but is transmuting it into an entirely different logical form. To effect: such a transmutation is not impossible—after all we can describe things which are not linguistic" (Bloch 1998: 15).

[40] Münzel (1986); Bloch (1998).

from oral cultures are using writing for their own purposes; however, Bloch argues they would not necessarily see literacy as such an important thing and even ridicule Westerners' dependency on written knowledge.[41] Besides, oral texts would be as complex and elaborate as written texts, with different distinguishable genres and narrative styles. This complexity may disappear partly in the process of transcription, as oral knowledge is inherently performative, transcending the mere literal content through the narrator's enactment.

It is true that oral knowledge constantly changes due to individual differences between the interpretations of each narrator, but it is doubtful whether the narrators are not aware of their different interpretations. The narrators know their oral knowledge by having assisted countless enactments performed by their elders before. There is no reason to assume they would make changes in their narrations unconsciously or due to false memory. Different interpretations of ancient oral texts, therefore, are as much an expression of reflexive reasoning as written interpretations of written texts. To associate oral knowledge with emotive reasoning and written knowledge with reflexive or rational reasoning would be misleading. No doubt both oral and written interpretations are equally reflexive, although they may represent different kinds of reflexivity, the former being more contextualised than the latter.[42] Actually, the very distinction between "emotive" and "reflexive" reasoning might reflect a particularly "Western" idea of "reasoning" as something completely separate from "feeling", while oral cultures simply might not make such a distinction.[43] This confusion seems to be as old as anthropology itself. Throughout its history, the magical power of words, that constantly mixes up wishes, dreams, and reality, has been attributed by Western anthropologists to "non-Western" (or "savage", "primitive", "traditional", "mythical", "magic", "oral"—you name it!) thought as a distinctive property and contrasted with "Western" ("modern", "rational", "logical", "scientific", "literate") reasoning.[44] But from the point of view of those "savages", reasoning may be more a business of the heart[45] than of the head, and they might even ask whether we Westerners have to learn to read first to be able to think and reflect.[46] Be it as it may, if literacy really is related to the separation of logical and emotive reasoning as seems to be

[41] Indigenous intellectuals frequently both read and write ethnographic accounts on their culture. Hence, oral traditions are increasingly influenced, and in some cases even largely constructed in direct reference to written transcriptions and interpretations (Clifford 1986; Linhart 2008).

[42] Hornbacher (2005).

[43] Münzel (1986); Hornbacher (2005).

[44] See previous passages.

[45] Castillo (2005); Linhart (2008); Soto (2019); CRIC (2021).

[46] Münzel (1986).

characteristic for the "West", this property would not necessarily be seen as an advantage by the "non-Western" Others.[47]

It seems also clear that writing has not been invented in order to free people and their minds, or to make them think in a more reflexive manner. As a rule, from a historical perspective, literacy always emerged in the context of expanding empires, serving as a means for power and control; for the control of mystic powers, as in early China, for eternalising and legitimising the divine power of some ruler, like in Egypt and Central America, or to impose and enhance bureaucratic structures, as in European and Mesopotamian antiquity.[48] Different usages of the written word may be attached to different power-relations or political systems. Sacred texts like the Bible or the Quran obviously will not contribute much to a more competitive mode of theorising, whereas the philosophical discourse in Greek antiquity was related to the *polis*, where open public discourse at the *agora*, ruled by the competition of the better argument, were core elements of the political system. But still, only educated, free, male Greek citizens had access to education, literacy, and politics.

Oral knowledge, in contrast, is by and large open to all members of the community. There may be some kinds of knowledge that are restricted to specific gender, age, or spiritual leadership, but in most cases the great majority of oral knowledge has no restrictions at all. Most myths and practical knowledge about hunting and planting will be known to every child in the community. It is a knowledge coming from all the ancestors that ever lived to be perpetuated and further developed by all living members of the community, and which will be handed over to all future generations to come. Oral knowledge, therefore, is a collective knowledge that stretches throughout time, guarantees continuity, and defines the identity of a "traditional" community, while continuously being adapted to changing needs and circumstances. This is the very meaning and importance of oral tradition. The written word, in contrast, is the product of an individual author, immutable in its content, and restricted to a limited group of readers.

The question may be, then, why literacy became so important for the Western self-image? According to Hornbacher,[49] one answer to this question could lie in the role literacy might have played concerning the development of some key notions of Western philosophy. As a text is the product of an individual author's mind, the truth of its content is also bound to the limits of reason, subjective experience, and the way ideas represent the objective outer world. So, the rise of literacy in early Greek antiquity may have been intimately related to the rise of the autonomous subject, rationalism, and representationalism.

In the time of Homer and Hesiod (700 B.C.) truth, or *aletheia*, was based on the oral knowledge of the myths and spiritual intuition. Literacy was beginning to be

[47] According to McGilchrist (2009), our exaggerated focus on logical reasoning may really be more a deficiency than an advantage.

[48] Crystal (1997); Lévi-Strauss (1999); Goody (2000).

[49] Hornbacher (2005).

used to write down the old mythic narrations,[50] which later other authors would comment on, giving birth to Western philosophical discourse. Now individual authors would propose their ideas and discuss those of their peers, becoming the prime source of wisdom. While in former times speech was perceived as an embodied enactment of collective memory, now the written word would represent just the ideas produced by the subject's intellect. Words turned into images of ideas, which in turn were images of the *logos*, or, generally, of the true, objective outer world. As a consequence, man's self-image changed, perceiving himself as a rational being, an intellect enclosed within a body.

Some 200 years later, Plato would go about reforming the Pre-Socratic concept of *aletheia* and privilege the concept of *logos*, demanding a new model of truth based on logical reasoning and reflection. The ancestors' wisdom would no longer be a guarantee for truth; instead the logical capacity of the subject's mind would be the final arbiter. "Myth" gradually became a synonym for an illusive, outdated knowledge, which would have to be overcome in order to illuminate people's minds.

However, Hornbacher also calls attention to the fact that by the time those changes in Western thought occurred not only had literacy become the main vehicle of knowledge, but there were also deep changes in the power relations that governed Greek society. At the same time as the subject happened to become the only source of knowledge, democracy also arose, handing over political power from the king to the citizen. While the former regime was based on tradition, the new regime was based on the better argument and rhetoric, thus changing in parallel with the notion of truth.

The attic enlightenment of Greek antiquity actually shows interesting parallels with seventeenth and eighteenth century enlightenment after the humanist renaissance and scientific revolution. There, too, the spread of literacy coincided with a democratisation of both political power and knowledge, and the rise of modern rationalism.[51] This historical coincidence may be less surprising if we consider the lessons taught by thinkers like Nietzsche, Heidegger, and Foucault, who called attention to the intimate relation between power and knowledge as the two sides of the same coin. But while other cultures openly admit this relationship as an obvious fact, the Western discourse on truth systematically negates it, holding to its foundationalist universalism based on subjectivism, rationalism, and representationalism. This may be another reason for the paradox of modern humanism, which declares human reason to be universal and then goes on to negate other cultures' knowledge as being irrational. And literacy may have played a crucial role in this story.

Summing up, there does not seem to be any solid ground for holding that literate culture would be more evolved than oral culture, or that written knowledge would facilitate a more reflexive and open mode of reasoning compared to performative or narrative knowledge. Performative and narrative knowledge has its own mode of

[50] Which were actually epic songs.

[51] Linhart (2008).

reflexive reasoning and is also open, as it continuously adapts to new circumstances, maybe even quicker and smoother than written knowledge.

On the other hand, there is also no evidence that literacy inevitably results in the same deep impacts as those we may observe in our own Western culture.[52] In Western history, however, literacy may have had an exceptional influence concerning the rise of some philosophical key notions which are fundamental for our particular "Western" worldview, and which differ quite radically from most other cultures. Rationalism, as the notion that all true knowledge is based on the logical reasoning and the experience of an autonomous subject whose ideas are representations of an objective outer world, also entails a particular anthropological image of man as a free, reasonable intellect jailed in a material body (the *cogito*). This notion may also have led us to distinguish between rational and emotive, or embodied knowledge, favouring the first and neglecting the latter, while oral cultures may not pay much attention to this distinction at all.

Literacy, therefore, may not be necessary for reasonable thought, but its particular role in Western history may make us believe so; it may even have had an important influence in the course of the development of our own modern/Western concept of rationality, our worldview, and the notion of ourselves as reasonable subjects. But there is no evidence that in the context of other times or cultures literacy automatically results in these same effects as well. Oral cultures may appear to *Us* as being inferior concerning their intellectual capacities, because for Us, "Westerners", literacy is of prime importance both for our own intellect and our self-image.

5.3.3 The Western Scope of Rationality

Given that we Western scientists are caught up within our supposedly "rational" mode of theorising, how can we understand the others, if they live in worlds made up by completely different ways of thinking, feeling, and knowing?

Stanley J. Tambiah[53] famously boiled this question down to the problem of "rationality". He held that the vast majority of Western interpretations of the non-Western Others would be constrained by one of two different Western concepts of rationality. The first one suggests the existence of just one universal rationality governed by the principles of logic: coherence, consistency, and non-contradiction. Tambiah called the adherents to this view "unifiers", as they suppose rationality to be a universal ground of understanding, serving as a yardstick for intercultural comparison. This position assumes the existence of a fixed point of reference for the interpretation of other cultures as well as for objective judgements concerning their degree of "rationality" or "irrationality". However, Tambiah pointed out that the unifiers' concept of rationality appears to be a Western phenomenon, itself just rep-

[52] Bloch (1998).

[53] Tambiah (1990).

resenting a particular culturally and historically determined disposition towards the world. Hence, to hold that culturally determined normative criteria for rationality would prove its universal validity would be circular. The Western concept of rationality and its logical attributes of coherence, consistency, and non-contradiction, therefore, would not do as a universal yardstick for intercultural comparison.

This argument would also be the point for those who advocate the second concept of rationality, whom Tambiah called the "relativisers". Following this view, there are many different rationalities with no fixed point of reference for any judgment or objective interpretation of other worldviews or cultures. Any aspect of a culture is equally meaningful and true, but only within its own context. The worldview produced by Western science, therefore, would be just one of countless other possible subjective realities and there would be no reason to assume its universal validity to measure or judge other rationalities. Moreover, the scientific view would not only be restricted to the modern "West", but also represent a very particular view of an even smaller group within modern Western society: the scientific community. However, Tambiah alluded to the problem that relativism absolutises incommensurability, while also leading to moral relativism.[54] Furthermore, the assumption of an absolute relativism in itself would violate its own relativistic supposition, as its non-judgment-taboo would be moral in character, too, and therefore equally relative and inadequate for serving as a neutral and at the same time absolute standard.

As an alternative, Tambiah suggests a more complex position in between the two extremes of universalism and relativism. Incommensurability is a very rigorous notion and may be employed all too easily in cases where in fact there might be just a difference in perception and not an absolute impossibility of translation.[55] Although any direct translation from alien concepts into our own would seem impossible, other perceptions could be understood from within those other "forms of life"[56] they originate from and be described in terms of our own concepts. This dialectical process of apprehension would eventually also change our own views and amplify our understanding of our own cultural context. However, some perceptions and concepts may in fact be incommensurable, while others may be translatable up to varying degrees. For example, two different propositions may refer to the same problem in different terms but on the basis of the same basic suppositions, sharing a common frame of reference. This could allow them to come to an agreement by applying their shared logical rules and arguments to come to a shared judgment about the validity of both propositions. In other cases, there may be different solutions to the same problem, with each solution referring to different basic suppositions, allowing only for a comparison of its practical implications, but not for a judgment about its

---

[54] "[I]f [...] we are prepared to argue that on a certain issue societies or cultures A and B hold different views, and each in its context is justified, true or meaningful, we should be prepared to defend this judgment as having absolute validity for us, and provide the necessary proof" (Tambiah 1990: 128).

[55] "To tell us that Galileo had 'incommensurable' notions and then to go on to describe them at length is totally incoherent" (Putnam 1981: 115).

[56] Tambiah borrows this expression from Wittgenstein (1969).

inner logic. However, there may also be cases of "exclusive incommensurability" where different views result from completely distinct forms of life, making any meaningful comparison impossible.

In sum, Western rationality, with modern science as its most articulated expression, represents just one of many viable "frames of reference" or "ways of worldmaking",[57] providing reasonable and meaningful explanations only within the context of the specific form of life they emerged from—in this case: modern Western science.

Nevertheless, Tambiah holds that this does not necessarily entail absolute relativism. Instead of trying to blur the differences between the "West" and the "Rest" by searching for supposed similarities between science and magic or the "savage mind", declaring the Others to be "rational" as well (in the style of Malinowski, Levi-Strauss or Horton),[58] Tambiah suggests a new demarcation line.[59] He champions Maurice Leenhardt's[60] interpretation of Lévy-Bruhl's concept of the *primitive mind* as a universal aspect of human cognition oriented towards *participation,* which goes together with *causality* as its complementary opposite. *Participation*, as a kind of perceptive mode or way of relating to the world, would aim at the establishment of relations to all things in a more transcendental manner, especially to those things and landscapes suffused by the ancestor's spirits; it would encompass notions of one-ness, unity, continuity in space and time, myths and ritual enactments. *Causality*, in contrast, would be represented best by the rules of positive sciences and mathematic-logical reasoning. Those two principles would never be strictly separated and rather appear in real life in mixed forms. Although our Western concept of rationality may be dominated by the principle of causality, the principle of participation may play some role in our perception, too, while causality is equally employed in other cultures, at least to some extent. So, there may be still some common ground of perception we share with other forms of life, even if they are oriented mainly by the principle of participation and therefore, appear to be completely incommensurable to us, at the first glance.

Tambiah holds that even in science both notions would be present, as demonstrated by the conflict between Einstein and Bohr concerning objective versus participatory reality in the light of Heisenberg's findings on indeterminism and uncertainty, and Bohr's principle of complementarity. Science, therefore, could be understood as a special kind of "mental province"[61] where causality is the dominant principle, while coexisting in parallel with other provinces like everyday perception

[57] Tambiah borrows these expressions from Nelson Goodman (1985).

[58] Latour (1993) also highlights that previous attempts of anthropologists like Levi-Strauss to construe some degree of continuity between Us and the Others tried to put them closer to science. By conflating science with nature, science itself becomes transcendental, and thus, universal and independent from culture, untouched by cultural relativism.

[59] See also Latour (1993) and Bourdieu's critique on this issue (Bourdieu 1987: 69).

[60] Tambiah refers to Leenhardt (1982).

[61] Like Berger and Luckmann (1991), Tambiah borrows this expression from Alfred Schutz (1962).

or religious experience, where participation might be the leading principle.[62] In the everyday life of modern Western society, however, causality-based rationality may play a much less important role in our perception than we imagine, being limited more or less to mental provinces like science and maybe some technical activities like engineering, and leaving considerable space for other participation-oriented provinces.[63]

So, in the end it is difficult to imagine a whole culture to be completely incommensurable to us. However, we may well encounter some particular phenomena in other cultures which emerge from perceptions or mental provinces that do not match with any of our own, and thus, will challenge our interpretative capacities to the limits when we try to make sense of them.

In any case, the Great Divide between the "rational" "West" and the "emotive" "Rest" has been further relativised by Tambiah's approach. First, because participation and causality both represent equally valid universal orienting principles present in every human mind, although with differently weighted importance, depending on a person's culturally induced mental dispositions. So, there would be no fundamental cognitive difference between the "West" and the "Rest", nor do we need to make the Others more rational than they actually might be. Secondly, by eliminating the Western concept of rationality both as a supposedly universal yardstick for objective value-judgements about other modes of reasoning and the relativist notion of multiple incommensurable rationalities. Although seemingly contradictory, both concepts of rationality are a consequence of representationalism, the unifiers' concept following the objectivist and the relativisers' the subjectivist point of view. As a corollary, it appears that most theoretical problems concerning the anthropological project of understanding and explaining cultural difference are not a consequence of incommensurability, but rather that incommensurability is a consequence of this particular Western concept of rationality, and ultimately of the epistemological presuppositions of Western philosophy and modern science.

---

[62] Compare also Atmanspacher and Primas (2006) on Pauli's ideas on mind and matter in the context of contemporary science.

[63] At this point Tambiah draws some parallels to Freud's concept of primary mental processes that would govern our unconsciousness and feminist descriptions of "female" reasoning within our own culture. Such notions would equally describe participation-oriented mental dispositions within Western society. I personally think it would also be interesting here to explore Bourdieu's notion of the Habitus as a universal, unconscious, and thus, irrational behavioural matrix of embodied knowledge. With his notion of the Habitus, Bourdieu goes a huge step further than Tambiah. He not only declares that, although dominated by causal rationality, we Westerners also may be influenced by participation oriented perceptions. Bourdieu's approach is much more radical, as the irrational rules of the Habitus are paramount for all social domains, in the "Rest" as well as in the "West", including modern science. Following Bourdieu, science would represent just one particular social "field" with its own academic Habitus, equally governed by unconscious embodied notions and perceptions (Bourdieu 1975, 1985, 1987, 1992, 2001). Compare the previous chapter.

Moreover, Tambiah holds (together with Max Weber,[64] Herbert Marcuse,[65] and other critical voices), that even the apparent successes of modern sciences in manipulating the physical world would not prove its objective superiority compared to other thought systems. In the face of its destructive effects, modern science may be questioned exactly because it is effective in only one particular way.[66] Unfortunately, due to its intrinsic entanglement with virtually every aspect of modern society, scientific knowledge occupies a truth monopoly infringing also on moral issues, excluding other world orientations as possible alternatives, while at the same time eliminating any meaningful explanation of the whole picture or sense of life. Tambiah alerts us to the risks of this universalistic scientism, as causality may not be the only rational framework and the repudiation of other participation-orientated views may block our understanding of the ultimate concerns of life. And he reminds us of Weber's conclusion, that even instrumental and absolutist rationalities are based on subjective grounds and legitimated truth values; this would be true for religion as well as for modern science.

5.4 The Ontological Turn: Beyond Nature and Culture

Tambiah's approach is part of a paradigmatic shift in anthropology which became visible during the 1990s. In the political climate of "the wind of change" after the fall of the Berlin wall and Soviet Union, (supposedly) bringing an end to more than 40 years of cold war and its threat of nuclear Armageddon, new agendas began to emerge. Boundaries shifted, expanding the "West" to the former "East", replacing the spectre of "communism" and nuclear war with the fear of ecological disaster caused by capitalism, globalisation, and modernity in general. The Great Divide between Us and Them, the "West" and the "Rest", "modern" and "premodern" cultures, was put into question. What is it that "really" differentiates Us compared to Them? Are we actually so different from all other cultures or do we only think so? And if our "modern" way of life threatens human survival on earth, what could we learn from other "non-modern" cultures?

---

[64] Tambiah refers to Weber's The Protestant Ethic and the Spirit of Capitalism (Weber 2006).

[65] Tambiah refers to Marcuse (1964).

[66] "There is in fact no reason to suppose that effective science does increase the survival-prospect of the species which carries it. The self-destruction of humanity, through nuclear or other war or ecological disasters perfectly possible and perhaps probable in the post-scientific age..." (Gellner 1985, *apud* Tambiah 1990: 152).

5.4.1 *The End of the Great Divide?*

It was in the context of these radically changing challenges that Bruno Latour[67] proposed his polemic hypotheses, that "we have never been modern". Based on his earlier work on science studies and his actor network theory,[68] Latour offered a quite unorthodox definition of modernity. He surmised that modernity is sustained by two interdependent, but contradictory sets of essentially different practices.

The first one, which he called *translation*, results in the continuous production of *hybrids* or *quasi-objects*, entities which are both natural and social, objects and subjects, and which interact with us and one another as actors within a network. Such hybrids can be material objects or technologies, like computers or mobile phones, or other, more abstract objects or scientific facts like the ozone hole, AIDS, or DNA, as well as humans, CEOs, politicians, ordinary people, or statistics and reports on their behaviour, news on TV, and articles in journals. They are hybrids because they are a result of social action while at the same time playing an active role in modern society.

The second fundamental practice, which Latour called *purification*, negates and obfuscates the work and even the existence of all those hybrids by producing a dual ontology through the exclusive categorisation of everything as either human or non-human, subject or object, natural or cultural/social. Latour emphasised that these two practices are mutually constitutive, depending on each other as two antagonistic forces, which, while being apparently contradictory, secretly reinforce each other's work.

But while We, moderns, share the practice of hybrid production with all other cultures, We differ from the Others in disavowing our hybrids. Since for Us moderns, what defines Our being so special and incomparable to all Other cultures, is precisely the ontological distinction between subject and object, nature and culture. And as We in fact never stopped mixing up these two realms and continue to produce ever more hybrids with whom We permanently interact, We never really have been modern in the sense We thought We were (hence the provocative title of Latour's book).

As a consequence, the only real difference between Us and the Others is that we think We are so different, while in fact We are much more like Them than We imagine. The Great Divide between Us and Them together with all Our triumphalist exceptionalism, therefore, turns out to be a result of modernity's internal Great Divide between culture/society and nature, subject and object, human and nonhuman. This internal Divide even cuts through Our own history, separating Us, moderns, from Our past, from the "Dark Ages" of the "Ancient Regime". Notions of linear time, revolutionary changes and progress, thus, are conceptual instruments of the work of purification and essential for maintaining the Great Divide between Us, the moderns, and the "premodern" Others. This intrinsic interdependence between

[67] Latour (1993).

[68] Latour and Woolgar (1986); Latour (1987); see the previous chapter.

the linear model of time and the dichotomist ontology as well as between the internal and the external Great Divide, offers an interesting explanation for the evolutionist identification of the Others as "primitives", still living in magical worlds full of spiritual entities, human-nonhuman-hybrids, subject-objects and object-subjects, unable to distinguish between nature and culture, human and nonhuman, subject and object.

However, the more powerful modern society gets, the more hybrids it produces, and the more difficult it becomes to hide their existence and its intrinsic contradictions embedded in the subject-object dichotomy. Latour showed how, throughout modern discourse, different philosophical approaches tried and failed to solve the predicaments of modernity. Neither the extreme dualism of positivism, nor dialectics, nor the linguistic or semiotic turn, nor phenomenology, nor Heidegger's isolation of the idea of Being would have been able to overcome the modern contradiction between translation and purification. On the contrary, all these attempts would have maintained the Great Divide both in its internal as well as in its external dimension. So-called post-modern and deconstructionist approaches have done even worse by simply applying the modern practice of debunking and purifying to modernity itself, producing kind of a "hyper-incommensurability" and thus deepening the gap instead of bridging it. As a consequence, anthropology, which absorbed all those philosophical impulses, continued to be asymmetrical, limiting itself by studying just one side of the whole picture, culture, while ignoring the other side, nature, thus being unable to cope with hybrids of any kind other than taking them for simulacra or symbols within socio-cultural structures of knowledge and power-relations.

Latour called for a new, more symmetrical anthropology,[69] which should surpass the limits of sociology of knowledge and epistemology, following a principle of generalised symmetry. Explanation should depart from a middle ground position to follow the attribution of human and nonhuman properties to entities in the world, neither explaining society via nature nor the other way round. Instead of studying "cultures", anthropologists should study "nature-cultures" and move down to the nonmodern dimension where the work of mediation emerges, which secretly constitutes our world made up by hybrids. Finally, we should accept that the "premoderns are like us" and drop the whole dichotomy between Us and Them altogether[70] with modern notions of relative cultures, on one side, and universal nature on the other.[71]

---

[69] Latour and Miranda (2017).

[70] As already suggested by Feyerabend (1993).

[71] Of course, my presentation of Latour's (1993) approach omits many critical questions. I am not really sure whether Latour's aphoristic assay is just one more example of the countless attempts to overcome the modern subject-object dichotomy that populate the endless swamp of modern and postmodern philosophy, or whether it really points to the essence of the whole problem. His attempt to boil modernity down to its cosmological Constitution contradicts the very solution he proposes, which is exactly to transcend essentialism, idealism and materialism. On the other hand, he suggested substituting the nature-culture dichotomy by networks made up of human and nonhuman actors, while the latter are material, or at least abstract objects (hybrids, machines, technologies) endowed with agency only by virtue of the creative practices of the former, as mediators—how

5.4.2 *Relational Epistemologies: Animism Revisited*

Latour's unconventional analysis of the modern Constitution opens new perspectives for comparative anthropology. Suppose the external Great Divide between Us and Them is in fact just a reflection of modernity's inner Great Divide between culture and nature, human and nonhuman, subject and object, and thus a modern construction while We actually share the practice of hybrid production with all Others, why then do We have to negate Our hybrids? And how do the Others deal with their hybrids? Are there Other ways of worldmaking beyond the nature-culture divide We could learn from?

Such questions were taken up by a number of anthropologists who developed a set of novel approaches, which have been discussed under titles like "New Animism"[72] and "Perspectivism",[73] and which would be fundamental to the "Ontological Turn"[74] in the humanities.

---

then, did he escape materialism and idealism, or dialectics? Then, he continued to maintain, that we have never been modern, while talking about the "moderns" and the "modern" Constitution all the time. Also, Latour's extremely theoretical approach, based on highly abstract concepts from Western philosophical discourse (immanence, transcendence, objectivity, subjectivity, etc.), and his attempt to distil this cocktail of abstract terms into a crystal-clear theoretical solution to the whole predicament of Western subject-object-dichotomy, is at least suspicious. This is even more the case, as he insisted on maintaining the separation of a transcendental nature and an immanent society while making the processes of its production more transparent (in total contradiction to his previous analysis, where he showed that the obfuscation of the practice of translation is at the core of the whole process). I think Latour's proposal would only be coherent if it took the Other's point of view seriously, including immaterial agents and material objects endowed with some kind of "personhood" or intention by their own virtue. It seems that Latour felt these shortcomings himself and so he resumed his project of an ethnography of the Moderns in later works (Latour 2013, 2016). His 2013 enquiry into modes of existence subjacent to the Modern's way of being and knowing is meant to serve as a preparatory step towards a comparative anthropology, allowing us to "renegotiate that 'we' from top to bottom— and thus also renegotiate what we might become with the 'others', as we face the new horizon of Gaia" (idem: 15). Standing on Whitehead's giant shoulders, Latour attempted to square ANT with a kind of object-oriented process ontology (however, without explicitly referring either to Whitehead's process ontology or to Harman's object-oriented ontology). While the identification and comparison of modes of existence is certainly a valuable research programme, I cannot but feel that Latour's insistence on ANT as an all-purpose tool for solving all of modernity's multiple dilemmas led him into category mistakes (e.g. identifying his own idiosyncratic theoretical concept of networks as a modern mode of existence [net]). More importantly, Latour's notion of translation seems to follow a rather vicarious mode of interaction, dismissing the fundamental role of prehension, thus missing the opportunity to close the chasm between mind and world and to bail out the full potential of Whitehead's philosophy (compare also Shaviro 2014; Harman 2016). I therefore chose not to refer to Latour's more recent works, since discussing them would take much more space than would be justified by the possible gains for the present purpose.

[72] Bird-David (1999); Harvey (2005); Ingold (2006); Garuba (2012); Halbmayer (2012); Harding (2014); Morrison (2014), et al.

[73] Castro (1996, 2004a, b, 2013a, b, 2015).

[74] Descola (1992, 2006); Cadena (2010, 2015); Pedersen (2012); Castro (2013b); Green (2013); Danowski and Castro (2017); Holbraad and Pedersen (2017); Cadena and Blaser (2018); Strathern (2018); Verran (2018); et al.

New Animism offers an alternative perspective on the metaphysical and ethical dimensions of Other, non-modern ways of being that hinges on a critical revision of Edward Taylor's concept of animism[75] and Irving Hallowell's[76] pioneering work on Ojibwa Ontology.

Edward Taylor, who was probably the first to use the term *animism* in the context of anthropology, had borrowed it from seventeenth/eighteenth century alchemist Georg Stahl to conceptualise "primitive" people's belief in an animated nature pervaded with life, full of wilful and spiritual beings. For Taylor, a convinced positivist, this attribution of a "soul", "spirit", or simply life to inanimate objects, was the expression of childish perception and false epistemology typical of the "primitives" as a sort of infancy of humanity. It was a "primitive" belief, as it represented the very origin of religion. However, religious belief was considered to be only a previous state to science, which, as a natural result of human progress, would eventually substitute all kinds of beliefs in the supernatural. Taylor's theory of animism was based on second-hand reports on "primitive" ritual, which he had read in his armchair, and on his own personal experiences with European spiritism in London, both of his sources having little or nothing to do with Indigenous realities.[77] Howsoever, animism became one of the most influential notions in anthropology, representing the image of the irrational "primitive" mind as antithesis to European scientific rationality. The concept of animism, therefore, has been instrumental to the construction and maintenance of the Great Divide.

Far from depicting animism as a childish false epistemology, in his description of Ojibwa[78] ontology Irving Hallowell[79] draws a quite different picture. Although he points out that the Ojibwa's worldview[80] was fundamentally different from the modernist view, this would not imply that it would not be equally consistent with experience. On the contrary, animistic worldviews would imply particular fundamental principles, thus constituting their own metaphysical systems. Although not being consciously articulated by Indigenous people themselves, they provide "a unified phenomenal field of thought, values, and action which is integral with the kind of world view that characterizes a society", the "behavioural environment" which

[75] See Bird-David (1999); Harvey (2010).

[76] Hallowell (1960).

[77] Harvey (2010). Also Tim Ingold (2006) holds that the whole notion of animism as a way of believing *about* the world appears to be an entirely European concept, in contrast to Indigenous notions of being *in* the world.

[78] The Ojibwa (also called Ojibwe) belong to the Anishinaabe nations of the North American Great Lake region.

[79] Hallowell (1960).

[80] Hallowell uses Robert Redfield's concept of *world view* as different from *culture*: "Of all that is connoted by 'culture,' 'world view' attends especially to the way a man, in a particular society, sees himself in relation to all else. It is the properties of existence as distinguished from and related to the self. It is, in short, a man's idea of the universe" (Redfield 1952: 30).

orients the self in a "world of objects rather than self".[81] These different ways of conceiving the world of being come with deep philosophical implications which have to be studied as a kind of "ethno-metaphysics". Hallowell's own fieldwork with the Ojibwa led him to believe that their "metaphysics of being" were oriented by the action of "persons", including "other than human persons". In western culture and folklore, "supernatural" beings are persons, too, but not so in science. Also, the concept of "supernatural" would be misleading, as it already presupposes the concept of *nature*, which does not exist in Ojibwa thought. As a consequence, Our objective approach is not adequate to study worldviews to which persons other than humans are central. It would be necessary to achieve a higher order of objectivity by adopting the perspective of the Other's worldviews to understand such cultures as a whole. But Hallowell also points out that "the Ojibwa are not animists in the sense that they dogmatically attribute living souls to inanimate objects such as stones":

> I once asked an old man: Are *all* the stones we see about us here alive? He reflected a long while and then replied, 'No! But *some* are' (Hallowell 1960: 24).

The attribution of a person-status to an entity rather depends on the experience with it. Only objects which behave like persons are treated as such. Persons, both human and nonhuman, permanently transform in myths, dreams, and visions, once appearing as humans and then in nonhuman form, while maintaining their inner essence or "soul", even beyond death. The concept of anthropomorphism, therefore, would not be sufficient to explain the attribution of a person-status to an entity in the world. It is not the form or appearance of an entity which makes it a person. Some persons are not only able to change their form, but even to leave their body behind while their vital part or "soul" travels to other places in time and space. All persons have such a vital part or "soul" in addition to their material body, they all have experiences, feelings, volition and understanding, and they all demand to be respected. Relations between persons are social in nature, and hence, essentially moral and based on reciprocity. Being made up of persons, the Ojibwa's world behaves and reacts like persons do. This, in turn, implies a different notion of causality based on personalistic explanations rather than deterministic natural laws. Whatever happens is caused by some person and the question is not *how* it happened, but *who* did it and *why?*; how shall one *relate* to the *causer* in order to influence their attitude?; should one offer a gift, apologise for one's own disrespectful behaviour, or, better, kill and eat them?

Hallowell's account of the Ojibwa's worldview in terms of a relational ontology was highly influential for almost all recent works on animism. However, although having published his challenging approach in 1960, it was only through Nurit Bird-David's[82] famous article *"Animism" Revisited: Personhood, Environment, and Relational Epistemology* that Hallowell's work got the attention it deserved. Bird-David follows Hallowell's description of the Ojibwa's way of relating to a world made up of persons and applies it to the generic concept of animism. Albeit hinging

[81] Hallowell (1960: 20).

[82] Bird-David (1999).

her own approach on Hallowell's work, she criticises that the term "other than human person" still includes the modern classification as either "human" or "not human". She herself would rather opt for the term "superpersons" instead to refer to such "persons with extrapowers".[83] Furthermore, it would be important to overcome the Western notion of person as an individual. Relational concepts like Strathern's[84] notion of the *dividual* would come closer to animistic realities, which would be based on *relational epistemologies* focussing on relations rather than on the essence of individual, isolated objects or subjects. The dividual is defined by its relatedness to me and others, and has to be activated through relationship, being essentially an event of mutual relatedness.

> Against 'I think, therefore I am' stand 'I relate, therefore I am' and 'I know as I relate' (Bird-David 1999: 79).

While the objectivist paradigm "involves acquiring knowledge *of* things through the separation of knower and known, and often by breaking the known down into its parts in order to know it", animistic epistemologies reach an understanding by talking, interacting, in short, by responsibly and attentively relating to entities in the world, turning attention to our "we-ness" rather than "otherness".

> If 'cutting trees into parts' epitomizes the modernist epistemology, 'talking with trees', I argue, epitomizes Nayaka animistic epistemology (Bird-David 1999: 77).

Knowing would stay for being *in* the world with whom one dividuates, rather than for attributing meaning *to* a world of discrete objects, an interactive action that allows for developing the skill of being in the world. A stone becomes a stone-person by interacting, dividuating with me, and I acquire knowledge about her in the course of our interaction.[85]

---

[83] Bird-David (1999) also stresses that "superpersons" are often seen as relatives and even termed "grandparents" or using other kinship designations, "superrelatives" with whom one relates in order to receive help. This intimate relationship between Indigenous people and their "superrelatives" would also become visible in the way they treat them during rituals, "including joking, teasing, bargaining".

[84] Bird-David (1999: 72) refers to Strathern (1988). However, as Castro observes: "Strathernian relations *separate*, while Bird-David's relatednesses are predicated on the *absorption* of difference by commonalities and togethernesses" (Castro's comment in Bird-David (1999: 80); italics from the original). Together with authors like Isabelle Stengers (2005a, 2018a), Marisol de la Cadena and Mario Blaser (2018), Strathern (2018) argues that divergence is in fact a necessary condition for relating to others, and that a certain degree of incommensurability between diverging ontological conceptions and practices of worldmaking may entail the not-knowing required for a non-universalist dialogue beyond commonly-accepted epistemic foundations.

[85] Bird-David refers here to Gibson's (1979) ecological approach, which is also fundamental to Tim Ingold's contributions to the discussion of animism. Ingold (2000, 2006) emphasises that animistic ontologies are not another belief *about* the world, but rather a particular way of *being* and experiencing as active bodies *in* the world; a world that is alive and in continuous birth along lines of relationships, which Ingold calls "dwelling-perspective". Similarly, Hornborg (2011) emphasises the performative character of relational epistemologies, which would not be representational, and therefore, rather ontologies. However, this would equally be true for objectivism, with the differ-

Bird-David argues that both ways of perceiving the world are equally true and valid. However, the question remains why and how We "Westerners" became so modern and estranged from our original, universal animism?

> Yet powerful as it is, the scientific way is neither good for studying everything nor the only way of studying everything (Bird-David 1999: 86).

Bird-David's revision of animism was paralleled by Philippe Descola's[86] work on the nature-culture divide. Initially, Descola set out to search for cultural invariants and consequently attempted to derive both *animism* and *totemism* from social structure as two different schemes of social objectification of nature. Totemism used animals and plants as signs to organise social order along metaphors, while animism used social order to organise relations between human and non-human persons, thus treating animals and plants like real persons, too. However, Descola later understood that such a semiotic approach would only reproduce Western nature-culture dualism, since social realities are analytically subordinated to ontological realities. Western concepts of nature and culture are themselves based on a much more fundamental and universal distinction between "interiority" and "physicality", resulting in four different types of ontologies, each representing particular basic assumptions about the interiority and physicality of the non-self compared to the self:

1. *Totemism* suggests a non-self with analogous internal and physical properties
2. *Animism* a non-self with similar interiority, but different physicality compared to the self
3. *Analogism* presumes a non-self with both interiority and physically being entirely distinct from the self
4. *Naturalism*, finally, sees the non-self as being physically of the same kind, but completely deprived of any interiority

Western nature-culture dualism is, of course, based on naturalism, thus representing one of four possible ontological configurations, and not a universal ontic principle.

The four idealised types of ontologies – totemism, analogism, animism and naturalism – "serve as a point of reference for contrasting forms of cosmologies, models of social links, and theories of identity and alterity".[87] Descola offers a universal matrix for reanalysing the vast and extremely heterogenic ethnographic account in terms of a "comparative ontology" in which "Western" naturalism plays no privileged role—it is simply one among four cognitive possibilities for dealing with the

---

ence that the letter denies this fact, resulting in alienation and the disembodiment of rationality. In this sense, we would be born "pre-modern" animists, but then alienated and deprived of our initial relatedness.

[86] Descola (1992, 2006, 2014).

[87] Descola (2014: 121).

universal duality of interiority and physicality. However, such a stark typological reductionism "requires a strong dose of ontological 'foundationalism', establishing the terra firma of basic ontological premises upon which to found the edifice of anthropological theorization".[88]

Differences and critiques notwithstanding, this revisiting of animism as a potentially liberating reconception allowing for provincialising the dominant "Western" metaphysics and its characteristic notions of "nature" and "culture" has been attracting more authors, like Eduardo Viveiros de Castro,[89] Graham Harvey[90] and Isabelle Stengers,[91] among others.[92]

5.4.3 *Perspectivism and Cannibal Metaphysics*

Eduardo Viveiros de Castro criticises Bird-David for holding on to modernist tradition in translating other cosmologies in terms of epistemologies, while in fact animism would rather be an ontology.[93] His intervention points to his own approach on

[88] Holbraad and Pedersen (2017).

[89] Castro (1996, 2015).

[90] Harvey (2005, 2010, 2014).

[91] Stengers (2012, 2018a, b).

[92] E.g. Alf Hornborg (2011), Stefan Harding (2014), Ernst Halbmayer (2012) or Kenneth Morrison (2014). Of course, there are also critical responses to these revised conceptions of animism. Harry Garuba (2012) argues that rather than representing the Others' worldview, "animism is the spectral Other that simultaneously constitutes and haunts the modern". Animism has not only served as a receptacle for anything considered non-modern; without animism, positivist science would be difficult to imagine. New Animism, like post-modernism and other attempts to overcome modernism, is presented as an advance in Western knowledge. However, Garuba points out, animism matters more as a Western construct of knowledge under the control of the Western subject than as an existing practice between non-Western people. Nevertheless, Garuba admits that New Animism might be helpful for the development of new alternatives. Stefan Harding (2014) suggests, that instead of looking at Indigenous supposedly "animistic" cultures, we should search for alternatives in Our Western culture, since this is where modern science breeds. Animism was present in western philosophy from its very beginnings in the times of Thales of Miletus, who believed that all matter is alive or "full of Gods". The idea of an omnipresent sentience in all matter was never completely lost in Western philosophy and reappeared during the Renaissance in the hermeneutic concept of the anima mundi, in Goethe's intuitive method and his pantheistic worldview, as well as in James Lovelock's Gaia theory (Lovelock and Margulis 1973). Animism, in this broad sense, is similar to panpsychism and idealism in general.

[93] In her response to the comments of her colleagues, Bird-David admits that Castro is right in saying that animism is an ontology, but we (moderns) would not be able to describe it in this term (Bird-David 1999).

"Amerindian" *perspectivism*[94] and what he calls "multinaturalism".[95] In accordance with Hallowell's, Bird-David's and Descola's animistic approaches, Castro argues that "Amerindian" cosmologies are populated by subjects or persons[96] of different species both human and nonhuman, each of them perceiving the world from their particular point of view. However, the difference between "Amerindian" perspectivism and Western naturalism would not merely be epistemological, but ontological.

While "Western" ontologies suggest a universal material nature/object/body in contrast to a relative culture/subject/mind, "Amerindian" perspectivism would suggest a universal personhood, or "generic type of soul"[97] instead, in contrast to exchangeable physical bodies, thus inverting the whole logic of "Western" dualism. In order to illustrate the difference between the "Western" and the "Amerindian" ontology, Castro cites Levi-Strauss:

> On the Greater Antilles, some years after the discovery of the Americas, while the Spanish were sending commissions to investigate whether the Indians had a soul or not, the latter dedicated themselves to drowning their white prisoners in order to verify, by means of a lengthy observation, whether their corpses would decompose or not (Lévi-Strauss 1976: 4).[98]

The important question for the Spanish was, of course, whether the "Indians" were real humans or not, with the soul being the necessary precondition. The "Indians", on the other hand, had no doubt that the Europeans would have souls—all beings, humans, animals and spirits have souls anyway—but they were interested in what kind of bodies these souls might have. Or to put it in a nutshell: While our "Western" cosmology suggests physical continuity in contrast to metaphysical discontinuity,

---

[94] Castro (1996) criticises the concept of animism for its relativist tendency. Animism would mostly be understood as a worldview based on the *attribution* of animic properties to animals or objects, and therefore not escape Western representationalism. However, Castro develops his ontological concept of perspectivism in close correspondence to Philippe Descola's work on animism. Castro's and Descola's approaches mutually influenced each other, while they also point to each other's limitations. In the face of Castro's perspectivistic approach, Descola (2006) later criticised himself for reproducing Western nature-culture dualism in his earlier attempts, which in fact would be of no concern for American natives. Rather, social realities would be analytically subordinated to ontological realities. However, albeit some apparent similarities between their approaches, Castro claims his approach to be much more radical than Descola's. While Descola would be obsessed by classifying and categorising in order to maintain some cosmic order, he, Eduardo Viveiros de Castro, would strive to decolonize anthropology by hooking into "Amerindian" perspectivism, and thus, to get rid of the whole Kantian representationalism (Latour 2009).

[95] Castro (1996, 2004a, 2015).

[96] Actually, in his texts, Castro uses the term "human" both to refer to "person", including other than human persons, and "human species". This terminological overlap does not seem very helpful to me, so I prefer to use the more generic term "person" here instead.

[97] Castro (2004b).

[98] My translation from Portuguese: "Nas Grandes Antilhas, alguns anos após a descoberta da América, enquanto os espanhóis enviavam comissões de investigação para indagar se os indígenas possuíam ou não alma, estes últimos dedicavam-se a afogar os brancos feitos prisioneiros para verificarem, através de uma vigilância prolongada, se o cadáver daqueles estava ou não sujeito à putrefação".

"Amerindian" cosmologies rather suggest metaphysical continuity in contrast to physical discontinuity.[99]

However, the categories *nature* and *culture* are not simply merged or symmetrically inverted, because in "Amerindian" cosmologies their distinction would be one of changing perspectives, while in the "Western" context they would apply to different regions of being. Perspective, in this sense, refers to (ontological) viewpoint, different perceptions rather than different ontological categories. The perspective of a person changes together with its physical form, but without changing its inner nature or essence. For example, a jaguar-person may look at a human-person and perceive them as prey. However, a shaman-person may transform into a jaguar and adopt the jaguar's physical form and/or perspective, seeing human-persons as prey, too, but still continue to be the same shaman-person (soul) just with a jaguar body/perspective and seeing a jaguar's world. This unchangeable internal form refers to what We "Westerners" would try to translate as "spirit" or "soul", an immaterial intentionality or subjectivity, which is formally identical to human consciousness and equally common to humans, animals, and spirits alike.[100]

Castro emphasises that his concept of perspectivism is not another relativism, but rather a multi-naturalism. Jaguar-persons and human-persons do not perceive *the world* in different ways, they rather perceive different *worlds*, although both share the same "culture" or subjectivity. For example, both jaguars and humans would like beer, but what would be beer for the jaguar-person would be blood from the human-person's perspective. Each perspective represents a particular world, not just a different representation of one and the same world. Thus, from the perspective of perspectivism, the difference between "Western" and "Amerindian" perspectives is not merely one of different thought-systems, but one of *different worlds* or *multiple natures*. The difference between different perspectives, therefore, is not an epistemological, but an *ontological* one.

Moreover, to be a jaguar-person or a human-person is not a question of distinct essences, but one of different relational perspectives, too. You are a jaguar-person or a human-person because other persons see you like this or like that, and because you see either a jaguar's world or a human's world. For the jaguar will perceive themself simply as a person, just as we humans perceive ourselves. It is through each other's perspective that one is either a human or a jaguar-person, and the physical form of a person mediates this relational constitution of different perspectives, worlds, or natures. Perspectivism, therefore, is not just another kind of relativism, but rather a *multi-naturalistic relationism*.

---

[99] Castro (1996, 2004a, 2015); Taylor and Castro (2019).

[100] Castro (2015) calls attention to the central importance of "supernatural" beings in "Amerindian" cosmologies, which we may translate as "spirits", and the double nature of persons, consisting of a material body and an immaterial "soul". Although "supernatural" would be a quite outworn concept, it would be difficult to substitute. More recently, however, Castro (together with Taylor 2019) seems to suggest a more symmetric relation between body and soul/spirit, the latter rather unfolding into the former, both being equally "images" and "material", just each in a different realm or viewpoint, so to say.

Hence, perspectivism (like animism) cannot be just another epistemology, because it is contrary to the very existence of any epistemology. Knowing, from the perspectivist perspective, is a process of relating with the other subject one seeks to understand and to assume their point of view, so that there is no "object" which could be objectivised by a subject. Furthermore, the knowing subject is not a solipsistic *cogito*, but a person perceiving and interacting according to the perspective of its physical form. The perspective itself, as a kind of embodied phenomenal experience, has an ontic status, so that there is no space for any epistemology to explain how some isolated *cogito* might represent a world of intangible things-in-themselves.[101]

The mediation between knower and known is not *representation*, but *transformation* in order to assume the other's point of view by putting on their body, their physical form, and hence, their perspective. This metamorphic ability is typical for the "shaman".[102] They are the mediator who interacts with persons other than

[101] As Castro (2022) puts it: Contrary to the Cartesian cogito ergo sum, the Indigenous cogito would rather state: "they exist, therefore they think".

[102] Castro (2015) seems to use the term "shaman" in the same generic sense as "Amerindian", referring to all American native nations, in-distinctively. "Shamanism" has long been criticised for being part of Western discourse on alterity and identity, having little to do with American native ritual practices (e.g. Greifeld and Schmidt 2003; von Stuckrad 2003; Landquist 2005). Having been described for the first time in 1692 by Nicolaes Witsen as a ritual practice of Siberian Tunguse people, "shamanism", like "animism", has become a cipher of counter-enlightenment movements since the eighteenth century serving as a negative matrix to rationalism and Christian monotheism. The concept has been fundamentally influenced by Mircea Eliade's (1956) writings, depicting "shamanism" as an archaic spiritual technique based on ecstasy and a pattern of ritualistic elements present in a huge range of different cultures all over the world. Although Eliade's thesis on "shamanism" has received harsh critique from anthropologists it continues to be influential for esoteric and New Age movements. His concept of "shamanism" as a spiritual technique to provoke altered states of consciousness has also been popularised by Anthropologists like Carlos Castaneda and Michael Harner (1972, 2002) whose writings became central for the so called "Neo-Shamanism" (Wallis 2000; von Stuckrad 2003; Landquist 2005; Curry 2006) or "White Shamanism" (Wernitznig 2003). All this notwithstanding, "shamanism" persists as a central concept in ethnographic literature, especially in the Amarican Native context (e.g. Reichel-Dolmatoff 1971; Reichel 1987; Faust 1989; Langdon and Bear 1992; Descola 1996; Taussig 1997; Narby 1998; Perruchon 2003; Cesarino 2006; et al.). "Shamanic" practices have been interpreted in many different terms including techniques to provoke altered states of consciousness (Langdon and Bear 1992), innate brain structures (Winkelmann 1999), keeping of tradition (Baker 1999) and socio-ecological equilibrium (Reichel 1987; Curry 2006), mediators between the material and the transcendental world (Descola 1996), mimetic techniques (Taussig 1997) of symbolic metaphor (Langdon and Bear 1992), healing practices (Faust 1989), witchcraft (Faust 1989, Descola 1996, Perruchon 2003), a form of psychotherapy (Harner 2002; Landquist 2005), or a way to acquire knowledge about the subtle structures of the universe (Narby 1998). While it is true that some ideas and ritual practices often hold to be typical elements of "shamanism" (like near death and rebirth experience during initiation, soul voyages during trance, sucking bad energy or blowing positive energy into the patient's body, an animistic view of nature and the belief in invisible "doubles" or "souls", the use of drums during ritual, between others) can be found in different cultural contexts throughout the world (e.g. Stoller and Olkes 1987 on their experiences with sorcery in Africa; also Hinderling 1981), these patterns of ritual and cosmological elements differ considerably from culture to culture. However, if there be a common element to all so-called "shamanic" practices, it would probably be some

humans by disconnecting from their body or assuming the form and the subjectivity of another species, becoming one of their kind, thus interacting and administrating relations between human and other than human persons. Our "Western" way of knowing, in contrast, is to objectify; the other is an object, a thing—anything that cannot be objectified appears to be unreal, intangible. The "shaman", on the other hand, strives for knowing the other by activating their subjectivity by means of relating and adopting the other's perspective, assuming their subjectivity and world. The self and the other interpenetrate, and thereby, constitute each other. By assuming the other's body and perspective, the "shaman" also assumes their skills and their power. This may also be the reason why "Amerindians" perceive knowledge and power as two sides of the same coin, while our modern epistemology systematically tries to hide this intrinsic relation.[103]

Finally, Castro suggests that metamorphoses, as a driving motive of perspectivism, also implies predation as a metaphysical principle, a kind of "cannibal metaphysics".[104] The incorporation of the other as an act of assimilating its powers and particular properties would also be constitutive for the practice of anthropophagy. Cannibalism, therefore, would be an omnipresent motive in "Amerindian" contexts, although only rarely being practiced as literally as among the (historical) Tupinamba. But even the apparently crude and extremely violent ritual of Tupinamba cannibalism would be guided by a deep respect for the victim[105] and the desire to incorporate them, to become one with the enemy. From the "Amerindian" perspective of perspectivism, "every vital activity is a form of predatory expansion".[106]

However, not being satisfied with describing the Others' point of view, Castro wants to transform anthropology by adopting a perspectivist perspective. A new anthropology, operating as a "comparative ontography", would be necessary to finally assume its true mission as a "theory-practice of decolonization". Anthropology would have to cease looking at Others just to see Us in Our magic mirror. As long as We continue to ask why the Others are *not* modern, *not* literate, *not* rational, *not* whatsoever as We are, in short, why They are *not like Us*, there will only remain the hollow space of some non-We, non-quite-as-human Other. The problem is the problem. Moreover, "Western" metaphysics would be the "*fons et origo*" of all kinds of colonialism. As a consequence, a new anthropology would have to be an "anti-occidental" "alter-anthropology" guided by the three principles of (1) interspecies

"animistic" view together with ritual practices aiming to act upon the invisible aspects of things, which are treated as "persons", thus blurring the distinction between human and extra-human (Langdon and Bear 1992; Perruchon 2003), nature and culture (see above). Anyhow, the term "shamanism" refers to a quite fuzzy set of concepts and suggests the existence of a transcultural pattern of ritual and cosmological elements which does not seem to be supported by ethnographic evidence (compare also Greifeld and Schmidt 2003).

[103] Compare also Linhart (2008).

[104] Castro (2015); also Taylor and Castro (2019).

[105] See also Hans Staden's (1557) description of Tupinamba ritual anthropophagy.

[106] My translation from the original: "[…] toda atividade vital é uma forma de expansão predatória" (Castro 2015: Chapter 9).

perspectivism, (2) ontological multi-naturalism, and (3) cannibal alterity. The problem would have to be inverted by radically assuming the Others' perspectivist point of view. The new problem would be: What are the Others' anthropologies like and how would They describe Us? In short, an inverted anthropology.

> A good translation is the one that manages to have the alien concepts deform and subvert the conceptual dispositives of the translator. [...] It is not about suggesting an interpretation of the Amerindian way of thinking, but about carrying out an experiment with it, and by doing so, with our own (Castro 2015: Chapters 4/12).[107]

In other words, we should take the risk of having the Others change Us. This would imply taking the Others' view for real, to believe in it. And why shouldn't we? Are "Amerindian" cosmologies not as fascinating philosophical approaches as Leibniz' monades? Of course, it is not possible to simply start thinking like American natives, but We can think *together* with Them. The objective would not be to become like the Others, but to set off on the adventure of *becoming* Them (much in the sense of Deleuze's *devir*), without ever really *being like* Them.[108]

5.4.4 Political Ontology

Eduardo Viveiros de Castro, with his insistence on the ontological dimensions entailed by our notions of "cultural" difference, has contributed in an important way to a turn towards ontology in anthropology, which also fecundated other fields in the humanities as well as in philosophy.[109] In more general terms, this Ontological Turn refers to a shift from epistemology, that is, the question about *how and what we know*, towards the question about *what is*, or better, *what might be* or *become*. This is also a turn away from the linguistic turn, away from representationalism, away from constructionism, and towards the ontological deep structures and the practices of worldmaking different epistemologies are derived from. The description of "cultures"[110] in terms of "worldviews", different socially constructed representations of a "world out there", is in itself the expression of a very particular epistemology and its underlying ontological framework: Our "Western", anthropocentric, bifurcated cosmology. Other cosmologies, however, may imply quite different ontological frameworks with different epistemological premises, making other things visible by enacting other worlds. That is, just because from the perspective of our epistemology Other cosmologies seem to be talking about "things" or "persons"

---

[107] My translation from the original: "A boa tradução é aquela que consegue fazer com que os conceitos alheios deformem e subvertam o dispositivo conceitual do tradutor" (Chapter 4) "Não se trata, enfim, de propor uma interpretação do pensamento ameríndio, mas de realizar uma experimentação com ele, e portanto com o nosso" (Chapter 12).

[108] Compare also: "Parece-me que essa irresolução é uma dimensão constitutiva do conceito de devir: o devir não termina nunca, assim como de certo modo ele não começa" (Castro 2018: 30).

[109] Holbraad and Pedersen (2017).

[110] Wagner and Ingold (2016).

that, for Us, do not exist, this does not mean that they might not exist at all—they might simply not be visible from Our epistemological vantage point because its ontological underpinning does not entail the possible existence of such "things" or "persons". In this sense, the Ontological Turn provincializes modern epistemology together with its ontological grounding.[111] Other worlds are possible, since Our epistemology does not prove in any way that Our "One-World World"[112] is the only "real" world; it is just one among many possible worlds, and probably not even the one with the most promising future. However, as John Law[113] explains, current scientific practices are constantly reproducing a One-World World by crafting *manifest absences*, thus *Othering* and finally annihilating anything (and anyone) that does not fit into its ontological framework.

Of course, from a decolonial perspective, the political dimension of cosmological differences is striking. The Indigenous struggle for their "land" and their call for respectful treatment of the "Earth" are both actually addressing entities that do not (and must not!) exist in Our One-World World. For what "land" is to Us is for Them a living being they relate to, the territory where their ancestors dwell, the soil that nurtures their bodies and their "souls", the place that retains their past and enables continuity, that bears their future. These disputes are not about different viewpoints, mere epistemological considerations of different representations or interpretations of a single immanent "nature". Those are ontological disputes, different worlds made up of different "things" and "persons", each with their particular *causes* and *obligations* that are being negotiated—at stake are different lifeforms fighting for their right to exist, struggles for life or death[114]!

The political dimension of ontological (rather than epistemological) divergence has been emphasised by authors like Annemarie Mol,[115] John Law,[116] Arturo Escobar,[117] Marisol de la Cadena[118] and Mario Blaser[119] together with Isabelle Stengers,[120] Helen Verran,[121] Marilyn Strathern,[122] Eduardo Viveiros de Castro and Déborah Danowski,[123] among others. The *Political Ontology*[124] put forth by these

[111] Blaser (2013); Holbraad and Pedersen (2017).

[112] Law (2011); Escobar (2020).

[113] Law (2004).

[114] Castro (2013a, b); Stengers (2018a, b).

[115] Mol (1999).

[116] Law (2004, 2011).

[117] Escobar (2007, 2011, 2018, 2020).

[118] Cadena (2010, 2015); Cadena and Blaser (2018).

[119] Blaser (2013, 2018).

[120] Stengers (2005a, b, 2018a, b).

[121] Verran (2018).

[122] Strathern (2018).

[123] Danowski and Castro (2017); Castro and Danowski (2018).

[124] For Cadena and Blaser (2018) "political ontology wants to enable political thought and practice beyond the onto-epistemic limits of modern politics and what its practice allows. […] [The] consideration of the pluriverse as a possibility […] operates on the presumption of divergent worldings

authors is being construed on top of the findings from a range of different fields, including science and technology studies (particularly ANT), (eco-)feminist approaches, post- and decolonial studies (particularly M/C), the ontological turn in anthropology (e.g. New Animism and perspectivism) and certain strands in philosophy, like post-structuralism, speculative realism,[125] new materialism[126] and particularly on Stengers'[127] cosmopolitical proposal and her reception of Lovelock's[128] Gaia hypotheses.

For Stengers,[129] Gaia is not "a good, nurturing mother, whose health [is] to be protected"; Stengers's Gaia is rather a mighty entity we are provoking with our disrespect, our lack of attention, and whose response "might well be without any measure to what we have done", sweeping away mercilessly all kinds of different species, regardless of their innocence, "a bit like a shrugging of the shoulder provoked when one is briefly touched by a midge".[130] Having been treated for too long as "nature", Gaia has now intruded into our modern world, urging us to find new answers together with all the other victims, both human and non-human, of our irresponsible actions. The "intrusion of Gaia"[131] as a mighty entity makes it impossible to ignore her, calling the nature-culture divide into question. Or as Castro[132] puts it, in the face of Gaia anthropocentrism in no longer tenable, since there is no gap between geopolitics and geophysics, between "human" and "natural" affairs. This is why geopolitics have to be cosmopolitics.[133] The menace of the world's approaching end is, therefore, the backdrop of a new consideration of alternative, "non-modern", "perspectivist", "animic" and, above all, "relational"[134] cosmovi-

---

constantly coming about through negotiations, enmeshments, crossings, and interruptions [...]" (idem: 23), "[...] conversations about what is might take place in a political field. [...] Considering that the power of modern disciplines and their knowledges to cancel the possibility of what emerges beyond their grasp was a historical event (the result of a coloniality that needs not be such), our proposal offers those disciplines the possibility to use their creative might differently: without the undisputable certainty of superiority, and accepting that rather than resting on colonial world-making, their prevalence could be achieved in constant negotiation with worlding practices that might not—or might not only—reflect them" (idem: 50).

[125] Shaviro (2014); Harman (2016).

[126] Barad (2007).

[127] Stengers (2005a).

[128] Lovelock and Margulis (1973).

[129] Stengers (2015, 2018a, b).

[130] Idem: 46.

[131] "But the intrusion of Gaia is not a crisis, in the sense of a transitional period that would allow us to envisage the post-crisis. She will be a permanent part of our future, raising the question: will this future be worth living?" (Stengers 2018a, b: position 2155).

[132] Castro (2013b).

[133] Castro (2013a) refers to Stengers's cosmopolitical proposal—compare also the previous chapter.

[134] Virtually all proponents of ontological politics identify these alternative cosmovisions as "relational" ontologies (e.g. Strathern 1988, 2018; Green 2013; Nhemachena 2013; Verran 2013, 2018; Holbraad and Pedersen 2017; Blaser 2018; Cadena 2019; Escobar 2020, 2021; Stengers 2015; Haraway 2016; Tanasescu 2022; Escobar et al. 2024; Huambachano 2024). However, as

sions of those who already went through several ends of their worlds[135] and finally learned to "live in the ruins".[136] Those people are, of course, the Indigenous people whose worlds have repeatedly been destroyed in the course of European invasions—be it via catastrophic epidemics, war, slavery, forced schooling, displacement from or the depletion of their territories. They who are struggling for the recognition of Their cosmovisions and the "earth beings"[137] dwelling in Their worlds, and who are urging Us to join Them in the construction of a "world where many worlds fit",[138] a "pluriverse"[139] of worlds where a "good living" (*buen vivir*) becomes possible, and in which We can (re-)learn how to live in an "Earth~Form of life", to "fell-think with the Earth".[140] Engaging together with Indigenous people and other "Terrans"[141] in a pluriversal,[142] onto-, "alter-" or cosmo-politics[143] enact-

---

Castro (2013b) points out, the term "relational" has been used in quite different ways by different authors, so there is probably no complete agreement about what "relational ontologies" actually defines as such. In recent years, "relationality" has gained popularity among academics and activists alike, serving as a kind of meta-concept for non-modern, non-dualist, non-anthropocentric cosmopractices. As a result, a wide variety of religious, spiritual and cultural traditions have been identified as examples of "relational ontologies"—including "Indigenous" knowledge and practices from the Americas, Africa, Asia, New Zeeland and Australia, Buddhism, Taoism, post-extractionism, the commons, and even quantum physics, just to name some examples. Of course, applying "relationality" so broadly risks both category mistakes and the essentialization of Otherness, thereby inadvertently reproducing the very Great Divide between "the West" and "the Rest" it seeks to overcome. I therefore use the term "relational ontologies" in a more restrictive sense, referring primarily to Viveiros de Castro's notion of perspectivist or multinaturalist "Amerindian metaphysics."

[135] Castro and Danowski (2018); Danowski and Castro (2017).

[136] Tsing (2015); Haraway (2016); Stengers (2018a, b); Stengers et al. (2023).

[137] Cadena (2015).

[138] EZLN (1996).

[139] The Zapatistas' declaration to aspire a world where many worlds fit has been recoined by decolonial intellectuals like Walter Mignolo and Arturo Escobar under the label of a "pluriverse" of worlds and as an ontopolitical counter approach to universalism—including universalist understandings of decoloniality: "The argument for decoloniality must at the same time work to wrestle decoloniality from the temptations of totalitarian totality. Decoloniality promotes pluriversality as a universal option—which means that what "should be" universal is in fact pluriversal, and not a single totality" (Mignolo and Walsh 2018: 147). Compare also Mignolo (2011, 2021); Escobar (2011, 2020); Walsh (2017); Cadena and Blaser (2018); Kothari et al. (2019); Stengers et al. (2023).

[140] Escobar (2020).

[141] Castro and Danowski (2018) use "Humans" and "Terrans" as terms to denominate those who are "thoroughly invested in the practices that generate the Anthropocene and those that are more or less forcefully dragged along. The authors identify the former as Humans; they call the latter Terrans" (Cadena and Blaser 2018: 46).

[142] Escobar (2020).

[143] Although Stengers's (2005a, b) cosmopolitical proposal has been received quite enthusiastically by the proponents of ontological politics, it is clear that political ontology exceeds Stengers' original concept "of opening modern politics to the possibility of divergence among collectives composed of humans and nonhumans that [...] agreed to gather around a concern" (Cadena and Blaser 2018: 37). "Cosmopolitics means that politics should proceed in the presence of those who will bear the consequences, who will be the victims of political decisions, in the presence not only of

ing an "ecology of worlds"[144] might, thus, not only be necessary for decolonising scientific and political practices, but also for escaping the apocalyptic outlook in the face of Gaia's intrusion into Our so called "Anthropocene",[145] the "Age of Humans" (and possibly human's disappearance). We need the Others (the "terrans"[146]) in these "Gaia Wars" to clean up the mess We (the "humans") provoked by splitting Ourselves from "nature" and becoming "Humans", thereby turning ourselves into a major geological force of self-destruction.[147]

> We cannot construct the postconflict (and postcarbon) world using the categories that created the conflict (Escobar 2020: 125).

'humans' but also of the multiple divergent worlds they belong to, which this decision threatens. From the ontological politics point of view, cosmopolitics is badly limited" (Stengers 2018a, b: 222). Cosmopolitics as ontological politics has to be diplomacy: "This is why I would take ontological politics as corresponding to the reverse situation, when 'causes' would not mean only the disruption of political deliberation. If politics is ontological, ontological clashes would have to be anticipated everywhere as no issue can any longer be considered as a matter of free deliberation, putting into brackets the worlds it implies and the way it matters in these worlds. It would be diplomacy all the way down" (Stengers 2018a, b: 223).

[144] Cadena (2015).

[145] I use the term here in a very critical way, acknowledging its technical and ideological inappropriateness as discussed e.g. by Haraway (2015), Stengers et al. (2023), and others. Since is was coined as the "current epoch in which humans and our societies have become a global geophysical force" (Steffen et al. 2007), the Anthropocene has been subject to a lot of discussion and critique. While eco-modernists (Asafu-Adjaye et al. 2015) painted a triumphalist view of the human capacities to transform and control nature—a "good Anthropocene" if you will (Danowski and Castro 2017; Hamilton 2017; Viveiros de Castro 2019)—others criticized the concept for its anthropocentrism, highlighting rather the danger of arrogant phantasies of human omni-potency threatening to draw us into Apocalypse (Stengers 2015, 2018a, b; Danowski and Castro 2017; Stengers et al. 2023; compare also Indigenous voices like Krenak 2019 and Kopenawa 2021). All the critiques and downplaying of the Anthropocene as rather a "disturbance" than a "geological force" (Stengers in Latour et al. 2018) notwithstanding, it has been orienting the work of its criticisers (e.g. Tsing 2015; Tsing and Bazzul 2022), too, giving rise to a number of interesting recoinages and counter approaches such as capitalo-, plantation- or Chthulucene (Haraway 2015, 2016), misanthropo- or entropocene (Viveiros de Castro 2019), anthropo-not-seen (Cadena 2019), and of course, Stengers's (2015) "intrusion of Gaia". What unites advocates and critiques of the Anthropocene is the notion that the relation between us "humans" and "nature" is undergoing fundamental changes. However, while some voices highlight the "human" ability to intervene in "nature", others point to "nature's" (or Gaia's) powerful reaction to our (human) "disturbance" and the necessity to re-feel-think our place within "nature". Compare also Cadena 2019: "Yes, 'the Anthropocene' is a place for debate, and as implied in the Manifesto, a place to displace the knowing anthropos, to enable knowing-feeling-thinking without it—or, better, not only against it. Perhaps more important: this moment of catastrophe may give us 'the courage to question our most basic cultural narratives'" (p. 477).

[146] Danowski and Castro (2017).

[147] For Stengers, Our world is not even worth be called a "world": "The global West is not a 'world' and recognizes no world. Referring to Deleuze and Guattari, I would rather characterize it as a 'machine,' destroying both politics and ontologies. No peace is possible with this hegemonic machine, […] Those who oppose modernization are just "backward" or "misled". […] Even their massacres were purely pedagogical! […] A world-destroying machine cannot fit with other worlds" (Stengers 2018a, b: 201–202).

The "Anthropocene", Our "catastrophic times", may thus represent an opportunity for Us to remake Our worlding practices by reclaiming magic or animism, that is, the existence of Other worlds populated by Other beings, thereby intentionally threatening Our own ontological existence as "progressive" "modern" "Westerners".

> The idea of ontological politics needs the transformative magic of tales, rituals, modes of palaver, ways of thinking-feeling with, which reworld our ruins and open them to partial connections with other worlds (Stengers 2018a,: 253).

While Our "universal" sciences stubbornly insist on a ontologically unified world, a cosmopolitical or "civilized" science "would participate in a 'world in the making' through the creation of connections with a specificity related to what commits them: the question of what, how, and under which conditions we can 'learn from' what we address".[148] Such a "civilised" science has to be *pluriversal politics*.[149] This demands a symmetric understanding of plural worlds. It demands recognising the socionatural (ontological) diversity while interconnecting these worlds without making them completely commensurable, maintaining divergencies, thus, generating the possibility of becoming *legitimate adversaries*.[150] In short, it demands taking the Others and Their worlds seriously together with the earth beings dwelling therein. The maintenance and cultivation of diversity is central to Ontological Politics, since only by acknowledging otherness in its own right – not as a procedure of othering, but fully respecting diverging worlding practices—can we recognise others as respectable political players capable of negotiating with us also our own onto-epistemo-ethical practices of worldmaking. Negotiating these practices, which is always about negotiating realities, truths and values, is not a matter of facts, but essentially a matter of concern.[151] When Andean Indigenous activists are defending non-human earth beings like trees, rivers, mountains, *pachamama* or Mother Earth, their concern is with the possible end not only of Their earth beings and Their world, but with the impending end of all life in any world.[152] For in the face of Gaia, our common concern should be with life in general. The question put for negotiation by these struggles is thus, what, in the end, is life about? What different worlds and kinds of life are being enacted through diverging worlding practices? Which worlds and worlding practices might promise what kind of futures[153]? Which modes of

[148] Idem: 212.

[149] Escobar (2020).

[150] Cadena (2010).

[151] Latour (2004a); Stengers (2018a, b); Stengers et al. (2023).

[152] E.g. Krenak (2019); Kopenawa (2021).

[153] Of course, "future" can mean quite different things, depending on the cultural and cosmological standpoint from where it is approached. As a "cultural fact" (Appadurai 2013), future can be understood in terms of different "capacities of future making", "aspiring" a "good life", either implying an "ethics of possibility" or "probability", each bring about particular worlds while destroying others. While there has been an inflectional increase in research on the possible futures that might be waiting for us, those are themselves an expression of a particular ideological project of "progress" and an ontological conception of linear time. Other cosmologies suggest diverging conceptions of future and time in general. For example, the Andean *pacha* collapses notions of

existence might help us and life on Earth to thrive? And what kind of end might particular worlding practices bring to the worlds they once brought into being? What, finally, does each ontological divergence mean to our lives?

Ontological Politics is, thus, about enabling a "dialogue of visions"[154] or "pluriversal dialogue"[155] aiming to make the implicit ethical premises entailed in particular ontological divergences explicit and to evaluate the implications these premises might have – not only on our *notion* of life, but also on what life on Earth might or should *be* or *become*. Engaging into a pluriversal dialogue of cosmovisions and -practices means relating with other worlds and their inhabitants and ways of inhabiting by enacting divergent *cosmopractices*[156] that allow for "feel-thinking" (*sentipensar*) through divergent worldings, thereby opening "pluriversal contact zones"[157] for the development of post-anthropocenic, post-humanist, biocentric utopias. From a pluriversal perspective, therefore, life itself is an expression of diversity,[158] or more precisely, of relations among divergent perspectives of different beings, some of them being humans, "but not only".[159] For this reason, "pluriversal politics" require practices of "being~doing~knowing" that entail "an entire different ethics of life".[160] But what might such a different ethics of life look like?

In many ways, (re-)claiming the pluriverse is itself a political act that alludes to particular values and ethical claims. Claiming the pluriverse means aspiring to a

---

time, space, nature and life in a single concept, with the "past" lying in front of us, guiding us through the unfolding of the *pacha* (time-space-living-cosmos-of-complementary-dualities), and the future rather building a background of possible unfoldings, unavoidably leading into the next *pachakuti*, the turning of time/cosmos, as part of a cyclical time-space-renewal (Estermann 2006; Macas 2014; Soto 2019). Hence, projecting futures is never an objective, neutral busyness, but always a "political act" (Tironi et al. 2024). Futures are "contested fields" of political negotiations among diverging claims about the possibility of certain, often mutually exclusive futures. At stake is the question which futures have a future and which don't.

[154] Escobar (2020).

[155] Dunford (2017); Hutchings (2019); Fitzgerald (2021); Behr and Shani (2021); Linhart et al. (forthcoming).

[156] The term "cosmopraxis" has been used occasionally by Eduardo Viveiros de Castro (2004a, b, 2013a, 2015) referring to "Amerindian" (perspectivist/relational/multinaturalist) cosmovisions and related practices. Some authors (e.g. Cesarino 2006; Pereira 2021) adopted a similarly unspecific use of the term "cosmopractices", while others (e.g. Munter and Note 2009; Querejazu 2022) developed "cosmopraxis" into a more specific concept referring to a particular type of relational ontologies and pluriversal practices of relating to/with and navigating in between different but interrelated worlds. Here, I use the term "cosmopractice(s)" as a more canny synonym of what I also call "onto-epistemo-ethic-aesthetic practices", referring to the multi-layered unity of ontological, epistemological, ethical and aesthetic dimensions of worldmaking practices or worldings. I developed this conception in close relation to Barad's (2007) *ethico-onto-epistemology*, Stengers's (2005a) *cosmopolitics* and later receptions by Latour (2004b), Castro (2013a), Cadena and Blaser (2018).

[157] Cadena and Escobar (2024).

[158] Castro (2013a).

[159] Cadena (2015).

[160] Escobar (2020: 27).

world where many worlds fit, and thus, fighting the One-World World that negates and destroys all the other worlds and which has been identified as being responsible for all the mess of the Anthropocene and the menace of a downing Apocalypse.

Of course, ecomodernists and transhumanists would vigorously object to such ungrounded pessimistic evaluations of the modern humanist heritage.[161] For them, the current ecological and social crises are just a deplorable but necessary step towards modernity's consummation, the coming crest of the "good Anthropocene", where "humans" (who might become transhuman cyborgs) finally rule "nature". Speculative realists and new materialists, on the other hand, have been emphasising the shortcomings of "correlationist"[162] metaphysics, and as a response, developed new "posthumanist"[163] ontologies on their own. However, while posthumanist philosophical approaches, in one way or another, aim to overcome the onto-epistemological subject-object-divide between the human and non-human, there is a tendency to eliminate the subject by attributing agency to material objects or matter in general[164] rather than invoking a person-like intentionality that moves the relations the universe is made of (as "relational", "animic" or "perspectivist" cosmovisions may suggest). More importantly, these "Western" approaches towards posthumanist metaphysics seek to overcome the outdated and pointless attempt to grasp a supposed "really real reality out there" by substituting "correlationism" with another, more "realist" onto-epistmological account of "reality"—a more encompassing "theory of everything", as Harman[165] puts it. Hence, instead of emphasising the transcendental, and thus, pluriversal or multinatural nature of "nature", these approaches are just another "Western" attempt to find the "true" foundations of *the* universe.[166]

---

[161] E.g. Asafu-Adjaye et al. (2015); Pinker (2018).

[162] Meillassoux (2008); also Shaviro (2014).

[163] E.g. Barad (2007); Castro (2018).

[164] E.g. Meillassoux's (2008) Speculative Materialism or Barad's (2007) Agential Realism; Latour's (2013) later conception of ANT may also serve as an example (Harman 2017; Holbraad and Pedersen 2017). Other authors, such as Harman's (2017) Object Oriented Ontology or Steven Shaviro (2014) explore Whitehead's (1978) Process Ontology and panpsychism, focusing rather on the inner nature of things and aesthetics as an ontological key concept.

[165] Harman (2017).

[166] Barad's (2007) Agential Realism might, at least to a certain extent, be considered an exception in this respect, since she emphasises the performative character of being in terms of "intra-action" between entangled phenomena as "ontologically primitive relations—relations without preexisting relata" (idem: 138). "In summary, the primary ontological units are not 'things' but phenomena—dynamic topological reconfigurings/entanglements/relationalities/(re)articulations of the world. And the primary semantic units are not 'words' but material-discursive practices through which (ontic and semantic) boundaries are constituted. This dynamism is agency. Agency is not an attribute but the ongoing reconfigurings of the world. The universe is agential intra-activity in its becoming" (idem. 141). Hence, one could argue with Barad that there is no "universe" as such to be explained, since it is permanently being re-enacted by "apparatuses" (specific, difference producing material-discursive practices), thereby incessantly becoming anew. However, as a dynamism with no concert form, the ontological core of existence is still described by Barad in universal terms.

> The key point [...] is that these diverse approaches and perspectives share a straightforwardly philosophical ambition to provide the outline of a new metaphysics and, indeed, an alternative ontology—a single conceptual framework that would account, once and for all, for everything that exists (Holbraad and Pedersen 2017: 35).

Proponents of Political Ontology, in contrast, unanimously emphasise that there is no single, universal "really real" world to be explained; instead there are many being enacted and negotiated through relations among hybrid, not quite "human" and not quite "non-human", "persons". But, what exactly does it mean to speak of a pluriverse of many worlds? Are we talking about different ontologies (*models of* the ontic nature of the universe) and (socionatural) practices producing different living worlds, or are we talking about different *ontic worlds*? Or is there, after all, no difference between ontological worldings and ontic worlds? The question whether or not the ontological turn itself tacitly presumes its own meta-ontology has been subject to controversial debates.[167]

First of all, a pluriverse of many worlds only makes sense from within a particular non-representationist, non-correlationist ontological meta-framework where the inner and outer worlds of subjects and objects are somehow collapsed into other ontic categories in such a way that phenomenal properties (thoughts, perceptions, intentions or prehensions) can be constitutive, causal events in the process of enacting different "worlds". In this sense, the ontological turn alludes to an alternative ontological meta-framework of its own – or at least, an onto-epistemo-ethic-aesthetical counter-paradigm that excludes anthropocentrism/dualism/ correlationism/representationism from the list of viable metaphysical frameworks (for being epistemologically, socially, ecologically, and thus, ethically untenable). However, this alternative onto-epistemo-ethical counter-framework in itself does not explicitly determine the ontic status of these multiple "worlds" and how they might relate to each other.

Some anthropologists insist that precisely this oscillation between two (apparently contradictory) conceptions of "ontology" as views/models of and claims about what exists is more of an advantage than a problem.[168] To them, the ontological turn should not be concerned with finding new foundations for alternative ontologies but rather open ways for other ontologies to show us how the world *could* be otherwise.[169]

---

[167] Holbraad and Pedersen (2017).

[168] For example, for Holbraad and Pedersen (2017) the Ontological Turn in Anthropology is "not concerned with what the 'really real' nature of the world is or similar metaphysical quests. Rather, it is a methodological project that poses ontological questions to solve epistemological problems" (idem.: 5). "We are left with an anthropological concept of ontology that does not confuse 'essence' and 'model', or 'reality' and its 'representations', but that denotes a single yet infinitely differentiated object of ethnographic study, which spans 'everything both actual and potential'" (Pedersen 2012).

[169] "Posing ethnography as a conduit for metaphysical contingency, anthropology turns to ontological questions without taking any single 'ontology' as an answer—its ultimate concern being not with what is, but with what could be" (Holbraad and Pedersen 2017: 68).

> Sometimes I have the impression that we anthropologists feel as if we were required to profess some ontological creed concerning the actual make-up of the world (human nature and culture included). I am not sure this is our business at all. Our business is to connect, period. We are metaphysical brokers. We strive to connect different ontologies, but we are not in the business of ontologising. We are especially not in the business of judging other people's ontologies—either 'our own' people, or other peoples (Castro 2013b: 275).

Instead of judging Ourselves or Others for being unrealistic or guilty of messing up our planet, pluriversality calls for taking Others and their worlds seriously, as valid options. Entering into a pluriversal dialogue demands *humility* and *respect*. However, the *urgency* of taking Others seriously derives not only from the moral imperative of *justice*, but also from judging ourselves *guilty* of provoking global disaster, coming to terms with our *failed beliefs* in "progress" and human control over nature, and maybe, also from our (always a bit messianic) *hope* that the Others will show us the way towards *a better life*. The Indigenous "trademark" of *buen vivir* is a frequent referent of such projections of "relational" ontologies that would point to an ethics of "care", "reparation" and "healing" [170]—and Indigenous discourses actively engage in the construction of these alternative conceptions. In short, pluriversality is governed by a whole range of implicit and explicit ethical suppositions. And that is all fine. One, should, however, draw a line between (1) the ethics that impose the pluriverse as a normative approach, (2) the ethics implied by pluriversality in terms of a dialogical practice of negotiating divergencies and (3) the ethics aspired by pluriversality as a utopian project towards post-anthropocenic futures oriented by diverging onto-epistemo-ethic-aesthetical practices.

While technically speaking, being a logical consequence of translating *cultural difference* into *ontological divergence*, the implied pluriverse of many (co-equal) worlds receives the normative character of a decolonial counter-paradigm to the universalising of modern/colonial Occi-/Eurocentric particularisms.[171] Claiming the pluriverse, thus, amounts to universalising equity among all worlds, cosmovisions and -practices, forms of knowing/doing/being. However, by universalising ontological equivalence, all universalistic One-World Worlds are banned, so to say, for violating the norm of pluriversality by negating and destroying other worlds. This is why the pluriverse ultimately entails a normative and universal imperative.[172] The ontological meta-question about the ontic status of those "many worlds" and the way in which they might be related to each other is secondary, but not unimportant to its normative power. As mentioned just before, much of the pluriverse's conceptual power hinges on (a) the possibility of Other worlds having the same ontological status as Ours, and (b) on the onto-epistemic potential for transcending correlationism/representationalism/dualism/anthropocentrism, and finally, for providing pathways towards post-anthropocenic futures. These latter demands, however, already dip into the second and third categories of the ethics that derive from the implications and aspirations of pluriversality.

---

[170] Haraway (2016); Escobar (2020, 2021); Cadena and Escobar (2024); Tironi et al. (2024).

[171] Mignolo (2011); Dunford (2017).

[172] Dunford (2017); Hutchings (2019).

The universal ethical imperative of ontological equivalence also demands for an ethics of coexistence that somehow regulates relations and negotiations among diverging worlds. However, in a pluriverse ethical norms cannot be derived from universal truths, but only from a pluriversal dialogue on the consequences of thinking, feeling, doing, dwelling in, and finally, making of worlds in particular ways. Pluriversality, therefore, amounts to the cosmopolitics of an *ecology of diverging worldings*,[173] which again demand for an *ecology of trust.*[174] Rather than ethical norms, pluriversal cosmopolitics require cultivating the kind of virtues[175] that facilitate mutual trust, understanding, collaboration, co-creation and co-existence, such as humility, respect, solidarity, mindfulness and care. Instead of sceptically deconstructing Our own and Others' cosmopractices, pluriversality demands building trust based on mutual respect for diverging cosmopractices and entering into a pluriversal dialogue about new forms of relating to Ourselves and Others, Our own and Other worlds, laying grounds for co-creating futures of co-existence. Hence, pluriversality, understood as a mode of co-existence that is based on a co-creative dialogue among diverging cosmopractices, points to a particular, however always provisional, set of *virtues* (rather than ethical norms) for a pragmatic evaluation of diverging cosmopractices concerning their effectiveness in bringing about particular worlds, while precluding others.

However, the imperative of coexistence and its dialogical operational mode alone do not exhaust the utopian vision aspired by pluriversality. The full ethical reach of current discourse on pluriversality unfolds against the backdrop of apocalyptical interpretations of anthropocenic socio-environmental crises in terms of an awakening Gaia. The (scientifically sustained) identification of Our (modern/colonial/"Western") triumphalist anthropocentric exceptionalism as the culprit for the menace of human self-extinction almost inevitably leads into the quest for alternative, non-anthropocentric, post-humanist ethics of care and reparation. So-called "aminic", "perspectivist" and/or "relational" cosmopractices have been identified as promising interlocutors in a pluriversal dialogue because they seem to evade the pitfalls of human exceptionalism by focusing on intentional processes of relating among human and non-human "persons" (rather than on deterministic atomism and its representation in human minds). So, in what concerns the possible outcome of pluriversal dialogues, pluriversality aims to pluralise future regimes, however, being driven by an ethics of hope in the face of impending Apocalypse—more precisely, the hope to mobilize Other worlds for Our need to find a new *ethics of life* capable of re-orienting Our modern/colonial worlding practices towards futures beyond anthropocenic distopias.

This vital role of ethics for the pluriversal endeavour, and for pluriversal dialogues on alternative futures in particular, corresponds to the absence of any universal yardstick for truth claims and related metaphysical suppositions. To avoid

[173] Cadena and Escobar (2024).

[174] Debaise and Stengers (2022).

[175] Hutchings (2019).

slipping into relativism, a pragmatic evaluation of diverging cosmopractices according to their objective effectiveness seems to be the only viable solution. Ethics is about bringing diverging views and demands to the test concerning their capability to bring about "better worlds" in the sense of "new modes of composing, maximizing the possibilities for coexistence of what in every epoch seem destined to exclude each other".[176] The conjoined perspective on ontological, epistemological, ethical, aesthetical and practical aspects entailed in the notions like "worldings", "worldmaking" or "cosmopractices" alludes to a re-unified consideration of the good, the beautiful and the true, however, guided by a dialogue about diverging ethics of life and how they might help us design more (co-)inhabitable futures.[177]

Summing Up: From Noble Savages to Noble Terrans?

As I outlined in this chapter, throughout modern history the image of the Other has been instrumental to the maintenance of the Great Divide, both in its internal and in its external dimension.[178] In its outer dimension, it sustained and legitimated European colonialism and capitalist expansion as well as scientific universalism. In its inner dimension, it served as a two-fold conceptual dispositive for the construction of the modern subject and society at large, with the Barbarian Savage justifying the conservative programme and the Noble Savage calling for progressive changes in "Western" society. Furthermore, the construction of the Other was essential for the definition of the relation between the modern rational subject and nature, and thus, central to the development of modern dualist metaphysics and its representational epistemology.

At its outset as a new scientific discipline during the nineteenth century, anthropology basically adopted the common sense and practice of its time, with rich, white, and (most importantly!) "rational" men of European descent studying the "irrational", "primitive" "races" of the European empires' remote colonies. Although it did not take too long for a new generation of anthropologists (like Boas and Malinowski) to appear and criticise early evolutionist accounts, and despite the countless engaged colleagues who would continue their endeavour during the next decades, none of their attempts to recognise the Others as equally intelligent and rational would overcome either relativism or the Great Divide between the (progressive) "West" and the (underdeveloped) "Rest". The problem, of course, was the problem of the anthropological research programme itself, which continued to ask why the (pre-modern) Others are not as "modern" and "rational" as We are, thus reproducing not only the external Great Divide between the "West" and the "Rest", but also the internal dualism between culture/subject/human/mind on the one side and nature/object/non-human/body on the other.

Although relativism did not define the Others as necessarily less "rational", their rationality would still be too different from ours to be translatable. The linguistic turn and post-modern de-constructivism further relativised knowledge per se,

[176] Stengers (2009: 18).

[177] Cadena and Escobar (2024); Tironi et al. (2024).

[178] As demonstrated by Latour (1993).

deepening the problem of incommensurability, instead of solving it. The resulting constructionist concept of knowledge and the (re-)turn to the interpretative method did not overcome modern epistemology, but quite the opposite. In a way, it was its' accomplishment, as it went right back to Kant's transcendental question and Dilthey's response to it, the foundation of the hermeneutic *Geisteswissenschaften*—it was the final cut between "objective" and "subjective" reality. Incommensurability had become an inherent condition of subjectivity, rendering any translation a hopeless enterprise. The difference between Us and the Others had not only become more relative, but more absolute, too, with each representing distinct (mental) worlds, mutually incommensurable by definition. As a consequence, other knowledge-systems might not be more or less true than science, but being too different to be translated into "Western" rationality, they would simply be *incommensurable*, and hence, *irrelevant* for Western science.

This stalemate situation would only change in the course of the geopolitical reorganisation during the 1980s and 1990s. Stanley Tambiah is certainly one of those who contributed to these changes. He made an important step by questioning the "Western" concept of rationality, thus inverting the problem by asking what kind of rationality we actually think we have? Instead of following his predecessors like Malinowski, Levi-Strauss, or Horton, who tried to show that the Others are as "rational" as we are, he demonstrated that Our "Western" concept of rationality is only a product of, and instrumental to "Western" dualist metaphysics and scientific universalism. More importantly, this is true for the universalist as much as for relativist concepts of rationalism, since both deny the full recognition of Indigenous knowledge. "Rationality" in itself is therefore a dispositive for creating the idea of a "rational" "West" by othering the "irrational" "Rest".

There has been a paradigmatic shift in anthropology during the last decades, indicating the necessity to fundamentally rethink our image of Us and the Others in terms of ontological divergences rather than "cultural" or epistemological differences. Bruno Latour's analysis of the modern Constitution provides a vivid account of the way in which Our idea of "culture" itself is the result of the same ontological cut that separates Us moderns from Our human-nonhuman hybrids, from Our past, from Nature, and ultimately, from the "Rest" of humanity. A number of anthropologists have been following this turn towards ontology, describing Other cultural practices in terms of diverging ontologies or worlding practices, each enacting a particular world with its particular set of (possible) beings. A core tenet of the Ontological Turn is its emphasis on the prevalence of the ontological deep structure over its epistemological (and ethical) implications. Accordingly, "cultural" differences are now understood in terms of ontological divergences, imbued with diverging epistemological, ethical and aesthetical inflections.

Probably the most important consequence of this turn towards ontology is that epistemological incommensurability is no argument for rejecting diverging worldviews, worlding practices or worlds, or the beings dwelling in those different worlds. Ontological divergence, on the other hand, might bear alternative solutions to Our epistemological limitations. It has been argued that certain non-modern (aminic/animistic, relational or pespectivist/multinaturalist) cosmopractices do not resemble the same nature-culture divide Our modern Constitution is based upon. Instead, these alternative worlds are populated by (almost but not quite) human and (almost but not quite) non-human persons who are constituted by relating to each other – be it through kinship, by dint of reciprocal exchange or communication, by taking on each other's form and perspective, or by devouring each other. And since the great ontological divide between culture and nature, subject and object, humans and non-humans, Us and Them has been identified as the metaphysical root of all those dark sides of modernity – from masculine domination to colonial racism and environmental disaster – other, non-modern and hitherto subalternised onto-epistemo-ethical practices might be a loophole or escape way out of the cul-de-sac of modern anthropocentrism/ /representationalism/universalism. Hence, while truth claims from different epistemologies cannot be compared or evaluated regarding their absolute truth value, diverging onto-epistemo-ethical cosmopractices can be compared according to their pragmatic implications regarding the objective socio-natural realities or worlds they may bring into being.[179]

Thus provincializing[180] scientific universalism together with "Western" and human exceptionalism without slipping into relativism, the Ontological Turn provides a powerful political tool in the hands of decolonial, feminist and other subaltern movements. In recent years, insights from philosophy of science, STS, (eco-) feminism, decolonial studies and anthropology have been converging into an increasingly coherent picture, bringing the essentially political dimension of ontological divergence to the fore. Facing the potentially apocalyptical intrusion of Gaia, proponents of Political Ontology are urging Us to take Other, diverging onto-epistemo-ethic-aesthetical practices seriously, to accept the invitation of Indigenous movements and join their fight against the devastating One-World World and for "a world where many worlds fit". Doing pluriversal cosmopolitics requires a symmetrical or inverted anthropology, a pluriversal dialogue of cosmopractices envisioning alternative worlds with different futures. Surviving the catastrophic times of the Anthropocene might require "post-humanist", "relational" and/or "pluriversal" cosmopractices – it might demand Us take sides by deciding to desist from being "humans" and become "terrans" instead.

Recalling scientific universalism's epistemological, social, geopolitical and ontological aspects, as discussed in this first section of this book, there seem to be clear tendencies towards a confluence of the different discourses on these issues. In particular, debates in philosophy, history and sociology of science as well as in feminist and decolonial studies, and in anthropology have all been increasingly

[179] In a way, the ontological turn reverts the whole modern hierarchy of truth. In modern thought, ethical maxims and ontological models derive from the rational subject and its ability to know about an outer world of objects. From an ontological perspective, however, the existence of a rational subject is just one among many possible metaphysical premises with no objective evidence, but with measurable objective consequences for our very lives. As a corollary, ethical and aesthetic questions about the good and beautiful are at the very basis of and inseparable from epistemological considerations about (possible) truth(s).

[180] Chakrabarty (2007).

emphasising the importance of ontology (over epistemology), suggesting relational, perspectivist, cosmopolitical or pluriversal and ultimately, *pragmatic* approaches as possible solutions to the predicaments of both universalism and relativism. Moreover, a growing number of authors has been calling for rethinking modern onto-epistemo-ethic-aesthetical practices—particularly concerning their colonial aspects, fundamental metaphysical presuppositions, and resulting epistemological shortcomings—based on an equitable dialogue with Other, subaltern forms of being and knowing. According to many authors, what is at stake is not only modern science's truth monopoly, but nothing less than the current world-system and the future of humankind. Scientific universalism, this blameful and antiquated myth, has to be finally discarded and substituted by a world of sciences, an ecology of knowledge/practices/diverging worldings, or a pluriversal cosmopolitics based on a dialogue among diverging cosmopractices, enabling Us to think together with the Others, to think beyond and from the borders, an inverted anthropology comparing different ontologies and ethics of life concerning their objective effects on our living.

Anyway, for those who find these arguments too pathetic, it may be enough to consider that scientific universalism has no defendable epistemological backing, and that it definitively accounts for othering, thus devaluing Indigenous worldviews together with their ways of living and their political demands for cultural autonomy. This alone should be a more than sufficient argument for making an effort to advance beyond blindly universalising the particularisms of Our modern/colonial worlding practices.

Of course, a lot of unsolved issues are hovering above these new and frankly revolutionary approaches. Conceptions of "the Others" as "animists", "perspectivists", "terrans", or whatever diverging attributes, are always subject to allegations of essentialism. Moreover, for Ontological or Pluriversal Politics to become a strong dispositive in a cosmopolitical struggle for a decolonised world, the ontological relations between the imaginary dimension of *cosmovisions* and the ontic status of those different *cosmoi*—that are related to and emerging from or together with those visions—has to be made explicit. What is needed is a coherent meta-ontological framework explaining what "enacting different worlds" actually means. For without such a comprehensive meta-ontological framework, most "modern" scientists, "bifurcated" as We are, will have difficulties in understanding the *cause* Ontological Politics are standing for.

Be this as it may, for my part, I consider the approaches discussed in this first section highly valuable, notwithstanding some inevitable inconsistencies and unsolved problems. I would also like to emphasise that, up to this point, I have not added anything substantially new to existing academic discourse; I just provided a summary of some of the many ideas that have been discussed within modern discourse which I though useful to elucidate what (from my perspective) scientific universalism is all about. Accordingly, I take these previous approaches as a fundament for my further considerations which, roughly speaking, will pursue the following rationale:

1. Both philosophy and sociology of science have clearly shown science and scientific method to be institutionalised social practices bound to a set of particular

metaphysical presumptions, which are also a constitutive element of the modern/colonial world view and world order

2. Of all the underlying metaphysical presumptions of modern/colonial science, universalism is the one responsible for the a priori invalidation and exclusion of Other cosmologies; however, universalism is itself precisely based on fundamental presuppositions that are at least questionable, sometimes incoherent, and in any case unprovable
3. However, debunking science's epistemological untenability, its socially construed and historically contingent character, and its geopolitical function as hegemonic discourse of a colonial system that divides the world into citizens fully eligible to human rights and those not quite so, only leads to relativism
4. Relativism, in turn, is not a solution, but rather a central part of the problem, for at least the following reasons:

   (a) Denouncing the illusiveness of any "truth" it reinforces the epistemological pitfalls of modern epistemology
   (b) It therefore continues neglecting the truth value of Other ways of knowing
   (c) It does not solve the problem of incommensurability, but to the contrary, rather further deepens the abyss between Us and the Others
   (d) And finally, it opens the Pandoras' box releasing not only the hope for equity, but also the horsemen of the Apocalypse: post-truth, irrationality, fundamentalism, and fascism

5. As an alternative, different kinds of knowing/feeling/being can be understood as diverging onto-epistemo-ethic-aesthetical or cosmopractices, each being situated within and (re-)worlding a particular world together with its particular set of enfolded potential futures and pointing towards a particular ethics of life with its own ontological underpinnings
6. From the vantage point of such pluriversal pragmatics, ontology is of vital importance for our concrete lives, while epistemology is rather about intellectual vanities of some unworldly philosophers hiding in their dusty libraries and reading old books about the impossibility of knowing
7. Nothing I said so far questions scientific objectivity nor its efficacy; but of course, these arguments expose its unjustified and noxious truth monopoly together with its undeniable entanglement with capitalism and the modern/colonial world-system. In other words, the problem is not that science is not effective or objective, but that its specific efficacy tends to produce realities and possible futures we might or might not desire
8. In addition, anthropological interpretations of "Amerindian" nature-cultures in terms of perspectivist, relational ontologies and worlding practices as well as the Indigenous self-understanding suggest that their cosmopractices and ethics of life could provide productive divergences for re-orienting Our ways of feel-thinking-doing and relating towards more inhabitable futures
9. As a corollary, and in the face of the ongoing crisis of modernity (actually modernity has always been a crisis!), We ("Western" modern/colonial scientists and philosophers) have to make up our minds (and hearts) and start listening to

and feel-thinking with Other (human and non-human) earthlings about their ways of being and knowing and the worlds they live in. In short, we need to engage in a pluriversal dialogue of cosmopractices for feel-thinking and experimenting with Others and their worlds, their worldings, diverging onto-epistemo-ethic-aesthetical perspectives and practices, inverting the perspective for a while and trying to understand how They see Us, enacting new forms of co-relating, co-existing and co-creating an ethics of life and the cosmopractices that might trigger the unfolding of more desirable futures beyond anthropocenic distopias

10. A dialogue is always about some matter of concern, and thus, demands mutual understanding of what is at stake. Ontological divergence, however, points to what cannot exist in Our world, what exceeds our onto-epistemic capacities of grasping.[181] The challenge of pluriversal dialogue is thus to turn divergence into an opportunity for allowing oneself to feel-think-experience what, in Our world, cannot be,[182] thereby making Other, hitherto muted worlds with Other futures visible, and thus, negotiable. However, this also means translating apparently incommensurable divergences into shared matters of concern
11. Hence, if the challenge is to overcome scientific universalism by inviting scientists to engage into a pluriversal dialogue with Other knowledge cultures, than it will be necessary to provide arguments against the assumption of a general and insurmountable incommensurability of those Other, excluded cosmopractices from the other side of colonial difference. And since epistemological arguments are ruled out, so to say, by recognising ontology as the more fundamental level of divergence, scientific claims to universalism could only find a hold in showing that Other cosmopractices refer to ontological referents that do not and *cannot* exists in the face of scientific evidence. So, paraphrasing Mannheim,[183] a (minimal) common ground of understanding for pluriversal dialogue between science and Other cosmopractices could be viable if:

---

[181] Stengers (2005a, b); Cadena and Escobar (2024).

[182] "Approaching a practice then means approaching it as it diverges, that is, feeling its borders, experimenting with the questions which practitioners may accept as relevant, even if they are not their own questions, rather than posing insulting questions that would lead them to mobilise and transform the border into a defence against their outside" (Stengers 2005a, b: 184).

[183] As suggested by Karl Mannheim (1954) a century ago with incredible far-sightedness, in order to get different (incommensurable) thought styles into a productive dialogue, there would be two possible alternative solutions, each coming with its particular challenges: (1) The first would be to accept the relational, situated, and contingent character of knowledge, and to adopt a pragmatic perspectivism, assuming all perspectives to be potentially equally true in their own right. However, to avoid relativism, a "common denominator" would be necessary to make the different perspectives commensurable, and thereby, comparable and accessible to an objective evaluation. In this way, different perspectives might be evaluated concerning their problem-solving capacity. (2) The second option was not to absolutise the situated and contingent character of knowledge, but instead to integrate the different viewpoints within a new, overarching meta-ontology. This would probably lead to increasingly abstract and formalised higher-level models of reality. Moreover, the construction of such a universal meta-ontology would be limited by the fundamental problem of interpretation and commensurability.

(a) the Other cosmology suggests fundamental ontic referents that, albeit being radically different, still share properties comparable to those described by evidence based scientific theories, thereby functioning as "common denominators"[184] and/or
(b) both scientific and Other ontologies can be allocated within some overarching meta-ontological framework (e.g., an ontological explanation for the co-existence of many diverging worlds in a pluriverse)

While the development of an overarching ontological meta-framework for the pluriverse would certainly be fun, I do not feel I am in the position to face this megalomanic challenge. I do feel, however, that it should be possible to submit particular ontologies to a comparative analysis concerning the aspects in which they either con- or diverge, and what each of these con- and divergences might tell us about different worlds and forms of worldmaking.

So, what I am going to investigate in the following two sections, is the question whether so-called "perspectivist" or "relational" cosmopractices actually amount to entirely incommensurable worlds made up by ontic referents with no identifiable counterpart in evidence based scientific theory, or not.

Having declared these tasks, in the following second part of this work I will present the Potiguara (as simply one example of a subaltern, non-hegemonic standpoint) and an analysis of the cosmological principles implied by their way of being and knowing. The third section provides a discussion of the different cosmological models that are currently being debated in the context of recent scientific and philosophical disputes on the "hard problem" of mind and related quantum theoretical issues (as examples of hegemonic, scientific discourse). A subsequent comparison may show potential points of convergence and divergence between Potiguara cosmopractice and particular evidence based ontological models as discussed within scientific discourse. In the event that significant points of convergence can be identified, incommensurability ceases to be an argument against a co-creative pluriversal dialogue on alternative, more inhabitable futures and the ethics and cosmopractices we might need to have for them to come true.

References

Appadurai A (ed) (2013) The future as cultural fact: essays on the global condition. Verso Books, London

Asafu-Adjaye J, Blomqvist L, Brand S et al (2015) An ecomodernist manifesto. www.ecomodernism.org. Accessed 30 Nov 2023

Atmanspacher H, Primas H (2006) Pauli's ideas on mind and matter in the context of contemporary science. J Conscious Stud 13:5–50

[184] Walter Mignolo (2011), in a similar context, calls attention of the importance of common "connectors", shared referents that orient pluriversal dialogues across colonial difference (e.g. "democracy" as a shared connector for a dialogue between Zapatistas and the Mexican government).

Baker JR (1999) Keepers of tradition, agents of change: shamanism, altered states of consciousness, and cultural adaptation. Currare 22:115–120
Barad K (2007) Meeting the universe halfway: quantum physics and the entanglement of matter and meaning. Duke University Press, Durham
Behr H, Shani G (2021) Rethinking emancipation in *a* critical IR: normativity, cosmology, and pluriversal dialogue. Millennium 49:368–391. https://doi.org/10.1177/03058298211031983
Berger PL, Luckmann T (1991) The social construction of reality: a treatise in the sociology of knowledge. Penguin, London
Bird-David N (1999) "Animism" revisited: personhood, environment, and relational epistemology. Curr Anthropol 40(Special issue Culture—a second chance?):67–91
Blaser M (2013) Ontological conflicts and the stories of peoples in spite of Europe: toward a conversation on political ontology. Curr Anthropol 54:547–568. https://doi.org/10.1086/672270
Blaser M (2018) ¿Es otra cosmopolítica posible? Anthropologica 36:115–144. https://doi.org/10.18800/anthropologica.201802.005
Bloch EFM (1998) How we think they think: anthropological approaches to cognition. Memory, and literacy. Westview, Oxford
Bourdieu P (1975) The specificity of the scientific field and the social conditions of the progress of reason. Soc Sci Info 14:19–47. https://doi.org/10.1177/053901847501400602
Bourdieu P (1985) Praktische Vernunft: Zur Theorie des Handelns. Suhrkamp, Frankfurt a.M
Bourdieu P (1987) Sozialer Sinn: Kritik der theoretischen Vernunft. Suhrkamp, Frankfurt a.M
Bourdieu P (1992) Homo Academicus. Suhrkamp, Frankfurt a.M
Bourdieu P (2001) Para uma Sociologia da Ciência. Edições, Lisboa
Cadena Mdl (2010) Indigenous cosmopolitics in the Andes: conceptual reflections beyond "politics." Cult Anthropol 25:334–370
Cadena Mdl (2015) Earth beings: ecologies of practice across Andean worlds. Duke University Press, Durham
Cadena Mdl (2019) An invitation to live together: making the "complex we." Environ Humanit 11:477–484
Cadena Mdl, Blaser M (eds) (2018) A world of many worlds. Duke University Press, Durham
Cadena Mdl, A (2024) Notes on excess: towards pluriversal design. In: Tironi M et al (eds) Design for more-than-human futures towards post-anthropocentric worlding. Routledge, New York, pp 29–50
Castillo MC (2005) Aprendiendo con el corazón: El tejido andino en la educación quechua. La Paz
Castro EVd (1996) Os pronomes cosmológicos e o perspectivismo ameríndio. Mana 2:115–144
Castro EVd (2004a) Perspectivismo e multinaturalismo na América indígena. O que nos faz pensar 018:225–254
Castro EVd (2004b) Perspectival anthropology and the method of controlled equivocation. Tipití J Soc Anthropol Lowland South Am 2(1):Article 1
Castro EVd (2013a) Economic development and cosmopolitical re-involvement: From necessity to sufficiency. In: Green L (ed) Contested ecologies: dialogues in the south on nature and knowledge. HSRC, Cape Town, pp 28–41
Castro EVd (2013b) Closing remarks from the conclusion of the contested ecologies writing workshop, September 2011. In: Green L (ed) Contested ecologies: dialogues in the south on nature and knowledge. HSRC, Cape Town, pp 271–277
Castro EVd (2015) Metafisicas Canibais: Elementos para uma Antropologia Pós-Estrutural. Cosac & Naify, São Paulo
Castro EVd (2018) Rosa e Clarice, a fera e o fora. Revista Letras 9–30
Castro EVd (2022) O medo dos outros. Concinnitas 23:28–52. https://doi.org/10.12957/concinnitas.2022.67434
Castro EVd, Danowski D (2018) Humans and terrans in the Gaia War. In: Cadena Mdl, Blaser M (eds) A world of many worlds. Duke University Press, Durham, pp 395–468
Cesarino PDN (2006) De duplos e estereoscópios: paralelismo e personificação nos cantos xamanísticos ameríndios. Mana 12:105–134. https://doi.org/10.1590/S0104-93132006000100004

Chakrabarty D (2007) Provincializing Europe: postcolonial thought and historical difference. Princeton University Press, Princeton
Clifford J (1986) On ethnographic allegory. In: Clifford J, Marcus G (eds) Writing culture: the poetics and politics of ethnography. University of California Press, Berkeley, pp 98–121
Comte IMAX (1974) Die Soziologie. Die positive Philosophie im Auszug ("Cours de philosophie positive"). Kröner, Stuttgart
CRIC CRIDC (2021) La Crianza y Siembra se Sabidurías y Conocimientos (Crissac): Sentir, Pensar y Hacer para Trascender la Investigación Convencional. Grupo Estelar Impresores, Popayán, Santiago de Cali
Crystal D (1997) The Cambridge encyclopedia of language, 2nd edn. Cambridge University Press, Cambridge
Curry P (2006) Research note: neo-shamanism. J Contemp Relig 21(1):99–101
Danowski D, Castro EVd (2017) The ends of the world. Polity, Cambridge
Debaise D, Stengers I (2022) An ecology of trust? Consenting to a pluralist universe. Sociol Rev 70:402–415. https://doi.org/10.1177/00380261221084794
Descola P (1992) Societies of nature and the nature of society. In: Kuper A (ed) Conceptualizing society. Routledge, London, pp 107–126
Descola P (1996) Leben und Sterben in Amazonien: Bei den Jívaro-Indianern. Klett-Cotta, Stuttgart
Descola P (2006) Radcliffe-Brown lecture in social anthropology: beyond nature and culture. In: Proceedings of the British Academy, pp 137–155
Descola P (2014) Modes of being and forms of predication. HAU J Ethnogr Theory 4:271–280
Dunford R (2017) Toward a decolonial global ethics. J Global Ethics 13:380–397. https://doi.org/10.1080/17449626.2017.1373140
Eliade M (1956) Schamanismus und Archaische Ekstasetechniken. Zürich, Stuttgart
Erdheim M (1990) Anthropologische Modelle des 16. Jahrhunderts: Oviedo. In: Marschall W (ed) Klassiker der Kulturanthropologie: von Montaigne bis Margaret Mead. Munich, Beck, pp 19–50
Escobar A (2007) The 'ontological turn' in social theory. A commentary on 'human geography without scale', by Sallie Marston, John Paul Jones II and Keith Woodward. Trans Inst Br Geog 32:106–111. https://doi.org/10.1111/j.1475-5661.2007.00243.x
Escobar A (2011) Sustainability: design for the pluriverse. Development 54:137–140. https://doi.org/10.1057/dev.2011.28
Escobar A (2018) Designs for the pluriverse: radical interdependence, autonomy, and the making of worlds. Duke University Press, Durham
Escobar A (2020) Pluriversal politics: the real and the possible. Duke University Press, Durham
Escobar A (2021) Reframing civilization(s): from critique to transitions. Globalizations 1–18. https://doi.org/10.1080/14747731.2021.2002673
Escobar A, Osterweil M, Sharma K (2024) Relationality: an emergent politics of life beyond the human. Bloomsbury Visual Arts, London, New York
Estermann J (2006) Filosofia andina: sabiduría indígena para un mundo nuevo, 2da ed. (reimp.). Instituto Superior Ecuménico Andino de Teología (ISEAT), La Paz, Bolivia
EZLN (1996) 4. Declaración de la Selve da Lacandona. https://palabra.ezln.org.mx/comunicados/1996/1996_01_01_a.htm. Accessed 21 Nov 2023
Faust FX (1989) Medizin Und Weltbild: Zur Ethnographie der Coyaima und Natagaima-Indianer Kolumbiens. Munich
Feyerabend P (1993) Against method: outline of an anarchist theory of knowledge. Verso, London
Fitzgerald G (2021) Pluriversal peacebuilding: peace beyond epistemic and ontological violence. E-International Relations. https://www.e-ir.info/2021/11/27/pluriversal-peacebuilding-peace-beyond-epistemic-and-ontological-violence/. Accessed 19 Dec 2023
Galeano E (2010) As Veias Abertas da America Latina. L&PM Etitora, Montevideo
Garuba H (2012) On animism, modernity/colonialism, and the African order of knowledge: provisional reflections. E-Flux J 36

Gellner E (1985) Malinowski go home: reflexions on the Malinowski century conference. Anthropol Today 5–7
Gibson JJ (1979) The ecological approach to visual perception. Houghton Mufflin, Boston
Goodman N (1985) Language of art: an approach to a theory of symbols. Hacket, Indianapolis
Goody J (1977) The domestication of the savage mind. Cambridge University Press, Cambridge
Goody J (2000) The power of written tradition. Smithsonian Institution Press, Washington
Greaber D, Wengrow D (2021) The dawn of everything: a new history of humanity. Penguim Random House, New York
Green L (ed) (2013) Contested ecologies: dialogues in the south on nature and knowledge. HSRC, Cape Town
Greifeld K, Schmidt BE (2003) Medizinische Systeme Süd- und Afroamerikas. In: Greifeld K (ed) Ritual und Heilung: Eine Einführung in die Medizinethnologie. Reimer, Berlin, pp 105–132
Halbmayer E (2012) Debating animism, perspectivism and the construction of ontologies. Indiana 29:9–23
Hallowell AI (1960) Ojibwa ontology, behavior and world view. In: Diamond S (ed) Culture in history: essays in honor of Paul Radin. Columbia University Press, New York
Hamilton C (2017) Defiant earth: the fate of humans in the anthropocene, Kindle edition. Polity, Cambridge
Haraway D (2015) Anthropocene, capitalocene, plantationocene, chthulucene: making kin. Environ Humanit 6:159–165. https://doi.org/10.1215/22011919-3615934
Haraway DJ (2016) Staying with the trouble: making kin in the Chthulucene. Duke University Press, Durham
Harding SG (1994) Is science multicultural?: Challenges, resources, opportunities, uncertainties. Configurations 2:301–330. https://doi.org/10.1353/con.1994.0019
Harding S (2014) Towards an animistic science of the earth. In: Harvey G (ed) The handbook of contemporary animism. Routledge, New York
Harman G (2016) A new occasionalism? In: Latour B (ed) Reset modernity! MIT Press, Cambridge, pp 129–138
Harman G (2017) Object-oriented ontology: a new theory of everything. Pelican/Penguin, London
Harner M (1972) The Jívaro, people of the Sacred Waterfalls. University of California Press, Berkeley
Harner M (2002) Der Weg des Schamanen: Das Praktische Grundlagenwerk zum Schamanismus. Wilhelm Heyne, Munich
Harvey G (2005) Animism: respecting the living world. Wakefield, Kent Town
Harvey G (2010) Animism rather than Shamanism: new approaches to what shamans do (for other animists). In: Schmidt B, Huskinson L (eds) Spirit possession and trance: new interdisciplinary perspectives.Continuum advances in religious studies. Continuum, London, pp 14–34
Harvey G (ed) (2014) The handbook of contemporary animism. Routledge, London
Hinderling P (1981) Kranksein in "Primitiven" und Traditionellen Kulturen, Norderstedt
Holbraad M, Pedersen MA (2017) The ontological turn: an anthropological exposition, 1st edn. Cambridge University Press, Cambridge
Hornbacher A (2005) Zuschreibung und Befremdung: Postmoderne Repräsentationskrise und verkörpertes Wissen im balinesischen Tanz. Reimer, Berlin
Hornborg A (2011) Animism, fetishism, and objectivism as strategies for knowing (or not knowing) the world. Ethos 71:21–32
Horton R (1967) African traditional thought and western science. Africa 37:155–187
Horton R (1993) Patterns of thought in Africa and the west: essays on magic, religion and science. Cambridge University Press, Cambridge
Huambachano M (2024) Recovering our ancestral foodways: indigenous traditions as a recipe for living well. University of California Press, Oakland, California
Hutchings K (2019) Decolonizing global ethics: thinking with the pluriverse. Ethics Int Aff 33:115–125. https://doi.org/10.1017/S0892679419000169

Ingold T (2000) The perception of the environment: essays on livelihood, dwelling and skill. Routledge, New York

Ingold T (2006) Rethinking the animate, re-animating thought. Ethos 71:9–20

Kopenawa D (2021) A queda do céu. Companhia das Letras, São Paulo, SP

Kothari A et al (2019) Pluriverse: A post-development dictionary. Tulika, New Delhi

Krenak A (2019) Ideias para adiar o fim do mundo, 1ª edição. Companhia das Letras, São Paulo, SP

Landquist G (2005) Bringing the soul back to the self: soul retrieval in neo-shamanism. Soc Anal 48:155–173

Langdon EJM, Bear G (eds) (1992) Portals of power: shamanism in South America. University of New Mexico Press, Albuquerque

Langness LL (1974) The study of culture. University of California, Los Angeles

Latour B (1987) Science in action: how to follow scientists and engineers through society. Harvard University Press, Cambridge

Latour B (1993) We have never been modern. Harvard University Press, Cambridge

Latour B (2004a) Why has critique run out of steam? From matters of fact to matters of concern. Crit Inq 30(2):225–248

Latour B (2004b) Whose cosmos, which cosmopolitics? Comments on the peace terms of Ulrich Beck. In: Symposium: talking peace with Gods, part I. Common knowledge, vol 10, no 3. Duke University Press, pp 450–462

Latour B (2009) Perspectivism: 'Type' or 'bomb'? Anthropol Today 25(2):21–22

Latour B (2013) An inquiry into modes of existence: an anthropology of the moderns. Harvard University Press, Cambridge

Latour B (2016) Reset modernity! MIT Press, Cambridge

Latour B, Miranda C (2017) A dialog about a new meaning of symmetric anthropology (with Carolina Miranda). In: Charbonnier P, Salmon G, Skafish P (eds) Comparative metaphysics—ontology after anthropology. Rowman & Littlefield, London, pp 327–345

Latour B, Woolgar S (1986) Laboratory life: the construction of scientific facts. Princeton University Press, Princeton

Latour B, Stengers I, Tsing A, Bubandt N (2018) Anthropologists are talking—about capitalism, ecology, and apocalypse. Ethnos 83:587–606. https://doi.org/10.1080/00141844.2018.1457703

Law J (2004) After method: mess in social science research. Routledge, London

Law J (2011) What's wrong with a one-world world. Presented to the Center for the Humanities, Wesleyan University, September 19, 2011

Leenhardt M (1982) Do Kamo: person and myth in the Melanesian world. University of California Press, Berkeley

Lery Jd (1580) Histoire d'un voyage faict en la terre du Bresil, autrement dite Amerique. Chippin, Geneve

Lery Jd (1992) History of a voyage to the land of Brazil, otherwise called America. University of California Press, Berkeley

Lévi-Strauss C (1973) Das Wilde Denken. Suhrkamp, Frankfurt a.M

Lévi-Strauss C (1976) Raça e História. In: Antropologia Estrutural II, Rio de Janeiro, Tempo Brasileiro, capítulo XVIII, pp 328–366

Lévi-Strauss C (1995) Mythos und Bedeutung: Vorträge. Surhkamp, Frankfurt a.M

Lévi-Strauss C (1999) Traurige Tropen. Suhrkamp, Frankfurt a.M

Lévy-Bruhl L (1927) Die geistige Welt der Primitiven. Bruckmann, Munich

Linhart J (2008) Universidades Indígenas: Programas de Educação Indígena Superior na América Latina: A Caminho de uma Ciência Intercultural? Master Thesis, LMU

Linhart J et al (forthcoming) Towards pluriversal dialogues—a report on current research. Third World Quarterly. York, UK

Lovelock JE, Margulis L (1973) Atmospheric Homeostasis by and for the biosphere: the gaia hypothesis. Tellus 26:2–10

Macas LFS (2014) El Paradigma educativo de Abya Yala: continuidad histórica, avances y desafíos. URACCAN, Managua
Malinowski B (1948) Magic, science and religion and other essays. Beacon, Boston
Mannheim K (1954) Ideology and utopia: an introduction to the sociology of knowledge. Routledge & Kegan Paul, New York
Marcuse H (1964) One dimensional man. Beacon, Boston
McGilchrist I (2009) The master and his emissary: the divided brain and the making of the western world. Yale University Press, New Haven
Meillassoux Q (2008) After finitude: an essay on the necessity of contingency. Continuum, London
Mendonça W (2014) Memorias de nos. Karioka Multimedia, Porto Alegre
Mignolo WD (2011) The darker side of western modernity—global futures, decolonial options. Duke University Press, Durham
Mignolo W (2021) The politics of decolonial investigations. Duke University Press, Durham
Mignolo W, Walsh CE (2018) On decoloniality: concepts, analytics, praxis. Duke University Press, Durham
Mol A (1999) Ontological politics. A word and some questions. Sociol Rev 47:74–89. https://doi.org/10.1111/j.1467-954X.1999.tb03483.x
Montaigne M de (1877) Essays of Michael, Seigneur de Montaigne. Translated by Charles Cotton Edited by William Carew Hazlitt. "Release date: October 26, 2004". "The Project Gutenberg eBook". https://www.gutenberg.org/ebooks/3600. Downloaded: 23.09.2025
Morrison KM (2014) Animism and a proposal for a post-Cartesian anthropology. In: Harvey G (ed) The handbook of contemporary animism. Routledge, New York, pp 38–52
Munter KD, Note N (2009) Cosmopraxis and contextualising among the contemporary Aymara. In: Note N, Fornet-Betancout R, Estermann J, Aerts D (eds) Worldviews and cultures. Springer, Dordrecht, pp 87–102
Münzel M (1986) Indianische Oralkultur der Gegenwart. In: Scharlau B, Münzel M (eds) Quellqay: Mündliche Kultur und Schrifttradition bei Indianern Lateinamerikas. Campus, Frankfurt a.M
Narby J (1998) The cosmic serpent: DNA and the origins of knowledge. Penguin, New York
Nhemachena A (2013) Are petitioners makers of rain? Rains, worlds and survival in conflict-torn Buhera, Zimbabwe. In: Green L (ed) Contested ecologies: dialogues in the south on nature and knowledge. HSRC, Cape Town, pp 110–125
Niess F (1991) Am Anfang war Kolumbus: Geschichte einer Unterentwicklung—Lateinamerika 1492 bis Heute. Munich
Pedersen MA (2012) Common nonsense: a review of certain recent reviews of the "ontological turn". Anthropol Century, issue 5
Pereira JRDS (2021) Movimento de Mulheres do Xingu (MMX). Margens 15:123. https://doi.org/10.18542/rmi.v15i24.10040
Perruchon M (2003) I am Tsunki: gender and shamanism among the shuar of Western Amazonia. Acta Universitatis Upsaliensis, Uppsala
Pinker S (2018) Aufklärung Jetzt: Für Vernunft, Wissenschaft, Humanismus und Fortschritt—Eine Verteidigung. Fischer, Frankfurt a.M
Putnam H (1981) Reason, truth and history. Cambridge University Press, Cambridge
Querejazu A (2022) Cosmopraxis: Relational methods for a pluriversal IR. Rev Int Stud 48:875–890. https://doi.org/10.1017/S0260210521000450
Redfield R (1952) The primitive world view. Proc Am Philos Soc 96:30–36
Reichel ED (1987) Die Ökopolitik im Schamanismus der Yukuna und Tanimuka vom Nordwestlichen Amazonas. In: Gottwald FT, Rätsch C (eds) Schamanische Wissenschaft, Ökologie, Naturwissenschaft und Kunst. Munich, pp 25–95
Reichel-Dolmatoff G (1971) Amazonian cosmos: the sexual and religious symbolism of the Tukano Indians. University of Chicago Press, Chicago
Rousseau JJ (2020) A discourse upon the origin and the foundation of the inequality among mankind. Project Gutenberg
Schutz A (1962) Collected papers 1: The problem of social reality. Martinus Nijhoff, The Hague

Shaviro S (2014) The universe of things: on speculative realism. University of Minneapolis Press, Minneapolis
Soto RRH (2019) ¿El entretejido de la pluriversidad?. Conocimientos en tensión y diálogo en universidades indígenas de Abya Yala: Amawtay Wasi (Ecuador), UAIIN-CRIC (Colombia) y Tupak Katari (Bolivia). PhD thesis, Universidad Andina Simón Bolívar
Staden H (1557) Warhaftige Historia und beschreibung eyner Landtschafft der Wilden/ Nacketen/ Grimmigen Menschfresser Leuthen. Marpurg
Steffen W, Crutzen PJ, McNeill JR (2007) The anthropocene: are humans now overwhelming the great forces of nature. Ambio 36(8):614–621
Stengers I (2005a) The cosmopolitical proposal. In: Latur B, Weibel P (eds) Making things public. Atmospheres of democracy. MIT Press, Cambridge
Stengers I (2005b) Introductory notes on: an ecology of practices. Cult Stud Rev 11(1):183–196
Stengers I (2009) William James—an ethics of thought? Radic Philos 157:9–19
Stengers I (2012) Reclaiming animism. E-Flus J 36:1–10
Stengers I (2015) In catastrophic times: resisting the coming barbarism. Open Humanities, London
Stengers I (2018a) The challenge of ontological politics. In: Cadena Mdl, Blaser M (eds) A world of many worlds. Duke University Press, Durham, pp 195–260
Stengers I (2018b) Another science is possible—a manifesto for slow science, Kindle version. Polity, Cambridge
Stengers I, Higgins M, Wallace M (2023) In conversation with Isabelle Stengers: ontological politics in catastrophic times. In: Tolbert S, Wallace MFG, Higgins M, Bazzul J (eds) Reimagining science education in the anthropocene, vol 2. Springer, Cham, pp 363–387
Stoller P, Olkes C (1987) In sorcery's shadow: a memoir of apprenticeship among the Songhay of Niger. University of Chicago Press, Chicago
Strathern M (1988) The gender of the gift: problems with women and problems with society in Melanesia. University of California Press, Berkeley
Strathern M (2018) Opening up relations. In: Cadena Mdl, Blaser M (eds) A world of many worlds. Duke University Press, Durham, pp 62–126
Tambiah SJ (1990) Magic, science, religion, and the scope of rationality. Cambridge University Press, Cambridge
Tanasescu M (2022) Ecocene politics. Open Book Publishers, Cambridge, UK
Taussig M (1997) Mimesis und Alterität: eine eigenwillige Geschichte der Sinne. Europäische Verlagsanstalt, Hamburg
Taylor AC, Castro EV (2019) Um corpo feito de olhares (Amazônia). Revista de Antropologia 62:769–818
Tironi M, Chilet M, Marín CU, Hermansen P (eds) (2024) Design for more-than-human futures; towards post-anthropocentric worlding. Routledge, Abingdon
Tsing AL (2015) The mushroom at the end of the world: on the possibility of life in capitalist ruins. Princeton University Press, Princeton
Tsing AL, Bazzul J (2022) A feral atlas for the anthropocene: an interview with Anna L. Tsing. In: Wallace MFG, Bazzul J, Higgins M, Tolbert S (eds) Reimagining science education in the anthropocene. Palgrave Macmillan, Cham, pp 309–320
Verran H (2013) Engagements between disparate knowledge traditions: Toward doing difference generatively and in good faith. In: Green L (ed) Contested ecologies: dialogues in the south an nature and knowledge. HSRC, Cape Town, pp 127–141
Verran H (2018) The politics of working cosmologies together while keeping them separate. In: Cadena Mdl, Blaser M (eds) A world of many worlds. Duke University Press, Durham, pp 262–304
Viveiros de Castro E (2019) On models and examples: engineers and bricoleurs in the anthropocene. Curr Anthropol 60:S296–S308. https://doi.org/10.1086/702787
von Stuckrad K (2003) Schamanismus und Esoterik: Kultur- und wissenschaftsgeschichtliche Betrachtung. Peeters, Leuven
Wagner R, Ingold T (2016) The invention of culture. University of Chicago Press, Chicago

Wallis JR (2000) Queer shamans: autoarcheology and neo-shamanism. World Archeol 32:252–262
Walsh C (ed) (2017) Pedagogías decoloniales: Prácticas insurgentes de resistir, (re)existir y (re) vivir. Tomo II. Ediciones Abya Yala, Quito
Weber M (2006) Die protestantische Ethik und der Geist des Kapitalismus. Munich
Wernitznig D (2003) Going native or going naive: white shamanism and the neo-noble savage. University Press of America, Lanham
Whitehead AN (1978) Process and reality: an essay in cosmology. Griffin DR (ed). Free Press, New York
Winkelmann M (1999) Shamanism as psychobiological structures of consciousness, cognition and healing. Currare 22:121–128
Wittgenstein L (1969) On certainty. Blackwell, Oxford
Wolf ER (2010) Europe and the people without history. University of California Press, Berkeley

Part II
The Potiguara

Chapter 6
On Method

This second part of this book is dedicated to the Potiguara, to their brave struggle for their ancestors' lands and for their way of being, and also to the enchanted beings dwelling among them. The years I was allowed to spend with them, the exciting experiences they let me partake in, their sincere friendship, the moments of joy we shared, and the many things I learned with them, all this will forever fill my heart with the sweet pain of remembrance. And I sincerely hope our work will, in the end, somehow contribute to their fight for cultural autonomy, social equity, or simply, a better life.

However, my personal feelings notwithstanding, here I will refer to the Potiguara just as representing an example of those countless Others, those subalternised colonial moderns, those "hybrids" populating the borders of our modern/colonial world-system, in short, all those that have no voice in scientific discourse because their knowledge has been radically disqualified by scientific universalism for being "irrational" or simply too different. Having shown that scientific universalism is nothing but a modern/colonial myth, I would like to compare the Potiguara's cosmovision and practice with those cosmological models being discussed by Us "Western" scientists and philosophers (which will be continued in Part III), and see how different and incommensurable they really are. Although the Potiguara share many aspects of their history, culture, and cosmovision with other subalternised groups, this is not important for my argument. On the contrary, my argument is that if only one, no matter which, of those Other visions turned out to be commensurable with Ours (or at least with one seriously discussed academic approach), then incommensurability would, in principle, no longer be a valid argument for an a priori exclusion of Other views from academic discourse. Moreover, "Other" in this context does not necessarily mean "different" from "Us" "moderns", "Europeans", "Westerners", "scientists", or "academics", but rather refers to the subalternised modern/colonial identities resulting from othering all those that have to be stigmatised as "Others" in order to be dominated.

Of course, identitary debates in ethnography are minefields, and since I discuss "the" Potiguara and "their" cosmovision as representing "the Others'" (or more

J. Linhart, *Science and the Other*, Schriften zu Leben und Gesellschaft - Series on Life and Society 2, https://doi.org/10.1007/978-3-032-03927-9_6

precisely, "an Other") point of view, my descriptions might be (mis-)interpreted as essentialisations of otherwise "hybrid" modern/colonial identities. However, despite the general linguistic limitations to a clear-cut separation from the objectively existing social category of the "Others" from actual differences between "Us", the representatives of the global centres, and the peripheral "Others", I would like to emphasise my efforts in avoiding any kind of essentialist concept of "the" Others or "the" Potiguara. And I apologise for any instance in my work where I might not have managed to make this point crystal clear.

Having said this, it is time now to come to the methodological instruments that guided my field work.

* * *

Doing anthropology, in my personal view, has always been an essentially political activity. Actually, my decision, as a young student of biology, to switch over to anthropology was motivated by my experiences with Indigenous activists in Ecuador fighting against international oil-companies and the socio-ecological disaster these companies have been causing in their territory. They clearly understood their subaltern position within a global hierarchical system and the importance of the forest for their cultural continuity and, hence, their ethnic identity as a weapon in the political game of ecologist and human rights discourse. There was nothing romantic about their situation, although they obviously used "Western" romantic notions of the Noble Savage, supposedly living in perfect harmony with nature,[1] in their own favour. However, it became also clear to me that their way of relating to the world was fundamentally different from our own. They openly ridiculed me as a budding biologist for trying to understand life by reading books and killing, dismembering and analysing the chemical components of living beings. For them, it was obvious that a living plant is something completely different from a dead one, and that to understand what being a plant is about one should rather chant and talk to her, or maybe ingest her, instead of reading books and doing chemical analysis in a laboratory[2]—and I, honestly, had to agree with them.

---

[1] Bargatzky (1998) argues that such notions are romantic Western constructions based on a concept of "nature" based on cartesian dualism, both of which would not exist in Indigenous cosmologies. However, Indigenous movements and their activists have long introduced environmentalist notions into their current cosmologies and self-understanding, be it for political reasons or some philosophical conviction (Linhart 2008). Moreover, as seen above, recent anthropological approaches suggest that it is exactly the lack of a Western-style human-nature-dualism which characterises "animistic" ontologies, with its implicit respect towards a world made up by persons rather than things.

[2] "Estuve en [...] Montpellier en un laboratorio muy famoso, dicho allí por el mismo doctor, el primer laboratorio mas grande en Europa. [...] Científicamente en el estudio bio-químico nosotros tenemos otros tipos de realidad, su composición, su aplicación, y sus efectos. Para nosotros no existe laboratorio. Entonces la planta procesada por supuesto tiene otros argumentos químicos, y la planta no procesada tiene otros argumentos químicos, la planta esta viva! Entonces nosotros aplicamos la planta desde el punto de vista activo, y en los laboratorios se aplica desde el punto de

6.1 Representing Others

There can be no doubt about the fact that ethnic identity is socially construed within political fields, delimiting social boundaries and thereby regulating relations of inequality.[3] Ethnography has played an important role in this process for a long time now, shaping our image of Us and the Other. The images of the Noble and the Barbarian Savage have been fundamental for legitimating and ordering power relations throughout modern history. This is not only true for the global and intercultural sphere, but also for all other social levels, from major ideological strands, national politics, down to family relationships and even our individual self-image.[4]

Meanwhile, the ethnographic representation of the Others has been subject to serious critiques leading to an ongoing crisis in anthropology.[5] The problem is complex and multi-layered, and certainly cannot be treated sufficiently here. For sake of conciseness, I will try to boil the issue down to two fundamental questions:

The first one, the question of *authenticity*, asks to what extent ethnography is really able to paint a picture of the Others which is more than just a narcissistic[6] allegory[7] of our own self-image?

Second, there is the question of *authority*, asking who actually has the right to represent whom and for what purpose?

While the first question concerns the *epistemological* dimension of the representation problem, the latter points to its *political* or *ethical* dimension. The two questions are closely related, both having deep methodological consequences for field work as much as for the production of written (or audio-visual) ethnographic accounts.

The epistemological problem of authenticity transcends the questions of objectivity and cultural essentialism, both of which having by and large been settled

---

vista inactivo, donde la ciencia tiene que buscar en sus laboratorios la composición—eso es la diferencia, y esto los científicos tienen que aceptar: que una planta viva es diferente que una planta muerta [...]" (Interview with Indigenous Shuar activist—Yawints, Ecuador, 20.12.2006. In: Linhart 2008: 183).

[3] Barth (1969); Hobsbowm and Ranger (1983); Hall (1992); Elias and Scotson (2000); Giddens (2003); Becker (2008); et al.

[4] James Clifford (1986) highlights the importance of ethnography, as it mediates powerful systems of meaning at the boundaries of diacritical categories like civilisation, culture, class or race, while itself being part of the historical and semiotic processes of decoding and recoding. Ethnographic texts, therefore, are "powerful lies" or "true fictions". "Power and history work through them, in ways their authors cannot fully control" (ibidem: 7).

[5] Huizer (1989); Clifford (1986); et al.

[6] Castro (2015).

[7] James Clifford (1986) called attention to the problem of ethnographic writing as a process of "writing cultures" in terms of allegories of our own Western self-image, inventing cultures much more than representing them, while obfuscating their authority.

during the second half of the twentieth century.[8] What is at stake is modern logocentrism, representationalism, and thus, epistemology itself.

In the previous chapters I have tried to show how deeply entangled our "Western"/modern self-image is with our image of the Others, and how difficult, if not impossible,[9] it is to really *see* the Others behind our magic mirror. Instead of a transparent image any time we try to look at Them, our mirror incessantly shows distorted images of our own unconscious self—with the Noble Savage epitomising everything we desire to be, and the Barbarian representing that part of ourselves we fear and abominate. Since there is no objective measure or record of what it is like to be someone else, ethnographic research remains dependent on subjective experiences and interpretations offered by anthropologists. The problem is, of course, that the relation between the cultural phenomenon of concern, the anthropologist's experience (including observation, conversation, participation and introspection) and their final interpretation is a complex process of construction, so that it is questionable to what extent the outcome of this whole process has to do with the initial input. There are no such phenomena as "cosmologies" one could observe or experience; there are people thinking, feeling, talking and acting, relating to the world in their particular manner. Moreover, the idea of interpreting or translating "cultures" is derived from a logocentric concept of culture as a semiotic system or text,[10] that is, a representation of the world rather than a way of being in it.[11] Hence, cosmolo-

[8] Positivistic claims for objective standards in Anthropology have long been replaced by a common agreement on the inevitable subjective character of ethnographic research. Being based on participatory observation as its main source of "data", the ethnologist's bias can only be relativised through self-reflection and peer review (e.g. Dammann 1991). The linguistic and semiotic turn, post-modern deconstructionism, cultural studies and feminist theory further fostered the establishment of the interpretative method based on hermeneutics as mainstream theoretical strand in Anthropology. Moreover, it has long become clear that essentialist notions of "original" "ancient" culture or tradition are as much social and historical constructions as the concepts of "culture" and "tradition" (see above). So that in a way, all "cultures" and "traditions" are equally authentic and invented at the same time.

[9] If Michael Taussig (1997) is right, alterity is always a mimetic product of our unconscious. Being a universal mode of human apprehension which is at work in magic as well as in modern commodity fetishism, photography and film, mimesis would incessantly produce self-similarity. Hence, ethnography would not be able to escape this mimetic trap either. However, Taussig's mimesis concept is trapped in post-modern hyper-representationalism, much like Baudrillard's (1982) simulacra, thus declaring reality or world to be just a mimetic sham.

[10] Geertz (2008).

[11] Talal Asad (1986) criticised the metaphor of culture as text as present in Clifford Geertz's hermeneutic approach of an interpretative Anthropology. Ethnography, understood as translation of cultural text, is an exegesis of the unwritten *noema* which the anthropologist has to read between the lines of the Other's symbolic performances and then transform it into a "dense description". However, culture is not a text, but people thinking, feeling, speaking and acting. By "reading" other cultures, the anthropologist offers interpretations of a phenomenal cultural surface, revealing its "true", hidden "sense" in terms of some coherent cosmology. But since the people are themselves unaware of this apparently coherent meaningful system, it becomes, in a way, culture's unconsciousness, with the anthropologist acting as cultural psychoanalyst to unravel the logic behind their seemingly irrational performances. One problem with this approach is that these inter-

gies, being a culture's core frame of reference, are conceptualised as representational systems or epistemologies. However, epistemology is itself a historical phenomenon of modern (or at least "Western") philosophical discourse, and thus, not a universal subjacent principle of perception or culture.[12] It has been argued, that instead of projecting our cultural history on to our image of the Others, we should rather submit our own modern worldview to an anthropological investigation of its historical constitution within social practice. Anthropology has to be decentralised, adopting different viewpoints and turning these new eyes on its own position within modernity/coloniality.[13]

The problem of authenticity, hence, is ultimately one of modern epistemology. In the face of these arguments, one way (if not the only one) to avoid the predicaments of ethnographic representation could be an inverted anthropology, as proposed by Viveiros de Castro, with Westerners and non-Westerners collectively experimenting with diverging ontologies or other anthropologies.

However, Western epistemology as employed by anthropologists not only distorts ethnographic representations of the Others, it also reproduces the unequal power relations which sustain the dominant World System. Being a direct result of Cartesian dualism, the modern concept of epistemology is unthinkable without the distinction between subject and object and, hence, intrinsic to scientific research per se. In social sciences, however, this epistemological distinction inevitably entails a political dimension, since both subjects and objects are human beings, and therefore all of them subjects alike. Moreover, the ethnographer would typically be a white man of European descent, from the upper or middle class with an academic education, while researching poor groups of non-European descent which occupy a subaltern position in relation to the dominant society. The classical research design implicated in modern epistemology, therefore, reproduces and naturalises the unequal power relations of the modern/colonial World System. As a consequence, the question of authenticity—how can we give an authentic account of the Others?—entails the question of authority—who is representing whom, with what right and for what purpose?

---

pretations cannot normally be contested by the people they describe. Geertz's cock fight puts him and his readers on top of the hierarchy of understanding, thus reproducing the hierarchical relations between the rational, reflexive "West" and the irrational, non-reflexive "Rest" (see also Crapanzano's (1986) contribution in the same volume).

[12] Richard Rorty (1979) argued, that epistemology as mental representation stems from the seventeenth century. Modern philosophy was born when Kant defined it as a theory of knowledge. In Greek antiquity, in contrast, there would have been no sharp division between inner representation and outer reality. This historical move in philosophical discourse went together with the rise of the regime of truth and falsity, which Foucault (1974) showed to be part of an overarching system of public social practice, order and power, which generated the conditions for the emergence of capitalism.

[13] Rabinow (1986); Huizer (1989); Castro (2015); et al.

From a (Post-)Marxist[14] or Gramscian[15] point of view, anthropologists, coming from upper and middle class, would obviously reproduce bourgeoise ideology. Hence, for an anthropologist to come to both an authentic and an authorised view of the Others they have to understand Them within their historical class struggles, while reflecting on their own privileged position within the modern/colonial World-System.[16] In addition to being upper- or middle-class intellectuals, subaltern groups "embody the most powerful critique of capitalism". They do not need to believe in the dominant ideology because they are forced to fulfil their function anyway, no matter whether they agree or not. Being immersed in a constant class struggle, their culture is, at least in part, a product of this struggle, too. Michael Taussig,[17] for example, showed how Colombian peasants and Bolivian miners manifest their protest through different symbolic channels, including magic ritual and myth. According to Taussig's interpretation, the "spirit of evil in capitalism" is symbolised through the image of the Devil, who is worshipped by those who seek economic wealth. Colombian peasants, still in the process of proletarisation, are aware of the unnaturalness of capitalist reification and commoditisation, thus mystifying this reification in their own terms of magical beliefs. Working as a "fetish of evil", the contract with the Devil implies the sale of the worker's soul in exchange for miserable money, which never lasts.

However fascinating and elucidating, Taussig's interpretations are still *his* representation of the Others. Still, taking critically into account both the Others' and his own historical position within the capitalist World System, he may have more authority than his (supposedly) unreflected "bourgeoise" colleagues. More importantly, Taussig not only wrote about those workers, but also militated together with them for several years. He became an active part of the process and the group he later represented in his text.

This kind of active engagement of the anthropologist to the advantage of the group they are studying had been proposed by Sol Tax in the 1940s.[18] As the story goes, Tax had been questioned by one of his "informants" among the Meskwaki about why he continued doing research on their culture while the Meskwaki community was facing so many serious problems. During the next decades, Tax implemented several projects together with his Indigenous friends and his students,

[14] Marx (1852, 1962).

[15] Gramsci (1982).

[16] George Marcus (1986) criticises that most ethnographic accounts do not pay much attention to the greater context of global political economy in which the realities they describe are embedded. He champions Wallerstein's (2004) World-System-Theory as a framework to re-associate history and social theory in ethnography by focussing on an understanding of capitalist political economy. He holds that Marxism would still be the "most sophisticated and coherent framework for conceptualizing modern societies to survive the nineteenth century" and that "Marxist system imagery remains the most convenient and comprehensive framework for embedding single-locale ethnography in political economy" (idem: 173).

[17] Taussig (2006).

[18] Tax (1988); Daubenmier (2003, 2008); Foley (2009).

resulting in what would later be known as a*ction anthropology*. Tax argued that anthropological research would inevitably have an impact on the group under study, and as human relations are intrinsically political in character, any attempt to maintain political neutrality would be an illusion anyway. Negating this fact would not enhance objectivity, but to the contrary, ignore important insights concerning the political dimension of a group's cultural expressions.

Despite all criticism and shortcomings, his experiences had a significant influence on anthropological research. However, the actively engaged anthropologist is still the author of the written representation of the Others. The Anthropologist is the subject who controls the research process as well as the text production, while the Others are passively being described, like objects. It is still them who are writing the Others' culture. Some anthropologists tried to attenuate this problem by experimenting with polyvocal or polyphone texts, giving a voice to their "informants".[19] However, though representing an important stylistic element for bringing the individual voices to the reader in a more direct and vivid way, it continues to be the author who chooses and arranges their voices in a way which is convenient for their purpose, so the Others' voices may contribute to the author's arguments.

> Once "informants" begin to be considered as co-authors, and the ethnographer as scribe and archivist as well as interpreting observer, we can ask new, critical questions of all ethnographies. However monological, dialogical, or polyphonic their form, they are hierarchical arrangements of discourses (Clifford 1986: 17).

Moreover, the question of authorship begins long before compiling the final result, during research itself. Who does research on whom? Who asks whom what kind of questions?

6.2 Acting Rather than Representing

While "Western" anthropologists have been debating on the aporia of representing the Others, Indigenous intellectuals have long begun to represent their own ethnic groups.[20] Auto-ethnographic research has become an important element in Indigenous activism, not only for the purpose of gaining plain authority over their own ethnic identity, but also as a means of self-understanding and cultural continuity. In many Indigenous groups the younger generations are losing touch with their "traditional" culture; in other cases the whole community may have lost considerable parts of their cultural and historical heritage. The Indigenous intellectuals then need to do research on their own culture and history first, and then transform this newly-acquired knowledge into a coherent set of historical and cosmological

[19] See Clifford (1986). Also Linhart (2008).

[20] Bolaños (2004); Ramos and Rappaport (2005); Linhart (2008, 2012); Ramos and Linhart (2012); Linhart et al. (2017a, b).

narrations. These "cosmovisions" serve as guiding principles for their political projections and as models for didactic material to be used in their schools.

However, the Indigenous intellectuals who instantiate such auto-ethnographic research are often themselves quite alienated from their Indigenous culture. Many of them are academics, forced to live in cities far from their community in order to visit high-schools and universities and to militate for Indigenous organisation—they are living at the cultural boundary, they are border intellectuals.[21] Hence, they are not really researching themselves but rather their elder relatives and "traditional" authorities who spend their whole lives in their rural communities, and who are the holders of "tradition". As a consequence, Indigenous intellectuals and militants have been accused by their communities of inventing their own "traditions", and the authenticity of their representations has been questioned. Auto-ethnography, therefore, offers a good solution to the question of authority,[22] but it faces similar problems concerning authenticity compared to external representations.[23]

Faced with such problems concerning the authenticity of their own auto-ethnographic research, Indigenous intellectuals in Latin America resorted on Paulo Freire's works on *Popular education* and Orlando Fals Borda's concept of *participatory action research.*

Paulo Freire's interest in research was mainly of pedagogical concern and was originally based on experiences with his literacy programme for the Brazilian underprivileged population during the 1960s. His *pedagogy of the oppressed*[24] takes education as a central dispositive in the struggle of the working classes, which would depend on the self-conscious recognition of Popular culture as equally rich and valuable compared to the hegemonic culture of the dominant classes.[25]

For Paulo Freire, there is no objective scientific neutrality. All knowledge, education and science are political, and hence, ideological in character. Education, therefore, is conceived as a dialogical investigative process based on the equality of all participants, aiming to achieve a conscious understanding of the cultural values and "traditional" knowledge within the particular historical situation of a class struggle.

In order to come to a critical understanding of one's own situation, its limits and possibilities, it is necessary to understand it in its totality, not just as separated parts, each being subject to different scientific disciplines. One has to understand the

---

[21] Rappaport (2005).

[22] Especially if the results are published under a collective authorship, either in the name of a collective or organisation, or naming all participants of the research as authors.

[23] For a more detailed discussion of this issue see Linhart (2008).

[24] Freire (1987).

[25] Paulo Freire's pedagogical approach heavily hinges on Antonio Gramsci's writings on the social role of intellectuals. Following Gramsci (1982), class struggles are also a struggle for hegemony, that is, over the dominant ideologies orienting value systems, political decisions and social behaviour. As a result, the subaltern classes need to breed their own "organic intellectuals" to transform their experiences into intellectual frameworks and effective political demands. Freire's work can be understood as an attempt to educate the subaltern classes to become organic intellectuals and to empower them to effectively articulate their own political demands.

"limiting situations" that sustain one's own oppression. These "generating themes" can neither be found within the subject, nor in objective reality, but in the relations between subject and world, leading to a dialectical perception of reality.

Both professional external and "Popular" local researchers are subjects in the process of identifying and investigating the generator themes. The research "objects" are not the subjects, but the total situation in which they are immersed. The researcher who, for the sake of scientific objectivity, transforms the living into a dead thing is afraid of change and reproduces the necrophile[26] logic of the dominating classes. Rather, what has to be investigated is the people's way of thinking and acting within their situatedness, seeking the *liberating moment* of consciously understanding their historical situation. Hence, in Freire's "problematising concept of education" as "dialogical practice", any thematic investigation is educational in character and any true education is an investigation.

Freire's work has been fundamental for Popular movements all over Latin America as well as in Africa and other parts of the world. His educational approach has been applied in landless peasant and homeless movements, leftist parties, labour unions, as well as Indigenous organisations and their schools, and it continues to be used as a guideline for the national educational systems of several countries.

Orlando Fals Borda was one of many Latin American intellectuals who were strongly influenced by Paulo Freire. He would further develop Freire's approach into what would become known as *Participatory Action Research (PAR)*.[27] As a social scientist who had studied at US universities during the 1940s and 1950s, Fals Borda developed his approach in contrast to Kurt Lewin's[28] conservative action research approach. In the face of the deep socio-political upheavals of the 1960s (e.g. Cuban Revolution, Cheguevarism, Sandinism and Colombian *violencia*) leftist social scientists felt their studies would have to be more useful to their proletarian brothers and sisters—Fals Borda's approach was a direct response to that situation.[29]

---

[26] Freire borrows this expression from Erich Fromm (1967).

[27] Borda (1971, 1981); also Thiollent (1986); Gabarón and Landa (1994); Brandão (1999); Baldissera (2001); Neves (2006); Brandão and Borges (2007); Faermam (2014); Linhart et al. (2017a, b); Pacheco (2017).

[28] Kurt Lewin (1946) suggested a more pragmatic social research approach focussing on the needs of social managers and social engineers to enhance intergroup relations, and which finally would result in concrete social action rather than mere theoretical conceptions. Action research should be based on a collective process which would involve participants in a "cycle of planning, executing and reconnaissance or fact-finding" in a "spiral of steps", including workshops as an important instrument in the whole process. Although Lewin's suggestions concerning the basic design of the participatory process probably have been influential for the conception of PAR, its focus on management rather than on concerns of the working class is of striking difference.

[29] Like Paulo Freire and many other Latin American leftist intellectuals, Borda was strongly influenced by Marxism and liberation theology. According to Pacheco (2017), Borda exemplifies the contradictions of the history of Marxism in Latin America and the constant tension between critical scientism, religious foundations and political activism that repudiates the extremism of violent revolution. Borda oscillated between Cuban revolution, popular movements and revolutionary guerrillas in Colombia, posterior disenchantment and crisis of Marxism, and the direct influence of theology of liberation. After his initial successful academic career, Borda changed his theoretical

Like Paulo Freire, Fals Borda developed his version of PAR as a tool for social transformation through decolonising the knowledge of the subaltern classes. Research should be oriented by the needs and the ways of learning and understanding of disadvantaged groups, and should articulate the voices of oppressed knowledge against the predominance of classic (modern) science. Borda contrasts "Popular science", the "science of the common man", with the "predominant classic science". While the latter would be an apparatus of the dominant classes which, by emphasising or neglecting certain facts or paradigms, contributes to the maintenance of the capitalist system as a "total constant process" with a huge negative impact, the first could show clues to alternative solutions. Consequently, Borda calls for a re-orientation of science towards the needs of the world's majority, who today are the victims of the unequal progress of science. Hence, the crucial question would be: *What kind of knowledge do we really need?*

Since its initial articulation by Freire and Borda, PAR has been further developed in the academic field.[30] But more importantly, it has proven to be a highly effective instrument for the intellectual empowerment of subaltern communities. Being more of a strategic social practice of social movements than an academic method, there have been manifold experiences of experimenting with countless different social contexts and processual designs. However, there is a common agreement about the basic principles and techniques which are central to PAR and which serve as a general guideline for practitioners:

Basic Principles of PAR[31]:

1. *Horizontality/participation:* Transformation of the subject-object relation between researcher and researched into a subject-subject relation. This includes the active participation and control over the whole research process by the participating local community. Rather than enacting their social superiority, academic researchers should leave their ivory tower to learn from subaltern communities and subject themselves to their judgment.

---

and political direction in the face of the assassination of ELN *guerrillero* Father Camilo Torres in 1966, towards a reinterpretation of Marxism within the Latin American context based on religious roots. While critical of dogmatic Marxism, Borda defended socialism as the only utopian project able to provide new imaginational scenarios of action. Change would be possible through "subversion", Borda's sociological concept of a historical situation in which the contradictions of the current system become obvious and new utopias start to challenge the dominant order.

[30] In 1977, the World Symposium on Critique and Politics in Social Science in Cartagena, Colombia, defined PAR as a transformative decolonisation process of scientific character. Its theoretical foundations are multiple and include major strands like historical materialism, structural functionalism, phenomenology, ethnomethodology, interactive symbolism, critical theory, and thinkers like Antonio Gramsci, Erich Fromm, Louis Althusser, Franz Fanon, Michel Foucault, Paul Feyerabend, Thomas Kuhn, Wright Mills, Edgar Morin, between many others (Thiollent 1986; Gabarón and Landa 1994).

[31] My own summary based on Borda (1971, 1981); Thiollent (1986); Freire (1987); Gabarón and Landa (1994); Brandão (1999); Baldissera (2001); Neves (2006); Brandão and Borges (2007); Pacheco (2017).

2. *Action-orientation:* Research aims at transformative collective practice and concrete action. Moreover, the dialogical research process itself represents an educational activity aiming at political awareness, empowerment and decolonisation.
3. *Commitment:* External intellectuals or activists have to accept existing differences, while assuming the projects of the groups to whom they dedicate their work. The main aim of the research project is to benefit the participating community and its members. Other, scientific objectives may exist, but they are secondary and may under no circumstances be imposed on or subdue the primal objective of empowering the local community. Finally, all results and products deriving from the research are returned to the community.
4. *Situatedness:* Contextualisation of the research problem according to local needs as articulated and felt by the participants. The entire research process, including its aims and central questions, is derived from local knowledge and the community's own demands. Furthermore, it seeks to raise the community's awareness about their historical situation and the limiting situations which are responsible for perpetuating their subordinated position.
5. *Decolonisation of knowledge:* Modern science's dominant position is based on power-relations rather than epistemological superiority. Subaltern (so called "local", "traditional", "Popular", "Indigenous") knowledge is recognised as equally valid compared to hegemonic modern/colonial science, providing the basic assumptions and problems of the research programme. The research project does not aim to reproduce either the dominant "scientific" paradigm or "traditional" subaltern knowledge, but to critically re-articulate both into a new, third contra-hegemonic kind of knowledge.
6. *Anti-dogmatism:* Following the basic principle of modern science, any kind of dogmatism, be it right or left wing, has to be avoided. Any knowledge gains its value by virtue of its dialogical openness, not by its dogmatic or supposedly intrinsic certainties. Progress in such an understanding goes hand in hand with abandoning positivism and objectivist dualism, as well as any foundationalist notion of one universal truth. It is necessary to understand and apply popular values while respecting their particular logic and practices in order to overcome the limitations of the dominant paradigm. Anti-dogmatism has nothing to do with extreme relativism or methodological anarchism. On the contrary, meta-theoretical openness demands methodological scrutiny while allowing for other than objectivist yardsticks to measure the truth-value of different ways of knowing and their particular propositions.

Common Techniques and Procedures Used in PAR Include:

1. Group discussions and seminars with community members
2. Building focus groups of organic intellectuals[32]
3. Literature research

---

[32] Gramsci (1982).

4. Participatory observation
5. Methodological workshops
6. "Culture circles" or research groups
7. Auto-ethnography (or "auto-investigation")
8. Collective publication and presentation of results and demands
9. Activism, educational programmes, creation of communal schools and libraries

Concerning the representational problems of authenticity and authority mentioned above, PAR joins several advantageous elements:

1. The problem of authenticity as essentially a problem of "Western"/modern epistemology is met, in Viveiros de Castro's sense, by applying alternative ontologies to recentre the viewpoint or basic assumption of the research programme.
2. The problem of authority is met both by auto-ethnography and the collective construction and authorship of the resulting representation.
3. Finally, PAR not only recognises the intrinsically political character of knowledge but also envisages its decolonisation by researching its historical situatedness within unequal power relations. The whole approach is not only heuristically consistent, but also methodologically coherent with its ethical principles.

From my personal perspective and research experience, PAR not only holds to highest ethical standards of transparency and compromise towards subaltern populations; it also represents a coherent answer to fundamental heuristic and methodological questions of ethnology and social sciences in general. PAR is frequently mentioned as one of the most important decolonial cosmopractices of the South.[33] Moreover, in Latin America, PAR has become a kind of a minimum standard which is expected to be complied with if a researcher wants to be accepted by a community. Hence, assuming PAR the guiding principle of my own research among the Potiguara was the most reasonable option.

References

Asad T (1986) The concept of cultural translation in British social anthropology. In: Clifford J, Marcus GE (eds) Writing culture: the poetics and politics of ethnography. University of California Press, Berkeley, pp 141–164

Baldissera A (2001) Pesquisa-Ação: Uma Metodologia do "Conhecer" e do "Agir" Coletivo. Sociedade em Debate, Pelotas 7:5–25

Bargatzky T (1998) Kulturökologie. In: Fischer H (ed) Ethnologie: Einführung und Überblick. Munich

Barth F (1969) Ethnic groups and boundaries: the social organization of cultural difference. Universitets Forlaget, Bergen

Baudrillard J (1982) Der symbolische Tausch und der Tod. Matthes & Seitz, Munich

Becker HS (2008) Outsiders: Estudos de sociologia do desvio. Maria Luiza X. de Borges. Jorge Zahar Ed, Rio de Janeiro, Tradução

[33] Walsh (2013); Harding (2015); Santos (2018); Escobar (2020); among others.

Bolaños (2004) ¿Que pensaria si la escuala ...?: 30 años de construcción de una educación própria. Bogotá

Borda OF (1981) Aspectos teóricos da pesquisa participante: considerações sobre o significado e o papel da ciência na participação popular. In: Brandão CR (ed) Pesquisa participante. Brasiliense, São Paulo, pp 42–62

Brandão CR (ed) (1999) Repensando a Pesquisa Participante. Brasiliense, Sao Paulo

Brandão CR, Borges MCA (2007) Pesquisa Participante: Um Momento da Educação Popular. Revista de Educação Popular 6(1):51–62

Castro EVd (2015) The relative native: essays on indigenous conceptual worlds. Hau, Chicago

Clifford J (1986) On ethnographic allegory. In: Clifford J, Marcus GE (eds) Writing culture: the poetics and politics of ethnography. University of California Press, Berkeley, pp 98–121

Crapanzano V (1986) Hermes' dilemma: the masking of subversion in ethnographic description. In: Clifford J, Marcus GE (eds) Writing culture: the poetics and politics of ethnography. University of California Press, Berkeley, pp 51–76

Dammann R (1991) Die Dialogische Praxis der Feldforschung. Der Ethnographische Blick als Paradigma der Erkenntnisgewinnung. Campus, Frankfurt a.M

Daubenmier JM (2003) Meskwaki remember action anthropology. Ann Iowa 62(4):427–464

Daubenmier JM (2008) The Meskwaki and anthropologists action anthropology reconsidered. University of Nebraska Press, Lincoln

Elias N, Scotson JL (2000) Os Estabelecidos e os Outsiders: Sociologia das relações de poder a partir de uma pequena comunidade. Vera Ribeiro

Escobar A (2020) Pluriversal politics: the real and the possible. Duke University Press, Durham

Faermam LA (2014) A Pesquisa Participante: Suas Contribuições no Âmbito das Ciências Sociais. Revista Ciências Humanas 7(1):41–56

Fals Borda O (1971) Ciencia propia y colonialismo intelectual (2ª ed). Oveja Negra, Bogotá

Foley D (2009) The Meskwaki and anthropologists: action anthropology reconsidered. Ann Iowa 68(3):331–333

Foucault M (1974) Die Ordnung der Dinge: Eine Archäologie der Humanwissenschaften. Suhrkamp, Frankfurt a.M

Freire P (1987) Pedagogia do Oprimido. Paz e Terra, Rio de Janeiro

Fromm E (1967) El Corazon del Hombre. Fondo de Cultura Economica, Breviario, Mexico

Gabarón LR, Landa LH (1994) Investigación Participativa. Madrid

Geertz C (2008) A Interpretação das Culturas. LTC, Rio de Janeiro

Giddens A (2003) A Construção da Sociedade. Martins Fontes, São Paulo

Gramsci A (1982) Os Intelectuais e a Organização da Cultura. Civilização Brasileira, Rio de Janeiro

Hall S (1992) A identidade cultural na pós-modernidade. DP&A Editora, Rio de Janeiro

Harding S (2015) Objectivity and diversity: another logic of scientific research. University of Chicago Press, Chicago

Hobsbowm E, Ranger T (1983) The invention of tradition. Cambridge University Press, Cambridge

Huizer G (1989) Anthropologie der Kriese, Aktionsforschung und Zauberei Trixter 7:81–111

Lewin K (1946) Action research and minority problems. Soc Issues 2:34–46

Linhart J (2008) Universidades Indígenas: Programas de Educação Indígena Superior na América Latina: A Caminho de uma Ciência Intercultural? Master Thesis, LMU

Linhart J (2012) A interculturalidade no contexto do ensino superior e as suas implicações epistemológicas. Cadernos de Educação Escolar Indígenas 10(1):35–51. https://doi.org/10.17851/2175-0998.2.0.268-285

Linhart J, Batista MNF, Felix ICG, Silva PRP (2017a) Auto-Etnografia Colaborativa entre os Potiguara e a Capacitação de Intelectuais Orgânicos. In: 2° Seminário Internacional do Núcleo de Extensão Multidisciplinar para o Desenvolvimento Rural (Nemdr), 27 de Julho de 2017, CCHSA, Campus III da Universidade Federal da Paraíba—UFPB. Bananeiras, PB, Brazil

Linhart J, Zampier MB, Kaaguasu et al (2017b) O Coletivo de Pesquisa pela Valorização dos Saberes Potiguara: Apropriação do Espaço Acadêmico pelos Indígenas Potiguara. In: Uma

Década de Expensão Universitaria: Estudos Sobre o Vale de Mamanguape. Editora CCTA, João Pessoa, pp 103–130
Marcus GE (1986) Contemporary problems of ethnography in the modern world system. In: Clifford J, Marcus GE (eds) Writing culture: the poetics and politics of ethnography. University of California Press, Berkeley, pp 156–193
Marx K (1852) Der achtzehnte Brumaire des Louis Bonaparte. In: Marx/Engels: Ausgewählte Werke. p 198
Marx K (1962) Das Kapital: Kritik der politischen Ökonomie. Dietz, Berlin
Neves VFA (2006) Pesquisa-Ação e Etnografia: Caminhos Cruzados. Pesquisas e Práticas Psicossociais 1(1)
Pacheco JAL (2017) Orlando Fals Borda: Del Cientificismo a la Subversión Moral. Tránsitos y Reconstrucciones de un Pensamiento Crític Ciencias Políticas 1:172–185
Rabinow P (1986) Representations are social facts: modernity and post-modernity in anthropology. In: Clifford J, Marcus GE (eds) Writing culture: the poetics and politics of ethnography. University of California Press, Berkeley, pp 234–261
Ramos I, Linhart J (2012) Educación Intercultural Indígena: El programa de educación propia del CRIC como un ejemplo de una propuesta integral para una educación alternativa. In: Anais do III. SECAMPO. UFPB, Mamanguape
Ramos A, Rappaport J (2005) Una Historia Colaborativa: Retos para el Diálogo Indígena-Academico. Historia Crítica 1(29):39–62
Rappaport J (2005) Intercultural utopias: public intellectuals, cultural experimentations, and ethnic pluralism in Colombia. Durham, London
Rorty R (1979) Philosophy and the mirror of nature. Princeton University Press, Princeton
Santos BdS (2018) The end of the cognitive empire: the coming of age of epistemologies of the South. Duke University Press, Durham
Taussig M (1997) Mimesis und Alterität: eine eigenwillige Geschichte der Sinne. Europäische Verlagsanstalt, Hamburg
Taussig M (2006) The devil and commodity fetishism in South America. University of Chicago Press, Chicago
Tax S (1988) Pride and puzzlement: a retro-introspective record of 60 years of anthropology. Annu Rev Anthropol 17:1–21
Thiollent M (1986) Metodologia Da Pesquisa-Ação, 2nd edn. São Paulo, Cortez
Wallerstein I (2004) World-system analysis: an introduction. Duke University Press, London
Walsh C (ed) (2013) Pedagogias Descoloniales: Prácticas insurgentes de resistir, (re)existir y (re) vivir—Tomo I. Ediciones Abya Yala, Quito

Chapter 7
Research in Action

It was in October 18, 2015 that I met with Pedro Kaaguasu Potiguara to talk about my idea to organise a research project together with him and his Potiguara community at the north-eastern Brazilian coast. Pedro and I had been friends for some years at that time, and I frequently visited him with my graduate students. As an Indigenous activist and "traditional" healer, he would receive my students kindly and explain things about his nation, its history and way of life to them. At that time, Pedro was one of about 30 students of a governmental undergraduate program for Indigenous schoolteachers, called PROLIND,[1] and my idea was to invite these students to participate in the research project I was proposing. A prerequisite for participating in the PROLIND was that candidates were nominated by their communities. Most of the students were already working as schoolteachers,[2] and many were also active members of the Indigenous movement, some as well-known political leaders or "traditional" authorities. To my eyes, this group represented a good example of what Antonio Gramsci famously called *organic intellectuals*[3] and would therefore perfectly fit as a focus group in a participatory action research project. Quite typically for Indigenous activists, they were border intellectuals with considerable knowledge of both their "traditional" culture and history, as well as of the dominant

---

[1] PROLIND (*Programa de Apoio à Formação Superior e Licenciaturas Interculturais Indígenas)* offers public funding to Brazilian universities for an undergraduate program (licenciate) for Indigenous schoolteachers. However, PROLIND does not offer funding for regular courses in Indigenous education, but only for one term courses for a limited number of students.

[2] In the rural areas of Brazil there are still many schoolteachers without any academic qualification. During recent decades the Government invested in professionalising courses, like the *magisterio*, and offered additional incentives for attending university courses in education.

[3] In his famous work on the social role of intellectuals, Antonio Gramsci (1982) calls those intellectuals "organic" who have been brought up by their own class and who are responsible for the ideological fight aiming to achieve hegemony. Organic intellectuals channel the experiences and feelings of the members of their class in a way to make it culturally and ideologically effective.

J. Linhart, *Science and the Other*, Schriften zu Leben und Gesellschaft - Series on Life and Society 2, https://doi.org/10.1007/978-3-032-03927-9_7

political discourse and scientific knowledge. My plan was to discuss my initial research project with this group of Indigenous intellectuals and to further develop and adjust it following their critical contributions, so it would become *their* project, too, primarily serving *their* needs and demands (even if this would mean adjusting my initial project aims). The discussions were realised during periodical meetings and workshops, focussing on the central questions and objectives of my research proposal and how to transform them into concrete actions addressing current local demands. To make things feasible, we boiled the project down to its core and I condensed it into a short project proposal to be presented to the Indigenous authorities for their approval and, afterwards, to the group of initial participants to be further discussed and adjusted.

This document, which also contained my declaration of commitment to the Potiguara and their struggle for cultural, educational and territorial autonomy, described the project as "participatory research to be articulated and developed in collaboration with the Potiguara" aiming to "come to a better understanding of the mechanisms that delegitimise Indigenous knowledge" compared to Western science.

The *problem* at stake was the central role of modern science concerning the reproduction and legitimation of hegemonic knowledge while being incapable of coherently explaining certain phenomena or integrating culturally different knowledge. As a result, Indigenous knowledge was misinterpreted and its own explanatory models disregarded, simultaneously devaluing Indigenous political demands for cultural recognition and autonomy. Moreover, this hierarchical relation between "Indigenous" and "scientific" knowledge had a significant impact on Indigenous schools, and thus, on the perpetuation of Potiguara culture and identity. Whereas both kinds of knowledge were taught to Indigenous pupils, only "scientific" knowledge was regarded as "universal", while their own "tradition" merely represented "local" knowledge and was treated like "folklore".

The *main objective* of the proposed research was to elaborate methods of knowledge integration that could work as hinges between the dominant "scientific" and "Indigenous" knowledge, seeking a plain recognition of Indigenous knowledge systems.

Concerning the research *method,* I underlined its participatory character so that all details would have to be defined collectively together with the participating Potiguara. However, I proposed three general methodological strands:

1. Theoretical analysis of the mechanisms responsible for the delegitimisation of Indigenous knowledge.
2. Participatory research based on meetings and workshops.
3. Field work including interviews.

In addition to declaring my commitment to the Potiguara as a nation, their interests and the security of all people involved, I also committed to respecting local rules and customs (especially concerning the condition of consulting local authorities before doing research in their territory), and to sharing all data produced in the course of the research, further reinforcing the participatory character of the project and its openness to any Potiguara who would like to participate.

The next day I went out to meet the *cacique geral* (general chief) and other important Indigenous authorities to ask for their consent to my proposal. To my surprise, all of them seemed to be very interested and did not hesitate to sign the document.[4] To this point I had felt a bit insecure, as I thought my proposal might be too theoretical, too academic, and too far from their worries about land conflicts and Indigenous politics. But, to my own shame, I had underestimated their consciousness about the geopolitics of knowledge and its impact on their daily efforts as Indigenous activists.

During my next stay a few weeks later, I had the opportunity to present my proposal to the students of the PROLIND. After my presentation, the group had many questions and we had an interesting discussion. Again, the students, all of them Indigenous teachers, agreed with my approach, by and large. Like the authorities before, their main concern was about the return the project would offer to the community and the control they would have over the research and its results. I did not succeed in convincing the group as a whole, but several members were interested and agreed to participate, or at least to attend a first planning session. Moreover, they indicated other potential participants. During the weeks to follow, I had many conversations with directors of Indigenous schools, activists, healers and local leaders.

A month later, on December 5th, 2015, we had the first group meeting with six participants. The order of the day was to discuss the project proposal and align it with local needs and demands, to define objectives and responsibilities, and above all, to get the project going. While the general objectives of our initial proposal were reaffirmed, the participants contributed with important suggestions and requests. Most importantly, it was decided to produce collective publications to call attention to our subject matter in academic circles, to create instruments for improving Indigenous education, and to keep our research group as open and transparent as possible. Moreover, we defined several research topics with one responsible member for each topic. The first research results should be presented at our next meeting which was planned for January 2016. However, it would take several months to reunite the group for another meeting. Most members were too busy with their political engagement and their jobs, making it difficult to find a date when all group members were free. In the meantime, I continued our planning during individual encounters with the most enthusiastic participants, visited further candidates to invite them to join our group, and did some field work and data collection among friends and group members.

[4] See copy in the Appendix. Their only doubt was concerning my retribution to their community, because, as they said, other researchers before went away leaving nothing to them. But in the face of my declaration of commitment they understood that the benefits would outweigh the risks.

At our next meeting, on May 28th, 2016, I found myself together with nine highly motivated participants planning our first seminar for June with the objective to involve a wider range of the Potiguara society. These included friends I already knew for some years and others I had met more recently. There was also a new non-Indigenous participant, Professor Thiago Romero from the Federal University of Campina Grande, who would become an important partner in our work and a good friend of mine.[5] On that day, the group decided to act under the name *Coletivo de Pesquisa pelos Saberes Potiguara* (Research Collective for Potiguara Knowledge), and also defined and signed its statutes. While the general objectives concerning the decolonisation of hegemonic science were reaffirmed, our brand-new statutes further detailed the Collective's objectives. The Collective would now support Indigenous intellectuals to occupy the academic field and establish their own counter-hegemonic discourse on science, and to elaborate an auto-ethnographic self-representation of Potiguara culture and knowledge. Moreover, the status of non-Potiguara members like me would be changed to the role of external assessors.[6] This was an important step on the Collective's way to become independent of external supporters.

I felt very happy and grateful for so much confidence and engagement. It was a great day and the beginning of an exciting and fruitful collective work. During the next 2 years, we had monthly meetings, realised two annual seminars in 2016 and 2017 with about 30 and 50 participants respectively (Fig. 7.1), published a number of scientific papers[7] and book chapters,[8] participated in several academic events, created a community library offering the Potiguara access to a major portion of the existing literature on their culture and history, and produced two didactic books[9] for their Indigenous schools, one on cosmology and another on their healing system.

This relative success notwithstanding, there were many challenges and obstacles to deal with. Most importantly, I have to admit that I did not achieve my main objective, which was to pass the project over to the Potiguara and have them run it without external help.

[5] While Thiago would become our constant partner, being present at every meeting, other friends from the Federal University of Paraíba would also join us in supporting the Collective as external assessors. They participated in several meetings and provided important assistance in the organisation of events and publications.

[6] The idea was to guarantee the Collective's autonomy in face of the growing interest it attracted from non-Indigenous academics. We needed their support, but the Collective should become an independent Indigenous endeavour. Giving them the role of external assessors, we could stay open to any external help while guaranteeing the Collectives independency as a representative of Indigenous interests.

[7] Gomes (2016); Linhart et al. (2016, 2017a).

[8] Dantas et al. (2017); Gomes (2017); Linhart et al. (2017b).

[9] Batista et al. (2021a, b).

Fig. 7.1 Second seminar of the Collective, September 02, 2017, Indigenous school of Brejinho, Paraíba, Brazil. This time we opted for a more dynamic format giving more space for ritual and creativity. The event was initiated by an intense *toré* lead by some of the most renowned *pagés* (healers/spiritual mediums) among the Potiguara. The participants were invited to reflect on the mythic *terra sem males* (world without suffering) as a utopian horizon for a better future. How would they wish to see the Potiguara live, what would have to change and what kind of knowledge would be needed to have this vision come true? As a result, participants showed a common agreement in highlighting the importance of the sacred nature and ancestral spirituality as fundamental elements for a better future. Hence, the ancestral knowledge and its perpetuation in the Indigenous schools were seen as essential to the continuity of Potiguara culture and society (image from private archive)

7.1 Some Challenges

Initially, my main concern was about the internal political cleavages of Potiguara society. There seemed to be a clear cut between those who supported the current *cacique*[10] *geral,* and his opponents. Typically, each group would accuse the other

[10] The *cacique* is the official representative of Potiguara society. Besides the *cacique geral*, there are local *caciques* in each community. The local *caciques* are elected by their communities for an indeterminate period and have almost complete autonomy within their community. Their main function is to solve local problems and conflicts. While they may solve smaller issues individually, issues that affect the community as a whole are discussed in the assemblies. Although the *caciques* do not have the legal authority to impose their will, in most cases their decisions will be accepted

side of being corrupt, incompetent and morally inferior, which is a recurrent theme I already knew from other Indigenous and rural communities.[11] Moreover, party politics had entered the territory and were increasingly infused with internal politics.[12] Quite obviously, my preoccupation was not to be instrumentalised by either side, which might have provoked resistance to our project from the other side.

Although I tried my best to include both sides as much as possible and despite the *cacique*'s official support for our project, I ended up working predominantly with people that were rather critical to the then-governing *cacique geral*. However, to my surprise, political boundaries turned out to be less rigid than I had expected. One reason was the Potiguara kinship-system,[13] which makes virtually everyone a relative of anyone else, at least to some, often very small, extent. So, one could be a fierce political opponent, but being also a brother-in-law, a cousin or an uncle, one would meet at feasts, drink together and enjoy family affairs. Another reason may be the awareness of a common external enemy that never sleeps and which will immediately take advantage of any internal division.

Be this as it may, political cleavage was a constant issue during my entire stay among the Potiguara and we did the best we could to stress our Collective's neutrality towards internal politics. Although some Potiguara may not have actively participated as members of the Collective due to internal political oppositions, I have

---

by the members of their community. The *cacique geral* is elected indirectly by the assembly of the elders and the local *caciques* for an indeterminate period of time, too. But his legitimacy can be questioned at any time by a public impeachment, if his behaviour raises the displeasure of the community. The office of the *cacique* substituted the *tuxá* from the times of the SPI, which again substituted the *regente dos índios* from imperial times. All of these offices have been imposed on the Indigenous communities as their official representatives with whom the colonial powers would address the issues of their community. However, while the *tuxá* and the *regente dos indios* were chosen by the colonial powers, the *cacique* is elected by the community itself (see also Palitot 2005).

[11] According to Münzel (1993), these cleavages reflect on diverging perceptions of personhood and authority. Since Indigenous "persons" are made up by a multiplicity of "souls" and since their conceptions of authority are bound to shifting alliances and collective decisions, in order to defend their interests against dominant society, Indigenous groups had to adopt essentialist identity and representative models of authority. However, contradictions between "traditional" perceptions and "modern" models of authority will lead into permanent conflict, cleavage and frequent abandonment of political leadership.

[12] Actually, the Potiguara are famous for their strategy to occupy important institutional positions with their Indigenous leaders (Vieira 2010; Oliveira 2013). They were organised in numerous associations, they had elected Potiguara for mayors and deputies, and the *cacique geral* became the Governor's assessor for Indigenous affairs. However, this institutional influence came with the price of conflicts between collective, individual and institutional interests. Moreover, all Indigenous candidates would be a member of some political party, mixing up internal with party politics. Traditionally, Potiguara elect their *caciques* following kin-relations, while party politics are based on individual voting. As a consequence, individual deviation from their kin during elections would result in internal conflict. Local elections, therefore, have become periods of turmoil and even violence, and complaints about the negative effects of party politics shattering internal unity are very frequent.

[13] Interestingly, this kinship based political system of contemporary Potiguara society still shows some parallels to the kindred-system of the historical Tupi nations, the Potiguara's ancestors (compare e.g. Noelli 1999).

no reason to suspect that anyone actively disturbed our activities for political reasons. On the contrary, I frequently met with the *cacique geral* and his backers, giving account of our activities and inviting them to participate, and they would always express their support and sympathy for our work.

Another, much more limiting problem, was time. To start with, I had to give classes during the week in João Pessoa, the state capital, located about 100 km from the Potiguara territory, and my colleague, Professor Thiago, was living in Campina Grande, more than 150 km away. Consequently, our presence among the Potiguara was limited to a couple of weekends per month. This situation only changed in April 2017, when I left João Pessoa to live among the Potiguara, making myself comfortable in a little mud hut at the farm of a chummy family I knew for several years. I continued to live in the territory until October 2018. Now, spending my days closely together with my local friends, I could finally participate in their daily affairs, helping them on their plantations while they helped me fixing my hut, participating in rituals; in short, doing classical field work and participatory observation.

However, my Potiguara fellows turned out to be even busier than I was. They were active members of the Indigenous movement, almost all of them were doing some university course, most of them were working as teachers, not to mention their obligations as family members. In practical terms, time management was certainly the biggest challenge of our endeavour. To tackle this problem, we tried out different modes of collaboration. At first we thought it would be enough to define some research topics, each of us working on one of them more or less independently, and then present and discuss our results at our meetings. But this model, which we basically had copied from academic research groups, did not work for us since everyone was busy with their own academic work and engagement in the Indigenous movement. Thus, we tried to do things the other way round and start with what each one was either already doing or planning to do. Many members of the Collective had to write some kind of academic work for their studies, and obviously were happy to work on subject matters that might contribute to their activism, too. Moreover, the acquisition of academic titles by Indigenous intellectuals was one of our declared objectives. Consequently, we redefined our mode of collaboration quite radically. Instead of focussing primarily on my own research topic (modern science), I would now invest my main effort in giving technical assistance to my Potiguara fellows in defining and elaborating their particular academic research projects which, we thought, in the end would all contribute to a common knowledge base. My own research for my thesis would be just one of several works contributing to this common endeavour. The Collective had become kind of an incubator for Potiguara academics. The idea was that once the first generation of academics had been formed, they themselves could help the next generation, and so on, similar to a mentoring programme.[14]

[14] Looking back, I think this was the right move, but as far as I can see, unfortunately we did not succeed much in this respect. There is no doubt that we helped some members of the Collective to graduate—one even concluded her master's during my stay, and another received a doctor *honoris causa* thanks to the support of our friends at the university. I also feel that we motivated the Collective members to go much further in their aspirations as academics and activists. But the

A further challenge was to align my initial expectations with reality. Quite ingenuously, I had formed a Collective of Indigenous academics hoping they would join me in comparing their "traditional" knowledge with modern "science", thereby contributing important insights from a viewpoint external to modern epistemology and its ugly old dualism (much in the sense of Viveiros de Castro's inverted anthropology). In my fantasy, these organic intellectuals would be holders of both their own Indigenous and academic knowledge. I would offer a systematic analysis of the epistemological and ontological structure of modern science, "my" knowledge, and they would compare it with the structure of "their" knowledge. Of course, things would not be that simple. It turned out that especially the younger intellectuals were not really holders of "their" knowledge, but were rather in the process of acquiring it. And the elder participants who had more profound "traditional" knowledge had problems with engaging in scientific discourse. Moreover, there was no systematic account of Potiguara knowledge, no complete ethnography of Potiguara culture and cosmopractices or anything similar.[15] The whole work of collecting and systematising Potiguara knowledge still had to be done. This would be necessary not only for our project, but even more for the members of the Collective and other activists, the Potiguara teachers and their pupils, and hence, the Potiguara as a nation. We decided to face this challenge and develop auto-ethnographic research. But this solution came with further problems. To write an ethnography, no matter who writes it, one has to refer to previous works on the subject. Although some of us had read a number of works on the Potiguara and their history, nobody knew all of them, and what was worse, we did not even know where to find them. There was no library in the whole region where we could get access to all these texts. Thus, we needed to build this library ourselves. This is why and how the construction of the Potiguara Library ended up on the list of our many objectives. And it would take us almost 2 years to identify, get access to, copy and finally present at least a portion of the total of approximately 150 texts about the Potiguara in the municipal library of Marcação, right at the centre of the Potiguara territory.[16]

Moreover, to do field work, one needs a minimum understanding of research methods and anthropological theory. So, we organised workshops to capacitate the members of the Collective before we went on to continue our training in the field.

---

process had no direct continuity. Maybe the Indigenous intellectuals we worked with will play some role in the formation of future generations of militants and academics we still do not know about.

[15] See also Palitot (2005).

[16] Although there was a stock of about a dozen texts most experts on Potiguara matters would normally use as reference, the vast majority of existing literature was unknown even to most professional scholars. We started by asking our friends at the university who had done research among the Potiguara during the last decades for bibliographic references and then went on tracking further references in this literature, researching in university libraries and online resources. But many texts were neither available online nor for sale, only existing as a few copies in private hands or local libraries. Some authors donated a copy, some friends allowed us to make copies of their books, others donated some money, a printer and some paper. But then the printer would break, parts would not be available, paper would run out, electric power would break down… it was to go bananas!

But in the end, our old enemy, time, prevented my Potiguara fellows doing much ethnographic field work themselves; too many were their responsibilities, too important their income for sustaining their families, their graduation, their master-degree, their children, their duties in the Indigenous movement. As a result, I had to do most of the field work myself. To avoid producing just another external representation of the Others, I made the move to a collective text edition together with the people in the communities.[17] For years I had been constructing an initial stock of data together with Potiguara elders, healers and leaders with whom I maintained a close personal relationship. We frequently met and talked about all kinds of things, including politics, family business, medical plants, rituals and the differences between the performances of each healer, cosmological notions, myths, Potiguara history, you name it. Of course, I took notes and discussed them with my friends. And they would make their critiques and contributions, enriching the picture which was gradually assembling before us. One day I felt we had come to a quite coherent idea of what could be called the Potiguara cosmovision and healing system, and so I wrote everything down into two nice little texts, and once again, presented it to my Potiguara friends. They seemed to be quite satisfied with the result, and so I went out to present our draft to others to see what they would have to say about it. I had been collecting names of elders, healers and midwifes who had been named by other Potiguara as those who could give some relevant contribution. There are more than 30 communities spread over the Potiguara territory (covering approximately 50,000 ha), each with its particular history, leadership, customs and religious groups.[18] Previously, certain communities had been researched disproportionally, while other communities have rarely or never been visited by any researcher. For this reason, I made an effort to identify and interview at least one or two people of reference in each community. For months, I spent my days motorcycling on dusty sand roads until I finally had discussed our little draft with all of them. Of course, my first stop was always the local *cacique* whom I had to ask for authorisation of my field work in their village. I would explain my intentions, and sometimes the *cacique* themself would contribute to the construction of our cosmological account, becoming one of its authors, too. The majority of the Potiguara elders are not literate, making it impossible to ask them to read the text and give some written feedback. So, I would patiently read all relevant parts of our draft to them and ask for their feedback, make changes where necessary, then read the modified version again and again until they were satisfied with the result and agreed to be named as one of its authors. To a healer I would read everything concerning healing, spiritual

[17] In a way I was forced to go one step back and give up our initial project of a fully fledged autonomous auto-ethnography under sole Indigenous control and authorship in favour of what Lassiter (2000) calls *collaborative ethnography*. Collaborative or reciprocal ethnography "seeks to resituate control and authority within the ongoing dialogue about the evolving ethnographic text. […] Ethnographers should choose to construct and re-construct their texts for and with local communities rather than solely for the academy. […] Collaborative ethnography presents scholars with the unique opportunity to elaborate culture from a truly 'native point of view'" (idem: 9).

[18] Barcellos (2012).

Fig. 7.2 Monthly meeting on November 25, 2017, indigenous school of Aldeia do Forte, Paraíba, Brazil (image from private archive)

concepts, death, birth, and whatever they considered interesting; to a midwife I would read everything concerning birth, midwifery, and whatever they would think interesting; and so we went on. This was the workaround I found to achieve a maximum of authenticity and authority in the face of our limited possibilities. The results were also discussed with the members of the Collective, and after some debate we came to the agreement that they should be published as didactic material for the Indigenous schools instead of producing yet another academic publication which only a few academics would read, if ever. And this was what we did (Fig. 7.2).[19]

Nothing happened as planned, but we did a lot of exciting and hopefully useful things. Our meetings were pleasant happenings, full of enthusiasm and harmony. Contributions and critiques were constructive, disputes and personal vanity did not disturb our happy gatherings. The younger activists, most of them women, took a leading role in our debates, growing visibly before our eyes, making us all feel proud of them. We were confident that these young women and men would soon assume control of the Collective and become completely independent from external support, and we felt lucky to accompany them on their way of becoming academic Indigenous leaders, real counter-hegemonic intellectuals. We felt united and we had

[19] Batista et al. (2021a, b). The two school books on Potiguara cosmology and healing system are freely available online: https://www.sabeh.org.br/?s=potiguara.

great plans. The success of our little mentorship programme of Potiguara university students and of our annual seminars, although still quite modest, motivated the members of the Collective to further redefine its objectives.[20]

At our monthly meeting in October 2017, the Collective's members decided it was time to do more for their community. During our previous seminar the contributions of the participants had emphasised the central importance of improving Indigenous education. The model of the Collective as an incubator for Potiguara intellectuals had worked quite well and could be applied wider, starting with the Indigenous schoolteachers. Although most schools in the Potiguara territory are Indigenous schools, thus valorising "traditional" knowledge, including classes in "traditional" handcraft and Tupi language, most teachers had no specific training in intercultural Indigenous education. As a result, the quality of the education offered by each school differed widely. The Potiguara had been fighting for decades to get courses in Indigenous intercultural education for their teachers, finally achieving the PROLIND in 2005. But more than a decade later, its thirty students had still not received their certification. Action was required! It was suggested to offer mini-courses to the teachers in the schools, to offer them mentoring for their academic career, amplifying the Collective as an incubator for the auto-capacitation of Potiguara by Potiguara. Further professors from universities could be invited to support us as volunteers, so more teachers could be mentored at the same time. Soon we were talking about an Intercultural Potiguara Academy, a network of engaged Indigenous and non-Indigenous professors together with Potiguara elders providing courses in intercultural Indigenous education. And why not go even further? Why not found the first Indigenous university of Brazil? We had many friends among the professors of the local Federal University of Paraiba, and we knew they would help us formatting regular courses for undergraduates and graduates, with real official academic titles but under the sole control of the Potiguara. On November 25th, 2017, we decided to found the *Universidade Intercultural Potiguara*. It was awesome! Everybody was very excited, although we all knew the magnitude of the problems we had just created for ourselves. In the next 2 months to follow, we had several extra-ordinal planning sessions. Everybody was extremely motivated, spending whole weekends discussing rather than relaxing with their families. Our friends from the university guaranteed their support, and even suggested launching the first course in 2018. The Indigenous authorities also supported our endeavour, offering locations where we could give the first classes. Everything seemed to be working perfectly.

However, 2 months later, some members expressed their doubts about the project. They argued it might be better to do more research on similar projects first and avoid repeating mistakes others had already committed before us. The members decided to concentrate in our previous tasks, to finish them first and do more research on the subject before facing the new, big project of creating university courses. But the question was not just a technical one; it was also an indicator of

[20] Since we began our mentoring, several members of the Collective successfully graduated, accomplished master degrees and advanced to PhD students—one member was even honored with a doctor *honoris causas*.

lost internal harmony within the group. In the aftermath of this drawback, the enthusiastic climate which had inspired us declined. Internal friction and personal differences had become visible. Some of the energetic younger members questioned the role of us external assessors and the influence we would have within the Collective, while other members feared our absence could paralyse the Collective. We externals had always emphasised our aim to help them create *their* projects and hand the whole thing over to *their* full responsibility as soon as *they* would feel ready to accept it. Hence, at that time, we had already passed over most of the organisational responsibilities, and in the face of these new demands, we decided not to interfere anymore unless we were explicitly asked to do so. We would be there if needed, giving a helping hand as much as we could, but taking no initiative.[21] This was, of course, a very delicate moment in our work with the Potiguara as we now had to see whether our comrades from the Collective would go on with what we had begun together.

The next point on the Collective's agenda was to finalise the library to provide the Potiguara with an easy access to the existing literature about their people. In April 2018 the Collective officially inaugurated the Potiguara Library inside the facilities of the public library of Marcação, right in the middle of the Potiguara's territory. However, although the Library was a great success, and despite the members' declared willingness to continue our work, after this event the Collective never met together again.

This sudden end of the Collective's activities had many reasons: some were of a more internal nature, while there were also determining external factors. Internally, the way in which some members had taken an explicit position against the protagonism of the external supporters had resulted in a climate of latent tension. In a sense, the harmony and friendship which had been our strength had weakened a bit. Furthermore, the great vision of an Indigenous university, which had raised our enthusiasm, had been set on ice, leading the ambitious younger leaders who had assumed the leadership of the group to invest their time in priorities other than the continuity of the Collective. Many of them had just received their academic titles and were now ready to initiate a professional career; some of them becoming school directors, some promoting "traditional" healing practices and others going into local politics or municipal administration. Several of the elder members asked us to reorganise the Collective, but once we had retreated from its leadership to take it back would be perceived as a dismissal of the young leaders. So we were left with no option but to reaffirm our availability for support if required.

[21] The moment of handing over a project to the target group is always very delicate, especially in our case for there was no external funding or substantial support from any official institution. In the past there had been a range of projects aiming to improve the Potiguara's lives, focussing on different aspects, and most, if not all of them, had failed to achieve sustained continuity. Moreover, in many cases external supporters who had initiated or supported those projects were later blamed for their (supposedly) selfish objectives or for having "abandoned" the Potiguara (e.g. the protagonism of the CIMI (Conselho Indigenista Missionário), or the ethnographer Franz Moonen, among many others I do not want to expose here for ethical reasons).

Moreover, Brazil was changing dramatically. After the constitutional coup d'état in 2015 the interim government had been rapidly eroding Indigenous rights and health services, questioning Indigenous lands, privatising public education, putting in question basically all that had been achieved during decades of struggle, and thus, changing priorities in the political agenda of Indigenous movements as well as the personal priorities of their activists. These activists had to defend their Indigenous schools, their legal territories, the social welfare programmes many Indigenous families depend on, and also their own jobs in public administration, education and health-services—everything was at stake. Political persecution, especially among teachers, was becoming a common practice in Brazil and many feared the comeback of a military dictatorship.

The presidential elections of 2018 were perceived as a turning point in Brazilian history which would decide the future of its still-young democracy. The election campaign split the land into two hostile camps, and everybody was busy in campaigning for one side or the other. After the election of Jair Bolsonaro it was clear that the progressive forces had lost the game. Most leftist activists entered a state of paralysing shock. Many of them had acquired jobs in leftist governments, were teachers or working for some social welfare or environmental programme; all of which was now at risk. As expected, Bolsonaro's neo-facist government was a complete disaster, leading to the de facto abolishment of Indigenous and ecological policies and threatening the right of free public health care and education. Furthermore, the government's open glorification of violence and its hate campaign against minority groups and social rights organisations provoked a dramatic increase in the number of assassinated Indigenous and leftist activists. Finally, the almost complete abandonment of the population by Bolsonaro's government during the COVID pandemic caused hundreds of thousands of unnecessary deaths and drove millions back into extreme poverty, particularly among Indigenous groups. Faced with this breakdown into chaos and threatened with poverty, violence and death, many activists reduced their political engagement and focused on their own survival.[22]

What remains is the hope that our experience contributed to the empowerment of some Indigenous intellectuals and that the few little products we left to the Potiguara will be of some use to the education of a new conscious generation ready for battle. Anyhow, we threw our drops into the sea—and who are we to think we could control the ocean with a few little drops?

References

Barcellos L (2012) Práticas Educativo-Religiosas dos Potiguara da Paraíba. Editora Universitária da UFPB, João Pessoa

Batista MNF, Conceição FMd, Pereira PE (2021a) Medicina Tradicional Potiguara. Sociedade Brasileira de Ecologia Humana—SABEH, Paulo Afonso, BA

[22] My own return to my home country, Germany, was a direct result of this hopeless situation and the lack of any foreseeable perspective in Brazil.

Batista MNF, Conceição FMd, Pereira PE (2021b) Cosmologia e Espiritualidade Potiguara. Sociedade Brasileira de Ecologia Humana—SABEH, Paulo Afonso, BA

Dantas MB, Barbosa MV, Santos SR (2017) Lendas e/ou Mitos Potiguaras? Tradição, Sacralidade, Mulheres Míticas e Riqueza Cultural. In: Batista AC (ed) Uma Década de Extensão Universitaria: Estudos Sobre o Vale de Mamanguape. Editora do Ccta, João Pessoa, pp 163–187

Gomes I (2016) Mangaba: Recursos Naturais e Fonte de Renda Para os Potiguara da Paraíba. In: Anais do V. SECAMPO 2016. UFPB, Mamanguape, pp 120–131

Gomes I (2017) A Contribuição do CCAE na Entrada dos Indígenas Potiguara no Ensino Superior. In: Batista AC (ed) Uma Década de Expensão Universitaria: Estudos Sobre o Vale de Mamanguape. Editora do CCTA, João Pessoa

Gramsci A (1982) Os Intelectuais e a Organização da Cultura. Civilização Brasileira, Rio de Janeiro

Lassiter LE (2000) Authoritative texts, collaborative ethnography, and native American studies. Am Indian Q Fall 24:601–614

Linhart J, Pereira PE, Zampier MB (2016) Escrita e Oralidade: Sobre o Papel Ambivalente do Uso da Escrita nas Escolas Indígenas. In: V. SECAMPO 2016. UFPB, Mamanguape, pp 153–169

Linhart J, Batista MNF, Felix ICG, Silva PRP (2017a) Auto-Etnografia Colaborativa entre os Potiguara e a Capacitação de Intelectuais Orgânicos. In: 2° Seminário Internacional do Núcleo de Extensão Multidisciplinar para o Desenvolvimento Rural (Nemdr), 27 de Julho de 2017, CCHSA, Campus III da Universidade Federal da Paraíba—UFPB. Bananeiras

Linhart J, Zampier MB, Kaaguasu et al (2017b) O Coletivo de Pesquisa pela Valorização dos Saberes Potiguara: Apropriação do Espaço Acadêmico pelos Indígenas Potiguara. In: Uma Década de Expensão Universitaria: Estudos Sobre o Vale de Mamanguape. Editora CCTA, João Pessoa, pp 103–130

Münzel M (1993) Traditionsbruch als Tradition: Indianisches in der indianischen ethnischen Bewegung Brasiliens. Ibero-Amerikanisches Archiv: Zeitschrift für Sozialwissenschaften und Geschichte 19:243–270

Noelli FS (1999) Curt Nimuendaju and Alfred Metraux: a invenção da busca da terra sem mal. Suplemento Antropologico XXXIV:123–166

Oliveira K (2013) Diga ao Povo que Avance! Movimento Indígena no Nordeste. Fundação Joaquim Nabuco, Recife

Palitot EM (2005) Os Potiguara da Baía da Traição e Monte-Mór: História, Etinicidade e Cultura. Master Thesis, UFPB

Vieira JG (2010) Amigos e Competidores: Política Faccional e Feitiçaria nos Potiguara da Paraíba. PhD Thesis, Universidade de São Paulo

Chapter 8
Changing Potiguara Worlds

The Potiguara were among the first original "American" nations to come in contact with the European invaders. It was probably between the years 1501 and 1505[1] that the Portuguese set anchor in the shallow waters of a natural harbour at the north-eastern Brazilian coast. The legend says that naked Potiguara women at the beach attracted and seduced the Portuguese while the Potiguara warriors were hiding in an ambush to kill and eat the poor, betrayed Europeans in a ritual of anthropophagy. This is why the place, originally known to the Potiguara as *Akajutibiró* (sour caju fruit), was later named *Baia da Traição* (Treason Bay) by the Portuguese, and is today occupied by a little town with the same name. The Potiguara fought the Portuguese for a century until, finally, they were defeated in 1590. Nevertheless, and in contrast to most other original inhabitants of the Brazilian coast, the Potiguara never left their homelands around Baia da Traição, or at least not all of them. Ethnohistorical studies suggest their uninterrupted presence in the region between Baia da Traição,[2] the city of Mamanguape, and the southern region of Rio Grande do Norte state. However, wars, slavery and European diseases drastically decimated the Potiguara. They had once been a great nation, inhabiting an area stretching for hundreds of kilometres along the coast and dozens of kilometres into the hinterlands, with an estimated population of about 100,000 souls. However, 400 years later, at the beginning of the twentieth century, there were only a few hundred Potiguara left.[3]

In part, this drastic decrease of their population was also a result of ethnic oppression and invisibilisation. After their final subjugation during the seventeenth century, the Portuguese had been gathering the surviving Potiguara in missions to be catechised by the Jesuits and later by the Carmelites. The missions guaranteed them rights over their land, intending to motivate them to submit themselves pacifically

[1] Baumann (1981); Moonen and Maia (1992); Palitot (2005); Moonen (2008).

[2] Idem.

[3] Idem; Amorim (1970).

J. Linhart, *Science and the Other*, Schriften zu Leben und Gesellschaft - Series on Life and Society 2, https://doi.org/10.1007/978-3-032-03927-9_8

under colonial rule and order.[4] The "Indios" in turn would have to assume the Christian faith and renounce their pagan beliefs, or otherwise be punished by prison or death.[5] Hence, the missions created a schizophrenic situation, connecting the Potiguara's right to their lands to their Indigenous identity, while simultaneously following an integrationist doctrine, forcing them to adopt the dominant culture, agriculture and the Portuguese language. Consequently, in order to survive within the new colonial order, they had to learn to be Us and Them at the same time.

However, no matter how much the Potiguara tried to adapt, their rights would be violated anyway by landlords and settlers who continued invading their lands and enslaving them, provoking an endless spiral of violence. Meanwhile, land rights stimulated poor non-Indigenous peasants to marry into Potiguara families so they could get access to their lands. The resulting ethic miscegenation provided another argument for those who wanted to grab their lands, holding there were no more "Indios", but only fake "*caboclos*",[6] cross-breed offspring with little or no Indigenous culture or identity.

During the 1920s, the Lundgrens,[7] a rich Swedish immigrant family, erected an industrial complex together with an entire new city right in the middle of the Potiguara territory. They illegally acquired land titles on a large scale on Indigenous

---

[4] The natives's right to be free and to own their lands had been determined several times by the Pope, the Spanish and the Portuguese kings. First with the papal bull from 1537, then with the royal laws from 1548, 1570, 1587, then again with the royal charters from 1680, 1700, 1740 and the laws from 1755 and 1758, being reformulated with the imperial decrees from 1831 and 1845, putting the "Indians" under the guardianship of the missions. With the law on "vacant lands" (*terras devolutas*) from 1850 the old missions are reviewed, liberating abandoned lands, and those where the Indigenous populations could not be distinguished from non-Indigenous citizens, for sale. In 1864, Don Pedro II finally confirms the permanence of the Potiguara in their old missions between Mamanguape and Baia da Traição, and guarantees their collective right over those lands, while explicitly precluding the right to register individual land titles or to sell the land. But the local authorities would never respect any of these laws and rather continue to favour the landlords' interests (idem).

[5] Indigenous rituals were seen as sorcery and worship of the devil, and were therefore persecuted by the Inquisition and punished with death. The Brazilian state persecuted Afro-Brazilian and Indigenous religions until 1966.

[6] The term "*caboclo*" has been used to denominate the christianised and "civilised" "Indios" of the Brazilian North-East. Interestingly, although fighting to be officially recognised as Indigenous ethnicities, the Potiguara and other original nations still call themselves "caboclos", thereby assuming both their Indigenous heritage and their history of miscegenation (Palitot 2005; Amorim 1970).

[7] The Lundgrens are an example of the Brazilian *Coronelismo*, the oppressive neo-feudalist model that governed the land during the Old Republic (1889–1930), transferring extensive competences to the private hand of capitalist oligarchy. After the Lundgrens had acquired textile industries in Recife, they quickly expanded their business and soon after controlled huge amounts of lands stretching along the coast between Recife and Rio Grande do Norte, thereby displacing and decimating not only the Potiguara, but also other Indigenous populations like the Tabajara in southern Paraiba. Although their cruel and illegal practices are well known, the Lundgrens continue to hold massive amounts of real estate. They are still the owners of some 80% of the city of Rio Tinto and of a major part of the surrounding lands, which they are leasing to the big sugar cane companies. Together with these companies, the Lundgrens are still trying to regain control over Potiguara ter-

territories, often by means of crude violence against their Indigenous owners, persecuting anyone who dared to call themself an "Indio"; they burned the Potiguara village of *Preguiça* down, built the town of Monte Mor on its ashes, and forced the Potiguara to work in their textile factory and to cut down the forests for timber supply to fuel their machines. As a result, many Potiguara emigrated to the neighbouring state, Rio Grande do Norte, and most of those who remained would deny their Indigenous identity. The Lundgrens governed the region for decades and their cruel regime of terror dug itself deeply into the Potiguara's collective memory.

Threatened by all this violent oppression, the Potiguara called the SPI (*Serviço de Proteção aos Índios*—Indian Protection Service)[8] for help and claimed their rights as an Indigenous ethnic group.[9] In the course of the following 100 years, their ethnic identity would become their most powerful weapon in their fight for land and ultimately for their survival, and consequently, be constantly disputed by their enemies.

But the officials of the SPI hesitated. It took the Potiguara another decade to convince those responsible that they were "Indios", until finally, in 1932, the SPI installed a permanent post in the Aldeia do Forte, at the edge of the little town of Baia da Traição. But instead of solving problems, the SPI became just another agent within the violent conflicts between the Potiguara, local peasants, landlords and the Lundgrens, trying to get control over the land, its resources, the local population and labour. Although the SPI initiated the demarcation of the Potiguara territory in 1948, never-ending violent conflicts between the SPI and the Potiguara made this task impossible. Meanwhile, the Potiguara continued negotiating their natural resources and labour with the different interested parties, selling timber to the factory, leasing land to peasants and sugar refineries, entering alliances with local peasants against powerful landlords.

Things would change in the 1970s with new actors entering the scene. Activists of the liberation theology movement, the newly founded FUNAI and engaged academics supported the Potiguara in their resistance. With their aid, the Potiguara organised large scale mobilisations and finally achieved the regularisation of at least a part of their territory.[10] During the intense mobilisation during the 1980s, 1990s

ritory by means of corruption, extortion, violence and by questioning their ethnic identity with false anthropological reports (see also Marques 2009).

[8] The SPI was a governmental institution, founded in 1910, with the mission to protect, civilise and integrate the native nations into the Brazilian civil society. The SPI would be substituted by the FUNAI (*Fundação Nacional do Índio*—National Indian Foundation) in 1967, which continues to be the responsible governmental organisation for Indigenous affairs in Brazil.

[9] Palitot (2005, 2011).

[10] The liberation theology movement had become a leading force in Latin American social rights movements and was also fundamental to the foundation of Indigenous organisations throughout the continent. In 1976, the FUNAI announced the demarcation of a territory extending over 57,000 ha, but soon after reconsider their initial estimation to a much smaller area, provoking further conflicts. The Federal University of Paraíba (UFPB) begins to actively support the demarcation project in 1979, but conflicts continue, and 2 years later, in 1981, the Potiguara decide to demarcate their lands by their own. However, the army intervened in favour for the big sugar cane

and 2000s, the Potiguara united and fought for their land, civil rights and cultural autonomy. They spent months together in occupation camps, sharing primitive shelters and suffering violent attacks, while singing and dancing the *toré*[11] to summon their ancestors to give them strength. They recovered and re-invented "traditional" attire and skin paintings to be proudly exposed during the *toré* and when they would march to claim their lands. To dance and sing the *toré* was more than just a symbol of Potiguara identity; it was the lived experience of the power of unity and spiritual connectedness with one's ancestors and the land soaked with their blood, the territory so many Potiguara had fought and given their lives for. It did not matter that they had lost much of their knowledge about the exact *toré* texts or the images of their "traditional" skin paintings—they invented their own versions within their concrete life-world, just as their ancestors did.[12] They also visited other Indigenous groups to make alliances and join forces, participating also in their mobilisations and their rituals, hereby exchanging all kinds of cultural elements across ethnic boundaries.[13]

It is true that the Potiguara, like many other Indigenous nations, have changed fundamentally since the Europeans invaded their lands five centuries ago. And it is equally true that their ethnic identity is the result of a process of negotiating social status and access to resources in the context of inter-societal friction.[14] But to oppress, enslave and decimate them, deprive them of their land, their religion, their language and their way of life for hundreds of years, and then to go on arguing they

plantations and the textile factory of Rio Tino, reducing the territory to 21,238 ha, provoking new mobilisations of the Indigenous movement for the demarcation and occupation of further lands. Although the Potiguara finally achieved the legalisation of some 33,757 ha, a considerable part of their territory is still in dispute (idem; see also Marques 2009; Soares 2009; Vale 2012).

[11] The *toré* is a term used to determine ritual collective dances practiced among the Indigenous communities of the Brazilian North-East. Typically, participants would chant and dance together in a circle following to the rhythm of their *maracás* (traditional sacred rattle) and other instruments, like flutes or drums. Today, the *toré* is the central symbolic denominator of Indigenous identity among these groups. However, the first records of the *toré* go back to the early twentieth century and have been associated only later to Indigenous culture. Although originally the *toré* had been observed only among some groups, like the Fulni'Ó, the Pankarurú or the Xucurú, the SPI would use the *toré* as a diacritical cultural element to define whether a community would be considered Indigenous or not, thus forcing *all* North-Eastern nations to enact their *toré*, regardlessly. Hence, each group would reconstruct its own *toré* based on the elders narratives, other traditional dances, like the *coco*, *cirandas,* and *catimbó* rituals, as well as mediumistic experiences. Moreover, since the times of the missions, North-Eastern nations had been in frequent contact with African slaves, exchanging spiritual and cultural patterns and melting them together in different kinds of Ancestral-Afro-Brazilian syncretism, like the *catimbó* or *jurema*-cults. The "new" tradition of the *toré* is the result of the re-interpretation of older traditions from various cultural origins within the context of an ethnicity-based political discourse (Oliveira 1998; Grünewald 2004; Palitot 2005).

[12] See also Paiva (2013).

[13] Oliveira (1998, 2013); Palitot (2005).

[14] This instrumentalist concept of ethnic identity, as proposed by Frederik Barth (1969), has also been applied to the Potiguara and other "emergent" ethnic groups (Palitot 2005; Oliveira 1998).

had no right to their lands because they changed too much to be recognised as "Indios" is nothing but an expression of the abysmal hypocrisy of the ruling classes.

Today (2025) there are about 25,000[15] Potiguara living in the territory at the north-eastern coast of Paraíba state. The territory consists of three official reserves, TI (*terra indigena*—Indigenous territory) Potiguara, TI Jacaré de São Domingos and TI Potiguara de Monte Mor, covering a total of 33,757 ha (plus the areas which have not yet been legalised). Moreover, many Potiguara are living in the adjacent towns of Mamanguape, Rio Tinto, Marcação and Baia da Traição, in the state capital João Pessoa, and there are Potiguara communities in the neighbouring states of Rio Grande do Norte and Ceará. Furthermore, in the majority of Potiguara families there are at least some relatives who went to the industrial centres of Rio de Janeiro or São Paulo to make their living—a destiny they share with most families in the North-East, which is Brazil's poorest region.

The foreigner who visits the Potiguara territory today will barely notice much difference compared to other rural communities in the region. Most houses in their villages are built from brick and the few remaining clay houses are covered with tile. There are new school buildings and medical stations, and many Potiguara work there as teachers, nurses, guards or cooks, making their living with a regular salary, while others live from the sugar cane plantations or shrimp farms that dominate the landscape. Today, they mainly use cars and motorcycles instead of horses or donkeys, and they love using their smart phones.

However, this picture is the result of deep demographic, social and economic changes which are actually quite recent. Ethnographic records from the 1980s[16] as well as local elders report a quite different reality. Until a few decades ago, the Potiguara had been living in straw huts entirely build by palm leaves; only the "richer" Potiguara could afford a clay house with a tile roof. The region was still covered by dense forests and most people made their living hunting, fishing, catching crabs in the mangroves, growing manioc, corn and sweet potatoes on their little plots. The babies were born with the assistance of the "traditional" midwife and children rarely had a school to go to. Those who had this privilege would walk hours through the dense woods to get there (Fig. 8.1).

The first deep ecological changes came with the textile factory of Rio Tinto, causing large-scale deforestation for firewood, followed by the massive expansion of alcohol production during the 1970s, resulting in further deforestation for new

[15] There are no exact figures on the current population. Different sources differ give very different figures. The official census of 2010, carried out by the IBGE (*Instituto Brasileiro de Geografia e Estatistica*—Brazilian Institute for Geography and Statistics) registered a total of 20,554 Potiguara living in and outside their official territory; the most recent census of 2022 registered around 18,000 Potiguara living in the official territories, but without registering Potiguara living in neighbouring places outside the official territories; Cardoso and Guimarães (2012) suggest a total of 19,000; the ISA (*Instituto Socioambiental*—the Socia-Ambiental Institute is Brazils leading indigenist NGO) indicates a population of 14,831 living inside the official territory in 2010 and a growth rate of more than 1000 per year. These data, when considered together, suggest a current (2025) population of around 25,000.

[16] Baumann (1981); Moonen and Maia (1992); Moonen (2008).

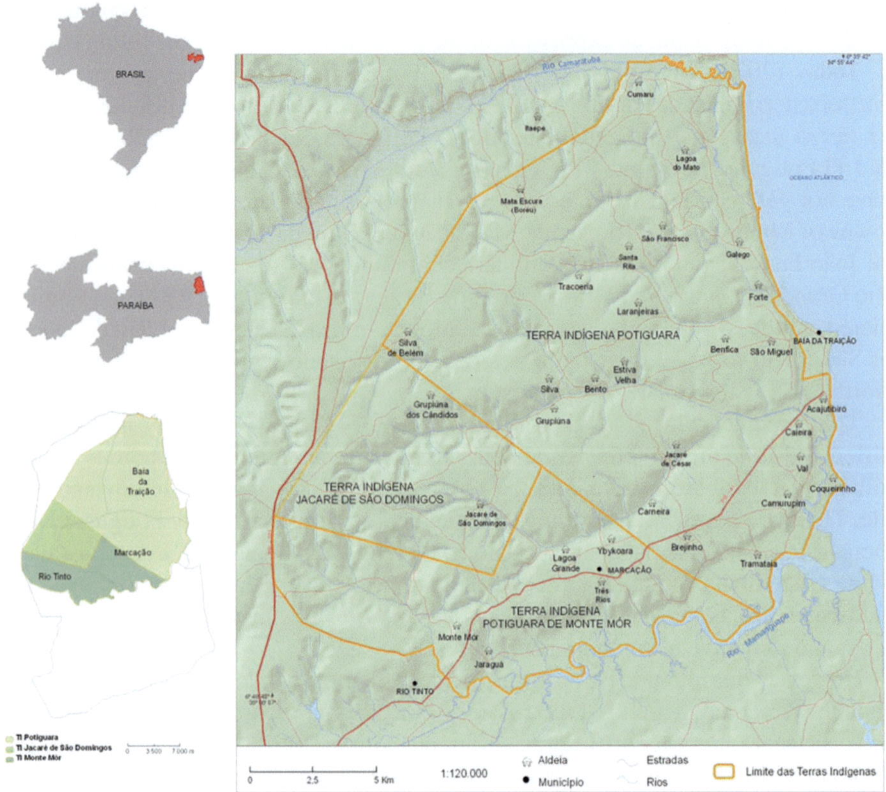

Fig. 8.1 Potiguara territory (source: Cardoso and Guimarães 2012 (With the kind permission of Thiago Motta Cardoso.))

sugar cane plantations.[17] Meanwhile, the population of the Potiguara would explode, growing from some 3000[18] in the 1970s to over 20,000 individuals.[19] As a result, natural resources became extremely scarce, making it impossible to survive by "traditional" extractivism and small-scale agriculture. Moreover, sugar cane monoculture and sugar refinery are causing a permanent ecological disaster, degrading soils, polluting rivers and mangroves. Although the recapture of their lands was explicitly connected with the task to make an end to the dreadful sugar cane plantations in favour of a comeback of "traditional" agriculture, economic pressure insidiously

[17] Cardoso and Guimarães (2012). With the kind permission of Thiago Motta Cardoso.

[18] Moonen (2008).

[19] Of course, these figures are also a result of migration and shifting ethnic identities. With the decline of the factory of Rio Tinto and the rise of the Indigenous movements during the 1970s, perspectives on the Potiguara changed considerably. Hence, many Potiguara who had been coerced to migrate or negate their Indigenous identity could now come back and claim their rights as Potiguara.

pushed the sugar cane back into Potiguara territory. Currently, about 70–80% of the area is covered with sugar cane, while only some 10–20% are still covered with natural vegetation and around 5–10% with "traditional" crops. The reasons are manyfold and the issue is far too complex to be discussed here. But due to its central importance for Potiguara life, I will point out at least some of what I think are the most important aspects of the problem. Sugar cane not only dominates the Potiguara territory, but also most, if not all aspects of their life. First of all, it is the main economic factor in the whole region. Most Potiguara depend on sugar cane either directly or indirectly. Those who have rights over some land will grow at least a few hectares of sugar cane, while others work on the plantations or for the distillation plants. The reason is that "traditional" crops, mainly different tubercles and fruits, are much more capital- and work-intensive than sugar cane, and hence, much riskier.[20] But sugar cane plantations become profitable only on a large scale, and therefore lead to a concentration of land in the hand of a small economic elite among the Potiguara, thus deepening social inequality and fuelling political disintegration within Potiguara society. As a consequence, sugar cane has become the most threatening challenge to Potiguara, exactly because they have become so dependent on it as an economic resource. This dependence goes hand in hand with the deep changes in their lifestyle. By re-conquering their lands, the Potiguara also get access to further rights and resources. Now, being officially recognised as an Indigenous nation with their own territory, they can get streets, electric energy, water-supply, medical centres, Indigenous schools, and access to higher education. As a consequence, a growing portion of the younger Potiguara no longer depend on agriculture or extractivism. Ironically, the more they advanced in their fight for their land, ethnic recognition and cultural autonomy, the more they became intricated with and dependent on the dominant society and capitalism.

These changes in the material dimension went together with complex transformations in their noosphere, too. While the elder generation still grew up with an oral tradition, most of them having little or no formal education, the great majority of the younger generations went to school, and many of them even attend university.[21] Of

[20] In order to get access to their lands, sugar industries established an economic scheme which provides fixed returns with minimal risks to the planters. Typically, the sugar company will make an estimate of the expected harvest and provide pesticides and credits to finance the plantation, while guaranteeing a more or less fixed price for the harvest. Moreover, once planted, sugar cane will grow for many years without the need to plant it again before each harvest, lowering labour costs enormously.

[21] Today, there are hundreds of Potiguara studying at the Federal University and other institutions of higher education, many of them already graduated, and some of them even obtained masters or doctor degrees. A few years ago, it would be very difficult, if not impossible for a Potiguara to enter university. There was no transport to get from their remote villages to the state capital João Pessoa and the low educational level at local schools would not allow them to pass the national qualifying exams (ENEM). Although the UFPB inaugurated a brand-new campus in Rio Tinto and Mamanguape in 2006, it would take more to enable the Potiguara to study there. Preparatory courses for local students between 2008 and 2010 enabled a number of Potiguara to enter university. But still, there were be only a dozen Potiguara among hundreds of non-Indigenous students at the campus, right in the middle of their lands. It was thanks to the work of some engaged professors

course, many Potiguara pursue an academic title to get access to better jobs, but some of them use their privilege to appropriate and occupy the academic sphere for their Indigenous militancy. Being supported by some engaged professors, they enact the *toré* at scientific events and focused their studies on Indigenous issues. They do research on their own history and culture, do fieldwork among their elders, and produce their own scientific accounts of Potiguara realities. This new generation of organic intellectuals lives in between the oral world of their parents and grandparents, and the literate world of academic knowledge. The symbolic and cultural capital provided by their academic titles, their theoretical knowledge and their capability of mastering the dominant political discourse is an indispensable weapon for current Indigenous militancy. However, all those years they spent studying texts and attending lessens were also years they had little time to participate in "traditional" activities, to go fishing, hunting, planting, or sitting together with their elders. Hence, their access to Potiguara "tradition" is not the same as that of their elder relatives, which was, above all, a question of daily practice and survival. The younger generation's way of reconstructing and living their Potiguara identity, culture and spirituality, in contrast, transcends the elders' pragmatic fight for fundamental rights and land, having a much more intellectual and spiritual horizon. They seek to experience the living presence of their ancestors and the sacredness of nature by experimenting with the reenactment of rituals and mediumistic experiences.

There are several young *pajés* practicing among the Potiguara, each developing their individual mediumship based on a range of doctrines, including orientations by older *pajés*, but also charismatic Catholicism, *umbanda*, kardecism, neo-shamanism and paganism. But it would be too simple to see their eclecticism as an illegitimate jumbling of all kinds of religious beliefs under the label of Potiguara spirituality. In fact, the syncretic junction of ancestral, African and European elements is a characteristic feature of the different ethnic groups in the Brazilian North-East.[22] Moreover, the appropriation of the mystified Other is a

that in 2010 the *PET Indigena* (a graduate program for Indigenous students) would motivate the Potiguara students to assume their Indigenous identity, to do research on their culture and to give classes at the schools in remote communities to support and motivate the younger Potiguara to enter university, too. Moreover, they promoted the AUP (Potiguara Students' Association), with currently counting about 100 members (Barcellos 2015).

[22] Actually, over the last 500 years there has been so much mutual influence between the different ethnic groups that it is virtually impossible to separate their cultures and religious beliefs from each other. First of all, Christianity has become kind of a common substrate of Afro-Brazilian, Indigenous and Spiritist cults alike. But this is also true for old European folk magic. Moreover, Indigenous myths and medical practices became part of Brazilian folk cosmopractices. This is also true for many elements of Afro-Brazilian religions, like *candomblé*. Moreover, indigneous and Quilombola (runaway slave communities) joined in resistance to their common enemies, living side by side for centuries, and consequently exchange a lot of cultural elements between these communities, resulting in Ancestral-Afro-Brazilian syncretisms, like the *catimbó* or *jurema*-cult. The Fusion of *candomblé* with Kardesist spiritualism, again, would result in the *umbanda* movement, which would later also appropriate the *jurema* cult from *catimbó* (Vandezande 1975; Oliveira 1998; Freyre 2003; Grünewald 2004; Mendonça 2013).

recurrent feature of spiritual practice.[23] The more exotic and mysterious, the more power is attributed to a magical practice. Hence, to appropriate the Others' magic is to increase one's power. But all this magical mingling notwithstanding, the principal source of spiritual force is always one's own ancestors. And whatever new practice one might adopt, it has to be adjusted to one's own ancestral heritage through mediumistic communication during dreams or ritual.

Though religion and cosmology are construed as a fundamental unifying element of ethnic identity, the reality of Potiguara society is quite the opposite; a patchwork of various religious groups, doctrines and syncretism. Roman Catholicism still dominates public life and the annual calendar of Potiguara society. There are several important religious festivals in honour of local patron saints throughout the year. However, while all Potiguara would call themselves Christians, individually they interpret "Christian" belief quite differently. Many of them have been practicing other magico-religious rites, like *catimbó*, *umbanda* or Kardecism, while equally claiming to do God's work. Especially the presence of the ancestral-Afro-Brazilian syncretism of *catimbó* seems to have a long history among the Potiguara. Although the majority is probably still Roman Catholic, Protestant congregations are growing rapidly in their communities. Since the 1960s, Protestant churches are gaining ever more followers. Today, there are at least nine different Protestant congregations present, in different proportions, in virtually all Potiguara communities; in some of them even representing the majority of its inhabitants,[24] including local *caciques* and other important Indigenous leaders. This situation is problematic because many priests condemn "traditional" rituals as satanic rites. There are countless stories about healers, midwifes and elders who abandoned their "traditional" practices or even cut down their sacred *jurema*[25] trees after having converted to protestantism. This open opposition to central elements of Potiguara culture and identity has been causing serious conflicts between priests and Indigenous authorities. Threatened with being sent away, many priests made a compromise with the demands of local leadership, allowing their followers to participate in the *toré*. However, their participation would be just a symbolic act of demonstrating their ethnic identity, thus neglecting the ritual's deep spiritual and cosmological dimension.

Like most other Indigenous peoples in post-Columbian times, the Potiguara have been living in-between different worlds. Their world has ever since been a "hybrid"[26] world, breeding in the interstices between their ancestral heritage and the dominant colonial/modern culture. This kind of in-betweenness, this existence along the borders is a core feature of coloniality as a "modern/colonial" state of

[23] Descola (1996); Bund (1997); Taussig (1997); Langford (1999); Perruchon (2003); Linhart (2008).

[24] Barcellos (2012).

[25] The *jurema* tree (*Mimosa tenuiflora*) is a sacred plant with psychotropic properties, which plays a central role in several Indigenous and Afro-Brazilian magico-religious traditions, like the *catimbó*, *umbanda* and *jurema*. Although experts and Indigenous practitioners are still debating its origins, the *jurema* is a central recurrent theme in Potiguara body paintings, their *toré* chants, and it is frequently served to the participants during rituals.

[26] Bhabha (1994).

feeling-thinking-being. While this has been recognised as a shared condition of most colonised and marginalised people in the Americas, Africa, Asia and Oceania, we tend to see US Europeans and other "Westerns" merely as "modern" colonisers. However, this dichotomous view ignores the brutal processes of marginalisation, dispossession, oppression, exploitation and persecution[27] to which varying segments of European populations have been subjected in the multiple, bloody histories that, eventually, transformed our "barbarian", "pagan" ancestors into slaves or subjects of the Roman Empire, Christians, and finally, "moderns". How many sacred trees had to be felled, witches and heretics be tortured and burned, peasant farmers be driven from their lands to become proletarian working poor, before We, "European" "moderns", finally renounced our "barbarian" Ancestors together with their "mythss" and "traditional" ways of feeling-thinking-being? These violent historical processes of internal and external Othering and systematic disruption of ancestral ties led to a painful and irreversible loss of Our ancestral heritage (and attempts to compensate these losses by taking recourse to Greek and Roman classics, Romanticism, nationalism or blatant Aryan racism.[28] From this perspective, "coloniality at large"[29] appears as a long and still ongoing historical process of classifying, marginalising and unrooting people across the world—at different times and places, and under very different conditions—from their ancestral heritages, transforming them into dwellers of intersecting subaltern and/or dominant positionalities, and into "hybrid" forms of existence within a racialised modern/colonial World-System. Essentialising Others as "pre-moderns", fundamentally different from Us "moderns", blinds us to the interconnectedness of these diverse histories within this long, global process of self-/colonisation and modernisation. The spirit of modernity has been fighting "tradition" and "myth" not only in its colonial peripheries, but also—perhaps above all—in its European homelands. Of course, participating in interconnected historical processes does not in any way diminish the grotesque asymmetries between colonisers and colonised and the fates of those living on either side of the colonial difference. There can be no excuse for Our ancestors' historical role as brutal colonisers and slaveholders, nor for the all-too-comfortable ignorance of the unbearable injustices and dehumanising living conditions that Our (upper-middle-class) "modern way of life" continues to impose on the subalternised, Othered majority of this planet. However, the difference between Us and Them might *not only* be conceived in terms of a colonial difference between dominant and subaltern positionalities, but *also* in Our coming to terms with finally identifying Ourselves as "moderns", while those recalcitrant Others persist in *resisting*, holding fast to their ancestral heritage against all (Our) external pressure. From this perspective, the insight that culture and identity are "hybrid" can take on the taste of inevitable cultural dilution or assimilation as a particular destiny of the colonised—and thus, in a way, risk reinforcing essentialism through the backdoor, so to

[27] Moore (2007).

[28] Dussel (2000).

[29] Mignolo and Ennis (2001).

speak. This point is important, since the "decolonial option"[30] to "re-exist"[31] one's own ancestral heritage is not about going backwards or essentialising ethnic identities. To re-exist is to resist the modern/colonial fate of living at the "End of Times",[32] and to revive one's ancestral legacy and territoriality as an essential resource for decolonising oneself and enabling self-determined future-building beyond modern/colonial categories of Otherness. To be Potiguara today does not mean to remain unchanged or to turn back to one's ancestors 500 years ago, but to be the heir to their territory, to their spiritual legacy, and to their struggle for a self-determined life that is more than merely a "mimicry" of the dominant modern/colonial way of being. For many, reclaiming their "Indigenous" identity and legal rights corresponds to a counter-hegemonic vision of living the utopia[33] of building self-determined, liveable futures grounded in spiritual unity with the Ancestors, the territory, and all the beings dwelling therein.

8.1 Ancestral Heritage and Changing "Traditions"

Historically, the Potiguara were one of several Tupi-speaking groups, but like many other colonized nations,[34] they lost their mother tongue some 250 years ago.[35] We do not know much about their original culture and worldview in the times of their first encounter with the Europeans. There are only a few documents, written by the chroniclers (European travellers and priests who wrote reports about the New World during the sixteenth century), suggesting they would have shared by and large the same cultural features as the Tupinambá, the Tupiniquim, and other Tupi-speaking nations at that time.[36]

According to these reports, the Tupi were nations of great warriors, constantly at war with other native groups in an endless circle of vengeance, seeking to capture their enemies for their anthropophagic feasts.[37] Both war and anthropophagy were organic elements of a wider ritual complex which was deeply embedded within the cosmology and fundamental to the social structure of these nations. Their anthropophagic rituals have been described in some detail by Hans Staden, Jean de Lery, Pedro Magalhães de Gandavo and other Europeans who had witnessed their customs during the sixteenth century.

[30] Mignolo and Walsh (2018).

[31] Walsh (2023).

[32] Latour and Porter (2017).

[33] Oliveira (1998); Rappaport (2005); Ramos and Linhart (2012); Linhart et al. (2017).

[34] This is especially true for the northeastern region of Brazil, were virtually all of the more than 20 Indigenous groups have lost their mother tongues, with the Fulni-ô being the only exception.

[35] Palitot (2005); Moonen (2008).

[36] Lopes (2003).

[37] Staden (1557); Gandavo (1575); Lery (1992); Fernandes (2006).

Following these reports, the warriors would return from battle bringing enemies as captives, destined to be ritually eaten in order to take revenge for all those relatives and Ancestors who had been previously killed and eaten by those enemies. The women would receive the victim shouting at and beating them, saying how much they desired to eat them in revenge for their murdered husbands, while the victim was expected to respond: “Here I am, your food!”, further affirming that they, too, had killed and eaten many of their relatives before. However, all this ostentation of hate and loathing notwithstanding, the Tupi would frequently have their captives live among them for months or even for years, treating them with honour and respect, before killing and eating them. After the initial demonstration of hostility performed by the women, the victim would be adorned and then dance with them, they would be fed with the best food and it was customary for the victim’s owner to give them a daughter or sister-in-law in marriage.[38] Sometimes, the owner would take their victim and go hunting together and even to war against their enemies, almost as if the captive had become one of their kind. But one day, they would decide it was time to kill and eat the captive and start preparing the *cauim*[39] for the big anthropophagic feast. Before being killed, however, their captive would be submitted to complex ceremonies of purification and protection. They would be washed, shaved and adorned with colourful feathers, be shackled with a rope around their neck, and then be paraded around the village, before being brought to the central place to be finally slain.

Despite knowing perfectly about his approaching death, the victim would not show any fear or despair, but to the contrary, proudly declare that he, too, had killed and eaten many of them, his enemies. On reaching the central place, the crowd would gather by the hundreds, surrounding the scene. The victim was now fixed with a rope around his abdomen, with two strong men holding him tight so he could not move to either side, but still leaving both of his hands free. Then, he would receive stones to defend himself, which he would start throwing furiously at the crowd around him. Meanwhile, the executioner would enter the scene, with his *tacapé*[40] in his hand, position himself behind the victim and ask him whether he was the one who had fought, killed and eaten so many of their relatives. The captive was expected to proudly respond that he is a great warrior and, indeed, it was him and his brothers who had done this to them, and that after he himself was killed and eaten, his brothers would come to avenge his death, probably killing and eating

[38] Actually, the widows of warriors who were killed in combat were not allowed to marry again until their husband’s death was avenged by capturing, marrying and killing an enemy. So, it was necessary for them to marry a captive in order be allowed to marry one of their own kind (normally one of her uncles or brothers-in-law). Hence, a warrior who had fallen in love with a widow would have to take a captive for her to marry first to be allowed to marry her after the captive’s death (Fernandes 2006).

[39] *Cauim* is the traditional fermented beverage made of manioc, corn or fruits. Staden, for example, tells us that the Tupinamba went out to war when their corn was ready for harvest so they had enough to make their *cauim* and prepare their anthropophagic feasts.

[40] Wooden club-sword.

many more of them. It was a great honour to be eaten and every warrior would wish to die this way. Once his part of the ceremony was finished, the victim was struck down by the executioner from behind with a precise blow of a club to his head. His ritual "wife" would come to her dead "husband" and perform some symbolic mourning before the body would be washed and cleaned by the other women, to be cut into pieces thereafter. The children of the fallen warriors were called and their mothers would rub them with the enemy's blood to avenge their fathers' death, before roasting the flesh and cooking the viscera together with maniac flour. The distribution of the different parts of the body between the participants of the feast received great attention, making sure that everyone present at the feast would get their portion, with each part of the body being designated to a specific group or person. Our European testimonies all emphasise that every part of the body was eaten except the brain,[41] the bones and the teeth, the latter being transformed into flutes and necklaces, respectively.[42] Nevertheless, one can imagine that all those hundreds of participants at the feast would not receive enough human meat to appease their hunger. Moreover, some parts of the body would be dried to be eaten later, further reducing the quantity of meat to be eaten at the feast. Hence, anthropophagy has never played any role in nutrition, at least not in the physiological sense, neither can it be fully explained as a ritual of vengeance, at least not in the physical sense; rather, it was a magic practice focussing on the victim's immaterial aspects (Figs. 8.2 and 8.3).

What was consumed during the ritual was not only the enemy's flesh, but also their immaterial dimension, their "vital energy" or "spirit", one could say, together with their skills and their strength as a warrior.[43] Moreover, as each victim themself had already eaten many of their relatives, who again had eaten many other enemies, and so on, by eating a part of their flesh one would also acquire the accumulated spiritual power of all those enemies and one's own Ancestors.[44] Hence, the preoccupation during the ritual to make sure the victim really was a great warrior who had eaten many of their kind.

---

[41] This is a very interesting detail, as it could explain why we have no reports of neuronal diseases among the Tupi caused by the ingestion of human flesh, as is reported about the Kuru disease between endo-anthropophagic groups of Papua New Guinea.

[42] The warriors used to display the skulls of their victims mounted on wooden posts in front of their houses. And when they went to war, they would adorn themselves with paintings, colourful bird-feathers and necklaces made of the teeth of their enemies, while playing on flutes made of their bones—doing everything to look as fierce as possible.

[43] This kind of "absorbing" the victim's vital energy can also be found among other original nations, like the Shuar and Ashuar from Peru and Ecuador, for example. After the killing of an enemy, the warrior would have to go to the woods in search for an encounter with the victim's *arutam* and fight him in a spiritual combat under the influence of powerful psychotropic plants. It is a fight for death or life, which can even cause his physical death. But if he wins the *arutam*, it will enter him and make him invincible. And the more *arutam* a warrior has absorbed, the more powerful he will become (my own experiences among the Shuar; see also Descola 1996).

[44] Pierri (2006).

Fig. 8.2 Lery (1580): 214 (source: https://gallica.bnf.fr, with permission of the National Library of France)

Fig. 8.3 Source: Thevet (1878): 202. Provided by https://fr.wikisource.org/ under creative commons licence (https://foundation.wikimedia.org/wiki/Terms_of_Use/en)

On the other hand, by destroying the enemy both physically and spiritually, their "spirit", that is, their immaterial aspect,[45] was prevented from taking revenge on his murderer.[46] However, the victim's executioner had to fear being haunted by the dead warrior's spirit. After beating the captive to death, the executioner retreated into their house where they received incisions all over their body and then had to stay in the hammock for several days, without touching the ground with the feet, without eating any meat or fish, and maintaining sexual abstinence.[47]

The vengeance of the victim's spirit is a common preoccupation among Indigenous people, including the spirit of animals killed during hunting. In fact, there are striking similarities between different concepts of war, anthropophagy and hunting in this respect.[48] All three categories are conceived as acts of predation in a cycle of lives being exchanged for other lives. Hence, by taking a life one happens to owe a life, too—and one who does not pay this debt will be charged. There is always a principle of reciprocity implicit in the relation between hunter and prey, warrior and defeated enemy. Consequently, it is no big surprise that rituals to prevent the prey's spirit from haunting the hunter often resemble rituals aiming to detain the spirit of anthropophagic victims from taking revenge on their murderers. According to Lery and Staden, the Tupinamba explicitly compared war with hunting and their captives with prey. Moreover, there are reports of rituals where the human sacrifice was substituted by a jaguar which would be submitted to the same ceremony as a captive enemy would.[49] And when Hans Staden rejected eating the human flesh offered to him by the chief Cunhambebe, arguing that even wild animals would not eat their own kind, Cunhambebe responded: "*Jau ware che!*—I am a jaguar, it tastes awesome![50]". There is no categorical difference between human or animal persons. A human can play the role of a jaguar and a jaguar can stand for a human. And as with their human victims, the consumption of the flesh of an animal would transfer

---

[45] The definition and terminology referring to this immaterial aspect of "persons", be they humans, animals, plants or certain objects, has been subject to some debate in anthropology. Virtually all existing cultures come with some concept of such kind, and in many cases these are translated using terms like "souls" or "spirits" (e.g. Harner 1972; Faust 1989; Descola 1996; Narby 1998; among others). But of course, these terms derive from the European context and are, therefore, encumbered with correspondent connotations. Moreover, the common use of these terms for denominating a countless number of cosmological concepts from different cultural contexts comes with the risk of levelling out important differences. Other anthropologists have used alternative terms, like "spiritual" (Guss 1980; Stoller and Olkes 1987) or "mimetic doubles" (Taussig 1997), "thoughts" (Reichel 1987), "knowledge" or "power" (Langdon and Bear 1992; compare also Linhart 2008 on this discussion). However, the problem of translating such cosmological concepts persists, as there is still no common terminology anthropologists would agree on. So, for the present purpose and the sake of simplicity, I will use the terms "immaterial aspect" or "dimension" as well as "spirit" (port.: *espírito*), for the latter being the term most often used by contemporary Potiguara themselves (and also for being much shorter than the first option).

[46] Fernandes (2006).

[47] E.g. Lery (1992); et al.

[48] Descola (1992, 1996); Fernandes (2006); Castro (2015).

[49] Fernandes (2006).

[50] Staden (1557).

its properties, and hence, a warrior would avoid eating certain animals and fishes considered to be slow or weak. To be a human or an animal person are interchangeable perspectives. The warrior takes the jaguar's perspective towards his enemy, who is consequently put into the prey's role. Moreover, the "spirits" or immaterial personhoods of both human and animal persons are included within this reciprocal relation of interchanging perspectives, as they, too, can take the role of the hunter/jaguar/warrior who goes hunting for the one who killed his respective material personhood.

Eduardo Viveiros de Castro has argued that these dualistic patterns of hunter-prey relations can even shift between the material and the immaterial dimension, while maintaining the essence of their inner logic. He refers to the transcendental funeral cannibalism of the Araweté (another recent Tupi-speaking group living in Pará) which transfers the physical anthropophagy of their Ancestors to the immaterial dimension, were the *Mai* deities devour the spirits of the dead so they might become one of their kind, immortal transcendental beings as well.[51] The underlying duality between predator and prey is at the same time a relation of equality, a mutual exchange of lives and interchanging perspectives through predation. Like the Tupinambas' victim who has to be an enemy, but at the same time has to be transformed into a relative through marriage before his essence can be absorbed by ingesting him. And while the Tupi nations were hunting and eating their enemies after having transformed them into relatives, other neighbouring nations called Tapuia were eating their own dead relatives. This endo-anthropophagic practices, too, aimed to incorporate the dead's immaterial properties by burying them within one's own body.[52] Similar cosmological patterns can also be found in distant regions. In Desana[53] cosmology, each life of a prey taken by a hunter has to be compensated by a human life in the immaterial dimension, reincarnating as an animal after their human death. Hence, the animals which the Desana hunt and eat are their Ancestors, that is, their dead relatives. From Viveiros de Castro's perspectivist view, thence, there is no fundamental difference between the cosmological principals underlying the physical anthropophagy of the historical Tupi nations and those other rituals of predation—be they physical or transcendental. What is ultimately consumed during these predatory transmutations are the *relations* between predator and prey, one's own kind and the Other, by assimilating the signs of alterity, and thus, consummating the fundamental relatedness of all kinds of persons—regardless of being Them or Us, humans, animals or immaterial entities. This perspectivist interpretation of Tupi anthropophagy comes close to the concepts of "new animism" and "relational ontologies" (as discussed above), relocating this quite particular cultural feature within a much more general cosmological framework.[54]

---

[51] Castro (2015).

[52] Gandavo (1575).

[53] A Tukano nation living in north-western Amazonia at the frontier between Brazil and Colombia (Reichel-Dolmatoff 1971; Descola 1992).

[54] See also Tânia Stolze Lima (1996) on the metaphysics of Juruna cosmology.

Quite notably, all those cycles of transformation and exchange are organised by means of rituals. The person who ministers these rituals, often referred to as "shaman",[55] is the one who mediates between the different worlds or perspectives of human, animal and immaterial persons by assuming the Other's perspective through mediumistic techniques or altered states of consciousness.[56] They are an expert in traveling along the borders between these worlds and have the ability to communicate with persons of different kinds which people during normal states of consciousness are not able to communicate with. Most importantly, they can talk and interact with the Ancestors and other immaterial persons who may reveal important information about the future, healing plants or distant events.[57]

Among the Tupi, there were two distinct kinds of such mediumistic experts. The *pajé* was a person with some psychic abilities and medical knowledge, who could be described as a "healer" or local "shaman". The *pajé* would be responsible for interpreting dreams and caring for injured or ill persons, making use of herbal medicine, trance (often under the effect of psychotropic plants), smoke and blasts.[58]

But there were also men called *caraíbas*, who were described as kind of "prophets" or "holy men" who enjoyed great prestige and the privilege of free transit between different hostile groups. They were responsible for the conduction of major rituals and their advice was decisive for the most important decisions and events in Tupi society. Jean de Lery provided us with an extraordinarily vivid impression of such a ritual:

> Now I had heard from the Norman interpreters who had lived a long time in that country that our Tupinamba held a solemn assembly every three or four years; since I once found myself by chance attending one of these, and there is what I can truthfully report. […] we saw the savages from the neighbouring regions arriving from all directions, and being met by people of the village, who were coming out of their houses; five or six hundred were soon assembled in a large open place. We stopped and turned back to find the purpose of the assembly, and saw them suddenly separate into three groups: all the men in one house, the women in another, and the children in a third. Seeing ten or twelve of these *caraibe* gentlemen who had joined the men, and suspecting that they would do something extraordinary, I urged my companions to stay with me to see this mystery, and they agreed. The *caraibes*, before leaving the women and children, had strictly forbidden them to go out of their houses; rather they were to listen attentively to the singing from there. They also ordered us to confine ourselves to the house where the women were. […] we began to hear in the men's house […] a very low murmur, like the muttering of someone reciting his hours. Upon hearing this, the women (about a hundred of them) all stood up and clustered together, listening

[55] The terms "shamanism" or "shaman", respectively, are often used in this context. However, due to its fuzzy meaning and its inflationary use in esoteric literature I prefer to avoid this term. Instead I will make use of terms like "ritual expert", "healer", "medium" or vernacular names like "*pajé*" (compare footnote above).

[56] Baker (1999).

[57] Compare Castro (2015).

[58] The blast (span.: *soplo*; port.: *sopro*) is a central technique in many curing rituals, where the healer uses his breath as a vehicle to transmit some beneficial "energy" or "force" to another person (e.g. Hinderling 1981; Faust 1989; Descola 1996; Wörrle 2004; et al.—also my own experiences among the Shuar in Ecuador and the Nasa in Colombia).

> intently. The men little by little raised their voices and were distinctly heard singing all together and repeating this syllable of exhortation. *He, he, he, he*: the women, to our amazement, answered them from their side, and with a trembling voice; reiterating that same interjection *He, he, he, he,* they let out such cries, for more than a quarter of an hour, that as we watched them we were utterly disconcerted. Not only did they howl, but also, leaping violently into the air, they made their breasts shake and they foamed at the mouth—in fact, some, like those who have the falling-sickness over here, fell in a dead faint; I can only believe that the devil entered their body and that they fell into a fit of madness. We heard the children similarly shaken and tormented in the house where they were kept, which was quite near us. […] after these chaotic noises and howls had ended and the men had taken a short pause (the women and children were now silent), we heard them once again singing and making their voices resound in a harmony so marvelous […] I wished to watch them from nearby. […] They stood close to each other, without holding hands or stirring from their place, but arranged in a circle, bending forward, keeping their bodies slightly stiff, moving only the right leg and foot, with the right hand placed on the buttocks, and the left hand and arm hanging: In that posture they sang and danced. Because there were so many of them, there were three circles, and in the middle of each circle there were three or four of these *caraibes*, richly decked in robes, headdresses, and bracelets made of beautiful natural feathers of various colours, holding in each hand a *maraca* or rattle made of fruit bigger than an ostrich-egg […]. So that (as they said) the spirit might thereafter speak through these rattles, to dedicate them to this use they made them sound incessantly. […] Moreover, these *caraibes,* advancing and leaping forward, then drawing back, did not always stay in one place as the others did. I noticed that they would frequently take a wooden cane four or five feet long, at the end of which was burning some of the dried herb *petun* […]; turning and blowing the smoke in all directions on the other savages, they would say to them. "So that you may overcome your enemies, receive all of you the spirit of strength." And thus these *caraibes* did several times (Lery 1992 (1575): 140–142).

In his text, Lery describes many important elements of Tupi ritual and spirituality in those times. The *caraibas* acted as mediators between the visible and the invisible world in order to assess the forces of the Ancestors and transfer them to the community of the living. For this purpose, they made use of several ritual instruments and techniques, like collective chanting and trance with "possession", circular dancing, the use of the *maracá*[59] and smoke, not to forget the collective use of alcohol in the form of *cauim* (although not mentioned in *this* passage). These ritual techniques have also been reported by several other European witnesses during the sixteenth century and continue to be practiced among contemporary Tupi nations until today, including the Potiguara.[60]

The *caraibas* have also been associated with the great migrations of the Tupi and Guarani nations, crossing the continent from central Amazonia to the Brazilian coast. Following this hypothesis, the *caraíbas* were great charismatic leaders who had been guiding the Tupi-Guaraní for thousands of years in the search for the "land without suffering" (*yby marã e'yma*—in Tupi) or "land where one does not die"

---

[59] The *maracá* was of great importance, as reported by several Europeans at that times, and continues to be central to Potiguara ritual until today. Following to Lery's report, the Tupinamba had special rituals dedicated to initiating the *maracas,* which would be adorned with feathers, giving them food and drink to inspire their power as mediators to the spirits (see also Assunção 2006).

[60] E.g. Gandavo (1575); Staden (1557); Fernandes (2006) (1952); Assunção (2006); Mendonça (2014); Palitot (2005); Palitot and Junior (2004); among others.

(*yvy marane'y*—in Guaraní).[61] Once they finally reached the coast, some 2000 years ago,[62] they eventually split into the Guarani nations going southwards down to northern Argentine, Paraguay and Uruguay, and the Tupi nations populating the Brazilian coast between São Paulo and Maranhão.

However, recent studies suggest that this view was based on the construction of a supposed cultural continuity between the pre-historic Tupi and recent Guarani, and hence, might be an artefact.[63] The first analyses offered by Nimuendaju[64] and Métraux[65] filled the vast lacunas in the chroniclers' reports on the Tupinambá of the sixteenth century with ethnographic data about the Guarani of the nineteenth and twentieth century, taking these two historically and ethnically different realms for one and the same immutable socio-cultural unit—the "Tupiguarani". But in fact, the reports on the sixteenth century Tupinamba do not offer much evidence for any messianic movement in search for some "world without suffering". Much to the contrary, the vast majority of the early chroniclers[66] explicitly associated the migrations of the Tupi with their colonial situation, being threatened by violence, slavery and terrible new diseases, while more recent migrations of some Guarani groups seem to have been mainly ecological reasons.[67]

While the chroniclers did not mention a "world without suffering" they repeatedly reported the Tupinamba's believe in the catastrophic end of the world and a place (beyond the mountains) where their dead relatives would go, which have erroneously been compared with Christian concepts of the Great Flood, Paradise and Armageddon. The French priest André Thevet provided us with several cosmogonic myths he transcribed, which refer to different mythic cataclysms. However, these ends of mythic worlds are always the beginning of new worlds, too, indicating a cyclic concept of time,[68] completely different from the linear time concept of Christian eschatology. In a similar way, the chroniclers used Christian concepts

[61] Nimuendaju (1914); Métraux (1927); Fernandes (2006) (1952); Lopes (2003); Navarro (1995); Andrade (2012); Castro (2015); Clastres (1976, 1978); among others.

[62] Noelli (1999).

[63] Pompa (1998, 2004); Noelli (1999).

[64] Nimuendaju (1914).

[65] Métraux (1927).

[66] With the only exception of Gandavo (1575), who mentions in one single sentence that the Tupi had no possessions and therefore were permanently searching for new lands, where they hoped to find immortality. However, there is plenty of archeological evidence that the Tupi used to stay decades or even centuries at a place, and although they expanded to distant regions through the millennia, they would not necessarily abandon their old territory in exchange for a new one (Noelli 1999). Moreover, Gandavo does not mention anything about the *caraíbas* or any other messianic leaders who would have motivated their migration. On the other hand, the Tupi seemed to believe that after death, their souls would go to a place "behind the high mountains" (Lery 1992), where they expected to meet their Ancestors. It is possible that Gandavo was referring to some information of this kind when he mentioned a place of immortality, although he does not make this point explicit.

[67] Pompa (1998, 2004); Noelli (1999).

[68] Pierri (2006).

when they reported the Tupinamba feared some "devil" or "daemon" called *Aignan*, a term probably referring to a more generic concept of immaterial actants which might have been better described as "spirits", "energies" or "sorcery".

So, we know little or nothing about the reasons for the pre-Columbian migrations of their ancestors starting some 3000–5000 years ago, and there are no consistent data for any messianic movement between the Tubinamba of the sixteenth century led by their *caraíbas*. What we do have is information about Jesuit priests who used their knowledge about the Tupinamba's culture to have them move into the missions. Father Antonio Pires was one of the first Jesuits to convince several Potiguara chiefs to submit themselves and their relatives to the rule and order of the church, in the middle of the sixteenth century.[69] He knew the importance of the habits of the *caraíbas* and adopted some of their customs, intending to be held for a *caraíba,* too—with considerable success. He would talk about paradise on earth, the reign of God, and behave much like a *caraíba*, ostensibly taking care of the diseased, offering cure, protection and land, and consequently being treated like a *caraíba* as well. Meanwhile, the traditional *caraíbas* had shown themselves unable to prevent the Potiguara from dying of the European diseases and from being enslaved by the Portuguese. Hence, the priest appeared as an alternative type of *caraíba*, offering new solutions to new problems. The priest acted as a mediator and protector against their new, uncontrollable colonial situation, thus convincing the Potiguara to move into his missions. Under the shadow of the cross, they would be legally protected, by virtue of royal law, from slavery and granted the right to own their lands.[70]

The missions not only joined people from different native groups in order to catechise them, they also established microcosms of mutual influence between the Jesuits and the Tupinambás, creating a kind of Tupinambá Catholicism on the one hand, and provoking the rise of new religions as an anti-colonial response, like the *Santidade*[71] movement, on the other.

Be this as it may, as far as I can see there is not enough reliable information about the Potiguara's ancestors to allow reaching a final conclusion about the supposed existence of some messianic element in their cosmovision. But what our sources do show quite clearly is that the Potiguara, like other Tupi nations, had been deeply affected right from the beginning of the European invasion. There is plenty of evidence indicating that many Indigenous groups left their traditional territory due to

---

[69] Lopes (2003); see also Pierri (2006) on Father André Thevet.

[70] Interestingly, in search of evidence for a messianic movement between the Tupi, Florestan Fernandes (2006) quotes Abbeville's report on a migration led by a European who had imposed himself on the Potiguara as a *caraíba*.

[71] The Santidade religion of the late sixteenth century appeared among the different subaltern groups living in close contact with each other, African slaves, christianised Tupinambas and peasants of European descent, all of them being confronted with the hybrid character of the colonial situation they were experiencing. The movement was led by a christianised Tupinamba called Antonio, who claimed to be Tamaduaré, one of the cultural heroes of Tupi cosmology who survived the mythic Flood. Although making use of Christian symbols, the Santidade movement had an anti-Christian character, and hence, would be persecuted and violently ended by the Inquisition in 1585 (Pompa 2004).

the European presence while other groups were joined under the control of the Jesuit missions, resulting in profound changes in their culture, their religious practices and their cosmovision.

Today, the Potiguara no longer eat their enemies; neither do they live in *malocas*, nor practice polygamy or follow some messianic leaders in search of a world without suffering, like their ancestors may have done (or not). Much to the contrary, the Potiguara maintain a deep attachment to their territory, their Ancestors' lands as they say, practice the Christian faith with great devotion, and adopt by and large the typical lifestyle of the rural population in the neighbouring communities. However, they also conserved many practices and beliefs thought to be of ancestral origin, and which together constitute what could be called the *contemporary "traditional" Potiguara culture.* All the profound changes suffered during the last 500 years notwithstanding, current "traditional" Potiguara culture and worldview still shows some fundamental differences compared to the hegemonic culture of dominant society.

Their current "tradition" emerged through changing historical processes of intersocial friction[72] and mutual exchange of cultural elements. For the sake of a comprehensive overview and at risk of oversimplifying, these historical processes could be summarised as follows:

1. Re-signification of their own cosmovision and practice in face of the catastrophic hecatomb caused by the European invasion.
2. Mutual influence and re-signification of Catholicism together with cosmopractices of different Indigenous groups gathered under the control of the Jesuit missions, resulting in "Tupi-Catholicisms" and other syncretisms, like the *Santidade* movement.
3. Further diffusion and mutual exchange of cultural and cosmological elements between the Potiguara and other local groups, such as peasants of European descent and Afro-Brazilian communities (*quilombolas*), ultimately resulting in new magico-religious traditions, like the *catimbó*, the *rezadeiras* (faith healers) and popular Catholicism, and a shared set of myths common among the rural populations living in the area covering the original territory of the Potiguara and their neighbouring "brother-enemies", the Tabajara (roughly along the coastline between Recife and Natal).
4. The "civilisation" of the Indigenous population during the nineteenth century promoted by the integrationist politics under a nationalist tenet, which followed Brazilian independency, aiming to create a national Brazilian identity. These integrationist public policies would give incentives for the privatising of collective Indigenous lands and mixed marriages between Potiguara and other peasant families in order to convert the Indigenous population into "ordinary" Brazilian citizens.[73]

---

[72] Palitot (2005).

[73] Idem 2013.

5. The violent silencing of their Indigenous identity during the first large-scale expansion of capitalist industry in Potiguara territory at the beginning of the twentieth century (most visibly represented by the Lundgren's Textile Factory of Rio Tinto).
6. The reconstruction of their Indigenous identity in the context of a new ethnicity-based political discourse on civil and land rights. Although this process was initiated in the 1920s, it would only develop into a fully fledged Indigenous movement during the 1960s, and with the support of the liberation theology movement. Besides its essentialist attempts to recover and revive their "original" traditions, this process of ethnic reconstruction was also characterised by the mutual exchange of cultural, cosmological and ritual elements between the different Indigenous groups which collaborated in their joined fight for their rights and their lands.
7. During the last three or four decades, Potiguara society has been undergoing further deep changes. A new expansion of agroindustrial (sugar cane) production, general public schooling, the intrusion of Protestant sects and the exponential growth of their own population, together, had deep and manyfold impacts. While the Potiguara finally succeeded in recovering at least a part of their territory, many of them adopted a "modern" lifestyle, just like their non-Indigenous neighbours did.

The result of these multiple historical processes was a fusion of different Indigenous, Afro-Brazilian and European traditions into what might be best called *regional popular culture*. This particular culture and cosmopractice is common to the poor rural populations living on the ancestral lands of the Tabajara and Potiguara, who are the descendants of these Indigenous nations, as well as of Afro-Brazilians and peasants of European descent alike. While the Potiguara by and large share this popular culture with their neighbouring communities, they emphasise their Indigenous heritage in this cultural amalgam and cultivate some additional practices of particular symbolic and spiritual value for the maintenance of Potiguara identity.

Although utterly different from the culture of their pre-Columbian ancestors, contemporary "traditional" Potiguara culture has been registered repeatedly since the nineteenth century and ever since it has conserved most of its core aspects, including a surprising amount of pre-Columbian elements. However, while the Potiguara had been living their "traditional" way of life until recently, today there is only a minority of elders and younger Indigenous militants holding on to and promoting their "traditions" as well as they can. These elders are the keepers of "tradition" and therefore called *troncos velhos* ("old trunks"), and are deeply respected by the younger generations. They are the ones who still grew up in the world of "traditional" Potiguara culture and who are expected to pass on their oral and practical knowledge to posterity.

In the next section, I will present a summary of the magico-religious practices and the cosmovision which nowadays is held by the Potiguara as "traditional", and whose reference are the narratives of the *troncos velhos*.

References

Amorim PMd (1970) Indios Camponeses: Os Potiguara da Baia da Traição. Master Thesis, Universidade Federal do Rio de Janeiro

Andrade TMd (2012) Povos Indígenas da Paraíba. Editora Grafset, João Pessoa

Assunção L (2006) O Reino Dos Mestres: A Tradição Da Jurema Na Umbanda Nordestina. Pallas, Rio de Janeiro

Baker JR (1999) Keepers of tradition, agents of change: shamanism, altered states of consciousness, and cultural adaptation. Currare 22:115–120

Barcellos L (2012) Práticas Educativo-Religiosas dos Potiguara da Paraíba. Editora Universitária da UFPB, João Pessoa

Barcellos L (2015) PET-Indígena Potiguara da Paraíba. In: Freitas AEdC (ed) Intelectuais Indígenas e a construção da universidade plurietnica no Brasil: Povos indígenas e os novos contornos do Programa de Educação Tutorial/Conexões de Saberes. e-papers, Rio de Janeiro

Barth F (1969) Ethic groups and boundaries: the social organization of cultural difference. Universitets Forlaget, Bergen

Bhabha H (1994) The location of culture. Routladge, London/NY

Baumann TdB (1981) Relatório Potiguara. Fundação Nacional do Índio, Rio de Janeiro

Bund M (1997) Imagining the other: Michael Taussig on mimesis, colonialism and identity. Crit Anthropol 17:103–112

Cardoso TM, Guimarães GC (eds) (2012) Etnomapeamento dos Potiguara da Paraíba. Funai/Cgmt/Cgetno/Cggam, Brasília

Castro EVd (2015) Metafisicas Canibais: Elementos Para Uma Antropologia Pós-Estrutural. Cosac & Naify, São Paulo

Clastres P (1976) Staatsfeinde (La société contre l'État, dt.): Studien zur politischen Anthropologie

Clastres H (1978) Terra Sem Mal. Editora Brasilense, São Paulo

Descola P (1992) Societies of nature and the nature of society. In: Kuper A (ed) Conceptualizing society. Routledge, London, pp 107–126

Descola P (1996) Leben und Sterben in Amazonien: Bei den Jívaro-Indianern. Klett-Cotta, Stuttgart

Dussel E (2000) Europa, modernidad y eurocentrismo. In: Lander E (ed) La colonialidad del saber: eurocentrismo y ciencias sociales - Perspectivas latinoamericanas. CLASCO, Buenos Aires, pp 41–54

Faust FX (1989) Medizin Und Weltbild: Zur Ethnographie der Coyaima und Natagaima-Indianer Kolumbiens. Munich

Fernandes F (2006) A função social da guerra na sociedade Tupinambá. Editora Globo, São Paulo

Freyre G (2003) Casa Grande e Senzala: Formação da familia brasileira sob o regime da economia patriarcal. Global, São Paulo

Gandavo PdM (1575) Historia da Provincia Sãcta Cruz a qui vulgarmente chamamos Brasil. Lisboa

Grünewald RdA (ed) (2004) Toré: Regime Encantado do Índio do Nordeste. Fundação Joaquim Nabuco, Recife

Guss DM (1980) Steering for dream: dream concept of the Makiritare. J Latina Am Lore 6:297–312

Harner M (1972) The Jívaro, poeple of the Sacret Waterfalls. University of California Press, London

Hinderling P (1981) Kranksein in "Primitiven" und Traditionellen Kulturen. Norderstedt

Langdon EJM, Bear G (eds) (1992) Portals of power: Shamanism in South America. University of New Mexico Press, Albuquerque

Langford JM (1999) Medical mimesis: healing signs of a cosmopolitan "quack". Am Ethnol 26:24–46

Latour B, Porter C (2017) Facing Gaia: eight lectures on the new climatic regime. Polity, Cambridge, UK; Medford, MA

Lery Jd (1580) Histoire d'un voyage faict en la terre du Bresil, autrement dite Amerique. Chippin, Geneve

Lery Jd (1992) History of a voyage to the land of Brazil, otherwise called America. University of California Press, London
Lima TS (1996) O Dois e seu Múltiplo: Reflexões sobre o Perspectivismo em uma Cosmologia Tupi. Mana 2:21–47
Linhart J (2008) Universidades Indígenas: Programas de Educação Indígena Superior na América Latina: A Caminho de uma Ciência Intercultural? Master thesis, LMU
Linhart J, Batista MNF, Felix ICG, Silva PRP (2017) Auto-Etnografia Colaborativa entre os Potiguara e a Capacitação de Intelectuais Orgânicos. In: 2° Seminário Internacional do Núcleo de Extensão Multidisciplinar para o Desenvolvimento Rural (Nemdr), 27 de Julho de 2017, CCHSA, Campus III da Universidade Federal da Paraíba—UFPB. Bananeiras
Lopes FM (2003) Índios, Colonos e Missionários na Colonização da Capitania do Rio Grande do Norte/Fátima Martins Lopes; Apresentação de Enélio Lima Petrovich. Instituto Histórico e Geográfico do Rio Grande do Norte, Natal
Marques ACN (2009) Território de Memória e Territorialidades da Vitória dos Potiguara da Aldeia Três Rios. Master thesis, UFPB, João Pessoa
Mendonça CFL (2013) Insurgência Política e Desobediência Epistêmica: Movimento Descolonial de Indígenas e Quilombolas na Serra Do Arapuá. PhD thesis, Universidade Federal de Pernambuco
Mendonça W (2014) Memorias de nos. Karioka Multimedia, Porto Alegre
Métraux A (1927) Migrations historiques des tupi-guarani. Librarie Orientale et Américaine, Paris
Mignolo W, Ennis M (2001) Coloniality at large: the Western Hemisphere in the Colonial Horizon of modernity. CR: The New Centennial Rev 1:19–54. https://doi.org/10.1353/ncr.2003.0057
Mignolo W, Walsh CE (2018) On decoloniality: concepts, analytics, praxis. Duke University Press, Durham
Moonen F (2008) Os Indios Potiguara da Paraiba, 2. digital edn. Recife
Moonen F, Maia LM (1992) Etnohistória Dos Índios Potiguara: Ensaios, Relatos, Documentos. Grafset, João Pessoa
Moore RI (2007) The formation of a persecuting society: authority and deviance in Western Europe, 2nd edn. Blackwell, Oxford, pp 950–1250
Narby J (1998) The cosmic serpent: DNA and the origins of knowledge. Penguin, New York
Navarro EA (1995) A Terra sem Mal, o Paraíso Tupi-Guarani. Cultura Vozes N° 2:61–71
Nimuendaju C (1914) Die Sagen von der Erschaffung und Vernichtung der Welt als Grundlagen der Religion der Apapocuva-Guarani. Zeitschrift für Ethnologie 46:284–403
Noelli FS (1999) Curt Nimuendaju and Alfred Metraux: a invenção da busca da terra sem mal. Suplemento Antropologico XXXIV:123–166
Oliveira JPd (1998) Uma Etnologia Dos "Índios Misturados"? Situação Colonial, Territorialização e Fluxos Culturais. Mana 4:47–77
Oliveira K (2013) Diga ao Povo que Avance! Movimento Indígena no Nordeste. Fundação Joaquim Nabuco, Recife
Paiva EB (2013) Narrativas Indígenas: construindo identidades e constituindo-se em fontes de informação. Doctoral thesis, UFPB, João Pessoa
Palitot EM (2005) Os Potiguara da Baía da Traição e Monte-Mór: História, Etinicidade e Cultura. Master thesis, UFPB
Palitot EM (2011) A Multidão Potiguara: Poder Tutelar e Conflito na Baía da Traição ao Longo do Século XX. Raízes 31(1):25–44
Palitot EM, Júnior FBS (2004) Todos os Pássaros do Céu: O Toré Potiguara. In: Grünewald R de A (ed) Toré: Regime Encantado do Índio do Nordeste. Fundação Joaquim Nabuco, Recife
Perruchon M (2003) I am Tsunki: gender and shamanism among the Shuar of Western Amazonia. Uppsala University Press, Uppsala
Pierri DC (2006) Por sobre os Ombros de um Viajante: Ensaio sobre o Movimento, o Perspectivismo e o Xamanismo da Cosmologia Tubinambá a Partir da Obra de André Thevet. São Paulo
Pompa C (1998) O Mito "Mito da Terra sem Mal": A Literatura 'Clássica' sobre o Profetismo Tupi-Guarani. Revista de Ciências Sociais 1:44–72
Pompa C (2004) O Profetismo Tupi-Guarani: A Construção de um Objeto Antropológico. Revista de Indias LXIV 230:141–174

Ramos I, Linhart J (2012) Educación Intercultural Indígena: El programa de educación propia del CRIC como un ejemplo de una propuesta integral para una educación alternativa. In: Anais do III. SECAMPO. UFPB, Mamanguape

Rappaport J (2005) Intercultural utopias: public intellectuals, cultural experimentations, and ethnic pluralism in Colombia. Duke University Press, Durham

Reichel ED (1987) Die Ökopolitik im Schamanismus der Yukuna und Tanimuka vom Nordwestlichen Amazonas. In: Gottwald FT, Rätsch C (eds) Schamanische Wissenschaft, Ökologie, Naturwissenschaft und Kunst. Munich, pp 25–95

Reichel-Dolmatoff G (1971) Amazonian cosmos: the sexual and religious symbolism of the Tukano Indians. University of Chicago Press, Chicago

Soares AS (2009) Direito à Terra e a "Viagem da Volta": Processos de Construção da Terra Indígena Potiguara de Monte-Mor. Master thesis, UFPB, João Pessoa

Staden H (1557) Warhaftige Historia und beschreibung eyner Landtschafft der Wilden/Nacketen/Grimmigen Menschfresser Leuthen. Marpurg

Stoller P, Olkes C (1987) In sorcery's shadow: A memoir of apprenticeship among the Songhay of Niger. University of Chicago Press, Chicago

Taussig M (1997) Mimesis und Alterität: eine eigenwillige Geschichte der Sinne. Europäische Verlagsanstalt, Hamburg

Thevet A (1878) Les singularitez de la france antarcique. Maisonneuve & cie, Paris

Vale EC (2012) "Da Aldeia aa Preguiça a Ativa Colmeia Operária": O Processo de Constituição da Cidade-fábrica Rio Tinto—Parahyba do Norte (1917–1924). Revista Crítica Histórica Ano III(5):60–80

Vandezande R (1975) Catimbó: Pesquisa Exploratoria da Forma Nordestina de Religião Mediúnica. Master thesis, Universidade Federal de Pernambuco

Walsh CE (2023) Rising up, living on: re-existences, sowings, and decolonial cracks. Duke University Press, Durham

Wörrle B (2004) Lateinamerika: Patienten und Heiler zwischen den medizinischen Systemen. Curare 27:115–127

Chapter 9
Contemporary Potiguara Cosmovision and Practice

9.1 An Enchanted Word

The "traditional" world of the Potiguara is an enchanted world, full of mystery and inhabited by invisible and mythic beings. This world is entirely permeated by the divine force of God Tupã,[1] who manifests himself in the vital force which moves all living beings, the earth and the heavens, and in the abundance and the mystery of Nature in general. It is a world made up by entities who demand respect and whom one has to relate to and communicate with, just like with persons. There are many

In contrast to most other Indigenous nations and their historical ancestors, contemporary Potiguara do not have any cosmogonic myths. However, their narrations and the rituals they practice tell a lot about their worldview. I made quite an effort to ensure our representation of their narrations would include as many opinions and "voices" as possible, offering a synthesis most Potiguara would assign to. Nonetheless, there can be no doubt that the "cosmovision" I am presenting here is a product of an interpretative process and that its result is an apparently coherent construct which will hardly be reported in these terms by any Potiguara. Hence, I ask the reader to take it for what it really is: an abstract representation of a much more complex socio-cultural reality.
This chapter is based on the results of the fieldwork we did together with the ***Coletivo de Pesquisa pela Valorização dos Saberes Potiguara*** and the many ***troncos velhos***, ***caciques***, ***rezadeiras, pajés*** and traditional midwives in the communities, which have been published in two volumes of didactic books for their schools (Batista et al. 2021a, b). However, while I heavily build on this work, emphasising its collective authorship, the descriptions and interpretations exposed here are my own and may be contested by someone among the Potiguara, for whatever reasons. Further readings on Potiguara cosmology and religion: Lima (1946); Vandezande (1975); Grünewald (2004); Palitot and Júnior (2004); Assunção (2006); Marques et al. (2009); Rosa (2009); Gerlic and Zoettl (2011); Sousa and Nascimento (2011); Barcellos (2012); Casemiro (2012); Silva and Nascimento (2013); Mendonça (2014); Dantas et al. (2017).

[1] Tupã means "thunder" in Tupi and was introduced by the missionaries in the sixteenth century as a vehicle to explain the meaning of the Christian God, which was entirely alien to the Tupi in those times (see Lery 1992). Actually, it seems that the Potiguara did not use the name "Tupã" until a few decades ago, when they adopted this term as a substitute for "God" in order to underline the Indigenous character of their faith.

J. Linhart, *Science and the Other*, Schriften zu Leben und Gesellschaft - Series on Life and Society 2, https://doi.org/10.1007/978-3-032-03927-9_9

different kinds of such persons, some of them being physical, some of them immaterial beings, each representing a certain aspect of the world or a natural ambient, and each endowed with its particular spirituality and needing to be addressed in the appropriate manner.

9.1.1 Tupã and Mother Nature[2]

Potiguara life is moved by a deep faith in *Tupã*, or *God*, which they express whenever they can, affirming that everything happens according to God's will. Their thoughts and speeches are characterised by a permanent reverence to God, but also to Nature, the sacred locus where He makes himself present in the material world. In fact, God and Nature are related in such a deep sense that both almost merge into one single divine entity, each representing one of two complementary aspects of life.

Tupã, or God, are the names used to refer to the one creative principle that pervades and determines everything that is; He is the primordial, immaterial, wilful force that emanates in the material form of Mother Nature. Tupã and Mother Nature seem to coalesce into a single vitality that constitutes the universe, with Tupã representing the male, immaterial divine order or thought, and Mother Nature representing its female, material manifestation of fertility and life.[3] While Tupã represents the order and the immaterial aspect of things, Mother Nature represents the vital energy of physical life. Hence, both are worshipped as the highest divinities, each representing one of the two constitutive cosmological principles.

---

[2] Some (but not all) Potiguara explicitly use the term *mãe natureza* (Mother Nature) to refer to Nature as a divine entity which is very closely related, for some of them even equivalent, with God.

[3] While some Potiguara explicitly identify Tupã with Mother Nature, others prefer to hold to the Biblical version of God who created Nature and then continues to be present in his creation by means of the holy spirit. However, although not explicitly put in this way by the elders themselves, there is an implicit androgyne character in this close relation between the male God of Christian origin and the female Mother Nature of (supposedly) Indigenous origin. Anyhow, the idea of an androgyne deity who created the world out of some immaterial dimension can also be found in other Indigenous cosmological models. According to Baumgartner (1994), the Kogi of Columbia believe that the world was created by an androgyne deity out of *aluna*, the hidden, immaterial realm of thoughts and vital energy. After creating the world, she transferred her male aspect to her sons, representing the immaterial aspects of all things, with her female aspect being present in (the physical aspect of) Nature and her vital energy, and particularly in the waters, rivers, lakes and the sea. Similarly, Guss (1980) reports that following the cosmogony of the Makiritare (living along the frontier between Brazil and Venezuela) the world emerged out of the metaphysical dreamtime, were animals could speak and transform into other beings (compare also Lukesch (1994) on the Kayapó in Brazil). The similarity between dreams and myth has also been observed by Descola (1996). Put in such general terms, the cosmic genesis of the current, physical world out of a mythical dreamtime appears as a general feature common to Indigenous cosmogonies (compare e.g. Lévi-Strauss' Mythologiques (Lévi-Strauss 2004)).

This intimate relation between Tupã and Nature implies a profound respect for all natural elements and the beings that live therein. The presence of Tupã can be experienced through the observation of and the contact with Nature. It is a common habit among the elders to go to the woods, the waterfalls or the seaside to get in contact with Mother Nature, and hence, with Tupã. Moreover, there are several rituals explicitly addressing Tupã, God and Mother Nature, like the *toré*, healing rituals, and of course, the Christian Masses, novenas and feasts.

However, God, Tupã and Mother Nature not only represent complementary cosmic principles, but also different religious traditions, as well as antithetical political positions within social hierarchy. These subjacent tensions are expressed by the diverging references to the three terms during different kinds of rituals and depending on the different spaces in which they take place. While Christian rituals almost exclusively refer to God and other Christian divinities, healing rituals and *toré* are characterised by a mixed reference to Christian divinities as well as to Mother Nature and other divine entities and natural elements, like Ancestor spirits, Mother Earth, the Sun or the Moon. Likewise, the use of the alternative terms "God" and "Tupã" for one and the same entity is bound to the particular political and cultural context. While in Church and every-day-life "God" will be the privileged naming, during rituals and political events making reference to the Potiguara's Indigenous identity the term "Tupã" will be preferred.

In any case, "traditional" rituals of different strands all call upon Tupã or God, often together with other Catholic and non-Christian entities which are all held to represent different aspects of His universal power. Hence, the explicit reference to a particular saint or enchanted being equally calls upon His intervention by dint of the invoked entity. In this same spirit, a healer does not cure by force of their own spiritual powers; they only serve as a medium for accessing and channelling the divine power of God. Likewise, the healing powers of medicine plants are explicitly attributed to Tupã and His manifest presence in Mother Nature.[4]

9.1.2 Earth, Sun and Moon

In Potiguara cosmovision and practice, the earth, the sun and the moon are entities representing the divine powers of Tupã and Mother Nature, each endowed with its particular functions and forces, demanding certain precautions.

The Earth

The Earth is one of the most complex sacred concepts in Potiguara cosmovision, as the Portuguese term "*terra*" can be understood in several quite distinct ways, meaning "earth", "soil", as well as "land" or "territory".

[4] It is important to hold this pantheist tendency in mind while we look at the apparently animistic aspects of Potiguara cosmopractice, with all its immaterial personhoods and enchanted beings that dwell in their natural environment.

First of all, there is the sacred dimension of Mother Earth as the principal representative of Mother Nature and Her infinite abundance and generosity (although the two are not synonymous, because Nature also includes the luminaries). Earth is the divine mother of all terrestrial life, of us all; She cares for us, providing nutrition; from Earth we have come to life and to Earth we will return. Sometimes, the Earth is also thought of in its planetary dimension, as a giant living being, a super-subject we all are a part of, thus demanding our utmost respect and care.[5]

The Earth represents the female aspect of the divine power of Tupã embodied, above all, in Mother Nature in a very immediate way and it has itself a highly sacred character. Hence, it demands a deep respect, gratitude and worship which goes far beyond a mere protection of natural resources. It is a divinity infinitely more powerful than we human beings, and any disrespect will inevitably result in negative consequences. Thus, it is important to maintain a good relationship with Mother Earth, especially in agriculture. The vast majority of Potiguara still practice some kind of agriculture or gardening, maintaining a direct connection with the soil. They say it is important to care for the soil with affection to keep it "alive"; otherwise it will "die", become barren and even bring bad fortune to the family.

The Earth as land or territory has another important meaning for the Potiguara. It is their ancestral territory, the land so many generations have fought and died for, the place where their Ancestors' spirits are dwelling. Thousands of brave warriors gave their lives for this land, for their people and their way of life. Earth, in this dimension, is inseparably connected with the fate of the Potiguara nation. It is the place where being Potiguara is possible.

The importance of the Earth becomes also visible in the *toré* performances. During the initial prayer, the authorities kneel down on the earth and touch it with their hands, asking for Her protection and Her strength. It is also important to dance the *toré* barefoot to stay connected and feel the Earth. And at the end of each *toré*, the participants will give their thanks to Mother Earth and the other elements of Nature.

The Sun

The Sun is a direct representative of the male strength of Tupã. He is the one who provides all vital energy and who determines the pulsing rhythm of life, night and day, winter and summer. The Sun gives us light, warmth, food and life. But the Sun's masculine energy is also dangerous, as it may burn plantations, cause droughts or do harm to one's health. This is why the Sun has to be kept under control by the night and the moon, his female counterparts.

Although some Potiguara say they venerate the Sun during their morning prayers, there are no specific rituals devoted to the Sun. But there are several rules

[5] I know this part of the story sounds much like the western Gaya-Theory or the Andean *pachamana* concept, but nonetheless, it is part of the imagery explicitly narrated and confirmed by many Potiguara. It is quite probable that this view is just another recent acquirement which has been introduced in the course of inter-ethnic exchanges within the Indigenous movement. However, historical authenticity in any essentialist sense is not my major concern.

determining the right hour for planting, harvesting and other activities that should be protected from exposure to the heat and light of the sun, like making oil from coconut or *dendé* (palm-oil).

The Moon

The Moon is the female counterpart of the Sun and the mistress of time. She is the one who moves the tides of the sea, who controls the cycles of menstruation, gestation and birth, and who determines the right time for planting, fishing, hunting, making coconut oil, dancing the *toré*, and even for cutting one's hair. As a rule, these things should be done during the waxing moon while the waning moon is not a good time for solving important things. The Moon is imagined as a kind of energy that pulls and impels not only the tides of the sea but things in general. The position of the Moon and the tides are so important for so many things that most Potiguara are aware of their phases at any time. One reason may be that most Potiguara used to go fishing, collecting shells and catching crabs in the mangroves, activities demanding a perfect knowledge of the exact position of the tides, and hence, of the Moon. It is quite common even for Potiguara from inland communities to read the position of the tide by a single glimpse at the Moon.

9.1.3 Living Beings

Among the many different kinds of persons that populate the Potiguara cosmos, there are "ordinary" living beings and "enchanted" beings.[6] While the first are biological beings, bound to a physical body which emerges with birth and disappears with death, the latter are not necessarily bound to a physical body, having either already died and passed to the afterlife, or become enchanted beings by some kind of magical transformation. For this reason, living beings are also called "incarnated" beings in contrast to the "disincarnated" character of their enchanted counterparts.

In this section I will first refer to incarnated living beings, basically plants, animals and humans, before referring to the different enchanted beings.

Plants

Plants play a central role in Potiguara life and cosmopractice. Most Potiguara still live (at least in part) from agriculture, and hence, depend on the wellbeing of their plants. Moreover, most work is still done by hand, so that the planter will maintain a direct physical contact with their plants, from sowing to harvest. If the plants do not go well, they will feel bad, too. But plants are not only important for subsistence; they are also appreciated for their healing powers. Every family will grow at

[6] The Potiguara themselves call them *encantados* ("enchanted ones"). I also feel that this term fits much better than "super-natural", which would imply those beings to be something unnatural, while they are actually as natural as any biological being—most of them dwell in the wilderness and some of them are even the guardians of certain natural environments.

least some medical plants in their yard and an adult Potiguara should be able to identify dozens of native plants and their medical properties. The healing powers of these plants are attributed to Tupã, Mother Earth and to the Ancestors who dwell in the territory and who may indicate the right plant during dreams and visions.

There is an intimate relationship between human and plant persons, and some Potiguara say they talk with the plants in their gardens as well as with trees in the woods. Like human persons, plants, too, have an immaterial dimension which may appear to a healer in a dream to reveal their healing potentials.[7] Accordingly, a healer has to treat their plant persons with care and respect, asking for permission before picking leaves, barks or roots, otherwise they cannot expect any cure. In some cases, it may even be necessary for both healer and patient to maintain sexual abstinence before using plants for healing. And it is important to collect medical plants from remote places, far from housing, trails and streets laden with the "heavy" energies of those people who have been passing along.

Some plants are addressed as "masters" and treated like ancestral divinities. This is especially true for the sacred *jurema* tree (*mimosa hostilis*), which is central to Potiguara identity and cosmopractice, but also for other plants frequently used during ritual. These divine plant persons are invoked during healing prayers and numerous *toré* chants.

Animals

Like plants and humans, animals are also persons endowed with an immaterial aspect or spirit. Although the Potiguara frequently hold some domestic animals, like horses, donkeys, dogs, chicken and, more rarely, cattle or pigs, the archetypical animals[8] in Potiguara cosmopractice are rather wildlife they use to hunt and catch, like birds, armadillos, capibaras, snakes, crabs or fish. These beings, who are populating the rivers, mangroves, bushes, woods and the sea, represent the vital force of Nature and maintain an intimate relation with the enchanted beings who are the protectors of these natural realms (*Comadre Florzinha, Pai do Mangue, Mãe d'Água*).[9] Wild animals are commanded, at least to a certain degree, by their protector deities, and will react according to the relations one has established with these enchanted beings. One who behaves disrespectfully will find no game, no crabs and might be attacked by some wild animal or an enchanted being. Some animals may directly serve an enchanted being, like the armadillo who is said to serve *Comadre Florzinha* as her horse, or the bird *pitiguari* who is a messenger. In other cases, an

[7] The active teaching by plant persons during visions and dreams seems to be a frequent phenomenon among Indigenous healers (e.g. Faust (1989) on the Coyaima and Natagaima of Columbia; Langdon and Bear (1992) on the Siona, also from Columbia; Narby (1998) on Ashaninka of Peru; Descola (1996) on the Ashuar of Peru; also my own experiences among the Shuar of Ecuador and the Nasa of Colombia).

[8] "Animal", here, does not stand for a biological category, but rather for a cognitive prototype or a typological category within Potiguara cosmovision.

[9] See below.

enchanted being itself may appear in the form of an animal; and some animals are themselves enchanted beings, like the dolphin and the whale.

Humans

Together with plants, animals and enchanted beings, humans are part of Nature. However, in contrast to those other beings, humans are endowed with reason and morality—they know about good and bad, and they are conscious of the moral value of their actions. However, this is not true for their spirit, which acts much like a little child, an animal or an enchanted being, following its immediate impulses and passions (or at least it may look like they would act this way from the human point of view). Accordingly, a human's immaterial aspect may not always act according to their conscious intents. This spiritual "schizophrenia" can result in incoherent behaviours of one's consciousness and one's spirit. For example, a human person may desire another person's possession or beauty, but still not wish to do any harm to them; however, their envy will grow to a negative "energy"[10] in their spirit, and thus, eventually cause harm to another person, without any conscious intention.[11] Hence, any kind of envy or other negative emotions, conscious or not, can cause "evil eye" (*olhado* or *olho gordo*).[12]

Some people are born with an extraordinary spiritual power, which may be so strong, that it may cause harm not only to other people around them, but also to themself. Such persons have to learn to get control over their immaterial aspect by means of mediumistic techniques, so they can use their abilities consciously in favour (or against) the wellbeing of other persons, thus, becoming healers or *pajés*. However, mediumship is a natural ability of all persons, including all human beings; it is just the intensity and its development which varies from person to person.

When someone dies, their spirit will leave the body, but continue to stay close to their relatives and connected with the territory. They are now an enchanted being or Ancestor, pertaining to the immaterial aspect of the world, a dimension beyond time and space, the limits of the material world. Hence, the territory is full of Ancestors who can be called upon for help and spiritual guidance. Having left their physical body, dead persons are still active family members. Socially, Potiguara personhood is constituted by the extensive kin-relations they maintain to hundreds of relatives,

[10] "Energy" is the term used by the Potiguara concerning to this subject. But of course, the term is all too laden with concepts of Western physics and esoterism to be used without quotes.

[11] The unconscious or involuntary impairment of others by such spiritual "energies" or "witchcraft" has been reported from many different cultural contexts all over the world (e.g. Evans-Pritchard 1976; Hinderling 1981; Descola 1996; et al.).

[12] For example, a person may come to another's garden and admire their plants, thus causing these plants to wither and die. Or someone may become attached to another's child and thereby cause the child to contract *olhado*, to get sick or even die. And a person who treats others with disrespect will attract negative energies, resulting in misfortune, illness or even death. Hence, it is important to avoid both attracting or passing such negative energies, to be polite, generous and respectful, and most importantly, not to envy. Therefore, if someone has a very beautiful plant, the other may comment: "What an ugly plant you have!", expressing both a compliment and the intention not to envy the plant.

including their Ancestors.[13] As a consequence, personhood is not only constituted by social relations, it also transcends time and is bound to the territory where one's Ancestors dwell.

9.1.4 Enchanted Beings

There are different kinds of enchanted beings in the Potiguara's world, most of whom have once been human persons. It follows that most, if not all enchanted beings are sort of Ancestors, too, although this is not always explicitly put this way. However, although utterly distinct from each other, this shared origin may explain why they still share some essential characteristics. In contrast to incarnated living beings, whose essential characteristics are primarily bound to their physical bodies, the essence of enchanted beings is immaterial—despite the fact that each of them has a typical appearance and may even take a physical form. Enchanted persons are neither "bad" nor "good" in any moral sense, although each one has their own personality. This means that one can call for their help both to do good or to do bad, to cure or to kill, while the invoked enchanted person will behave according to the relation one has established with them. To receive an enchanted being's support, one has to become their ally by treating them with respect and doing favours for them. The rules and the means to establish such a reciprocal relation differ and depend on the personality of each enchanted being, but once the ritualistic protocol has been accomplished properly, one can count on their help, no matter what one's purpose.

The Role of Ancestors

The Ancestors are the ultimate reference for Potiguara culture and identity; they are the guardians of "traditional" wisdom and territory; they are the uniting element of Potiguara society and the source of spiritual strength. These invisible spirits of their departed relatives are crowding the territory, where they will stay until the end of the world, offering their support and their wisdom to all generations to come. They may appear in dreams or visions, or be invoked by means of mediumistic rituals. However, as with all enchanted beings, the Ancestors, too, can be called either to

[13] As mentioned above, family ties also play a crucial role in the political organisation of Potiguara society, as it is expected from the individual to vote according to their patriarch. Moreover, many of the important political leaders pertain to certain lineages, tracing back to great leaders in Potiguara history. These characteristics of contemporary Potiguara kinship and political organisation show some parallels compared to the kindreds of historical Tupi nations, suggesting a certain cultural continuity in this respect. However, such social features are also typical of the traditional rural society in the region in general, which is of both European and Indigenous descent, so that it would be difficult to figure out what its exact origins might be. Independently, there might also be another historical explanation for these extended families among the Potiguara, which is based on demography. While at the beginning of the twentieth century there were only a few hundred Potiguara left, three or four generations later there were more than 20,000, all of them descended from a handful of families, sharing the same ancestors.

heal or to cause harm, depending on the intentions of the one who invokes them. Moreover, their presence can be dangerous, especially when the spirit of a late relative refuses to leave their family, as they may draw upon one of their relatives, causing *encosto*, a particularly serious spiritual ailment. Hence, the right place for the Ancestors to stay is the wilderness, to become part of the territory where they are dwelling in the soil, the plants, the animals, the rivers; in short, in Nature. Consequently, the best places to get in contact with the Ancestors are the woods, the waterfalls, rivers and lakes. There are several sacred places in the woods where the Potiguara conduct rituals to call their Ancestors for advice, protection and support. The most emblematic public rituals to conjure the Ancestors are the *toré* and the annual ritual at the "*furnas*", caves where the Ancestors hid from their enemies in mythic times. Moreover, there are several other ritualistic traditions being practiced among the Potiguara, like the *pajelancia,* the *catimbó* and *umbanda*, equally aiming to summon the Ancestors' spirits.

9.1.5 The Enchanted Kingdoms and Their Patrons

The territory of the Potiguara is characterised by its natural diversity, joining distinct environments, each with its particular importance for Potiguara subsistence. First of all, there are the woods, a patchwork of velds and forests (although most of them have been destroyed for the expanding sugar cane monocultures). Then, there are the mangroves, covering the huge deltas of the Mamanguape river at the southern margins of their territory, and the Camaratuba at its northern limits. Finally, there are the rivers, lakes and the sea, representing another aquatic world. Together, these different realms represent wilderness, the part of Nature where humans are just visitors and where they are subject to the mysterious laws of the enchanted beings ruling therein. Each of these three natural environments, also called the "three enchanted kingdoms", has its own patron spirit, enchanted beings who protect their "kingdom" and its (non-human) inhabitants from abusive human intruders.

Comadre Florzinha: Protector of the Woods

The woods are the terrestrial realm of Nature, with all its plants and animals. They are the place to go for hunting and for collecting medicine plants. But they are also the home of the Ancestors' spirits, an enchanted world protected by *Comadre Florzinha*,[14] its patron spirit.

According to the Potiguara, the Comadre is a little Indigenous girl with long, black hair covering most of her naked little body, who lives alone in the woods, caring for and protecting the animals and plants, which she is especially fond of. Many Potiguara can tell stories about encounters with the Comadre and it is very common

[14] Comadre Florzinha means something like "Crony Little Flower", having a slightly ironic, but also a tender and intimate connotation. The Comadre is not only known to the Potiguara, but also to the rural population of the region in general.

to hear her whistle or to find the horses with dreadlocks in their manes, which are put down to the Comadre playing with them. However, the Comadre has not always been an enchanted being. In mythic times, she was a human girl who got lost in the woods, where she finally died. Since then, her spirit has been roaming the woods.

Despite her innocent appearance, Comadre Florzinha is a powerful enchanted being and deserves great respect and caution. A good hunter should never forget to bring her some tobacco or porridge, asking for her permission before hunting, and should avoid cursing in the forest, as his fortune depends on the Comadre's sympathy and consent.[15] Encounters with the Comadre can get really dangerous if she feels disrespected. There are countless stories of hunters who got lost in the wilderness or who were beaten by the Comadre, causing serious disease and even the hunter's death. In other narrations, she will appear to the hunter as a beautiful woman to seduce and take him (that is, his spirit, while his material aspect will die) with her to the enchanted kingdom. But the Comadre is also a spiritual guide who appears in dreams and visions, and which may be incorporated during ritual. There are many *toré* chants evoking a female warrior or guardian of the sacred *jurema* tree,[16] which are also identified with the Comadre as a kind of ancestral *pajé*.

Pai do Mangue: Protector of the Mangroves

The mangroves are mysterious and dangerous places, made up of foul-smelling mud and intertwined roots full of razor-sharp oysters, with myriads of mosquitos attacking whoever dares to enter this inhospitable wilderness. Here in the mangroves, where Nature's dominance becomes evident, humans are only visitors who may be accepted as long as they submit themselves to Her rules. It is a magic realm where the boundaries of reality may shift, where the senses and the mind may be fooled, and where it is easy to get lost.

The *Pai do Mangue*[17] ("Father of the Mangroves") is the guardian of this magic wilderness and all the fishes, crabs and mosquitos living there. He is described as an old man wearing a huge hat and smoking corn husk cigarettes, sometimes dressed like a fisherman, sometimes walking naked, exposing the typical appearance of the traditional crab-collector; and sometimes he may take the form of a crab or another inhabitant of the mangroves. He, too, had once been an ordinary man who got lost and died in the mangroves. There are many stories about encounters with the Pai do

[15] Some hunters even hold it necessary to maintain sexual abstinence before hunting in order to prevent the Comadre from becoming jealous.

[16] Of course, these female characters are reminiscent of Brazilian popular mythology about Iracema, inspired by a romance by José Alencar from 1865 (Alencar 2003), mixing up historical characters and fact with pure fiction. However, such popular myths were also the source of Alencar's writings. Moreover, chroniclers like Lery reported on the important role of the women during ritual, and it is a common feature among several Indigenous cultures for women to become powerful spiritual mediums (e.g. Faust 1994; Perruchon 2003), which is also the case of the Potiguara.

[17] Like the Comadre Florzinha, the Pai do Mangue is not only known to the Potiguara, but also to the rural population between Recife and Natal.

Fig. 9.1 Waterfall (image from private archive)

Mangue and people whom he led astray in the mangroves. And if one listens or perceives something strange, or even encounters the Pai do Mange, one should talk to him showing no fear, expressing one's respect and good intentions, before leaving the mangroves as quickly as possible. However, despite his scary appearance, he is not a malevolent being, although he may punish disrespectful intruders. One who offers him some tobacco and *cachaça* (sugar cane brandy), showing respect to him and the other beings of the mangroves, will find plenty of crabs and fishes, and get home safely (Fig. 9.1).

Mãe d'Água: Protector of the Waters

Water is a very important element for the Potiguara, a famous nation of fishermen and navigators[18] living surrounded by rivers, lakes and the sea. The waters are the

[18] Most etymologies suggest that the name Potiguara comes from an Tupi expression meaning "shrimp-eaters" and the first Europeans described them as great fishermen and navigators (e.g. Lery 1992). Even today, many Potiguara make their living working on ships as sea- or fishermen, or collecting crabs and mussels.

kingdom of abundance and prosperity, reigned by the *Mãe d'Água* ("mother of the waters"), also known as the mermaid.[19] Just like the Comadre and the Pai do Mangue, the Mãe d'Água is an ambiguous being who provides protection to the beings living in her underwater kingdom and decides the fishermen's success, requesting respect and gifts.

There are different individual opinions among the Potiguara about the identity of the Mãe d'Água and the mermaid. While some hold that they are two distinct entities, others argue that they are one and the same entity, with the Mãe d'Água assuming the form of a mermaid when she goes from the river to the sea. And while some witnesses say they saw the Mãe d'Água with a fishtail, like a mermaid, others say she has normal human legs. Be this as it may, both entities are described as beautiful Potiguara women with long, black hair, who may enchant the fishermen with their charm and their voices to take them to the underwater world. But the Mãe d'Água can also be dangerous for children. There are many stories about children who were taken to her underwater world or fell ill with *olhado* caused by her attachment. Even if they are cured by means of a healing ritual, such persons will have to avoid staying too long at the river, especially if they continue to dream of the Mãe d'Água, as she may come for them once again.[20]

---

[19] The Mãe d'Água, also known as *Iara*, is an enchanted being known to rural populations in different parts of Brazil, which has been appropriated by the Brazilian romantics to be presented as part of Brazilian national culture. While it is generally held to trace back to mythologic entities of Indigenous origin, like other divinities of the (sweet) waters (e.g. the myth of serpent Boiuna or the dolphin-spirit between the Tanimuka and Yukuna (Reichel 1987)), it has also been argued that Iara is a character primarily based on European folklore and myths on sirens or mermaids (Casemiro 2012). However, in many Indigenous cosmovisions, water is the element of the underworld where the spirits, first "shamans" and the mythical anaconda serpent dwell (e.g. Reichel 1987; Faust 1989; Langdon and Bear 1992; Baumgartner 1994; Descola 1996; Narby 1998; et al.—compare also Stoller and Olkes 1987 concerning similar concepts in the African contexts). So, although the image of the siren may be of European origin, the idea of an enchanted under-water-world inhabited by powerful entities is certainly a common feature among Indigenous (and other non-modern) cosmopractices. Accordingly, water is an ambivalent element, representing at once life, spiritual power and danger. The one who seeks spiritual knowledge or power may do rituals at lakes, waterfalls or the seaside, while vulnerable persons like children or menstruating women shall avoid coming too close to the waters (also Vieira (2010) explicitly draws a parallel between the Potiguara's image of Mãe d'Água and similarities to recurrent patterns in Amazonian cosmopractices).

[20] While stories about enchanted entities seducing and kidnapping children, young women and fishermen are a recurrent theme in (Latin) American ethnography, Xaver Faust's (1989) description of the Coyaima and Natagaima's cosmology shows particular similarities compared to the Potiguara's stories about the dangers related to encounters with the Mãe d'Água. According to Faust, these people believe that water (a cold element) and its enchanted inhabitants may extract (hot) vital energy from vulnerable persons, like children, menstruating or young women, and those especially exposed to the water, like fishermen and their wives. The inappropriate exposition of children to water may cause "*coco*", an illness similar to the Potiguara's "*olhado*", while young women may dream of underwater spirits resulting in a desire to go and live with them in their underwater world, a phenomenon called "*persecución del água*". However, Faust explicitly highlights the importance of the distinction between "hot" and "cold" aspects as a transversal principle

9.1.6 *Other Mythic Beings*

The different natural and enchanted beings I represented so far can be considered constitutive elements within a more or less coherent cosmological system and are essential for various ritual practices. However, there are several myths about other enchanted beings which are definitively part of Potiguara oral tradition and worldview, but do not play any important role in ritual or represent a systematic category in Potiguara cosmovision—at least not in any explicit way. Nonetheless, these beings do exist in the conception of many Potiguara who frequently refer to these myths and report experiences they had with those enchanted beings.

There are some beings stemming from European mythology which have become part of general Brazilian popular culture with apparently no direct nexus to the Potiguara's cosmological system (if one assumes there really to be such a "system", as I am suggesting here). For example, there are many stories about werewolfs. Some people may indicate neighbours from their villages who made a contract with the devil to transform themselves into such monsters at nights of a full moon and others may even report scary encounters they had with them.[21] Also frequently reported are witches who come at night to steal the little children from their beds, and some Potiguara are convinced there are still women among them who are witches. There is also a local myth about witches who used to live in a village in the Mamanguape delta called Coqueirinho. According to this narration, these witches used to travel in canoes, returning with many unknown plants from far away which can still be found there. This local myth may trace back to the historical persecution of "witches" by the Inquisition, as there is even a graveyard in Coqueirinho called the "witches' cemetery".[22]

A quite popular local myth tells the story of *Compadre Aibino*, a boy who died in the woods and whose spirit may appear in form of a little fireball, called *batatão* ("big potato"). Lost alone in the woods, Aibino wants to be close to other people, doing no harm to them, but if someone calls him "*Batatão*" instead of "Aibino" he may get angry and burn them.

Another important local myth about St Michael goes back to a dead Potiguara child, too. A long time ago, the grave of a dead boy at the local cemetery cracked in the form of a cross. When his grave was opened to see what had happened, his body had not decomposed, and was thus declared to be the living image of St Michael, which would be exhibited during centuries in the Church of the village São Miguel. When the old church finally tumbled down in the 1980s, the Saint was brought to

of the Coyaima's and Natagaima's cosmology, with water being a "cold" element and adolescence and menstruation being "hot" states etc., which is a principle almost entirely missing in the Potiguara's contexts.

[21] Actually, one of my interlocutors with mediumistic abilities even told me in detail how one of his drunken pals turned into a werewolf and then attacked him. Following his narration, he defended himself with a knife, injuring the monster, and the next day his friend had a wound at the very same part of his body.

[22] Dantas et al. (2017).

Rome, where he remains until this day. In exchange for the original Saint, another image made of wood was sent back to be exhibited in the church of São Francisco.[23]

Some animals, like the dolphin and the whale, have also once been human beings who went to live in the sea. There are many other local myths, like one about an entity called the "screamer" (*gritador*), who is said to be the spirit of a murderer screaming for someone he can throw his guilt upon; about a procession of the dead passing through the village at midnight by full moon; about a hairy hand that pushes swimmers into the depth of lakes and rivers; about hidden treasures in an enchanted lake; along with other mysterious stories of this kind.[24]

Although these narratives do not show much direct relation with each other, most of them share the common theme of some metamorphoses from human form into an enchanted being. The first two myths on werewolfs and witches, both belonging to Brazilian popular culture of European origin, ascribe the metamorphoses to a contract with the devil, transforming human beings temporarily into malevolent daemons at midnight and at the full moon. In the local myths, humans are permanently transformed into enchanted beings through death. Hence, the local narrations are basically about mythical Ancestor spirits, thus sharing some parallels with the myths of the Comadre Florzinha, Pai do Mangue and Mãe d'Água.

9.1.7 Immaterial Agency

In Potiguara cosmopractice, the material world is moved by different immaterial agents, all of them ultimately representing different aspects of Tupã, the immaterial force or order out of which the material universe of Mother Nature is continuously emanating. The idea of different "forces" or "energies" is very present in the Potiguara's narrations about cosmological concepts and may throw some light on the relation between material and immaterial aspects.

Generally speaking, all that is has some immaterial dimension or aspect, while, on the other hand, some immaterial entities may have no fixed material form. Such immaterial aspects can be called by different names, like "energy", "force", "spirit", "soul", and so on, depending on the context in which they become relevant, but they all have in common that they are autonomous actants who do not just react mechanically to outer stimuli.

[23] In another version of this myth, the body of the boy was brought to the church by his parents. But the next day, his body had disappeared from the church and mysteriously returned to his grave. The priest saw the miracle and brought the body to Rome and returned with the image of St Michael. There are many other stories about the origin of the image of the St Michael, but all of them agree that he goes back to a dead Potiguara, and hence, is an enchanted Ancestor.

[24] Further readings on Potiguara mythology: Palitot (2005); Marques et al. (2009); Vieira (2010); Gerlic and Zoettl (2011); Barcellos (2012); Mendonça (2014); Dantas et al. (2017); Batista et al. (2021a).

Spirit, Thought and Faith

When we talk about "beings" or "persons", we assume the existence of some subject-like entity, gifted with at least some kind of "will". Such wilful beings will always have a "soul" or "spirit", but not necessarily a physical body. In other words, "persons", in this sense, are subject-like immaterial entities some of whom can be connected to a physical body for a period of time. This means that such persons not only *have* a spirit, they *are* spirits in the first place, and they may assume a physical form under certain circumstances. Moreover, all persons share some common features: they demand to be respected, they enter in reciprocal relations with each other, they can provoke positive or negative effects in each other which may be reflected in the physical dimension, resulting both in cure or sickness, and so on. This is true for enchanted beings as much as for living beings like humans, animals or plants. As a consequence, there is no fundamental difference between the spirits of humans and those of animals, plants, dead Ancestors or other enchanted beings—they are all persons alike. However, as long as such an immaterial personhood is bound to a particular physical form, it will also assume the particular way of being and perceiving related to it.[25] From a human point of view, the greatest difference between human persons and non-human persons seems to be our moral *consciousness* about good and bad deeds. Our human consciousness is, therefore, a particular perspective bound to our human body, and hence, both disappear together after death, while the spirit persists. However, our conscious thoughts and emotions are equally understood as some kind of immaterial "energy", or agency, able to provoke effects in the real world. To think or feel negatively will have negative effects and to think positively will have positive results. Thought itself is an immaterial actant with the power to evoke other immaterial forces like enchanted beings or Tupã by means of faith, which can be understood as kind of an alignment of one's conscious thoughts and emotions with one's (normally unconscious) spirit. Faith, in this sense, is the bridge which connects consciousness with the spirit, giving access to the mysteries and hidden powers of the invisible world where the enchanted beings dwell. In other words, faith is the key to magic.[26]

---

[25] Notably, this relation is inverted during the intermittent incarnation of a disincarnated person, who will take control over the body and behave in its individual characteristic manner while in this body. This is also the reason why I am careful not to simply apply Viveiros de Castro's perspectivistic concept of "shamanism" to the context of the Potiguara, although there are some important similarities.

[26] This is, of course, a quite far-reaching interpretation, which is why I was careful to discuss these ideas with several *pajés* and local experts on Potiguara cosmopractices, and I can say that all of them agreed with this interpretation. I use the term "magic" here in the sense of parapsychological abilities to foresee or interfere in the course of events by means of non-causal, or "spiritual" operations, as usually attributed to the *pajés* and other mediumistic practitioners, often referred to as "shamans", "witch-doctors", "medicine-men", and the like.

Words
Words have power. They are the objectivised manifestation of thought in the material world. As such, words are means to reinforce the effects of thoughts and faith. This is the meaning of sacred chants, prayers and magic spells. And it is for this reason that it makes a difference whether or not we talk about the dreams or visions we had. For once a dream is being pronounced and revealed to others, it is said to come true more likely, gaining in predictive power through the physical manifestation of thoughts in the form of vocal enunciation.

Wind
Just like earth and water, the air we breathe is a life-giving natural element. It also constitutes the wind that controls the weather, that brings rain or sun, heat or cooling, thus deciding the success or misfortune of the plantations as well as fishing, both being fundamental to the subsistence of Potiguara families. However, in its immaterial dimension, the wind may also bring new thoughts and serve as a vehicle for both positive and negative "energies", eventually causing healing or illness, bringing good or bad news. Such "energies" may have their origin in suffering persons or obsessive spirits. Hence, some Potiguara hide from certain kinds of wind to prevent being affected by the bad "energies" it might bring. But the wind is also mentioned in some *toré* chants and it plays an important role in healing ritual where the *pajé* transfers good "energies" to the patient and expels the bad ones by his breath (*sopro*).

9.1.8 Birth and Death

The birth of a child is the beginning of a new life, both physically and spiritually, a new body and a new spirit, a new person and a new relative. However, this new person is also the heir of an ancestral lineage and tradition, and will 1 day become an Ancestor, too. Birth is always part of a cycle and from the very beginning, the child is part of and a result of a collective which transcends time as well as the boundary between the material and the immaterial dimension.

There is no collective narration or commonly-shared opinion among the Potiguara which would explain the provenience of a new-born's spirit. But there is quite clear agreement that once the child is born, the life of this person will depend on the healthy coexistence of their spirit and body. If either should be harmed or taken away, their life as a living being will end, leaving their disincarnated immaterial aspect behind. As discussed before, their reasonable, conscious self will die together with their body, while their immaterial aspect will remain and continue behaving according to its amoral emotions and affections. In this aspect, the dead's spirits or Ancestors may have more in common with the spirit of a new-born child than with an adult person. On the other hand, the Ancestors are also the holders of great wisdom, resembling more the image of the elders. But, maybe wisdom has less in common with reason than with emotive experience?

Anyhow, the life and wellbeing of a living person depends on the integrity of their physical as much as their immaterial aspect, while their identity depends on their conscious self-perception and position within a time-transcending network of kin-relations. The disincarnated person, on the other hand, exists fundamentally through their relations to living beings, and particularly, to their progeny.[27]

9.2 Health and Sickness

In Potiguara cosmopractice, material and immaterial dimensions are intimately related in such a way that any event in the immaterial dimension will inevitably impinge on the material dimension, and vice versa. As a consequence, the health of an incarnated being, like a human person, will depend on the integrity of both their material and their immaterial aspects. Once either of these aspects is affected or taken away, the person will get sick or die. Hence, there are both material and immaterial causes resulting in different kinds of diseases. While some ailments have their causes in the material dimension, having a direct effect on the physical body, others may be caused by some immaterial agent, affecting primarily (but not only) the immaterial aspect of a person. Accordingly, the Potiguara distinguish (more or less explicitly) between bodily (*doença do corpo*) and spiritual diseases (*doença d'alma*).[28]

This seems to be a clear-cut distinction at first sight. However, it turns out to be quite fuzzy when looked at in more detail. Despite most afflictions being conceived in terms of bodily diseases, this does not necessarily exclude immaterial causes. Actually, some apparently physical ailments may be caused—more or less directly—by spiritual diseases or some immaterial agent. Also, a person whose immaterial aspect is debilitated for any reason may get ill more easily than a spiritually strong person, without this spiritual weakness being necessarily the primary cause of a physical ailment. The defining point seems to be that bodily diseases *primarily* manifest in the physical aspect of a person and that they have a "natural" *cause*, that is, they are not provoked by any "person".[29]

[27] There is an interesting contradiction between the general image of the Ancestors as elders or grandparents, and the myths about enchanted beings like the Cumadre Florzinha, Mãe d'Água, Cumpadre Aibino and St Michael who are said to be spirits of deceased children, but nevertheless representing important ancestral entities who may also appear in the form of adult humans.

[28] Of course, this traditional distinction between bodily and spiritual diseases is not a fixed taxonomic system and there are some cases where different healers would suggest different definitions. However, in most cases, there was a surprising correspondence between the opinions of the traditional specialists who collaborated with our research. Similar distinctions between "natural" and "spiritual" causes of sickness are also common in a range of other non-modern medical systems (e.g. Hinderling 1981; Greifeld and Schmidt 2003; Kutalek 2003).

[29] Such diagnostic distinctions along etiological parameters rather than symptoms appear to be a common feature among non-modern medical systems (Hinderling 1981). Etiologies, that is the systematic attribution of supposed causes to certain symptomatic patterns or syndromes, are deeply rooted in the particular cosmological models and their social and cultural contexts (Greifeld 2003).

Bodily Diseases

Bodily diseases[30] comprise all kinds of different maladies with a variety of symptoms. However, though many of them show symptoms comparable to those we find among the diagnostic categories of modern biomedicine, they may be associated with quite different causes, differing in the etiological explanations, and hence, indicate different kinds of therapy, too.

Table 9.1 Headache

Diagnosis	**Headache**
Cause	Ray of sun- or moonlight entered the head; negative thoughts or preoccupation; spiritual disease
Therapy	Magic prayer with symbolic gestures using plant leaves and/or a bottle filled with water (the bottle is put on the patient's head until the water begins to bubble by force of the magic prayer); plants (tea, wet pack, bath, incense/smoke) prepared according to the position of moon
Curing principle	The words of the prayer together with faith release the spiritual power of the healer and invoke benevolent spirits; the water in the bottle, wet pack and plant leaves absorb noxious energies; vital forces of the plants inspired by Nature/Tupã, the Ancestors and the Moon; smoke invokes benevolent spirits and expels the bad ones

Table 9.2 Injury

Diagnosis	**Injury**
Cause	Physical lesion
Therapy	Magic prayer/chanting with ritual (using *maracá* and pipe); plants (tea, wet pack, unguent, incense/smoke) prepared according to the position of moon
Curing principle	The words of the prayer together with faith release the spiritual power of the healer and invoke benevolent spirits; vital forces of the plants inspired by Nature/Tupã, the Ancestors and the Moon

Table 9.3 Fracture

Diagnosis	**Fracture**
Cause	Physical lesion
Therapy	Stone powder (internal use); plants (sap, tea, wet pack)
Curing principle	Hardness of the stone transferred to the broken bone; vital forces of the plants inspired by Nature/Tupã and the Ancestors

Table 9.4 Infection or parasites

Diagnosis	**Infection or parasites**
Cause	Noxious energy brought by someone
Therapy	Plants (tea, bath, syrup, incense/smoke) prepared according to the position of the moon; prayer to thank the enchanted being for their help
Curing principle	Vital forces of the plants inspired by Nature/Tupã, the Ancestors and the Moon; smoke invokes benevolent spirits and expels the bad ones; the words of the prayer together with faith release the spiritual power of the healer to invoke God's help

[30] Tables 9.1, 9.2, 9.3, 9.4, 9.5, 9.6, 9.7, 9.8, 9.9 and 9.10.

Table 9.5 Herpes zoster (*cobreiro*)

Diagnosis	**Herpes zoster (*cobreiro*)**
Cause	Inflammation of the skin
Therapy	Magic prayer with symbolic gestures using plant leave; necklace made of castor beans confected according to the position of the Moon
Curing principle	The words of the prayer together with faith release the spiritual power of the healer to invoke God's help; vital forces of the plants inspired by Nature/Tupã and the Ancestors

Table 9.6 Diarrhoea

Diagnosis	**Diarrhoea**
Cause	Wrong alimentation; helminthiasis; virus infection
Therapy	Plants (tea); tapioca diluted in water; preparation according to the position of the Moon
Curing principle	Vital forces of the plants inspired by Nature/Tupã, the Ancestors and the Moon

Table 9.7 Female infertility

Diagnosis	**Female infertility**
Cause	Disfunction of the body; lack of energy
Therapy	Fat from the opossum (*Didelphis albiventris*) prepared according to the position of the Moon
Curing principle	The animal's vital energy; vital forces of the plants inspired by Nature/Tupã and the Ancestors

Table 9.8 "Choking" (*engasgo*)

Diagnosis	**"Choking" (*engasgo*)**
Cause	Something got stuck in one's throat (fish bone, etc.)
Therapy	Magic prayer with symbolic gestures using plant leaves, and a cup of water
Curing principle	The words of the prayer together with faith release the spiritual power of the healer to invoke God's help; water helps to flush the harmful object down

Table 9.9 "New/thick blood" (*Sangue Novo*)

Diagnosis	**"New/thick blood" (*Sangue Novo*)**
Cause	Too much blood (=energy)
Therapy	Clay/earth from an anthill (internal use); Plants (tea) preparation according to the position of the Moon; coconut oil to thin the blood
Curing principle	Earth is a cool element and the source, but also the end of life, so the clay will equilibrate the excess of vital energy; the earth from the anthill comes from deep down in the earth and is therefore pure and cool

Table 9.10 "Dropped sternum" (*Espinhela Caida*)

Diagnosis	**"Dropped sternum" (*Espinhela Caida*)**[a]; Symptoms are flabbiness, fatigue, pains in the back and in the chest
Cause	Exaggerated or inadequate physical exertion
Therapy	Magic prayer with symbolic gestures using plant leaves and ritual: the chest is measured with a rope for diagnosis. If positive, the patient is fastened with his hands up during the ritual; finally, a special massage is applied to "close" the thorax and the fingers and toes are pushed; additionally, a cup with hot air on the chest may push the thorax into the right position
Curing principle	The words of the prayer together with faith release the spiritual power of the healer to invoke help of God and enchanted beings; physical effect of therapeutic treatment

[a]This diagnosis is part of traditional folk medicine all over Brazil (Vargas 2005; Hutchinson 1981; Almeida 2013); among others), including Afro-Brazilian traditions, spiritism and Indigenous groups, as well as in Portugal (Gallop 1961). It seems very likely that this diagnostic concept, which is actually a syndrome of a complex of different symptoms, is rooted in Portuguese folk medicine and was brought from there to Brazil, were it has been registered since the seventeenth century (Almeida 2013)

For a better understanding, I will list some examples together with the suggested possible causes (etiology), indicated therapies and supposed curing principles.[31]

It is easy to see the great mismatch between the Potiguara way of understanding sickness and healing compared to the biomedical approach we are normally used to. Although some "traditional" diagnoses may at first sight seem to share some similarities with bio-medical diagnosis (like injury, fraction, infertility, diarrhoea or herpes zoster), equally indicating physical causes, the difference comes with the indicated therapeutic provisions. In contrast to biomedicine's straightforward approach of curing physical maladies by physical means, "traditional" Potiguara therapy aims to activate some immaterial curing principle instead. Moreover, there are diagnostic categories completely unknown to biomedicine, like "dropped sternum" or "new blood". And even in those cases where the "traditional" therapy simply consists of the application of medical plants, the curing principle is not some chemical compound, but the vital energy of the plant as a living being, that is, the plant's immaterial principle or aspect. These differences in the conception of sickness and healing compared to biomedical concepts are embedded within the general cosmological model, where the physical realm of Nature is understood as an emanation of the immaterial dimension constituted by Tupã and all those enchanted beings that represent his multiple aspects. This cosmological principle becomes even more evident in the second category of maladies, the spiritual diseases.

Spiritual Diseases

In contrast to bodily diseases, spiritual diseases[32] are caused by immaterial agents acting primarily on the victim's immaterial aspect. However, once the immaterial aspect has been affected, the person's material aspect will be harmed, too, showing

[31] Tables 9.1, 9.2, 9.3, 9.4, 9.5, 9.6, 9.7, 9.8, 9.9, 9.10, 9.11, 9.12, 9.13 and 9.14.

[32] Tables 9.11, 9.12, 9.13 and 9.14.

Table 9.11 "Evil eye" (*olhado/olho gordo*)

Diagnosis	**"Evil eye" (*olhado/olho gordo*)**[a]
Cause	Envy, jealousy, desire or passion experienced by some living or enchanted person towards the victim, thus "sucking" their immaterial aspect or transferring "bad energy" to them
Therapy	Magic prayer with symbolic gestures using plant leaves; mediumistic ritual with an embodied entity; mediumistic ritual under trance to get in contact with ancestor spirits and discover appropriate remedy; sacred plants (tobacco smoke & jurema wine)
Curing principle	The words of the prayer together with faith release the spiritual power of the healer to invoke help of God and enchanted beings; mediumistic ability of the healer to act upon the immaterial dimension; spiritual power of the incorporated enchanted being or Ancestor spirit; spiritual power of sacred plants

[a]"Evil eye" is, of course, a category of spiritual diseases known all over Latin America as well as in European folk medicine. Similar concepts can also be found in other Indigenous contexts all over the world and refer to what has been termed "witchcraft" by Evans-Pritchard (1976) in the African context (compare also Hinderling 1981)

Table 9.12 "Persecution" (*encosto*)

Diagnosis	**"Persecution" (*encosto*)**[a]
Cause	A disincarnated being leaps on the victim, taking their vital energy
Therapy	Magic prayer with symbolic gestures using plant leaves; mediumistic ritual with an embodied entity; plants (baths, smoke)
Curing principle	The words of the prayer together with faith release the spiritual power of the healer to invoke help of God and enchanted beings; mediumistic ability of the healer to act upon the immaterial dimension; spiritual power of the incorporated enchanted being or Ancestor spirit; spiritual power of the sacred plants

[a]The idea that the spirits of dead relatives may want to stay close to their relatives thereby (involuntarily) "sucking" their vital energy or "kidnapping" their "soul" is a widespread concept among Indigenous nations (e.g. Faust 1989; Descola 1996; among others). Similar ideas about creeping spirits who may leap on the living are also common among Afro-Brazilian religious groups as well as Kardecist spiritism

Table 9.13 "Curse" (*botado, quebrante*)

Diagnosis	**"Curse" (*botado, quebrante*)**[a]
Cause	Purposeful use of mediumistic abilities to invoke enchanted beings to do harm to the victim; sorcery, also described as magic "arrow"
Therapy	Magic prayer with symbolic gestures using plant leaves; mediumistic ritual with an embodied entity; plants (tobacco smoke & jurema wine)
Curing principle	The words of the prayer together with faith release the spiritual power of the healer to invoke help of God and enchanted beings; mediumistic ability of the healer to act upon the immaterial dimension; spiritual power of the incorporated enchanted being or Ancestor spirit; spiritual power of the sacred plants

[a]This is probably the prototypical case of "sorcery" or "black magic", as described in countless ethnographic accounts on such practices all over the world. The belief in sorcery, that is in the intentional use of mediumistic abilities to harm other persons, is a common feature of Indigenous cosmopractices and a major reason for warfare and vendetta (Hinderling 1981; Faust 1989; Descola 1996; Narby 1998; Greifeld and Schmidt 2003; Perruchon 2003; Wörrle 2004; Fernandes 2006; among others). Similar concepts can also be found among other ethnic and religious groups in Brazil, especially in Afro-Brazilian religions like *cantomblé* and *umbanda*

Table 9.14 "Break down" (*enguiço*)

Diagnosis	**"Break down" (*enguiço*)**[a]
Cause	Passing across the victim or one of their belongings by a menstruating[b] woman or a man who just had sexual intercourse with a menstruating woman, thus transferring (wilfully or not) impure negative energy to the victim
Therapy	Magic prayer and ritual using plant incenses to discover the causer, followed by a ritual to undo the crossing by having the causer redo the pass across the victim in the opposite direction (and other secret procedures)
Curing principle	The words of the prayer together with faith release the spiritual power of the healer to invoke help of God and enchanted beings; inverted crossing reverts the situation, the causer takes their bad energies back; plant incenses attract good energies and expel the negative ones

[a]"*Enguiço*" is also an expression common to Brazilian and Portuguese folk knowledge, although by far less popular in use than concepts like "*olhado*" or "*botado*". However, it is generally used in a similar sense as being "cursed" or "bewitched". The use of the term in the specific meaning as described by the Potiguara, (with its explicit reference to menstruating women as its cause) seems to be a regional adaptation

[b]Menstruation is perceived as a moment of "openness" of the woman. This means that menstruating woman is vulnerable to external "energies", but also to exuding her excessive "energies" (remembering that blood represents vital energy, as discussed above). For this reason there are several taboos concerning menstruating women, like sexual abstinence, alimentary restrictions, and basically staying away from any kind of important activity or object. Conceptions of menstruation as both a state of vulnerability and impurity, representing danger for others, together with respective taboos, are very common among Indigenous people (e.g. Faust 1989; also my own observations among Indigenous groups in Brazil, Bolivia, Ecuador and Colombia)

all different kinds of physical and psychiatric symptoms, including headache, flabbiness, diarrhoea, depression, loss of appetite, and even death. As a general characteristic, symptoms of spiritual diseases cannot be attributed to a specific "natural" cause in any trivial way. Despite the great variety of possibly related symptoms, they can be traced back to one of four different types of spiritual diseases:

What immediately calls attention is the fact that despite each type of spiritual disease being attributed to a specific group of possible causes, three out of the four of them will receive the same therapeutic care[33] (only "break down" receives a special treatment). Furthermore, there are parallels between the methods to cure both bodily and spiritual diseases, with both generally including prayers, ritual and the use of plants. The reason is, of course, that from the viewpoint of Potiguara cosmovision everything and every event is ultimately related to events in the immaterial dimension, and hence, demands a response within this realm, too. Accordingly, bodily diseases with "natural" causes may also receive care directed to their immaterial aspect. However, even though some "natural" causes may include immaterial principles (e.g. sun-rays; negative, excessive or insufficient "energy"), they do not result from the actions of a "person", that is, some intentional subjectivity acting in the immaterial dimension, as is the case with spiritual diseases. Nevertheless, this does not mean that those "persons" necessarily act with the intention to harm the

[33]Note that the quoted therapeutic treatments are optional or complementary and may not necessarily be applied all together. The mediumistic techniques of incarnation and trance in particular are rarely enacted during the same ritual.

victim. As already mentioned above, in the immaterial dimension, human moral categories of good and bad are insignificant. Disincarnated beings may well become harmful exactly because they feel passionately for an incarnated person, as typically occurs in the case of "persecution", often caused by deceased relatives who feel too attached to their family to go away. Similarly, "evil eye" may be caused by a person who feels attracted to the victim, thus feeling jealousy or envy, but not necessarily intending to harm the victim. And even in the case of "curse", where an enchanted person has intentionally been activated in order to harm the victim, the enchanted being will simply obey their role within the reciprocal relation with the person who asked them for a favour. Hence, it is not the disincarnated person who is the "bad" one, but the incarnated person who activated them to do harm. Similarly, "cruising" can be used to do harm, but it can also be an unintended accident, and it can be reverted by the person responsible. Just like mediumistic rituals or magic prayers, "cruising" someone or someone's belongings is just another dispositive to operate some immaterial agency for whatever purpose, be it for good or for bad.

9.3 Spiritual Practices and Healing Rituals

Rituals are probably the most visible and intense expressions of cosmological beliefs and ideas. For a long time, the Potiguara have been practicing a wide range of rituals stemming from various religious and spiritual traditions. While the vast majority was born Catholic, many became Protestants in recent years. Yet most of them also still participate in ancestral ritual, too. Moreover, the historical presence of the *catimbó* and other spiritual traditions, like the *jurema*, *umbanda* and Kardecism remains. It is quite common for a person to participate in two or more different religious or spiritual cults in the course of their life or even to practice several religions in parallel (a common habit among the Brazilian population in general). Consequently, there has always been considerable transfer between different rituals. Of course, it is not possible to offer a clear definition concerning which of those rituals and its elements should be considered as "traditional", especially because there is no consensus between the Potiguara themselves. All of this confusion notwithstanding, I will give a brief overview of different rituals and spiritual practices following the typological categories used by the Potiguara themselves.

The Toré

The *toré* is certainly the most prominent and emblematic manifestation of Potiguara cultural identity as well as of Indigenous groups of the Brazilian northeast in general. It has been argued that the *toré* resulted from more recent historical processes of cultural exchange within an ethnicity-based political discourse[34]; but it is also clear that it follows the tradition of the circular dances of their Ancestors, the historical Tupi nations, as described by the chroniclers.[35] While the *toré* of the Potiguara

[34] E.g. Nascimento (1994); Oliveira (1998).

[35] E.g. Lery (1992), as mentioned above.

was first mentioned in 1913,[36] it probably emerged centuries before in the context of the missions, as a result of a process of mutual adaptation between Catholicism and ancestral spiritual practices. As far as written documents and the elder's memory reach back the Potiguara have been dancing the *toré* during the feast of their Patron St Michael, and several of its chants refer to God, Jesus Christ, the Virgin Mary and different Catholic saints. As with St Michael, who was turned into an Ancestor by Potiguara mythology, the *toré* has been serving as a means for appropriating and adapting Catholicism to the Potiguara's ancestral heritage. But in the melting pots of the missions, there was also cultural exchange between different Indigenous nations and Afro-Brazilians. Hence, the Potiguara also used to dance the *coco* (a regional circular dance of Afro-Brazilian origin), adopted the *zabumba* (an African drum) to their *toré*, and introduced the *jurema*-cult (probably from neighbouring Indigenous nations). Due to the violent persecution of Indigenous and Afro-Brazilian cults and religions during the twentieth century, most Potiguara ceased to practice the *toré* and other "traditional" rituals, which were later only revived in the course of the reinvigorating Indigenous movement and the struggle for their lands since the 1980s. Interethnic collaboration with Indigenous brother nations from all over Brazil influenced the way the Potiguara enacted their *toré* once again. Moreover, motivated by this powerful revival of their cultural identity and ritual practices, some Potiguara introduced new vocals to their *toré*, which they had received from the Ancestors during dreams and mediumistic experiences.

Be this as it may, the *toré* is a living tradition of great symbolic value, not only for the Potiguara's ethnic identity, but also for their spirituality, which is the reason why I present it in the first place. Currently, the *toré* is being practiced in many Potiguara communities and during all kinds of different events, including graduation ceremonies, political demonstrations, academic events, internal assemblies, full-moon rituals, along with the big annual ritual of the official "Indians' Day" (*dia do índio*) on the 19th of April and the festivals of St Michael in September (Figs. 9.2, 9.3 and 9.4). The significance of the *toré* is multilayered; some elders say at times they would dance the *toré* as a playful game ("*brincadeira*"), together with other popular dances like the *coco* and the *ciranda*; but the *toré* owes its importance to its role as a means to invoke the Ancestor's spirits, and as a symbol for ethnic identity and unity. The enactment of a *toré* may vary depending on occasion, location, community, participants and the leading group which "pulls" the ritual. However, a *toré* will generally follow the same basic ritual protocol and choreography.

There are no restrictions or distinctions to the participation in a *toré* concerning age or sex, so that typically men, women, children and elders will sing and dance together, following the same choreography. Frequently, even non-Indigenous spectators are invited to participate. However, there is always a group of persons with higher social status who will "pull" the ritual, generally including a *pajé*, some *caciques, troncos velhos* (respectable elder leaders) and younger leaders from the Indigenous movement.[37] The leading group will take its position in the centre of the

[36] Palitot and Júnior (2004).

[37] External visitors of higher status, like politicians or important indigenists, may also be invited to the leading group in the centre.

Fig. 9.2 Regional conference on Indigenous education, Fortaleza, 2017 (image from private archive)

Fig. 9.3 Aldeia do Forte, Baia da Traição, 2016 (image from private archive)

Fig. 9.4 Annual Potiguara assembly, Aldeia São Francisco, 2018 (image from private archive)

location, while the other participants will form one or more circles around their leaders. The leaders and those participants who wish to demonstrate their commitment with their tradition and ethnic identity will use a typical dress and body paintings made with (red) *urucum* and (black) *jenipapo* ink.

The *toré* begins with an opening ritual, all participants kneeling down, touching the ground with their hands and remaining in silence. Meanwhile, the spiritual leaders at the centre will enkindle incenses and ritual pipes with sacred herbs, blowing smoke on their *maracas*, and beginning their prayer—sometimes in loud voice, sometimes in silence. After the initial prayer, the *pajé* may speak up, praising Tupã, Mother Nature, the Ancestors and other sacred entities. Frequently, *jurema* wine[38] is offered to the participants, before the *maracas* begin rattling, followed by the drum, the flute, and the chanting and then dancing begins. There are many different vocals, all with their own characteristic melody, a few of them with their own choreography, but most following the same repetitive steps. Most

[38] There are many different recipes for the preparation of this sacred liquid, always including *jurema* together with other herbs, often also honey and alcohol. However, some Potiguara object to the use of *jurema*, arguing that in old times the Potiguara would have used *caui* instead and that the use of *jurema* has been imported from other Indigenous nations, or that it is related to Afro-Brazilian cults. There is an ongoing discussion on this subject, with as many different opinions being defended as there are spokespersons.

chants are composed by two pairs of short verses, each pair being repeated two times before passing on with the next pair, reiterating the text in this sequence several times. Here are some examples:

Caboquinha da jurema, eu dancei o seu toré, *Para me livrar da flecha dos tapuias Canindé.* *Reis Canindé, oh Reis Canindé,* *Palmas de jurema pra Reis Canindé.*	Little *Caboca*[39] of the *jurema* tree, I danced your *toré,* To free myself from the arrows[40] of the savage *Canindé.*[41] Oh, kings of the *Canindé*, oh kings of the *Canindé*, Smacking with *jurema* at the kings of *Canindé.*
Eu tava sentado na Pedra Fina, o Rei dos índios mandei chamar, *Caboca índia, índia guerreira, caboca índia do jurema.* *Com meu bodoque eu sacudo a flecha, com meu bodoque eu vou atirar,* *Caboca índia, índia guerreira, caboca índia do jurema.*	I was sitting at the fine stone, calling for the king of the indians, Indian woman, indian warrior, woman of the *jurema* tree. With my bow I shatter the arrow, with my bow I will shoot, Indian woman, indian warrior, woman of the *jurema* tree.
Ai, Caboca de Pena,[42] *ai Caboca de Pena,* *Tem pena de mim, tem dó.* *Minhas Caboca de Pena, eu chamei ela pra vir me ajudar,* *Pra ver a força da jurema, cadê a força que a jurema dá?!*	Oh, *Caboca* of the feathers, oh, *Caboca* of the feathers, Have a heart for me, have a heart. My *Caboca* of the feathers, I called her to come for help, To see the power of the *jurema* tree, where is the force the *jurema* gives?!

The repetitive drumming, rattling, singing and dancing may go on for hours, creating a strong synesthetic experience (together with the effect of the alkaloids contained in the *jurema* wine), inducing a state of trance among the more sensitive participants. One may easily get into a meditative state of exclusively situational awareness, and suddenly experience only the *toré* with its magic chants, calling for the Ancestors. Sometimes, when everyone reaches such a mediumistic state of consciousness, feeling the Ancestors' presence, the Potiguara say it was a "strong" (*forte*) *toré*. During a strong *toré*, sensitive participants frequently get "manifested", falling into states of deep trance or even possession by an enchanted entity, depending on their personal mediumistic tendency.

Some *torés* are even led by an incorporated Ancestor, also called "master", which entered the body of the *pajé*. During such *torés*, several participants may incorporate different "masters". Once manifested, they will speak with the voice of an old man or woman, using the typical frumpy speech of the masters. From time to time they will dance wildly, fidgeting with their lance or bow, and yell like a bird or an animal. Once they calm down again, the masters begin their "work", curing those

[39] Here, the term *Caboca*, meaning "indian woman", refers to a female Ancestor spirit.

[40] Here, the "arrows" refer to magic arrows or sorcery.

[41] The *Canindé* are a so called *tapuia,* that is, a non-Tupi nation which were among the historical enemies of the Potiguara.

[42] "*Pena*" is a homonym meaning both "feather" and "pity".

who need help, blowing smoke through their inverted pipes on the patient's body, giving good advice, alerting them to the envy of their enemies.[43] On such occasions, the entities will be treated with a mixture of great respect and cheerful complicity, as one would expect to treat an elder relative. It is a celebration of unity between the generations, including those who already passed away a long time ago.

In sum, the *toré* is much more than a political symbol for their ethnicity or a practice with the function of producing social unity; it is an instrument to get into contact with the Ancestors and to benefit from their strength, their wisdom and to receive a cure.

Healing Rituals

The *pajes'* leading role during the *toré* as a public enactment of mediumistic unity with the Ancestors is certainly the most visible proof of their importance as spiritual leaders. However, the *pajés* also have an important role as healers. Their healing rituals are realised in private, involving only themselves, the patient and, sometimes, an assistant. During these rituals, which are also called *pajelancia*, the *pajé* will make use of different ritualistic dispositives, including smoke (in the form of incants and a pipe to blow smoke on the patient), trance, magic prayers,[44] chants, baths, plants, the *maracá*, and sometimes, a drum. Each *pajé* has their own doctrine and style, and will apply these elements in different combinations, depending on their intuition and the individual needs concerning each case. However, no matter

[43] Such particularly intense *torés* are mostly enacted at night within a circle of participants who are interested in mediumistic experiences and who may also practice *umbanda* or *catimbó*. In fact, there are strong parallels between the "traditional" *toré* and these syncretistic cults. But while some Potiguara defend the *catimbó* as an old "tradition" among the Potiguara, stressing its ancestral origin, others point to Afro-Brazilian elements of *catimbó* and its close relation to *umbanda*. Following the latter argument, both the *jurema*-cult and the incorporation of spiritual entities belong to these external traditions, being alien to "original" Potiguara "tradition". Historically, the *catimbó* probably had its origins in the region between João Pessoa and Recife, which was also the former territory of the Tabaja, another historical Tupi nation. The *catimbó* is part of the "jurema-complex", a set of ritualistic practices common to many Indigenous groups and Afro-Brazilian religions of the Brazilian northeast (Vandezande 1975; Nascimento 1994; Palitot and Júnior 2004; Assunção 2006; Vieira 2010; Sousa and Nascimento 2011; among others). The use of *jurema* had its origins between the non-Tupi nations (which the Tupi called *tapuia*) living in the arid hinterlands (*sertão* and *cariri*) from where it probably diffused to Afro-Brazilian religions (*candomblé* and *umbanda*), while the population of Indigenous descent adopted Afro-Brazilian elements into their ritualistic practices. There can be no doubt that the *catimbó* has been a widespread practice among the Potiguara for at least a century, and that they were using *jurema* and incorporating spirits when they were dancing the *toré* hiding in the woods. It is, therefore, virtually impossible to dissociate Afro-Brazilian elements from "original" Potiguara "tradition". However, both Indigenous and Afro-Brazilian spiritual cosmopractices have always been demonised as worship of the devil or witchcraft, being violently persecuted until the 1960s. As a result, *catimbó* and *macumba* (a pejorative name for *candomblé* and *umbanda*) are still used as synonyms for sorcery and black magic, and hence, rejected by the majority of Potiguara—at least in public.

[44] Such prayers, which may make reference to Jesus Christ, Mary, God or Tupã, or else enchanted beings, have the function of magic spells or incantations, either invoking God and certain immaterial persons to cure the patient, to expel whatever malignant "energy" from the patient's body, or to activate the healing powers of the plants and objects used during ritual.

what the exact procedures in the material world may be, they will always focus on the manipulation of the immaterial domain. Hence, the smoke serves to expel evil energies, to blow positive energies into the patient and to "close" their body; the bath is to wash away negative energies; the plants shall transfer their inherent healing powers stemming from Tupã, Nature and the Ancestors; the drum, the *maracá* and the magic words invoke the Ancestors' support in the struggle against the invisible enemies, envy, evil eye and malefic deeds. However, a *pajé* will always emphasise that their healing powers come from Tupã and Nature; they are only an instrument of these divine forces, who will talk to them through the Ancestors, the messengers and guardians of their sacred secrets. They are the ones who identify the cause of the patient's malady, indicate the right plants for cure and help the *pajé* fight the invisible enemies. The Ancestors will manifest themselves during trance, either entering the *pajé*'s body and speaking through their mouth, or appearing to their inner eye. It should be emphasised how different these two kinds of mediumistic experiences are.

Visions of enchanted beings, future or distant events during dreams and altered states of consciousness are a common phenomenon among the Potiguara, and are by no means restricted to the *pajés*. Interpreting dreams is a common habit, and there are many sensitive persons among the Potiguara who have visions or spontaneously fall into trance. However, the *pajés* not only have a special mediumistic gift, they are also trained to remember the details and even to consciously act in their dreams and visions, which are conceived as a kind of portals to the immaterial dimension.[45] Moreover, they master ritual techniques to provoke such altered states of consciousness at will and leave their bodies behind to travel through time and space, seeing future or distant events, finding healing plants, fighting evil deeds or obsessive spirits. In other words, the *pajés* are able to visit the invisible world of the enchanted beings and even to share some of their magic abilities. During these mediumistic experiences, the body of the *pajé* will stay asleep, showing no action at all, while their spirit is extremely active. Although their body will not be harmed, such spiritual voyages are not without any risk, as their immaterial aspect may be attacked by an enemy, provoking sickness or even death, as the material body cannot live without its immaterial aspect. Hence, support is needed, which comes from enchanted beings with whom the *pajé* established a sympathetic relationship.[46]

[45] This perception of dreams and visions during trance in terms of voyages to another aspect or dimension of the world, invisible to normal perception, is a common feature among many Indigenous cultures. While everybody dreams and also interprets their dreams as a means of divination, the *pajés* and other ritual experts with trained mediumistic abilities are able to maintain control over their dream voyages to consciously act in the other dimension in order to influence the course of events by manipulating the hidden aspect of reality (e.g. Descola (1996) on the Ashuar of Peru; Perruchon (2003) on the Shuar of Ecuador; Guss (1980) on the Makiritare of Venezuela; Langdon and Bear (1992) on the Siona of Columbia; also my own experiences among the Shuar of Ecuador, the Nasa of Colombia, the Iranxe, the Pataxó and the Potiguara of Brazil, among others).

[46] The acquisition of spirit-guides is also a common feature among so-called "shamans" from many different ethnic groups all over the world (Eliade 1956; Faust 1989; Descola 1996; Narby 1998; among others).

During incorporation just the opposite happens; while the body is in action, the mind is asleep. The manifesting entity is taking control of the medium's body, their mind will be set on standby, leaving their unconscious and with no or only very fuzzy memories of their bodily actions. This procedure, too, is not without risk for the *pajé*, as the incorporated entity may be careless and harm their body. Sensitive people, therefore, have to learn to identify and educate the spirits who may call upon them. Generally, a *pajé* will not simply receive whatever spirit who may wish to manifest, but only one or a few entities with whom they maintain an intimate relationship, which may last a lifetime. Frequently, these entities are the same friendly spirits who may support the *pajé* during their spiritual journeys in the invisible world.

The two mediumistic techniques both provide access to the immaterial dimension through intermediation by the Ancestors, and both are based on a temporary dissociation of the medium's material and immaterial aspect; but they do this by making inverse use of each. The first technique inactivates the body to unleash the spirit's faculty to communicate with the disincarnated beings; the latter inactivates the mind to vacate the body for the reception of a disincarnated being. In the first case, the immaterial aspect is the medium, in the latter, it is the material body.[47]

But not all "traditional" healers are *pajés*. There are *rezadeiras* and *rezadores* ("prayers") practicing among the Potiguara. Although sharing many similarities with the *pajés*,[48] their healing practices differ in some important points. First of all, this healing tradition is part of common Brazilian popular culture (rooted in yet older Portuguese traditions), and hence, does not make any effort to revive its

---

[47] Moreover, there is also a symbolic difference: while the first technique is associated with Indigenous spiritual and healing practices (often called "shamanism"), the latter is associated with the syncretic *catimbó* and Afro-Brazilian religions like *umbanda* and *candomblé*. So, while the first one may be understood as a symbol of "Indigenous" culture and identity, the latter stands for miscegenation, witchcraft and black magic. Of course, these are prejudices, as both techniques are employed in American as well as in African contexts, and both can be used for good as well as for bad. In fact, the chroniclers explicitly described such states of "possession" between the Tupinambá and repeatedly pointed out how much they feared the "sorcery" of their *pajés*. However, as a result of these prejudices, many Potiguara associate rituals of incorporation with *catimbó*, black magic and Afro-Brazilian tradition, and hence, repudiate them.

[48] In fact, contemporary *pajés* among the Potiguara are strongly influenced by the tradition of the *rezadeiras*, as well as by other spiritual traditions, including *catimbó*, *umbanda*, Kardecism, popular Catholicism and neo-shamanism. Although the *pajés* are the heirs of a millenary tradition, they had disappeared for centuries. The tradition of the historical *pajés* had been absorbed by syncretic traditions like the *catimbó* and by the *rezadeiras*. The *catimbozeiros* (practitioners of *catimbó*) and rezadeiras would substitute the old *pajés*, while preserving much of their knowledge and ritual practices. These oral traditions were handed over from one generation to another, but due to the violent persecution and the deep socio-cultural transformations during the twentieth century, many younger Potiguara refused to assume these offices, as they were seen more as a burden than a blessing, as they exposed the practitioner to the noxious energies of their patients for no pay in return. As a consequence, most of the old *rezadeiras* and *catimbozeiros* died without having passed their knowledge to the new generation. However, to become a spiritual medium is not always a question of choice. Persons with a very strong mediumistic sensibility may spontaneously fall into trance or get seriously sick, being haunted by the spirits, and the only way to survive may be to assume this

Indigenous heritage. The typical healing prayer (*reza*) is a quite simple ritual, basically consisting of reciting a prayer or a spell, and waving a green twig crosswise before the patient until its leaves begin to wilt, signalling that the evil has been extracted. The lines of the prayer vary depending on the ailment to be cured, and each practitioner has their own set of prayers, which they may have received from another practitioner, often their own mother, or from an enchanted entity during a vision or a dream. While some *rezadeiras* may also use canonical prayers (Lord's Prayer, Ave Maria, etc.), most lines are composed by enigmatic allegories, allusions to biblical psalms, and invocations of God, Jesus Christ, the Virgin Mary, different Catholic saints and other entities.

In contrast to the *pajés*, the *rezadeiras* generally do not use drums, *maracás* or pipes during their ritual, nor do they play any important role during the *toré*. Yet, several *rezadeiras* incorporate enchanted beings while they are praying, and some are also practitioners of *catimbó*. Just like the *pajés*, they mediate the divine powers to interfere in the immaterial aspect of reality. Although the *rezadeiras* also know and apply a great variety of plants, most people will consult them to cure spiritual diseases, like "evil eye" or "curse". Also, most of them received a "calling" and many learned their art from the Ancestors during mediumistic experiences. In fact, there are more similarities than differences between *rezadeiras* and *pajés*. The greatest difference is probably a symbolic one: the *rezadeiras* basically substituted the ancients *pajés* and certainly preserved much of their practices, but covered this Indigenous knowledge with Catholic symbolism, while contemporary *pajés* do just the opposite, deliberately exposing the symbols of their Ancestors, which of course, is also a political act.

Birth and Baptism

The moment of delivery represents an extraordinarily vulnerable situation for both mother and child, demanding great caution and protection. Until recently, most Potiguara were born at home under the care of a "traditional" midwife,[49] who would

"gift" and learn to use it in a beneficial way. Most contemporary *pajés* and rezaderias had such a calling and some are the sons and daughters of *rezadeiras*. The old practitioners died before they could pass their knowledge to their children, so they had to learn from the Ancestors, who would teach them during mediumistic experiences. They also learned from *pajés* from other Indigenous nations, as well as from other spiritual schools, like *catimbó*, *umbanda*, neo-shamanism, and Kardecism. Each *pajé* among the Potiguara has an individual life-history which made them assume and further develop their mediumship, resulting in notably different styles and practices, and there is a continuous dispute about their divergences. However, despite this historical rupture and the resulting external influences, all *pajés* share the same cosmological framework as well as most of their ritualistic practices. Moreover, this kind of introduction and mixed use of elements from different medical and spiritual traditions within the frameworks of traditional cosmopractices is a very common phenomenon among Indigenous groups in Latin America (e.g. Langford 1999; Greifeld and Schmidt 2003).

[49] Many "traditional" midwives are also *pajés* or *rezadeiras*, but most of them simply assumed this office due to the immediate necessity to help with the birth of some relative or neighbour. Once becoming known as a midwife, others would call her, too, and she would learn by doing and with

not only be responsible for the physical, but also for the spiritual wellbeing of the mother and her child. Like the *pajés* and the *rezadeiras*, the midwives know many medical plants to facilitate the accouchement and to care for the health and the security of mother and child thereafter, but they also use prayers and incants to tend to the delicate spiritual aspects of birth. During the process of parturition, their bodies are "open", leaving their immaterial aspects unprotected, so that external immaterial agents might easily affect them. Apart from various measures to facilitate the parturition and to prevent haemorrhages or infections, the midwife would also conduct rituals to "close" the bodies of the mother and her child to protect their immaterial aspects.

During a "traditional" birth, the midwife will give support and comfort to the expectant mother, who bears her child sitting on her haunches. The midwife may prepare an infusion with herbs and apply a massage with coconut oil to facilitate delivery, but she may also recite a special spell for this purpose. Once the child is born, it is washed and incenses of aromatic herbs are lit to purify the ambient and to protect the child by passing it crosswise through the smoke, and thus, close their body. This procedure is called "baptism", although the child will later also receive a Christian baptism at church. However, this "traditional" baptism is important to protect the child's immaterial aspect from being attacked by some disincarnated being, to guarantee the unity of their material and immaterial aspect, and to introduce them to the time-transcending kinship network of the living and the disincarnated.[50]

The midwife will also prepare a wet pack with medical plants (with strong antiseptic properties) to close the mother's body, and additionally to prevent postnatal infections. If the mother suffers from haemorrhage, the midwife will pronounce a prayer and apply another infusion to stop the bleeding. Once mother and child are safe, the placenta is handed over to the father to be buried under a tree in the yard. In the same way, the umbilical cord may be buried later, or stored for later medical use.

Moreover, the mother will have to maintain several taboos and restrictions. During a period of 40 days, counted from a week before parturition, she may not execute any heavy work, and must eschew certain victuals (like red or pork meat, fish, crustacea, etc.), avoid stress and negative emotions, and stay indoors, away from curious eyes which might cause "evil eye" and dry her lactation.

---

the aid of God and the Ancestors. During the last decades, most "traditional" midwives had the opportunity to participate in governmental professionalizing programs, receiving some basic medical instructions. But today, most of them are too old to practice. Also, most Potiguara prefer to have their babies in hospital, as they learned to consider it more secure. But there are still some active midwives and mothers who make demands on their services, which of course, are free of charge.

[50] Faust (1989) reports about similar ritual among the Coyaima and Natagaima aiming to "close" the body of the newborn.

Funeral

"Traditionally",[51] when a person died their body would be exposed in their house and the whole family would come to pay them their last respect. The women would sing sad songs of farewell, so the spirit of the deceased might depart in peace and stay together with the other Ancestors. But the singing was also to send the dead's spirit away and to prevent them from staying too close to the living, as they might become attached to one of their relatives, causing sickness or even death. While the women were singing, the men were drinking and telling funny stories about their memories of the beloved person who had just passed away. This singing and drinking would go on through the night until in the early morning, when the corpse was placed in a hammock to be carried to the church. The hammock was fixed to a beam which was carried by the men, running with it quickly and shouting out loudly: "Here s/he comes!" Often, the next graveyard would be several miles away and the cortege would pass through other villages on its way. The body would be exposed a second time in the church next to the cemetery, and again, the women would intone the chanting, before the mortal remains were finally buried.

Catholic Rituals

Despite the fact that, if asked, virtually all Potiguara would call themselves Christians, it is not easy to allocate Christian ritual within their "traditional" spiritual practices and cosmological imagery. The reason may be that the relation between Christian religion and Indigenous cosmology has never been one of a smooth fusion into a coherent syncretism, but rather one of continuous conflict and friction.[52] Both Catholic and Protestant[53] priests have always more or less openly demonised anything other than Christian spiritual practices, although the Catholic church may have shown more flexibility in this respect. On the other hand, for a long time the Potiguara had been largely abandoned by the Catholic church, which would only provide a single priest for the whole region. Consequently, the Potiguara had to organise their Christian cults and ceremonies on their own. "Traditionally", the annual patron feasts have always been the business of the local leadership (today represented by the *caciques*) and many liturgies are still read by local laymen. One result of this situation was that the Potiguara developed their own popular version of "Catholicism" with their own interpretation of Christian religion; another was that they introduced Indigenous elements into Christian ritual, like dancing the *toré* during patron feasts. Moreover, "Potiguara religion" is by no means a coherent

[51] Today, most funerals among the Potiguara follow more or less the common regional habits of Christian ceremony. But until a generation ago, the dead would be buried according to their old traditions.

[52] Compare also Barcellos (2012) on this subject.

[53] Protestant churches have been growing rapidly since the 1970s, but they have never played a constructive role in "traditional" Potiguara spirituality, but to the contrary, rigorously demonised it. Many Potiguara have abandoned their old "traditions" due to pressure from their Protestant priests. Although some Protestant *caciques* and members of the Indigenous movement still participate in the *toré*, they do it only to reaffirm their ethnic identity, while rejecting its spiritual dimension.

institution, but, on the contrary, a patchwork of different overlapping religious and spiritual traditions, including Catholicism, *catimbó*, *umbanda,* kardecism, and more recently, a growing number of Protestant congregations, and it is quite common for one and the same person to practice several different religions in parallel.[54] So, even though all Potiguara will affirm their faith in God, not all of them will necessarily be active practitioners of Roman Catholicism. For example, it is still quite common to "marry" just by moving together into a shared household, without necessarily celebrating a Christian wedding in church; similarly, many "Catholic" Potiguara have never been formally baptised by a priest; and only a small portion of "Catholic" Potiguara go to church.[55] Hence, in fact, active Roman Catholics represent just one of several other religious groups in Potiguara society. Nevertheless, Catholicism has greatly influenced the Potiguara culture and worldview, and their "traditional" calendar is still organised by Catholic dates and rituals.

The most prominent Catholic ritual is certainly the celebration in honour of St Michael, patron of the Potiguara, which takes place each year in September. The profane feast is anticipated by 9 days of novenas, which occur in parallel in the two villages of São Miguel and São Francisco, finalised by the great Mass on the ninth day. While the participation during the novenas is rather limited, the final Mass has hundreds of spectators from different Potiguara communities. "Traditionally", the ceremony was followed by circular dances and a final *toré,* but today the profane feast is more like a commercial fun fair. Another important novena with considerable participation is held in December in honour of *Nossa Senhora da Conceição* (The Immaculate Conception), also taking place in São Francisco, along with other celebrations of local patron saints in other villages, which are also followed by profane feast at night, attracting many Potiguara for drinking and dancing. However, most Christian rituals do not involve any symbols or attributes of their Indigenous ethnicity, culture or spirituality, but rather maintain and reinforce the deepening separation between the Potiguara's Christian and their ancestral heritage.[56]

---

[54] Actually, some of the most respected and vigorous defenders of Potiguara "tradition" are also active Catholics, there are *pajés* who are also *pais de santo* (*umbanda* priests), several *caciques* are active Protestants, and some Indigenous activists have become Christian priests.

[55] Interestingly, most participants and lay-practitioners in Catholic ritual, like Masses, novenas and processions, are women with their children, while men only very rarely participate (compare also Barcellos 2012). And when I asked some elders whether they went to church, several of them affirmed they did not, because the priests would only tell "nonsense" (*besteiras*); they said they would rather go to the river or to the woods to speak with God, and that nature would be their "church".

[56] During the last decades, agents of the Catholic church invested in the charismatic movement, whose growing influence on the celebrations reinforced the exclusively Catholic character of these dates. On the other hand, there is an increasing consciousness among many younger Potiguara (especially among university students) concerning their ancestral roots and the importance of their Ancestor's spirituality.

There is a more profane ritual, but nevertheless associated with a Christian date, which may be more significant in the life of most Potiguara. Each year, during Holy Week, the Potiguara prepare lots of *beju* (the delicious "traditional" manioc bread with coconut); the production of *beju* involves a lengthy collective preparation in the "traditional" *casas de farinha* (local manioc flour workshops), joining the neighbourhood working together during several days. They also prepare other "traditional" dishes, like crabs and fish, and visit all their relatives to share the food with them. During their visits, the younger ones kneel down before their elders and ask for their blessing, showing their deep respect. Then, the families join together at the house of some elder relative and pass the day eating, drinking and enjoying themselves. This annual renewal of family bonds and ancient tradition has little to do with Roman Catholicism, but for the Potiguara it is a form of commemorating one of the most important Christian dates.

9.4 Recapitulating Potiguara Cosmovision and Practice

I know this short ethnographic sketch of the Potiguara is neither extensive nor profound enough to be called an ethnography; but this has never been my task. Rather, my research interest was merely focussing on cosmological aspects within historical and geopolitical context, and analysing them concerning possible analogies compared to scientific concepts.[57] It is also clear that the concept of a "traditional" Potiguara cosmovision is an abstraction from a very particular, and in part, quite hypothetical reality, even though this abstraction has been construed in collaboration with numerous Potiguara. However, having these rather inevitable restrictions in mind, the cosmological scheme outlined here should provide a sufficient notion of the most salient metaphysical conceptions to be compared to current ontological models from academic discourse.

There are two aspects of Potiguara cosmovision to which I would like to call attention. First, is its strikingly hybrid character. Potiguara cosmovision is not only an abstraction, it is also a historical product of mutual influence and exchange between different religious and spiritual traditions, which resulted in a confusing pattern of Indigenous, Afro-Brazilian, Catholic, Brazilian folklore, as well as popular beliefs in magic and healing practices. Despite all the deep changes, the Potiguara still maintain some fundamental aspects of the culture of their Ancestors, the historical Tupi. Just to name some, the Potiguara still use the *maracá* and practice circular dances to call on their Ancestors, provoking states of altered consciousness and incarnation of spirits; they still believe in immaterial agents who may cure or cause sickness; they use the pipe to blow smoke on the patients for cures; they believe that plants and animals also have spirits; that their *pajés* are able to act in the

[57] See comparative analysis in Part III, Chap. 3.

immaterial world of the Ancestors; that these *pajés* had a calling in the form of a near death experience[58]; along with many other views and practices. The confusing thing about all this is that these "original" elements are indistinguishably fused with those "external" influences. And despite this obvious hybridism, the resulting set of beliefs and practices is perceived by the Potiguara as their very own "tradition".

This last point leads me to the second aspect I would like to highlight. Once one assumes the existence of such a "Potiguara tradition", no matter what its provenience, it also suggests a more or less coherent system, based on some quite clearly definable basic cosmological assumptions. These basic assumptions could be summarised as follows:

1. There is a supreme deity called God or Tupã, who is the source of everything that is, and which continues to be present as the immaterial aspect of Nature (hence, the sacred character of Nature and Earth as manifestations of Tupã).
2. Everything that exists or happens in the material world has also an immaterial aspect (called "soul", "spirit", "Ancestor", "enchanted being" or "energy"). But while the material aspects of all things and living beings are ephemeral, their immaterial aspects will persist and continue to influence the material world.[59]
3. Such immaterial aspects, be they incarnated or disincarnated, are subject-like, that is, they act intentionally, and therefore, are treated like "persons" who can be manipulated by establishing reciprocal relations with them.
4. All events in the material world are accompanied by events in the immaterial world. This is also true for diseases, which may be caused by immaterial agents or not, but always receive some therapy aiming at the immaterial aspect of the problem.
5. The material and the immaterial aspects of the world are separated by the limits of the perception of our "normal" consciousness, but we may be able to access the immaterial realm during altered states of consciousness, like dreams, visions or trance, which can be conceived as "soul journeys". While on such occasions the immaterial aspect may temporarily separate from its material aspect, in other moments an external immaterial "person" may enter the body and take control over it.
6. Although these kind of mediumistic abilities are intrinsic to all human beings, only some people can dominate the techniques to consciously visit and act in the immaterial realm. Such persons are called *pajés, rezadeiras* or *catimbozeiros;* they are the ones responsible for the health of individuals as well as for the well-being of the community.

[58]This "calling" in form of a disease during childhood as well as near death experiences during initiation are also a common features of so-called "shamans" among other Indigenous nations (e.g. Faust (1989) on the *teguas* of the Coyaima and Natagaima; Descola (1996) on the *uwishin* of the Ashuar; Langdon and Bear (1992) on the Siona; et al.)

[59]This also implies a concept of the body as a kind of physical receptacle of its immaterial aspect, which seems to be at odds with the notion the physical being a manifestation of the non-physical aspects—sea discussion in the next chapter.

Of course, this is a very gross reduction and there are many other fascinating aspects of Potiguara cosmovision and practice which could also be mentioned, but this little selection may be enough to show the apparent coherence between these cosmological assumptions and why I was talking about a cosmological "system". This alone would not be surprising, as in the social sciences "systems" are always constructed by social scientists. But I was surprised how easy it was to "find" such a system in the particularly hybrid context of the Potiguara's reality. Is it not astonishing how seamlessly all these parts from different religious and spiritual traditions are assembled into a (more or less) coherent whole? There are certainly many disputes between the Potiguara concerning the "right" ritualistic techniques and whether or not they are "original" or "imported"; but those who are disputing such details are arguing within a common cosmological frame of reference. To make a comparison to Our world of modern science, these disputes are like physicists discussing the best technical approach to measure the impact of a quark, rather than disputing its existence. However, We, modern scientists would very well doubt the existence of immaterial persons. The reason is that modern sciences apparently do not share the same basic cosmological assumptions about the structure of reality. But what about our neo-shamanic neighbour, the Protestant fundamentalist next door, and all the other "Westerners" who hold onto different religious and spiritual beliefs? Hence, the coherence between the different elements of Potiguara cosmopractices might have its reason in some common basic assumptions, which are fundamentally different from those sustained by modern sciences, but are equally present in most cultures and societies—and maybe even in Us, the scientists.

For a very long time, anthropology has been reproducing the image of the Others as being the diametrical opposite to Us, the "moderns". It has, therefore, contributed to the maintenance of the Great Divide, which is probably one of modernity's grand narrations and essential for both its legitimation and its self-understanding. Hence, ethnographic representations of the Others as modern hybrids are not new, but still somehow disturbing—especially if they continue to be essentially different from our learned representation of "modernity". Moreover, this situation is not only disturbing for Us, but also for Them, the Potiguara and other Indigenous groups who suffered from deep changes in the course of colonial oppression. There is an ongoing debate between the Potiguara about the "right" way of being Potiguara, a highly conflictual and contradictory process of constructing a new way of being "traditional". Moreover, this collective process on the ethnic and spiritual identity of some 20,000 Potiguara is constituted by almost as many individual opinions, which are loosely joined in different subgroups, and so on. All of this sounds very much like a typical "modern" society. Nevertheless, these manyfold debates seem to have one common referent, which is Potiguara "tradition" and "culture". This "tradition" is represented by the *troncos velhos*, the generation of elders who grew up in a time when the Potiguara were still living their "own" "traditions". In fact, this group of highly respected elders really seem to share a set of common beliefs and practices, which can be described as a common "tradition" or "culture", and which is referred to as "traditional Potiguara culture" by most Potiguara. However, many Potiguara do not live in this "traditional" world any longer, but probably share a life world quite similar to the common rural Brazilian population. And one might ask why the Potiguara chose to hold this "traditional" aspect of their reality and not, for example, the one they live as Protestant sugar cane planters or Catholic academics. The reason is, of course, a political one: due to the political situation during the last decades, claiming their ethnic identity was a more successful strategy than fighting for their rights from the position of common rural workers. That is not to say that Potiguara "tradition" is an invention (although invention has also been part of the dynamic process of constructing their ethnic identity), it is more the construction of a collective *utopia*, a better way of life, which by definition has to be somehow different from dominant society and at the same time rooted in their past. The reference for their past is provided by their elders, their Ancestors and the historical Tupi nations, while the reference for their otherness is everything that is generally held to be "Indigenous".[60] However, both of these references also imply a worldview which differs considerably compared to the hegemonic view defended by modern sciences, even though a growing number of Potiguara are scientists, too. So, if the Potiguara opted for their "traditional" cosmovision in the interest of a better way of life, why should we not do the same? Are we not confronted with a generalised global crisis, which has long been associated with the negative effects of "modernity"? The problem is, of course, that we do not share the same frame of reference. Science simply does not (want to) understand the Others, who are talking about such crazy things as "spirits" or "enchanted" beings. But is there really no common language we could share, are we really so different? What are the basic metaphysical assumptions that keep us from accepting other cosmological approaches, and why do we think they are incompatible with modern science?

To answer these questions, I will take Potiguara cosmopractice as just one example of a cosmological approach which is (apparently) incommensurable to the basic metaphysical assumptions of modern science. To do so, I will try to boil Potiguara cosmology down to its fundamental ontological categories.

References

Alencar Jd (2003) Iracema. Biblioteca Virtual Miguel de Cervantes, Alicante

Almeida AV (2013) Espinhela Caída: Referencias Históricas e Práticas de Cura Populares. EDUFRPE, Recife

Assunção L (2006) O Reino Dos Mestres: A Tradição Da Jurema Na Umbanda Nordestina. Pallas, Rio de Janeiro

Barcellos L (2012) Práticas Educativo-Religiosas dos Potiguara da Paraíba. Editora Universitária da UFPB, João Pessoa

[60] Including all kinds of cliché symbols, like dreamcatchers and North American Indian style plumages.

Batista MNF, Conceição FMd, Pereira PE et al (2021a) Cosmologia e Espiritualidade Potiguara. Sociedade Brasileira de Ecologia Humana—SABEH, Paulo Afonso, BA

Batista MNF, Conceição FMd, Pereira PE et al (2021b) Medicina Tradicional Potiguara. Sociedade Brasileira de Ecologia Humana—SABEH, Paulo Afonso, BA

Baumgartner D (1994) Das Priesterwesen der Kogi. Jahrbuch für Ethnomedizin und Beweußtseinsforschung, Currare 1994–3:170–191

Casemiro SR (2012) A lenda da Iara: nacionalismo literário e folclore. Master thesis, USP

Dantas MB, Barbosa MV, Santos SR (2017) Lendas e/ou Mitos Potiguaras? Tradição, Sacralidade, Mulheres Míticas e Riqueza Cultural. In: Batista AC (ed) Uma Década de Expensão Universitaria: Estudos Sobre o Vale de Mamanguape. Editora do Ccta, João Pessoa, pp 163–187

Descola P (1996) Leben und Sterben in Amazonien: Bei den Jívaro-Indianern. Klett-Cotta, Stuttgart

Eliade M (1956) Schamanismus und Archaische Ekstasetechniken. Zürich, Stuttgart

Evans-Pritchard EE (1976) Witchcraft, oracles, and magic among the Azande. Clarendon, Oxford

Faust FX (1989) Medizin Und Weltbild: Zur Ethnographie der Coyaima und Natagaima-Indianer Kolumbiens. Trickster Wissenschaft, Munich

Faust FX (1994) Kultur, ein durch Fraktale determiniertes Chaos. Jahrbuch für Ethnomedizin 25–41

Fernandes F (2006) A função social da guerra na sociedade Tupinambá. Editora Globo, São Paulo

Gallop R (1961) Portugal: a book of falk-ways. Cambridge University Press, Cambridge

Gerlic S, Zoettl PA (eds) (2011) Índios Na Visão Dos Índios: Potiguara. Thydêwá, Salvador

Greifeld K (ed) (2003) Ritual und Heilung: Eine Einführung in die Medizinethnologie. Reimer, Berlin

Greifeld K, Schmidt BE (2003) Medizinische Systeme Süd- und Afroamerikas. In: Greifeld K (ed) Ritual und Heilung: Eine Einführung in die Medizinethnologie. Reimer, Berlin, pp 105–132

Grünewald RdA (ed) (2004) Toré: Regime Encantado do Índio do Nordeste. Fundação Joaquim Nabuco, Recife

Guss DM (1980) Steering for dream: dream concept of the Makiritare. J Latina Am Lore 6:297–312

Hinderling P (1981) Kranksein in "Primitiven" und Traditionellen Kulturen. Verlag für Ethnologie, Norderstedt

Hutchinson HW (1981) Research report: Espinhela caida: A Brazilian folk illness. Med Anthropol Newsl 12:9

Kutalek R (2003) Medizinische system in Afrika. In: Greifeld K (ed) Ritual und Heilung: Eine Einführung in die Medizinethnologie. Reimer, Berlin, pp 39–68

Langdon EJM, Bear G (eds) (1992) Portals of power: shamanism in South America. University of New Mexico Press, Albuquerque

Langford JM (1999) Medical mimesis: healing signs of a cosmopolitan "quack". Am Ethnol 26:24–46

Lery Jd (1992) History of a voyage to the land of Brazil, otherwise called America. University of California Press, Berkeley

Lévi-Strauss C (2004) Mitologica. Cosac Naifa, São Paulo

Lima OGd (1946) Observações sobre o Vinho da Juremah Utilizado pelos Índios Pancarú de Tacaratú. Arquivos do Instituto de Pesquisas Argonómicas 4:45–80

Lukesch A (1994) Der Tapir der an der Himmelsstütze nagt: Mythos und Leben der Kayapó-Indianer. Böhlau, Wien

Marques CF, Araujo IX, Simas HCP (2009) Lendas e Causos do Povo Potiguara. Editora da Ufpb, João Pessoa

Mendonça JBSdS (2014) Entre o Tronco e o Monte: Convergências e Divergências nas Espiritualidades dos Indígenas Potiguara e Do Carmelo Monástico da Paraíba. Master thesis, Universidade Federal da Paraíba

Narby J (1998) The cosmic serpent: DNA and the origins of knowledge. Penguin, New York

Nascimento MTdS (1994) O Tronco da Jurema: Ritual e etnicidade entre os povos indígenas do nordeste—o caso Kiriri. Master thesis, Universidade Federal da Bahia

Oliveira JPd (1998) Uma Etnologia Dos "Índios Misturados"? Situação Colonial, Territorialização e Fluxos Culturais. Mana 4:47–77

Palitot EM (2005) Os Potiguara da Baía da Traição e Monte-Mór: História, Etinicidade e Cultura. Master thesis, UFPB

Palitot EM, Júnior FBS (2004) Todos os Pássaros do Céu: O Toré Potiguara. In: Grünewald RdA (ed) Toré: Regime Encantado do Índio do Nordeste. Fundação Joaquim Nabuco, Recife

Perruchon M (2003) I am Tsunki: gender and shamanism among the Shuar of Western Amazonia. Acta Universitatis Upsaliensis, Uppsala

Reichel ED (1987) Die Ökopolitik im Schamanismus der Yukuna und Tanimuka vom Nordwestlichen Amazonas. In: Gottwald FT, Rätsch C (eds) Schamanische Wissenschaft. Ökologie, Naturwissenschaft und Kunst, Munich, pp 25–95

Rosa LAC (2009) As juremeiras da nação Xambá (Olinda, PE): músicas, performances, representações de feminino e relações de gênero na jurema sagrada. Doctoral thesis, UFBA

Silva PRP, Nascimento JM (2013) Educação e movimentos sociais: registro do Toré Potiguara—a força da espiritualidade. Cronos R Pós Grad Ci Soc UFRN Natal 14(2):216–221

Sousa RMM, Nascimento JM (2011) A Jurema no Ritual Toré dos Potiguara. Colóquio Internacional "Educaçnao e Contemporaneidade". São Cristovão, Brazil, pp 1–9

Stoller P, Olkes C (1987) In sorcery's shadow: a memoir of apprenticeship among the Songhay of Niger. University of Chicago Press, Chicago

Vandezande R (1975) Catimbó: Pesquisa Exploratoria da Forma Nordestina de Religião Mediúnica. Master thesis, Universidade Federal de Pernambuco

Vargas A (2005) Medicina Popular. Instituto Estadual do Patrimônio Cultural, Rio de Janeiro

Vieira JG (2010) Amigos e Competidores: Política Faccional e Feitiçaria nos Potiguara da Paraíba. PhD thesis, Universidade de São Paulo

Wörrle B (2004) Lateinamerika: Patienten und Heiler zwischen den medizinischen Systemen. Curare 27:115–127

Chapter 10
Potiguara Ontology

When we, as ethnographers, write about "cosmologies" of Other nations, we often do this as if we were describing fictions. Of course, such cosmologies are fictions, as we, the anthropologists, are the ones who invented them by abstracting from a set of narrations and lived practices we had the opportunity to observe and partake in. But in fact, what we are trying to describe are different metaphysical models of the existing world. It's just that we describe these metaphysical approaches using terminologies that differ from the philosophical terminology we use in our own meta-scientific discourses. What if we take the Others' metaphysics as being equally applicable to reality and try to find a more generic meta-scientific terminology that could be applicable to both Our own and the Others' metaphysical models? One might object that applying Western concepts to explain alien categories would be to westernise, and hence, to misinterpret them. This argument is true if we treat these metaphysical models as different "views". However, this implies the epistemological presumption that our "views" are representations of the "real" world. But the underlying representational epistemology is itself an implication of Our particular "modern" or "Western" ontological model of the universe. My guess would be, therefore, that one way to find a common meta-language for an intercultural or pluriversal comparison of different cosmopractices could be to reduce them to their basic ontological structures. I am well aware that this might just shift the problem of translation to another discursive dimension. But this is only true if we leave this debate on the Others' ontologies to Us "Westerners". The endeavour I am proposing can only work if we include the Others in this discourse as equal partners. Hence my efforts to include the Potiguara as deeply as possible in the (re-)construction of their cosmology as well as in my reflections on its ontological implications. Of course, this dialogue cannot end here and has to continue if we are to get any further than presenting just another collaborative ethnographic account. The present work cannot be more than one little step on a long journey towards a scientific practice and ethos based on pluriversal dialogues.

In order to facilitate a comparison between different cosmopractices, the ontological categories to be compared have to be as fundamental as possible. As far as I

J. Linhart, *Science and the Other*, Schriften zu Leben und Gesellschaft - Series on Life and Society 2, https://doi.org/10.1007/978-3-032-03927-9_10

can see, most conflicts between modern science and other worldviews concern the relations between dual categories like mind and matter, object and subject, human and nature, sacred and profane, space and time, and the resulting casuistic and moral principles. My analysis of Potiguara cosmopractices concerning its ontological principles will, therefore, focus on these questions and attempt to reduce these ontological categories to concepts that are translatable to those we use in Our scientific meta-discourse.

10.1 The Immaterial and the Material Realm

One of the first aspects of the Potiguara's way of understanding their world to call Our (the scientists') attention is probably the existence of an invisible, immaterial realm made up by "persons", and the great importance they attribute to it. The most prominent expression of its importance is, of course, their concept of God Tupã and his relation to Nature. Tupã is the immaterial principle of all existence, with Nature representing its material manifestation.[1] Moreover, the Potiguara say that everything happens according to Tupã's will, which implies a subject or person-like concept of this omnipresent immaterial principle. In sum, these attributes of Tupã and Nature suggest an ontological structure of the universe as fundamentally consisting of an immaterial, subject-like principle (called God or Tupã) and its material manifestation (called Nature). The most salient "subject-like" property of this immaterial principle is its *intentionality*, which is expressed in Tupã's almighty will and creative power. Of course, this is a very far-reaching reduction and I shall analyse whether this universal principle can be traced through all the other different expressions of Potiguara cosmopractice.

Another notion that is central to the world of the Potiguara is their concept of the Ancestors. According to the Potiguara, they are the spirits of their dead relatives. However, in a broader sense, all the other enchanted beings, like the *Pai do Mangue*, the *Comadre Florzinha*, the *Mãe d'Água* or St Michael (and even the whales and the dolphins), are also Ancestors and share more or less the same properties. All of these entities have once been living human beings who were transformed into enchanted beings through the passage of physical death and, thus, represent Ancestors of the living Potiguara. Death, as the process of disincarnation, separated their spirit from the body, resulting in the latter's deterioration while releasing the full potential of the former. Freed from the restrictions of their material existence, disincarnated beings are able to transit through the immaterial realm, transcending time and space, but also to influence the material realm. Hence, the Ancestors can

[1] However, Nature is not limited to the material realm, but also encompasses its immaterial aspect, so that there is no clear ontological distinction between Tupã and Nature. If there is a difference between the two, it is rather one of succession or hierarchy, as Nature is a consequence of God's existence, and not the other way round. Otherwise, God and Nature seem to be the two sides of the same coin, one representing its immaterial and the other its material aspect.

also be understood as representing a more generic ontological category of immaterial agents.

Despite their human provenience and their immaterial character, enchanted beings belong to the realm of Nature and are, therefore, an expression of God's universal presence. They are the guardians of the natural environments, of Mother Earth and the territory, and they are a potential danger for human beings, much like wild animals. Moreover, all living beings, including humans, animals and plants alike, have spirits, that is, an immaterial aspect, which persists after death.[2] The life and health of an incarnated being depend on the unity of their immaterial and material aspects. If this unity is threatened, sickness or death may be the consequence. In this respect, the spirit appears as the animating principle of life and the body just as its material receptacle. Such a container concept of the body is also supported by mediumistic practices of incorporating discarnate beings, where an external immaterial person enters a living person's body, or during "soul journeys", when the spirit leaves its senseless body behind.[3]

So far, there seems to be quite a clear cut between the material and the immaterial realm, suggesting two different substances rather than two aspects of one universal substance. While the immaterial substance is characterised as subject-like and eternal, the material substance is just its ephemeral emanation.

10.2 The Underdetermined Character of Consciousness and the Overdetermination of the Body

This picture becomes more fuzzy when we try to analyse the role of consciousness in Potiguara cosmopractice. As discussed above, consciousness clearly belongs to the immaterial realm, as it shares most of its properties with the spirit. First of all, consciousness is the prototype of subjectivity, one of the most important attributes of any immaterial entity, which is also one of the reasons why I chose to refer to them as "persons". Furthermore, different states and emotions of the conscious mind may cause effects in the immaterial realm, as typically exemplified by the phenomenon of "evil eye". And it is possible to visit the immaterial realm during dreams and trance, although it is necessary to dominate certain techniques to do this consciously.

However, our conscious mind distinguishes between good and bad, and in contrast to the spirit, this moral consciousness dies together with the body. Moreover, the behaviour of the spirit seems to be more similar to animals or infants, driven by immediate impulses and affections rather than rational thought. So, there seems to be quite a difference between the subjectivity of the conscious mind and the

[2] In fact, most Potiguara would not spontaneously mention the spirits of dead animals or plants, but if asked about them, most will affirm that they probably exist, just like the human Ancestors do.

[3] Actually, the term "medium" already implies such a cognitive container scheme (Lakoff 1987).

subjectivity of the spirit, which might be better termed "conscience" or "intentionality" instead. And to make it even more confusing, our conscious mind is often not even aware of our spiritual activities, which may do harm to a beloved person without our knowledge.[4] It also appears that the conscious mind can only get access to the immaterial realm if it reaches a state of consonance with the spirit, for example, during trance or through the power of faith—as if it would need the spirit as a vehicle or mediator to access the immaterial realm. On the other hand, faith and trance are also essentially embodied experiences, not a conscious decision, and it is quite common to feel the presence of immaterial entities via somatic sensations, like horripilation or cold (also called "signs"). So, in this respect, the body seems to be more susceptible to events in the immaterial realm than the mind. Similarly, physical ailments may be cured by spiritual rituals, that is by acting upon the immaterial realm, without necessarily involving either the spirit or the conscious mind of the diseased body, and there may well be a direct effect of external immaterial actants on the body. And finally, apart from God Tupã, all immaterial entities were once born as living beings with material bodies. Although the spirit continues to exist after death, it only comes into existence with the birth of a living being. There is no cycle of rebirth with eternal "souls" being reincarnated in a succession of different lives (as we know it, for example, from Asian religions), but rather an endless emergence of new bodies with new spirits. One might wonder what the heck happens with all those spirits accumulating around the living? Actually, the Potiguara would not have any concrete answer either, suggesting that all the Ancestors will stay in their territory, accumulating endlessly, until the day of the Last Judgement. I try to recapitulate:

1. There are immaterial spirits and immaterial minds, both of which are born as subject-like properties of living, material bodies, and both of which act on their respective body.
2. However, the "subject-like" properties of mind and spirit differ considerably: the mind is associated with our conscious, embodied perception of the physical world, and rational reasoning in moral categories of "good" and "bad"; the spirit, on the other hand, is associated with a rather unconscious intentionality and supposed to perceive the immaterial aspect of the world.
3. Both mind and spirit somehow act in parallel, not always being in harmony with each other, and it is never completely clear to what extent the body is controlled by either of these two immaterial principles. Moreover, the body itself seems to react to events both in the material and the immaterial realms. In this sense, the body seems to be somehow overdetermined.
4. On the other hand, the mind is bound to a waking, living body, while the spirit is able to leave the body temporarily or permanently; although both mind and body are immaterial principles, the mind dies together with the body, while the spirit remains as a permanent element of the immaterial realm; hence, the mind seems to be rather kind of an hybrid property of a living body, neither physical nor part

[4] Compare the causes of maladies as discussed above.

of the immaterial realm, and with no clearly identifiable function; in this sense, the mind seems to be a strangely underdetermined ontic category.

In the face of this confusing pattern, Potiguara cosmopractice does not seem to make a clear line between body, mind and spirit, and hence, between the material and immaterial realms. But maybe there is another aspect of the cosmological concepts discussed above that can shed some light on this issue.

10.3 Intentionality and Relational Causation

So far, I have discussed the immaterial and the material realms as two, mutually effective aspects of the world. However, there has been little about the causal mechanisms responsible for this mutual effectiveness. How exactly do immaterial entities cause effects in the material realm and vice versa? One reason for this omission is that the Potiguara do not have any concrete theory concerning this question. For them, it is good and fair enough to know that there is an immaterial domain that interferes in the material world and how to manipulate it in their favour. However, for the present purpose it would be helpful to come to a better understanding concerning the nature of the inter-relatedness between material and immaterial aspects of the world.

So, if the Potiguara use certain ritualistic instruments to influence the immaterial sphere, a close look at these practices might reveal something about the causal principles they imply. As discussed above, most rituals will establish relations with different kinds of persons. Such persons may be enchanted beings as well as plants or God Himself. The *rezadeira* will ask God and the Catholic saints for a cure, the *pajé* will invoke the Ancestors, their allied spirits and the plant masters, the hunter will make an offer to the *Comadre* for good hunting fortune, the crab collector will offer some tobacco to the *Pai do Mangue* and the fisherman some perfume to the *Mãe d'Água*, the Indigenous militant will dance the *toré* to call upon the Ancestors. These immaterial persons will function as intermediaries between the material and the immaterial worlds. It is a flip-flop game of influencing immaterial actants to make them achieve the desired results in the material world. But why should this metaphysical flip-flop be more efficient than trying to directly influence things in the material realm? If asked such a question, the Potiguara would probably answer that everything ultimately happens according to God's will and with the help of the Ancestors. Hence, everything happens according to the intention of some immaterial subjectivity, and the best way to influence another subject is to establish a relationship with them. In the same way, many maladies are caused by other persons' intentions, be they enchanted beings, humans or even animals, which is another way to say sickness is a result of disturbed or negative relations. Likewise, immaterial entities who become manifest during ritual will almost exclusively talk about relations and intentions, about envy, jealousy, anger, fear and the need to react in a reciprocal manner. *Intentionality* may be the very essence of the immaterial realm and the principle of its effectiveness—in this sense, God himself is ultimately a universalised intentionality. However, an intention only exists towards another object or person, and thus, is always relational. Intentionality, therefore, could be called the "vector" of relation. Consequently, the best way to influence reality is by establishing and manipulating relations, and hence, the intentions of persons. From this perspective, it becomes important to transform as many other persons as possible into allies, relatives, or friends. The anthropomorphic imagery of guardian spirits of game and the natural environments—like the *Comadre*, the *Pai do Mangue* and the *Mãe d'Água*—not only facilitate an understanding of their supposed subjectivity; they also relocate them within a network of kinship by transforming them into Ancestors. The great importance the Potiguara give to kinship is not restricted to the immaterial realm. As mentioned earlier, the Potiguara person is constituted by their kin-relations, including their dead relatives and their ancient Ancestors, and there also are rituals to transform friends into relatives.[5] The same is true for the Ancestors, too, who are essentially defined by their relations to their living offspring. One could even say they only exist because there are living relatives who relate to them, and they may cease to exist when there is nobody left to call upon them.[6] In the same way, the spirit only comes into being with the birth of its body, which is also the beginning of its relations to other persons as well as between body and spirit. Because these relations transcend physical death, the spirit will persist as an Ancestor as long as others continue to relate to them. From this relational perspective, discarnate persons are like immaterial "vestiges", patterns of relations within the virtually endless relational network that constitutes the immaterial realm, and hence, God Himself, representing the universal node everything is related to. Moreover, in a wider sense, kinship is an expression of equality—it says: "You are of the same kind as I am, and hence, we are related to each other." Similarity is also fundamental to many rituals, which frequently use mimetic techniques to establish a relation to some entity, and by virtue of this relation, invoke their "magic" capacities. "Magic", in this sense, is the immediate effect which inevitably results from any relation, be it positive or negative. However, this relational "magic" is nothing "supernatural", but rather a universal principle of mutual influence, which may be even more fundamental than physical causality. Hence, the great care for everything that is in some way related to oneself and the ones we love. The umbilical cord and placenta of a newborn child have to be buried because it matters what happens to these objects, which have been so intimately related to the child, and hence, will

[5] Besides the North-East-Brazilian tradition of the "*Madrinha/Padrinho de Fogueira*" (ritual godfather/mother), the Potiguara also have a ritual to transform a friend into one's cousin. This tendency to establish some kin-relation is not limited to the Potiguara, but a quite generalised phenomenon between many Indigenous groups. And it can be equally found in the cannibalistic habits of the historical Tupi, the Potiguara's ancestors, who used to transform their victims into sons-in-law, before eating them.

[6] I once interviewed a former *rezadeira* who had abandoned her office after converting, together with her husband, to a Protestant congregation. She told me that after she and her husband had stopped calling upon the enchanted beings, they would have never appeared again. She and her husband did not think these beings do not exist, but that they ended their relations with them.

stay connected to their destiny. It would be wrong to simply throw them away, or to let the animals eat these objects, as this kind of disrespectful relations could be harmful for the child. Likewise, to bury a body is a symbol of respect towards a defunct relative, and symbols are instrumental to the establishment of relations. Seen from this angle, the typical allegoric and mimetic symbolism of rituals can be understood as a means to establish relations, invoking the aid of immaterial actants, which are themselves essentially made up of relations.

In sum, the underlying rationale of Potiguara ritual and cosmology seems to suggest an intentional, and thus, relational causal principle. One could even say that the immaterial realm (essentially represented by the God Tupã) is nothing other than a network of infinite relations with their resulting intentions (immaterial actants). There are nodes of converging relations in this network (e.g. kinship), forming intentional entities (which I have referred to as "persons", "immaterial aspects" or "spirits"), which may become manifest in the material realm. Considering the previous discussion on the material and the immaterial realms, the former is the manifestation of the latter; in other words, the material world is the manifestation of these intentional relations. Hence, any change of the immaterial relations also implies an immediate change of its material aspect. There is no chain of events, no time lapse between changes in the immaterial realm and the emergence of its corresponding effects in the material world. Intentions themselves are actions, and thus, changes in the relations, in the immaterial aspects that govern the material realm. Moreover, relational causality is by no means deterministic, although it follows general rules. There are no "objects" in the immaterial realm, but only persons, intentional entities, which react to each other according to their reciprocal relations; but the quality of a relation only suggests a range of probable intentional changes; they do not determine a particular reaction.

What does this tell us about the underdetermined nature of consciousness and the relation between body, mind, and spirit? The physical body is the manifestation of its constitutive relations, represented by its spirit, which is by definition intentional. However, this immaterial aspect does not seem to be "conscious" in the way our conscious mind is; the spirit may have some experience we cannot directly access, but what we actually know from its behavioural patterns only tells us that it behaves person-like in the sense that it acts intentionally and according to its relations to other persons. So, while it seems evident that spirit and mind are two different immaterial actants, it is also evident that both are intimately related to the same material body. The body is born together with its spirit and depends on its presence, and hence, "feels" its intentions. The conscious mind, in contrast, appears to be rather bound to the body, despite its immaterial nature; it is not there from birth on, it develops together with the body and functions as a kind of instrumental perceptivity in the material realm (or the immaterial aspect of the senses and the nervous system?). The mind is, however, not the source of our intentions, it only rationalises them in the contexts of the material realm. Nonetheless, it is possible to bridge the gap between mind and spirit by fading out the body during altered states of consciousness, like trance or dreams. But it is also possible to get information about the immaterial realm by paying attention to the sensitivity of the body to its immaterial aspect, that is, to read the "signs".

I admit, there does not seem to be any crystal clear, coherent way of defining the exact ontological status of the (conscious) mind and the (intentional/relational) spirit, nor of their relations to the (material) body. But maybe this is exactly the important information we need to come to a better understanding of the underlying ontological categories. Since, if they cannot be separated, they might be representing aspects of a unity rather than of different substances.

10.4 Time and Space

So far as my interpretations as presented above are acceptable, "reality" would be the outcome of related intentions and their material manifestation. But what about the nature of time and space in the face of relational causality? Quite obviously, relations develop in a temporal succession, as a chain of interactions of intentional actants. This evolution of relational networks finds its expression in the Potiguara's kindredships, stretching throughout time, from the mythic Ancestors (called "masters" or "*caboclos*"), over the "old trunks" (*troncos velhos*), to the "young twigs" (*ramos novos*) and, finally, to future generations, representing the Potiguara's *utopia* to be realised on their territory. The Ancestors are like hermetic mediators in this time-transcending scheme, establishing a permanent channel between past, present, and future. Through their mediation during mediumistic experience, the living generation is able to get into contact with the past and to receive information about the future. In a certain way, the Ancestors represent the most accessible (for being kin, and thus, the most closely related) connection to the immaterial realm, where time and space obey different laws than in the material realm.

However, the nature of the immaterial realm can also be experienced during dreams and trance. These experiences are conceived as instances of harmonising spirit and mind, allowing for more or less conscious voyages through the immaterial realm. Here, it is possible to visit distant places and persons, to see future or past events, and to interact with immaterial actants, like Ancestors, enchanted beings, or the spirits of plants, animals or humans. It seems the restrictions of linear time, extended space, and physical form do not apply in this realm. However, there may be other restrictions, and time and space are not totally irrelevant. For example, the Potiguara hold their Ancestors would dwell in their territory as they are related to the land and to their relatives living therein. Consequently, it is considered to be easier to get into contact with the Ancestors from within the territory. Nevertheless, it is also possible to call upon them from distant places, as long as a relation is established by means of ritual (e.g. a *toré* together with many relatives). So, here again, the important factor is relation, not time or distance. The same seems to be true for healing rituals. Of course, most rituals require the physical presence of the patient, but a *pajé* is also able to visit and heal at a distance during trance or dream, or to summon a helpful spirit to do the job. Since there is not necessarily a pre-existing relation between healer and patient, physical presence is the easiest way to establish a connection. This may be the reason why most reports I heard about distant healing were concerning relatives of the healer.

Be this as it may, it is evident that the immaterial realm is governed by totally different laws than we know from the material world, and that categories like time, space, form, or causality do not have the same meaning in these two realms. It seems time and space simply do not apply in the material realm, where relations define the distances as well as the events, implying a relational causality instead of a deterministic one. The same seems to be true for the form of entities, which determines their physical properties in the material world, but are rather symbolic appearances in the immaterial realm, indicating their position within the relational network.[7]

The big question is, of course, how the material world obeys totally different laws if it is a manifestation of the immaterial realm? And I am sorry to admit that I have no answer to this question and neither do the Potiguara, who would probably answer: "It is God's will that Nature is this way".

10.5 Conclusive Remarks on the Potiguara and Their Cosmopractices

To be sure, the Potiguara are certainly not an exotic culture living deep down in the jungle and in perfect harmony with nature. They rather represent a typical socio-cultural group of our modern/colonial world, full of contradictions and cleavages, permanently subjected to the grinding stones of modern/colonial capitalism, racist prejudice and social division—and of course, "typical" in this usage means "subaltern", since We privileged members of the global centres represent the fortunate exception. As a typical subaltern group, the Potiguara also represent some typical features they share with other subalternised groups in both Latin America and also in other parts of the world. On the other hand, they probably share as much with Us as with our neglected past, while being separated from Us by the Great Divide of the racial, social, and geo- and cosmopolitical borders incessantly being drawn by the colonial difference. They are Others primarily for being excluded from being Us. However, by assuming the negated identity of the subalternised, "Indigenous" Other, they assume the construction of their own identity and worldview in continuity with their ancestors, and in more or less radical opposition to the hegemonic modern/colonial worldview, while assuming the ancient cultural heritage that We were forced to neglect in order to be accepted in Our glorious club of the privileged, "developed", "modern", "rational", "civilised", "white" men. Of course, there is no

[7] For example, the *Pai do Mangue* appears as an old *caboclo* to the Potiguara, while the non-Indigenous population in the region would describe him as a black man. In the same way, other entities, which are known to the non-Indigenous populations, like the *Comadre Florzinha* or Saint Miguel, are also imagined as Indians by the Potiguara.

return to the past, since nobody even knows what this past was actually like. Potiguara "tradition" and culture is, to be sure, a construction of a certain socio-political group among the Potiguara, and by no means a "pure" historical heritage. Moreover, Potiguara society is extremely diverse, socio-economically and politically stratified, uniting many different religious groups, modernists and traditionalists, and even the traditionalist wing will disagree in many cosmological questions. However, what is more important is that Potiguara "tradition" and culture represent a subaltern, counter-hegemonic project, in open opposition to the hegemonic "truths" of the dominant sectors of modern/colonial society. Hence, the "Potiguara cosmopractice" I presented here is clearly an artefact, but it is an artefact which has at least been construed in collaboration with many Potiguara following, as much as possible, the high standards of Participatory Action Research. So, at least as far as it concerns the participants of our research project, I should be confident that many Potiguara would agree with my presentation of their cosmology and practice.

The ontological principles I extracted from the Potiguara cosmopractices are certainly not the way a Potiguara would present their cosmology. What I termed "Potiguara ontology" here is rather the result of an abstract analysis of the ontological implications of their cosmopractices, taking them as an expression of a philosophical system. The idea behind all this is, of course, to see whether or not the ontological presumptions implicit in Potiguara cosmopractices really are as incommensurable with scientific findings - as the advocates of cultural relativism would have it. In the first part of this work I discussed some of the metaphysical presumptions held by scientism that are responsible for the a priori dismissal of Other kinds of knowledge, which is still a common habit among scientists. In the following third and final part, I will try to sketch out some of the more serious ontological discussions currently being put forth in academic discourse. A final comparative analysis shall show whether the ontological assumptions implied by Potiguara cosmopractices could be articulated in terms of ontological conceptions from academic discourse, or not, and if so, if this can be done in a way that does not disrespect *emic* explanations provided by the Potiguara themselves.

Reference

Lakoff G (1987) Women, fire and dangerous things: what categories reveal about the mind. University of Chicago Press, Chicago

Part III
The Hard Problem of Modern Science

Chapter 11
The Hard Problem of Consciousness

11.1 The Hard Problem of Modern Science

In Part I, I spent many pages resuming all those discussions from modern philosophy, history and sociology of science, and anthropology which have been pointing, quite unanimously, to the metaphysical and ideological character of scientific universalism. The discussion revealed a somehow paradoxical character of modern science: On the one hand, universalism weaponises "Western" rationality and science's supposed epistemological superiority to sustain and reproduce a modern/colonial world-system based on social and racial inequalities and the reckless commodification and exploitation human and more-than-human "nature". On the other hand, however, its own meta-discourses have been denouncing the historically contingent, socially construed, and untenable metaphysical fundaments of scientific knowledge, and thus, of its universal truth claims. Following a number of other authors,[1] I argued that this vexing inconsistency within scientific discourse is based on a mystifying view of science as a quasi-religious belief-system, *scientism*, which has proven astonishingly resistant to any kind of scientific evidence or sound logical argument. I then took a closer look at the metaphysical suppositions that sustain scientistic beliefs in the incontestable superiority of modern science, and the arguments used to justify the a priori rejection of any diverging, alternative views as "unscientific". This inquiry revealed not only the metaphysical character of those arguments, but also their particular weaknesses in terms of scientific evidence, logical consistency and epistemological strength. In sum, scientific universalism is a myth based on outdated theoretical supposition sustained by scientistic creed, but not necessarily by science proper.

Science proper, on the other hand, is facing some serious theoretical problems, not only concerning its unsatisfying epistemological constitution, but also the

[1] E.g. Fleck (1981); James (1981); Lorimer (2019); Walach (2019); Latour (2001, 2004), among others.

J. Linhart, *Science and the Other*, Schriften zu Leben und Gesellschaft - Series on Life and Society 2, https://doi.org/10.1007/978-3-032-03927-9_11

difficulty of integrating its own empirical findings into a single, coherent theoretical framework. Both problem clusters are related to a number of fundamental metaphysical suppositions that ultimately lead into different, and partly contradictory, ontological models about the fundamental structure of the universe. This is particularly evident in the utterly incompatible scientific theories about the nature of mind and matter. This lack of a consistent, unified ontological framework capable of providing a solid metaphysical embedding for both its own findings and the epistemic processes behind them amounts to what I will call the *hard problem of modern science*. However, due to the dogmatic exclusion of metaphysical questions from scientific agenda, as still defended by a significant part of scientific mainstream (particularly by adherents of the scientistic creed), this task has not gained the priority it actually deserves. Nevertheless, there is a growing, albeit still marginal, interest in these issues. There are two research fields that are dealing with particularly stubborn phenomena and that have been investing a lot of ink and brainpower discussing different ontological models to come to a coherent theoretical explanation for recalcitrant "evidence" that simply cannot be ignored. The first one concerns the old mind-body problem in the face of more recent neurological evidence; the other concerns primarily the nature of fundamental physical observables in the face of quantum physics. However, it turns out that both problems ultimately add up to questions about the ontological roles of mind and matter. A number of authors have made an effort to develop, analyse, and systematise different ontological frameworks concerning their consistency and explanatory power. Of course, "evidence" allows for many different ontological interpretations, all of them with their particular weaknesses and strengths, but *in principle* it should be possible to imagine ontological models, beyond scientistic myths, providing a more coherent metaphysical embedding of current scientific evidence and at the potential of new points of convergence with Other cosmologies from different cultural contexts.

In this third and last part of this work I will explore some of the ontological models that are being discussed in scientific discourse as potential candidates for a coherent metaphysical framework to live up to current scientific development, and their potential to bridge the ontological gap between Us and Them. Potiguara cosmovision and practice, as depicted in the previous, second part of this volume, will serve as an example of one among many different subalternised, othered ways of knowing, with its particular ontological model to be compared with some of the most promising proposals from scientific discourse. My bet would be that *if* scientific evidence can be convincingly interpreted in cosmological terms that do not directly contradict or preclude the subjacent ontological categories traceable in Potiguara cosmopractices, *then* incommensurability is no longer an argument for any a priori dismissal of Other forms of knowledge. Even though Potiguara cosmopractice may differ radically compared other cultural contexts, incommensurability would have to be shown in every single case. Moreover, in principle, further interpretations of scientific evidence are thinkable that do not conflict with further cosmopractices from different cultural contexts. This outlook of a possible (if only partial) commensurability between modern science and Other knowledge cultures at their ontological level by itself does not amount either to equal validity or to complete commensurability; it does, however, offer a common ground of understanding, for once our fundamental ontological categories are comparable we are at least talking about the same "things" (or "persons"); and my suggestion is that this basic commensurability could open ways to an equitable dialogue between modern science and Other forms of knowing, which is a necessary precondition for an inter-scientific, pluriversal impact assessment of different ways of being and practices of world-making related to those different ontological concepts (as suggested by Santos' *ecology of knowledge,* Stengers' *cosmopolitical ecology of practices,* Castro's *inverted anthropology* or Escobar's *pluriversal dialogue of visions*). In this sense, a partial ontological commensurability could allow for transcending both foundationalism and relativism, and thus, lay the cornerstone for a relational notion of knowledge based on a comparative evaluation of the benefits we (humans from different social and cultural contexts) can expect from different forms of knowing in terms of the possible futures they promise.

11.1.1 The Ontological Bottleneck

> [T]he Cartesian anxiety requires not only that we believe in a self that we know cannot be found but also that we believe in a world to which we have no access. And once again, the logic of such a predicament leads inevitably to a condition of nihilism (Varela et al. 1993: 143).[2]

Although the limits of scientific knowledge for the most part have been discussed in terms of epistemological shortcomings concerning its truth value, these epistemological limitations have predominantly been attributed to implicit metaphysical presumptions entailed in Cartesian dualism. Particularly its ontological dualism has been held responsible for contributing to the Great Divide between mind and body, subject and object, human and non-human, culture and nature, humanities and natural sciences, and eventually, between Us and Them. I think it would be no exaggeration to state that Cartesian dualism has been identified as the most central problem of modern science as well as of modern/colonial world view in general, particularly in the face of its tremendous impact on the unfolding of modern history.[3]

While Descartes' dualist model has been subject to harsh critique from the day he published his *Meditations*, the predictive power of Newton's laws seemed to sustain at least its mechanistic understanding of nature. During the following three

[2] "This feeling of anxiety arises from the craving for an absolute ground. When this craving cannot be satisfied, the only other possibility seems to be nihilism or anarchy. The search for a ground can take many forms, but given the basic logic of representationism, the tendency is to search either for an outer ground in the world or an inner ground in the mind. By treating mind and world as opposed subjective and objective poles, the Cartesian anxiety oscillates endlessly between the two in search of a ground" (idem: 141).

[3] Whitehead (1925); Heidegger (1954); Husserl (1962); Rorty (1979); Latour (1993); Collingwood (1998); Morin (2005); Maxwell (2017, 2021); and many others.

centuries, natural scientists would explain more and more phenomena by deterministic natural laws, giving rise to a physicalist picture of the natural universe, including life, the origin of humanity, and finally, the human mind. However, by the turn of the twentieth century, modern science would be drowning in a profound and multi-dimensional crisis. On the one hand, the experimental method of natural sciences had proven inappropriate to cope with social and psychological phenomena, eventually resulting in the "two culture" divide between the humanities and the natural sciences. As discussed in Part I of this work, the humanities' perspective would denounce the contingent and construed character of science as well as the alienating, reifying, and disenchanting effects of its underlying metaphysical presuppositions. However, the humanities themselves continued trapped by the spell of the critical, disembodied Cartesian subject, only discovering, again and again, the illusiveness of reality lurking behind every single of its critical inquiries. Being unable to bridge the yawning gap between subject and object, mind and body, individual and society, the humanities got lost somewhere in the no man's land in between matters of fact and matters of concern. In the natural sciences, on the other hand, new findings in physics had shown the explanatory limits of Newtonian physics and its unified cosmology. Particularly, Einstein's relativity theory and the rise of quantum physics, as the two irreconsiliable pillars of modern physics, imposed an intolerably disunited picture of the universe, violating central principles of scientific theory building, like parsimony and non-contradiction. Moreover, quantum physics seemed to threaten the objectivist notion of a "neutral" observer, further exacerbating the epistemological crisis of positivism and empiricism.

At first sight the problems highlighted by the humanities and those encountered by modern physics do not seem to have much in common. While the epistemological crisis issued by the humanities primarily drew on a problematic notion of the subject as implied by rationalism, relativity and quantum physics rather emphasised the problematic ontological patterns of the physical universe as revealed by empirical evidence. But of course, the modern notions of the rational subject and empirical evidence are intrinsically related, since they derive from the same dualist ontology that defines these two poles as two separable "things": the first representing the sole thinking "stuff" observing and manipulating the blind matter represented by the latter. Ironically, it is exactly this separation between mind and matter that renders experience, and hence, "evidence" a pure business of the mind with no determinable relation to the material world "out there". Natural sciences had been "neutralising" this implicit illusiveness of its empirical evidence, more or less successfully, by reducing the mind to a cumbrous byproduct of matter, trying to explain it away so to say, supposing that matter would be a much simpler thing to handle than this inscrutable thing called "mind" (or "consciousness", "psyche", "experience", "subjectivity", "phenomenal", you name it!—nobody even knows how to name this annoying something!). However, relativity theory and quantum physics revealed that matter is at least as mysterious as the mind. In fact, there is no "matter" in the classical sense, only empty, flexing time-space pervaded by probability waves manifesting as particles in-deterministically, or something like that—actually, the "evidence" produced by scientists in their laboratories was so fuzzy and confusing, that a clear picture of what matter might be was almost impossible to be drawn (let alone what a mind might be!). Also, while relativity and quantum theory suggested equally weird pictures of matter, the two were utterly irreconcilable, allowing for no unified theory of the physical universe. And finally, quantum physics suggested that matter itself might have some properties that thitherto had been ascribed exclusively to the mind. On its fundamental level, matter is constituted by quanta (discrete portions) of the same "stuff" as light or other kinds of electromagnetic radiation, equalling rather a kind of informed energy than classical material objects. These quanta behave probabilistically and depending on the type of measurement, that is, the intervention an observer decided to apply in order to yield a physically detectable manifestation of those quanta, showing either wave-like or particle-like properties. While particle-like manifestations of quanta resemble properties we would expect from classical objects, their wave-like behaviour alludes rather to a kind of "active information".[4] This wave-particle dualism at the very fundament of the physical universe was soon associated with the mind-body problem, with some of the leading quantum physicists[5] suggesting that the wave-like properties of quanta might somehow be related to the emergence of conscious experience and free will. There have been many attempts to get the wave-particle dualism into a single coherent ontological framework, resulting in a confusing variety of (often incredibly odd) proposals concerning the place and role of mind and matter in our physical universe. So, notwithstanding all the attempts to keep the physical realm clear from this recalcitrant phenomenon called mind, with quantum physics it intruded on the scene again through the "backdoor" of wave-particle dualism—but this time right in the heart of fundamental physics. Now, the ontological roles of mind and matter would not only be decisive for the epistemological status of empirical evidence, as highlighted by the humanities, but also for making sense of it in terms of a unified theory of the physical universe. Despite the numerous efforts to come up with a convincing ontological interpretation of quantum theory, to date none have attained consensus. There are still many different proposals in the running, suggesting radically different worlds, with different roles for waves and particles, mind(s) and matter. So, quantum physics (still?) does not explain what mind and matter actually might be, nor how they emerge, or how they are connected with each other.

However, there is yet another scientific field of research particularly concerned with questions of this kind, located somewhere between cognitive sciences, neurosciences, and philosophy, and which is generally referred to as philosophy of mind. While neurosciences have been rather explaining consciousness away, reducing it to a mere epiphenomenon of neuronal activity, recent contributions in philosophy of mind have been insisting on the ontological status of consciousness as an irreducible observable. David Chalmers (1995) famously argues that the *hard problem of consciousness* is not about tracing all neuronal processes and their correlation with cognitive processes, but about explaining why such physical activity is accompanied by phenomenal experience at all. So, again, the mind-body problem has to be treated at its ontological level to make sense of our empirical evidence. And, again, there are many

[4] Bohm (1990).

[5] E.g. Bohr (1928); Oppenheimer (1954); Heisenberg et al. (1963).

radically different worlds in the run, suggesting different ontological roles of mind and matter. Conspicuously, the ontological frameworks discussed in philosophy of mind reveal some fundamental parallels compared to ontological interpretations discussed in quantum physics. Of course, these convergences have long been noticed and some authors made an effort to evaluate, compare, and where possible, to integrate different models into a coherent, unified ontological framework able to do justice both to the findings from quantum physics and philosophy of mind.

It goes without saying that all this is work in progress and will need a lot more discussion and research before anything definitive can be said about the possibility to really accomplish this ambitious objective. However, the persistence of the mind-body problem, representing the core of an *ontological bottleneck* science has to go through before it can finally transcend the limitations it inherited from Cartesian dualism, dictates that we must never give up trying. As a reminder: Without a fundamental theory of mind and matter we do not know how and what we know (due to the induction problem and relativism); the knowledge we produce makes no sense to us (due to the epistemic gap between objective description and phenomenal experience); we do not know exactly what kind of knowledge we are producing and for what purpose (since we are not aware of our metaphysical suppositions and their objective impacts); and we have no access to other kinds of knowledge (since we think we think too differently to talk to each other). This is why the *hard problem of consciousness* ultimately amounts to the real *hard problem of modern science*.[6]

Moreover, while the preliminary character of the ontological models that are currently being discussed is something these proposals share with any other scientific hypothesis, they are based on extraordinarily solid empirical evidence (from

---

[6] "In unserem wissenschaftlichen Weltbild, sowohl dem geisteswissenschaftlichen als auch, noch eklatanter, dem naturwissenschaftlichen, offenbart sich an zentraler Stelle ein fundamentaler Konflikt: Das 'Medium', durch das wir all unsere Erkenntnisse über 'die Welt' überhaupt erst erlangen, nämlich das Bewusstsein, fügt sich in das aus diesen Erkenntnissen abgeleitete Weltbild nicht ein. So gut unsere theoretischen Modelle der Realität uns in die Lage versetzen, ihre Prozesse zu verstehen, vorherzusagen und sogar zu gestalten, so unbefriedigend und herausfordernd ist, zumindest für mich, dieser fundamentale weiße Fleck auf der epistemologischen Landkarte" (von Stillfried 2018: 4). Compare also David Chalmers (2010: 39): "The problem of explaining first-person data is the hard problem"; Bertrand Russell (2007: 402): "Percepts are the only part of the physical world that we know otherwise than abstractly"; Thomas Nagel (1974: 5): "The less it depends on a specifically human viewpoint, the more objective is our description. […] If the subjective character of experience is fully comprehensible only from one point of view, then any shift to greater objectivity—that is, less attachment to a specific viewpoint—does not take us nearer to the real nature of the phenomenon: it takes us farther away from it"; or Whitehead (1925): "We are aware of nature as an interplay of bodies, colours, sounds, scents, tastes, touches and other various bodily feelings, displayed as in space, in patterns of mutual separation by intervening volumes, and of individual shape. Also the whole is a flux, changing with the lapse of time. This systematic totality is disclosed to us as one complex of things. But the seventeenth century dualism cuts straight across it. The objective world of science was confined to mere spatial material with simple location in space and time, and subjected to definite rules as to its locomotion" (idem: 180). "Also the assumption of the bare valuelessness of mere matter led to a lack of reverence in the treatment of natural or artistic beauty" (idem: 243). "The two evils are: one, the ignoration of the true relation of each organism to its environment; and the other, the habit of ignoring the intrinsic worth of the environment which must be allowed its weight in any consideration of final ends" (idem: 244).

experimental physics) and on logical arguments approved in the course of a long-lasting academic discourse (philosophy of mind).

Anyhow, what counts for my purpose here is the intuition that some of the most promising proposals for a unified ontological framework capable of serving as a fundamental scientific theory of mind and matter may be more commensurable with Other ontological conceptions than scientistic prejudice.

In the following chapter I will provide a brief summary of recent debates on the ontological status of consciousness before I turn to ontological interpretations of quantum physics and what they can tell us about the possible nature of mind and matter. The whole issue has been treated in great detail by others before me, so that I will rather lean on these second-hand summaries than on my own research in these vast discursive fields. Particularly, I will refer to David Chalmers's's[7] groundbreaking contributions to a more comprehensive, unified discussion of the hard problem of consciousness, and to Nikolaus von Stillfried's[8] recent monumental effort to synthesise both ontological interpretations derived from the philosophy of mind and quantum physics into a single coherent theory of mind and matter.

* * *

> The really hard problem of consciousness is the problem of *experience*. When we think and perceive, there is a whir of information processing, but there is also a subjective aspect. As Nagel (1974) has put it, there is *something it is like* to be a conscious organism. This subjective aspect is experience (Chalmers 2010: 5).

If asked about the source of our experience, our feelings, impressions, and thoughts, most of us would probably reply that they are a product of our brain activity. We believe that our mind is somehow the output of neuronal activity, because we were told so in school, in documentaries on TV, and maybe even in lectures at university. Neuroscience has invested great effort to associate particular cognitive activities

---

[7] David Chalmers and his definition of the hard problem of consciousness have become a central point of reference in contemporary philosophy of mind. Chalmers had been publishing extensively on the problem of consciousness since 1993, outlining his core ideas on the hard problem of consciousness in his 1995 The Conscious Mind and in his 2010 The Character of Consciousness. I will use these two publications as basic references when I refer to Chalmers's general approach. The great advantage of Chalmers' earlier work is that he primarily reframes an old problem in a new way rather than offering a solution to it. He began his research by elaborating on the epistemological, ontological, and logical implications of the various proposals of other authors and categorising them into different types of ontological constellations (e.g. different types of monism and dualism). This generic approach to possible ways of dealing with the hard problem provides a solid foundation for comparison with other ontological debates, such as those in quantum physics.

[8] Nikolaus von Stillfried's 2018 habilitation thesis (forthcoming publication), is one of the most in-depth comparative analyses of the entire discourse surrounding the hard problem of consciousness and quantum-theoretically informed attempts to develop a natural theory of mind and matter. His work and countless personal conversations have shaped much of the discussions on this topic presented here. Consequently, the third part of this book can be read as a commentary on Chalmers' and von Stillfried's accounts.

and abilities, perceptions, feelings, and even memories with precisely defined neuronal processes, neurons firing and neurotransmitters stimulating synaptic activity in particular brain areas, and so on. Today there is copious empirical evidence giving proof of the tight correlation between our subjective experience and physical processes in our nervous system. We know which brain areas are active when we see, listen, speak, think in symbols or signs, when we are waking or asleep, and a lot more.[9] And although our conscious self does not seem to be related to a particular locus in the brain, we may content ourselves with explaining it by some "re-entry" processes between distant active brain areas,[10] or simply explain it away—do we not have many "selves" anyway? Isn't consciousness just a flux of sequenced instances of being aware of particular thoughts, impressions, and sensations, each being related to certain brain areas[11]? However, even if we are prepared to give up our precious self, we still think, feel love, pain and joy, experience the beauty of colours we see and music we listen to, that is, there would still be *qualia*. Supposed we would know exactly which neuronal process is responsible for every single qualium we experience, and suppose we would communicate our feelings referring to our "c-fibres firing" when we get frightened, like Rorty's (1979) Antipodians might do, even then we would still experience *fear*. And suppose the Antipodeans would be experiencing a different kind of qualium when their c-fibres are firing than we do, it would be impossible for us to know how the Antipodians feel when their c-fibres are firing, just as we will never know what it is like to be a bat, even though we may have precise knowledge about the physical properties of their sonar system.[12] It actually does not matter what we call the qualia we experience or which particular neuronal process might be responsible for them or not; the only way to know what it is like to have those qualia, that is, what kind of phenomenal qualities they actually have, is to experience them. This train of thought led some authors[13] to the conclusion, that conscious experience is an undeniable fact, and that no materialist account will ever be able to sufficiently explain consciousness (or to explain it away). The explanatory gap between physical and phenomenal accounts is, of course, an old topic which has been discussed for centuries in terms of the mind-body problem. Though all human beings may have the perception of an inner and an outer world, the mind-body problem in its particular modern fashion goes back to Descartes's interactionist ontological dualism and the mechanistic worldview of his time.[14] Previously, scholastic scholars like Thomas Aquinas had been propagating Aristotle's view, suggesting rather some kind of ontological monism than a dualistic

---

[9] Varela et al. (1993); Edelman (2004); Walach (2014).

[10] Dennett (1991); Edelman (2004).

[11] Hume (2017) already suggested that there no self in the sense of Descartes's *cogito*, only a flux of impressions and ideas, including memories of past impressions, leading to the fiction of a self-identity. Other scholars that refused the notion of the conscious self are, for example, Rorty (1979), Dennett (1991), Varela et al. (1993), James (1996), Nietzsche (2002).

[12] Nagel (1974).

[13] Chalmers (1995, 2010); Walach and Römer (2011); von Stillfried (2018); among others.

[14] Husserl (1962); Rorty (1979); Walach (2014); among others.

model.[15] With the modern problematisation of the mind and its relation to reality, as put forth in different ways by Descartes, Locke, Berkeley, Hume, and Kant, the mind-body problem advanced to the central question of epistemology and of modern philosophy in general. However, while some scholars, like Locke and Boyle, would propagate physicalist models of mind, others, like Berkeley, Hume and Kant, would more or less radically contest that it is in principle possible to acquire any reliable knowledge about the physical world. The physical and the phenomenal realms were put at war, so to say, since one could stay only with either of these mutually exclusive aspects: either reducing the mind to an epiphenomenon of the physical, or reducing the physical to phenomenal representations in the mind. But, there were also alternative views trying to keep things together. Spinoza's neutral monism and Leibniz's monadology, for example, can be understood as attempts to avoid a rupture between the physical and the phenomenal.[16] However fascinating those philosophical systems, they were based on purely logical speculation with no noteworthy empirical evidence concerning the possible physical correlates of conscious experience. In fact, available evidence would rather sustain some kind of idealism or solipsism, since from a representational view, inner experience was the only irrefutable fact, while the existence of the physical world was a mere metaphysical supposition. Nonetheless, history turned out to give more credit to the physicalists, and with the rise of biology and neurosciences during the nineteenth and twentieth century an increasingly detailed picture of neuronal processes could be associated with mental states, promising the possibility of a purely physical explanation both of our experience and our behaviour. For quite a time now physicalism has been the hegemonic paradigm, though critical voices never ceased questioning its explanatory power. But until recently, these alternative views were rather marginal and isolated, barely forming a unified discursive field.[17] This situation

[15] According to Aristotle's holomorphism, matter has no independent existence, but rather the character of a potentiality whose actual "form" (*eidos*) as an object has to be activated though its relation to the actuality of other things or beings. The "form" of living things is the "soul", representing kind of a vitalist principle actualising the matter providing the form of the living body. Hence, for Aristotle there is no soul-body duality, since both constitute a unity (Walach 2014). However, Rorty (1979) insists that although the Greek viewed the body and the soul as something separated, they saw the sensations as something pertaining to the body, while the intellect or reason would be something divine and separated from the physical body. It was Descartes and later Locke who lumped the sensory and the intellectual contents of inner experience together, thus creating the modern use of the term "idea" as inner representation before the mind's eye. Only then epistemology became the central question of modern philosophy. Also, by lumping together emotions, sensations and thoughts, the new concept of consciousness is created, something untranslatable into ancient Greek: "The paradigm of the 'epistemological turn' taken by philosophy in the seventeenth century was what Kant called 'the physiology of the human understanding of the celebrated Mr. Locke'—a causal account of mental processes which is supposed to criticize and justify knowledge-claims. To get this notion off the ground required the Cartesian replacement of the ancient and medieval problem of reason by the modern problem of consciousness" (idem: 126).

[16] Walach and Römer (2011); compare also Whitehead (1925) and Husserl (1962).

[17] Von Stillfried (2018). If not marked otherwise, in the following discussion I will refer to von Stillfried (2018).

would change during the 1990s with David Chalmers's contributions and his formulation of the *Hard Problem of Consciousness*.[18] After his initial purpose to prove physicalism had been frustrated, Chalmers boiled the whole discussion down to what he felt was its ontological core:

> The really hard problem of consciousness is the problem of experience. [...] As Nagel (1974) has put it, there is something it is like to be a conscious organism. This subjective aspect is experience (Chalmers 2010: 5).

Of course, in its essence, this definition was not really new; Descartes had already followed a similar rationale and, as mentioned by Chalmers himself, also later authors like Thomas Nagel (1974) had pointed to the irreducibility of experience (in this case of "what it is like to be a bat").[19] However, Chalmers reformulated the mind-body problem in the face of current findings from cognitive and neurosciences while pointing to its metaphysical dimension, and he provided a systematic comparative analysis of many different ontological approaches concerning both their logical and empirical tenability. It is important to note that Chalmers came from physicalism to ultimately discover its untenability, thus constructing his arguments with physicalism as its central point of reference.[20] This reference to physicalism resides also in his definition of the "hard problem" in contrast to "easy problems" of

[18] "Even in the science of the mind, much progress has been made. Recent work in cognitive science and neuroscience is leading us to a better understanding of human behavior and of the processes that drive it. We do not have many detailed theories of cognition, to be sure, but there are few problems of principle; the details cannot be too far off. But consciousness is as perplexing as it ever was. It still seems utterly mysterious that the causation of behavior should be accompanied by conscious experience. We do not just lack a detailed theory; we are in the dark about what a theory of consciousness would even look like. [...] We are entirely in the dark about how it fits into the natural order. This means that a correct theory of consciousness is likely to affect our conception of the universe more profoundly than any other new scientific development. Consciousness is both fundamental and unexplained; this makes for a potent cocktail" (Chalmers 1995: ix). "We can say that a being is conscious if there is something it is like to be that being, to use a phrase made famous by Thomas Nagel. Similarly, a mental state is conscious if there is something it is like to be in that mental state. Equivalently, we can say that a mental state is conscious if it has a qualitative feel—an associated quality of experience. These qualitative feels are also known as phenomenal qualities, or qualia for short. The problem of explaining these phenomenal qualities is just the problem of explaining consciousness. This is the really hard part of the mind–body problem" (Chalmers 1995: 4).

[19] However, Nagel thought this would not prove physicalism to be false, but only that it needs more investigation. Nagel also associated the mind-body problem with the subject-object dichotomy, suggesting that some kind of "objective phenomenology" might overcome the limitations of reductionism. But his proposal would probably not stand the knowledge argument (see below).

[20] "The hard problem of consciousness [...] is that of explaining how and *why physical processes give rise to phenomenal consciousness* [sic!]. A solution to the hard problem would involve an account of the relation between physical processes and consciousness, explaining on the basis of natural principles how and why it is that physical processes are associated with states of experience" (Chalmers 2010: 105—italics inserted by myself). Note, that the expression to "give rise" already points to some sort of supervenience of the phenomenal on the physical.

consciousness.[21] According to Chalmers, questions concerning the structure and function of cognition, or the psychological aspects of consciousness in terms of awareness and information processing as usually treated by cognitive and neurosciences refer to "easy problems". Such problems are "easy", because they are, at least in principle, neurophysiologically explainable without the need for any changes in the underlying metaphysical framework. The "hard problem of consciousness", in contrast, refers to the question why neurophysical processes are correlated by qualitative experience (qualia), that is, the phenomenal aspect of consciousness, and how this correlation might be explained. So, the fact that there is something it is like to be me, you, or a bat, demands an explanation, and since physicalism cannot provide such an explanation, the solution of the "hard problem of consciousness" requires radical changes in the ontological framework modern science is currently based upon. However, Chalmers's definition of the hard problem of consciousness presupposes a number of hypotheses concerning the natures of mind and matter[22]:

- A: Consciousness (Q) exists
- B: The physical (P) exists
- C: Naturalism counts, or Q and P are naturally and lawfully correlated
- D: Q is not reducible to P
- E: P is not reducible to Q

Since these hypotheses depend on further assumptions and definitions, I would like to have a short look at each of them before I come to possible solutions to the hard problem of consciousness.

(A) Consciousness Exists

Although modern epistemology is entirely based on the idea of an autonomous, thinking subject, a significant number of scientists and philosophers seem to be prepared to assume that the self and its free will is an illusive notion, entirely explainable in terms of neuronal and cognitive processes.[23] Moreover, one should suppose that physicalists experience the same rich and lively qualia as, let's say, dualists or idealists, and still they seem prepared to assume that their experience is just a meaningless byproduct of their brain activity. How come if consciousness is such an obvious and undeniable fact? Chalmers admits that the existence of consciousness is not logically necessary once we suppose that our behaviour and even the content of our thoughts might be explainable by solving all the "easy problems"

---

[21] "The hard problem is that of explaining conscious experience. Where the easy problems are concerned, it suffices to explain how a function is performed, and to do this it suffices to specify an appropriate neural or computational mechanism. But where the hard problem is concerned, explaining cognitive and behavioral functions always leaves a further open question: why is the performance of these functions accompanied by experience? Because of this, the standard reductive methods of neuroscience and cognitive science that work for the easy problems do not work for the hard problem" (Chalmers 2010: xiv).

[22] This systematic analysis of Chalmers implicit presumptions has been elaborated by von Stillfried (2018), not by Chalmers himself.

[23] Particularly Daniel Dennett (1991).

of neurosciences. However, Chalmers insists that such a view would be "utterly unsatisfying", since his own experience is so "baffling" and imbued with phenomenal qualities that they simply demand an explanation. So, if people with phenomenal experience cannot ignore it, this would lead to the conclusion that physicalists do not have any phenomenal qualia, just like Chalmers's "zombie twin in the universe next door".[24] According to Chalmers's conceivability argument (which I will treat in more detail in a moment), there should be absolutely no way to actually distinguish "zombie"-philosophers-of-mind from their conscious mates, since their behaviour would be exactly the same and we cannot, per definition, know what it is like to be a "zombie" who does not at all know what is like to be.

Be this as it may, one could also ask why Chalmers spends so much effort in proving the evidence of something which is either too evident to be ignored by anyone who experiences it, or neither evident nor logically necessary at all, simply depending on the experiencer's worldview. Conspicuously though, in Descartes's days, philosophers of all different schools of thought would agree, quite unanimously, that they have phenomenal experience, and that experience is the only access to reality—independently from their different theories concerning the possible nature of experience. This is why for those philosophers the problem was rather to avoid solipsism than to prove the existence of consciousness. So, once oneself happens to experience qualia and feels this deep conviction that there is something demanding to be explained, it does not matter much whether other people are "zombies" or not, since this is something we cannot, by definition, ever know.[25] The only thing which one knows for sure is that there are qualia popping up before one's inner eye.[26] Of course, if a significant number of other people report sharing similar kinds of experience, and if one is prepared to accept the hypotheses that they and the physical world around exist (even though there is no absolute proof of that), one may easily come to the conclusion that consciousness might be a general property of human beings and maybe even of the universe in general.[27] However, this still leaves us with the question of what consciousness is. Chalmers himself does not offer a clear definition of consciousness, but rather identifies consciousness

[24] Chalmers (1995): 167. In fact, Daniel Dennett (1991) prefers to be rather a zombie than to believe in consciousness: "Are zombies possible? They're not just possible, they're actual. We're all zombies. Nobody is conscious — not in the systematically mysterious way that supports such doctrines as epiphenomenalism" (idem: 406).

[25] Much like in Kurt Vonnegut's famous novel "Breakfast for Champions", where the main protagonist, Dwayne Hoover, becomes convinced that he is the only being with free will and that all other people around him are in fact machines made by the creator of the universe to test him (Vonnegut 1973).

[26] Nikolaus von Stillfried (2018), for example, emphasises that, differently from Chalmers, he does not see how one could doubt the existence of consciousness, because for him (von Stillfried) experience is a fundamental empirical fact, making solipsism more plausible than physicalism.

[27] Of course, as mentioned above, the existence of people who deny having phenomenal consciousness would imply a universe were some living beings have consciousness while others do not, which would complicate the whole problem quite a bit. However, for the sake of parsimony it makes more sense to treat consciousness-deniers as "anomalia".

with the phenomenal character of conscious states or qualia, which ultimately amount to the part of reality that cannot be described in terms of physical properties. Though one can doubt this definition, it might be a good strategy, since it avoids the Cartesian identification of consciousness with the self, and thus, also avoids criticism from those who argue against the Cartesian self.[28] Another strategy might be to follow Bertrand Russell (2007) in defining experience as simply incorrigible since "intrinsic" in contrast to the relational description of physical properties.[29] Anyhow, since the bare, and by definition "incorrigible" ascertainment of the existence of experience by itself does not reveal much about its intrinsic essence, other determinants will have to be defined before more can be said.

(B) The Physical World Exists

It may not surprise that Chalmers, as a former physicalist, initialle[30] took the existence of the physical world for granted and that he constructs his arguments rather to convince himself about the irreducibility of consciousness to the physical than against scepticism. However, logically speaking, the existence of the physical is at least as hard a problem as the problem of consciousness. Once consciousness is taken for the only incorrigible and intrinsic evidence, the Cartesian problem of solipsism emerges as the "hard problem of the physical". In the absence of solid arguments from Chalmers, von Stillfried (2018) comes to his aid pointing to the continuity of the physical in the face of the discontinuity of consciousness. Our continuous flux of experience is interrupted by periods of unconsciousness during sleep or coma while the physical world continues both stable and moving as evidenced by our own experience, when we wake up again, and the observation of others who stood awake while we were sleeping. Thus, continuity and intersubjectivity are definitively properties that allude to the existence of the physical and that differentiate it from phenomenal experience. However, these arguments are not

[28] E.g. Rorty (1979); James (1981); Hume (2017).

[29] "Physics, in itself, is exceedingly abstract, and reveals only certain mathematical characteristics of the material with which it deals. It does not tell us anything as to the intrinsic character of this material. Psychology is preferable in this respect, but is not causally autonomous: if we assume that psychical events are subject, completely, to causal laws, we are compelled to postulate apparently extra-psychical causes for some of them. But by bringing physics and perception together, we are able to include psychical events in the material of physics, and to give to physics the greater concreteness which results from our more intimate acquaintance with the subject-matter of our own experience. To show that the traditional separation between physics and psychology, mind and matter, is not metaphysically defensible. will be one of the purposes of this work; but the two will be brought together, not by subordinating either to the other, but by displaying each as a logical structure composed of what, following Dr H. M. Sheffer,* we shall call "neutral stuff" (Russell 2007: 12). "Percepts are the only part of the physical world that we know otherwise than abstractly. As regards the world in general, both physical and mental, everything that we know of its intrinsic character is derived from the mental side, and almost everything that we know of its causal laws is derived from the physical side. But from the standpoint of philosophy the distinction between physical and mental is superficial and unreal" (idem: 402).

[30] Inspired by the metaphysical implications of the 1999 film The Matrix, Chalmers (2003, 2022) went on to develop the idea of "simulation realism".

sufficient proof, for both aspects, my own experience of the physical and its continuity, and the others and their report, might only exist in my imagination. But of course, if we relegate the burden of proof against solipsism to the physical, we will inevitably end up with idealism. So, for the sake of horse-sense, let us assume the physical to exist without demanding further proof.

Anyhow, given the ontological existence of the physical, what then is its essence compared to the phenomenal realm of consciousness? Chalmers himself seems to follow different argumentations, mixing them up at times, but does not provide a single, consistent definition.[31] One strategy to differentiate the physical from the phenomenal might be to associate the first with spatiality while defining the latter as non-spatial. However, Chalmers himself observes that some physical phenomena might not comply with the requirement of spatiality, rendering this aspect a problematic candidate for a solid definition of the physical. But also Chalmers's analytical definition of the physical as the part of reality which can be described in terms of structure and function might face some problems, since cognition can be conceptualised in similar terms.[32] A third strategy Chalmers pursues is to combine the two properties of spatiality and structural/functional description to define the physical, associating structure to the spatiotemporal aspect of the physical and function to its "causal role in the production of a system's behaviour".[33] This solution, however, restricts the causal role to the physical while precluding interactionist interpretations without any further justification.[34] Another attempt by Chalmers to define the physical follows Russell's[35] observation that experience is our only access to the intrinsic character of reality in contrast to the relational character of the physical as described by causal laws. But again, this would run parallel to the relational character of qualia. Of course, one could counter that consciousness cannot be reduced to its content, however, what then should be the ontic status of qualia? On the other hand, if phenomenal experience is the only intrinsic access to reality, and if this experience is characterised by a certain relational structure as well, this could either be interpreted in terms of the immanent relational structure of the physical realm reflecting into our mind, or as a projection of our transcendental structure of perception onto external reality. Thus, the intrinsicness of experience would stay against the extrinsicness of the physical, while still saying nothing about the structure or existence of the latter. Such a distinction seems to be the subjacent assumption of yet another attempt to define the physical. Chalmers associates the physical with

[31] von Stillfried (2018).

[32] Actually, once we assume experience to be the only intrinsic evidence, the apparently causal structure of time-space cannot be differentiated from our cognitive structures. This problem has been most famously and in great detail demonstrated by Hume and, in particular, by Kant. Accordingly, von Stillfried suggests that Chalmers' definition is circular. Accordingly, von Stillfried portends that Chalmers definition is circular. Similar arguments can also be found in Rorty (1979).

[33] Chalmers (2002).

[34] von Stillfried (2018).

[35] Russell (2007).

those properties which can be sufficiently described from a third-person perspective in contrast to phenomenal properties which can only be described from a first-person view. This distinction amounts simply to the subject-object dichotomy, which certainly continues to have an important heuristic value; but since it does not provide any analytical distinction between phenomenal and physical objects, it rather leads back to the problem of solipsism than to a solid definition of the physical. So, while the first-person perspective is the only direct experience we have, and thus holds as a strong argument for the existence of consciousness, third-person perspectives are nothing but first-person perspectives of others concerning a material world of which nobody has direct experience. Due to this circularity, third-person perspectives do not prove anything about the physical world, not even about its existence (at least as long as one holds to representational epistemology).[36]

In sum, the discussion shows that there does not seem to be any direct evidence nor any logical proof of the existence of the physical realm beyond our subjective experience as long as we do not make some additional (metaphysical) assumption about the nature of mind and matter. Or to put it simply: Although we are generally told that our mind is somehow caused by matter, it turns out to be much harder to provide solid proof for the existence of the physical than for the existence of mind. And even if we are prepared to follow Chalmers in "bypassing this sort of skeptical problem by giving [us] the physical world for free",[37] we are still left in the dark about the essential character of this physical world and about how it might be related to our experience.

(C) Naturalism Counts

Although Chalmers suggests that consciousness might not follow the same causal laws we know from physics, he assumes that it is a natural phenomenon as any other, following some universal principles or "laws". However, naturalism in this sense is not the same as materialism or physicalism,[38] since the phenomenal properties of consciousness might represent a separate ontic category obeying "psychophysical principles" that differ radically from those governing physical properties, while at the same time "specifying how phenomenal (or protophenomenal) properties depend on physical properties".[39] Thus, Chalmers's notion of a "naturalist" theory of consciousness already presumes consciousness to represent a fundamental property with an ontic status of its own and in addition to the physical realm. The presumed irreducibility of the phenomenal character of experience to physical properties implies an additional ontic category, however, it does not necessarily imply an additional non-physical ontic "stuff" (since it allows for certain non-dualistic

---

[36] Interestingly, Chalmers (1995) does not seem to follow this train of thought, insisting rather in the solidity of intersubjectively testable third-person accounts and the weak character of subjective first-person account, which can neither be tested, nor shared, or compared according to any objective standard.

[37] Chalmers (1995: 68).

[38] Compare also Part I, Chap. 2 of this volume.

[39] Chalmers (1995: 112). Chalmers uses the same definition in (2010: 17).

interpretations). Any naturalistic theory of mind, in the spirit of Chalmers's, demands alternative interpretations of existing evidence from neuroscience and physics in terms of new ontological models of mind and matter. Chalmers himself admits the necessarily speculative character of such a metaphysical assumption about fundamental ontological categories like mind and matter. Since it is in principle impossible to come to any final conclusion about the true nature of reality, there are always different possible ontological interpretations of existing data depending on the metaphysical presupposition involved. However, in saying this, Chalmers explicitly does not follow a sceptic rationale, instead he insists that although any interpretation of experience is based on metaphysical presupposition, our notion of reality is still no illusion. To illustrate his point Chalmers refers to the well-known movie "the Matrix"[40] and its subjacent philosophical figure of a "brain in a vat".[41] While the film rather suggests a sceptic interpretation of the "matrix" as an illusive reality in contrast to the true reality where humans are only brains in vats, so to say, Chalmers proposes a metaphysical interpretation of the situation. Accordingly, the "reality" within the matrix is as real as the one outside of it; however, the two "realities" operate with different metaphysical premises concerning the ontological nature of the phenomenal and the physical, the resulting kind of "world" we think we live in, and how and what we can know about it. The same goes for any metaphysical framework, and therefore, also for a fundamental theory of consciousness.

(D) Phenomenal Properties Are Not Reducible to Physical Properties

The irreducibility of consciousness to physical properties is the core assumption of Chalmers's "hard problem of consciousness". Would consciousness be reducible to, that is, sufficiently explainable in terms of, physical properties, there would be no hard problem about consciousness. But what exactly does it mean for a phenomenon to be reducible, or irreducible to the physical? Unfortunately, "reducibility" is not a trivial concept and Chalmers hints at several possible definitions.[42] By and large, he uses "irreducibility" to come to a more precise definition of the explanatory gap[43] between phenomenal experience (how it feels to be), and physical accounts of neuronal activity, cognition, and behaviour. In this quite general sense, for consciousness to be reducible would mean that a description of the causal chain, that might somehow lead from photons with a 550 nm wavelength hitting our retina all the way through complex neuronal processing in our brains to our sensation of

---

[40] The Matrix is a 1999 science fiction film by Lena and Lilly Wachowski. It basically paints the picture of a distopic future where mankind is being bred by machines for energy supply, while their minds are connected to a virtual world, called "The Matrix", where they live and interact as if it was the real world. People do not know they are within the Matrix as long as they do not exit to the real world. In his later work, Chalmers further developed the idea of a metaphysics of virtual reality (Chalmers 2022).The same as the one to which I referred in Part I, Chap. 2.

[41] Chalmers (2010: 455).

[42] For a more detailed discussion of Chalmers different usages of the term see von Stillfried (2018).

[43] Chalmers refers to Joseph Levine (1983) (quoted in Chalmers 1995, 2010, and von Stillfried 2018).

seeing "green" at the traffic light, and finally, having us move our legs to cross the street, would amount to a complete and sufficient explanation of consciousness. Since this physical account does not explain *how it feels* to see green and to move one's legs, it does not provide a sufficient *explanation* of consciousness either, and hence, consciousness is irreducible. According to this general use of the term, reducibility is an epistemological concept in the first place. However, Chalmers also associates reducibility with supervenience, which is rather an ontological concept. In this respect, he distinguishes between *logical* and *natural* supervenience. While *logical* supervenience of A on B implies A as a necessary consequence of B, *natural* supervenience requires an additional rule or principle (not entailed in B) to establish the dependency between A and B. Chalmers defines reducibility as a kind of logical supervenience, since a sufficient description of B will necessarily entail a sufficient description of A. On the other hand, a non-reductive naturalistic theory of consciousness may well suggest some kind of natural supervenience of the phenomenal on the physical, given that it is based on additional natural principles not entailed in physical law. It follows, that a non-reductive account of consciousness necessarily demands alternative ontological models that differ from physicalist monism in suggesting additional ontic categories (such as the "phenomenal") for a sufficient explanation of consciousness. With this move, Chalmers transforms the *epistemological* explanatory gap into an *ontological* gap between physical and phenomenal properties.[44]

Another famous argument by Chalmers to substantiate his irreducibility thesis of consciousness leads us into a hypothetical zombie-world. This so-called conceivability argument builds on a modal thought experiment, imagining the existence of a parallel universe which is an exact copy of ours, with the only difference being that it completely lacks phenomenal properties. Hence, there is a clone of each of us in this parallel universe, but a zombie clone who has no idea what it is like to be. Chalmers argues that since it is in principle possible to explain behaviour in purely physical terms, our zombie-twins might well behave exactly as we do, despite having no phenomenal experience. This means that such a universe is perfectly conceivable, at least from a physicalist point of view. However, since we know from our own experience that there definitively is something it is like to be us, consciousness cannot be explained in terms of physical properties, and thus, has to be based on some kind of irreducible fundamental non-physical ontic category.[45] Their odd-

---

[44] Historically, there have been similar observation of an explanatory gap between the physical and phenomenal accounts of consciousness, with Leibniz's mills argument being one of the earliest and most prominent ones. Leibniz famously argued that if the mind was produced by a machine, like a windmill, even the most detailed description of the mechanical movements inside the mill would never give a sufficient account of our phenomenal experience (Leibniz 1965). Similarly, Bois-Reymond (1974) emphasised that physical processes in the brain cannot explain the existence of consciousness (both examples quoted in von Stillfried 2018).

[45] Again, this argument has historical antecedents like Descartes's "zombie"-animals with no phenomenal experience. Since Descartes's zombie-animals share the same world as human beings with phenomenal experience, Descartes had to introduce an additional principle to explain consciousness, which was, of course, God. However, once God is excluded from this model, there is

ness[46] notwithstanding, Chalmers's zombies have become a standard element in recent discussions on consciousness.

A third argument Chalmers often quotes in support of his irreducibility thesis is known as the "knowledge argument". In its essence, the argument follows the same rationale as the two previous arguments, namely that knowledge about the physical correlates of phenomenal experience does not amount to knowledge about what it feels like to have experience. The argument has been articulated by several authors[47] using different anecdotes, with Jackson's (1982)[48] probably being the most famous example. According to this example, Mary spent her whole life in a black and white room, without ever having seen a colour. However, Mary has a complete knowledge about all psychophysiological processes as well as about optics, that is, about all physical correlates of colour perception. One day Mary is released from her room and, for the first time in her life, she experiences colours. The argument maintains that despite all the theoretical knowledge Mary has about colour perception, in the moment she first sees colours she learns something essentially new: what it is like to see colours. Of course, Nagel's example of the impossibility of knowing what it feels like to be a bat goes in the same direction, too. Chalmers himself observes, however, the knowledge argument by itself does not refute physicalism, since experience might supervene on the physical, and thus, be explicable in terms of physical facts. Thus, physicalists may hold that Mary already knows everything about experience, since it somehow results from physical facts. Thus, for the knowledge argument to hold against physicalism further definitions would be necessary to distinguish between "narrowly" and "broadly" physical facts. However, this might be an artificial problem resulting from Chalmers's misplaced equation of knowledge with deducibility, for even if Mary was able to deduce what experience is, she

no explanation for consciousness. Von Stillfried (2018) notes that this problem has long been perceived by other authors like George Frederick Stout (1931), who demonstrated that physicalism leads to epiphenomenalism and thus is inviable. Philosophical zombies have also been introduced previous to Chalmers by other authors (e.g. Kirk 1974; Squires 1974).

[46] Personally I do not follow Chalmers argument, since I do not think it logically conceivable for zombies to behave like us, since our behaviour is most probable influenced by our experience of what it is like to be, and most importantly, to feel the consequences of our action. Chalmers's underlying premise that behaviour might be explainable exclusively in terms of physical processes is, at least for me, as odd as Descartes's thesis that animals are just bio-machines with no phenomenal experience. Chalmers admits that "Zombies are probably not naturally possible: they probably cannot exist in our world, with its laws of nature. But the argument holds that zombies could have existed, perhaps in a very different sort of universe. For example, it is sometimes suggested that God could have created a zombie world, if he had so chosen" (Chalmers 2010; 107). But still, if in our world it is not logically conceivable for a conscious being to behave as if it would have no notion of what it is like to be, then I do not see why it should be logically conceivable in any other logically possible world. Thus, Chalmers modal argument would only hold if in our world Descartes's zombie-animals were conceivable—which I think is not the case.

[47] Broad (1925); Feigl (1967); Jackson (1982).

[48] Quoted e.g. in Chalmers (1995, 2002, 2010); von Stillfried (2018).

would still only have theoretical knowledge *about* experience, but not *how* it is to have an experience.[49]

Be this as it may, it should have become clear that ultimately all three arguments are postulating an explanatory gap between physical and phenomenal accounts of consciousness, rendering the latter irreducible to the former, finally claiming that this epistemological irreducibility implicates an ontological distinction between phenomenal and physical properties. As von Stillfried observes, Chalmers does not seem to distinguish between the fact of the incorrigible phenomenal *experiencing* what it is like to be and the supposed *existence* of "the phenomenal" as an irreducible ontic category. Howsoever, von Stillfried concludes that there are good reasons for Chalmers's transition from the epistemological to the ontological gap. In sum, Chalmers's arguments suggest that his irreducibility thesis is a comprehensible assumption, although it might not hold as a logically necessary conclusion (as Chalmers would have it).

(E) Physical Properties Are Not Reducible to the Phenomenal

Although Chalmers does not seem to be preoccupied with this point, it might be relevant for the hard problem of consciousness. Strictly speaking, if all premises from A to D be true, then it is logically conceivable that the physical world supervenes logically on the phenomenal, which would basically be equivalent to some kind of idealist monism or solipsism. In such a case, there would be no ontological gap, and thus, no hard problem of consciousness. Initially, Chalmers (1995, 2010) did not seem to seriously consider this problem, and therefore, did not offer any considerable solutions either.[50] This may seem even more surprising since Chalmers himself discussed natural supervenience of the physical on the phenomenal (panprotopsychism) as a possible solution to the hard problem of consciousness. The similarity between the two questions of irreducibility of the phenomenal and irreducibility of the physical suggests that an inverse reading of Chalmers's arguments for the former should also sustain the latter.[51] This would read: Since it is equally conceivable that there be a world equal to the one I perceive, but with other physical properties or no physical properties at all, the physical cannot be reduced to the phenomenal. There is, however, a fundamental difference between the hard problem

[49] Compare also von Stillfried's (2018).

[50] In his later works, Chalmers (2022) further explores the idea of taking virtual realities, such as that depicted in the 1999 film The Matrix, at their metaphysical face value, developing an information theoretical "it-from-bit" view of reality. However, he clearly emphasises his realist stance: "Our minds are part of reality, but there's a great deal of reality outside our minds. Reality contains our world and it may contain many others. […] Most importantly: Reality exists, independently of us. The truth matters. There are truths about reality, and we can try to find them" (p. 18). "The it-from-bit view is closer to materialism—at least, if we think of bits as the fundamental components of matter. But it is a distinctive and special form of materialism" (p. 158). However, according to Chalmers, his 2022 book does not specifically address the hard problem of consciousness.

[51] Compare also von Stillfried (2018).

of consciousness and the hard problem of the physical. As discussed above, there seem to be more arguments for the incorrigibility or intrinsicness of the phenomenal than for any a priori proof of the existence of the physical. Accordingly, the conceivability of a phenomenal world without any physical correlatum does not necessarily imply irreducibility of the physical, but rather its non-existence as an equally logical corollary. This asymmetry is, of course, a result of the representational model as implied by Cartesian dualism. Accordingly, the only hope to get rid of scepticism and the spectre of solipsism would be to come to a non-representational epistemology. This, in turn, would demand a non-dualist ontological framework. However, some solutions that have been suggested to solve the hard problem of consciousness entail non-dualist models, so that there might be reason for hope that the epistemological implications of the solutions being discussed concerning the hard problem of consciousness will possibly also contribute to the solution of the hard problem of the physical.

Summing up, the premises (A to E) we need to assume for a coherent formulation of the hard problem of consciousness are rather conclusive presumptions than logically necessary conclusions. However, the discussion also showed that all available arguments one could invoke to disprove the existence of a hard problem of consciousness will either entail the elimination of phenomenal experience or of the physical world, thus, leading either into physicalism or idealism/solipsism. And since physicalism is ultimately untenable, due to the sceptic arguments comprised in representationalism, and because solipsism is so utterly unattractive that for most people living in such an illusive world would make little or no sense, there are good reasons to face the hard problem of consciousness—particularly because it comes with the (albeit remote) hope of a solution to the epistemological predicaments of representationalism.

11.2 Possible Solutions to the Hard Problem of Consciousness

So, once we decide to face the hard problem of consciousness (and be it for the lack of a better option) and to accept its premises (at least as preliminary working hypotheses), we have to further specify our problem and the resulting subquestions.

In general terms, the hard problem of consciousness comprises the question about the nature of the correlation between phenomenal and physical properties of consciousness. This problem already entails the question *why* psychophysical processes are correlated with phenomenal experience, that is, *why consciousness actually exists*, as well as the inverse question about the reason for the existence of physical correlata of experience, that is, *why the physical world exists*. And even if we came to know the reason why we experience a world, the question would still remain about the particular quality of all the different, unique qualia that constitute our experience, that is, *why it is exactly like this* to see green right now and not somehow different, while it actually might feel different to see the "same"[52] green in another moment or context?

Ideally, a solution to the hard problem of consciousness should provide convincing answers to at least these questions, which also means that it should also answer the hard problem of the physical. In more concrete terms, this means that any attempt at a solution to the hard problem of consciousness/the physical will amount to a proposal for a fundamental theory of mind and matter. There is a quite confusing variety of ontological models which have been discussed in this respect, and which can be classified along different parameters.[53] In any case, however, the most central and defining aspect is grounded in the particular role and ontological status of the phenomenal and/or physical properties that constitute our universe, and the specific way they relate to each other. Accordingly, the most fundamental distinction divides *monist* ontologies from *dualisms*, while roughly speaking, monisms (sensu stricto) fall into materialisms[54] and idealisms, and dualisms into *substance dualisms* and *aspect dualisms*. One can easily see that monisms will have a hard time to comply with the basic premises (A to E) the hard problem is derived from, since they eliminate either phenomenal experience or the physical world, or at least suggest that one is reducible to the other.[55] Accordingly, monist approaches will not

[52] Strictly speaking, there is no equal phenomenal green, even if it has the same wavelength, since each perception is a unique confluence of countless impressions within a particular moment and biographical context in our life (compare also Chalmers 2010).

[53] Although there have been earlier influential proposals, such as Broad's 1925), Chalmers's (2002) classification (distinguishing between type-A/B/C/Q materialisms, type-D/E dualisms, type-F monism) has certainly advanced to a kind of standard reference in recent philosophy of mind. However, his heavy focus on materialism (and its refutation) does not appear to me to be the most appropriate option for my purposes here, since non-materialist approaches turned out to offer by far the more interesting solutions. Von Stillfried (2018) offers a slightly different classification (differentiating between "positive" and "negative" approaches), although still largely following Chalmers's approach, following rather a hierarchy of propensity to success or usefulness concerning the problems at stake. My own presentation will by and large follow von Stillfried's and Chalmers's, though it may slightly differ in some aspects.

[54] The meaning of "materialism" I use here is not interchangeable with "physicalism". Materialism, in the sense I use it refers to the classical physical concept of a universe constituted by known physical forces governed by known deterministic causal laws. Physicalism, in contrast, includes the findings of quantum physics, suggesting that physical observables behave non-deterministically and interact non-locally, allowing for different ontological interpretations, including models that introduce further ontic categories or principles to explain those physical observables. Such an additional ontic category or principle within a physical framework might also help explain the existence of phenomenal properties. Thus, a naturalistic theory of consciousness may (although it does not need to) amount to a "physicalist" account of consciousness, while not being "materialist".

[55] Of course, there are ontologies which are sometimes treated as "monisms" that do not face this problem, since they suggest that both physical and phenomenal properties supervene on, or are aspects of some even more fundamental ontic category or principle. However, these "monisms" still assume the physical and the phenomenal to represent two different existing categories, either representing two complementary aspects, or emergent properties of one underlying fundamental

be of further interest for my purpose here, since they have already been excluded a priori from the list of candidates for solving the hard problem of consciousness once its premises were accepted as valid working hypotheses.[56]

11.2.1 Substance Dualism

Given the existence of both phenomenal and physical properties as two irreducible ontic categories, the question is how these two categories relate to each other, which ultimately also requires some explanation of what these categories might be and why they exist. One way to face this question is to assume that mind and matter represent two fundamentally different kinds of "stuff" or "substance" which coexist more or less independently of each other, although representing two complementary properties of one individual (mind and body).[57] This poses the question whether these two substances somehow interact, and if so, how?. And if not, how can their tight correlation be explained?

---

unity. Due to their ambivalent character, such ontological models are at times referred to in terms of "monism" (e.g. "neutral monism", "dual aspect monism", "type-F monism", "Russell's monism") or "dualism" (e.g. "aspect-dualism", "naturalistic dualism"). The naming rather depends on the interpretation of the two properties in terms of *aspects* or emergent *ontic categories*. For the sake of simplicity and to avoid this confusing wording, I will use the term "monism" only for eliminative monisms ("negative approaches" in von Stillfried's (2018) terminology), while treating any non-eliminative ontology (von Stillfried's "positive approaches") as different types of dualism, distinguishing between substance and aspect dualism.

[56] It goes without saying that I do not maintain that monist ontologies are logically untenable or impossible to reflect the "real" structure of the universe—all fundamental ontological models are metaphysical, and thus, per definition unfalsifiable. However, monist ontologies appear to offer the least promising options if we want to find solutions to the hard problem of consciousness as defined above, which is also the hard problem of matter, and which ultimately entails the hard problem of modern science (as shown above). For an in-depth discussion of different versions of materialism and the reasons for their (supposed) invalidity concerning the solution of the hard problem of consciousness see Chalmers (1995, 2002, 2010).

[57] Chalmers (1995, 2002, 2010) holds that "substance dualism" leads to implications comparable to "property dualism", however, I do not think that this equation contributes to a comparative analysis concerning the viability of the different ontological models. Particularly so, because the problems and arguments discussed in this respect are based on abstract thought experiments, bearing a high risk of slipping into category mistakes. "Properties" are attributes of entities, thus a "property dualism" suggests the existence of one entity with two fundamentally different properties. On the one hand, Chalmers (1995: 110) relates "property dualism" to phenomenal and physical properties of an individual, on the other, to emergent ontic properties of an underlying, more fundamental ontic substance (idem 1995, 2002, 2010), thus mixing up two entirely different categories of entities. While the former definition simply restates the mind-body problem, thus embracing any type of dualism, the latter rather suggests some kind of emergentism (if one property naturally supervenes on the other) or aspect dualism (if both properties somehow supervene on a third fundamental substance or principle). Considering the fuzziness of Chalmers's definition, I will abstain from using the term "property dualism".

Interactionism

If we embrace the idea that mind and body interact, that is, that to explain the functioning of the one we have to understand the functioning of the other, we may either suppose a mutual influence between the two, or a one-way influence of the physical on phenomenal, or the other way round. However, most authors seem to take physical influence on the phenomenal for granted, while the assumption that consciousness might induce or at least somehow influence physical events demands solid proof.[58] Accordingly, "interactionism" came to refer primarily to approaches that attribute a causal role to consciousness, while those denying any kind of influence of the mind on the body are generally subsumed under the tag "epiphenomenalism".

Of course, an interactionist's main problem will be to show how two fundamentally different, non-reducible ontic substances may interact. The epiphenomenalist, on the other hand, will have to convince us that our experience of taking the decision to move our hand or talk about our ideas concerning the hard problem of consciousness is just an illusive *ex post* attribution of causal agency to unconscious psychophysical processes. Additionally, both interactionist and epiphenomenalists are charged with explaining how phenomenal experience may emerge from physical processes. Since both are irreducible to each other, there is neither a simple causal mechanism nor any kind of "weak" emergence available to solve the problem, for both would amount to reductionist accounts of consciousness, and hence, to monism. At best, one might assume some kind of "strong" emergence of the phenomenal as a new, separate fundamental ontic category emerging from physical systems under certain conditions. However, strong emergence is a very strong assumption, demanding strong arguments, too. All this may seem quite confusing, and it really is, so let me begin with having a closer look at interactionism and some of the problems it faces.

First of all, the lack of a causal connection poses the question what other kind of non-causal mechanism might be responsible for a supposed influence of consciousness on physical processes. Of course, causation is itself a problematic concept[59] which has also proven insufficient to cope with certain kinds of physical events.[60] Alternatively, one could postulate an additional fundamental natural principle to explain some kind of lawful impact of consciousness on physical events; however, since known natural laws already seem to provide a sufficient explanation for all physical events, an additional influence of the phenomenal would be redundant, either violating causal closeness of the physical or leading to overdetermination. Anyhow, despite its oddness, there seems to be no forceful argument against overdetermination. The causal closeness of the physical realm, on the other hand, is deduced from conservation laws in closed systems. However, if mind and body

[58] von Stillfried (2018).

[59] Chalmers (2010) refers to Humes sceptical analysis of causation. Compare also Chap. 3 in Part I in this volume on the metaphysical conception of causation.

[60] E.g. non-local character of gravity and quantum events.

interact with each other they will constitute a single system and energy exchange between the two will not necessarily result in a violation of conservation laws. In addition, there could also be some sort of non-energetic forms of interaction between phenomenal and physical relata. It has been proposed that consciousness might somehow influence indeterministic quantum events within our nervous system without necessarily involving energy exchange. Some of these micro-events might trigger cascades of further events, finally leading to measurable macro-events, implying measurable change in overall stochastic distribution of indeterministic quantum events.[61] Thus, an influence of the phenomenal at quantum level could result in a significant and constant impact on brain activity without being traceable by means of current measuring methods.[62] There are other arguments against interactionism[63] that could be mentioned here, however, none of them seems to be strong enough to prove it invalid. However, even if we accepted interactionism for the time being, it would not solve the hard problem, since it does not explain how interaction occurs. This is not only true for the causal role of consciousness, but also for the (taken for granted) physical influence on consciousness and causation in general. When it comes to the details, the problem of causation is revealed as being as mysterious as that of non-causal correlation. In the case of interactionism, the problem is worsened by the fact that it is based on a substance dualism, thus having to explain how two fundamentally different and mutually irreducible kinds of "stuff" may "interact" across this ontological boundary.

[61] E.g. Hameroff and Penrose (1996, 2003); Beck and Eccles (1992).

[62] "[W]e present now the hypothesis that the mental intention (the volition) becomes neurally effective by momentarily increasing the probability of exocytosis in selected cortical areas [...]. In the language of quantum mechanics this means a selection of events [...]. Effectively this selection mechanism increases the probability for exocytosis, and in this way generates increased EPSPs [exitatory post synapic potentials] without violation of the conservation laws. Furthermore, the interaction of mental events with the quantum probability amplitudes for exocytosis introduces a coherent coupling of a large number of individual amplitudes of the hundreds of thousands of boutons in a dendron. This then leads to an overwhelming variety of actualities, or modes, in brain activity" (Beck and Eccles 1992: 11360).

[63] For example, Chalmers mentions that a functional role of the phenomenal would collide with the (supposed) non-functionality of consciousness. However, this is rather a problem of definition, since "functional" can be defined in different ways and is not absolutely necessary to define the distinction between physical and phenomenal properties, since there are other possible candidates, like intrinsicness, relationality, spatiality, etc. The whole problem rather results from the assumption that physical influence on the phenomenal is not problematic while the inverse has to be proven—however, once we assume that both directions are equally probable the problem ceases to exist. Von Stillfried mentions his discomfort with substance-like concepts of consciousness as implied by interactionism and substance dualism in general. The suggested idea of a mind-stuff, which exists separately from physical matter, would imply that a physical system may act differently, depending on whether it interacts with some mind-stuff or not. But what determines when and where consciousness is involved? Von Stillfried suggests two possible option to deal with this question: either physical and phenomenal properties might be always intrinsically correlated, ultimately leading to panpsychism, or the phenomenal might be an intrinsic essence of the physical, as suggested by Russellian monism (a type of aspect dualism, which I will discuss in more detail in the next section).

Epiphenomenalism[64]

Although it may be argued that there is no knockout argument against interactionism, some authors[65] still thought it improbable enough to suggest that there be no interaction at all, or at least no phenomenal influence on the physical. Consciousness, this view holds, is rather an "epiphenomenon" somehow emerging from brain activity, but with no causal role whatsoever. In other words, we experience qualia, we think and take decisions to effectuate certain actions or not, however, our impression that our conscious decisions were the *cause* of our acting is completely illusive; instead, unconscious, psychophysiological processes did the whole processing of sensory information that ultimately commanded our thoughts as much as our behaviour entirely in the dark, so to say, a couple of instances before we would have the impression of "deciding" to do something. In fact, there is strong empirical support[66] for such a view, notwithstanding its utterly odd consequences. However, while we might accept that our behaviour is largely governed by cognitive routines and reflex actions, it is much more difficult to imagine that Descartes's meditations about his thinking hence being were simply an illusive and ultimately useless exercise of his nervous system. It has been argued that this kind of reflexive reasoning about one's phenomenal experience adds up to a paradox,[67] particularly if our reflexive reasoning results in physical action, like talking or writing things like "cogito ergo sum". According to epiphenomenalism, there should be no fundamental difference between my jerking reflex in response to the heat of a cup, my "decision" to lift my left arm, or the act of writing these lines about the hard problem of consciousness—all this should happen exclusively as a result of psychophysical processes in my brain, while my phenomenal self only thinks that it was in charge, following the illusive notion that my thoughts and "decisions" were the cause of my actions. However, it is very hard to accept the idea that my subjective impression of reflecting and talking about my reflections are two completely independent events, one exclusively phenomenal and the other exclusively physical, with no causal nexus between the two of them. There simply seems to be no explanation for my act of writing this here without referring to my experience. Now, the oddness of epiphenomenalism has reached a really paradoxical character. Chalmers has put considerable emphasis on the importance of such "direct phenomenal judgments", since

---

[64] Type-E Dualism in Chalmers (2002) categorisation.

[65] Occasionalism and parallelistic views such as Leibniz's or Spinoza's proposed some kind of Divine principle to explain the correlation between mental and physical states, circumventing the problems of a naturalistic explanation. According to von Stillfried (2018), in recent decades such views have been substituted by emergentist proposals (Huxley 1874; Campbell 1970; Jackson 1982; Robinson 1988; Bieri 1992). Von Stillfried distinguishes between "strong" and "weak" epiphenomenalism, the former denying any kind of interaction between mind and body, the latter only denying the causal role of consciousness.

[66] Although epiphenomenalism remains the dominant view among scholars, it is based on an overinterpretation of empirical studies. However, there is no solid proof against it (see also Stillfried 2018).

[67] Chalmers (1995).

they would best exemplify what he called the "paradox of phenomenal judgments".[68] Particularly, he pointed to the double character of direct phenomenal judgments which are both phenomenal (experiencing qualia) and physical (uttering one's thoughts about experience) events, thus providing a bridge between the two realms. The explanatory irrelevance of consciousness claimed by epiphenomenalism is obviously at odds with its explanatory relevance as suggested by direct phenomenal judgments. However, further in-depth reviews of the problem revealed, that in the last analysis, there is no mandatory logical argument strong enough to disprove epiphenomenalism. Direct phenomenal judgments and the tight correlation between our experience of deciding to talk about our experience and the physical act of utterance may still be explained by an inexplicable coincidence or some equally inexplicable pre-established law of correspondence. In the face of this outrageous counter-intuitiveness, however, it might be easier to imagine a more fundamental principle both physical and phenomenal properties are based upon than to imagine such an arbitrary additional principle of correspondence.[69]

[68] Chalmers coined this expression in his 1995 The Conscious Mind but later submitted his views to a revision: "The paradox is a consequence of the facts that (1) The physical domain is causally closed; (2) Judgments about consciousness are logically supervenient on the physical; (3) Consciousness is not logically supervenient on the physical; and (4) We know we are conscious. From (1) and (2) it follows that judgments about consciousness can be reductively explained. In combination with (3), this implies that consciousness is explanatorily irrelevant to our judgments, which lies in tension with (4). Thus we have the paradox. One might try to escape the paradox by denying any one of these premises" (ibidem: 170). In later publications (e.g. 2010) he rather speaks about "phenomenal beliefs" and relinquishes using the strong term "paradox": "In The Conscious Mind I called this 'the paradox of phenomenal judgment' and argued that, while it is strange (many strange things happen in other possible worlds), it does nothing to undermine the coherence of zombies. [...] I argue that an appropriate account of the content and epistemology of our phenomenal judgments shows that there is no problem here" (idem: 156–157). However, in his discussion of the Meta-Problem of Consciousness (Chalmers 2018), Chalmers attributes a central role to "phenomenal reports", which are closely related to his earlier notion of phenomenal judgments: "There is nevertheless one behavioural function that has an especially close tie to the hard problem. This behavioural function involves phenomenal reports: the things we say about consciousness (that is, about phenomenal consciousness). More specifically, many people make problem reports expressing our sense that consciousness poses a hard problem. I say things like 'There is a hard problem of consciousness', 'It is hard to see how consciousness could be physical', 'Explaining behaviour does not explain consciousness', and so on. ... The meta-problem of consciousness is (to a second approximation) the problem of explaining these problem reports. Problem reports are a fact of human behaviour. Because of this, the meta-problem of explaining them is strictly speaking one of the easy problems of consciousness. Although the meta-problem is strictly speaking an easy problem, it is deeply connected to the hard problem. We can reasonably hope that a solution to the meta-problem will shed significant light on the hard problem" (Chalmers 2018: 7–8).

[69] Despite Chalmers's (2010) later reluctance concerning his earlier writings on *direct phenomenal judgments* (DPJ), von Stillfried (2018) still attributes a central importance to DPJ as a key argument against epiphenomenalism. He defines DPJ following Chalmers's (1995) definition of second order phenomenal judgments that relate to the existence (not quality) of phenomenal experience (in contrast to first order phenomenal judgments about the content of experience, and to third order judgments on meta-reflections on consciousness). A typical example would be a situation like when I experience that I have experience and utter: "I have experience". Although Chalmers shows that DPJ do not fundamentally differ from other judgments, von Stillfried argues that they would

In summary, it can be asserted that substance dualisms such as interactionism and epiphenomenalism seem to be logically possible, albeit facing serious objections. The central problem of interactionism is, of course, to explain how two irreducible substances, each following its own intrinsic principles, may act upon each other. Recourse to indeterministic quantum processes with no net energy exchange might at least outline an explanation for the principal possibility of a causal role of consciousness. However, such approaches still do not define under which conditions the mind may interfere in physical processes nor how, and based on which natural principle, such an interference might be possible. In fact, the same goes for the often taken for granted "causation" of consciousness by physical processes, which turns out to be equally mysterious. Thus, the standard epiphenomenalist attempt to elude the problems of interactionism by denying consciousness any causal role only solves half of the problem, since it still has to explain how consciousness might possibly emerge from the physical, without reducing the former to the latter. Moreover, epiphenomenalism presents an even worse problem, since it cannot offer any explanations for the correspondence between direct phenomenal judgments and phenomenal states other than suggesting an "outrageous coincidence"[70] or some not further deducible fundamental "law of correspondence". In Chalmers words:

> A completed theory of mind must provide both a (nonreductive) account of consciousness and a (reductive) account of why we judge that we are conscious, and it is reasonable to expect that these two accounts will cohere with each other (Chalmers 1995: 289).

While both types of substance dualism (interactionism and epiphenomenalism) only offer dissatisfactory (however logically possible) "accounts of why we judge that we are conscious", neither of them offers an explanation concerning the emergence of the phenomenal from the physical as a distinct ontic substance. But what if both phenomenal and physical properties supervened on some more fundamental principle or ontic category?

---

still give no answer to the question *why* we should make DPJ? Also, Chalmers's introduction of the concept of *acquaintance* would only solve the epistemological question *how* I can know that I really have consciousness, but the ontological question about *why* there is concordance and whether consciousness is explanatorily relevant would remain unsolved. More precisely, von Stillfried argues that if epiphenomenalism be true, consciousness cannot effectuate physical events, thus DPJ are impossible. Hence, acquaintance is explanatorily irrelevant for the ontological question of DPJ, since my zombie twin would utter the same phrases, anyway. As a result, acquaintance proves the existence of one's own experience, but it does not explain DPJ. The same goes for Chalmers's example of intelligent systems. In sum, the ontological problem of concordance between phenomenal experience and physical correlata cannot be explained. Epiphenomenalism has, therefore, to assume either a random or an arbitrary emergence of concordance between physical processes and phenomenal judgments, implicating enormous metaphysical consequences.

[70] Chalmers (1995: 271).

11.2.2 Aspect Dualism[71]

The problems related to substance dualism led some authors to the suggestion that mind and matter might not be two different substances, but rather two aspects or properties of one universal principle or substance. Hence, if mind and body be just aspects or properties of one and the same "thing", their correlation should be taken for granted without having to take recourse to any causal mechanism. Also, phenomenal "stuff" would not have to mysteriously *emerge* from physical "stuff", since the two are no "stuffs" at all, but rather *properties* of a yet more fundamental universal "stuff", and thus, the presence of phenomenal properties will necessarily imply the co-presence of physical properties, and vice versa. So, prima facie, aspect dualism avoids the most serious problems substance dualisms are facing.

Spinoza's pantheism and Leibniz's monads can be understood as early examples of cosmological models of this type, and also Russell's thinking has been interpreted in similar ways. These models are generally treated as neutral monisms, since they suggest that there is a fundamental universal principle or substance which is neither phenomenal nor physical, but of some third and completely inscrutable quality we can only deduce indirectly from its phenomenal and physical manifestations. This is why aspect dualism and neutral monism are often used as synonym term to refer to Chalmers's Type-F monism (which is a regrettably confusing convention). Anyhow, in practice, the postulated fundamental substance has been associated rather with properties like non-locality, intrinsicness, information and indeterminacy, than with matter-like properties, like spatiotemporal location, mass, energy and causal determination. In fact, some versions of aspect dualism suggest that the fundamental intrinsic essence of both mind and matter might be identical to phenomenal, mind-like properties. Hence, in contrast to most versions of substance dualism that presuppose consciousness to somehow emerge from a physical substrate, these approaches assume that the physical world might be the manifestation of some ubiquitous phenomenal or *proto*phenomenal essence. Of course, this will result in a quite different picture than initially suggested by neutral monism, since there is no *neutral* fundamental substance or essence, but instead the phenomenal is now supposed to be fundamental to the physical. Such views are often treated under the label of *panpsychism* for holding that everything is (at least potentially) associated with some kind of psychic state. However, panpsychism allows for a range of quite different cosmological models, each with its particular implications concerning the mind-body problem. For example, we might think of the phenomenal essence as of a universal substance or God (like Spinoza did), or in terms of

[71] Chalmers also refers to aspect dualism using different terms, like "Type-F monism" (2002), "Russellian monism" (2010), or "property dualism" (1995). In fact, when it comes to this class of ontological models, terms like "dualism" and "monism" appear to be insufficient descriptions. Finally, Chalmers (2016a) comes to the conclusion that this distinction is "a largely verbal question". Hence, it would be perfectly justifiable to use any of these labels here, however, I opted for *aspect dualism* to emphasise the ontological difference between phenomenal and physical properties as the decisive distinction compared to eliminativist monisms.

"microexperiences"[72] had by microphysical entities adding up to macroexperiences had by certain macrophysical entities (e.g. bats and human beings). In the first case, our mind would be an instantiation of a universal super-mind or God, while following the latter, *constitutive* view, it would be the result of a particular structural arrangement of microexperiences and their corresponding microphysical instantiations. It is not difficult to see that *constitutive panpsychism* is a promising option if we are looking for a naturalistic solution to the hard problem of consciousness which is maximally coherent with current scientific evidence and theory.

Chalmers[73] hopes to show how the macrophenomenal could be lawfully reduced to microphenomenal properties, thus allowing for a naturalistic aspect dualism. He argues that evidence from neuroscience suggests a lawful relationship between physical process and conscious experience; however, since these represent two irreducible ontic categories, the responsible natural law cannot be entailed by physical law. Accordingly, there has to be a contingent non-physical fundamental law that explains how and why physical processes are related to microphenomenal properties. Fully-fledged consciousness, on the other hand, should follow a priori from such law, and thus, logically supervene on microphenomenal properties.[74] In search of such a naturalistic theory, Chalmers develops a naturalistic aspect dualist interpretation of *Russellian Monism*, which he also calls "Type-F Monism", and which combines aspects of both interactionism and epiphenomenalism, while solving some of their main problems.[75]

Russell[76] had famously pointed to the structuralism of physical theory and its incapacity to grasp the intrinsic essence of things themselves. According to Russell, the abstract description of relations within spatiotemporal structure as produced by physics would reveal nothing about the inscrutable nature of the relata it describes, while "percepts are the only part of the physical world that we know otherwise than abstractly".[77] Although Russell himself interpreted his findings in terms of a neutral

---

[72] Chalmers (2016a).

[73] Chalmers (1995, 2016a, b).

[74] Chalmers (2016b).

[75] Particularly, Russellian monism is not affected either by the conceivability or the knowledge argument, and thus, solves most problems physicalism and dualism are facing, while supporting a naturalist view on consciousness (e.g. Chalmers 2010, 2016a; compare also Alter and Nagasawa 2012, or von Stillfried 2018). "This view holds the promise of integrating phenomenal and physical properties very tightly in the natural world. Here, nature consists of entities with intrinsic (proto)phenomenal qualities standing in causal relations within a space-time manifold. Physics as we know it emerges from the relations between these entities, whereas consciousness as we know it emerges from their intrinsic nature. As a bonus, this view is perfectly compatible with the causal closure of the microphysical and indeed with existing physical laws. The view can retain the structure of physical theory as it already exists; it simply supplements this structure with an intrinsic nature. Furthermore, the view acknowledges a clear causal role for consciousness in the physical world: (proto)phenomenal properties serve as the ultimate categorical basis of all physical causation" (Chalmers 2010: 134).

[76] Russell (2007).

[77] Idem: 402.

monism,[78] Chalmers finds the propinquity between percepts and intrinsic essence might rather suggest that "the intrinsic properties of the physical world are themselves phenomenal properties". From this perspective, Russellian monism would also allow for a panpsychist interpretation, however, Chalmers (initially) rather favoured a pan*proto*psychist approach.[79]

A plain panpsychism would ultimately imply that *everything* has consciousness, including entities such as trees, rocks, bananas, single cells of an organism, and even each single quantum.[80] However, Chalmers uses a much more restricted definition of panpsychism "as the thesis that some fundamental physical entities have mental states. For example, if quarks or photons have mental states, that suffices for panpsychism to be true, even if rocks and numbers do not have mental states".[81] Nonetheless, the idea that quarks or photons think and feel still "provokes an incredulous stare".[82] Besides its oddness, constitutive panpsychism faces its particular problems. For example, it would have to explain the absence of consciousness during sleep or coma, while being the intrinsic essence of the physical body. Attempts to remedy this problem by assuming additional necessary conditions for the presence of consciousness, like complexity or self-referentiality of conscious systems, however, come down to the even worse problem of constitution. Now, one has to explain how and under which exact conditions those nano-consciousnesses of

[78] According to Russell's (2007) neutral monism the intrinsic essence is neither physical nor phenomenal. However, his writings have been interpreted by later authors (e.g. Chalmers 1995, 2002, 2010; Stoljar 2020; see Alter and Nagasawa 2012 for more details) in quite different ways. Alter and Nagasawa (2012) note that, all the differences notwithstanding, most interpretations amount to an understanding "of Russellian monism as a conjunction of three claims: [1.] Structuralism about physics: the basic properties physics describes are structural/relational properties. [2.] Realism about inscrutables: there are inscrutables, the natures of which are not wholly structural/relational. [3.] (Proto)phenomenal foundationalism: at least some inscrutables are either phenomenal or protophenomenal properties" (idem: 70/71). In sum, "we are led to Russellian monism by combining Russell's structuralism about physics with a view he held about knowledge and perception" (ibidem). Although the distinction between the "intrinsic" properties of relata and their "extrinsic" physical description is not absolute and rather vague, it still suggests that relata (or "inscrutables") are not reducible to their relations/structure. However, it allows for different possible relationships between relata and phenomenal properties. Inscrutables could either be identical with, be somehow constituted by, or supervene on phenomenal properties. Depending on the presumed relationship, Russellian monism might be interpreted as a kind of physicalism (if relata are taken for (non-standard) physical properties), as aspect dualism (if relata are taken for phenomenal properties that do not constitute physical properties), or idealism (if relata be phenomena properties that constitute both phenomenal and physical properties).

[79] Chalmers (1995, 2002, 2010). However, in his later publications (2016a, b) on this issue he seems to treat both options as more or less equivalent possibilities, each with its particular pros and cons.

[80] Stoljar 2020.

[81] Chalmers (2016a: 19).

[82] Stoljar (2020: 6).

quanta merge into consciousnesses of our cells, and finally, those of cells to consciousnesses of macro-organisms, like ourselves.[83]

Pan*proto*psychism, in contrast, suggests a gradual presence of consciousness associated with different kinds of entities. For example, a quantum may have some kind of *proto*phenomenal properties which, however, would *not* amount to anything it is like to be a quantum.[84] Hence, according to a constitutive panprotopsychism, protophenomenal properties are conceived of as a "raw material" of experience, kind of "mind-quanta" which may add up to fully-fledged consciousness, just as the microphysical properties of quanta add up to macroscopic material objects with macrophysical properties. In other words, the protophenomenal properties of quanta might then, under certain circumstances yet to be defined, instantiate macrophenomenal conscious states. Moreover, Chalmers suggests that mircophysical properties as well as their causal roles might be instantiations of some kind of protophenomenal "quiddities". As a corollary, the physical realm together with its causal determination would eventually supervene on, or at least be somehow constituted by the same protophenomenal properties that also amount to conscious experience. Von Stillfried (2018) observes that such a radical interpretation of Russell's ideas might be the necessary step to explain direct phenomenal judgements, and thus, solve yet another problem epiphenomenalism and interactionism cannot. Particularly, Chalmers's claim that his interpretation of Russellian monism should allow for ascribing a causal role to consciousness, if true, would be a considerable step forward in this respect. A modal argument based on the supposition of a parallel world that is physically identical with ours, but lacking phenomenal properties, would therefore lose its logical basis, since if radical Russellian monism be true, such a world is logically impossible. Thus, Chalmers's interpretation of Russellian monism probably explains the correlation between phenomenal and physical properties. However, since the causal nexus kind of bifurcates at the microlevel, going from the proto-/microphenomenal to the microphysical to macrophysical, on one hand, and to the macrophenomenal on the other, it rather amounts to a parallelism on the macro-level. In other words, it does not necessarily explain why our insight of having consciousness could be causally relevant to our physical act of writing: "cogito ergo sum!" Chalmers argues that macrophenomenal consciousness might inherit the causal role of its constituent microphenomenal properties or quiddities. However, the burden of proof has now been committed to the question about the

[83] Chalmers (2016a) notes the possibility to conceive also non-constitutive forms of panpsychism, which might suggest "that there is microexperience and macroexperience, but the microexperience does not ground the macroexperience" (idem: 27). However, since non-constitutive panpsychism will have to presume some kind of strong emergence, is inherits many of the problems substance dualism is struggling with. Moreover, Chalmers holds that "Non-Russellian panpsychism faces obvious problems with mental causation" (idem: 39).

[84] "Protophenomenal properties are special properties that are not themselves phenomenal (there is nothing it is like to have them) but that can collectively constitute phenomenal properties" (Chalmers 2016b: 183).

constitution of consciousness out of proto-/microphenomenal properties and the resulting causal relations between the two magnitude orders.

The remaining problem with pan(proto)phenomenal views is, thus, to explain the emergence of consciousness out of such, still not quite conscious, proto-/microphenomenal "quanta", so to say, without reducing one (phenomenal) ontic category to another, different one (*proto*phenomenal).[85] This problem has been debated at large for a couple of decades now, and there seems to be a consensus that this so-called *combination problem*[86] represents the single most serious objection to constitutive pan(proto)psychism. Considering the serious problems substance dualism is facing, constitutive pan(proto)psychism bears the promise of solving the hard problem of consciousness, since it seems not to be affected by the problems interactionism and epiphenomenalism are facing. However, the combination problem appears to be a serious threat to panpsychism. Consequently, the solution of the combination problem might entail the solution of the hard problem of consciousness. Due to this decisive role in the whole debate on the hard problem of consciousness, Chalmers has spent considerable effort in discussing the issue. One of Chalmers's formulations of the combination problem goes as follows:

> [...] how do microexperiences combine to yield macro-experiences? It is at least very hard to see how a number of separate experiences had by separate entities could combine to yield a distinct experience had by a composite entity. It is especially hard to see how they could

[85] Stoljar (2020) refers to this problem calling it the "exclusion argument". In order to avoid this and other problems of panpsychism, he offers a non-standard materialist interpretation of Russell's ideas. Following this approach, the intrinsic essence of relata might be some inscrutable fundamental non-standard, since non-dispositional and non-structural, physical properties which all standard properties would derive from. According to Stoljar's comparison with Chalmers panprotopsychist approach, phenomenal or protophenomenal properties might be conflated into inscrutable non-standard physical properties, thus avoiding its oddness, the conceivability and the exclusion argument, all together. In fact, if Chalmers protophenomenal properties could be identified with physical observables, his panprotopsychism would actually amount to a kind of physicalism. The further discussion of the wave-particle dualism in quantum physics in the next section will show that an identification of panprotophenomenl properties with the wave function is possible, however, still rather points to panpsychism than to materialism. Anyhow, Stoljar's wording might also rather confuse the issue than clarify it, since it speaks about "non-standards *materialism*" instead of "physicalism", while his definition of non-standard physical properties as non-structural and non-dispositional rather resemble mind-like than matter-like properties. That means, that the mysterious fundamental essence of both mind and matter is certainly not anything matter-like, but rather something mind-like, even if this fundamental mind-like something can be reasonably associated with physical observables (e.g. the wave function of quanta). So, panprotophenomenalism might be interpreted as a type of "*broad physicalism*", but not as *materialism* or "*narrow physicalism*" (Chalmers 2016a). And since "protophenomenal" and "non-standard-physical" properties share the two decisive attributes of (1.) *not* being standard physical properties and (2.) being constitutive for both physical and phenomenal properties, the wording does not change the essence of the model.

[86] Between 2002 and 2016, Chalmers has spent great effort in trying to solve this problem, without much success, before he finally decided to leave the solution to others. His reference to the "combination problem" goes back to William Seager's (1995) coinage of the term, while William James (1895) might be the first one to articulate the problem.

combine to yield the distinctive kind of macroexperience that we find in our own case (Chalmers 2016b: 36).

According to Chalmers (2016b), the combination problem falls into a whole range of subproblems, that can roughly be joined under three main branches:

1. The *subject* combination problem concerning the question how "microsubjects combine to yield macrosubjects?", which is also associated with:
   (a) The *unity* problem of how "microexperiences come together to yield a *unified* consciousness?"
   (b) The *boundary* problem of how "microexperiences come together to yield a *bounded* consciousness?"
   (c) The *awareness* problem of how "microexperiences come together to yield *awareness of qualities*?"
2. The *quality* combination problem of how "micro*qualities* combine to yield macro*qualities*?", entailing two further subproblems:
   (a) The *palette* problem of how a "*limited palette* of microqualities combine to yield the *vast array of macroqualities*?"
   (b) The *grain* problem of how "microexperiences come together to yield *homogeneous* macroexperiences, such as a homogeneous experience of red, instead of an enormous jagged array of distinct qualities?"
3. And finally, the *structural* combination problem of how "microexperiential structure (and microphysical structure) combine to yield macroexperiential structure?", also containing:
   (a) The *structural mismatch* problem of why and how phenomenal microstructures do not combine into macrostructures analogues to macrophysical structures, but instead combine to yield completely disanalogous macrophenomenal structure?

Additionally, Chalmers observes that the combination problem as well as most of its subproblems equally apply to all versions of constitutive panpsychism, including its panprotophenomenal interpretations. Hence, a satisfactory solution to the combination problem would require solving each single subproblem. However, panprotopsychism might be less vulnerable to the subject combination problem, while facing the additional problem of having to explain how micro-*non*-experiences might constitute macroexperiences?

After a thorough discussion of the different possible solution to each subproblem, Chalmers finally comes to the conclusion that none of them can be regarded as definitively solved. In general terms, it seems safe to say that the obvious attempt to avoid the problem of combination by suggesting non-constitutive versions of panpsychism will lead into problems similar to those substance dualism is facing. Constitutive Russellian pan(proto)psychist attempts to solve the problems, on the other hand, will encounter great difficulties when it comes to show how and why microphenomenal properties, subjects, awarenesses, qualities and structures might *necessarily* combine into fully fledged macrophenomenal conscious subjects being aware of countless qualia. However, some subproblems might be more propitious to be solved than others. While Chalmers sees some prospects for solving the *subject* and the *quality* combination problem and their subproblems (by phenomenal bounding,[87] deflating the awareness[88] and suggesting small qualitative palettes[89]), the *structural mismatch problem* appears to pose the most serious challenge to pan(proto)psychism. Looking back to almost three decades of intensive work on the hard problem of consciousness with no solid solution to the combination problem in sight, Chalmers finally comes to a rather pessimistic outlook concerning its solution, which would be "a little like trying to juggle seven balls in the air with both hands tied behind one's back".[90]

[87] Phenomenal bounding is the idea that "microsubjects constitute macrosubjects in virtue of certain phenomenal relations between the microsubjects. [...] On this view, the subject-summing argument is generated in part by thinking of microsubjects as being merely related spatiotemporally or causally. Once we acknowledge distinctively phenomenal relations between microsubjects and their phenomenal states, we can see how all this might constitute a macrosubject and macrophenomenal states" (Chalmers 2016b: 200).

[88] Deflation of awareness suggests that consciousness can be seen as awareness of qualities, so that an explanation of the constitution of awareness by microexperiences might solve the combination problem (as suggested by e.g. James's elimination of both subject and awareness: there are only qualities). However, Chalmers (2016b) points out that awareness is important to explain our knowledge of qualities. So, ultimately, the awareness problem is related to the subject problem (what is that something that has consciousness/qualia and how can it result from a collective of smaller entities?). "A view like this has the potential to answer the subject combination problem. Anything that is aware of a quality is a subject, so if this approach can show how brains or organisms stand in the awareness relation to qualities, then it will show how brains or organisms can be subjects. On the other hand, the fact that awareness requires subjects might simply suggest that the awareness combination problem is just as hard as the subject combination problem and is subject to the same sort of worries" (idem: 203). From my perspective, however, neither microexperiences nor microphysical properties are "entities" but only "properties" or "aspects" of inscrutable quiddities. Hence, the "subject" can only be the quiddity behind the mind-body-individual, so that the question would rather be how microquiddities might combine into a macroquiddity, while it should be taken for granted that both its constituent microphysical and its microphenomenal properties will show equally irreducible, and thus, incomparable properties as its macrophysical/phenomenal properties—and since the underlying quiddities or essences are per definition inscrutable, it seem odd to worry about the difficulty of explaining how microquiddities might combine into macroquiddities, since we will never know what they are; we only know they exist because they manifest in certain ways, some of which we can partially describe by contingent "natural" laws; hence, if there are aspects we can yet not explain, we should try out further possible contingent "laws". But of course, compared to Chalmers, I am just a visitor to consciousness studies, and I might look at the problem in too simplistic terms to grasp the depth of the issues at stake.

[89] "Small-palette solutions argue that all macroqualities can be generated from just a few microqualities, if we find the right underlying microqualities with sufficient flexibility and generality. It is far from obvious that such a class can be found, but it is also not obviously out of the question. Small-palette solutions are very much subject to the previous problem of how quality combination works, however" (idem: 206).

[90] Idem: 209. In fact, Chalmers stopped writing on the issue ever since, which makes it look like he had thrown in the towel.

Anyhow, I am rather inclined to follow von Stillfried[91] in taking a more optimistic view. First of all, the progress that has been made in consciousness studies during the last decades, particularly due to Chalmers's contributions, should not be underestimated. If Chalmers and his followers are right in maintaining that panpsychism avoids *all* the serious problems monist materialism, interactionism and epiphenomenalism are facing, we should be prepared to further invest in the solution to the combination problem. Even more so, since the combination problem is not restricted to panpsychism, but also applies to interactionism and epiphenomenalism. In fact, materialism avoids the problem by simply eliminating consciousness, while substance dualism either postulates its emergence out of nowhere, or assumes some kind of strong emergence of consciousness from physical structures, without spending much effort in explaining how microphysical processes may possibly scale up to macrophenomenal experience and why its structure does not match with the structure of its physical correlates? Hence, if compared to the huge problems materialist and substance dualist approaches are facing, the combination problem of panpsychism appears much less serious.

Last but not least, part of the problem might be grounded in its definition. Just to recall: Chalmers went out to search for a naturalist theory of consciousness to show how microphenomenal processes are lawfully related to both microphysical and macrophenomenal processes. Since phenomenal and physical processes belong to distinct irreducible ontic categories, the correlation between microphenomenal and microphysical processes ought to be based on some *contingent* principle (not entailed in standard physical law), while the emergence of macrophenomenal properties should be *logically entailed* by the nature of micro-/protophenomenal properties. Interestingly, Chalmers eventually boils his analysis of the combination problem down precisely to the lack of any logical a priori necessity of consciousness entailed by micro-/protophenomenal properties. Particularly, he rejects his own earlier interpretation of phenomenal properties in terms of information structure as a possible solution of the structural mismatch problem, because "it is not easy to see how these will be metaphysically necessary rather than brute nomic principles".[92] However, von Stillfried argues that such an

[91] von Stillfried (2018).

[92] "I suggested in *The Conscious Mind* that the principles of phenomenal composition more closely reflect the constitution of information than the constitution of standard macrophysical structure. Again, I think that something like this is perhaps the only viable line for a panpsychist or panprotopsychist. But it is not at all clear why or how phenomenal composition could work this way, and still be a sort of constitutive composition. Certainly one could articulate laws of informational structure for phenomenology, but it is not easy to see how these will be metaphysically necessary rather than brute nomic principles" (idem: 208). Personally, I disagree with Chalmers, since the requirement of a logical necessity for the existence of compound holistic systems would preclude a whole range of obviously existing observables. For example, the existence of life does not logically follow from natural laws of physics and chemistry. On the contrary, from the vantage point of physics, life appears to be something completely unexpected, as it inverts entropy, one of the fundamental laws of the universe; but still, most scientists would insist that life can be explained by natural law alone. Similarly, societies or cultures do not logically follow from the existence of

a priori entailment of macrophenomenal in microphenomenal properties might not be a necessary requirement for a coherent naturalist interpretation of Russellian panpsychism. A quantum theoretical interpretation of phenomenal properties in terms of quantum wave functions might explain why microphenomenal properties *must* fuse into holistic macrophenomenal properties. Evidence from quantum physics shows that, as a rule, interfering wave functions aggregate into higher dimensional total wave functions with new holistic properties. Accordingly, phenomenal combination would have to occur in parallel to physical combination, simply following contingent natural principles of quantum wave-particle dualism. However, now the really decisive requirement for Russellian panpsychism (and the hard problem at large) would be to find a logically necessary relation between physical and protophenomenal properties. Only such a logically necessary principle would preclude the possibility of zombies, and thus, solve the conceivability argument, for if physical properties be logically entailed by phenomenal properties, then a physically identical world without consciousness is logically unconceivable. Chalmers, however, does not rate such an a priori entailment a necessary requirement for his theory of consciousness, but rather contents himself with some contingent principle to explain the relation between phenomenal and physical properties.[93] Although he admits that the existence of relational structure and disposition as evidenced by physics points to the conclusion that there are intrinsic relata or quiddities, this would not amount to a logical necessity. Of course, a world with quiddities gives a more coherent picture than a world made up of relations between "empty" relata, so it seems reasonable to follow von Stillfried's suggestion and assume them logically necessary. On the other hand, Chalmers's identification of phenomenal properties with the intrinsic essence or quiddities of relata is certainly not logically necessary. It might be true that they be the only candidates we know about, and hence, appear to be the most likely ones, however, there might be others we simple do not know. Anyhow, von Stillfried emphasises that even if the identity-thesis of the intrinsic essence and the phenomenal be true, this would not explain why we experience things in exactly the way we do, or to put it otherwise, to which extent the relation between the physical and the phenomenal is contingent or not? However, if we assume the intrinsic essence to be logically necessary, this assumption alone would suffice to preclude the existence of zombies, since there can be no physically identical world without phenomenal properties.

individuals, since they display holistic properties that cannot be explained by simply summing up individual properties; and still, they are obviously constituted by individuals. Thus, as long as we do not discover some deep law in the structure of the universe that logically implies the emergence of holistic systems out of collectives of more primitive systems, we should be prepared to accept contingent principles, at least as long as they appear to be coherent with known facts.

[93] Of course, on the face of it, such a logical entailment of the phenomenal by the physical would equal reductionism, and thus, physicalism. However, von Stillfried (2018) argues that this need not be the case, since a logical implication of the existence of an ontic category by the existence of another need not imply that the one must supervene on the other.

Chalmers's pessimism notwithstanding, I think constitutive panpsychism is still the most promising ontological framework for a possible naturalist theory of consciousness. Particularly if compared to existing alternative approaches, their stunning oddness, and the logical problems they are facing. If, as Chalmers holds, the combination problem is the only serious problem on the way to a solution to the hard problem of consciousness, and if von Stillfried is right in suggesting that a quantum theoretical interpretation of the phenomenal-physical dualism as an analogy of the wave-particle duality might help solving the combination problem, then it should be worth exploring the potential contributions of quantum physics to the mind-body problem.

References

Alter T, Nagasawa Y (2012) What is Russelian monism? J Conscious Stud 19:67–95

Beck F, Eccles JC (1992) Quantum aspects of brain activity and the role of consciousness. Proc Nadl Acad Sci 89:11357–11361

Bieri P (1992) Trying out epiphenomenalism. Erkenntnis 36:283–309

Bohm DJ (1990) A new theory of the relationship of mind and matter. Philos Psychol 3:271–286

Bohr N (1928) The quantum postulate and the recent development of atomic theory. Nature 121:580–591

Bois-Reymond E (ed) (1974) Über die Grenzen des Naturerkennens. Vorträge über Philosophie und Gesellschaft. Meiner, Hamburg

Broad CD (1925) The mind and its place in nature. K. Paul, Trench, Trubner, London

Campbell K (1970) Body and mind. MacMillan, London

Chalmers DJ (1995) The conscious mind: in search of a theory of conscious experience. Department of Philosophy, University of California, Santa Cruz

Chalmers DJ (2002) Consciousness and its place in nature. In: Chalmers DJ (ed) Philosophy of mind: classical and contemporary readings. Oxford University Press, Oxford

Chalmers DJ (2010) The character of consciousness. Oxford University Press, Oxford

Chalmers DJ (2016a) Panpsychism and panprotopsychism. In: Bruntrup G, Jaskolla L (eds) Panpsychism. Oxford University Press, Oxford, pp 19–47

Chalmers DJ (2016b) The combination problem for panpsychism. In: Bruntrup G, Jaskolla L (eds) Panpsychism. Oxford University Press, Oxford, pp 179–214

Chalmers DJ (2018) The meta-problem of consciousness. J Conscious Stud 25(9–10):6–61

Chalmers DJ (2022) Reality+ virtual worlds and the problems of philosophy. W.W. Norton and Co.

Collingwood RG (1998) An essay on metaphysics, revised. Clarendon, Oxford

Dennett DC (1991) Consciousness explained. Little, Brown, Boston

Edelman GM (2004) Das Licht des Geistes: Wie Bewusstsein entsteht. Zürich, Düsseldorf

Feigl H (1967) The mental and the physical: The essay and a postscript. University of Minnesota Press, Minneapolis

Fleck L (1981) Genesis and development of a scientific fact. University of Chicago Press, Chicago

Heidegger M (1954) Vorträge und Aufsätze. Tübingen

Heisenberg W, Bohr N, Herrmann A (1963) Die Kopenhagener Deutung der Quantentheorie. Battenberg, Stuttgart

Hameroff S, Penrose R (1996) Orchestrated reduction of quantum coherence in brain microtubules: a model for consciousness. Math Comput Simul 40:453–480

Hameroff S, Penrose R (2003) Conscious events as orchestrated space-time selections. NeuroQuantology 1:10–35

Hume D (2017) Treatise of human nature. Bennet N (ed). https://www.earlymoderntexts.com/assets/pdfs/hume1739book1_4.pdf. Accessed 12.11.2023
Husserl E (1962) Hesserliana. Köln
Huxley TH (1874) On the hypothesis that animals are automata, and its history. Method Results Essays Thomas H 16:555–580
Jackson F (1982) Epiphenomenal qualia. Philos Q 32:127–136
James W (1895) The principles of psychology, Reprinted 1950. Dover, New York
James W (1981) Pragmatism: a new name for some old ways of thinking. Hackett, Indianapolis
James W (1996) Essays in radical empiricism, Reprint. University of Nebraska Press, Lincoln
Kirk R (1974) Zombies vs materialists. Proc Aristotelian Soc 48:135–152
Latour B (1993) We have never been modern. Harvard University Press, Cambridge
Latour B (2001) A Esperança de Pandora: Ensaios sobre a Realidade dos Estudos Cinetificos. Edusc, Bauru
Latour B (2004) Why has critique run out of steam? From matters of fact to matters of concern. Crit Inq 30(2):225–248
Leibniz GW (1965) Monadology and other philosophical essays. Bobbs-Merril, Indianapolis
Levine J (1983) Materialism and qualia: the explanatory gap. Pac Philos Q 64:354–361
Lorimer D (2019) Towards a post-materialist science. In: Walach H (ed) The Galileo commission report: beyond a materialist worldview: towards an expanded science. Scientific Medical Network pp 88–93
Maxwell N (2017) In praise of natural philosophy: a revolution for thought and life. Kindle. McGill-Queen's University Press, Quebec
Maxwell N (2021) The world crisis—and what to do about it: a revolution for thought and action. University College, London
Morin E (2005) Ciência com Consciência. Editora Bertrand Brasil, Rio de Janeiro
Nagel T (1974) What is it like to be a bat. Philos Rev LXXXIII(4):435–450
Nietzsche F (2002) Jenseits von Gut und Böse. Genealogie der Moral, Stuttgart
Oppenheimer JR (1954) Science and common understanding. Theoria Int J Theory Hist Found Sci 2:225–232
Robinson WS (1988) Brains and people: an essay on mentality and its causal conditions. Temple University Press, Philadelphia
Rorty R (1979) Philosophy and the mirror of nature. Princeton University Press, Princeton
Russell B (2007) The analysis of matter. Russell, Nottingham
Seager W (1995) Consciousness, information, and panpsychism. J Conscious Stud 2:272–288
Squires R (1974) Zombies vs materialists II. Proc Aristotelian Soc 48:153–163
Stoljar D (2020) Panpsychism and non-standard materialism: some comparative remarks. In: Seager W (ed) The Routledge handbook of panpsychism. Routledge, London
Stout GF (1931) Mind and matter. Cambridge University Press, Cambridge
Varela FJ, Thompson E, Rosch A (1993) The embodied mind. Cognitive science and human experience. MIT Press, Cambridge
von Stillfried N (2018) Vom Innen der Dinge: Das "Bewusstsein-Körper-Problem" und die "Welle-Teilchen-Dualität": Interdisziplinäre Impulse zwischen Quantentheorie und analytischer Philosophie des Geistes. Habilitation thesis, University of Trier
Vonnegut K (1973) Breakfast for champions. Delacorte, New York
Walach H (2014) Towards an epistemology of inner experience. In: Schmidt S, Walach H (eds) Meditation—neuroscientific approaches and philosophical implications. Springer, Cham, pp 7–22
Walach H (2019) The Galileo Commission Report: beyond a materialist worldview: towards an expanded science. Scientific Medical Network
Walach H, Römer H (2011) Generalized entanglement—a nonreductive option for a phenomenologically dualist and ontologically monist view of consciousness. In: Walach H, Schmidt S, Jonas WB (eds) Neuroscience, consciousness and spirituality. Springer, Dordrecht, pp 81–95
Whitehead AN (1925) Science and the modern world. Cambridge University Press, London

Chapter 12
What Quantum Physics May Tell Us About Mind and Matter

The development of quantum physics is often attributed to Max Planck's[1] (1899/1900) work on black-body radiation and his postulation of the so-called Planck constant *h*. To make a long story short, *h* describes the minimum *quantum* of energy transmitted by electromagnetic radiation, including light. His finding that electromagnetic radiation is the sum of discrete quantities of energy and Einsteins (1905) subsequent photoelectric work strongly suggested that light is constituted by particles, such as electrons and photons. However, at that time, light was being conceived in terms of waves. The nature of light has been subject to disputes in modern science since the times of Newton and Huygens, the latter defending that light was a wave while the former thought it might be rather constituted by particles. However, since Thomas Young's (1804) experiments on the interference of light, there seemed to be no doubt about its wave-like character. So, while Planck's findings were shaking a century old "truth" about light and electromagnetism in general, evidence for the wave-like character of light was too strong to be ignored. Thus, physicists were left with the puzzling situation that evidence seemed to prove that light is simultaneously constituted by waves and by particles. Further contributions by Nils Bohr[2] and Luis de Broglie[3] suggested that this double nature was not restricted to light, but also applied to electrons and other fundamental constituents of atoms. The introduction of quantum physics in Bohr's atom model and de Broglie's works on the wave character of electrons gave way to a much broader understanding of the double character underlying quantum physics as a universal cosmic principle. What was still missing, however, was a mathematical formalism to precisely describe and predict the observed double nature of "quanta". This final step towards a real "quantum theory" was achieved by Erwin Schrödinger's[4] wave-mechanics and the matrix

[1] Planck (1899, 1900).

[2] Bohr (1913a, b, c).

[3] Broglie (1923, 2004).

[4] Schrödinger (1926a, b, c, d).

J. Linhart, *Science and the Other*, Schriften zu Leben und Gesellschaft - Series on Life and Society 2, https://doi.org/10.1007/978-3-032-03927-9_12

mechanics of particle-like quantum behaviour developed by Werner Heisenberg[5] together with Max Born and Pascual Jordan.[6] While Schrödinger's approach was based on de Broglie's wave-like description of electrons, Heisenberg and his colleagues further developed Bohr's earlier works on the particle-like behaviour of electrons in his atom model. Despite their harsh conceptual differences, both mathematical models came to the same predictions on quantum behaviour.[7] Moreover, the predictions provided by these mathematical models matched so precisely with empirical evidence, that to this day, no contrary proof has been observed. Quantum physics is, therefore, often called the best proven scientific theory ever, since there is no evidence against its predictions. Given the recalcitrant and enigmatic persistence of wave-particle dualism in both quantum theory and empirical evidence, one is left to wonder what kind of strange ontic structure the mathematical formalisms of quantum physics are actually describing? In fact, there is still no consensus about the ontological consequences of quantum physics, instead there are countless different heuristic and ontological interpretations. At the least, however, the classical concept of matter has been diluted by quantum physics, suggesting that at their fundamental bases physical objects are constituted by a lot of "empty" space pervaded by interfering "waves", eventually collapsing into "particles" with an infinitely small spatial extension (or whatever that something we try to describe using metaphors like "waves" or "particles" may be).

However, most of these sweeping theoretical inferences are based on a relatively small number of different experimental setups. Since quantum physics has been inspiring all kinds of mystical ideas, it might be interesting to call to mind what kind of evidence actually gave rise to which particular finding, and the possible interpretations these findings may permit (Fig. 12.1).

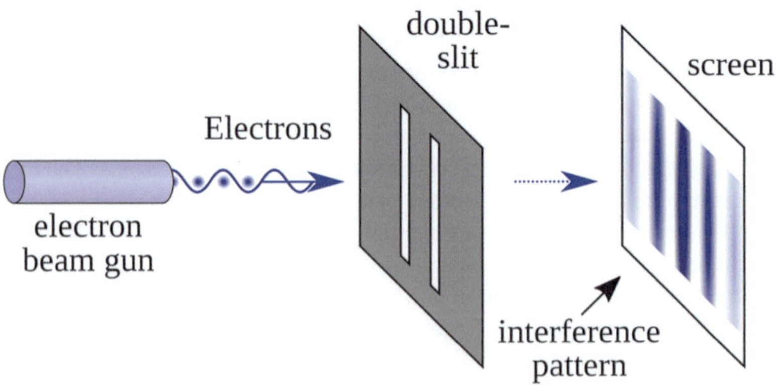

Fig. 12.1 Illustration of a double slit experiment (original: NekoJaNekoJa Vector: Johannes Kalliauer, https://commons.wikimedia.org/wiki/File:Double-slit.svg, https://creativecommons.org/licenses/by-sa/4.0/legalcode)

[5] Heisenberg (1925, 1927).

[6] Born and Jordan (1925).

[7] Born (1954).

The earliest and by far the most important experiment that led to quantum physics is the so-called double-slit experiment, first published by Thomas Young in 1804. In its simplest form this experimental set-up is constituted by a coherent source of light (nowadays e.g. a laser) illuminating a lightproof shade pierced by two parallel slits a small distance from each other, and a highly photosensitive screen behind the shade to detect the light that passed through the slits. If light was constituted by particles, they would pass the slits along two straight lines and display two parallel rows at the screen. What Young observed with his still quite limited equipment, however, were several parallel rows with decreasing intensity from the central to the outer rows. Young inferred that light, like sound, might be a wave, and not a beam of particles. Accordingly, after passing the slits, the two resulting waves would interfere with each other, which would explain the patterns on the screen. So, until this point in time, the double-slit experiment provided evidence for a wave-like behaviour of light. However, a century later, technical developments allowed for emitting and measuring single quanta (typically photons, or electrons). This technical improvement of the experimental set-up resulted in yet another insight. Now, the emitted quanta would hit the screen displaying a pattern of discrete dots, thus, showing particle-like behaviour. Nevertheless, with more quanta being emitted and absorbed by the screen, the little dots would, once again, gradually sum up to parallel rows, resembling just the same patterns as observed by Young a century before. It follows that there must be discrete "particles" exchanging energy with the molecules at the screen, while their distribution follows wave-like interference patterns. In other words, the quanta behave like "waves" until they hit the screen, when they suddenly behave like "particles". But there is more we can learn from this experiment. Since the distribution of hits at the screen depends on the precise number and size of slits in the shade, each hit represents a quantum which had to "know" of all the slits and their position in order to "decide" where to hit the screen. Alternatively, one could also suggest that each quantum passed all the slits at once, behaving like a "wave", before it instantiated as a "particle"-like quantum of energy when hitting the screen. In any case, it appears that quanta are not limited to a particle-sized region of space before hitting the screen. Moreover, the exact location where a quantum will hit the screen does not follow any deterministic rule, but only a probabilistic distribution along interference patterns. In sum, the double-slit experiment provides evidence for a double character of quanta, showing both "wave"-like and "particle"-like properties. Of course, "waves" and "particles" are only clumsy metaphors to describe the inscrutable nature of that something we cannot grasp by means of any imaging method for simply being too small. Still, the evidence provided by the double-slit experiment gives proof of a pattern of properties quanta show under certain conditions that can be arranged into two radically distinct groups: the first joining properties like deterministic behaviour, mass, linear movement in timespace, locality, and causal roles via energy exchange; the second combining properties like indeterministic behaviour, non-locality, field-like distribution in spacetime, no mass, and non-causal instant correlations without energy exchange. Obviously, the former group resembles rather matter- or particle-like properties, while the latter shows properties almost entirely unknown to macroscopic physics, which might be described as "wave"-like properties (particularly due to the observed interference-patterns). Other experiments, like the Mach-Zehnder-interferometer, allow for comparable conclusions about the double character of quanta.

There is, however, another class of experiments that sheds light on yet another aspect of quantum behaviour, which is also known as "entanglement" or "EPR-correlation" (named after Albert **E**instein, Boris **P**odolsky and Nathan **R**osen). To put it simply, quantum mechanics predicts that quanta that are systemically bound together (e.g. due to common origin) will behave in a correlated way, as long as their systemic relation is not interrupted through interaction with an external system. According to Bohr and Heisenberg, such *entangled* quanta would have no defined eigenstates until measurement (= interaction with an external system) provoked their instantiation. In other words, entangled quanta would "happen" to manifest individual properties in a particular and correlated way only at the moment of (and not previously to) measurement. As a corollary, this assumption precludes a local, causal explanation of this correlated behaviour of entangled quanta, when the measurements of the properties of the entangled quanta occur simultaneously or within such a short timeframe that no causal influence (propagating at a maximum velocity of the speed of light) can reach from the location of one of the quanta to the location of the other.

In 1935, Einstein and his colleagues (EPR) published a thought experiment intended to disprove the quantum-theoretical hypotheses of quantum indeterminacy and non-local behaviour. In contrast, EPR argued that quantum physics were still incomplete, however, once the missing element (or "hidden variables") were discovered, the correlated quantum values should turn out to be determined by a common, local cause, just as any other physical event. Further responses from Bohr and Bohm held against EPR's arguments for local realism, again invoking arguments from further thought experiments. There seemed to be no way of empirically testing the opposing hypotheses, until in the 1960s John Bell[8] developed a mathematical model (the so-called *Bell inequalities*) predicting different (joint) probability distributions for deterministic and indeterministic behaviour of entangled quanta. Subsequent experiments produced a considerable stock of data violating Bell's inequality and thus confirming non-localism as predicted by standard quantum mechanics and providing strong evidence against local realism.[9] Although Bell tests may follow a range of different experimental setups, most of them follow a more or less generic basic scheme (Fig. 12.2).

In its simplest version, an entangled pair of quanta is produced generally by "splitting" a single quantum into two entangled quanta on a crystal, each single quantum heading in opposite directions. At the end of each of the two different trajectories there is a detector with a polarising filter in front of it. It is an empirical fact

[8] Bell (1964).

[9] Hensen et al. (2015); Giustina et al. (2015); Shalm et al. (2015); Handsteiner et al. (2017); Rauch et al. (2018); Keiser (2022).

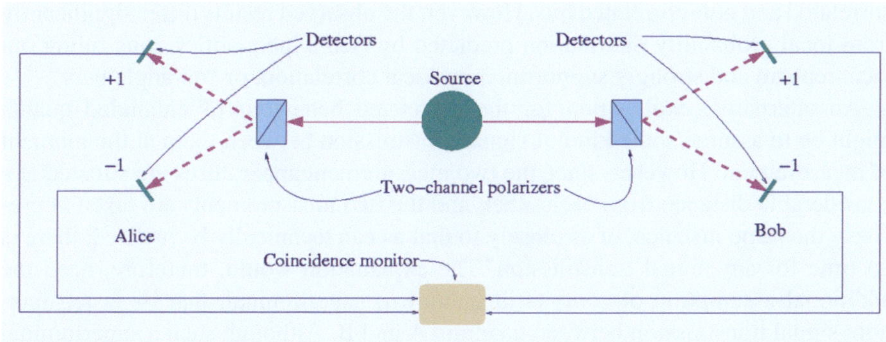

Fig. 12.2 Scheme of a "two-channel" Bell test (Anonym, https://commons.wikimedia.org/wiki/File:Bell-test-photon-analyer.png. "Bell-test-photon-analyer", https://creativecommons.org/licenses/by-sa/3.0/legalcode)

that entangled quanta will always have opposite properties if spin is measured, such as up- or down spins or orthogonal polarisations. Thus, if the polarisation filters are adjusted in orthogonal angles (turned 90° apart), either both or none of the quanta should pass the filters and hit the detectors. If, on the other hand, the filters are adjusted exactly in parallel, only one of the two entangled quanta will pass one of the filters, while the other will be absorbed. At intermediary angles there is a certain probability for one of the quanta to pass the polarisation filter if the other quantum has passed the other polarisation filter. In an experimental setting for testing Bell's theorem one may now change the direction of both polarisation filters, switching randomly between different angles before each emission of an entangled pair of quanta. After repeating this operation many times, the hits detected at the two detectors behind the two filters will amount to reproducible probability distributions. According to Bell's theorem, the number of detected quanta at the two detectors should show a particular ratio, if local realism be true, and another, clearly distinguishable ratio, if local realism be false. Since a considerable number of experiments of this type have confirmed Bell's predictions, they seem to support the non-local indeterminacy hypothesis rather than local determinism. But what exactly does indeterministic behaviour and non-locality mean in this setting? Just to summarise the observable results produced by Bell test-type experiments: We can observe that after emitting two quanta as a result of a single quantum event, these two "sister"-quanta will follow distinct trajectories through space and time until each of them encounter a measurement apparatus. Measurements will show that the eigenstates of both quanta are correlated. Hence, there is strong evidence for some kind of strict correlation between the behaviour of quantum A and quantum B. The question is, thus, how to explain this correlation?

The most obvious avenue is, of course, to assume that the behaviour of both A and B is being determined at the moment of emission, that is, previous to, and independent of later measurement. According to Bell's inequalities, this would imply specific local bounds on the joint statistics—that is, a characteristic distribution of correlated and non-correlated hits. However, the observed results differ significantly from local probability distribution predicted by Bell's inequalities, thus ruling out local realism and strongly supporting non-local correlation, or "entanglement".

An alternative explanation for the correlated behaviour of entangled quanta might be to assume some kind of signal transmission between them at the moment of measurement. However, since the two measurement apparatuses are situated at a considerable distance from each other, and the two measurements are taken at precisely the same instance, or as closely to that as can technically be realised, there is no time for any signal transmission. The explanation would, therefore, need the additional assumption of some (still unknown) superluminal, that is, faster-than-light signal transmission between quantum A and B. Although such a superluminal signal cannot be excluded, this option has little support in physics, as it violates linear causation and special relativity (allowing for retro-causality).[10]

Once all local causes are excluded, the only remaining "cause" might be the Big Bang or God. Following such a superdeterministic conspiracy thesis, the universe is entirely governed by strictly deterministic laws, so that all past, current and future events are nothing but instants of an entirely predetermined cosmic unfolding. As a consequence, there would be no free will, no contingent events, and no possibility of changing our future. Although this view cannot be falsified, it is obviously not very attractive, for being utterly counterintuitive and suggesting a very unsatisfactory picture of reality.

Finally, we are left with a picture in which quantum-systems show non-local behaviour. Unlike particle-like properties (as described by matrix mechanics), their wave-like properties (as described by the wave function) evolve in a higher-dimensional configuration space, allowing for interferences and non-local correlations between distant parts of a system, however, without energy exchange or (faster-than-light) signal transfer. When measured, entangled quanta are observed in correlated particle-like "eigenstates" selected from an array of "superposed" (potential) states predicted by their shared wave function. According to the standard interpretation, this manifestation of particle-like properties is described in terms of a "collapse" of the wave function upon interaction with an external system (e.g. measurement apparatus), resulting in discrete eigenstates with particle-like properties. In addition, upon interaction with the environment, a coherent quantum system (with an interference pattern of superpositions as defined by its wave function) will get "mixed" with an infinite number of other quantum systems, leading to "decoherence" and consequential loss of its unitary interference pattern and respective superpositions. This explains why the system behaves as if classically once observed. However, what exactly happens between the emission of the quanta and their detection is not empirically observable, since the wave-like properties are not directly

[10] Meanwhile, such Bell-tests have been carried out over large distances, for instance below Lake Geneva, have used starlight emanating from stars light-years away to trigger the choice of polarisation angles, thus closing loopholes for hidden variable interpretations (Salart et al. 2008; Handsteiner et al. 2017; Hensen et al. 2015; Giustina et al. 2015; Shalm et al. 2015; Rauch et al. 2018; Keiser 2022).

observable but only indirectly inferable from the quantum-behaviour evidenced through measurement (= instantiations as particle-like properties due to contact with an external system and subsequent energy exchange with a molecule at the measurement apparatus). Attempts to identify the trajectories by detecting quanta on their way to the terminal detector did not yield much information about their wave-like behaviour either, since such measurements resulted in the "disappearance" of their wave-like properties.[11] This effect reveals yet another strange aspect of quantum wave-particle dualism, which finds its expression in Heisenberg's uncertainty principle and Bohr's notion of complementarity. Paraphrasing uncertainty, the principle predicts that the more precisely one of two complementary properties of a quantum state is measured (e.g. position), the less precisely the other (e.g. momentum) can be known, and vice versa. Complementarity makes similar predictions about the mutually exclusive relation of wave-like and particle-like properties, however, on quite different albeit closely related theoretical grounds.[12] For example, measurement of the trajectory of one of two entangled quanta will annihilate the wave-like, non-local properties of the other.[13] This, in turn, implies a non-commutativity of measurements at quantum systems, that is, a measurement of one observable will alter the results of subsequent measurements of other observables. In other words, measurement at quantum-systems amount to an irreversible intervention, and thus, results in changes within the system, so that the same

[11] For example, the measurement of trajectories in a double-slit experiment will result in the disappearance of interference patterns.

[12] Heisenberg's uncertainty principle refers to inevitable disturbances caused by measurement of one property and the resulting impossibility to cancel out these disturbances from subsequent measurements of other properties. It thus establishes an epistemological principle of unsurmountable limitations to the completeness of obtainable knowledge about quantum states. Bohr, in contrast, understood measurement in terms of an interaction which inevitably becomes a part of the observed phenomenon. His notion of complementarity goes much further: "Thus, a sentence like 'we cannot know both the momentum and position of an atomic object' raises at once questions as to the physical reality of two such attributes of the object, which can be answered only by referring to the conditions for the unambiguous use of space-time concepts, on the one hand, and dynamical conservation laws, on the other hand." (Bohr (1963) [1949 essay: 'Discussion with Einstein on Epistemological Problems in Atomic Physics'], The Philosophical Writings of Niels Bohr, Vol. II, Essays, 1933–1957 On Atomic Physics and Human Knowledge, Woodbridge, CT: Ox Bow Press, pp. 40–41.; quoted in Barad 2022: 1035). For Bohr, quantum observables cannot be regarded as intrinsic properties of independent objects; they acquire meaning only within specific experimental contexts. Heisenberg's uncertainty highlights epistemological limits to knowledge, but Bohr's complementarity emphasizes a deeper ontological indeterminacy (Barad 2022).

[13] This effect has been observed during measurement at Mach-Zehnder interferometers. In this experiment, a quantum is "split" and projected into different directions. Mirrors reflect the two separate trajectories towards a second splitter, and detectors measuring the quanta passing the splitter in either direction. Measurement will show a wave-like (interference induced) behaviour of quanta. However, this so-called "which-path-measurement" at one of the two trajectories will lead to particle-like behaviour of the other quantum, even if no quantum has been detected. This effect has been interpreted as clear evidence for non-local behaviour (Elitzur and Vaidman 1993; quoted in von Stillfried 2018).

two subsequent measurements will lead to different results if applied in inverse succession.

Be this as it may, this little outline of the kind of evidence quantum physics is based on should have demonstrated at least two important, and somehow contradictory, aspects of quantum physics: On the one hand, there is extremely solid experimental evidence for the accuracy and reliability of the predictions made by the mathematical formalisms that constitute the core of quantum theory; on the other hand, neither the mathematical models nor the observations made during experiment provide a clear picture of the entities and events they are actually describing. "Quanta", "waves", "particles", "spins", "entangled systems", and the like, are at best scanty metaphors for those obscure objects quantum physics is investigating, leaving an enormous space for all kinds of speculative interpretations when it comes to the ontic categories they might possibly refer to. In fact, many physcists refuse to interpret quantum physics ontically but use it operationally. Of course, it can be argued that such speculations are unnecessary, since quantum theory simply works, and because their metaphysical character should exclude them from the agenda of science, anyway. Nonetheless, to simply slur over the cosmological riddles implied by quantum physics seems to be almost impossible, since it is dealing with nothing less than the very essence of matter, including ourselves, life, the universe and, well, of quite *everything*. Moreover, the persisting incoherencies between relativity theory and quantum physics are at least unsatisfactory, since a unified "theory of everything" has always been a chief objective of modern science.[14] And finally, from a more technical perspective, a unified fundamental theory of physics should be expected to contribute to the solution of many open questions, ranging from nanophysics to artificial intelligence, astrophysics, and maybe even the mind-body problem.

12.1 Interpreting Quantum Physics in Search of Mind

Quantum theory is the most useful and powerful theory physicists have ever devised. Yet today, nearly 90 years after its formulation, disagreement about the meaning of the theory is stronger than ever. New interpretations appear every day. None ever disappear (Mermin 2012: 8).

Although many physicists seem to feel comfortable with a pragmatic or heuristic interpretation of quantum theory in terms of a functional approximation, others have been investing considerable time and effort in developing a great variety of different epistemological and ontological interpretations. In fact, there are so many different approaches that even a superficial presentation of all of them would easily

[14] Although there have been innumerable attempts to adapt Quantum Theory to Relativity or vice versa, there is still no consensus on this issue. See for example Laloë 2022 or Szczeciniarz and Kounheiher (2022) (both in the same volume).

cram a whole volume.[15] It seems that quantum physical findings open a space for all kinds of metaphysical ideas, ranging from super-deterministic realism[16] to anti-realist idealisms,[17] along with some particularly weird ideas, like the famous many-worlds interpretation, and other curiosities.[18] One might get the impression that quantum physics serves to justify whatever worldview one prefers. But a closer look reveals that this is not quite the case. Although deep "feelings" about the fundamental constitution of the universe, ourselves and our free will certainly impinge on motivation and argumentation of most authors, however, each proposed interpretation features particular solutions and shortcomings to the problems posed by quantum theory.

Traditionally, the debate has been organising along the distinction between realist and anti-realist, that is, ontological versus epistemological interpretations of the observed quantum wave-particle dualism. In other words, for many authors the central question has been whether waves and particles are real existing entities, either coexisting simultaneously or diachronically transforming into each other, or whether "waves" and "particles" are rather metaphors describing instrumental formalisms with no clearly definable ontic referent. Epistemological interpretation may either interpret the wave-particle dualism as a regrettable, but possibly unavoidable shortcoming of current formalisms, or as two complementary aspects of a common, really existing referent (quanta). Ontological interpretations, on the other hand, will have to explain how, when and why waves "collapse" into particles, or, alternatively, explain how quanta may possibly be waves and particles simultaneously, and why they seem to behave differently depending on the kind of measurement applied. However, complementarity might be interpreted in terms of an ontological principle while non-collapse interpretations may treat "waves" and "particles" rather as aspects of a common ontic referent. Hence, the epistemological versus ontological distinction may at times get rather fuzzy. Alternatively, one could opt for a categorisation in terms of dualist and monist interpretations, that is, concerning the question whether waves and particles should be interpreted as two distinct fundamental ontic entities, or the one as an aspect or property of the other, with only waves *or* particles representing a fundamental ontic category. Such a categorisation would obviously also facilitate a comparison with the ontological models discussed in the context of the hard problem of consciousness, however, here again, the distinction between monism and aspect dualism may easily get blurred, too. A third touchstone might

[15] For a comprehensive overview see The Oxford Handbook of the History of Quantum Interpretations, edited by Olival Freire (2022).

[16] E.g. Einstein et al. (1935); Born (1954); Ballentine (1998).

[17] E.g. Wheeler (1990a).

[18] Surveys among physicists actually shows that there is still considerable confusion about the different interpretations of quantum physics even among physicists. According to Sivasundaram and Nielsen (2016), a majority of physicists rather holds to epistemological interpretations while at the same time emphasising the importance of a coherent ontological framework for physics. Among the different ontological interpretations, many-worlds theory and information-theoretical approaches seem to be the most popular.

be, then, to distinguish collapse from collapse-free interpretations. This distinction concerns the question whether quanta are simultaneously waves and particles, or, rather, waves that collapse into particles under certain conditions. Although this is a rather technical definition with little direct reference to philosophy of mind, it has important implications on possible contributions from quantum physics to the mind-body problem. Here, I will follow von Stillfried's combination of the three criteria, suggesting the following categorisation[19]:

I. Epistemic-dualistic interpretations: "Waves" and "particles" are only epistemological models of inscrutable ontic referents.
   1. Complementarity interpretations[20]: "Waves" and "particles" are complementary and mutually exclusive "images" describing two, ultimately inscrutable, aspects of the quanta.[21]
   2. Epistemic minimalist interpretations: "Waves" and "particles" are purely arbitrary models referring to mathematical formalisms of wave function and quantum mechanics, which coincidentally happen to provide sufficiently reliable predictions, and which do not necessarily need to have ontic referents.[22]
   3. Probability (or ensemble) interpretations[23]: The wave function describes a probability space of possible measurement events.[24]

---

[19] Von Stillfried's (2018) overview is not a complete enumeration of all existing interpretations, but only refers to some of the most prominent proposals. There are further interesting approaches that could be mentioned here, like Rovelli's (1996) relational quantum mechanics, or quantum Bayesianism or Qbism (Wheeler 1990b; Zwrin 2022).

[20] Bohr (1928); Oppenheimer (1954); Heisenberg et al. (1963). Complementarity interpretations are sometimes subsumed under the so-called "Copenhagen interpretation", following Heisenberg's coinage for views he had developed during his collaboration with Nils Bohr in Copenhagen during the 1920s. However, since there is no unified definition of the exact content of such a "Copenhagen interpretation", and since Heisenberg's views diverge from Bohr's views in some important aspects, I follow von Stillfried (2018) in refraining from listing the "Copenhagen interpretation" as a clearly definable view among others (for a detailed discussion on this issue see also Howard 2022).

[21] Complementarity interpretations have been discussed by several authors in quite different ways, often diverging considerably from Bohr's initial approach, some of them rather tending to ontological interpretations of wave-particle dualism, and even more frequently, acting on the assumption of wave function collapse. So, complementarity interpretations might well be classified as an ontic-dualistic collapse interpretation, however, since this detail is of no importance for my argument here, I simply reproduce von Stillfried's classification without any change.

[22] This view does actually not refer to any particular theoretical approach, but rather to a widespread view among physicians, which has famously been paraphrased by David Mermin's "shut up and calculate!" (an expression often erroneously attributed to Richard Feynman—see Mermin 2004). Since this view holds that any speculation about ontological interpretations of quantum physics is nonsense, there is no elaborated approach on this view either (von Stillfried 2021, personal communication).

[23] Born (1926a, b).

[24] Agnostic position providing no ontological explanation for mathematically predicted effects like interference on non-local correlations.

II. Ontic-dualistic interpretations: Both wave and particle properties are ontic categories.

1. Collapse interpretations: The transition from super-positioned probability wave-like quantum-states into particle-like defined eigenstates results from "collapse" of the wave function caused by measurement-like events.[25]

   (a) Collapse through consciousness[26]: The transition from indeterministic wave-like to deterministic particle-like behaviour is effectuated by conscious apprehension of measurement result.[27]
   (b) Collapse through decoherence[28]: Super-positioned wave-like states depend on operational closure of quantum-systems, wherefore interaction with other systems results in decoherence and collapse of the wave function.[29]
   (c) Spontaneous collapse[30]: Ontic indeterministic spontaneous collapse of a quantum leads to collapse of all superposed quanta of the same system, thereby instantiating deterministic objects.[31]

[25] In general terms, collapse interpretations provide a unified approach for both quantum nanoscopic and classical macroscopic systems, since it explains the transition from the first to the latter as a result of wave function collapse. The underlying mathematical formalism predicts an increase of collapse events in direct correlation to an increase in complexity and interdependence of quantum systems, thus resulting in a de facto deterministic behaviour of macro-objects.

[26] von Neumann (1996).

[27] According to Johann von Neumann (idem), quantum behaviour shows two distinct kinds of processes: non-linear indeterministic (manifestation of one local state) processes followed by a linear-deterministic processes (changes of the non-measured quant). However, measurement result is only instantiated after its conscious apprehension by an observer, hence, collapse is caused by consciousness. Schrödinger famously demonstrated the oddness of such views in a thought experiment known as "Schrödinger's cat". Here, a hypothetical cat in a closed box has been poisoned and opening the box to see whether the cat survived the poisoning or not would equal to a measurement event. According to "normal" perception, the cat should be either dead or alive before opening the box, however, according to von Neumann's observer-induced collapse the cat would rather exist in a superposed state between death and life until an observer opens the box. Curiously, popular receptions of Schrödinger's reflexions lead to the idea that quantum physics had proven that consciousness creates reality by actualising wave potentiality. Anyhow, von Neumann's interpretation leads into the problem of how the universe could emerge without the previous presence of consciousness?

[28] Zeh (1970); Zurek (1981).

[29] Macroscopic objects (e.g. measurement apparatus) are open systems that interact continuously with their environment. This interaction between a closed quantum system in superposition and apparatus therefore disperses quantum coherence, so that interference between different states of the apparatus–quantum system becomes unobservable. Decoherence allows one to calculate, with high precision, the timescale over which this occurs, but it does not explain why a single definite outcome is realized.

[30] Also called GRW-theory (after Ghirardi, Rimini and Weber) or "Quantum Mechanics with Spontaneous Localisations" (Friebe 2015; similar approach also discussed in Penrose 1996).

[31] Accordingly, less complex isolated quantum-systems (like in quantum physical experiments) will maintain superposition for some time, while larger systems (like macrophysical objects) will

2. Collapse-free interpretation: Waves and particles correspond to two different, but permanently correlated ontic categories.
   (a) Pilot-wave (or De-Broglie-Bohm) Interpretation[32]: Each quantum particle is "guided" by a corresponding "pilot wave", whereas interfering individual pilot waves amount to higher dimensional waves systems, ultimately forming a single wave function of the entire universe.[33]

III. Ontic-monistic interpretations: Only waves *or* particles correspond to ontic categories.

1. Wave-only interpretations[34]: All superposed states of the wave function correspond to actually existing ontic realities.
   (a) Many worlds interpretation[35]: Each interaction with a quantum system results in the instantiation of *all* possible events in its probability space, thus continuously splitting into countless independent, parallel "worlds".[36]
   (b) Many minds interpretation[37]: There is only one physical world, but each super-positioned quantum state corresponds to a particular mind being instantiated at each measurement-like event, thus permanently splitting into countless new minds, each perceiving other measurement results (=one of several super-positioned states of one existing world).
2. Particle-only interpretations: Quanta are just particles and their apparently wave-like behaviour is only an illusive effect of some deeper determinism.
   (a) Superdeterminism: All past and future events have been strictly predetermined from the moment of creation (Big Bang or God's creation); observed wave-like behaviour (interference, non-local correlation, etc.) have in fact been predetermined in a parallelistic manner.

---

collapse almost immediately. However, this interpretation comes with the disadvantage that new ad hoc constants are necessary.

[32] Bohm (1952); Broglie (2004).

[33] The universal interconnectedness may explain how quanta of a subsystem are entangled, while collapse is made obsolete by assuming a quasi-deterministic behaviour of complex systems. Despite its differences, Bohmian interpretation provides predictions identical to collapse theories.

[34] Everett (1957, 1973).

[35] DeWitt and Graham (1973).

[36] Thanks to its fascinating weirdness, many-worlds interpretations have received considerable attention. However, as von Stillfried (2018) emphasises, it is difficult to see how such an outrageous permanent *creatio ex nihilo* of infinite new universes should be imagined, besides other conceptual problems implied by this approach.

[37] Albert and Loewer (1988); Lockwood (1991).

(b) Retro-causality[38]: Observed indeterminacy of quantum-events is in fact determined by some retro-causal effectiveness of measurement-like events.

Apart from these very general distinctions between the different interpretations, they also differ concerning their responses to further questions left open by the evidence quantum theory is based on. For example:

1. *Determinism* versus *indeterminism*: Is the observed indeterminism of quantum behaviour an ontic property or just an illusory "appearance" based on some deterministic "hidden variables" or a fundamental superdeterminsm?
2. *Locality* versus *non-locality*: Is the observed non-local behaviour an ontic property of entangled quantum-systems (or their wave functions) or is there another local, causal principle responsible for the observed correlations?
3. *Measurement* versus *observation*: Is the observed non-commutative effect of measurements a result of the physical intervention (measurement) on quantum behaviour or is the observation, that is, the intentional consciousness of an observer, the actual cause of the observed quantum events (e.g. collapse of the wave function or decoherence of entangled systems).

While there are many different interpretations and theoretical responses to the questions posed by empirical evidence from quantum physics, all these interpretations make the same predictions. Empirical evidence alone, therefore, does not allow for deciding which of all these alternative interpretations is most likely to describe "real" structures of the universe. At the same time, each individual interpretation bears different, so far unsolved theoretical problems. In any case, the astonishing variations between the cosmological models suggested by the different interpretations of quantum physics give proof of the limited descriptive, let alone explanatory power of experimental evidence when it comes to the fundamental ontic principles of nature. On the face of it, matter is as mysterious a thing as mind, and it turns out that even the most fundamental principle of scientific method, causation, is by no means an evident principle of nature, but rather a fuzzy heuristic concept. However, quantum theory is not a blank cheque for a Feyerabendian "anything goes" science anarchism. Empirical evidence, together with the powerful mathematical formalisms provided by quantum theory, still impose considerable constrains on interpretative freedom, since they pose a number of defined questions with a limited range of possible answers.

So far, the interpretations mentioned were only constrained by the demands imposed by the task to find a fundamental theory of matter. If we now introduce the additional task to also account for phenomenal properties, this will also amount to additional theoretical requirements for such a fundamental theory of mind and matter.

[38] E.g. "Time Symmetric Quantum Mechanics" (Aharonov et al. 2010) or John G. Cramer's "transactional interpretation of quantum mechanics" (Cramer 1986).

Regarding the present purpose, I will choose only some of those interpretations of quantum theory that have been proposed as possible contributions to the mind-body problem, and particularly those containing ontological concepts that might be comparable to those I have previously extracted from the Potiguara's cosmopractices.[39]

12.1.1 Complementarity as a Fundamental Principle of Mind and Matter

Nils Bohr was one of the first to call attention to the similarities he saw between wave-particle dualism and mind-body dualism. According to Bohr, the common denominator was the complementarity principle, which he understood as a core characteristic of both dualities. Bohr's reflexions on complementarity inspired most later contributions to the issue, which may explain the comparably huge number of complementarity-based approaches to a general theory of mind and matter. However, Bohr's own writings on the mind-body problem remained noticeably vague and superficial. His complementarity principle held that the descriptions of the wave and particle properties were mutually exclusive but necessary for a complete description of quantum behaviour. However, he never provided a coherent definition of his principle. Bohr was rather fascinated by his impression that the wave-particle complementary relation, which had just been discovered to form the fundamental basis of everything, seemed to pop up everywhere around us in our macroscopic world. For example, he mentioned complementary pairs like love versus justice, thought versus feeling, acting versus reflecting, among others, and also physical versus psychological, determinism versus free will, and subject versus object.[40] Although some of his remarks on the complementarity relation between physical and psychological properties seemed to suggest a deeper relation to the wave-particle complementarity, Bohr never came up with any coherent quantum theoretical approach to mind.[41]

Despite the vagueness of Bohr's own statements on this issue, several renowned physicists of his time, like Schrödinger, Pauli, Fierz and Oppenheimer, took his ideas seriously and further developed the complementarity approach. Wolfgang Pauli may have been one of the most emphatic proponents of complementarity as a universal principle underlying both wave-particle and mind-body dualism:

[39] Concerning quantum theoretical approaches that have been discussed as possible solutions to the mind-body problem I will follow von Stillfried's (2018) large scale analysis of the issue. Additionally, I will discuss the Generalised Quantum Theory (Walach 2005, 2014a; Walach and Römer 2011; Walach and Stillfried 2011; Walach et al. 2014), since this interpretation of quantum theory provides some possible explanations for so-called spiritual or para-psychological phenomena, and thus, might offer an additional nexus to Potiguara cosmology.

[40] Examples quoted in von Stillfried (2018).

[41] Fahrenberg (2013).

The situation called 'complementarity' by N. Bohr is explained with the aid of the example furnished by the spheres of application of the contrasting concepts of 'wave' and 'particle' in modern atomic physics. It consists in the fact that the experimental arrangements to which the one or the other of these intuitive pictures is applied necessarily are mutually exclusive as a consequence of the fundamentally never completely determinable interaction between instruments of observation and observed system. The analogy is pointed out between this complementary situation and the paradoxes in the relation 'subject-object' in general, as well as the pair of opposites employed in more recent psychology, 'conscious-unconscious', in particular (Pauli 1950: 75).

His interest in the issue of consciousness also found an expression in his collaboration with Carl Gustav Jung. Together they developed a kind of a Platonic-Pythagorean idealism, with symbols indicating an "objective order of the cosmos". Their conception of *unus mundus* suggested a universal symbolic or archetypical reality, with mind and matter being complementary aspects of that same underlying reality. "The laws of this world would then be the physical manifestations of the archetypes, [...] as Plato's 'ideas' share the notion of a concept and of a force of nature (they create actions out of themselves)".[42] Pauli was driven by a deep conviction that physical descriptions were necessarily incomplete and needed to be amplified to include the inherent psychological aspects of reality.[43] Similarly, Robert Oppenheimer pointed to the core of the hard problem of consciousness when he observed:

Whether a physico-chemical description of the material counterpart of consciousness will in fact ever be possible, whether physiological or psychological observation will ever permit with any relevant confidence the prediction of our behaviour in moments of decision and in moments of challenge, we may be sure that these analyses and these understandings, even should they exist, will be as irrelevant to the acts of decision and the castings of the will as are the trajectories of molecules to the entropy of a gas. To be touched with awe, or humour, to be moved by beauty, to make a commitment or a determination, to understand some truth these are complementary modes of the human spirit (Oppenheimer 1954: 228).

In the face of these peremptory statements of such brilliant physicists there should be little doubt about the fundamental role of complementarity on the way to a unified theory of mind and matter. And indeed, their views have been taken seriously

---

[42] Pauli in a letter to Fierz of January 7, 1948. Letter 929 in von Meyenn (1993, pp. 496, 497); translated and quoted by Atmanspacher and Primas (2006: 18). More precisely, "Pauli emphasized that this ultimate reality is impersonal and proposed that mind and matter can be considered to emerge by a breakdown of the psychophysical symmetry of the unus mundus" (ibidem).

[43] "The general problem of the relation between psyche and physis, between inside and outside, can hardly be regarded as solved by the term 'psychophysical parallelism' advanced in the last century. Yet, perhaps, modern science has brought us closer to a more satisfying conception of this relationship, as it has established the notion of complementarity within physics. It would be most satisfactory if physis and psyche could be conceived as complementary aspects of the same reality" (Pauli 1952: 164; translated and quoted in Atmanspacher and Primas 2006: 17).

by a number of more recent authors[44] who endeavoured to further develop the complementarity approach. However, all the enthusiasm notwithstanding, the definition of complementarity as a common principle underlying both wave-particle and mind-body dualisms turned out to be much harder than initially imagined by Bohr and his followers. Authors like Peter Alexander[45] called attention to the problems involved in an application of the quantum-theoretical concept of complementarity to the mind-body distinction, since the two realms were significantly different, and thus, overrating the analogies might lead into category mistake. Subsequent attempts[46] to provide a single coherent definition of complementarity applicable to both realms had a hard time and finally would have to come to terms with the fundamental disanalogy between the two realms. Particularly, there seems to be no generalisable definition of *incompatibility*, which has been a central requirement ever since Bohr's introduction of his complementarity concept. Wave and particle properties of quanta, on the one hand, are incompatible for (1) manifesting *behavioural patterns* not reducible to each other (neither do particle-like properties follow logically from wave-like properties nor vice versa), which (2) can be *observed only separately from each other* (due to uncertainty relation), and which (3) are *inevitably affected* by any observation, thus, altering any subsequent observation (due to non-commuting observables).[47] Phenomenal properties of consciousness and their physical correlates, on the other hand, may (1) manifest *two fundamentally different phenomena* not reducible to each other, while (2) being co-present (apart from unconscious states) and *simultaneously observable*, and (3) *not necessarily* being affected by observation (at least as long as the observed subject does not take notice of the observer).[48] So, looking at the details, considerable disanalogies become apparent. Hence, the *incompatible* aspects of quantum behaviour cannot simply be applied to mind-body dualism. Another disanalogy lies in the fact that wave-properties of quanta can be inferred from the particle properties, and they must be

[44] There have been important contributions from MacKay (1957); Bedau and Oppenheim (1961); Hoche (1990); Velmans (1991, 1993); Atmanspacher and Primas (2006); Von Stillfried (2010); Walach and Römer (2011); Walach (2014a, b) and others. For in depth analysis of different complementarity interpretations see Fahrenberg (2013) and von Stillfried (2018).

[45] Alexander (1956).

[46] MacKay (1957); Bedau and Oppenheim (1961); Brody and Oppenheim (1969); Velmans (1991); von Stillfried (2010); et al.

[47] Of course, it is possible to further differentiate these incompatible aspects of the wave-particle dualism into more than three points (von Stillfried 2010, for example, lists six different incompatibility aspects). However, summing up Fahrenberg's (2013) and von Stillfried's (2018) analysis, these three may join the central points of the issue.

[48] Of course, two subsequent measurements of both physical *and* phenomenal states will have non-commutative results, since any "measurement" of *subjective* experience equals an *intervention,* just like measurements of quantum systems. This obvious analogy has generally been interpreted in support of comparability interpretations of mind-body dualism. However, the non-commutativity of measurement of quantum systems is a result of an irreversible "loss" of wave-like properties, maybe even its collapse into particles, and thus, the elimination of the wave function. "Measurement" of conscious states, in contrast, only results in different conscious states, but by no means in any "loss" or "collapse" of phenomenal into physical states or anything similar.

inferred in this way because only quantum-particles are empirically observable, while quantum-waves are not. In contrast, consciousness is irreducible to its physical correlates due to its intrinsic phenomenal quality, which cannot be deduced from descriptions of physical events.

Given these disanalogies, some authors[49] have taken recourse to the first-/third-person view distinction, arguing that these two "points of views" are complementary in an analogous sense as wave-/particle-like quantum behaviour. However, this is misleading in at least two important aspects: first, as mentioned earlier,[50] a third-person view is, in the last consequence, always also a first-person view, and thus, equally based on a subject's perception of qualia[51]; second, both wave- and particle-like behaviour are observable *only* from a third-person view, since there is no wave or particle that could report their experience of what it is like to be a wave or particle.[52] In other words, first- and third-person perspectives refer to an *epistemic* difference, while mind and matter represent distinct *ontic* categories.

As von Stillfried (2018) observes, these disanalogies are, at least in part, owing to the fact that (1.) complementarity is generally defined epistemologically in terms of incompatible *descriptions*, and (2.) because most authors act on the implicit or explicit assumption of a collapse of the wave function. An epistemological definition (1) of complementarity refers to "waves" and "particles" in terms of mutually exclusive *descriptions* of one single, yet inscrutable, ontic referent (a quantum). Collapse interpretations (2), however, imply an irreversible transition from one ontic state (wave) to another (particle). While (1) seems to support a comparison

---

[49] E.g. Velmans (1991); Atmanspacher and Primas (2006).

[50] Compare previous chapter: "[First-/third-person] distinction amounts simply to the subject-object dichotomy, which certainly continues to have an important heuristic value; but since it does not provide any analytical distinction between phenomenal and physical objects, it rather leads back to the problem of solipsism than to a solid definition of the physical. So, while first-person perspective equals to the only direct experience we have, and thus, holds as a strong argument for the existence of consciousness, third-person perspectives equal to first-person perspectives of others concerning a material world of which nobody has direct experience. Due to this circularity, third-person perspectives do not prove anything about the physical world, not even about its existence (at least as long as one holds to representational epistemology)."

[51] Likewise, von Stillfried (2018) observes: "Einen solchen Ansatz scheint Chalmers zu implizieren, wenn er gelegentlich eine weitere Charakterisierung des Physikalischen verwendet, die auf dieser Unterscheidung aufbaut, z. B. in Formulierungen wie "if we set consciousness aside and take a third-person view of the world" (Chalmers 1997, o. S.). Dabei wird demnach alles als physikalisch bezeichnet, was durch eine "Dritte-Person-Perspektive" vollständig beschrieben werden kann. Allerdings setzt diese Unterscheidung bereits voraus, dass andere Beobachtende und deren Aussagen über ihre Wahrnehmungen unabhängig von meinem Bewusstsein existieren. Es liegt also ein Zirkelschluss vor. Um von intersubjektiver Übereinstimmung und Dritte- Person-Perspektive sprechen zu können, muss ich bereits annehmen, dass die anderen Menschen "da draußen" existieren und nicht nur Strukturen in meinem Bewusstsein sind. Damit setze ich die Existenz einer externen physikalischen Realität voraus, um sie zu belegen" (idem 2018:36).

[52] "It should be stressed that psychological complementarity of (first- and third-person perspective observations) is not the wave-particle complementarity of quantum mechanics [...]; in electrons, wave and particle-like behaviour are both observable from a third-person perspective" (Velmans 1993: 540).

with first-/third-person perspectives, (2) suggests a mutually exclusive presence of either wave- or particle-like properties. The difference between mind and body, in contrast, is not only an epistemological, but an ontological one. Unlike wave-like properties of a superposed quantum system, consciousness does not diminish or disappear upon "measurement".

After all, and notwithstanding the enthusiastic contributions by Bohr and his numerous followers, complementarity does not seem to be a concept strong enough to lay the cornerstone of a unified theory of mind and matter. However, since its main shortcomings are related to epistemological and collapse interpretations, it might attain some importance if applied together with ontological non-collapse interpretations (I will come back to this point in a moment).

12.1.2 Mind-Induced Collapse

Several interpretations of quantum theory suggest that the collapse of the wave function is induced by a "measurement", while "measurement" may be (implicitly or explicitly) identified with conscious observation, thus attributing a causal role to consciousness. This general possibility of a causal nexus between mind and matter at the most fundamental level motivated some authors to speculate about quantum processes that might be responsible for the correlation between consciousness and its physical correlates in the nervous system. It has been suggested, for example, that "mind-fields" might somehow act on certain quantum events in synaptic signal transition, eventually resulting in significant influence on overall brain activity.[53] Like other interactionist theories of mind, however, nothing explains where consciousness comes from, what it actually is, and why it should have a causal role at all. Alternatively, it has been suggested that *all* collapse events are, and have always been, induced by consciousness or measurement-like events.[54] Consciousness may, according to some proposals,[55] "choose" to induce quantum-zeno-effect-like[56]

[53] Eccles (1986).

[54] The reason for such an apparently odd assumption is grounded in a lacuna of existing quantum formalisms which cannot predict the precise moment of collapse. In fact, the mathematical models would rather suggest that interaction of a wave function with a measurement apparatus would induce a state of superposition of the whole apparatus, instead of the observed collapse of the wave function. Hence the conclusion, that consciousness might be responsible for the instantiation of just one of several probable events (von Neumann 1996).

[55] Stapp (2001).

[56] The Quantum Zeno Effect refers to an apparently paradoxical phenomenon predicted by quantum mechanics: If a quantum system is submitted to continuous (=sufficiently frequent) measurement (=interaction with a macroscopic system), its evolution (e.g. decay of an unstable system) may be "frozen" (Sudarshan and Misra 1977). The Quantum Zeno Effect was later experimentally confirmed (Itano et al. 1990). However, Chalmers and McQueen (2020: 19) argue, that "the Zeno problem is a serious problem for almost any measurement-collapse interpretation of quantum mechanics. Any such interpretation faces the question of whether measurement itself can enter

stabilisation of certain brain states, thereby influencing neuronal processes together with correlated cognitive states. Other authors[57] conjecture that certain, particularly complex, systems may acquire superposition-resistant measurement properties capable of inducing collapse, and that these measurement properties might be equivalent to protophenomenal properties.

Of course, such speculations raise a lot of recalcitrant questions, particularly: Why and how should consciousness be the cause of collapse and not some (still unknown) physical property? How could the whole universe possibly have emerged from collapse induced by consciousness-like properties? Where did consciousness emerge from, if it was prior to anything else? Why does an omnipresent consciousness not result in immediate collapse of all wave functions? And: Why should the universe contain consciousness at all?

Although, at bottom, the idea of consciousness-induced collapse is based on postulating a causal role of consciousness, it is difficult to see why and how collapse should be induced by consciousness, and if so, how such a theory should contribute to a solution of the hard problem of consciousness.

12.1.3 Many Minds Instead of Many Worlds?

In order to bypass the measurement problem resulting from collapse interpretations, Hugh Everett[58] had famously suggested his relative state formulation, holding that unitary quantum mechanics might provide a complete description of the world. Everett's approach basically suggested that instead of collapsing the wave function and thereby instantiating only one of several probable states entailed in a quantum superposition, measurement events might instantiate all superposed states at once, however, in different "branches" or "worlds". Accordingly, the material world is not the result of individual wave functions collapsing into particle-like states, but rather one universal wave function (the composite constellation of all individual wave functions and all their superpositions) in a permanent state of superposition instantiating an infinite number of parallel "worlds" (one for each branch of superposed quantum events)—which is why this view became known as "many-worlds interpretation". Of course, in these strictly deterministic multiverses, there is no space for any explanatorily relevant concept of consciousness.

However, there is also an alternative interpretation of Everett's idea. Instead of instantiating an infinite number of "worlds", the universal wave function might instantiate just one "world", but many observers, each perceiving one branch of an

quantum superpositions. If measurement can enter superpositions, the standard dynamics of collapse upon measurement is ill-defined, and new dynamics is required. If measurement cannot enter superpositions, the quantum Zeno effect suggests that measurements can never start or finish, at least if measurement is an observable."

[57] Chalmers and McQueen (2020).

[58] Everett (1957).

infinite number of states in superposition. This ideas seems to be foreshadowed in Everett's own words:

> [...] after the interaction has taken place there will not, generally, exist a single observer state. There will, however, be a superposition of the composite system states, each element of which contains a definite observer state and a definite relative object-system state [...] Thus, each element of the resulting superposition describes an observer who perceived a definite and generally different result, and to whom it appears that the object-system state has been transformed into the corresponding eigenstate (Everett 1973: 10).

In other words, "the world" is identified with the wave function of the universe in all its superpositions, while "our worlds" correspond to instantiations of single branches, each perceived by an observer. Here, "instantiation" can be understood either in terms of actuality (I just happen to perceive *this* branch) or actualisation (my mind chooses to actualise *this* branch and not another). Von Stillfried (2018) calls attention to the undefined ontic status of fundamental categories like "world", "wave function", "particle", and "observer". At first glance, they all seem to belong to the same ontic category, since there are no isolated "waves" collapsing into "particles", but rather only one wave function instantiating through different minds. Of course, this poses the question whether "the world" should be regarded as a physical reality or rather a phenomenal one, and thus, whether wave and mind should be regarded as ontologically different or not. Lockwood,[59] for example, proposes a Russellian interpretation of the many-minds view, suggesting that phenomenal properties are ontologically identical with their physical correlates. Lockwood interprets Everett's relative states in terms of perspectives being selected by points of view, thus leading to a conception of world as a sum of different perspectives. By selecting between an infinity of superposed brain states, consciousness actualises particular perspectives or branches of superposed states of the universe.

Both Chalmers (1995) and von Stillfried (2018) consider many-minds interpretations as potentially promising approaches to the hard problem of consciousness, however, without further developing the idea. As with the collapse interpretations mentioned just before, there are a lot of unsolved important questions, particularly concerning the ontological status of "waves", "minds", and "matter". Should "minds" be considered as an ontic category of their own, or are they rather expressions of a unitary universal "wave"? And if the world only exists in the form of perspectives being actualised by our minds, does this mean that it only exists within our minds, or does it somehow "materialise" due to our perception? What happens with the world when we are asleep? What is the precise relationship between the universal wave and the many minds? How and why do our minds "select" between those infinite superposed states? And so forth…

It may be true that further advancements of a many-minds interpretation might bring some palpable results, however, in its present state it does not seem to be of much help for solving the hard problem of consciousness. Despite its shortcomings and its outrageous weirdness, Lockwood's perspectival interpretation might

---

[59] Lockwood (1991).

comprise a potential nexus to perspectivist interpretations of Indigenous cosmopractices.

12.1.4 Mind and Matter as Unfoldings of a Multi-Dimensional Wave Function?

The approaches discussed so far are (implicitly or explicitly) based on the assumption that a quantum will display *either* wave-like *or* particle-like properties or something in-between, but never both properties at the same time and with full expressivity. The interaction with a macroscopic measurement device will always result in complete loss of the wave-like properties and full actualisation of the particle-like properties. This mysterious transformation from one ontic state into another was explained in terms of a collapse of the wave function into a particle-like state. Besides monistic interpretations that explain the whole universe as an expression of *either* particles *or* waves, there seems to be just one interpretation proposing a simultaneous co-existence of both wave- and particle-like properties of quanta, without ever collapsing or transforming from one into another ontic state.

According to David Bohm,[60] quanta consist of two inseparable but ontologically different aspects: waves and particles. In this model, the wave function "guides" the particle, that is, it describes the particle's trajectory determined by the quantum potential. In a double-slit experiment, for example, the wave aspect of a quantum will pass both slits and then interfere with itself, resembling the typical interference patterns; the quantum's particle aspect, however, will follow a predetermined trajectory along the interference patterns determined by the wave function. Bohm's interpretation, therefore, predicts a deterministic particle trajectories, since both wave evolution and particle trajectory are determined at the onset and not by measurement.[61] However, it also predicts non-local behaviour of quanta, since interfering waves evolve expanding in space-time,[62] while being non-locally effective throughout their entire configuration space, thus solving the EPR paradox. In other words, an interaction with the wave function of a quantum system at any point of its evolution will result in an instantaneous change of its potential behaviour at any other (however distant) point within its extension. This explains why entangled quanta behave in a correlated manner (without assuming any "spooky action at a

[60] Bohm (1952).

[61] However, the wave does not determine particle behaviour entirely, since the "choice" of its actual trajectory among many different possible alternatives entailed in the form of the wave function ultimately depends on its random initial position. "The notion of 'determinism' in Bohm's interpretation, then, is different from the Copenhagen interpretation which tacitly identifies determinism with exact predictability and controllability" (Maleeh 2015: 319).

[62] Actually, wave systems evolve within a $3N$-dimensional configuration space, with N being the sum of all interacting quanta in a system.

distance"[63]); but it also explains why measurement (=interaction with larger systems) apparently results in a loss of wave-like properties: for if an isolated quantum system interferes with a larger compound system, its wave function does not collapse, but gets entangled with all constituent wave functions of the compound system, thus melting into a higher-dimensional wave function. Since all entangled quanta of a compound system are constrained by the overall wave function of the system, their interconnectedness results in quasi-deterministic overall system behaviour. In other words, the former isolated system loses its independence (wave-like properties), now being orchestrated by the operational mode (quasi-deterministic behaviour) of the compound system (measurement apparatus/observer/environment) it got entangled with. Moreover, since quantum waves evolve in $3N$-dimensional configuration space, eventually interfering with external systems and thereby forming higher-dimensional wave functions, it can be assumed that in the course of their evolution all existing wave functions will finally interact, adding up to an infinitely higher dimensional wave function of the entire universe. Hence, from a top-down point of view, so to say, all lower dimensional wave functions appear to be subsystems of the unitary wave function of the entire universe.

All of this leads to the same empirically testable predictions as those resulting from collapse interpretations, however, with considerably different theoretical, and in particular, ontological implications. While most of the problems collapse interpretations are faced with do not even appear in a Bohmian universe, Bohmian quantum physics are confronted with its own strange implications. For example, since all particle trajectories are at any moment completely determined by the wave functions, a quantum in superposition will contain just one "active" wave branch guiding an actual particle, but many "empty" waves-branches, so to say, with no particle associated with them. Hence, such empty waves represent all the potential events of a probability space which will never instantiate in the material world, but only exist as a kind of vestige of lost opportunity. It appears, however, that such empty waves remain coherent with active branches as long as no interaction with an external system occurs; once such an interaction happens, environmental entanglement induces decoherence, so the empty branches cease to have any observable effect on the active branch—and thus on particle behaviour—i.e., the state behaves as if a collapse had occurred, even though no physical collapse is assumed.[64]

---

[63] Einstein and Born (2005).

[64] Nevertheless, in principle it would still be possible for an empty wave to become effective again, although the probability of such an event is so remote, that it is generally not taken into account. "Our argument is that if the particle interacted with the environment, it would produce further separated wave-packets in which only one would be occupied. This scattered particle would then collide with another particle which would be scattered, occupying yet another separating wave packet and so on. Interference would only return if at least one each of the empty scattered wave packets could be returned to overlap. Since the scattering of the environmental particles was random, the chances of this happening would be remote. Thus the QP would never return spontaneously to its original form and interference would not reappear. Of course it may be possible, in principle, to exactly reverse everything but such a possibility is very hard to achieve so the system will behave as if the wave packet has collapsed, but no collapse has actually taken place" (Hiley 2010: 8).

In later publications, Bohm extended his theory introducing the additional concepts of *holomovement, implicate* and *explicate order*,[65] *active information*,[66] and *layers of reality*,[67] which he thought particularly useful for exploring the potential applicability of his quantum theoretical approach to the mind-body problem.

The concept of *implicate order* was originally developed with the aim of overcoming contradictions between relativity and quantum theory. It states that both the causal/local principles of relativity and the non-local/non-causal principles of quantum theory describe different existing *explicate orders*, both of which are, however, aspects (or "unfoldings") of a unitary *implicate order*. This *implicate order* is the expression of the "undivided wholeness" of the universe, which is evolving as a *holomovement* of a multi-dimensional reality, and which can be mathematically represented in terms of a 3N-dimensional wave function. One can also say, that the *implicate order* entails the "enfolded" potential of all possible "unfoldings" in the *explicate order* described by classical physics.

Bohm claimed that his concept of implicate order could equally be applied to both mind and matter, representing two aspects of the same underlying undivided wholeness or holomovement described by the universal wave function. Thus, mind and matter are conceived as "projections" of the universal implicate order into the (ontologically different) explicate orders presented by physical and mental (=phenomenal)[68] properties. Of course, in these terms, Bohm's proposal would amount to an aspect-dualist theory of mind and matter.[69] However, the common origin of both mind and matter in an underlying implicate order does not explain anything about the nature of phenomenal and physical properties, nor how the two ontic categories are related to each other.

In order to explain how mind and matter actually relate to each other, Bohm[70] later introduced his concept of *active information*. In his earlier proposals, Bohm interpreted the wave function in terms of a *quantum potential* that guides the particle along its trajectory, however, without energy exchange.[71] Hence, quantum

---

[65] Bohm (1980).

[66] Idem 1990.

[67] Idem.

[68] Bohm actually refers to "mental" rather than "phenomenal" properties. But for our purpose, the meaning of both terms can be considered synonymous here.

[69] Von Stillfried (2018) observes that, according to Bohm's (1980) conception, mind and matter are not two different substances mutually influencing each other (as suggested by interactionism), but rather projections of a common higher dimensional reality behaving in a strictly correlated way due to their common origin (as suggested by occasionalist or parallelist neutral monism).

[70] Bohm (1990).

[71] If the quantum potential was a classical force acting on the particle, the resulting energy exchange between the wave's quantum potential and the particle would result in violating conservation of energy. In order to avoid this problem, Bohm (1952) suggested that the quantum potential is derived from the wave's form, not its frequency. The overall effectiveness of a quantum potential is, therefore, not depending on its energy but merely deriving from its informational structure. However, it is not clear whether the quantum potential should be understood as a special kind of physical force with at least some very little energy, or as pure form of the wave with no energy at

potential is not a classical physical force, but rather a kind of pure information "acting to put form" into the particle's motion. Since the wave functions of related particles interact, forming higher dimensional wave functions, and thereby resulting in instantaneous changes of their entire configuration space (=3*N*-dimensional space, including its projections into three-dimensional space), they act as a kind of active information orchestrating all associated (*N*) particles to perform in a strictly correlated, non-local way. In sum, active information seems to display properties that are rather contrary to those generally associated with matter: it has no mass nor energy, it does not even seem to qualify as a "substance", it is pure information, and it "decides" about the behaviour of will-less particles. As Bohm noted, these are properties rather associated with consciousness. Accordingly, his concept of active information suggests a mind-like quality of waves, and thus, of matter.[72] In other words, at the fundamental level of quantum physics, everything has a mind-like and a matter-like pole. Hence, there can be no physical object without any mind-like property, which would perfectly explain why something like phenomenal consciousness might emerge together with a complex material organism. Moreover, active information is defined precisely by having an important causal role in the behaviour of particles, and thus, must exercise at least some influence on the material world including, but not limited to brain activity.

> It seems clear from all this that at least in the context of the processes of thought, there is a kind of active information that is simultaneously physical and mental in nature. Active information can thus serve as a kind of link or 'bridge' between these two sides of reality as a whole. These two sides are inseparable, in the sense that information contained in thought, which we feel to be on the 'mental' side, is at the same time a related neurophysiological, chemical, and physical activity [...] (Bohm 1990: 282).

It follows, that the mental poles of quanta on the fundamental level must somehow add up to more subtle levels of mind-like (phenomenal) properties, until they finally constitute what we know as conscious experience. Bohm argued that this would naturally result from the gradual increase of complexity of compound systems—like quanta forming atoms, forming molecules, cells, organs, and living organisms—representing *layers* of increasing *subtleness* of the underlying active information. Hence, phenomenal properties will evolve together with their physical correlates, with active information mediating between the two poles. Accordingly, the formation of complex physical systems should be expected to be concomitant with the emergence of increasingly subtle phenomenal properties, since both can be understood as "projections" out of the same underlying information structure (=compound 3N-dimensional wave function) into our three-dimensional realm. In other words, Bohm's model suggests that protophenomenal properties *naturally* add

---

all. As von Stillfried (2018) observes, some of Bohm's writing seem to suggest the first option, while later interpretations by Bohm's collaborators, Hiley and Pylkkänen, rather defended the second option.

[72] "[..] the whole notion of active information suggests a rudimentary mind-like behaviour of matter" (Bohm 1990: 281).

up to higher layers of subtleness just as physical entities like quanta and atoms add up to ever more subtle compound systems.[73]

The relevance of Bohm's approach to the hard problem of consciousness has been further explored by his former collaborators, Basil Hiley and Paavo Pylkkänen,[74] who explicitly refer to Chalmers and his formulation of related problems. Particularly, Pylkkänen[75] tried to provide a coherent model of (1) the mechanisms responsible for the causal role of consciousness and (2) the way in which consciousness might be affected by physical events. In fact, Bohm's writings are inconclusive regarding the exact relation between the wave function, quantum potential, active information, and consciousness. At times, it seems the terms refer to different referents, with one somehow emerging from the other, while other statements of Bohm's seem to use them as synonyms referring to one and the same referent. For example, he seems to suggest that active information unfolds as both mind and matter rather than representing only the mind-like pole of matter. This raises the question how exactly the resulting three ontic categories might act on each other. Pylkkänen attempts to tackle the problem by suggesting an indirect causation taking the loop-way through neuronal processes being influenced by quantum potential, which in turn might be orchestrated via active information, which again has been influenced by consciousness. It flies in the face that these speculations (much like those proposed by Eccles mentioned above) about quantum effects on neuronal processes only shift the attention from the hard problem about a possible causal role of phenomenal processes as such to the easy problems of physical (quantum) processes acting on (classical) physical processes. However, the question concerning the (causal?) relation between phenomenal (consciousness) and physical (active information/quantum potential/wave function) properties remains mysterious.

On the whole, Bohm's pilot-wave interpretation allows for interesting comparisons between wave-particle and mind-body dualities, particularly because it avoids most of the troubling problems related to collapse interpretations of quantum theory. At first sight, the suggested co-presence of both wave- and particle properties and their identification with mental and physical poles of matter seems to point to

---

[73] "One may then ask what is the relationship of these 2 processes? The answer that I want to propose here is that there are not 2 processes. Rather, I would suggest that both are essentially the same. This means that that which we experience as mind in its movement through various levels of subtlety will—in a natural way—ultimately move the body by reaching the level of the quantum potential and of the 'dance' of the particles. There is no unbridgeable gap or barrier between any of these levels. Rather, at each stage some kind of information is the bridge. This implies that the quantum potential acting on atomic particles, for example, represents only one stage in the process. The content of our own consciousness is then some part of this overall process. It is thus implied that in some sense a rudimentary mind-like quality is present even at the level of particle physics. And that as we go to subtler levels, this mind-like quality becomes stronger and more developed. Each kind and level of mind may have a relative autonomy and stability. One may then describe the essential mode of relationship of all these as participation, recalling that this word has 2 basic meanings—to partake of and to take part in" (Bohm 1990: 283).

[74] Hiley and Pylkkänen (2005).

[75] Pylkkänen (2007).

an interactionist model of mind and matter as two different substances. On the other hand, the assumption of an underlying higher-dimensional reality (implicate order/holomovement/3*N*-dimensional wave function/active information/quantum potential[76]) out of which both mind and matter unfold would rather suggest some kind of aspect-dualism or neutral monism, thereby explaining the correlation between mind and matter, but only in terms of a parallelism with no direct causal role to each other. This problem might be mitigated, however, if active information was identified with phenomenal properties, since this would establish a direct causal role of consciousness. Unfortunately, most proponents of the Bohmian approach to mind and matter seem to waver on this issue.[77]

12.1.5 The Wave Function as the Intrinsic Mind-Side of Matter?

In view of its promising prospects for the development of a unified theory of mind and matter, Nikolaus von Stillfried[78] endeavours to further consolidate the Bohmian approach with the requirements resulting from the hard problem of consciousness as defined by David Chalmers. According to von Stillfried's appraisal, Bohm's proposals are limited by a number of shortcomings that should be addressed to make them fit for responding to the theoretical challenges posed by the hard problem of consciousness: First of all, Bohm (as well as other proponents of a Bohmian theory of mind and matter, like Pylkkänen and Hiley) proposed a number of rather fuzzy and potentially redundant concepts, like "holomovement", "implicate order", "quantum potential", "active information", and "layers of reality", demanding a more coherent and, if possible, a more comprehensive definition. Moreover, there

[76] The terms are often used in a more or less synonymous way, making it difficult to understand precisely how they may relate to each other (von Stillfried 2018).

[77] In fact, there are some statements of Bohm's (1990) and Hiley's (1993) and Pylkkänen's (2005, 2007) equalling mental properties with the wave function and active information. However, in other places, they hold that consciousness might emerge from or contain active information on, or act via active information on waves and/or on particles, thus coming to no clear definition of the ontic status of these categories, nor how they actually relate to each other. Von Stillfried (2018) observes that even if such an identity hypothesis was assumed, Bohm's theory would rather parallel Chalmers's panprotopsychism, together with its (unsolved) combination problem. While von Stillfried (2018) is quite pessimistic on this issue, my own feeling is that Bohm's approach might contain some promising elements for a solution to the combination problem. Bohm actually addressed the problem, albeit not calling it the "combination problem", when he suggested that the experience resembles the multi-dimensional complexity of the underlying implicate order, thus transcending the limited qualities entailed in its physical unfoldings (and thus proposing a solution to Chalmers's quality combination problem). Moreover, I cannot see how Bohm's model could lead to a structural mismatch between macro-phenomenal and macro-physical structures, since both are unfoldings of the same underlying implicate order. But of course, these issues would have to be addressed in a more straightforward way to come to any definitive conclusion.

[78] von Stillfried (2018).

are contradictory statements about the exact relation between these concepts, the wave function, and phenomenal properties. And finally, the assumption of "empty" waves leads to problematic questions concerning their role in relation to phenomenal properties.

Following this analysis, von Stillfried proposes to further exploit a minimalist version of Bohm's approach based on an identity hypothesis equating active[79] wave branches to protophenomenal properties[80] out of which phenomenal properties can emerge. The physical world would, in contrast, be identified with the particles being guided by these protophenomenal waves. Since Bohm provides only weak arguments for why quantum waves and protophenomenal properties should be seen as identical, von Stillfried explores the possibility of grounding Bohm's identity theory in Chalmers's version of a Russellian panprotopsychism. Accordingly, von Stillfried baptises this new approach "RBI-thesis" (Russell-Bohm-Identity-Thesis), a Russellian adaptation of a wave-consciousness identity theory against the backdrop of the ontology of a Bohmian interpretation of quantum theory.

The resulting ontological view pictures a universe constituted by a Russellian type inscrutable intrinsic essence, now represented by protophenomenal (3*N*-dimensional) pilot waves (as kind of a collapsed equivalent to different, but closely related Bohmian concepts of implicate order, active information, quantum potential, and mental pole), manifesting in the three-dimensional reality of observable physical properties, represented by particles being "guided" by those pilot-waves/proto-phenomenal properties. The coexistence of and interaction between pilot waves and particles would thus explain both the wave-like and particle-like properties of quanta as well as the correlation between consciousness (consisting of waves) and the body (consisting of particles). In other words, the physical world would refer to relationally describable particles that are guided by the quantum potentials of ultimately inscrutable (since not directly observable) pilot waves, while the waves themselves rather present intrinsic (proto-)phenomenal properties. Due to their non-local character, individual waves interfere and thereby merge with other waves into higher dimensional waves, being paralleled by the emergence of correlated physical systems made up by particles associated with the active branches of the total wave. One can now imagine, that increasing dimensions of those interfering waves will correspond to increasingly complex, integrated, and potentially also self-referential phenomenal states (e.g. human consciousness) that are intrinsically correlated to equally complex, integrated, and potentially self-referential physical systems (e.g. human brains). Such levels of operational closure or

[79] Von Stillfried introduces the additional (preliminary) convention, that only actually effective ("active") waves are related to (proto-)phenomenal properties, while "dead" or "empty" branches of mere potentialities are not associated with phenomenal properties. The reason is, that we perceive only one, localised reality (the one actually being manifested by active waves and associated particles), while empty wave branches suggest the existence of parallel "worlds" within the universal 3*N*-dimensional wave function.

[80] According to von Stillfried (2018), Bohm and Pylkkänen have been the only ones to suggest a similar identity hypothesis, albeit not as straight forward; hence the novelty of his approach.

integrated information have already been discussed by other authors.[81] Von Stillfried argues, however, that, albeit yielding interesting models for a possible principle of weak emergence, there is still no sufficient evidence to sustain any concrete definition of such a principle. He therefore coins the fantasy term "selfcomplexigratedness" (*Selbstkomplexigriertheit*) instead, as a provisional place holder for such a principle of weak emergence yet to be defined. Hence, the more complex a quantum system gets, the more waves get entangled, the higher dimensional the resulting compound wave, and the more *selfcomplexigrated* will be both the resulting phenomenal states and the correlated physical processes.

From this vantage point, the wave function fills the two-fold gap left by the logical necessity of an intrinsic essence, on the one hand, and the missing natural principle of consciousness, on the other.[82] The RBI-thesis, therefore, comes with prospects of a framework for a unified naturalist theory of mind and matter.

Compared to other proposals discussed above, the RBI-thesis might solve (or avoid) some of their most critical issues. For example, approaches based on collapse interpretations of quantum theory will generally have great difficulties in drawing a coherent analogy between wave-particle and mind-body dualities, since the first rather refers to switching ontic states, while the latter describes two concomitant ontic properties. The RBI-thesis, in contrast, suggest a continuous co-existence of wave-/mind-like and particle-/matter-like properties. And while mind-induced collapse theories ascribe a causal role to consciousness, they do not explain what (proto)consciousness is, why it exists, and where it comes from. The RBI-thesis, however, uses the Russelian monist argument that the existence of protophenomenal intrinsic essence is a logically necessary corollary of the existence of purely

[81] E.g. Chalmers and McQueen (2020).

[82] Of course, one might question this identification of waves with protophenomenal properties, on the one hand, and the intrinsic essence, on the other. While there is an extensive discussion of Russellian panprotopsychism and the reasons for and against an identification of Russell's intrinsic essence with protophenomenal properties, its identification with quantum-waves is an almost entirely new proposal. On the face of it, quantum waves are physical properties, and thus, cannot be (proto-)phenomenal. Von Stillfried explicitly refers to this issue, pointing to the difficulty other authors demonstrated in defining the wave-like aspects of quanta as either physical or not. On the one hand, "waves" refer to particular aspects of quanta, which are obviously physical entities. On the other hand, these wave-like properties are completely different if compared to any other physical property. For example, there is no direct causal interaction between other physical entities and waves (but just between the particles associate to waves and other entities), which has led to the assumption "waves" might represent rather a natural order or laws, than an entity or substance. Also, Bohmian wave functions expand in a $3N$-dimensional space, not being describable in terms of conventional spacetime. And although waves influence particle behaviour, they do not carry a classical physical force (there is no measurable energy exchange between waves and particles). Consequently, some authors have come to the conclusion, that quantum waves might not pertain to the physical realm, but rather represent a non-physical ontic category of their own. The question is complicated by the fact that there is neither a consensus on the definition of physical nor of phenomenal properties. Finally, von Stillfried comes to the conclusion that there seem to be good reasons for assigning quantum waves to an ontic category of their own, while there are at least no obvious reasons against an identification with phenomenal properties and/or an intrinsic essence. However, the whole issue deserves more attention.

relational physical properties and subsequently explains consciousness as a natural result of fundamental natural principles (wave-like/protophenomenal properties + selfcomplexigratedness = phenomenal properties) via weak emergence. Additionally, the RBI-thesis not only ascribes a fundamental causal role to consciousness, it also predicts an interactionist relation between particle/matter-like and wave/mind-like aspects of quanta and quantum-systems,[83] thereby providing the necessary causal mechanisms to explain, at least in principle, direct phenomenal judgments.[84]

So far, it would seem that von Stillfried's approach elicits the advantages of Bohm's approach over other quantum-theoretical models of consciousness, and the advantages of a Russellian panprotopsychism over alternative solutions to the hard problem of consciousness, and joins them together. But what about the specific problems arising from panprotopsychism? Particularly, can the RBI-thesis solve the combination problem? Von Stillfried himself emphasises the tentative character of his RBI-thesis and submits it to a thorough examination, spending particular effort in analysing its implications for each of the different sub-problems associated to the combination problem.[85] It appears that the RBI-thesis should at least relativise the combination problem. Bohmian quantum physics predicts that, in contrast to particles, interacting waves merge into new holistic composite systems whose properties cannot be entirely derived from their constituents, and particularly so, if they form operationally closed systems (like organisms). In other words, the RBI-thesis predicts the emergence of holistic phenomenal properties in direct correlation with non-holistic, albeit structurally analogous, physical properties.[86] So, on the whole,

---

[83] According to Bohmian quantum mechanics, the wave function and the position of the particle on the wave together determine particle behaviour. Although, the particle position does not directly impinge on the wave form, it influences the activation of future (still inactive) wave branches, thus determining potential future unfoldings (Bohm 1980; Szczeciniarz & Kounheiher 2022; von Stillfried 2018).

[84] More precisely, von Stillfried argues that, according to his new approach, there is no special status for direct phenomenal judgments (DPJs), since all interacting quantum processes are always mutually effective. DPJs are not necessarily produced by phenomenal properties, but can be the result of particularly selfcomplexigrated physical systems. Hence, DPJs can be interpreted in terms of judgments of a system concerning its level of selfcomplexigratedness. However, this definition would also have to explain why such a judgement is necessarily related to the presence of consciousness, which is still an open question (ibidem).

[85] As discussed by Chalmers (2016b).

[86] Other authors (e.g. Chalmers 1995, 2016a, b; Kaufman 2014; Seager 2016) have pointed to quantum entanglement as possible solution to the combination problem. But they act on the assumption of quantum collapse, and therefore, have not been able to build on an identity-thesis between wave and protophenomenal. Chalmers (2016b) points to rapid decoherence and resulting loss of entangled states. However, decoherence does not necessarily imply disentanglement. On the contrary, decoherence of a system can be interpreted as a result of increasing entanglement with external quanta/systems, ultimately interrupting internal closure and integrity of the system. Moreover, Chalmers criticises that the universal wave function amounts to cosmophychism, however, this is not correct either, since the constituting individual conditional wave functions continue to exist even though being part of a holistic higher dimensional structure. And finally, von Stillfried (2018) argues, that no quantum system is completely closed or isolated, since all of them sum up to the wave of the universe.

the RBI-thesis seems to provide a comparably good basis for handling the combination problem, although a conclusive evaluation of this issue will certainly require further analysis.[87]

Of course, von Stillfried's RBI-thesis has not yet received much critical scrutiny (except for von Stillfried's own critical analysis), but I think it can already be said that it has the potential for providing a basis for a coherent naturalist and non-reductionist theory of mind and matter.

12.2 Generalised Quantum Theory

The theoretical approaches I have been discussing so far exclusively aim to solve the so-called mind-body problem in the light of quantum theory. Accordingly, these approaches aim to explain primarily the phenomenal properties associated with normal wakeful states of human consciousness which everybody is familiar with. These phenomenal states are strictly correlated to a living human body, and particularly, to its nervous system. Therefore, none of the theories discussed so far considers a causal role of consciousness beyond our neuronal processes and resulting bodily movements (like lifting an arm or uttering direct phenomenal judgements)—even though some of the proposals would in principle allow for consciousness to exist and be causally active even independently of a human body. It goes without saying that such a limited definition of phenomenal properties and their causal role imposes considerable restrictions on any attempt to draw a parallel to Other ontological models, such as those deriving from Potiguara cosmopractice, particularly when it comes to a causal role of phenomenal properties to external reality, let alone purely phenomenal (immaterial) "persons".

There is, however, yet another class of interpretations of quantum theory which has been suggested as a possible explanation for non-local macro-phenomena, and which has been discussed under the label *Generalised Quantum Theory* (GQT).[88]

[87] Von Stillfried himself comes to the conclusion, that his new approach might be able to solve some of its sub-problems, but not all of them. According to his in-depth analysis, the emergence of holistic quantum-systems predicted by the RBI-thesis should allow for providing quite convincing solutions to the subject summing problem and the unity problem, at least if we accept selfcomplexigratedness (whatever real system-theoretical principle this place holder may turn out to hold place for) as a sufficient explanation for weak emergence of phenomenal out of protophenomenal properties. Von Stillfried is also positive about solving the boundary problem and the awareness problem. Although for some problems, like the palette problem, structural mismatch problem, and particularly the grain problem, he has no fully elaborated solutions to offer, von Stillfried is still optimistic that RBI-thesis should provide the necessary basis for a sufficient solution to all relevant problems. Of course, according to Chalmers, only the solution of all of its sub-problems will solve the combination problem. Nevertheless, it can be stated that RBI-thesis might provide a more promising theoretical bases for solving the central aspects of the combination problem than any other comparable approach.

[88] Atmanspacher et al. (2002); Walach (2005); Filk and Römer (2010); Von Stillfried (2010); Walach and Stillfried (2011); Walach et al. (2014).

The intuition behind GQT is that since the macroscopic world of classical physics ultimately is made up of non-local, indeterministic quantum events, this may, in principle, entail a possible manifestation of quantum-like behaviour in macroscopic events—at least under certain circumstances.

However, most interpretations of quantum physics do not attribute properties such as indeterminate states or non-local entanglement to macroscopic objects, since they follow a *reductionist* explanation of classical physical events as a sum of innumerable quantum events. The apparent local-causal determinism of macroscopic objects is interpreted in terms of a "quasi-classical" behaviour resulting from decoherence processes on the quantum level. In fact, quantum behaviour can only be "observed" in carefully isolated systems, as they are typically prepared in laboratory experiments. As soon as the isolated quantum system interacts with an external system, such as a detector for example, it loses its internal coherence, and thereby, also its indeterministic and non-local behaviour. The reason for this decoherence is that the formerly isolated system and all its constituent quanta get entangled with all the quanta of the measurement apparatus, thus losing its former operational closure, resulting in classical behaviour. In contrast to isolated experimental setups, natural systems are normally in permanent contact with each other, and therefore, in a decohered state. As a consequence, no particular entangled correlation can be detected, since there are just too many of them. Moreover, interaction will occur almost immediately after every quantum event, so that an emergent superposition will immediately instantiate a definite eigenstate (often interpreted in terms of a collapse of the wave function). What remains, is the quasi-deterministic behaviour of a macroscopic object acting as a holistic system, although on its fundamental level, it represents the average result of countless probabilistic non-local quantum events orchestrated by a kind of generalised or ubiquitous entanglement among uncountable interacting quantum systems.[89] Furthermore, quantum behaviour is determined by measurement-like events, which ultimately amounts to an entanglement not only with the measurement apparatus, but also with the observing scientist who is conducting the measurement. In other words, upon measurement the observer becomes a part of the observed system.[90] Again, the effect of observation on classical objects is generally considered irrelevant, however, quantum physics suggest that there must be at least some howsoever tiny interdependence between observer and observed event.

In sum, a reductionist picture of nature in the light of quantum physics suggests that the objective, deterministic, causal description of classical objects is only a very good approximation, while in fact they are constituted by indeterministic, non-local, and observer-dependent quantum processes. Of course, there is a broad consensus about the fact that in most situations this approximation should provide sufficiently reliable results to predict and control macroscopic events with great precision. On the other hand, it has been suggested that quantum events at the microlevel might

[89] Von Stillfried (2010).

[90] E.g. Stapp (1979).

trigger measurable macroscopic events if these quantum events occur at decisive points in a sufficiently sensitive system. Actually, the experimental measurement of quantum behaviour is a perfect example of such a systemic amplification of a single quantum event. However, there might be similar processes in natural systems, too. For example, quantum events might influence synaptic activity, spurring cascades of neuronal processes, and finally resulting in changes in overall mental states.[91] Despite its apparent plausibility, it will be difficult to provide the necessary experimental evidence to prove such a claim, because the responsible quantum events cannot be isolated from the total system without changing its constitutional conditions. Anyhow, speculations like these may demonstrate why a unified theory of quantum and classical physics should be a desirable task, particularly concerning the place of "strange" quantum properties like indeterminism and entanglement in such a unified picture of nature.

Pauli and Jung were among the first to go about bridging the gap between classical and quantum physics. As a psychologist, Jung was frequently confronted with situations that were difficult to explain in terms of causal relations. He observed, for example, that the more he would get connected to a patient, meaningful intuitions would pop up in his mind,[92] or things would happen in an inexplicably meaningful way, coinciding with obviously correlated events despite having no traceable causal nexus. Jung speculated, therefore, that there must be some universal principle accountable for such non-causal correlations. As mentioned earlier, Jung, together with Pauli, developed the idea of a *unus mundus*, a kind of "invisible reality"[93] or implicate order, if you will, constituted by (Platonic idea-like) archetypes, which would instantiate both in mental and in physical reality as two complementary aspects of the one underlying archetypical reality. Accordingly, mind and matter should be expected to be synchronically correlated. Jung and Pauli reasoned that the same principle of *synchronicity* might be responsible for the non-causal correlations they observed at quantum level as well as in certain macroscopic events that might occur whenever two events were meaningfully connected by their common provenience from the same unitary archetypical reality.[94] Pauli was particularly interested

[91] E.g. Stapp (2001); Howard (2022).

[92] An effect known as "counter-transference" in psychology.

[93] "For the *invisible reality*, of which we have small pieces of evidence in both quantum physics and the psychology of the unconscious, a symbolic, psychophysical unitary language must *ultimately* be adequate, and this is the far goal which I actually aspire. I am quite confident that the final objective is the same, independent of whether one starts from the psyche (ideas) or from physis (matter). Therefore, I consider the old distinction between materialism and idealism as obsolete" (Letter by Pauli to Rosenfeld of April 1, 1952. Letter 1391 in von Meyenn 1996: 593. Translated and quoted by Atmanspacher and Primas 2006).

[94] "An unexpected content which unmediatedly or mediatedly relates to an objective outer event coincides with a common psychological state: this event I call synchronicity. I use the generic term synchronicity in the special sense of temporal coincidence of two or more events, which, however, are not causally related with each other and which have the same or similar content of meaning... Thus synchronicity in the first place refers to simultaneity of a certain psychological state with one or more outer events, which appear as meaningful parallels to the momentaneous subjective state

in a unified theory of nature, capable of integrating quantum and classical physics as well as mind and matter, which would also require a generic explanation of non-local correlations both at the micro- and the macroscopic level, preferably by a common underlying principle. However, Pauli and Jung never provided a detailed explanation for the analogy between *synchronicity* and non-causal quantum events, probably also because at that time there was still no substantiated proof of the ontological status of the observed indeterminism and non-local correlations of quantum events.

This situation would change with Bell's theorem and its empirical proof provided by Alain Aspect.[95] Bell's[96] findings and its experimental vindications suggest that, on its fundamental level, physical reality is not only constituted by indeterministic processes, but also by non-local correlations. Physicists like Henry Stapp[97] would soon note that this situation demands a revision of classical concepts of causality in the face of its non-local fundaments. In contrast to pragmatic, merely epistemic accounts of quantum physics, an ontological interpretation would have to provide a unified ontological model of nature based on the principles of quantum physics. However, according to Stapp, none of the existing proposals for an ontological interpretation of quantum physics would provide a coherent, unified picture of nature. He, therefore, proposed a new approach based on Whitehead's[98] process ontology and his theory of relativity. According to Whitehead, events are conceived as *prehensions* that actualise relationships from among a realm of possibilities, or *potentias*, resulting from previous events, so that ultimately the potentia of any event is conditioned by the past actualisations of the entire universe. Stapp reasoned that this view would also accord with Heisenberg's definition of quantum events as actualisations of the wave function as a probability space. Whitehead's events, however, have a physical and a mental pole, thus suggesting some mind-like character, although not being necessarily bound to consciousness of higher life-forms (in contrast, for example, to mind-induced collapse or many minds' interpretations). Hence, if all events have some primitive mental or (proto-)phenomenal property, the approach might provide a basis for a unified theory of nature.[99]

---

and vice versa" (Jung 1952: 31, 26—translated and quoted in Walach 2000). "Jung's notion of a synchronicity of pairwise arranged events in the mental and the material domains, correlated by a common meaning, is tightly related to the idea of a broken symmetry of the unus mundus. The synchronistic correlation between the events can be regarded as a retrospective indication, a remnant as it were, of the unity of the archetypal reality of the unus mundus from which they emerge" (Atmanspacher and Primas 2006).

[95] Aspect et al. (1982).

[96] Bell (1964).

[97] Stapp (1979).

[98] Whitehead (1978).

[99] There have been different approaches to a quantum physical interpretation of Whitehead's thinking. Michael Epperson (2004), for example, emphasises the potential of Whitehead's philosophy to "span the chasm separating classical and quantum mechanics". Atmanspacher and Primas (2006: 27), on the other hand, come to a rather pessimistic conclusion: "It turns out that the imple-

Of course, all this gives the impression of rather mysterious fundamental principles of nature, providing little or no explanation about how and when non-local macroscopic events might actually occur. What exactly are non-local macroscopic events and what are their necessary conditions? In fact, we still know too little about the ontology of quantum physics to give a complete account of the entire process-chain starting from countless entangled quantum events until finally adding up to macroscopic reality. And in view of the impossibility of observing all events in natural, complex multi-entangled quantum systems, this might turn out to be a permanent limitation.

There is, however, still another way to envisage quantum behaviour that might offer a bridge to the behaviour of macro-events, without necessarily constructing the latter as a result of the former, but rather conceptualising both as resulting from a common scale invariant principle. As mentioned before, quantum behaviour depends on *systemic* relations. A quantum behaves as part of a system, and quantum systems behave according to correlated probabilities entailed in their corresponding wave function and its entanglement with the wave functions of other systems, finally amounting to more and more complex systems of entangled subsystems. Walter von Lucadou and Klaus Kornwachs[100] describe non-locality as a general feature of nature related to meaningful relations between subsystems of a compound system. According to their Model of Pragmatic Information (MPI), the meaningfulness of information can be measured in terms of degrees of effectivity to its receiver. A subsystem will be increasingly meaningful to another subsystem if both are part of a highly integrated, self-referential, that is, an organisationally or operationally closed system.[101] Hence, the non-locality and indeterminism observed in isolated (=organisationally closed) quantum systems might be the result of a universal principle according to which subsystems of a system may start acting probabilistically and non-locally depending on the degree of operational closure of the total system they are part of. This principle is scale invariant, and therefore applies to both micro- and macroscopic systems, indifferently. Based on this assumption, the MPI postu-

mentation of events in Whitehead's sense into quantum theory is everything else than straightforward. The even more difficult inclusion of mental time remains mostly unaddressed".

[100] Kornwachs and Lucadou (1985).

[101] Maturana and Varela (1980); Varela (1981); Varela et al. (1993). "An organizationally closed unity is defined as a composite unity by a network of interactions of components that (i) through their interactions recursively regenerate the network of interactions that produced them, and (ii) realize the network as a unity in the space in which the components exist by constituting and specifying the unity's boundaries as a cleavage from the background" (Varela 1981: 15).

"A system that has operational closure is one in which the results of its processes are those processes themselves. The notion of operational closure is thus a way of specifying classes of processes that, in their very operation, tum back upon themselves to form autonomous networks. Such networks do not fall into the class of systems defined by external mechanisms of control (heteronomy) but rather into the class of systems defined by internal mechanisms of self-organization (autonomy). The key point is that such systems do not operate by representation. Instead of representing an independent world, they enact a world as a domain of distinctions that is inseparable from the structure embodied by the cognitive system" (Varela et al. 1993: 139).

lates that non-local correlations are induced by pragmatic information produced by operational closure. However, such non-local correlations can, in principle, never be used for signal transfer, since any attempt to do so will eliminate these correlations.[102] In other words, "quantum-like" behaviour would be equal to a system-theoretical principle emerging from specific organisational patterns of a system and its subsystems. Accordingly, MPI predicts that any system, be it micro- or macroscopic, should be expected to show indeterministic and non-local behaviour, if these systemic conditions are met.

More recently, Harald Atmanspacher, Hartman Römer, Harald Walach, and others[103] further advanced the system theoretical core of MPI to a novel approach, which they first termed *Weak Quantum Theory*, later using the more generic label of *General Quantum Theory* (GQT) to refer to their own theoretical contributions.[104] GQT (re-)introduces the notion of complementarity as one of several system-theoretical requirements for non-local correlations, which are now articulated in the form of a mathematical formalism derived from quantum physics proper.[105] In sum, GQT predicts non-local correlations between two observables under the following conditions:

- There is an operationally closed, holistic system identifiable by a *global observable*
- The system is constituted by mutually compatible subsystems identifiable by clearly separated *local observables*
- *Local* and *global observables* are complementary to each other, while complementarity is defined by:
  - Mutual incompatibility between the descriptions of two observables A and B
  - Non-commutativity, that is, measurement at A will alter a subsequent measurement result at B and vice versa
  - Necessity of both complementary descriptions of A and B to account for a complete description of a holistic system
- Non-local correlation cannot be used for signal transmission

[102] The reason for this restriction is derived from quantum physics, where signal transfer amounts to a measurement event, thus braking operational closure, thereby inducing decoherence of the observed system.

[103] Atmanspacher et al. (2002); Filk and Römer (2010); von Stillfried (2010).

[104] Filk and Römer (2010).

[105] The original formalism had been derived from a reduction of quantum theoretical formalism to define the conditions and relations between complementary systems. "The weak version of quantum theory is based on a minimal set of axioms. The basic structure of the resulting mathematical framework is that of a monoid.

Ordinary quantum theory can be recovered from this framework by additional axioms, restrictions, and specifications. For example, the weak version does not necessarily entail a Hilbert space representation or a probabilistic interpretation. The non-commutativity of observables is not necessarily quantified by Planck's constant. Bell-type inequalities cannot necessarily be formulated in weak quantum theory" (Atmanspacher et al. 2002: 23). The formalism has been updated in Filk and Römer (2010).

There have been several attempts to apply GQT to a range of different phenomena, including mind-body correlation,[106] homeopathy and alternative healing practices,[107] placebo and psychological effects,[108] spiritual concepts,[109] and even psychic experiences.[110] None of these phenomena seem to be explicable in terms of causal relations, which is why some of them have been simply excluded from the research agenda of scientific mainstream. Despite this disavowal by a considerable part of the scientific community, however, there is a huge corpus of interesting and thorough research on PSI phenomena. The results of scientific experiments that have been conducted in the field over the last 100 years strongly suggest that these phenomena actually exist, but that replication turns out to be very difficult.[111] My aim is not to advocate in favour or against such claims, however, it is obvious that a coherent quantum theoretical explanation for phenomena like precognition, telepathy, or telekinesis could provide useful models to bridge the ontological gap between modern science and Other cosmopractices.[112]

According to its proponents, the formalism provided by GQT might help explain and predict such phenomena in terms of generalised entanglement, that is, quantum-like indeterministic and non-local correlations. Equipped with their formalism, they went out in search of complementary global and local observables, identifying complementary pairs such as mind and body,[113] original substance and actual dilution of a homeopathic remedy,[114] collective and individual unconscious of therapist and patient,[115] verum/placebo groups and a clinical trial,[116] union and individuality (or

[106] Von Stillfried (2010); Walach and Römer (2011); Uzan (2014, 2016); Walach (2014b).

[107] Walach (2005).

[108] Atmanspacher et al. (2002); Walach (2005, 2021); Uzan (2014).

[109] Walach et al. (2009); Walach (2021).

[110] Walach (2005, 2014b); Walach et al. (2009, 2014); von Stillfried (2010); Walach and Römer (2011); Walach and Stillfried (2011).

[111] Particularly, the famous experiments conducted by U.S. intelligence reveal a stock of fascinating results (Puthoff 1996; Targ 1996; Utts 1996; May and Marwaha 2018). For an analysis of different experimental evidence in PSI research see also von Stillfried (2010). It is noteworthy, that observed difficulties to reliably reproduce PSI phenomena in controlled experiments might be due to the very nature of these phenomena (Walach et al. 2014; von Stillfried 2010). Conventional experiments are based on extracting causal signals, however, non-local events, like PSI phenomena, are precisely defined by the impossibility of signal transfer (Walach and Stillfried 2011). Moreover, classical systems are not (significantly) affected by measurement, but consciousness, just like quantum-events are inevitably affected by observation (Walach 2014a, b). All this suggests that there might be a whole class of phenomena that cannot, in principle, be proven via replicable, controlled experiment.

[112] As discussed in Chap. 3, Part I.

[113] Walach and Römer (2011).

[114] Walach (2005).

[115] Atmanspacher et al. (2002).

[116] Von Stillfried (2010). Harald Walach suggests that, in this case, the underlying complementarity derives from the definitive allocation and ignorance of an allocation due to blinding in placebo-controlled, randomised clinical trials (personal communication, 2021).

separation) among healer and patient,[117] an organism and its subsystems,[118] individual consciousness and universal oneness of the transcendental reality (for spiritual experiences),[119] separation and individuality,[120] connectedness and individuality,[121] or actuality and potentiality (for PSI phenomena and native healing rituals),[122] just to name a few examples.

As can be seen, these complementary pairs tend to draw oppositions along two superposed distinctions: first, between part and whole; second, between mental and physical. The first opposition, between part and whole, is explicitly defined as a general feature of entangled systems:

This alignment of an individual with a whole would, by necessity and as per definition of WQT [=GQT], lead to a non-local correlatedness between the individual and the whole. For 'part' and 'whole' are similarly complementary notions as 'individual/ community' and 'connectedness/separation' (Walach et al. 2009: 298).

As von Stillfried[123] notes, such a broad use of complementarity in terms of an opposition between a system and its elements ultimately predicts a non-local behaviour for any system with identifiable subsystems. As a consequence, a sufficiently stringent "generalized notion of complementarity and non-commutativity" is a major challenge of GQT, making it "harder to match to quantum theory and to interpret in a way which is both generalized and at the same time concrete and applicable".[124] He therefore proposes a system-theoretical adaptation of GQT, however, without considering complementarity a necessary requirement for the occurrence of non-local events:

We can thus predict that (possibly among other features) such parapsychological phenomena should occur in systems which are characterized by (1) a conserved global variable (whatever that might be) and (2) a high degree of freedom of the corresponding variables in the correlated subsystems. Furthermore (3) it should be impossible to use these phenomena for signal transmission and as such they should occur primarily in systems where this possibility is excluded in principle (von Stillfried 2010: 116).

However, such a systems theoretical definition hinges heavily on the existence of clearly identifiable systems as bounded and enduring unities with conserved global and local variables. In contrast to reductionist explanations of macroscopic entanglement based on ontological interpretations of quantum physics, GQT provides a rather phenomenological and explicitly formal framework, which is not linked to a particular interpretation of quantum physics. Nevertheless, GQT gives rise to the

---

[117] Idem.

[118] Idem.

[119] Walach et al. (2009).

[120] Walach et al. (2014).

[121] Idem.

[122] Idem.

[123] Von Stillfried (2010).

[124] Idem: 108.

ontological presumption that, on some underlying fundamental level, everything is connected.[125] Although GQT makes no statement concerning the ontological nature of this underlying reality, entanglement is sometimes depicted as a non-local correlation between two (complementary) aspects of an underlying monist reality.[126] Unfortunately, the implications of this ontological supposition are not discussed to their full range by the proponents of GQT. However, one of the more frequently addressed problems resulting from such a neutral or dual-aspect monism concerns the question of the identification of individual systems and subsystems that are ultimately all part of a single unitary reality. Since all systems are in some way part of a single whole, the identification of a system is unavoidably a creative act of ascription or asymptotic approximation rather than a purely objective description of objectively existing units.[127] This somehow subjective and approximative definition

[125] This assumption may be derived from an ontological interpretation of the quantum theoretical view of interfering wave functions, potentially amounting to a single higher-dimensional wave function of the entire universe. But to my knowledge, the authors do not explicitly refer to such a quantum physical explanation. Instead Walach et al. (2009) draw a parallel to the central notion of "oneness" in several spiritual traditions: "If we now assume that generalised entanglement is a rather general and ubiquitous process as suggested by the model of WQT [=GQT], then we have a rather natural understanding at hand. Such effects as healing, as telepathic connections or psychokinetic influences would be the natural result of entanglement correlations within a natural system. The systems in question would always include the conscious activity of a person that strives to be aligned with a higher, transcendent reality, thereby creating both the feeling of wholeness and connectedness. This alignment of an individual with a whole would, by necessity and as per definition of WQT, lead to a non-local correlatedness between the individual and the whole. For "part" and "whole" are similarly complementary notions as 'individual/community' and 'connectedness/separation' (Von Stillfried and Walach 2006). We can therefore assume that an alignment of the 'part', in that case a particular individual's consciousness, with a 'whole', in that case some absolute, transcendent reality, would generate or reinforce such a non-local correlation also with other 'parts' of the 'whole', or with other individuals" (idem: 298).

[126] "[…] we can combine a phenomenological duality with an ontological monism. We may assume that the underlying reality is one, beyond the distinction between mind and matter. Atmanspacher has formally shown that it is possible to construe the two systems as derived from one underlying unity through a spontaneous breaking of time-reversal symmetries (Atmanspacher 2003). This first breaking of an underlying symmetry would yield the distinction of two phenomenologically different systems, mind and matter, or material and conscious systems. Within one human being these systems might be coordinated with each other through the "mechanism" of generalized entanglement, or in other words, these two systems might be non-locally correlated" (Walach and Römer 2011: 92).

[127] "A system is anything which can be (imagined to be) isolated from the rest of the world and be subject to an investigation. A system can be as general as an object or a school of art together with all persons involved in production and interpretation. Unlike the situation in, e.g., classical mechanics the identification of a system is not always a trivial procedure but sometimes a creative act, in particular in view of the possibility of entanglement with other systems to be described in Sect. 4 In many cases it is possible to define subsystems inside a system. […] A system must have the capacity to reside in different states without losing its identity as a system. One may differentiate between pure states, which correspond to maximal possible knowledge of the system and mixed states corresponding to incomplete knowledge. Notice that the notion of a mixed state contains an epistemic element. We shall see later that this also applies to some extent to pure states" (Filk and Römer 2010: 212). According to Harald Walach, this dual-aspect-monist notion derives

of macroscopic system boundaries is paralleled by the impossibility of isolating experimental quantum systems from the observing experimenter. However, from a systems-theoretical point of view, systems are considered as operationally closed precisely if their operations are self-referential, and thereby, reproducing the conditions of their own operational continuity together with their systemic boundaries, distinguishing them from their environment. This self-reproducing or *autopoietic*[128] property is a typical feature of living systems, suggesting that indeterministic and non-local events should be expected to occur most likely in connection with increasingly complex, living organisms. In other words, while in the microcosm of quanta entropy leads to their almost immediate entanglement with the environment (making artificial isolation necessary for detecting non-local events), operationally closed autopoietic systems, like organisms, produce *negentropic* spaces within their boundaries, thus possibly re-establishing the ordered relations between clearly bounded subsystems which are a precondition for identifiable non-local events.

According to the authors of GQT, system boundaries might be established through similarity, contact, ritual, mental imagination, or strong emotions, while similarity and contact are understood as symbolic ascriptions rather than objective attributes. This strongly suggests the presence of a conscious subject, and hence a living autopoietic system, as a necessary condition for the establishment of operationally closed macrosystems. However, since GQT does not refer to the ontological nature of mental properties, the allusion to "imagination" or "emotions" remains very vague. For a better understanding consider the following example of a *poltergeist* phenomenon given by Walach, von Lucadou and Römer:

Phenomenologically speaking, such situations seem to require an 'agent', someone who suffers from a—usually—unconscious conflict that cannot be and must not be known and expressed. In such a situation the poltergeist phenomenon seems to 'express' the mental content phenomenologically. One of us was involved in a poltergeist-resolution where a young female secretary was strongly focused on her boss, a relationship which was impossible to express, because the boss was happily married and had no interest in pursuing a relationship. In short: The spuk started when the boss had to go on a business trip. He said to his employees: 'Only call me if there is fire!' Sure enough, after the boss had gone on his trip, fires started in his office. The boss had to return. Later, the shutters of the windows, without anybody setting them ablaze began to burn when his wife came to the office. As a funny aside, the German word for shutters is jalousie, derived from the French, meaning jealous. Thus, this particular poltergeist also had the phenomenological wisdom to express the inner dynamics of the jealous secretary, who likely was jealous of the wife.

How can such a strange situation be conceptualized? Again, we have a strong systemic closure (OC) that ties together various systemic elements. We normally

---

from the quantum mechanical formalism, which describes entanglement as a property of part-whole relations. Hence, the assumption of an underlying wholeness is a logical consequence of quantum formalism (personal communication, 2021).

[128] Maturana and Varela (1980).

have poltergeist phenomena within families. Here we have it within a company and within a subsystem of the company formed by the boss and his secretary, who, however, has no chance of expressing and fulfilling, perhaps not even admitting or being aware of her feelings. This forms a strong subsystem between the secretary and her boss. Again, complementarity between connectedness and individuality holds, describing the global and the local observables. Strong emotional material, usually disavowed or disconnected from the inner life, seeks some form of expression. As it happens, the expression is found in the outer reality that bears some symbolic connectedness with the total system. Thus, a nonlocal correlation becomes operative that exists between elements of a system by virtue of a strong systemic boundary (Walach et al. 2014: 621).

It would be important to understand how mental processes can be capable of establishing systemic ties to physical systems strong enough to constitute a shared operationally closed system, eventually provoking non-locally correlated physical events. In short, what kind of ontic categories are mind and matter, and how do they relate to each other? GQT is silent on the ontic definitions, as it is a purely phenomenal model.

So, in addition to the part-whole distinction, the complementary pairs identified by GQT generally comprise a mental and further mental and/or physical systems. The overall system boundaries are established by virtue of mental activity, eventually evoking entanglement between two or more components of the system. While two entangled mental systems might be meaningfully related to each other non-locally, a physical system which is entangled with a mental system, in contrast, will only be passively influenced by the mental system. This implicit pattern suggests a more or less explicit conception of mind and body as two complementary aspects of one underlying unitary reality. As discussed earlier, complementary conceptions of mind-body duality are faced with disanalogies, since quantum physics suggest a mutually exclusive presence of either wave or particle properties, while experience should be expected to be co-present with its physical correlates. However, the discussion of this problem also showed that this limitation results from an implicit assumption of a collapse of the wave function. Since GQT does not directly build on a particular interpretation of quantum theory, it should be possible to assume a non-collapse interpretation without further implications for GQT's overall conceptual framework. In fact, Walach and Römer[129] explicitly propose a dual-aspect monist solution to the mind-body problem based on GQT, suggesting that mind and body might be two complementary "phenomenologically different systems", both deriving "from one underlying unity". This view seems to fit nicely with a Bohmian non-collapse interpretation, with mind and matter representing mental and physical unfoldings of a unitary implicit order. However, according to Walach and Römer, the correlation between mental and brain activity should be explicable in terms of non-local correlation between two entangled subsystems (mind and brain) with an

[129] Walach and Römer (2011).

underlying unity (an individual). The hypotheses of a parallelism between mind and body is explicitly excluded and substituted by the notion of entanglement.

Moreover, this GQT-based model of non-local mind-body correlation has also been expanded by a mathematical model derived from GQT formalism.[130] This mathematical approach follows Bell's idea that causal correlations must lead to different probability distributions than non-local correlations. Accordingly, statistical testing of correlations between quantifiable psychological and somatic observables, like degrees of irritability and hormonal or cardiovascular variables, should allow for calculating whether the two observables are causally related, or not, and also whether they commute, or not. First results of such tests strongly suggest that "the psychosomatic correlations must be understood in terms of an entanglement relation".[131] This can be interpreted as a strong argument against both materialism and interactionism.

However, the definition of mind and body as two entangled *systems* seems to be at odds with the notion of mind and body as two *phenomenal actualities* of one underlying reality. In other words, there might be a crossover of the notions of phenomenal actuality and system, which deserves further explanation to avoid category mistake. The inconsistency becomes clear when we try to apply the same rationale to quantum physics proper: Quantum systems are constituted by interfering wave functions, which, upon measurement, become indirectly manifest in non-locally correlated, or entangled, particle behaviour. Hence, entanglement primarily occurs between wave systems in the form of interference, however resulting in the detection of non-locally correlated particle behaviour. Thus, strictly speaking, there is no entanglement between waves and particles; neither are there two complementary systems, one constituted by waves and another by particles. Rather, particle behaviour is strictly correlated with corresponding wave functions, since particles are generally interpreted as resembling complementary instantiations of wave functions, manifesting upon measurement. Likewise, particles are not entangled with each other, but indeterministically orchestrated by entangled wave functions. It follows that if isomorphic complementarity relations exist between waves and particles, on the one hand, and mind and matter, on the other, then, according to the formalism of GQT, entanglement should occur between two mental processes, possibly resulting in entangled behaviour of correlated physical observables, but never directly between a mental and a physical system. Given the dual-aspect monist grounding, a correlation between mental and physical properties would rather represent some kind of parallelism.

The problem with such a conceptual crossover between the system-theoretical assumption of GQT and the proposal by Walach and Römer[132] regarding the mind-body problem is that it mixes up two ontologically different kinds of correlations: while two subsystems of a common composite system may be non-locally corre-

---

130 Uzan (2014, 2016).

131 Uzan (2014: 32).

132 Walach and Römer (2011).

lated due to entanglement, a dual aspect monist interpretation would rather imply a parallelism between two different instantiations of one fundamental reality. Consequently, mind and matter would be epiphenomenal to each other, allowing for neither classical interaction nor quantum-like entanglement. A similar problem has already been discussed earlier in the context of the Bohmian model of mind and matter as two different phenomenologically explicate unfoldings of an underlying phenomenologically enfolded implicate order. The examination of the issue has shown that one option for avoiding parallelism might be a Russellian interpretation of physical properties as instantiations of an underlying fundamental phenomenal reality, as proposed by von Stillfried's RBI-thesis. A solution to the conceptual shortcomings of the current GQT approach to the mind-body problem might, therefore, be to combine the phenomenological GQT model with an RBI-like ontology. Of course, this solution would explain the correlation between mind and body in terms of physical (particle-like) properties emerging or unfolding from (proto-)phenomenal (wave-like) properties, and not as a result of entanglement. It will be necessary to investigate the consequences of this solution for the whole GQT framework and its formalism. Off hand, I would not expect too many conflicts, since the formalism of GQT predicts entanglement between local observables, one of which will generally be a conscious person responsible for establishing the systemic preconditions of entanglement. According to the RBI-thesis, the person's consciousness would be equal to a highly selfcomplexigrated phenomenal wave system, a kind of autopoietic active information, if you will, which is part of countless higher dimensional wave systems. In this picture, it is perfectly conceivable that a person's mind/wave system may act on other wave systems in a way which can be described in terms of entanglement. Since all active wave branches are orchestrating correlated particle-like actualities, such mind-induced entangled wave systems may influence other person's minds or even events in the actuality of the physical world. Moreover, QGT and the RBI-thesis converge in a crucial point concerning the explanation of the emergence of entanglement, on the one hand, and consciousness, on the other, which are both explained in terms of systemic properties like operational closure or "selfcomplexigratedness". This convergence might point to a common underlying principle responsible for the emergence of all kinds of indeterministic and non-local phenomena, including quantum entanglement, macroscopic non-causality, consciousness and the mind-body correlation.

Be this as it may, this is not the place to continue these speculations, but I think the discussion I presented so far has pointed to some crucial aspects of GQT. By now it should have become clear that GQT is still in an early stage of development, offering a lot of space for further theorising and empirical research. However, all the open questions notwithstanding, GQT is based on two very strong intuitions: First of all, the reductionist insight that the macroscopic world is made up of indeterministic non-local events suggests that our macrocosm might not be quite as deterministic and causal as supposed by classical physics. Second, the even bolder intuition that the non-local and indeterministic behaviour of microscopic quantum systems might be governed by a universal and scale-invariant natural principle that is also responsible for non-local events in our macroscopic reality. The phenomenal description of this universal principle in terms of a formalism has the great advantage of presenting a framework which should work with different ontological interpretations of quantum physics. However, the discussion also shows that the formalism alone might not allow for sufficiently convincing explanations of non-causal macro-phenomena, particularly so because of the general scepticism common to the scientific mainstream about the very existence of such phenomena.[133] It has also become apparent that the formalism of GQT in its current version is still in an early stage of development, with different authors proposing different solutions and interpretations. From my own limited point of view, most current limitations result from a problematic conception of complementarity and the lack of an ontological grounding capable of providing the formalism with a more explanatory grip. A solution might be to build the formalism on a merely system-theoretical basis and to combine the GQT framework with a coherent ontological interpretation of quantum theory. I think von Stillfried's RBI-thesis might be a promising candidate, but in principle, any other comparably coherent ontologies would do as well.

12.3 Summing Up Current Approaches to a Unified Theory of Mind and Matter

Of course, the brief overview I offered here of the debates on the so-called hard problem of consciousness and related attempts to derive a unified theory of mind and matter from quantum physics does not give a full account of the whole issue. But I hope the problems and suggested solutions discussed so far provided a notion

[133] Interestingly, GQT implies, at least according to some authors (e.g. Walach et al. 2009; von Stillfried 2010; Walach and Stillfried 2011), that macroscopic entanglement-like non-local phenomena—if they actually exist and occur in people's lives—will not be empirically verifiable by reproducible experimental studies under controlled conditions. This is due to the quantum-theoretical "no-signaling principle" which has to be obeyed by entanglement between quanta in narrow sense (subatomic particles etc.) and by quanta in the generalized sense of GQT (e.g. macroscopic systems with a sufficient degree of organizational closure). Due to the no-signaling principle, which is experimentally well confirmed in quantum physics, superluminal correlations are possible *within* an entangled system only as long as these correlations cannot be used from *outside* the system. Since for correlations in macroscopic systems the possibility to use them for transmitting information arises as soon as these systems are placed in controlled settings, and given that experimental settings are by definition controlled settings, it would follow that empirical verification of macroscopic entanglement-like correlations via experiments is in principle impossible. If this assumption is correct, it would explain the lack of experimental evidence due to which many empirical scientists remain unconvinced about the existence of non-local macro-phenomena. At the least, the proposal seems to show that theoretically it could be possible that phenomena exist and occur under the uncontrolled conditions of daily life, but their existence cannot be corroborated using the established procedures of experimental science. Therefore, the science-theoretical truism that the absence of proof for something does not equal the proof for the absence of that thing might be of particular importance when discussing the existence of macroscopic non-local phenomena.

of the depth and the astonishing complexity of the questions involved, and of how far We (modern scientists and philosophers) still seem to be from finding convincing answers to those questions.

Chalmers's[134] redefinition of the hard problem of consciousness as essentially the question of the relation between physical and phenomenal properties has certainly been an important step towards a better analytical understanding of the underlying ontological questions. This analytical perspective on the ontic relations between phenomenal and physical properties provides important arguments for the irreducibility of these two ontic categories, and hence, against materialist reductionism. Accordingly, the question of the fundamental structure of the universe and the place of phenomenal and physical properties within such a cosmological model calls for a naturalist theory of mind and matter.

On the whole, there seem to be good arguments suggesting that some kind of Russellian monism or pan(proto)psychism might provide a coherent ontological framework for such a naturalist theory. However, although Chalmers[135] himself has repeatedly pointed to the advantages of panpsychist models over other alternatives, he comes to a rather pessimistic conclusion concerning the possibility of solving the combination problem, which he identifies as the most challenging stumbling block on the way to a coherent pan(proto)psychist solution to the hard problem of consciousness.

According to Nikolaus von Stillfried's in-depth analysis of quantum-theoretical considerations of the ontic nature of mind and matter, however, a Russellian interpretation of Bohm's approach could provide a possible solution to the combination problem (and other challenges, such as the possibility of direct phenomenal judgments). In short, von Stillfried's RBI-thesis suggests that Chalmers's protophenomenal properties, the (Bohmian concept of) wave function and Russell's inscrutable essence all refer to the same ontic category; physical properties on the other hand, are represented by particle-like properties of quanta and quantum systems of varying degrees of complexity and operational closure (or other still undefined system-theoretical parameters von Stillfried provisionally summarises under the fantasy name "selfcomplexigratedness"). While every quantum has some kind of protophenomenal property, increasingly selfcomplexigrated systems might develop fully-fledged phenomenal experience. Accordingly, the RBI-thesis envisages providing an ontological framework for a naturalist (quantum-theoretical) approach to mind and matter, ascribing essential roles to both physical and phenomenal properties within fundamental physics.

Despite the promising prospects von Stillfried's approach seems to offer, it has to be emphasised that his RBI-thesis is just one among many different speculative proposals currently being discussed in this still very marginal field of academic discourse. Metaphysical questions, such as the ontology of mind, are still far from being perceived by the scientific mainstream as a central problem deserving serious

134 Chalmers (1995, 2002, 2010).

135 Chalmers (2016a, b).

scientific investigation. Also the Bohmian approach, on which von Stillfried's own RBI-thesis is based, only represents one among a huge range of radically different ontological interpretations of quantum physics, all of which are representing rather marginal views among physicists (where epistemological, so-called "Copenhagen" interpretations still seem to dominate the scene).[136] Hence, many scientists will probably not agree with these views, and there is no guarantee that von Stillfried's RBI-thesis will ever make it into scientific mainstream discourse.

Nonetheless, the great variety of different ontological interpretations of quantum physics that are being discussed within scientific discourse still shows the importance of the issue. Moreover, the proposed ontological models of reality not only radically differ from each other, many of them are also utterly counterintuitive, and at times, disturbingly weird.

In sum, the whole discussion shows at least that:

1. Modern science still has no coherent fundamental theory of mind and matter to offer,
2. Rather, current scientific evidence and theory seem to allow for a great variety of very different ontological models,
3. Many of the suggested solutions imply cosmological models that are at least as contrary to naive materialism as those suggested by Other kinds of knowledge,
4. Some of the apparently most promising academic models suggest that both mind and matter occupy equally essential roles within fundamental physics.

Given the wide interpretative scope left by current scientific evidence it might be pertinent to revisit the supposed a priori incommensurability between evidence-based "scientific" theory and Other cosmological models. An analysis of the apparent analogies and disanalogies between at least one comprehensive quantum-theoretical model of mind and matter and at least one Other, supposedly "unscientific", cosmology should provide a more concrete view of this question. In the following chapter I will provide such a tentative analysis, using the examples of Bohmian theory of mind and matter and Potiguara ontology to make a speculative comparison between "scientific" and Other ontological conceptions.

References

Aharonov A, Popescu S, Tollaksen J (2010) A time-symmetric formulation of quantum mechanics. Phys Today 63(11). https://doi.org/10.1063/1.3518209

Albert D, Loewer B (1988) Interpreting the many worlds interpretation. Synthese 77:195–213

Alexander P (1956) Complementary descriptions. Mind 65:145–165

Aspect A, Dalibard J, Roger G (1982) Experimental test of Bell's inequalities using time- varying analyzers. Phys Rev Lett 49:1804–1807

Atmanspacher H (2003) Mind and matter as asymptotically disjoint, inequivalent representations with broken time-reversal symmetry. Biosystems 68:19–30

[136] Sivasundaram and Nielsen (2016).

Atmanspacher H, Primas H (2006) Pauli's ideas on mind and matter in the context of contemporary science. J Conscious Stud 13:5–50
Atmanspacher H, Römer H, Walach H (2002) Weak quantum theory: complementarity and entanglement in physics and beyond. Found Phys 32:379–406. https://doi.org/10.1023/A:1014809312397
Ballentine LE (1998) Quantum mechanics: a modern development. World Scientific, Singapore
Barad K (2022) Agential realism—a relational ontology interpretation of quantum physics. In: Freire O Jr (ed) The Oxford Handbook of the history of quantum interpretations. Oxford University Press, pp 1031–1054
Bedau H, Oppenheim P (1961) Complementarity in quantum mechanics: A logical analysis. Synthese 13:201–232
Bell JS (1964) On the Einstein Podolsky Rosen paradox. Physics 1:195–200
Bohm DJ (1952) A suggested interpretation of the quantum theory in terms of 'hidden' variables, I and II. Phys Rev 85:166–193
Bohm DJ (1980) Wholeness and the implicate order. Routledge & Kegan Paul, London
Bohm DJ (1990) A new theory of the relationship of mind and matter. Philos Psychol 3:271–286
Bohm DJ, Hiley BJ (1993) The undivided universe: An ontological interpretation of quantum theory. Routledge, London
Bohr N (1913a) On the constitution of atoms and molecules I. Philos Mag Ser 26:1–25
Bohr N (1913b) On the constitution of atoms and molecules II. Philos Mag Ser 26:476–502
Bohr N (1913c) On the constitution of atoms and molecules III. Philos Mag Ser 26:857–875
Bohr N (1928) The quantum postulate and the recent development of atomic theory. Nature 121:580–591
Born M (1926a) Zur Quantenmechanik der Stoßvorgänge. Zeitschrift für Physik A Hadrons Nuclei 37:863–867
Born M (1926b) Quantenmechanik der Stoßvorgänge. Zeitschrift für Physik A Hadrons Nuclei 38:803–827
Born M (1954) The statistical interpretation of quantum mechanics. Nobel Lecture
Born M, Jordan P (1925) Zur Quantenmechanik. Zeitschrift für Physik 34:858–888
Brody N, Oppenheim P (1969) Application of Bohr's principle of complementarity to the mind-body problem. J Philos 66:97–113
Broglie Ld (1923) Waves and quanta. Nature 112:540–540
Broglie Ld (2004) On the Theory of Quanta. A translation of: Recherches sur la théorie des quanta. Ann. de Phys., 10e série, t. III (Janvier-Février 1925). Annales de physique 3:22–128
Chalmers DJ (1995) The conscious mind: in search of a theory of conscious experience. Department of Philosophy University of California, Santa Cruz
Chalmers DJ (1997) Moving forward on the problem of consciousness. J Conscious Stud 4(1):3–46
Chalmers DJ (2002) Consciousness and its place in nature. In: Chalmers DJ (ed) Philosophy of mind: classical and contemporary readings. Oxford University Press, Oxford
Chalmers DJ (2010) The character of consciousness. Oxford University Press, Oxford
Chalmers DJ (2016a) The combination problem for panpsychism. In: Bruntrup G, Jaskolla L (eds) Panpsychism. Oxford University Press, Oxford, pp 179–214
Chalmers DJ (2016b) Panpsychism and panprotopsychism. In: Bruntrup G, Jaskolla L (eds) Panpsychism. Oxford University Press, Oxford, pp 19–47
Chalmers DJ, McQueen KJ (2020) Consciousness and the collapse of the wave function. New York University/Chapman University, July 3, 2020. http://www.consc.net/papers/collapse.pdf. Accessed 29 Apr 2021
Cramer JG (1986) The transactional interpretation of quantum mechanics. Rev Mod Phys 58:647–688
DeWitt BS, Graham N (1973) The many worlds interpretation of quantum mechanics. Princeton University Press, Princeton

Eccles JC (1986) Do mental events cause neural events analogously to the probability fields of quantum mechanics? Proc R Soc Lon Ser B Biol Sci 227:411–428

Einstein A (1905) Über einen die Erzeugung und Verwandlung des Lichtes betreffenden heuristischen Gesichtspunkt. Annalen der Physik (ser. 4) 17:132–148. https://doi.org/10.1002/andp.19053220607

Einstein A, Born M (2005) Alber Einstein Max Born, Briefwechsel 1916-1955. Nymphenburger Verlagshandlung, Munich

Einstein A, Podolsky B, Rosen N (1935) Can quantum-mechanical description of reality be considered complete? Phys Rev 47:777–780

Elitzur AC, Vaidman L (1993) Interaction-free quantum measurements. Found Phys 23:987–997

Epperson M (2004) Quantum mechanics and the philosophy of Alfred North Whitehead. Fordham University Press, New York

Everett H (1957) "Relative state" formulation of quantum mechanics. Rev Mod Phys 29:454–462

Everett H (1973) The theory of the universal wave function. In: DeWitt B, Graham RN (eds) The many-worlds interpretation of quantum mechanics. Princeton University Press, Princeton, pp 3–140

Fahrenberg J (2013) Zur Kategorienlehre der Psychologie. Komplementaritätsprinzip. Perspektiven und Perspektiven-Wechsel. Pabst Science, Lengerich

Filk T, Römer H (2010) Generalized quantum theory: overview and latest developments. Axiomathes 21:211–220

Freire O Jr (ed) (2022) The Oxford Handbook of the history of quantum interpretations. Oxford University Press

Friebe C (2015) Messproblem, Minimal- und Kollapsinterpretationen. In: Friebe C et al (eds) Philosophie der Quantenphysik. Springer, Berlin, pp 45–78

Giustina M et al. (2015) Significant loophole-free test of Bell's theorem. Phys Rev Lett 115:250401

Handsteiner J, Friedman SA, Rauch D, Gallicchio J (2017) Cosmic Bell test: Measurement settings from Milky Way stars. Phys Rev Lett 118. https://doi.org/10.1103/PhysRevLett.118.060401

Heisenberg W (1925) Über quantentheoretische Umdeutung kinematischer und mechanischer Beziehungen. Zeitschrift für Physik A Hadrons Nuclei 33:879–893

Heisenberg W (1927) Über den anschaulichen Inhalt der quantentheoretischen Kinematik and Mechanik. Zeitschrift für Physik 43(172–198):62–84

Heisenberg W, Bohr N, Herrmann A (1963) Die Kopenhagener Deutung der Quantentheorie. Battenberg, Stuttgart

Hensen B et al. (2015) Loophole-free Bell violation. Nature 526:682–686

Hiley BJ (2010) The Bohm approach reassessed. Published online only. http://www.bbk.ac.uk/tpru/BasilHiley/BohmReassed1.pdf. Accessed 30 Apr 2021

Hiley BJ, Pylkkanen P (2005) Can mind affect matter via active information? Mind Matter 3:8–27

Hoche HU (1990) Anthropologische Komplementarität und die "Einheit der Sache". Versuch einer skeptischen Lösung eines skeptischen Zweifels. In: Hoche HU (ed) Einführung in das sprachanalytische Philosophieren. Wissenschaftliche Buchgesellschaft, Darmstadt, pp 107–129

Howard D (2022) The Copenhagen interpretation. In: Freire O Jr (ed) The Oxford Handbook of the history of quantum interpretations. Oxford University Press, pp 521–541

Itano WM, Heinzen DJ, Bollinger, JJ Wineland DJ (1990) Quantum Zeno effect. Phys Rev A 41(5):2295–2300. https://doi.org/10.1103/PhysRevA.41.2295

Jung CG, Pauli W (eds) (1952) Naturerklärung und Psyche. Rascher, Zürich

Kaufman S (2014) Beyond the stalemate: conscious mind-body—quantum mechanics—free will—possible panpsychism—possible interpretation of quantum enigma. Cosmos Hist J Nat Soc Philos 10:149–169

Keiser DI (2022) Tackling Loopholes in experimental tests of Bell's inequality. In: Freire O Jr (ed) The Oxford Handbook of the history of quantum interpretations. Oxford University Press, pp 339–370

Kornwachs K, Lucadou W (1985) Pragmatic information as a nonclassical concept to describe cognitive processes. Cogn Syst 1:79–94

Laloë F (2022) Quantum mechanics is routinely used in laboratories with great success, but no consensus on its interpretation has emerged. In: Freire O Jr (ed) The Oxford Handbook of the history of quantum interpretations. Oxford University Press, pp 7–51
Lockwood M (1991) Mind, brain and the quantum: the compound "I". B. Blackwell, Oxford
MacKay DM (1957) Complementary descriptions. Mind 66:390–394
Maleeh R (2015) Mind, matter, information and quantum interpretations. Information 6:314–338
Maturana HR, Varela FJ (1980) Autopoiesis and cognition: the realization of the living. D. Reidel, Dordrecht
May EC, Marwaha SB (eds) (2018) The Star Gate Archives. Reports of the United States Government Sponsored Psi Program, 1972–1995. McFarland, Jefferson
Mermin ND (2004) Could Feynman have said this? Phys Today 57:10–11
Mermin ND (2012) Quantum mechanics: Fixing the shifty split. Phys Today 65:8–10
Oppenheimer JR (1954) Science and common understanding. Theoria Int J Theory Hist Found Sci 2:225–232
Pauli W (1950) Die philosophische Bedeutung der Idee der Komplementarität. Cell Mol Life Sci CMLS 6:72–75
Penrose R (1996) On gravity's role in quantum state reduction. Gen Relativ Gravit 28:581–600
Planck M (1899) Über irreversible Strahlungsvorgänge. In: Sitzungsberichte der Königlich Preußischen Akademie der Wissenschaften zu Berlin, Berlin, pp 440–480
Planck M (1900) Entropy and Temperature of Radiant Heat. Annalen der Physik 1:719–737
Puthoff HE (1996) CIA-initiated remote viewing program at Stanford Research Institute. J Sci Explor 10:63–76
Pylkkänen P (2007) Mind, matter and the implicate order. Springer, Berlin
Rauch D et al. (2018) Cosmic Bell test (high-redshift quasars). Phys Rev Lett 121:080403
Rovelli C (1996) Relational quantum mechanics. Int J Theor Phys 35:1637–1678
Salart D, Baas A, Branciard C, Zbinden H (2008) Testing spooky actions at a distance. Nature 454:861–864
Schrödinger E (1926a) Quantisierung als Eigenwertproblem. Dritte Mitteilung. Annalen der Physik 80:437–490
Schrödinger E (1926b) Quantisierung als Eigenwertproblem. Erste Mitteilung Annalen der Physik 79:361–376
Schrödinger E (1926c) Quantisierung als Eigenwertproblem. Vierte Mitteilung. Annalen der Physik 81:109–139
Schrödinger E (1926d) Quantisierung als Eigenwertproblem. Zweite Mitteilung Annalen der Physik 79:489–527
Seager W (2016) Theories of consciousness: An introduction and assessment, 2nd edn. Routledge, New York
Sivasundaram S, Nielsen K (2016) Surveying the attitudes of physicists concerning foundational issues of quantum mechanics. physics.hist.ph 1–20
Shalm LK et al. (2015) Strong loophole-free test of local realism. Phys Rev Lett 115:250402
Stapp HP (1979) Whiteheadian approach to quantum theory and the generalized Bell's theorem. Found Phys 9:1–25
Stapp HP (2001) Quantum theory and the role of mind in nature. Found Phys 31:1465–1499
Sudarshan ECG, Misra B (1977) The Zeno's paradox in quantum theory. J Math Phys 18:756–763
Szczeciniarz K, Kounheiher J (2022) The philosophy of wholeness and the general and new order: Bohm's and Penrose's points of view. In: Freire O Jr (ed) The Oxford Handbook of the history of quantum interpretations. Oxford University Press, pp 1073–1101
Targ R (1996) Remote viewing at Stanford Research Institute in the 1970s: A memoir. J Sci Explor 10:77–88
Utts J (1996) An assessment of the evidence for psychic functioning. J Sci Explor 10:3–39
Uzan P (2014) On the nature of psychophysical correlations. Mind Matter 12:7–36

Uzan P (2016) Deciding the mind–body problem experimentally. Axiomathes 27:333–354. Springer
Varela FJ (1981) Autonomy and autopoiesis. In: Roth G, Schwengler H (eds) Self-organizing systems. Campus, Frankfurt, pp 14–23
Varela FJ, Thompson E, Rosch A (1993) The embodied mind. Cognitive science and human experience. MIT Press, Cambridge
Velmans M (1991) Is human information processing conscious? Behav Brain Sci 14:651–726
Velmans M (1993) Consciousness, causality and complementarity. Behav Brain Sci 16:409–416
von Meyenn K (ed) (1993) Wolfgang Pauli—Wissenschaftlicher Briefwechsel—1940–1949. Springer, Berlin
von Meyenn K (ed) (1996) Wolfgang Pauli—Wissenschaftlicher Briefwechsel—1950–1952. Springer, Berlin
von Neumann J (1996) Mathematische Grundlagen der Quantenmechanik, 2nd edn. Springer, Berlin
von Stillfried N (2010) Theoretical and experimental explorations of "generalized quantum theory." PhD thesis, European University Viadrina
von Stillfried N (2018) Vom Innen der Dinge: Das "Bewusstsein-Körper-Problem" und die "Welle-Teilchen-Dualität": Interdisziplinäre Impulse zwischen Quantentheorie und analytischer Philosophie des Geistes. Habilitation thesis, University of Trier
Von Stillfried N, Walach H (2006) The whole and its parts: Are complementarity and nonlocality intrinsic to closed systems? Int J Comput Anticip Syst 17:137–146
Walach H (2000) Magic of signs: a non-local interpretation of homeopathy. Br Homoeopath J 89:127–140
Walach H (2005) Generalized entanglement: a new theoretical model for understanding the effects of complementary and alternative medicine. J Altern Complement Med 11:549–559. https://doi.org/10.1089/acm.2005.11.549
Walach H (2014a) Geist in der Flasche—Vulgärer Materialismus auf dem Tisch: Kategorienfehler, unbequeme Daten und ein bescheidener Beitrag zum Leib-Seele-Problem. In: Weinzirl J, Heusser P (eds) Was Ist Geist? Wittener Kolloquium für Humanismus, Medizin und Philosophie. Verlag Königshausen und Neumann, Würzburg
Walach H (2014b) Towards an epistemology of inner experience. In: Schmidt S, Walach H (eds) Meditation—neuroscientific approaches and philosophical implications. Springer, Cham, pp 7–22
Walach H (2021) Brücken zwischen Psychotherapie und Spiritualität. Schattauer, Stuttgart
Walach H, Römer H (2011) Generalized entanglement—a nonreductive option for a phenomenologically dualist and ontologically monist view of consciousness. In: Walach H, Schmidt S, Jonas WB (eds) Neuroscience, consciousness and spirituality. Springer, Netherlands, pp 81–95
Walach H, Stillfried N (2011) Generalised quantum theory: basic idea and general intuition: a background story and overview. Axiomathes 21:185–209
Walach H, Kohls N, Von Stillfried N et al (2009) Spirituality: the legacy of parapsychology. Arch Psychol Relig 31:277–308. https://doi.org/10.1163/008467209X12499946199407
Walach H, von Lucadou W, Römer H (2014) Parapsychological phenomena as examples of generalized nonlocal correlations—a theoretical framework. J Sci Explor 28(4):605–631
Wheeler JA (1990a) A journey into gravity and spacetime. Scientific American Library, New York
Wheeler JA (1990b) Information, physics, quantum: the search for links. In: Zurek W (ed) Complexity, entropy, and the physics of information: proceedings of the SFI Workshop entitled, complexity, entropy, and the physics of information, held May 29 to June 10, 1989. CRC Press, London, pp 3–28
Whitehead AN (1978) Process and reality: an essay in cosmology. Griffin DR (ed). Free Press, New York
Young T (1804) The Bakerian lecture: Experiments and calculations relative to physical optics. Philos Trans R Soc Lond 94:1–16
Zeh HD (1970) On the interpretation of measurement in quantum theory. Found Phys 1:69–76

Zurek WH (1981) Pointer basis of quantum apparatus: into what mixture does the wave packet collapse. Phys Rev D 24:1516–1525

Zwrin H (2022) Is QBism a possible solution to the conceptual problems of QM? In: Freire O Jr (ed) The Oxford Handbook of the history of quantum interpretations. Oxford University Press, pp 1007–1029

Chapter 13
Of Ancestors and Wave Functions: A Tentative Comparability Analysis

If we analyse the principles of thought on which magic is based, they will probably be found to resolve themselves into two: first, that like produces like, or that an effect resembles its cause; and, second, that things which have once been in contact with each other continue to act on each other at a distance after the physical contact has been severed.

— Frazer (1922: 11)

Frazer's famous definition of magic was, to be sure, meant to show that magic was based upon *wrong* metaphysical presumptions, obviously violating natural laws of physics, and therefore coming to *wrong* conclusions. However, in the face of quantum physics, the latter part of his definition of magic strangely resembles the definition of quantum entanglement. Are Other kinds of knowledge really as incommensurable with the findings and theoretical concepts of modern science as commonly held by academic scholars? Maybe in our current world made up by quanta and their indeterministic and non-local "spooky action at a distance" Other metaphysics are not quite as incommensurable with modern science as it seemed in the world of nineteenth century classical physics?

Although my short presentation of current academic discourse on the fundamental nature of mind and matter was certainly very superficial, I hope it was sufficient to illustrate that the current state of scientific evidence and theory still allows for a wide range of different ontological interpretations. Moreover, personally I am astonished by the weirdness of some of the cosmological models that are seriously being discussed by scientific mainstream. It makes me wonder why the idea of living in one of infinite interlaced universes that are multiplying every second by the billions should be easier to accept than the idea of living in a world crowded by invisible Ancestor spirits. From the viewpoint of intuitive evidence, approaches like many-worlds or many-minds interpretations of quantum theory seem to be at least as odd as the enchanted worlds suggested by Other cosmopractices. I sometimes imagine a physicist who is an ardent defender of physicalism and many-world theory arguing that Potiguara cosmopractice is "unscientific" because it is at odds with scientific theory and evidence: "Look at those superstitious primitives! They say

J. Linhart, *Science and the Other*, Schriften zu Leben und Gesellschaft - Series on Life and Society 2, https://doi.org/10.1007/978-3-032-03927-9_13

there is another invisible world in a hidden dimension—what a nonsense! There are billions and trillions of invisible worlds popping up every second!"

But fun apart, I honestly think we should analyse Other views better and see whether they really are in conflict with scientific evidence before we simply dismiss those views for supposedly being "unscientific". In this last chapter of this book, I will offer a tentative comparative analysis concerning apparent analogies and disanalogies between the fundamental ontological categories suggested by Potiguara cosmopractice compared to those suggested by current academic theories of mind and matter. Of course, the few approaches from philosophy of mind and from quantum physics I have discussed here do not provide a complete account of the entire debate on these issues. There are other interesting proposals I could have taken into account, and there certainly will be new developments in the near future. And although I followed the discussion offered by von Stillfried showing that certain interpretations of quantum theory might be particularly helpful for the development of a unified theory of mind and matter, there is no consensus on this issue either. So, in principle, any or none of the discussed approaches might turn out to be the most accepted and/or most appropriate solution to the issues at stake. Accordingly, for my purpose here, any significant analogy between a central aspect of Potiguara ontology and at least one of the discussed academic ontological models will hold as an argument against incommensurability.[1] I will consider two concepts as analogues, if they can be understood as metaphors referring to isomorphic ontic categories, as far as their properties are concerned.[2] It goes without saying, that even a complete isomorphy between the properties of all categories of two alternative cosmological models will not necessarily result in identical worldviews, since each may use different metaphors to refer to a common ontic referent with isomorphic properties, and therefore, paint quite different pictures of "reality". Anyhow, analogous ontologies will "talk" about comparable existing "things", so to say, although referring to them by means of different terminology and imagery. In some ontologies, in contrast, such "things" may simply not exist, which would render them incommensurable (at least in regard to that aspect), since there is no common referent they could address. In other words, I am by no means trying to show that, deep down in their hearts, the Potiguara believe in quantum physics, or that quantum physics has proven magic to be real. An analogy between categories from two different cosmologies simply allows for exchanging ideas about a common referent, and hence,

[1] Although it would be preferable to identify a single coherent theory of mind and matter that converges in all aspects with Potiguara cosmology, this is not a necessary requirement, since currently there is no widely accepted coherent approach. Accordingly, isomorphy between different aspects of Potiguara cosmology and certain aspects of different academic approaches should suffice to argue against the universalist argument of a priori incommensurability between "scientific" and Other kinds of knowledge.

[2] For example, the RBI-theses postulates isomorphy between wave-like and proto-phenomenal properties, hence, both "wave functions" and "conscious states" refer to common ontic category.

suggests a minimum of commensurability.[3] However, commensurability also entails the possibility of disagreement. We can discuss a common issue and still come to different conclusions.

Traditionally, such a comparative analysis would probably try to "translate" Potiguara concepts into "Western" academic concepts. While this is certainly a possibility, this procedure will have to "squeeze" the Other's concepts into Our academic concepts. However, as discussed earlier,[4] such "translations" come with the risk of category mistake when we try to equate two actually incommensurable concepts as if they were referring to the same ontic referent, while in fact they are not. Moreover, there is little chance to learn something essentially new from Our own interpretations of the Other's view, since we are using Our own worn-out categories and metaphors.

But what about flipping things to the Potiguara's side and asking how they might "translate" Our concepts into theirs? My bet would be that the perspective of such an "inverted anthropology", as suggested by Eduardo Viveiros de Castro,[5] might reveal something new about Our own conceptions. Of course, I am neither a quantum physicist nor a Potiguara, and the ultimate aim should certainly be to get physicists into a dialogue with the Potiguara and see what *they* actually think about each other's ideas of the constitution of the universe.[6] However, in the absence of a group

[3] For example, a Moslem and a Christian may disagree about many religious questions, but both will talk about the same God referring to an entity with basically the same fundamental properties (almighty, omnipresent, invisible, creator of the universe, etc.). Likewise, quantum physicists may debate whether there is an ontic collapse of the wave function or not, but both will agree that quantum observables seem to behave in either a wave-like or particle-like way. However, some physicists may hold that there are only waves and no ontic particles, while others hold that the wave function is merely an epistemic description with no ontic referent, and only particles are "real". So strictly speaking, some interpretations of quantum physics suggest mutually incommensurable ontological models of reality because they do not refer to the same ontic categories, although they still describe the same phenomena with the same observable properties. Nevertheless, both may provide more or less equally coherent mathematical descriptions of experimental evidence. So, even here incommensurability seems to be an all too heavy ordnance of a concept, since all physicists will still be able to understand each other's ontological interpretation of their empirical data and the resulting mathematical models.

[4] Chapters 4, 5, and 6.

[5] Castro (2015)

[6] In fact, my plan was to realise this kind of dialogues in the course of our research project together with the Potiguara. However, there were so many things to do that there was simply not enough time to comply with the transfer of the specific knowledge to the group members, as necessary to go into such a discussion on quantum physics together with my Potiguara peers. I had the opportunity to check the fundamental ontological categories back with the Potiguara members of our research group, so I can hope that the account I presented here should at least provide an acceptable outline of the Potiguara's ideas. Since I am not a physicist either, my account of quantum physics is likewise a secondhand account, depending on the accounts of other authors. Hence, my own tentative comparison should be understood as a preparatory step towards a horizontal dialogue between "modern/colonial" discourse and the excluded Others.

of Potiguara and physicists, I will take our Potiguara ontology at face value and, by way of trial, pretend it would represent the view of a hypothetical Potiguara who is also a quantum physicist. How would this Potiguara physicist explain quantum physics to other Potiguara?

For the present purpose, I will follow a two-way comparison: first, looking at the fundamental categories of Potiguara ontology from a quantum physical perspective, and then, inverting the perspective, looking at quantum physics from a (hypothetical) Potiguara perspective.

13.1 Potiguara Cosmopractice Through the Lens of Quantum Physics

In the last chapter of Part II, I tried to boil the enormous diversity of the Potiguara's Pantheon of enchanted beings down to a small number of fundamental ontological principles. The resulting ontological framework is certainly a gross reduction of the colourful and enchanted world the Potiguara share with all those mythical beings dwelling in their Ancestral territory. The few fundamental principles I extracted, therefore, do not give a complete account of all ontological principles one could possibly extract from Potiguara cosmopractice, but rather exemplify just some of its core elements. However, a comprehensive demonstration of potential analogies between these central ontic categories and quantum theoretical models of reality should suffice as an argument against an a priori assumption that Other kinds of knowledge contradict scientific evidence, and consequently, are fundamentally incommensurable with scientific concepts of reality. In other words, if such a sample of Other ontological categories could be shown *not* to be explicitly incommensurable with ontic categories being discussed in Our academic discourse, then we should be prepared to analyse each individual case of those countless different Other views before dismissing one of them for being completely incommensurable and /or in conflict with scientific evidence.

The first and most fundamental aspect of Potiguara ontology is certainly the existence of two realms or dimensions, one comprising the visible, physical world, and the other an invisible, immaterial dimension populated by invisible, immaterial, *intentional* entities or "persons". The relation between the material and the immaterial realms is prototypically represented by Mother Nature and God Tupã, while Nature is either understood as an emanation or a creation of Tupã. Ontologically speaking, this constellation would point to an aspect-dualist panpsychism, however, not necessarily to neutral monism, since the material world is understood as an actualisation or manifestation of the immaterial realm. Among the various interpretations of quantum theory, this picture apparently shows some parallels to the complementarity interpretation suggested by Jung and Pauli, as well as to pan(proto) psychist interpretations of Bohm's pilot-wave theory, such as Bohm's own approach and von Stillfried's RBI-thesis.[7]

On the face of it, pan(proto)psychism offers strong analogies with so-called "animistic" cosmologies. Both are fundamentally based on the idea that everything is (at least potentially) endowed with some kind of person-like properties. Hence, panpsychist quantum interpretations should provide a good basis for "translating" Potiguara cosmopractice into quantum theoretical terms. At first glance, the analogy between wave particle dualism and mind-body dualism as two complementary aspects of the *unus mundus*—the fundamental reality made up by symbolic archetypes—depicted by Jung and Pauli could also provide a nice counterpart to the Potiguara's conception of a world emanating from and being governed by an invisible realm. Moreover, both conceptions are fundamentally based on experiences with altered states of consciousness, such as dreams and visions, suggesting that archetypes might connect physical events independently from time and space, thereby causing the phenomenon of *synchronicity* between two causally independent events. However, as mentioned before, Pauli never provided an ontological model of the underlying quantum physical mechanisms.

Bohm's[8] approach on the other hand, provides a quantum mechanical model describing an aspect-dualist reality, suggesting a fundamental *implicate order* or *holomovement* (mathematically modelled by the $3N$-dimensional wave function) which unfolds into an *explicate order* made up by physical observables (describable as "particles") acting in strict correlation to the form of the wave. However, since Bohm does not seem to provide an unambiguous definition of the relation between "implicate order", "wave function", "quantum potential", "active information", "mental pole", and "mind", it is difficult to draw a clear-cut association between one of his concepts and (proto)phenomenal properties. Von Stillfried's[9] RBI-Thesis suggests that "quantum potential", "active information", "mental pole" and (proto)phenomenality are referring to the same ontic referent. Further, he suggests that "quantum potential" / "active information" is a part of the "wave function" and he defines phenomenality as the property of mind that requires explanation, following Chalmers' delineation of the hard problem of consciousness. According to the Russellian aspect of his RBI-thesis, the wave function is additionally viewed as the mathematical representation of an inscrutable, intrinsic, (proto-)phenomenal essence. My first intuition is that this model might show interesting parallels to the Potiguara's conceptions of an invisible, immaterial realm, which is constituted by subject-like entities or "persons".

[7] Since both physical and immaterial realms permanently exist as two parallel realities, it would be difficult to draw an analogy to collapse-interpretations. Due to the almost instantaneous collapse of wave functions, they do not exist long enough to amount to a parallel realm, and hence, the there is only one physical dimension of reality. Everett's wave-only interpretation and derivates, like many-worlds and many-mind theories, on the other hand, suggest a parallel existence of a multiplicity of either physical or mental worlds, but not both physical and mental worlds in parallel.

[8] Bohm (1980, 1990).

[9] von Stillfried (2018).

According to Bohmian quantum physics, N quanta interfere, melting into interlaced systems of growing complexity, finally amounting to one universal wave function with $3N$ dimensions. Von Stillfried's system-theoretical explanation for the weak emergence of consciousness suggests that the protophenomenal properties of entangled wave systems can combine into phenomenal properties of higher order, given the necessary (hitherto unknown) system-theoretical parameters (or "self-complexigratedness"). Hence, von Stillfried's interpretation of Bohm's model in principle allows for the possibility of other than human physical systems to have some kind of higher order phenomenal property. Accordingly, if we consider the universe to present some kind of complex, self-referential order, its wave function could have some kind of phenomenal property, even though not comparable to our human consciousness. This provides room for an additional potential analogy to the Potiguara concept of God Tupã as the immaterial, intentionally creative essence of both immaterial and physical nature. This analogy also applies to the Potiguara's conception of immaterial actants, such as spirits or Ancestors, that are conceived of as elements of the same immaterial essence, and therefore ultimately all expressing Tupã's almighty and omnipresent creative will. Of course, all immaterial entities or forces, including Tupã, are intentional, subject-like beings or "persons", which seems to contradict the claim that all immaterial entities are part of the one essence represented by Tupã. However, Bohm's model also offers a possible explanation for this apparently contradictory idea: although all wave systems are ultimately subsystems of the one pilot wave of the entire universal wave function or "holomovement", each subsystem conserves its own individuality.[10] In sum, the two ontological conceptions represented by the Potiguara's concept of Tupã and von Stillfried's interpretation of Bohm's universal wave function seem to share a number of essential properties:

1. Both constitute an immaterial, implicate order out of which the physical, explicate realm "unfolds"
2. Both are characterised by mind-like, non-matter-like properties
3. Both are divisible into a virtually infinite number of bounded, holistic subsystems with a certain degree of freedom, each acting according to their own self-referential, meaningful order while also acting as parts of a whole

These apparent isomorphies between some of the core properties of the two concepts seem to allow for suggesting that both might refer to a common ontic referent, albeit using radically different metaphors (e.g. "God Tupã" and "spirits" vs. "wave functions" and "implicate order").

There are, however, also aspects of the two conceptions that are more difficult to match. For example, according to the Potiguara, spirits and other immaterial actants, sometimes called "energies", seem to exist more or less independently of the physical realm, but may still play a causal role in physical events. Consequently, if

[10] Additionally, one could evoke system-theoretical concepts of operational closure and self-referentiality as an explanation for the maintenance of these systemic boundaries, or some kind of "selfcomplexigratedness" yet to be defined.

"spirits" refer to the same ontic referent as "wave systems", there should be wave systems that are not bound to a particular physical system, but may still instantiate or influence physical events (if not as a rule, then at least under certain exceptional conditions). In fact, Bohm's model predicts the existence of "inactive" wave branches that refer to all those superposed wave branches that are not "piloting" a particle.[11] However, the existence of inactive wave branches is important for particle behaviour, too, they form part of a shared wave function or quantum field, thus being co-constitutive to the overall interference patterns that "(in-)form" the active branches that guide the actual particle trajectories.[12] However, Bohm's model is deterministic as far as it concerns the wave function, so that particle trajectories are predefined (by initial particle positioning according to quantum equilibrium—typically distributed per Born rule) *before* a measurement-like event occurs. Inactive branches are decoupled from active branches as a consequence of interaction with an external system (equalling "measurement", "scattering" or "decoherence"), and their further interactions with other wave systems will have no (direct) influence on the active wave branches. It appears, however, that in principle, there still exists a remote possibility of a future interaction between active and inactive wave branches. But for this to happen would require the resynchronisation of the separated wave branches, bringing them to overlap once again, which cannot be expected to occur spontaneously.[13] One might speculate now that highly organised, operationally closed, or howsoever "selfcomplexigrated" systems (e.g. a person's mind or spirit) might be able to re-establish a systemic connection to formerly related inactive branches, thereby somehow re-synchronising and having them act on active branches, and thus, on correlated physical systems. But such speculations are lacking empirical substantiation, and will, therefore, not hold as a solid analogy, although there might be no evidence against such an assumption either.[14]

Alternatively, one could search for an explanation of such immaterial actants in Bohm's notion of the wave function and its $3N$-dimensional configuration space as mathematical expression of a deeper reality of an implicate order within an infinite-dimensional holomovement. According to this definition, the unfolding or projection of a higher-dimensional (invisible) implicate order into the three-dimensional space (or four-dimensional spacetime) of the explicate order that constitutes our visible, material worlds, reflects just a tiny (although the only

[11] A discussed in the previous chapter.

[12] Basically evolving according to Schrödinger equation.

[13] Hiley (2010).

[14] "Nevertheless one may raise the question of what would happen if the channels were made to overlap again. For example, in two or three dimensions the experiment could be arranged to reflect both of the quantum fields into the same region of space. When this happened, the larger field would overwhelm the smaller one and the behaviour of the particle would be radically altered. In other words while the information in an 'empty' channel may not actually be active on the particle at a given moment, it may have the potentiality to become active later. Therefore one cannot say that the transmitted particle is in a state that is entirely independent of the reflected channel" (Bohm and Hiley 1993: 84).

objective physical) aspect of a much deeper, immaterial, invisible, holistic reality.[15] Likewise, the dynamics of the holomovement of the entire universe, including all physical dynamics, are orchestrated by the wave-dynamics in all its infinite dimensions. It is at least difficult to imagine what that means. However, Bohm's model seems to suggest that there are many interlaced and interconnected dimensions of enfolded, "invisible" wave systems with at least some kind of (proto-) phenomenal properties or mind-like aspect (attributed to quantum potential and/ or active information), only some of which are actively involved in the unfolding of the "visible", physical world. To my limited understanding, the ontological status of all those dimensions and layers of waves therein as well as their relation to the dimensions of the world accessible to our normal perception remain a mystery (what exactly are those "dimension" anyway, apart from representing a mathematical formalism?).[16] One could speculate that "spirits" and those mysterious, invisible dimensions of wave systems might refer to the same ontic referent, but due to the nebulous ontic status of Bohm's 3*N* wave-dimensions/implicate order/ holomovement, this identification of the two conceptions would not contribute much to their clarification either.

Another way of looking at the issue might be to conceive "spirits" in terms of "traces" of past events. Because in Bohm's model waves do not collapse, they never really vanish, but rather melt into a single whole, represented by the wave function of the universe. Accordingly, actual and future events are a result of all past events. Every event is the actualisation of a particular wave-pattern which will continue interfering with other waves, finally dispersing into countless new wave-patterns, and so on, ad infinitum. Hence, all past events leave their traces in the holomovement of the universe. Such traces of past events are neither inactive wave branches, nor active branches correlated with particular particles, but rather an informational inprints of the past which is pervading and interfusing other wave systems, imbuing particularly those active wave systems that have been somehow related to the

[15] "[…] one is to begin with the holomovement, in which there is the immense 'sea' of energy […] to be understood in terms of a multidimensional implicate order […], while the entire universe of matter as we generally observe it is to be treated as a comparatively small pattern of excitation. This excitation pattern is relatively autonomous and gives rise to approximately recurrent, stable and separable projections into a three-dimensional explicate order of manifestation, which is more or less equivalent to that of space as we commonly experience it" (Bohm 1980: 243).

[16] There is an ongoing debate about the possible ontological status of the wave function and/or configuration space. In Bohm's interpretation, the wave function is treated realistically as carrying active information that guides particle motion, whereas configuration space itself is not taken as physically real but rather as a mathematical domain (although Bohm introduces wholeness, implicate order, and holomovement — frameworks that move beyond ordinary space–time, but not in the sense of reifying configuration space). Other interpretations, however, such as configuration-space realism, do treat configuration space as fundamental (Solé and Hoefer 2015; Bohm 1980, 1990).

respective past events. Supposing "spirits" and such "traces" of the past would refer to the same ontic referent, what would this tell us about spirits[17]?

First of all, spirits would be something like the remains of actual events, or temporarily persisting systems. If such a system was a human being, every one of their actions will leave its ineffaceable traces in the holomovement of the universe; these traces will persist forever, even after the individual's death. Moreover, these traces are non-locally distributed along all those wave-patterns the individual interacted with during their lifetime, leaving its imprints on all those wave-patterns. The sum of all these traces in related wave systems would amount to the vestiges, or the Ancestor spirit of a defunct person. Accordingly, related systems, like relatives or friends (or more precisely their spirits/wave systems), will forever stay connected to, or imbued with, and thus, influenced by those Ancestor spirits. This connectedness between the spirits (=active wave functions) of the living and their Ancestors (=vestiges in the holomovement) would also explain how mediumistic experiences with such Ancestors may provide access to past, distant, or even future events. For Ancestor-vestiges are ultimately connected with, or rather dispersed throughout the entire holomovement (=universe), including its past and possible future states.

So, this might be an interesting hint to a possible analogy between the Potiguara concept of Ancestor spirits as a prototype of immaterial actants and an attempt at a quantum physical explanation for phenomena with comparable properties.

But what about other aspects of Potiguara spirituality, like the manifestation of a spirit by taking control over the body of a *pajé*, or appearances of the *Pai do Mangue* to a crab-collecting Potiguara in the mangroves? One would have to be very creative to construe plausible analogies between such phenomena and quantum theoretical concepts like wave systems or active information.

Although I feel that, compared to the former proposals (Ancestors = inactive wave branches or ($3N$ - 3)-dimensions), the latter train of thought (Ancestors = "traces") might be slightly less farfetched, it is still very speculative and far from representing an *obvious* isomorphy between the properties Bohmian quantum physics would predict for wave systems and the Potiguara's ideas about their Ancestors. Nevertheless, these speculations also show that such a comparison between "spirits" and quantum theoretical concepts should, at least in principle, be possible. But our understanding of the ontology implied by quantum physics and the possible relation to the ontology of consciousness is still too rudimentary to allow for a detailed analysis concerning a possible isomorphy between the properties of the different conceptions. Moreover, quantum physics, like physics in general, is primarily concerned with explaining the behaviour of physical observables. It took a long time for physicists to develop and accept non-material conceptions like "fields" and "waves", and for most physicists there is little reason to think of "immaterial

[17] It is interesting to note that in some Spanish-speaking regions of Latin America—particularly in the Andes—it is common to refer to the ancestors' huellas ("traces", "tracks" or "footprints"), and sometimes even to use huellas metonymically as a synonym for "ancestors." This expression reflects the notion that the ancestors precede us, walking ahead, while we are meant to follow in their footprints (e.g. Sarango Macas 2014; Huanca Soto 2019, CRIC 2021).

actants" as a possible explanation for macroscopic physical events. In other words, for most physicists, immaterial actants are not an explanandum, and hence, there is no need for a physical theory explaining them.

In the face of this lack of a detailed quantum physical model capable of giving a clear account of the existence or non-existence of independent immaterial actants, one could also try to take recourse to the system-theoretical framework provided by GQT. GQT explicitly acknowledges the existence of non-causal interaction between macroscopic subsystems as a result of certain systemic relations (e.g. operational closure and/or complementarity). Moreover, the respective phenomena typically involve one or more subject-like subsystems correlating either with each other or with a physical subsystem. Hence, subject-like systems should be expected to be able to establish the necessary systemic boundaries for becoming effective to other, including physical systems. If subject-like systems be understood in terms of wave systems, as suggested by RBI-thesis, the analogies with the Potiguara's Ancestor spirits in the light of GQT might explain a possible causal role of immaterial actants. Suppose there is an Ancestor-like wave system (whatever that may be) lounging around their neighbouring wave systems, some of whom correlate with physical systems, while others do not. How could this Ancestor-like system, which is obviously lacking a correlated physical system, provoke a physical event? According to GQT, system boundaries can be established by common origin, such as family ties, or strong emotional focus, such as love or sexual desire. Additional requirements of generalised entanglement, like a sufficient degree of freedom and exclusion of signal transmission, are intrinsic properties of any quantum-wave systems, such as "Ancestors", and therefore fulfilled per definition.[18] An Ancestor-like system should therefore be expected to be entangled with all their relatives and beloved, abhorred, or envied persons. Since entanglement occurs in higher-dimensional space, orchestrating events throughout time and space, it would not matter whether the Ancestor is bound to a distant territory or dwelling in another dimension, they still would have an effect on the entangled systems. Such a constellation would probably come close the Potiguara's ideas about their relation to their Ancestors. Moreover, other subject-like systems should be able to establish systemic relations with an Ancestor-like and a third, physical systems, thereby possibly influencing them in a way to have them entangle and start acting on each other. This model seems to provide an elegant explanation for rituals aiming to invoke Ancestor-spirits in order to have them help achieve a particular goal (e.g. curing or sickening someone else). So, as a formal framework, GQT offers an explanatory structure for a wide range of Potiguara conceptions and practices, that otherwise are difficult to "translate" into well-defined quantum physical models of comparable ontic principles.

The problem with this train of thought is, however, precisely that quantum mechanics does not make any *explicit* reference to wave systems with no directly correlated physical system that would be expected to provoke any effect on physical

[18] For simplicity, and due to the unsolved issues related to the definition of "complementarity", I will assume that von Stillfried's (2010) reduced requirements are sufficient (see previous chapter).

systems. Yet, my speculative analysis of possible traces in Bohmian quantum mechanics of comparable ontic referents for such immaterial actants indicates that further research could, in principle, provide the necessary evidence for a more specific definition of some kind of "Ancestor-like" wave-patterns (be they "inactive" wave branches, "traces", "multiple dimensions", or otherwise conceptualised). However, this would require the necessary research interest among quantum physicists. As long as immaterial actants are not being perceived as an important explanandum, this will probably not happen. In fact, even the authors of GQT rather explain *poltergeist* phenomena in terms of psychokinetic effects provoked by "unconscious conflict" that is somehow expressed "phenomenologically",[19] instead of conceiving the *poltergeist* themselves as an immaterial actant. This example shows Our difficulty in thinking outside the box of physicalism, even if we try to make sense of non-causal phenomena. A Potiguara, on the other hand, would probably not agree with such psychological explanations. Maybe, it will require a Potiguara physicist to do the necessary research?

On the whole, a quantum physical gaze on the Potiguara's cosmopractices seems to allow for "translating" some of their more general ontological conceptions into scientific concepts with comparable ontic referents. While the most fundamental ontic categories, like the aspect-dualist conception of a material nature emanating from a subject-like immaterial realm, seem to show relatively clear-cut analogies with a Russellian version of Bohmian quantum mechanics, other conceptions and practices will probably require more "creative" interpretations of quantum physics for constructing possible analogies. However, the circumstance that (my understanding of) currently available and possibly comparable quantum-theoretical conceptions (like inactive wave branches, 3*N*-dimensions, or "traces" in the wave function) apparently do not allow for a more conclusive analysis of analogies and/or disanalogies between Potiguara notions like immaterial actants and ontic categories suggested by quantum physical evidence does not prove that such ontic categories do not exist. Further efforts to identify corresponding phenomena in quantum physics could possibly allow for new theoretical developments, and ideally for empirically testable hypotheses providing evidence for or against the existence of such comparable ontic referents. As long as such testable theoretical models do not exist, there is also no evidence against the existence of the ontic categories in question.

As a result, it can be concluded that based on the currently available scientific evidence and my current understanding of Potiguara cosmovision and practice, an assertion of a fundamental incommensurability or a concrete contradiction between the two cannot be justified.

---

[19] Walach et al. (2014); see example in the previous chapter.

13.2 What Potiguara Ancestors Might Tell Us About Quantum Physics

> A good translation is the one that manages to have the alien concepts deform and subvert the conceptual dispositives of the translator. [...] It is not about suggesting an interpretation of the Amerindian way of thinking, but about carrying out an experiment with it, and by doing so, with our own (Castro 2015).[20]

Every translation is constrained by Our limited access to the Other's perception, and by Our own concepts. However, every attempt to translate the Other's ideas into Our own also reveals a lot about Our own limits of understanding, and thereby, about Ourselves. But, we learn even more about Ourselves and the Others if we listen to Them and Their understanding of Our views and practices.[21] How would our hypothetical Potiguara physicist explain quantum physics, let's say, to one of their elders?

---

[20] My translation from the original: "A boa tradução é aquela que consegue fazer com que os conceitos alheios deformem e subvertam o dispositivo conceitual do tradutor" (idem.: 103) "Não se trata, enfim, de propor uma interpretação do pensamento ameríndio, mas de realizar uma experimentação com ele, e portanto com o nosso" (idem: 266/267).

[21] Malinowski (1932) famously emphasised how this flip-flop change of viewpoints enhances Our understanding of the Others by understanding Ourselves through the glasses of the Other's standpoint, and vice versa: "When, after a six years' absence in the South Seas and Australia, I returned to Europe and did my first bit of sight-seeing in Edinburgh Castle, I was shown the Crown jewels. The keeper told many stories of how they were worn by this or that king or queen on such and such occasion, of how some of them had been taken over to London, to the great and just indignation of the whole Scottish nation, how they were restored, and how now everyone can be pleased, since they are safe under lock and key, and no one can touch them. As I was looking at them and thinking how ugly, useless, ungainly, even tawdry they were, I had the feeling that something similar had been told to me of late, and that I had seen many other objects of this sort, which made a similar impression on me. And then arose before me the vision of a native village on coral soil, and a small, rickety platform temporarily erected under a pandanus thatch, surrounded by a number of brown, naked men, and one of them showing me long, thin red strings, and big, white, worn-out objects, clumsy to sight and greasy to touch. With reverence he also would name them, and tell their history, and by whom and when they were worn, and how they changed hands, and how their temporary possession was a great sign of the importance and glory of the village. The analogy between the European and the Trobriand vaygu'a (valuables) must be delimited with more precision. The Crown Jewels, in fact, any heirlooms too valuable and too cumbersome to be worn, represent the same type as vaygu'a in that they are merely possessed for the sake of possession itself, and the ownership of them with the ensuing renown is the main source of their value. Also both heirlooms and vaygu'a are cherished because of the historical sentiment which surrounds them. However ugly, useless, and according to current standards valueless an object may be, if it has figured in historical scenes and passed through the hands of historic persons, and is therefore an unfailing vehicle of important sentimental associations, it cannot but be precious to us. This historic sentimentalism, which indeed has a large share in our general interest in studies of past events, exists also in the South Seas. Every really good Kula article has its individual name, round each there is a sort of history and romance in the traditions of the natives. Crown jewels or heirlooms are insignia of rank and symbols of wealth respectively, and in olden days with us, and in New Guinea up till a few years ago, both rank and wealth went together. The main point of difference is that the Kula goods are only in possession for a time, whereas the European treasure must be permanently owned in order to have full value" (idem: 88–89).

How would they translate Our concepts into Their's? Is there an equivalent for quanta, waves, or particles in Potiguara cosmopractice?

First of all, the notion of "quanta" is derived from an atomistic worldview, describing the world as an ensemble of very, very tiny, and in fact, invisible pieces of matter or energy. Obviously, atomistic cosmologies are rarely found outside Europe,[22] and certainly are not part of Potiguara cosmovision. Of course, most of today's Potiguara elders have heard about modern physics and atomic theory, so they may have some notion of a "particle", but it will probably not make much difference to their overall worldview. What does it matter, anyway, if the world is made up by invisible, tiny particles, or not? Presumably, for them, the more interesting information would come from the quantum theoretical insight that these tiny portions of reality might be constituted by two different aspects, called "particles" and "waves", the former presenting matter-like properties and the latter rather inscrutable, immaterial and somehow mind-like properties. Depending on the different hypotheses proposed by the physicists the particles arise from the waves upon "measurement" or coexist with the waves and are guided by them. In any case, it seems that the matter-like aspect is governed by the immaterial aspect rather than the other way round, and that quantum systems do not follow causal determinism, but instead "decide" in each individual occasion how to behave in a given situation (e.g. an experimental setting). Moreover, these decisions depend on the relations "waves" maintain to each other, including at a distance, all of them being ultimately interconnected throughout time and space, thus forming a universal wholeness, also called "wave function of the universe".

My guess would be that our hypothetical Potiguara physicist will take recourse to the analogies I mentioned just before, and describe "waves" as kinds of immaterial micro-spirits with a certain potential to manifest as material particles. The Potiguara physicist will thus probably also attribute quite a high a priori plausibility to hypotheses like the Bohmian proposal or the RBI-Thesis that regard the quantum waves as mind-like or (proto)phenomenal aspects of quanta. Whether, when, and how those micro-spirits manifest in the material realm depends on their interaction with other immaterial and/or material entities; these interactions are called "measurement events", since they result in an observable manifestation (called "particles" or "observables") of the invisible micro-spirits (called "waves"). Since micro-spirits (re-)act with a certain degree of freedom (indeterministically) and in correlation to each other at a distance (non-locally), "measurement-events" can be

[22] To my knowledge, atomistic theories are not common among Indigenous nations. However, it seems that early Indian philosophy developed atomistic theories even before Greek philosophers. "Two systems of Indian thought propound physical theories suggestively similar to those of Greece. Kanada, founder of the Vaisheshika philosophy, held that the world was composed of atoms as many in kind as the various elements more nearly approximated to Democritus by teaching that all atoms were of the same kind, producing different effects by diverse modes of combinations. The Vaisheshika believed light and heat to be varieties of the same substance; Udayana taught that all heat comes from the sun; and Vachaspati, like Newton, interpreted light as composed of minute particles emitted by substances and striking the eye" (Durant 1935: 528). Compare also Gangopadhyaya (1981).

conceived of as *intentional* interactions, that is, acts of relating to each other in a meaningful way. Depending on how a physicist decides to "measure" the behaviour of a particular set of "quanta", they will manifest differently, showing either spirit-like or matter-like properties. Likewise, an observable entity, which is obviously made up by a lot of those micro-spirits manifesting in a particular way, will show different properties, depending on how those micro-spirits relate to each other. If they relate to each other in a way to form an identifiable entity, physicists will say they constitute a "system". More precisely, "systems" appear as a result of meaningful relations between their constituent subunits, or "subsystems". In other words, those micro-spirits will manifest as identifiable material entities, if they are related to each other in a meaningful way, acting as a single whole. This meaningful, mutual relationship can be compared with the relations between organs of a living being, or between members of a family. Due to their common origin, they maintain meaningful, reciprocal relations to each other, and whatever happens with one of the members will affect the whole family, possibly even at distant times and places. The same goes for those little, invisible mirco-spirits. Physicists call this kind of non-local relatedness "entanglement". Since everything is made up of micro-spirits and their manifestations, it would be logical to assume "entanglement" to occur among micro-spirits as much as between family members. Curiously though, most physicists insist that only micro-spirits relate in this way, while the bigger entities of the visible world follow deterministic causal laws. Our hypothetical Potiguara physicist might add:

> Of course, we Potiguara know that this is not true, since all entities have a spirit, and because ultimately everything occurs according to God Tupã's will. Interestingly, some physicists think that all those micro-spirits and the larger families they form are all part of one big spirit (they call 'wave function of the universe' or 'holomovement'), who entails everything that is, that has happened, and that possibly may happen in the future—much like our God Tupã. But since physicists do not belief in 'Gods' and 'spirits', they treat them as if they were merely 'physical', that is, being no persons, giving no importance to their relations with Tupã and all the other beings around them. This is why they think our rituals are nonsense. But we Potiguara know that everything happens according to the way we relate to Him, to Mother Nature, to our Ancestors, and to our living brothers and sisters. Although it appears that each single physical event follows deterministic rules, what the physicists call 'probability' is in fact the actualisation of one of infinite potential futures according to Tupã's will. Hence, the best thing we can do to influence His will is to call upon Him and the enchanted beings for help and wisdom.

All this may sound odd to the ears of a physicist (at least if they are not Potiguara), but in fact I just changed the metaphors, while describing ontic referents with properties that are (roughly) isomorphic compared to those described by certain quantum-physical models. However, the little fictitious comment added by our hypothetical Potiguara physicist also shows that by changing the metaphors our perception of the underlying ontic referents may change quite dramatically, even though their properties remain by and large the same. By adopting Other metaphors, new perspectives become visible. In the present case, Our metaphors describe everything as if it were a physical mechanism, while the Other's metaphors describe everything as if it were a subject or person. This important shift in perception also implies different conceptions of contingency. Although both views acknowledge the existence of indeterminacy and classical causation as two fundamental principles of nature, they come to very different evaluations concerning the fundamental logic of nature. While Our materialist perception interprets indeterminacy in terms of probability, the Potiguara's view perceives indeterminacy in terms of intentionality, and thereby, causation rather as the overall result of all the "decisions" that have been taken by God as well as by all the subunits or other persons that constitute His wholeness, in all times, and throughout the universe. Of course, from the viewpoint of classical physics intentionality is an exclusive property of living beings with a at least a minimum of "consciousness". However, in the light of the fundamental ontic indeterminism suggested by quantum physical evidence, the Potiguara's perception of contingency might not be as misleading as commonly assumed by many scientists.

> Bohm's sketch of a mind-matter theory implies that the laws of quantum mechanics (and the Born rule) can be violated in those processes where higher order fields (including thoughts) act on the first-order quantum field. This means that human free will (in so far as it is possible for it to operate at the higher levels of information) can genuinely guide physical action (Pylkkänen 2019: 2).

In this sense, a Potiguara view on quantum physics might reveal new perspectives on existing evidence. Can it be that We could learn something from the Potiguara about quantum physics, maybe even inspiring the development of new interpretations of the empirical observations made in quantum physics? To see what all this might mean to quantum physics proper, we have to translate the (hypothetical) Potiguara view of quantum physics back into Our own metaphors.

First of all, a Potiguara view of quantum physics could tell us that the presumably "mind-like" and "protophenomenal" properties represented by the wave function are primarily characterised as "persons" or "(micro-)spirits" with some kind of intentionality. The indeterministic behaviour of such a "person-" or "spirit-like" wave system can be interpreted in terms of a manifestation of its intentionality, which is ultimately an expression of its meaninful inter-relatedness with all other existing waves/persons/(micro-)spirits. As a result, the physical realm can be understood as the actualisation of all meaningful relations among existing quantum systems, the sum of which are represented by the wave function of the universe. Accordingly, the potentialities entailed in a superpositioned quantum state are actualised according to the overall constellation of the mutual relations of a system's subsystems. Due to the intrinsic intentionality represented by the wave aspect of quantum-systems, each interaction with another quantum-system will be equal to the establishment of new intentionally directed, and thus, meaningful relations between all interacting systems. As a corollary, a "measurement event" would be equal to an active change in the overall relatedness of a system and its overall intentionality, resulting in the actualisation of new observables (represented by the measurable interaction of correlated "particles"). In other words, a measurement event would be something like a quantum system's intentional "decision" to relate in a particular, potentially meaningful manner. Macroscopic events are, thus, the total result of all previous decisions taken by the involved systems to relate to each other in a particular, meaningful[23] way. Due to the sheer plethora of such decisions, the arbitrariness of individual decisions is cancelled out, so that macroscopic events seem to be governed by deterministic causation, while in fact, they are instantiations of intentional decisions.[24] Arguably, such an interpretation of indeterminacy in terms of some kind of intentional, relation-driven decision should, at least in principle, be compatible with the findings from quantum physics.

From such an alternative perspective on quantum physics would probably also follow a particular view on the concept of entanglement. One could speculate, for example, that entanglement could be understood as a synchronised actualisation of systemically, and therefore, meaningfully correlated eigenstates out of a number of superpositioned states, resulting in non-locally correlated observables. Since all events, including apparently causal macroscopic events, are ultimately the result of decision-driven actualisations of meaningful relations among members of a system, all events should equally be expected to be orchestrated non-locally by the meaningful relations between their underlying wave functions (now identified with spirits or person-like properties) as well as by the overall relations represented by the wave function of the entire universe (now identified with God Tupã).

Although these speculations do not prove anything by themselves, there seem to be no evident objections to the possibility that such an alternative interpretation of entanglement might turn out to be largely coherent with quantum physics proper (particularly with Bohmian or RBI interpretation), and possibly also with extended models of non-locality as suggested by GQT.

Of course, this little outlook I briefly sketched out here in a couple of lines is not intended to provide a comprehensive theoretical approach. But I hope my speculations are at least sufficient to illustrate that, in principle, it might be possible to think quantum physics anew from alternative perspectives deriving from alternative metaphors applied to ontic referents with comparably analogous properties, without necessarily violating existing scientific theory or contradicting empirical evidence.

---

[23] E.g. Kornwachs and Lucadou (1985) describe non-locality as a general feature of nature related to meaningful relations between subsystems of a compound system (see previous chapter).

[24] At first glance, this relational definition of the underlying subject-like reality seems to be at odds with Russell's definition of the intrinsic essence as precisely being not relational, but intrinsic, in contrast to the relational description of physical properties. However, Russell's (2007) definition of physical properties as merely relational referred to their *description* as offered by modern physics. The *description* of physical properties in terms of their mutual relations in spacetime is deficient, since it does not touch the intrinsic essence of things in themselves, while, according to RBI thesis, intrinsic essence can be understood as that "something it is like to be" Thomas Nagel (1974) and Micheal Chalmers (1995, 2010) have been talking about. The *intentional* relations mentioned here are precisely the logical corollary of things having such an intrinsic, mind-like essence.

13.3 The Mind-Body Problem Revisited from a Potiguara Perspective

So far I emphasised the possible analogies between Potiguara ontology and modern discourse on the nature of mind and matter, in particular in the form of the so-called hard problem of (phenomenal) consciousness. However, my comparative analysis also revealed some apparent disanalogies. While any disanalogy could be interpreted in terms of potentially incommensurable categories, I would like to argue that different categories might also offer an opportunity to rethink Our own fundamental categorical framework (at least as long as there are enough other analogies to provide a common ground of understanding for discussing those disanalogies). Of course, rethinking Our fundamental categories demands a high degree of open-mindedness, since we have to free ourselves from our beloved "truths"; or to put it differently: in order to learn thinking differently we have to unlearn what we already (think we) know. In the end, we can only learn something new from the Others if their knowledge differs from Our own at least in some aspects. In this last section I would like to point out one such disanalogy and deliberate a bit on the possible implications of these Other categories on Our own metaphysical framework. It goes without saying that this sort of reflections require quite wild speculations on a range of very profound theoretical and metaphysical questions, none of which I am able to treat with the due diligence on these few pages. What follows is, thus, to be understood rather as an outlook on possible future investigations than an in-depth analysis with robust conclusions.

The critical reader already noted that our hypothetical Potiguara physicist identified the wave-like properties of quanta with their concept of "spirits" or "Ancestor", while the "Western"/"modern" scholars I discussed rather tend to identify them with "mind-like", or more specifically "(proto-)phenomenal" properties. The reason for this difference is that for Us, "Western"/"modern" scholars, the fundamental explanandum is the "mind" (and particularly phenomenal consciousness), while the Potiguara are more concerned about "spirits". So far I simply treated both notions as equally referring to some kind of "mind-" or "person-like" property including both intentionality and a phenomenal "something it is like to be". However, intentionality might not necessarily be related to conscious experience. Moreover, a closer look at the Potiguara's notions of spirit, mind, and body reveals a complex pattern of apparently overlapping material and immaterial properties, which does not map easily onto western distinctions between e.g. phenomenality, volition, cognition and psyche. So, there might in fact be a considerable disanalogy between our concepts of mind and body and the Potiguara's notions of mind and body, besides their additional concept of a spirit. I already discussed the rather underdetermined Potiguara notion of "mind", the overdetermined role of the body, and the person-like character of spirits in the last chapter of Part II, and I would like to explore a little of what these particular Potiguara notions might reveal about Our "modern" perception of mind and matter.

First of all, in modern academic discourse, concepts of mind, spirit and soul have been developing over the last centuries in a way that merged them into a psychological conception of "mind" in terms of cognition,[25] with conscious and unconscious layers, so to say. Although "*psyche*" (*ψυχή*) actually means "soul", the notion of an immaterial soul that enlivens the body and persists after its death has long been relegated from scientific to religious discourse.[26]

The Potiguara, in contrast, seem to make no explicit distinction between the "mind" and the "spirit", or "soul".[27] In fact, the Potiguara will frequently talk about spirits and souls (using them more or less as synonyms), but only rarely, if ever, mention the mind at all. However, certain ideas of the Potiguara about the causal role of thoughts and conscious emotions (like envy, jealousy, affection, or hate) reveal some implicit differences, for example, between "thoughts" and "spirit".[28] Although both thoughts and the movements of the spirit can be the cause of physical events (e.g. illness or cure), thoughts are rather considered part of conscious experience, while the movements of the spirit are normally not. Hence, there seems to be a difference between the conscious mind and the (unconscious?) spirit. Also, mind and spirit are supposed to represent quite radically different kinds of subjective perceptions, the former perceiving the material world of physical entities, with its linear space-time structure and within moral categories, the latter perceiving an immaterial world populated by "person"-like entities and governed by time- and space-transcending relations. Of course, since it is in principle impossible to know any other consciousness except one's own, it is also impossible to know "what it is like to be" a spirit, or whether spirits actually have phenomenal properties comparable to our conscious experience. And although mind and spirit both represent sorts of immaterial aspects of a living being, their relations to the material body are utterly different: both mind and spirit come into being with the birth of a material body, however, the former vanishes with the death of the body, while the latter persists as a part of the immaterial realm. Moreover, the presence of the spirit is a necessary condition for the health and life of a living being, while the conscious mind is not (e.g. we do not get sick just because we are asleep). And finally, the

[25] As discussed before, more recently Chalmers and others further distinguished the psychological notion of cognition from that of conscious experience or the "conscious mind", that is, the fact that that there is something it is like to be, arguing that cognition does not necessarily entail phenomenal properties. However, for the most, in modern discourse on the mind-body problem notions of consciousness, the self, cognition, and rational thought have been muddled in varying combinations into the modern concept of "mind".

[26] However, the German expressions for mind-body problem are still "*Körper-Geist-*" or "*Leib-Seele-Problem*", literally meaning "spirit-/soul-body problem", indicating that the process of separating the concepts of spirit/soul from consciousness has still not been fully concluded.

[27] For simplicity, I will use spirit and soul as synonymous, since in the context of the Potiguara, both term refer to roughly the same ontic referent.

[28] In fact, I spent many hours reflecting on this issue together with different Potiguara healers, *pajés*, and renowned authorities in Potiguara culture. None of them had a simple answer to the complex relations between mind, spirit and body, but all of them agreed quite unanimously on the scheme I am presenting here.

body seems to be moved by both mind and spirit, but the body also has its own intrinsic (instinctive?) active principle.

At first glance, this seems to be a pretty confusing pattern of material and immaterial properties: on the one hand mind and spirit both share the properties of an immaterial actant (capable of non-locally influencing physical events), but on the other the mind seems to be rather a property of the material body than an independently-existing immaterial substance. However, the material body appears to be more sensitive to the immaterial spirit and its own intrinsic impulses, and it is by no means clear to which extent it actually obeys the mind. In fact, if taken at face value, the general assumption that everything is ultimately governed by God Tupã and the spirits rather suggest a sort of quasi epiphenomenal conception of mind.

Our current academic concepts of mind and matter do not seem to be of much help for making sense of the Potiguara's notions of spirit, mind and body. But maybe other conceptions of Other ways of being can shed some light on the issue?

According to Eduardo Viveiros de Castro's (1996, 2004a, b, 2015) conception of "Amerindian" *perspectivism*, all beings are persons endowed with a spirit, while the perspective of a spirit is defined by its body.[29] Hence, a spirit with a human body will perceive the world from a human person's perspective, while a spirit with an animal body will perceive an animal perspective of the world, a plant person a plant perspective, a stone a stone person's perspective, and a disincarnated spirit will perceive things from the perspective of an immaterial enchanted being (whatever that may be), and so on. Castro emphasises that different spirits incarnating different bodies not only perceive the same material nature differently, but they rather perceive different *natures*. Accordingly, perspectives could be described as a sort of different layers of reality being actualised by the particular perspective deriving from a person's physical form or body. Paraphrasing Castro, all spirits share the same "culture", but their physical form impinges on the nature of things, resulting in a category shift, and thus, in different kinds of nature. From the "cultural" perspective of their own species, all person's live in villages, marry, go hunting, and drink beer; however, what from a human person's perspective *is* "blood", *is* "beer" from a jaguar person's perspective. In other words, different kinds of persons are defined by virtue of their different bodies, implying different minds perceiving different worlds; however, all person's share the same kind of spirit. Ontologically speaking, spirits represent a more or less uniform immaterial and somehow person-like essence actualising in multiple physical forms, each with its peculiar perspective, and thereby constituting a particular world or nature. Castro, therefore, also calls this view "*multi-naturalism*".

To make myself clear, I do not think that his concept of perspectivism/multi-naturalism can be applied to the Potiguara's cosmopractice without any restrictions. In particular, Castro conceives metamorphoses and predation as driving motives "Amerindian" of perspectivism. Although such motives are part of

[29] Compare Chap. 5.

Potiguara narratives about enchanted beings, these aspects do not occupy the same central role as in the mythologies of other Indigenous cultures (e.g. their ancestors, the historical Tupi). Nevertheless, the general scheme of rather generic spirits assuming a specific kind of conscious perception as a property bearing on the physical form in which they manifest, shows some interesting parallels compared to the Potiguara's notion of spirit, body, and mind. For example, among the Potiguara a person with mediumistic abilities who places their body to be used to receive a disincarnated spirit is called an "apparatus" ("*aparelho*"), since their body serves as an instrument to the spirit. The manifested spirit will perceive and act through their body, feel its sensations, smell, see, and taste, eat, drink and smoke, listen to music and dance, and speak through their mouth. Although each kind of spirit has their own character, displaying a typical pattern of habits and ritual performances, their particular behaviour will vary depending on the "apparatus" through which they are manifesting. Moreover, from a perspectivist view, the apparently confusing pattern of material and immaterial properties of a person's spirit, body, and mind, as suggested by Potiguara cosmopractice, suddenly seems to make sense: it makes sense that the conscious mind is bound to a living body, while the spirit persists after death, because the spirit has an independent immaterial existence while the mind is rather a property of the material body; and it also makes sense that the conscious mind of a human person perceives the world in a particular human way, with human moral categories and human reason, since it reflects the typical human form of life deriving from a human bodily existence. Likewise, one can also see why disincarnated spirits do not seem to follow human moral categories of "good" and "bad", but rather to relational principles of reciprocity and meaningful relatedness that govern the immaterial realm they are part of. And even more generally, it becomes understandable why all beings are conceived of as persons, since being a person is not bound to being human or having a human-like conscious mind, but rather to being a spirit. So, there is reason to suggest that such a perspectivist view might help to come to a better understanding of the Potiguara concepts of spirit, mind, and body. I will, therefore, assume such a perspectivist interpretation of Potiguara concepts of spirit, mind, and body as a tentative hypothesis to further explore the possible implications of the resulting ontological conceptions.

Castro emphasises the ontological dimension of perspectivism, but he also points to its epistemological consequences. From a perspectivist perspective, the world is made up of persons, more precisely, of different perceptions of different persons. Accordingly, in order to understand and manipulate the world, one has to assume the Other's perspective and enter into a reciprocal relation with them. Consequently, Castro proposes following perspectivist epistemology and engaging in an experimental inverted anthropology, trying to understand Their understanding of Our perspectives.

What could all this tell our hypothetical Potiguara physicists, now that they have also become ("inverted") anthropologists? What might a perspectivist Potiguara interpretation of quantum physics be like[30]? And what might all this tell Us about Our problem with Our mind, Our body, and maybe also with Our spirit or soul?

Once we take (the perspectivist interpretation of) the Potiguara's conviction of the existence of a spirit as a necessary ontic category in addition to mind and body at face value, both mind- and spirit-like properties should also appear in our quantum-theoretical models of reality. For example, if (as suggested by Bohm, von Stillfried, and others) the apparently non-matter-like character of quantum waves points to a possible association or even identity with mind-like or (proto-)phenomenal properties, these might alternatively also be conceivable in terms of "spirit-like" instead of "mind-like" properties. I have already discussed to what extent Bohmian wave systems and Potiguara conception of spirits may display isomorphic properties. Although there seem to be no insurmountable empirical or logical objections to construing this analogy, at firstglance, an identification of "spirits" with mind-like aspect of a quantum system represented by the wave function also revealed some notable disanalogies. However, *if* the spirit is represented by the wave function of a system, and *if* spirit and mind are two different ontic categories (as suggested by a perspectivist interpretation of Potiguara ontology), and *if* the mind is not reducible to physical properties (as suggested by Chalmers and others), *then* it would follow that the mind is neither physical nor represented by the wave function. So, what kind of thing should the mind be at last?

First of all, in order to seriously face this question, it would be necessary to unscramble the muddled notion of "mind" by differentiating between implicit notions like "the self", "cognition", "conscious experience", "the unconscious", "(free?) will", or "intentionality", and then analyse which of these notions might possibly match with the (perspectivist) Potiguara notions of either mind or spirit. Unfortunately, such an analysis would require a lot more space than I can offer here.

---

[30]There are probably several different interpretations of quantum physics that might show more or less obvious parallels to a perspectivist ontology as delineated above. If compared to the various interpretations of quantum physics already discussed herein, at first sight, Castro's multi-naturalism may be evocative of a many-minds interpretation of Everett's unitary wave function, with all those minds splitting into ever more different mind-worlds. However, there seems to be no link from perspectivism to the quantum-dynamical mechanism of superpositions actualising into countless parallel minds, so that this path will probably lead into a dead end. On the other hand, the notion that all those different natures are basically actualisations of perspectives could also be interpreted as "prehensions" in terms of a Whiteheadean process ontology and corresponding interpretations of quantum physics (e.g. Stapp 1979; Epperson 2004). A close analysis may well reveal significant analogies between one or several of these quantum-theoretical approaches and a perspectivist interpretation of the Potiguara's conceptions of spirit, mind, and body. However, without discarding any of such possible analogies, I will return to a comparison with Bohmian approaches, simply by reason of economy, since I already spend some pages discussing their theoretical implications and possible analogies with Potiguara notions of material and immaterial entities. I can, therefore, expect the reader to be somewhat familiar with the deeper theoretical implications of Bohmian quantum physics, with no need for further explanations of an entire theoretical framework. Moreover, Bohmian approaches (including von Stillfried's RBI-thesis) seem to be among the most promising interpretations of quantum physics on the way to a unified theory of mind and matter.

Hence, for the present purpose of providing just a first tentative outlook on possible directions for future investigation, I will follow Chalmers' suggestion in assuming *consciousness* (in the sense of phenomenality="the something it is like to be") to be the central property of "mind", and the (hypothetical) perspectivist Potiguara's notion of some kind of relational *intentionality* as the most salient person-like property ascribed to the "spirit".

As suggested previously, a Bohmian interpretation of quantum physics might allow for analogous properties of the wave function and the Potiguara concept of spirit (and maybe also of God Tupã). According to Bohm, the wave function is the mathematical representation of an implicate order that unfolds into the explicate order of our observable reality. Moreover, each unfolding in the explicate order has a mental and a physical pole, both of which are mediated by active information represented by the quantum potential Q, which in turn represents the form of the wave function (and not the wave function itself). Bohm explicitly associates active information and the mental pole of a physical system with some kind of mind-like properties. In fact, one could suggest that only the active information is identical with (proto)phenomenality while the wave as a whole includes spirit-like characteristics such as intentionality but not necessarily (proto)phenomenality. In sum, a Bohmian quantum-theoretical description of spirit, mind, and body could assume an ontic identity of spirit and wave function (or implicate order), while mind and body might represent the mental and the physical pole of the wave function's (=spirit's) unfolding in the explicate order.

Of course, this distinction between spirit and mind goes contrary to von Stillfried's identity interpretation of Bohm's approach, since wave function and active information now represent two distinguishable ontic referents, and hence, cannot be conflated. As a consequence, the model sketched out here would rather comply with a more "conventional" reading of Bohm's model in terms of a neutral monism and a resulting (quasi) parallelism between phenomenal and physical correlates. Von Stillfried rightly objects that such a parallelism would render mind and body epiphenomenal to each other.[31] Accordingly, there should be no interaction between physical and phenomenal correlates, and hence, no direct phenomenal judgments. As a solution to this problem, von Stillfried suggests a Russellian type aspect dualist identity thesis, collapsing (proto-)phenomenal properties, Russellian intrinsic essence, the wave function, and active information into a single ontic referent. However, the problem of parallelism only arises if consciousness is conflated with other attributes of a person's subjectivity, such as reasoning, intentionality, or will, thus necessarily attributing a causal role to consciousness. Obviously, if there are only two ontic categories, a physical and a phenomenal, either the phenomenal is causally relevant or it is epiphenomenal, thus precluding phenomenal judgments and rendering our perception of being an acting person an illusion. However, once the causal role of a person's subjectivity is represented by the spirit (and not by consciousness), the spirit is defined as the active, causal principle of both mental

[31] Compare the previous chapter.

(phenomenal) and bodily (physical) movements. Consequently, phenomenal judgements should be possible again, since our spirit's intentional movements are affected by our conscious embodied experience (including our human reasoning within social and moral categories etc.), sort of enfolding it into the implicate order of the spirit, thereby resulting in the unfolding of the spirit's intentional movements from the implicate into the explicate order of our bodily movements and our embodied phenomenal experience, and so on.[32] Such an incessant ping-pong-like dynamic of unfolding and enfolding from implicate to explicate order and back again is described by Bohm[33] in great detail. Moreover, there should be no combination problem, since neither the spirit nor the mind are defined as a compound system made up by more primitive subunits, but rather as representing holistic phenomena, so that the idea of "proto-spirits" combining into a "full-fledged" spirit will probably make no sense. Rather, all kinds of spirits are likewise bounded entities *and* parts of a unitary wholeness.[34]

All this seems to suggest that, in principle, it should be possible to integrate a perspectivist Potiguara notion of spirit, mind and body into a Bohmian quantum-theoretical framework. Actually, the depicted ontological scheme seems to allow for a surprisingly straightforward association of Potiguara concepts of spirit, mind and matter with basic conceptions from Bohm's ontological interpretation of quantum physics. Furthermore, the identification of the wave function/implicate order with the additional ontic category of "spirit" might even bear the potential of clarifying the relevance of the difference between the concept "wave function" and its subset "quantum potential"/"active information" for theories of consciousness. This is something that von Stillfried's RBI thesis did not achieve because there the concept "wave function" and "quantum potential"/"active information" are not differentiated. One might even further speculate that such a triadic model of spirit, mind and matter could also bear the potential of obviating other more general problems many dualist models of the phenomenal and physical are facing.

For example, the discussion of the hard problem of consciousness shows that dualist models tend to either lead into parallelism, or into some sort of aspect-dualism. While a parallelism generally leads into epiphenomenalism, most dual aspect theories have to explain the "strong" emergence of one ontic category out of the other, which is logically problematic.[35] The introduction of a third ontic category

---

[32] Suppose every phenomenal state of my mind and its neuronal correlata are instantaneous unfoldings of the volitious movements of my spirit, my utterance of a phenomenal judgement would have the same cause as the reflections it expresses. My spirit, that is, *I* as a thinking and felling subject, am causally responsible for both my thoughts and my corresponding actions. Hence, phenomenal judgments are given.

[33] Bohm (1980).

[34] In principle, von Stillfried's (2018) arguments concerning a possible solution of the combination problem by Bohmian quantum physics underlying the RBI-thesis should equally hold for this interpretation of Bohm's approach.

[35] Although some versions of Russelian monism, like von Stillfried's RBI-thesis for example, suggest a weak emergence of phenomenal properties from a protophenomenal intrinsic essence, they neither provide a suggestion on what this protophenomenal essence could be, nor why and how

which is neither physical nor phenomenal, but still not neutral, since it represents another essential aspect of subjectivity (e.g. intentionality) could solve both the problem of parallelism and of strong emergence.

Moreover, as mentioned earlier, the reduction of the concept of "mind" to phenomenal properties omits other important aspects of subjectivity, like the self, intentionality, (free?) will, and cognition, since these issues are relegated to the "easy problems" of consciousness. Building on the possibility offered by hypotheses like the RBI thesis for phenomenal properties to have a causal role within a causal chain, one would probably also need to assume a causal role of "thoughts" and endow them with "intentionality" or "will", as seems to be suggested by the Potiguara's concept of an intentional spirit.

And finally, it is difficult to see how any sort of dualism should be able to solve the predicaments of modern epistemology. As long as there are only phenomenal experience and physical objects, the first continues to be a sort of mirror of the latter, implying a representational model of reality. If, on the other hand, the active principle is assumed to be some kind of person-like, intentional property that is fundamental to both physical and phenomenal properties, other-than-representational ways of knowing might become possible. Russellian panpsychism, however, will tend to suggest an underlying *phenomenal* essence, but no particular active *intentional* principle. Hence, a merely phenomenal essence would imply nothing other than deterministic causation, and thus, provide no reason to assume that an understanding of *what* "it is like to be" another entity should possibly allow for predicting or controlling its behaviour.[36] Consequently, a phenomenal-physical aspect dualism will probably not help to overcome the predicaments of representationalism.

Of course, these assumptions will need far more scrutiny than I was able to provide in this volume, and other authors or future investigation may provide proof of the contrary. However, if at least some of my speculations should turn out to hold, they would still give reason for the hope that Other perspectives could give rise to new interpretations of quantum mechanics, possibly allowing for an alternative framework for a unified theory of mind and matter—e.g. by assuming an additional spirit-like, intentional ontic category. Even if further investigations show that Potiguara cosmopractices offer fewer analogies to evidence-based scientific ontological models than I have suggested, this does not preclude other Other(ed) cosmopractices from exhibiting more salient ones. In any case, my main point is that scientists should not dismiss such practices out of hand, but analyse each case and consider what it might teach us about our most challenging questions.

---

physical properties should emerge from protophenomenal properties. Of course, from a pragmatic point of view these ontological details might not matter, assuming that both physical and phenomenal properties are simply there. But from a cosmological perspective this solution is not completely satisfactory.

[36] This is precisely why Chalmers argues that zombies would behave as if they were conscious despite lacking a sense of 'what it is like to be'. This assumption also lies at the heart of the difficulty in explaining direct phenomenal judgements and, more generally, the causal role of consciousness.

As I argued in the introduction to this third part, the hard problem of consciousness and the underlying ontological question about the fundamental structure of the universe are at the core of the epistemological dilemma of modern science and philosophy. I therefore proposed that the hard problem of consciousness ultimately represents the central question of the real hard problem of modern science in general. I think it is not too far-fetched to draw a parallel to the epistemological problems resulting from the modern notions of a rational subject and the so-called Cartesian dualism, and the related representational concepts of reality and truth. It would be tempting to analyse the epistemological implications of Other ontological frameworks. However, this is not the place to offer a deep analysis. For the present purpose I will have to be content to recall some observations made by anthropologists like Latour, Hallowell, Bird-Davis, Descola, and Castro.[37] As Latour[38] suggests, the Great Divide between Us and Them may have its deepest metaphysical roots in the boundaries We "moderns" have been drawing between Us and Nature. Accordingly, the "modern" disavowal of the hybridity of a world made up by social entities finds its expression in a rational *subject* observing a passive nature made up by *objects*. A perspectivist or animist[39] view on the other hand, presupposes a world consisting of "persons", that is, an intrinsically "hybrid" (in Latour's sense) world of entities that are both material objects and (quasi) subjects. The perspectivist Potiguara interpretation of Bohmian quantum physics sketched out above suggests a relational ontology of spirit-like wave functions basically being constituted by meaningful, intentional relations among their subsystems, unfolding into hybrid mind/matter entities or "persons". This relational ontology also implies a relational epistemology, for "mind" refers to the peculiar perspective of a person's material form or unfolding. Hence, to understand another person-entity is to understand their peculiar perspective. Of course, the perspective is not an objectively observable property (such as position and extension in spacetime), but an intrinsic phenomenal property. Another perspective is only accessible indirectly via communication, empathy, and by trying to assume the other's standpoint. Traditionally, this is often done by means of mediumistic ritual, either having a spirit-person manifest and communicate through another person's body (serving as a "medium"), or by detaching one's own spirit from the body to communicate and relate more or less directly with other spirits. Although this may seem exotic, there is an interesting parallel to the human sciences, which are equally trying to understand other person's perspectives (in this case only human persons) by communicating, participating, and taking the others' perspective. The difference is, of course, that from a perspectivist/animist point of view, all entities are person-object hybrids. Hence, any "observation" is a form of relating to persons and their different perspectives. As a corollary, observation is never neutral, since it is always intrinsically qualified by the peculiar

[37] For a more detailed discussion see Chap. 5.

[38] Latour (1993).

[39] In the sense of new animism as discussed by Hallowell (1960); Descola (1992, 2006); Bird-David (1999).

perspective or gaze that conditions our relating to other person-object hybrids in a specific, qualified way. Furthermore, due to the ontic dimension of relations, the observer's gaze or perspective amounts to an actualisation of a particular aspect or response of the observed person-object. In other words, the world shows itself to us according to our gaze, our way of relating to it—not only in a merely epistemological, but in an essentially ontological sense. It follows that if we relate to the world as if it was a mechanism, it will present itself to us as a mechanism—in fact, Castro's notion of mutli-naturalism would suggest that an objectivist gaze will "create" or actualise a passive nature of objects. Applied to scientific knowledge, this conclusion might provide a possible answer to the "Two Cultures" divide between natural and human sciences. For if the world is actually made up by person-object hybrids, it makes sense to apply both objective and subjective methods in all fields of research, including the natural sciences. On the other hand, we should also be attentive to the ontological dimension of this conclusion: to treat the world as an object will actualise a different world than relating to it with respect and reverence, and the resulting knowledge will have a different impact, too. In this sense, knowing is literally a form of world-making. Consequently, perspectivism is by no means equal to a social constructionist relativism, with different mutually incommensurable social representations of an inscrutable objective reality. To the contrary, perspectivism suggests a universal understandability of all perspectives, including those of non-human person-objects, through relating to them in a meaningful way, and understanding their particular relatedness and resulting intentionality.

In summary, the reflections presented in this chapter suggest that a perspectivist Potiguara interpretation of quantum physics might not only provide a fresh look and possible solutions on the way to a unified theory of spirit, mind, and matter, it might also hint at a unified epistemology beyond the Great Divide between the "Two Cultures" of modern science, and beyond the two extremes of objectivism and relativism.

If my reflections hold, all this should by and large square with findings from philosophical, sociological, and anthropological research on the nature of knowledge as well as with current academic debates on the nature of mind and matter in the light of quantum physics. Moreover, Other ways of knowing and relating to the world may not only turn out to be more commensurable than presumed, they might also help us solve some of the most pressing challenges of science as a core element of our modern/colonial world.

It goes without saying that these rather wild speculations I presented in this last chapter do not present any claim to truth.

It is, therefore, important to emphasise the preliminary and illustrative character of my reflections on possible analogies between the Potiguara's way of knowing, quantum physics and the mind-body problem. I am utterly aware of the speculative and hypothetical character of the ontological scheme I extracted from my fieldwork with the Potiguara. And all good reasons I recited notwithstanding, my choice to compare these hypothetical Potiguara views precisely with Bohmian interpretations of quantum physics was a rather arbitrary result of my own limited readings in the field of quantum physics and philosophy of consciousness. There are certainly many different possible ways of interpreting quantum physics from different Other perspectives and vice versa, and I do not hold my speculations here to present any definite solution. I am sure other, more comprehensive and convincing analogies can be drawn, allowing for more sweeping reflexions on Our own metaphysical conceptions. On the other hand, further investigations may show that some of my suggested analogies between the Potiguara's cosmopractice and quantum physics to be untenable.

However, such an in-depth comparative analysis of the analogies and disanalogies between modern scientific and Other ways of knowing can only be accomplished with the *active participation of the Others* (e.g. the Potiguara) together with academic experts (e.g. philosophers and quantum physicists). For my present purpose it is actually not decisive if precisely the Potiguara´s way of knowing and being will eventually give rise to substantial improvements of academic theories on fundamental structures of the universes, or not. The important point I would like to have demonstrated is that it should, in principle, be possible to rethink Our own concerns together with the hitherto dismissed—since othered—"Others", thereby treating them as equals and transforming existing differences and divergences into potential insights for genuinely new perspectives on old problems. To make such a cross-fertilizing pluriversal dialogue possible, we must take different and diverging views seriously; only then can we learn something new - not only about different ways of making sense of the world, but also about ourselves, our own limits of understanding and related worlding practices.

References

Bird-David N (1999) "Animism" revisited: personhood, environment, and relational epistemology. Curr Anthropol 40(Special issue culture—a second chance?):67–91

Bohm DJ (1980) Wholeness and the Implicate Order. Routledge & Kegan Paul, London

Bohm DJ (1990) A new theory of the relationship of mind and matter. Philos Psychol 3:271–286

Bohm DJ, Hiley BJ (1993) The undivided universe: an ontological interpretation of quantum theory. Routledge, London/New York

Castro EVd (1996) Os pronomes cosmológicos e o perspectivismo ameríndio. Mana 2:115–144

Castro EVd (2004a) Perspectival anthropology and the method of controlled equivocation. Tipití: J Soc Anthropol Lowland S Am 2(1):Article 1

Castro EVe (2004b) Perspectivismo e multinaturalismo na América indígena. O que nos fazpensar 018:225–254

Castro EVd (2015) Metafisicas Canibais: Elementos Para Uma Antropologia Pós-Estrutural. Cosac & Naify, São Paulo

Chalmers DJ (1995) The conscious mind: in search of a theory of conscious experience. Department of Philosophy, University of California, Santa Cruz

Chalmers DJ (2010) The character of consciousness. Oxford University Press, Oxford

Consejo Regional Indígena del Cauca - CRIC (2021) La Crianza y Siembra de Sabidurías y Conocimientos (CRISSAC): Sentir, Pensar y Hacer para Trascender la Investigación Convencional. Programa de Educación Bilingüe Intercultural –PEBI, Universidad Autónoma Indígena Intercultural – UAIIN, Popayán

Descola P (1992) Societies of nature and the nature of society. In: Kuper A (ed) Conceptualizing society. Routledge, London, pp 107–126

Descola P (2006) Radcliffe-Brown lecture in social anthropology: beyond nature and culture. In: Proceedings of the British Academy, pp 137–155

Durant W (1935) Our oriental heritage: the story of civilization. Simon & Schuster, New York

Epperson M (2004) Quantum mechanics and the philosophy of Alfred North Whitehead. Fordham University Press, New York

Frazer JG (1922) The golden bow: a study in magic and religion. MacMillan, New York

Gangopadhyaya M (1981) Indian atomism: history and sources. Humanities Press, Atlantic Highlands

Hallowell AI (1960) Ojibwa ontology, behavior and world view. In: Diamond S (ed) Culture in history: essays in honor of Paul Radin. Columbia University Press, New York

Hiley BJ (2010) The Bohm approach reassessed. http://www7.bbk.ac.uk/tpru/BasilHiley/BohmReassed1.pdf. Accessed 12.1.2024

Huanca Soto RR (2019) ¿El entretejido de la pluriversidad?. Conocimientos en tensión y diálogo en universidades indígenas de Abya Yala: Amawtay Wasi (Ecuador), UAIIN-CRIC (Colombia) y Tupak Katari (Bolivia). Doctoral Thesis, Universidad Andina Simón Bolívar, Quito

Kornwachs K, Lucadou W (1985) Pragmatic information as a nonclassical concept to describe cognitive processes. Cogn Syst 1:79–94

Latour B (1993) We have never been modern. Harvard University Press, Cambridge

Malinowski B (1932) Argonauts of the Western Pacific. Routledge and Kegan Paul, London

Nagel T (1974) What is it like to be a bat. Philos Rev LXXXIII(4):435–450

Pylkkänen P (2019) Henry Stapp vs. David Bohm on mind, matter, and quantum mechanics. Act Nerv Super 61:48–50. https://doi.org/10.1007/s41470-019-00035-2

Russell B (2007) The analysis of matter. Russell, Nottingham

Sarango Macas LF (2014) El Paradigma educativo de Abya Yala: continuidad histórica, avances y desafíos. URACCAN, Managua

Solé A, Hoefer C (2015) Introduction: space–time and the wave function. Synthese 192(10): 3055–3070. https://doi.org/10.1007/s11229-015-0826-x

Stapp HP (1979) Whiteheadian approach to quantum theory and the generalized Bell's theorem. Found Phys 9:1–25

Von Stillfried N (2010) Theoretical and experimental explorations of "Generalized Quantum Theory." PhD Thesis, European University Viadrina

von Stillfried N (2018) Vom Innen der Dinge: Das "Bewusstsein-Körper-Problem" und die "Welle-Teilchen-Dualität": Interdisziplinäre Impulse zwischen Quantentheorie und analytischer Philosophie des Geistes. Habilitation thesis, University of Trier

Walach H, von Lucadou W, Römer H (2014) Parapsychological phenomena as examples of generalized nonlocal correlations—a theoretical framework. J Sci Explor 28(4):605–631

Chapter 14
Conclusion and Outlook

In the course of this inquiry, I invited the reader on a long journey, starting with the historical, epistemological, metaphysical, sociological, geopolitical, and anthropological aspects of scientific universalism, then continuing with Potiguara history and cosmopractice, finally visiting the current philosophical and quantum physical approaches to a unified theory of mind and matter. It was necessary to bring these apparently independent topics together in a larger picture in order to make their coalescences visible, as they would otherwise go unnoticed.

My analysis of the different perspectives of the universalism of modern science and its relation to Other kinds of knowledge, as discussed in Part I, primarily focussed on the instrumental character of universalism within a larger historical context of a global system of domination and exploitation.

Historically, scientific universalism is an anachronism inherited from the religious and institutional universalism of scholasticism and early Catholic universities, which is ideologically sustained by rationalism and a foundationalist notion of truth. However, the universalist truth monopoly of modern science is based on an epistemologically untenable myth of "objective" knowledge. Objectivism is untenable because rationalism implies representationalism, leading into the unbridgeable epistemological gap between the *inner* world of the knowing subject and the *external* world of objects, thereby precluding any direct access to "objective" reality, and thus, leading either into solipsism or constructionism. Hence, representationalism precludes foundationalism, since any truth is based on metaphysical presuppositions which are socially construed and historically contingent, being both the result and an instrument of particular historical power structures, rendering knowledge at large *ideological*.

From a social, economic, historical, and geopolitical perspective, modern science emerged as a central element of the modern/colonial world-system, which has its origins in the conquest of the New World and rising capitalism at the beginning of the sixteenth century. As such, modern/colonial science (including anthropology) was essential to the maintenance of the Great Divide between Us (rational, civilised, "Western", developed, white, male, etc.) and the (irrational, savage, "non-Western",

J. Linhart, *Science and the Other*, Schriften zu Leben und Gesellschaft - Series on Life and Society 2, https://doi.org/10.1007/978-3-032-03927-9_14

underdeveloped, non-white, female, etc.) Others, which is at the root of an ultimately racist *colonial difference* between hegemonic and subaltern identities, and the a priori disqualification of Other, subalternised kinds of knowledge as "unscientific". Moreover, (eco-)feminist, subaltern, and anthropological studies emphasise the intrinsic connection of the Great Divide between Us and Them to the underlying dichotomies between human and nature, subject and object, mind and body, and the resulting reification of nature, the body, and the Others as mere objects of scientific investigation and economic exploitation.

Taken together, these findings suggest that there is no epistemological difference concerning the objective truth value which would differentiate Our "scientific" from Other kinds of knowledge, but rather a global system of unequal power relations (or a modern/colonial world-system) sustained by a set of mystifying metaphysical presumptions, also known as "scientism".

All this calls for decolonising modern science by assuming a pragmatic concept of truth in terms of (different and often diverging) cosmovisions and related worldings or cosmopractices, bringing forth a pluriverse of different worlds with different possible futures. Hence, instead of benchmarking different kinds of knowledge according to their universal truth value—which is impossible—diverging cosmopractices have to be put to the test concerning their potential of coping with matters of common concern. Facing Gaia, currently our major concern would certainly be to bring about more co-inhabitable, post-anthropocenic futures. However, defining what matters, what is of concern, and finally, what might be desirable cannot be the business of experts talking and writing about others' practices; it has to be subject to *cosmopolitical* negotiations in the course of *pluriversal dialogues* of cosmopractices. While negotiating requires virtues typical of diplomats rather than of experts, building a pluriverse of many co-equally dwelling worlds imposes pluriversality as a universal value and challenges Us (particularly those who define themselves as "humans" separate from "nature") to come to a new *ethics of life*—an ethics that redefines our place among and our relations to other "critters" (as Donna Haraway would have it) and earthbeings.

However, the lack of epistemological foundations of any universal truth claim has been (mis-)interpreted in terms of an anti-realist relativism, thereby conceptualising different kinds of knowledge as fundamentally incommensurable and equally illusive worldviews. Philosophers and sociologists of science have repeatedly come to the conclusion that a pragmatic, relational evaluation of different kinds of knowledge, if taken as equally "objective" (since effective) *perspectives*, might be an alternative to the epistemological dead-end of foundationalism, representationalism, and the predicaments of the resulting relativism. Meanwhile, anthropologists have come to perspectivist, relational, or "animistic" interpretations of Other kinds of world-making, emphasising the ultimately ontological character of apparently epistemological differences between different ways of knowing. So there seems to be a surprising coalescence between the identified need for a more pragmatic, relational, perspectivist comprehension of knowledge in terms of different sets of metaphysical presumptions, each with its particular effectiveness, and the anthropological identification of Other kinds of knowledge as precisely representing such perspectivist, relational ontologies. A pragmatic and perspectivist conception of truth should in principle allow for transcending relativism by comparing the overall objective effects resulting from particular sets of practices and related fundamental metaphysical presumptions. However, a dialogue between different cosmopractices would require a minimum of commensurability between their underlying fundamental ontological categories. Accordingly, if it could be shown that at least one example of such Other, subalternised kinds of knowledge does not contradict evidence based scientific theories about the fundamental structures of the uni-/pluri-/multiverse (We do not even agree on that!), the last argument for an a priori exclusion of Other kinds of knowledge from "scientific" discourse on "truth" would fall.

In Part II, I presented the Potiguara, their cultural practices, and their cosmological conceptions, as one such example of a subalternised kind of knowledge. The Potiguara represent a typical modern/colonial subalternised ethnic group, with all the contradictory and hybrid social and cultural patterns that are incessantly being produced at the borders along the colonial difference between Us and Them. Hence, the Potiguara are both Us and Them, while maintaining their own ethnic and cultural identity. Potiguara culture is, thus, the product of and a weapon in a political struggle against oppression and negation, and for civil rights, natural resources, and cultural recognition and autonomy; but it is also a spiritual link to their past, to their ancestors, to their territory, to their identity, and to their own utopian project of a better future beyond the limits of hegemonic modern/colonial cultural norms. Moreover, their "traditional" culture is still present in the lives of many elders, Indigenous authorities, and younger activists, as well as in their political organisation, spiritual and religious faith, rituals at public and community events, and their school education. This "traditional" Potiguara culture consists of a set of relatively well-defined practices, mythical narratives, and cosmological conceptions that are known by most, if not all Potiguara (although today for many Potiguara these practices and narratives are of a more folkloric character). This "traditional" Potiguara world is constituted by a living Nature pervaded by the divine power of God Tupã, and populated by different kinds of enchanted beings, with Ancestor spirits representing sort of a prototypical model of enchanted beings in general.

My analysis of the underlying ontological concepts of "traditional" Potiguara cosmopractices suggests that God Tupã represents the universal and omnipresent immaterial principle of the material universe, represented by Mother Nature, while Ancestors and other immaterial actants are understood as resembling individual, person-like aspects of the universal immaterial principle represented by Tupã. Hence, everything, including physical entities and apparently causal events, are ultimately actualisations of the underlying immaterial principle represented by Tupã and His instantiation in the form of individual spirits or immaterial "persons". As a consequence, events are "caused" by virtue of relationships among different persons rather than by some deterministic laws of causation.

Of course, the universe pictured by Potiguara cosmopractices seems to differ quite radically from the one we know from classical physics, and therefore, should be expected to be incommensurable with scientific evidence and resulting theoretical conceptions. However, classical physics have long ceased to be the basis of our scientific understanding of the fundamental structures of the universe, having been substituted by relativity and quantum theory about a century ago.

In Part III, I provided a brief overview of some of the current attempts to come to a unified naturalist theory of mind and matter in view of the empirical findings from experimental physics. Particularly, I referred to the mind-body problem and the current debates on the "hard problem of consciousness" in the light of different quantum theoretical models of mind and matter. However, the epistemological predicaments of scientific knowledge, as well as its problematic role in driving epistemic injustice and socio-ecological exploitation, are closely linked to the Cartesian notion of the autonomous subject (or *cogito*) and the resulting subject-object dichotomy (also evident in the Great Divide between Us and Them). This is why the hard problem of consciousness ultimately comes down to the real hard problem of modern/colonial science. In other words, a coherent naturalist theory of consciousness in the light of scientific evidence could also provide the metaphysical basis for a more coherent theory of knowledge. However, the overall discussion of these topics showed that:

1. There is still no generally approved scientific theory capable of coherently explaining the existence of conscious experience, rather there are different and mutually exclusive proposals, most, if not all, of them suffering from more or less fatal logical inconsistencies
2. There is still no coherent scientific theory capable of explaining the existence of the physical universe, rather there are a range of utterly counterintuitive interpretations of empirical evidence from fundamental physics, some of which suggest a central role of consciousness or some mind-like properties in the fundamental structure of the universe
3. There is by far no consensus about how a unified naturalist theory of mind and matter might look, but at least there are some promising attempts to lay new grounds for further discussions on the issue and
4. Most, if not all, current proposals for a naturalist theory of mind and matter picture a universe that differs radically from the one drawn by classical physics

Some of the more promising proposals pont to different kinds of panpsychism or aspect dualism. Corresponding ontological models suggest the existence of an inscrutable essence or mind-like property that somehow manifests or actualises in the physical body, and conscious experience, both representing two different aspects of one underlying reality. Several physicists proposed that this mind-like essence or property might be represented by the wave function of quanta, while the physical aspects of reality are constituted by particle-like observables. Particularly, David Bohm's proposals of a quantum-physical theory of mind and matter seem to match with panpsychist solutions to the hard problem of consciousness as discussed by David Chalmers (and demonstrated by Nikolaus von Stillfried and his RBI-thesis).

Finally, my tentative comparability analysis of Potiguara cosmopractice and current scientific proposals for a unified theory of mind and matter suggested that:

1. Central ontological categories from Potiguara cosmopractice seem to be "translatable" into or describable in terms of (Bohmian) quantum-theoretical conceptions, and that
2. A Potiguara perspective on quantum physics could reveal alternative ontological interpretations that might entail new pathways to possible solutions to yet unsolved theoretical problems

The Potiguara notion of God Tupã as the person-like, immaterial aspect of physical Nature seems to show identifyable analogies compared to Bohmian and/or Russellian conceptions of an inscrutable essence or implicate order represented by a 3N-dimensional wave function. Moreover, individual immaterial actants like Ancestor spirits seem to share ontic properties that have been attributed to individual wave systems (e.g. (proto)phenomenality, immateriality, representing subsystems or instantiations of a universal wholeness, etc.). These apparent analogies seem to suggest that Potiguara cosmopractice and (Bohmian) quantum physics are using different metaphors while referring to a set of comparable ontic referents characterised by largely isomorphic properties. Different metaphors, however, paint a different picture of reality, with considerable metaphysical consequences. Hence, looking at the same ontic referents, but through the lenses of Potiguara metaphors, could, for example, point to relational conceptions of contingency and causation.

Of course, these preliminary and highly speculative results will need a lot more investigation. However, even though future inquiries may possibly show that my speculative comparative analysis cannot be sustained, revealing additional disanalogies I am currently not aware of, such possible incommensurabilities have to be shown first and not presumed without any proof. Hence, Potiguara cosmovision and ritual practices cannot be said to be a priori incommensurable with scientific theory or inconsistent with scientific evidence.

Moreover, if We want to learn something essentially new from the Other's views, there have to be at least some divergences compared to Our own notions. For example, from a Potiguara point of view, person-like properties are primarily ascribed to the "spirit" or "soul", while Our "Western" understanding rather defines the "mind" as the central instance of subjectivity, eliminating the notion of "spirit" or "soul" from its metaphysical inventory. Accordingly, "Western" academic discourse focusses on phenomenal properties, identifying *subjectivity* with conscious perception or *phenomenality*, while the Potiguara rather highlight the *intentionality* of the spirit as the defining property of a *person*. Despite this apparent disanalogy between Potiguara and "Western" conceptions of mind and spirit, the Potiguara notion of spirit is not necessarily at odds with scientific theory. In fact, it might even point to alternative solutions to Our mind-body problem. A first speculative sketch of a perspectivist interpretation of David Bohm's quantum-theoretical model of mind and matter in the light of the Potiguara's triadic notion of spirit, mind and body suggests a surprising degree of compatibility. More precisely, there seem to be identifiable isomorphies between the concepts of spirit-like intentional properties and the wave function on the one hand, and mind-like (proto)phenomenal properties and active information/quantum potential Q on the other, while the physical properties of the body are represented by the particle-like properties of quanta. Moreover, the resulting triadic model of spirit, mind and body might also imply considerable impacts on the resulting metaphysical framework. On the one hand, an identification of "spirit" (instead of "mind") with Bohmian wave functions could provide a new perspective on the mind-body problem; both mind and body would now appear as explicit actualisations of an underlying inscrutable reality represented by the wave-/spirit-like aspect, without facing the problems of a parallelism between physical and (proto) phenomenal properties. On the other hand, such a personhood-centered ontology would also imply a new *relational* and *perspectivist* epistemology. Although it would be rash to suggest any definite conclusions, this ontological shift from a "free-floating", rational knowing *cogito* to an embodied perspective of a person-like "spirit", which is ultimately an intentionality resulting from meaningful relations, will inevitably result in radically different concepts of "knowledge" and "truth". At the least, there will be no Cartesian subject-object dichotomy, since everything is a "person" in the first place, and hence not an object being passively represented in our mind; rather perceiving is always a form of relating to another person in a particular meaningful way and from a particular embodied perspective. And since there is no "objective" reality beyond the different perspectives, a foundationalist notion of truth does not make much sense either.

Of course, all this is still no more than wild speculations. However, if these tentative reflections hold, a Potiguara view on quantum physics could indicate an alternative way to a solution to the hard problem of consciousness, and thereby, also to the epistemological hard problem of science.

Unfortunately, I cannot offer an in-depth analysis of all the possible epistemological consequences of such a relational, perspectivist ontology. Not only because this would probably afford writing another volume, but also because the development of new metaphysical approaches will require more detailed quantum physical models of mind and matter, and of course, the active participation of the subaltern Other (and not just a *hypothetical* Other as employed in my tentative comparisons above). In this sense, I can only hope that my contribution will serve as an instrument and incentive for further investigations, and more importantly, for an active involvement of representatives of diverging, subalternised knowledge- or cosmo-practices in a pluriversal academic meta-discourse on the nature of "truth". For my own part, I am looking forward to another opportunity to discuss my results with the Potiguara, and maybe, with other interested subalternised groups.

However, there is still a long way to go before Other voices will be heard and accepted in the academic discourse on truth. The experiences we had during our action research clearly show the enormous barriers for subalternised groups, such as the Potiguara, to access university and partake in scientific discourse, let alone for their views to be truly taken seriously. More efforts will have to be made to support Indigenous and other subalternised groups in occupying and appropriating the academic space as a platform for their demands for a truly pluriversal, decolonial science. Of course, the problem is not merely one of limited resources and access, or of a universalist notion of scientific "truth". Below these rather political aspects of scientific universalism there is a still deeper layer, which concerns the notion of knowledge as content rather than as an activity or practice of knowing. As mentioned earlier,[1] the transcription of performative and narrative knowledge into written account amounts to a transformation into a different kind of knowledge practice, even though the content may remain unchanged. For the sake of comparability, I treated Potiguara cosmopractices as a mere ensemble of ontic categories, but of course, Potiguara knowledge is much more than this. In this way I was able to show that the *ontology* expressed by Potiguara cosmopractices does not necessarily contradict scientific *theory* and evidence. However, while this was a sufficient argument against an a priori exclusion of Other kinds of knowledge from scientific discourse for being supposedly "unscientific", such a reduction dismisses the full dimension of the Potiguara's cosmovision and practices of worldmaking. Potiguara knowledge is essentially an expression of a particular way of being through narrative and ritual performances. Knowing is feeling and doing rather than memorising content. So, too, is scientific knowledge, but we pretend our teaching in lecture halls, manipulating laboratory apparatus, and writing scientific papers is nothing but applied theory. But in so doing, we ignore the performative and onto-epistemo-ethic-aesthetic dimension of our own cosmopractices. And these cosmopractices differ radically from those of Potiguara practices of knowing and being. For example, it is impossible to know the precise amount of energy carried by a photon by means of incorporating an Ancestor spirit, just as much as it is impossible to know about Ancestors from manipulating and staring at technical devices in a laboratory. Different kinds of knowledge have different effects exactly because knowing is an activity. Knowing differently not only makes us act differently; knowing itself is an activity, a way of inter- and intra-acting[2] with and upon ourselves, other beings and (en- and unfolded) worlds. As a consequence, a mere change of the content of knowledge will hardly result in a different kind of knowledge, and therefore, probably not lead to a significant change of its overall effects either. In other words, thinking together with Others must mean feeling and acting together, sharing the practices and experiences that constitute their ways of knowing and worldmaking, and developing new cosmopractices together. Moreover, each practice of knowing demands appropriate spaces of knowing. A laboratory is not appropriate for realising ritual and the woods are not appropriate for doing quantum physical experiments. This is why an ecology of knowledge[3] will ultimately have to be an ecology of worlding practices.[4] Such changes in our practices and spaces of knowing will demand a very profound change in our deepest notions of knowledge, science, and education. My suggestion would be to start by revisiting existing experiences in Indigenous intercultural education and learn from their solutions and limitations. During the last three decades, a range of "intercultural" or "pluriversal" educational and research formats have been developed and tested, accumulating a vast stock of didactic and research methods,

---

[1] Part I, Chaps. 4 and 5.

[2] Barad (2007).

[3] Santos (2007).

[4] Stengers (2010).

and evaluational data. They all show that a pluriversal dialogue between modern sciences and Other ways of knowing will have to go far beyond the limits of Our conceptions of universities, libraries, and laboratories as spaces of scientific knowledge production. Generally speaking, once universalist prejudices are put aside, integrating and having all those different practices and spaces meaningfully interact turns out to be one of the biggest challenges on the way towards an intercultural or pluriversal knowledge production.[5]

Anyhow, we are still far away from vanquishing scientism and its universalistic myth. Despite all the striking evidence from philosophy, history and sociology of science, from decolonial, subaltern and feminist science studies, and from anthropology, debunking the untenability of scientific objectivism and universalism, the final battle in these science wars has still not been won by either side. Instead, critical voices have been misinterpreted as defenders of an anti-realist relativism, and thereby, misused for discrediting scientific knowledge in a political mud wrestling in favour of extremist and blatantly absurd positions from the far right and religious fundamentalisms. It is, therefore, time for a strategy change in science wars towards a more constructive dialogue among scientists on the limits of "objectivity", but also on the risks of relativism. One important element in the establishment of this new meta-discourse is to shift attention from epistemological to ontological questions and to the pragmatic evaluation of the concrete effects of particular metaphysical presuppositions and related practices of knowing. As discussed in Part I, philosophers and scientists from different fields have increasingly been emphasising the importance of such an ontological turn and of a pragmatic, relational, and perspectivist notion of knowledge, transcending the limitations of Cartesian subjectivism and the Great Divide between "West" and "Rest", Us and Them, human and nature, subject and object. Interestingly, a number of authors who advocate this return to metaphysics take more or less explicit recourse to Whitehead's[6] process ontology. Whitehead was not only one of the major critics of conventional epistemology in the pre-WWII-era, he also developed one of the most fascinating philosophical frameworks for a unified natural theory of mind and matter in the face of the (then brand new) insights from relativity and quantum theory. In recent decades, his approach has called the attention of researchers of science, such as Isabelle Stengers,[7] Bruno Latour,[8] and Michael Epperson,[9] as well as of physicists like

[5] Linhart (2008).

[6] Whitehead (1925, 1978).

[7] Stengers (2011, 2023).

[8] Latour (2004): "Of all the modern philosophers who tried to overcome matters of fact, Whitehead is the only one who, instead of taking the path of critique and directing his attention away from facts to what makes them possible as Kant did; or adding something to their bare bones as Husserl did; or avoiding the fate of their domination, their *Gestell*, as much as possible as Heidegger did; tried to get closer to them or, more exactly, to see through them the reality that requested a new respectful realist attitude" (idem: 244).

[9] Epperson (2004).

Henry Stapp[10] and Rudolf Haag.[11] Whitehead's philosophy unites several central requirements of a unified theory of mind and matter: He offers a metaphysical model that avoids the Cartesian subject-object dichotomy and the pitfalls of representationalism, without, however, slipping into phenomenology, constructionism, relativism, or anti-realism. He, thus, avoids epistemology and the Great Divide (or "bifurcation", as he calls it) between culture and nature by stepping behind it, so to say, and building his concept of reality directly into his ontological framework. Moreover, his ontology also offers a framework for an alternative interpretation of fundamental physics which is (at least in principle) both coherent with quantum and with relativity theory, and which provides a place for both mind and matter in a unified theoretical approach.

Due to a lack of space and time, it was not possible to go into this exciting discourse in the course of the present volume. However, I think it would be worth further exploring the potential of Whitehead's philosophy as a conceptual dispositive for the elaboration of an alternative metaphysical groundwork of a new, decolonised science beyond the limits of universalism, the Great Divide, the shortcomings of representational epistemology and relativism, and which is based on a pluriversal dialogue of cosmopractices. But this philosophical adventure will have to be endeavoured elsewhere.

I also think that, more important than satisfying Our logocentric thirst for theoretical coherence, will be to put hands on, going into practice and start doing/feeling/thinking together with Others. This will demand descending from our ivory towers, putting our precious books aside for a while, engaging with our hearts and bodies—not only our minds—into pluriversal dialogues of cosmo*practices*. We need to co-create pluriversal spaces or contact zones within academia, inserting the excluded Others together with their cosmopractices within the colonial structures of Science (with a capital S), causing decolonial cracks in the massive colonial systems that still dominate Our One-World World. This will require new *methods* of co-feel-thinking-doing-creating as well as new *virtues* and a new *ethics of life*, all of which can only derive from us engaging together, as feel-thinking bodies (not only as brains in vats), in the building of new relations to ourselves, other critters and earth beings.

So, as can be seen, there is plenty of work awaiting, and important work, I hold, since the ways we know determine the lives we live and the possible futures we bequeath to our children.

References

Barad K (2007) Meeting the universe halfway: quantum physics and the entanglement of matter and meaning. Duke University Press, Durham

Epperson M (2004) Quantum mechanics and the philosophy of Alfred North Whitehead. Fordham University Press, New York

---

[10] Stapp (1979).

[11] Haag (2004).

Haag R (2004) Quantum theory and the division of the world. Mind Matter 2:43–66

Latour B (2004) Why has critique run out of steam? From matters of fact to matters of concern. Crit Inq 30(2):225–248

Linhart J (2008) Universidades Indígenas: Programas de Educação Indígena Superior na América Latina: A Caminho de uma Ciência Intercultural? Master thesis, LMU

Santos BDS (2007) Para além do pensamento abissal: das linhas globais a uma ecologia de saberes. Novos estud CEBRAP 71–94. https://doi.org/10.1590/S0101-33002007000300004

Stapp HP (1979) Whiteheadian approach to quantum theory and the generalized Bell's theorem. Found Phys 9:1–25

Stengers I (2010) Cosmopolitics I/II. University of Minneapolis Press, Minneapolis

Stengers I (2011) Thinking with whitehead: a free and wild creation of concepts. Harvard University Press, Cambridge

Stengers I (2023) Making sense in common: a reading of whitehead in times of collapse. University of Minnesota Press, Minneapolis

Whitehead AN (1925) Science and the modern world. Cambridge University Press, London

Whitehead AN (1978) Process and reality: an essay in cosmology. Griffin DR, Sherburne DW (eds). Free Press, New York

MIX
Papier aus verantwortungsvollen Quellen
Paper from responsible sources
FSC® C105338

If you have any concerns about our products,
you can contact us on
ProductSafety@springernature.com

In case Publisher is established outside the EU,
the EU authorized representative is:
Springer Nature Customer Service Center GmbH
Europaplatz 3, 69115 Heidelberg, Germany

Printed by Libri Plureos GmbH
in Hamburg, Germany